SINGER
sewing book

SINGER
sewing book

Jessie Hutton
Gladys Cunningham
Claire Brekke
Stella Baines

HAMLYN
LONDON · NEW YORK · SYDNEY · TORONTO

Fifth Impression 1979
This edition published by
The Hamlyn Publishing Group Limited,
Astronaut House, Feltham, Middlesex, England.

ISBN 0 601 08662 7
Printed in Czechoslovakia by P. Z. Bratislava
52042/2

You are about to begin an adventure in creativity: you are going to sew. And you are going to sew well. You may open this book as a beginner, eager to make an absolutely marvellous dress; or you may open it as an experienced dressmaker, determined to master tailoring. Whatever your reason, we believe the book will satisfy you, for it aims to teach the novice basic sewing skills and help the advanced seamstress perfect her ability.

Sewing today is an exciting and rewarding pastime. Whether you sew for economy or fashion, you have at your disposal superb fabrics in brilliant colours and interesting textures and weaves; you have patterns by famous designers; and you have a versatile and compliant friend – your sewing machine.

Begin your adventure with a simple dress, and follow the rules implicitly. When you have mastered them, decide where you can cut corners without sacrificing good workmanship. (Many of the basic principles of sewing must never be omitted.) Each time you make a dress select a design that is a little more difficult. Gradually work up to bound buttonholes, set-in pockets, and finally suits and coats. Follow the same principle when sewing for your home. Start with a simple curtain or bedspread and advance to curtains, loose covers, and designs featuring decorative detail. If you are skilled in sewing use this book to broaden your knowledge – to acquaint yourself with the new construction methods that today's fabrics and fashions demand.

Sewing is an art and, as such, demands the discipline of an art. Bring to it desire, enthusiasm, and imagination, and it will give you in return a satisfaction that is unique: the joy of creating something that is truly yours.

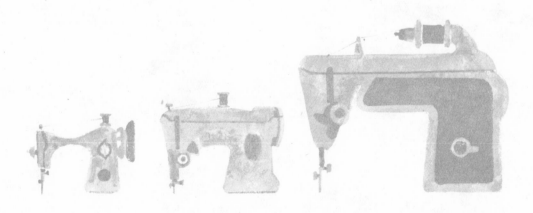

Acknowledgements

Many talented people have applied their skills and abilities to make this book informative, useful and attractive

Special thanks are due to Mary Skemp Perkins, who provided creative editorial assistance to Miss Cunningham in the preparation of the first edition of the SINGER SEWING BOOK

Text Illustration
Drawings for the text were made by A. Bernasconi, Sr., Helen Disbrow, Ralph Castenir, Derek Moore, Anthony Schmidt and Edward Hauser

Fashion colour photographs – Alphaplus Ltd., Leatherhead, Surrey
Other colour photography – Rudy Miller Studio (USA)

Colour wheel – Charles Palmer

Permission to reproduce the beautiful wedding dress and interior photographs is gratefully acknowledged. The source is given under each illustration.

THE SINGER COMPANY

Table of Contents

and Armhole Facing · Faced Slash Opening · Bound and Piped Neckline Finishes · Double-Fold Bias Binding · Single-Fold Bias Binding · Piped Neckline · Collars · Collar with Bias Facing · Collar and Revers with Back Facing · One-Piece Collar · Two-Piece Collar · Collar and Revers without Back Facing · Velvet Overcollar

Waistline Seams and Waistbands 153

To Join Bodice to Plain or Gored Skirt · To Join Bodice to Gathered Skirt · To Stay the Waistline · To Attach Waistband to Skirt · To Attach Waistband to Knitted Fabric · To Attach Elastic at the Waistline ·

Sleeve Styles and Finishes 158

Constructing Different Sleeve Styles · Set-In Sleeve · Raglan Sleeve · Epaulette Sleeve · Puff Sleeve · Magyar Sleeve without Gusset · Magyar Sleeve with Gusset · Armhole with Fitted Facing · Finishing the Sleeve · Hemmed Edge – Short Sleeve · Wrist Opening · Zip Opening · Vent Opening · Hemmed Cuff · Turn-Back Cuff · French Cuff · Cut in One with the Sleeve · Double-Fold Bias Binding

Homeward Bound: Zips, Hems, Belts and Buttons 176

Zips and Plackets · Dress Placket Zip in Lapped Seam · Hand-Finished Zip Insertion · Bindstitched Zip Insertion · No-Pin, No Tack Method · Skirt Placket Zip in Lapped Seam · Neckline or Sleeve Zip in Channel Seam · Zip in Centre Back Lapped Seam · Continuous Bound Placket · Placket in a Seam · Hems and Hem Finishes · Checking the Fit of the Dress · Preparing the Hem · Edge-Stitched Hem · Pinked Hem – Blind Herringbone · Bound Hem · Blindstitched Hem · Herringboned Hem · Zig-Zag Hem · Double Knit Fabric · Gored and Semi-Flared Skirts · Hem across Pleat in Skirt · Hem in Slit Skirt · Hem in Circular Skirt · Spliced Hem · Double-Stitched Hem · Soft Hemline · Hem at Corners · Hem with Mitred Corner · Narrow Hem Finishes · Machine-Stitched Hem · Hand-Rolled Hem · Blouse Hems · Belts and Belt Carriers · Belt with Stiffening · Lined Soft Belt · Contour Belt · Narrow Tie Belt · Sash Belt · Corded Belt · Cummerbund with Featherboning · Belt Carriers · Blanket-Stitch Carriers · Chain-Stitch Carriers · Fabric Carriers · Buttons and Fastenings · Positioning Buttons · Sewing on Buttons · Buttons without a Shank · Buttons with Thread Shank · Reinforced Buttons · Machine-Stitched Buttons · Press Fasteners · Lingerie Strap Holder · Hooks and Eyes · Thread Eye · Thread Loops · French Tacks · Eyelets

Pleats and Godets 209

Pleats · Knife or Wrap Pleats · Inverted Pleat with Underlay · Dior Pleat · Box Pleats · Pleated Skirt · Stitching Pleats · Pleated Ruffles · Inserting Godets · Godet in a Cut-Out · Godet in a Seam

Fabrics that Require Special Handling 215

Silk Fabrics · Knitted Fabrics · Stretch Fabrics · Bonded Fabrics · Laminated Fabrics · Drip-Dry Fabrics · Velvet, Velveteen, and Corduroy · Lace Fabrics · Soft Leather and Suede · Glass Fibre

Hand Sewing – Plain and Fancy 228

A Word About Thread · Slip Stitch · Blind Hemming Stitch · Hemming · Whipping · Herringbone · Backstitch · Running Stitch · Handpicked Stitch · Padding Stitch · Buttonhole Stitch · Blanket Stitch · Chain Stitch · Cross Stitch · Featherstitch · French Knot · Lazy Daisy · Outline or Stem Stitch · Hand Hemstitching · Faggoting

Decorative Touches 235

Tucks · To Estimate Fabric Width Requirements · To Mark the Position of Tucks · Pin Tucks · Hand-Stitched Tucks · Tucks and Space of Equal Width · Blind Tucks · Decorative Tucks · Tucks with Lace · Smocked Tucking · Shell Tucks · Scalloped Tucks · To Press Tucks · Frills · To Prepare the Fabric ·

List of Colour Plates

A Place to Sew

To find in sewing the pleasure that is waiting there, you need a cheerful, comfortable, neatly organised sewing area where you can keep your sewing machine and sewing supplies. The ideal place, of course, is a room where you can leave the machine open, the ironing board up, and the work spread out when you have to stop. But most women have to compromise and find a corner where they can.

Much, of course, depends on the space available and the time you spend in sewing. If you sew in the evening you may be able to find a place in the dining-room where you can work while the rest of the household is busy with television, a record player, homework, reading or a hobby. A large cupboard might be fitted with your sewing and pressing equipment and the dining-room table might double as your cutting table. Or, if you have a light and modern laundry room that is large enough for all your sewing equipment, you could make that your 'sewing studio'.

Study the layout of your own house. You may come up with several good ideas. If you cannot have a room of your own for sewing, make the best compromise – one that offers the most convenience to you with the least disruption to family life. Remember, if you have only a short time to sew, you do not want to spend most of it getting out your sewing and putting it away. And the pleasure possible in sewing will certainly be diminished if you have to sew in one room, press in another, and store your sewing supplies in still another.

Arranging Your Sewing Area

Wherever the space you have found for your sewing corner, you can, with skilful planning, arrange your sewing equipment and tools for long sewing sessions. The success with which you do this will be apparent in your sewing results.

Sewing and Pressing Area

Place your sewing machine near a window if possible so that you may have the benefit of natural daylight. Use a stool or straight chair without arms so that you can move your own arms and body freely as you work.

Since pressing as you sew is essential, place the ironing board and other pressing equipment close to the machine. Be sure the section is well lighted. The light on your machine is focused on the stitching area; to illuminate the section for both sewing and pressing, place a standard or table lamp nearby.

Keep a wastebasket handy for scraps and threads. If you keep your working area neat as you go along, you will find that you can quickly clean up when you have finished sewing.

If you have a dress stand, place it near the sewing unit so that it is handy for fitting your garments. (Store it in the cupboard when you have finished.)

Pattern Layout and Cutting Area

You will need a smooth surface. A bedboard, which can be supported with two trestles, or a ping-pong table is quite satisfactory since both are about 152·5 cm (60 inches) long. The bedboard can be stored between the mattress and bed base and the ping-pong table can be folded when not in use.

Place the table so that you can walk around at least two sides. Use it not only when laying out the pattern and cutting but also when marking the garment and when tacking the sections together.

If you have to use the dining-room table, protect it with heavy brown paper or a stiff table pad.

For fitting you will need a full-length mirror (a three-way mirror is better) so that you can inspect the fit of your garments as you try them on during various stages of construction. A mirror on a door solves this nicely. Other members of the family will probably appreciate it too when they are dressing.

Storage Area

The storage area should be near the sewing area if possible. The amount of space needed will depend on your sewing supplies and tools and the kind of sewing you do. You may need two or three drawers in a chest or cupboard to store fabrics, interfacings, trimmings, patterns, and related items. A sewing basket or sewing box is ideal for the smaller items such as scissors, needles, pins, bobbins, thread, thimbles, pin cushion, press-fasteners, tape measure and the like. You can keep the basket on a cupboard shelf.

All your pressing equipment should be stored together so that it is readily accessible when you are sewing.

You should have cupboard space for hanging dresses, coats and suits that are under construction, and for hanging lengths of fabric that you may buy to make up later. You should also have several padded hangers. As soon as darts are tacked, pin the seam edges of the dress together and hang the dress on the padded hanger instead of folding or laying it on the table or bed. This will keep the fabric free of creases and save you time later because you will not have to press the dress before you start working on it again.

Store sewing books on the cupboard shelf or in a bookcase; store fashion magazines on a shelf or in a magazine rack.

When storage space is limited, you might consider a storage wall. Secure a pegboard with hooks inside a cupboard door and use it for small tools such as a metre or yard stick, tape measures, scissors and the like.

Equipment and Supplies

Besides a good sewing machine, your place to sew should have many small tools and sewing accessories. They will facilitate your sewing and help you attain a professional look in your finished product. Buy good quality tools and supplies, take care of them properly, and store them so that you can quickly find what you need when you start to sew. You will be rewarded with good service, convenience, and satisfying sewing results.

The following are essential for good sewing:

Thread. Have in stock silk, mercerised, and synthetic thread in an assortment of colours for sewing, tacking, and making tailor's tacks. Also have a large spool of white tacking thread as well as thread that matches the colour of the fabric you are sewing. (Leftover spools of thread may be used for tailor's tacks.)

Hand-sewing needles. Buy good-quality steel needles and keep them in the package to prevent rust. Needles are available in sizes from 1 to 12; the selection depends on the weight and character of the fabric. You will find sizes 3 to 9 the most useful for general sewing. There are also many types of needles to choose from; here the selection depends on the kind of stitching you expect to do. The following will guide you:

Straw and Milliner's needles are long and slender with round eyes. Because of their length, slender shaping and flexibility, they produce good results when multiple stitches are taken on to the needle as in hand shirring, overcasting and similar stitching.

The *Betweens* are the very short, round-eyed needles. Use them, as tailors do, to make the fine, short, sturdy, invisible stitches that are a mark of good tailoring.

The all-purpose *Sharps* are medium-length, round-eyed needles. Use them for general sewing.

Crewel needles are similar to the Sharps in length but have a long, oval eye for easy threading and for carrying multiple strands as in hand embroidery.

Darners are long needles with long, oval eyes that are designed to carry multiple strands of thread. Because of their length, many stitches can be woven on to the needle with a single stroke.

Upholstery needles are curved and are made for stitching into a cushioned surface. The curved needle rises out of the cushion with each stitch, thus facilitating stitching that would be difficult with a straight needle.

Machine needles. Keep an assortment of sizes from 9 to 18. Select the size that is suited to the weight and character of your fabric. *Fabric, Thread and Needle Chart*, page 24, gives complete information on selecting the proper needle for the fabric used. A machine needle should be changed after it has been used to stitch two or three garments since it becomes bent and blunt from use.

Pins. Select fine, slender dressmaking pins with needle-like points and smooth blades. Always keep them separate from household pins since they will become bent and blunt if used for purposes other than sewing.

Tape measure. Select a tape measure with metal tips, 152·5 cm (60 inches) in length, reversible and numbered to read from each end. Linen, plastic and plastic-coated tape measures are best because they will not stretch.

Gauges. Keep several 15-cm (6-inch) sewing and knitting gauges for measuring short distances.

Rulers. Have one 45-cm (18-inch) ruler and a metre or yard stick for measuring fabric grain line on pattern layout, and a *folding ruler* or *steel tape* for measuring windows for curtains.

Thimbles. Be sure that thimbles fit well, and use one for all hand sewing and tacking.

Scissors. You will use three kinds: (1) *Bent-handle dressmaker's shears* with 15- or 18-cm (6- or 7-inch) blades for cutting. These shears have a small ring handle for the thumb and a large ring for two or three fingers. (2) *Light trimmers* for trimming seams and for small jobs.

These have a small ring handle for the thumb and a large ring for two or three fingers. (3) *Small embroidery scissors* for cutting threads and buttonholes. Left-handed dressmakers should use *left-handed shears* for greater ease and accuracy in cutting.

Pinking shears. Use them only for finishing seam edges. Not for cutting out.

Pressing equipment. You will need a steam iron, sleeveboard, seamboard, ironing board, pressing-mitt and tailor's ham, three kinds of pressing cloths, sponge, paintbrush, clothes brush and pressing pad. *Pressing as You Sew,* on page 64, explains how you will use this equipment.

Pin cushion. Use for needles and a few pins.

Extra bobbins. Keep a good supply on hand for your machine. Always have one bobbin wound with black thread and one with white ready to use in mending.

Awl or stiletto. Use it to punch holes for eyelets.

Tweezers. They are handy for removing tailor's tacks and short tacking threads.

Bodkin. Have one for inserting cord or elastic into a casing. It is also useful when you are forming a thread shank while sewing on buttons.

Skirt marker. It is a must for marking hemlines.

Embroidery hoops. Keep two or more 15 cm (6 inches) and smaller, for darning and embroidery.

Tailor's chalk or chalk pencil. You will need this for transferring pattern markings to some fabrics, for marking adjustments in garments, and for marking the width of hems.

Tracing wheel and dressmaker's tracing paper. These are useful for transferring pattern markings on interfacing, mounting and some fabrics.

Beeswax. Keep a piece on hand for waxing thread before you sew buttons on coats, jackets, waistbands and thick fabrics. It strengthens the thread and prevents twisting and fraying. Use it also for smoothing the surface of the iron.

Basic haberdashery. Keep an assortment of press fasteners, hooks and eyes, elastic, straight seam binding and zips.

Buttons. It is wise to have several cards of pearl buttons of various sizes, which can be used for blouses and children's clothes and for many mending jobs. Also, keep a box for buttons that you have removed from discarded garments; they may be used again.

Besides these supplies, a small 'reference' library is strongly recommended. It should contain: (1) The instruction book for your machine. (2) This sewing book. (3) A scrap book or folder of fashion clippings and features from newspapers and magazines for ideas that you would love to copy or use for inspiration. Also, watch for new sewing aids to appear on haberdashery counters from time to time. You may find some item that can help you save time and make your sewing more professional.

Your Sewing Machine

If you are an experienced dressmaker, you know how valuable and essential a good sewing machine is to a well-run home. You also know how important it is to keep your machine in first-class condition. (Information on caring for your machine appears at the end of this chapter.)

In addition, you should realize that advances in fabrics have caused many changes in your stitching needs. To the familiar fabrics woven from natural fibres – cotton, silk, wool and linen – have been added many man-made or synthetic fibres. The blending of natural and synthetic fibres and new finishing methods have revolutionised the appearance and properties of fabrics. Double-knit, stretch, bonded, crease-resistant and many other fabrics have increased the stitching range you will require from your machine.

Added to all these fabric developments are the ever fickle whims of fashion, which have changed sewing methods.

Fashion emphasis on simple, straight seams places emphasis, in turn, on the quality of stitching that holds the seam. Knitted (Jersey) and stretch fabrics, for example, require greater seam strength and flexibility. In loosely woven and textured fabrics, the seam should be finished by machine to prevent fraying and eliminate bulk. (Machine finishing will also save time.) Mounting and lining, which are now widely used to help retain the shape of the fabric and give added body, require stitching through several layers of different fabrics. This makes the quality of the feed of your machine very important.

Your sewing is simplified if your machine is easy to thread and if you can adjust the needle-thread tension, pressure and stitch length with a minimum of effort. You should be able, with minor adjustments of one or more of these, to stitch the newest fabrics without puckered seams or skipped stitches.

Sewing machine manufacturers have kept pace with fabrics, fashion sewing and modern living. And sewing machines today offer many features to make your sewing easier.

De-luxe zig-zag machines offer finger-tip switch from straight stitching to zig-zag stitching for finishing seams, buttonholing, blindstitching hems, sewing buttons and mending as well as doing decorative stitching. Simple zig-zag machines have limited zig-zag features and are less expensive. Straight stitch machines are designed to do excellent straight stitching and top stitching and to make buttonholes with the aid of a Buttonhole attachment.

Some machines have other features that make sewing more pleasant – for example, a slant needle for maximum vision, a horizontal spool pin that permits the thread to unwind without drag from the spool and a push-button bobbin that lets you fill the bobbin directly from the needle. Some machines will even chain stitch for easy-to-remove temporary stitching. In fact, modern sewing machines do more practical stitching jobs than you can imagine. Many machines are light enough to carry as portables; or they can be placed in attractive cabinets that match or blend with your furniture.

The type of machine you need will depend on the extent to which you use a machine and the kind of sewing you do. Remember that your sewing machine is the main equipment in your place to sew. Arrange all sewing tools and supplies around it.

Caring for Your Machine

Just as a good craftsman is meticulous about the care of his tools, so should you be about the care of your sewing machine. By getting into the habit of removing dust and lint regularly, to oiling the machine frequently and to having it cleaned at reasonable intervals, you will be assured of a faithful sewing companion – one that will give you pleasure, satisfaction and service. Suggestions on dusting and oiling the machine are given below; as for cleaning, your Singer Centre can give this service whenever you wish.

REMOVING DUST AND LINT

Many fabrics, when stitched, drop lint and particles of fibre or filling. These, mixed with dust and moisture from the air, collect around the bobbin case and feed dog. Lint and dust also collect around the moving parts of the machine.

Expose the working parts by removing the throat plate and face plate (on some machines the slide plate

4

should be removed), and brush away the dust and lint. A special lint brush and a piece of muslin are ideal for this job.

OILING THE MACHINE

Oiling keeps the machine running freely and prevents friction and wear. If the machine is used all day and every day, it should be oiled daily. If it is used moderately, it should be oiled every week or two. *Always remove the dust and lint before oiling the machine.* If the machine has not been used for some time, oil it the day before you start to sew to be sure that no oil will mark the fabric.

To find the oiling points, refer to the diagram in the instruction book. Use just a drop or two of oil at each point; never flood the machine with oil. After the machine has been thoroughly oiled, run it slowly for several minutes to allow the oil to work into the moving parts. Then remove the excess oil from the thread-handling parts with clean muslin or any other lint-less fabric. Polish the take-up lever, the thread guides, and the area around the needle and presser foot. Pass the cloth between the tension discs, being careful to avoid catching the take-up spring.

If you are going to give the machine an extended rest, remove the lint and oil the machine before placing it in storage. Lint absorbs moisture from the air and holds it against the metal parts, increasing the risk of rust damage in a humid atmosphere or over a long period of storage.

Some machines have gears that are lubricated instead of oiled; motors equipped for gear drive should be lubricated only once a year. Motors with grease tubes require lubrication every six months, however. On many machines, the motor is sealed and requires no lubrication.

Read carefully the instruction book accompanying your machine. It will tell you exactly how to care for it – whether to oil or lubricate it, where to apply the lubricant, and how often. A word of caution: always buy a high-quality oil or lubricant made specifically for sewing machines.

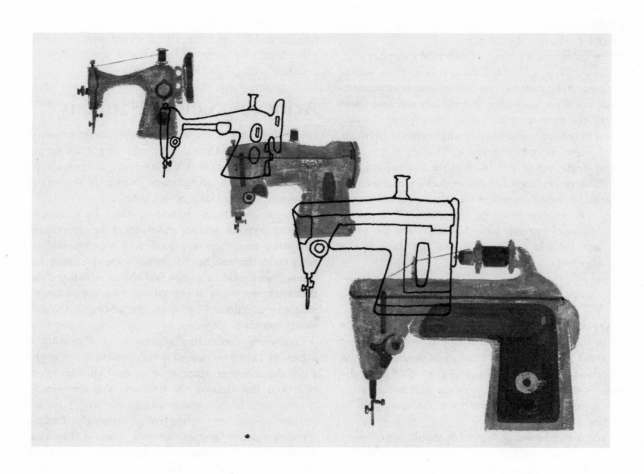

What You Should Know About Colour and Fabric

Eager as you may be to start sewing, you should sit back for a moment and consider where you are going. Essential to planning a wardrobe is a knowledge of colour and fabrics. This chapter will give you basic information. Then you are on your own.

About Colour

Colour can be exciting. Used wisely – and imaginatively – it will give your wardrobe a lift, contribute to the elegance of your outfit, and enhance your appearance by flattering your eyes and adding a glow to your skin tone and a radiance to your hair.

Since colour has a strong influence on everyday life, you should know a few facts about it before you begin. Then you can be your own watchdog. Simply explained, colour has three attributes: hue, shade and tint. Hue denotes the pure or 'true' colour, which may be described as red, yellow or blue, or intermediates between two of these, as orange, green and violet. If you add varying degrees of grey or black to the true colour, you get a shade or a colour value darker than the true colour; if you add varying degrees of white, you get a tint or a colour value lighter than the true colour. The colour wheel, Plate 21 opposite page 340, illustrates the principle, and the text on page 338 tells you many of the rules of colour.

Selecting the Right Colour

One season's fashions may be a splash of colour, another's may be subdued. Although it is easy to be carried away by a vivid, brilliant, or new shade, you should resist the temptation until you have satisfied yourself that the colour is right for you. Put personal preferences aside for a moment. Here are some tests you can apply in selecting a colour.

Is the colour becoming to you? It should compliment your skin tone, hair and eyes. Let your mirror be the judge. At the fabric counter, drape the fabric over one shoulder; study yourself in both natural and artificial light to see what the colour does for you. Or buy a package of assorted colours of tissue paper. Cut out a section to fit your neckline and try different colours against your face to decide which are the most becoming. Make a note of those colours in your sewing notebook, or on the colour bibs.

Is the colour flattering to your figure? Light, bright or vivid shades of almost any colour tend to make the figure appear larger or heavier; on the other hand, darker, subdued tones of the same colour have a slimming effect. This does not mean that if you are stocky or overweight, you must always choose dull colours. Rather, you should select fashion lines that minimise your figure.

Remember, too, that the little black dress is always in fashion and is a must in almost every woman's wardrobe. It can be worn all year round and changed or accented with colourful jewelry or a scarf.

Achieving Colour Harmony

Colour harmony is important to the attractiveness of your costume and the rules for achieving it are simple.

Of the many types of colour harmony, the best known is perhaps the monochromatic, which is the use of various shades and tints of one colour.

You can also obtain interesting effects by combining different textures, weaves and fibres of the same colour, but make sure that they look well together and are comparable in weight. Be cautious about mixing two prints, two checks or a print and check. Also make sure that your repetition of one colour does not produce a monotonous effect. If it does, try adding a slight or strong contrast.

Combining contrasting colours is another way of achieving a richness in your dress. Two colours may give a pleasing contrast; three or more may introduce complications that destroy the harmony you are seeking. A sharp contrast in colour is usually effective; however, use the strong, contrasting colour sparingly. Complementary colours lie opposite each other in the colour wheel, Plate 21. Combining two of these colours produces a striking effect with proper balance of colour, and a negative effect with improper balance.

These then, are the rules. But like all rules, fashion occasionally breaks them and combines clashing colours and prints. In this she is being true to her role of shocking the eye once in a while to jolt her followers into a new awareness of the beauty and possibilities of colour.

To use such shocks skilfully, however, first learn the rules. Then you are at liberty to break them just as the modern painter does when he splashes colour on a canvas, apparently heedless of line and form.

A WORD ABOUT ACCESSORIES AND COSMETICS

Accessories play a major role in colour harmony. Rather than have all your accessories of a contrasting colour, choose shoes and handbag to match, or hat and gloves to match, or hat, shoes and handbag to match. Vivid colours are often more dramatic when worn with conventional black accessories.

If a limited budget prevents you from having several sets of accessories, the wise thing is to choose a colour for your coat and accessories which will blend with the other colours you choose for dresses and suits. This basic colour will enable you to achieve colour harmony without exceeding your budget. It will also co-ordinate your wardrobe.

About cosmetics: train yourself to select them as carefully as the colours you wear, for they can upset an otherwise harmonious appearance. As skin tone and fashion colours change, so should make-up. Manufacturers of cosmetics keep pace with fashion colours; beauty consultants at cosmetic counters know how to match shades of cosmetics with skin tone and colours. Do not hesitate to seek their advice at regular intervals.

Always remember this: if you learn to use colour to your best advantage in every way, friends will compliment you and not the dress.

About Fabrics

You cannot sew successfully without a knowledge of fabrics, for fashion is found in fabrics as surely as it is found in pattern designs. Fabrics are available in a variety of weaves, textures and colours. Often they are so exciting that you must choose a simple pattern design that will not detract from them.

Unlike choosing a colour, however, choosing a fabric calls for more than your eye or common sense to guide you. You must know whether the fabric is suitable for your use, whether it is worth your expenditure of time and money, whether its upkeep is practical for your situation.

Without being too technical, this section will give you some fabric facts that will help you select the fabric best suited to your requirements.

Fibres

Fabric is made up of either *natural fibres* or *man-made fibres* that are spun into yarns and woven together on various types of looms. The natural fibres are *cotton, linen, silk* and *wool*. Cotton fibre is made from the cotton plant, linen fibre from the flax plant, silk fibre from the cocoon of the silkworm, and wool fibre from the fleece of sheep or lamb or the hair of certain goats or camels.

Man-made fibres are those synthetic or manufactured fibres that are produced through chemistry. Their list is long and, since new types appear on the market almost every year, never quite complete. The chart that follows gives the generic classification, the trade-mark name, and the manufacturer of some of the more familiar fibres or yarns. (The manufacturers listed produce only the basic fibres; they do not make the fabric containing these fibres.)

It is wise to make a note of the fibre content of the fabrics you buy and file it for future reference. You should know what special qualities or service you may expect from the fabric and whether it has any special finish. Look for this information on the label. It is important in the care and handling of the fabric, particularly in dry cleaning or washing and in pressing. Also, stitching techniques and the type of thread used depend to a large extent on the fabric – and the behaviour of the fabric depends on the fibres and the finish.

MAN-MADE FIBRES OR YARNS

(Synthetics)

Type	Trade-name	Manufacturer
Acrylic	Acrilan	Monsanto Textiles Ltd.
	Courtelle	Courtaulds Ltd.
	Orlon	Du Pont Co. (U.K.) Ltd.
Elastofibres	Spanzelle	Courtaulds Ltd.
	Lycra	Du Pont Co. (U.K.) Ltd.
Metallic Yarns	Lurex	Lurex Co. Ltd.
Modacrylic	Teklan	Courtaulds Ltd.
Nylon	Bri-nylon	I.C.I. Fibres
	Blue C nylon	Monsanto Textiles Ltd.
	Celon	Courtaulds Ltd.
	Enkalon	British Enkalon Ltd.
Olefin	Cournova	British Celanese Ltd.
	Courlene	
	Spunstran	I.C.I. Fibres

MAN-MADE FIBRES OR YARNS

(*Synthetics*)

Type	*Trade-name*	*Manufacturer*
Polyester	Crimplene Terylene	I.C.I. Fibres
	Diolen Terlenka	British Enkalon Ltd.
	Lirelle	Courtaulds Ltd.
	Trevira	Hoechst (U.K.) Ltd.
Rayon (Acetate)	Celafibre Celesta Dicel	British Celanese Ltd.
	Lansil	Lansil Ltd.
Rayon (Triacetate)	Tricel Tricelon	British Celanese Ltd.
Rayon (Viscose)	Evlan Darelle Sarille Vincel	Courtaulds Ltd.

Yarns

Next fibres are spun into yarns. Yarns may be made from short or 'staple' fibres or from long or 'filament' fibres and the construction may be simple or complex. One of the natural fibres or one of the man-made fibres may be used alone; or two or more fibres may be blended or mixed to give durability and beauty to the fabric or to facilitate the manufacturing process. The number and size of the fibres, the tightness of the twist, the roughness or smoothness of the yarn are some of the many factors that determine the characteristics of the fabric made from the yarn.

Processing techniques can be varied to produce novelty yarns such as bouclé, ratiné, slub, spiral or corkscrew, or looped, which are unusual in texture or appearance or both. Textured yarns may be formed from man-made fibres. Through certain processing techniques the filaments are coiled, crimped, curled, or looped. These yarns are called textured, bulk, or stretch yarns.

Woven Fabrics

Each fabric begins with the yarn threaded lengthwise on the weaving loom. Next, the filler yarn is woven crosswise, over and under the lengthwise threads. The lengthwise yarn is called the 'warp', and the crosswise or filler yarn is called the 'weft' (old term 'woof'). The extreme outside finished edges, which are parallel to the lengthwise yarns, are called 'selvedge'. These woven threads form the true lengthwise and crosswise grains of the fabric.

By varying the number of yarns on a loom, it is possible to produce many different weaves and achieve interesting textures and effects. It is often difficult to distinguish one man-made fibre from another or from the natural fibres because the weaves are so much alike. Rayon may look like silk, cotton may look like wool tweed. The weave of the fabric plays a greater part in determining the appearance of the final product than fibre or finish.

FAMILIAR TYPES OF WEAVES

Here is a description of the common types of weaves that you may be using in your sewing. These standard weaves can be varied to produce many interesting effects.
Plain weave. In this, the simplest and most common of all weaves, the horizontal threads (weft or filler) pass alternately over and under successive vertical threads (warp). Muslin and taffeta are examples. Variations are the basket weave and the rib weave.

Twill weave. This is more closely woven than a plain weave. In it, the warp and filler threads are interlaced to form a diagonal ridge or rib on the face of the fabric. Gaberdine is an example. Fancy designs can also be produced; the herringbone is a common variation.

Satin weave. Threads are interlaced at irregular intervals, with one set of threads floating over the opposite set of threads. The floats lie parallel to each other thus forming a smooth lustrous finish. Cotton sateen and damask are examples.

Leno weave. This is a porous, open-looking weave used to produce lightweight, gauzy fabrics – for example, marquisette.

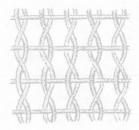

Jacquard weave. This is an intricate, figured weave made on a Jacquard loom. Examples are damasks, brocades and tapestries.

Dobby weave. This weave is produced by placing a dobby attachment on the loom. It is simpler and less expensive than the Jacquard weave and consists of small, geometric designs that are repeated frequently throughout the fabric.

Double-cloth weave. More than one set of warp and filler yarns are used in weaving to produce a fabric with two distinct faces – for example, double damask.

Pile weave. Three sets of yarns are interlaced in such a manner that the third set forms cut loops that stand up densely on the surface. Examples are velvet, velveteen, corduroy and plush. An exception is towelling, which has uncut loops, usually on both sides of the fabric.

Finishes

Many fabrics are given a 'finish' after they are woven to increase their body, to prevent shrinkage (sanforized) or wrinkling (crease-resistant), to impart crispness to the surface, or to make them drip-dry, water-repellent, stain-resistant or mothproof. It is unnecessary – and almost impossible to list the many finishes manufacturers are able to produce; however, they can be described as dull, shiny, stretch, rough, soft, smooth, coarse, fine, lustrous, hard, laminated or napped.

Napped fabrics (such as wool broadcloth, facecloth, doeskin and flannel) have hairlike fibres lying in one direction. This effect is achieved in the finishing process by a revolving brush that is used to raise the fibres of the cloth to the surface.

Stretch Fabrics

Stretch fabrics are woven fabrics that have been made to 'give' with the body and then recover their normal dimensions. Do not confuse them with knit fabrics.

Stretch characteristic can be given to classic fabrics such as denim, tweed, gaberdine, twill, corduroy, seersucker, batiste and broadcloth, as well as to many of the newer fabrics. It can also be given to all-cotton fabrics; to blends with natural fibres, rayon or acetate; or to all wool.

The amount of stretch a fabric will give varies; so do the processes of achieving stretch.

There are three kinds of stretch fabrics:

Lengthwise (warp) stretch, which is recommended for pants and slacks.

Crosswise (filling) stretch, which is used for blouses, shirts, jackets, coats, sport dresses, skirts and shorts.

Lengthwise and crosswise or two-way stretch, which is used mostly in swimsuits.

Some of the stretch fabrics are woven to look the same lengthwise as crosswise even though they stretch only in one direction. They can be used in any garment. Always examine the fabric carefully before buying it to be sure that the stretch goes in the direction you want. See page 218.

Stretch fabrics can be given drip-dry or water-repellent qualities.

Knit Fabrics

Knit fabrics are made of interlocking loops of yarn. The two types are warp and weft knits.

Warp knits, which are made on flat-bed machines, are generally tighter, flatter and less elastic than weft knits. In warp knitting, multiple yarns (all part of a single system of yarns) run vertically and parallel to each other. The fabric is constructed by manipulating all of these warp yarns at the same time into loops that are interconnected. Tricot and raschel are common types.

Weft knits, which are made on either circular or flat-bed knitting machines, are constructed in much the same way as hand knits, with one yarn at a time running in a horizontal direction. The most familiar types are jersey, rib knits, double knits and jacquards. See *The Many Faces of Knitted Fabrics*, page 417.

Blends and Combinations

Techniques of blending and combining fibres have revolutionised the fabric world and simplified in many ways the homemaker's life. Although most consumers apply the term 'blend' to any fabric containing more than one kind of fibre or yarn, there is a difference between blends and combinations. *Blended fabrics* are made of yarns in which two or more fibres have been mixed before spinning; the yarns may be used either as warp or filler or as both. *Combination fabrics* are made by combining different yarns, each of a single fibre, in the weaving process. In other words, the warp yarn may be of one fibre and the filler of another. Examples are silk/wool; silk/cotton/linen (two or more natural fibres); cotton/Dacron polyester (natural and man-made fibres); or Orlon acrylic/rayon/nylon (two or more man-made fibres).

11

Bonded and Laminated Fabrics

Like blends and combinations, the terms 'bonded' and 'laminated' are often used interchangeably by the shopper. And they are similar in one respect – both describe fabrics that are made of two layers.

In *bonded* fabrics, two layers of fabric are permanently joined either by an adhesive or by a thin layer of urethane foam, which is heat-set to form a bond.

Although almost any fabrics can be bonded, the most common bonds are of lining and face fabric. Acetate tricot seems to be favoured for the lining; the face fabric may be wool, synthetic, a blend of wool and man-made fibres, loopy tweed with a mohair look and knits. Bonding makes lace suitable for a tailored costume; the bonded lining adds stability to the fabric and prevents stretching.

Bonded fabrics are appropriate for dresses, coats, suits and sportswear. See page 220.

In *laminated* fabrics a backing of synthetic *foam* is bonded, or heat-set, to adhere permanently to a *face fabric*. Laminates have warmth without weight and require no interfacing; however, they should be lined to protect the foam backing. You will find laminated wool, jersey, cotton and synthetic fabrics that are appropriate for jackets, coats, sportswear, rainwear, children's wear and coat linings. Most of them can be washed or dry-cleaned. See page 221.

Non-woven Fabrics

Non-woven fabrics have no grain. They are made by pressing fibres together. Examples are felt, plastic film and Vilene interfacing.

Selecting Fabric

The judgment and taste you exercise in co-ordinating the fabric with the pattern can determine the success of your finished product. On the back of the pattern envelope you will find a list of fabrics appropriate for the design. This is a good guide if you are in doubt.

Suits and tailored dresses require firm fabrics with body. Dresses with shirring, draping or gathers require soft fabrics.

Remember too that a print, check or design should be in proportion to your figure. A small figure should not wear large stripes, checks or prints. A large figure may wear large prints; however, a large check will emphasize figure proportions. Narrow stripes will make the figure appear taller, broad stripes will make it appear shorter. Large prints and checks on the tall, thin figure will break the height.

The finish of the fabric also affects the appearance of your figure. For slimness, choose fabrics with a smooth dull finish. The bulk of heavy-weight or rough-finished fabrics makes the figure look larger. If handled with too much fullness, such fabrics may overpower a small figure and add weight to a full figure; simply handled they may be very flattering.

The following list will help you select suitable fabrics for various garments.

DAY AND TAILORED DRESSES

Jersey	Corduroy
Silk	Velveteen
Gingham	Linen
Broadcloth	Surah
Dotted Swiss	Barathea
Crêpe – Silk or Rayon	Shantung
Wool Crêpe	Cotton
Cotton Poplin	Honan
Raw Silk	Piqué
Heavy Sheers	Tie Silk
Cotton and Dacron	Faille
Blend	Double Knit

SOFT DRAPED DRESSES

Sheer Woollens	Chiffon
Soft Silk	Surah
Jersey	Lace
Voile	Velvet
Nylon	
Blends or Combinations of	
Natural and Synthetic Fibres	

SPORTSWEAR

Flannel	Velveteen
Denim	Gingham
Sailcloth	Seersucker
Cottons	Polished Cotton
Woollens	Stretch Fabrics
Corduroy	Bonded Fabrics
Blends or Combinations of	Madras Cotton
Natural and Synthetic Fibres	

COCKTAIL OR 'AFTER 6'

Suits	*Dresses*
Moiré	Taffeta
Peau de Soie	Brocade
Satin	Faille Taffeta
Taffeta	Peau de Soie
Ottoman	Heavy or Firm Lace
Brocade	Velvet
Velvet	Velveteen
Velveteen	Matelassé
Lurex	Lurex
Matelassé	Surah
Wild or Raw Silk	Chiffon
	Moiré

EVENING DRESSES

Lace	Peau de Soie
Chiffon	Dotted Swiss
Taffeta	Organdie
Velvet	Net
Velveteen	Brocade
Piqué	Lurex
Cottons	Surah
Sheers	Moiré
Silks	Satin

DRESSMAKER SUITS

Linen	Tussah
Faille	Heavy Cottons
Silk and Wool Blends or Combinations	Corduroy
Silk and Cotton Blends or Combinations	Face cloth
	Seersucker
Lightweight Wool	Double Knit

TAILORED SUITS

Woollens – Medium- or Heavy-weight	Ottoman
Tweed	Barathea
Wool Broadcloth	Wild or Raw Silk
Twill	Gaberdine
Flannel	Glen Checks
Linen	Tussah
Heavy Cottons	Worsted
Silk and Wool Blends or Combinations	Double Knit

COATS

Coating	Corduroy
Wool Broadcloth	Velveteen
Flannel	Suede Fabric
Camel Hair	Fur Fabric
Vicuna	Brocade
Cashmere	Jersey Coating
Silk Faille	Worsted
Ottoman	Tweed
Nubbed Wool	

Fabric Width

Fabric widths vary greatly, and before buying a fabric you should refer to the back of the pattern envelope to see what length you will need of the fabric width you have chosen.

Linens, velveteens and corduroys are 90 cm (36 inches) wide; cottons 90 cm (36 inches) wide; silks 84 cm (33 inches) wide; lightweight woven synthetics 115 cm (45 inches) wide; wools 138–154 cm (54–60 inches) wide; Jersey is usually a circular knit about 143 cm (56 inches) all round; double jersey is a flat knit usually 138 cm (54 inches) wide. Synthetic jersey can be 143 cm (56 inches), 173 cm (68 inches) or 183 cm (72 inches) wide. Interfacings range from 60 cm (24 inches) wide to 112 cm (44 inches) wide. Felts 90 cm (36 inches) to 183 cm (72 inches) wide. Imported fabrics can vary considerably in width.

Know the Right Side of the Fabric

Simple as it may seem, knowing the right side of the fabric can be tricky.

In satins and polished cottons, the lustrous face is on the right side; in pile and napped fabrics, the longer threads or pile is on the right side. Cottons and linens are usually folded right side out. The weave of many fabrics will help you identify the right side; so will the selvedge, which is smoother on the right side than on the wrong. Often you must examine the selvedge closely, however, to detect the 'smoother' side. Many cottons, checks and solid colours can be used on either side.

Grain Lines

In all your sewing you must consider the grain lines of the fabric because they have a direct influence on the way the garment fits and hangs.

The *lengthwise grain* of the fabric is the thread parallel to the selvedge and is known as the 'warp' thread in weaving. It is marked on all pattern sections and must be observed when laying and cutting any garment or article.

The *crosswise grain* is at a right angle to the lengthwise grain; it runs from selvedge to selvedge and is known as the 'weft' thread in weaving. In most fabrics there is some 'give' in the crosswise grain, but very little in the lengthwise grain.

The *true bias* of the fabric is the diagonal line formed by folding the lengthwise grain parallel to the crosswise grain. The maximum amount of 'give' in any fabric is found in the true bias.

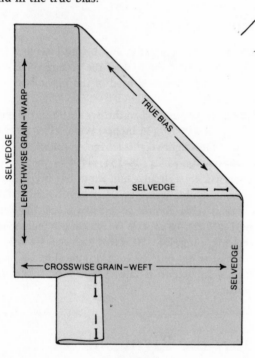

Preparing the Fabric for Cutting

Here you are concerned with three questions:
1. Are the fabric ends (crosswise grain) straight?
2. Does the lengthwise grain need straightening?
3. Has the fabric been shrunk?

STRAIGHTENING FABRIC GRAIN

In the manufacturing process – perhaps during finishing, printing or rolling – some fabrics are pulled 'off grain', and you must straighten them before cutting the gar-

ment so that the grain lines are correct; otherwise your garment will not fit and hang as it should.

To straighten the fabric ends, find the crosswise grain of the fabric as follows:
  – Snip through the selvedge edge with scissors.
  – With the fingers, grasp one thread that runs across the weave.
  – Pull it gently, allowing the fabric to gather on the thread.
  – Cut carefully along this pulled thread only as far as you can follow it clearly.
  – Grasp it again (or the one next to it) in your fingers and repeat the pulling and cutting until you have reached the other selvedge.

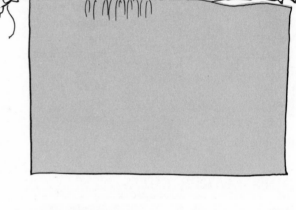

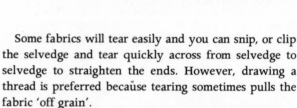

Some fabrics will tear easily and you can snip, or clip the selvedge and tear quickly across from selvedge to selvedge to straighten the ends. However, drawing a thread is preferred because tearing sometimes pulls the fabric 'off grain'.

To determine whether the fabric grain needs straightening, place the fabric on a flat surface and fold it with the selvedges together. Pin the edges together along the straightened end. If the fabric lies flat when the selvedges are together, the two grains are at a right angle and need no further attention. If not, the fabric must be straightened.

To straighten the fabric grain is simple:
  – First straighten the ends as explained above.
  – Then, gently pull the fabric on the true bias (as illustrated at the top of opposite page) and gradually work down the full length of the fabric.
  – Repeat along the length, if necessary.

Pressing with steam is helpful in straightening some fabrics; or you may have to dampen the fabric and then straighten it.

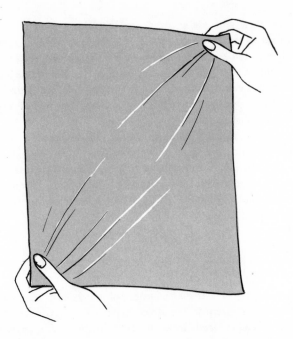

If a print or check is finished 'off grain', the design will not match at the seamline when the garment is cut on the true grain. Examine the fabric closely before making a purchase. If it is printed 'off grain', do not buy it.

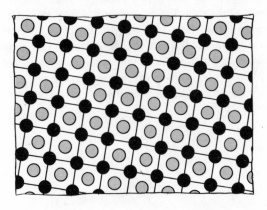

If dampening is necessary, proceed as follows:

On cotton and linens, use a damp sponge to moisten the fabric, then pull gently.

On woollens, place a wet sheet over the fabric and leave it long enough to moisten the wool (about two or three hours). Take care the fabric lies flat and that there are no creases in either the fabric or the sheet. Pull gently to straighten the fabric.

If fabrics such as chintz, polished cotton, and those with crease-resistant finish cannot be straightened because of their finish, square off the crosswise grain with a ruler. Place the fabric flat on a table with the selvedge parallel to the side of the table. Lay a ruler across the cut end of the fabric so that it forms a right angle with the selvedge, and draw a line with chalk from selvedge to selvedge; then cut on this line. Use only the lengthwise grain as a guide when cutting the garment. These fabrics are quite satisfactory as they will not lose their shape in wearing, hanging or pressing.

CHECKING THE FABRIC FOR SHRINKAGE

Most fabrics are pre-shrunk and information to that effect usually appears on the descriptive label or on the selvedge. Look for the labels 'pre-shrunk' or 'Sanforized'.

If one of them is used, it means that the fabric will not shrink more than 2·5 cm (1 inch) per 90 cm (1 yard); if you fail to find any information, ask the saleswoman. Fabrics that have not been pre-shrunk must be shrunk before cutting except wool crêpe and silk crêpe.

To shrink a fabric, snip or clip the edge every 5–7·5 cm (2–3 inches) along each selvedge. If the selvedge is not cut, it will draw up in the shrinking process.

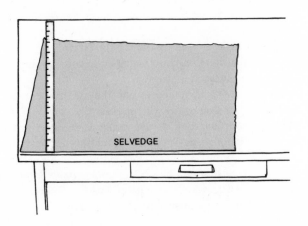

SELVEDGE

SELVEDGE

For *cottons*, *linens* and other *washable fabrics*, open the fabric its full width and form deep folds of about 46 cm (18 inches) on the crosswise grain. Place the fabric in the bathtub, cover it with lukewarm water, and leave it soaking for an hour. At the end of an hour, drain the water from the bath. Then press the water out of the fabric with your hands. (Do not wring or twist the fabric.) Hang the fabric lengthwise over the clotheshorse or line. Make sure that it is straight and smooth. Remove as much water as you can with a towel. Before the fabric is completely dry, press it on the wrong side. Glide the iron with the lengthwise grain. Press out the centre fold.

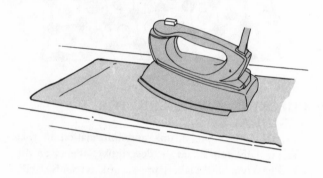

If you are uncertain about the necessity of shrinking washable fabrics, make a test: cut a swatch on the true lengthwise and crosswise grains and make a note of its length and width. Shrink the swatch as instructed above. After pressing, measure again. If the swatch is smaller than the original size, you will have to shrink the fabric.

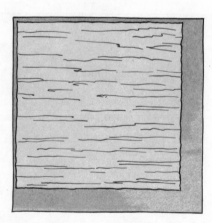

For *woollens*, fold the fabric lengthwise on the straight grain and place it between the folds of a wet sheet. Fold on the crosswise grain in deep folds. Avoid creases in the fabric and wet sheet. Cover the folded sheet with a towel so that the top section will not dry, and leave for eight or ten hours. Then remove the sheet and spread the fabric on a flat surface to dry. Be sure that the grains are straight. When dry, press on the wrong side with a press cloth or cheesecloth between the fabric and iron. Press out the centre fold.

(Woollens can also be shrunk by a dry cleaner if you can find one prepared to do it for you.)

Shrink *woven interfacings* that are not pre-shrunk as well as petersham for waistbands which will be used in washable garments. Follow the immersion method described above.

Interfacings

Interfacing is a third thickness of a carefully selected fabric that is cut in the same shape as the section interfaced and placed between the facing and garment section.

An interfacing adds body to the collars, cuffs, facings and peplums of dresses, blouses, suits and coats, and it adds strength to the areas around buttonholes and buttons. It is also used to mould and hold the shape in certain sections of the garment. It gives a professional look to anything that is well made.

Pattern envelopes usually include a separate pattern for the interfacing or instruct you to cut it the same as the garment section. Woven interfacing, which has a lengthwise and crosswise grain, must be cut with the same grain as the garment; non-woven interfacing has no grain and can be cut with the pattern laid in any direction.

Interfacing is available in a variety of textures and weights and should be selected with care. Consider the firmness and weight of the fabric to be interfaced as well as the style of the garment. Lay the interfacing between two layers of your fabric and manipulate the materials so that you can judge the final effect. Before buying interfacing make sure that:

    – It can be washed or dry-cleaned as the rest of the garment.

    – The weight is appropriate for the fabric.

    – The quality of the interfacing equals the quality of the garment fabric.

The following table shows you the variety of interfacing fabrics that are on the market. Use it as a guide only in shopping; you should examine the interfacing carefully before you buy, for several types may be correct for your garment, depending on the effect desired. Note that one fabric is missing from the list – that is self fabric, which is frequently used as interfacing, especially if the garment fabric is sheer.

16

FABRICS FOR INTERFACING

Fabric	Type	Description	Colours	Weight	Use	Care
Hair Canvas	Woven	Horse hair and cotton	Natural	Medium	Suits, medium-weight coats	Dry-clean only
Hair Canvas	Woven	Worsted	Natural	Medium	Suits and coats	Dry-clean only
Hair Canvas	Woven	Cotton, wool and fibro	Natural	Heavy	Coats	Dry-clean only
Hair Canvas	Woven	Cotton, wool and fibro	Natural	Medium	Suits and medium-weight coats	Dry-clean only
Linen Canvas	Woven	Linen	Black Natural White	Stiff	Coats	Dry-clean only
Linen Canvas	Woven	Linen	Black Natural White	Soft	Lightweight coats, suits	Dry-clean only
Holland	Woven	Linen	Black	Medium	Lightweight coats, suits	Dry-clean only
Sheer Canvas	Woven	Has true grain	Cream	Medium	Ties	Dry-clean only
Mull	Woven	Cotton	Black White	Light	Soft wool dresses	Dry-clean only
Victoria Lawn	Woven	Cotton (fine)	White	Light (stiff)	Cotton or linen suits, dresses	Wash or dry-clean
Lawn	Woven	Cotton	All colours	Light	Soft, lightweight dresses and blouses	Washable
Batiste	Woven	Cotton (very fine)	All colours	Light (soft)	Silk, cotton, linen dresses and blouses	Washable

(Continued)   17

Fabric	Type	Description	Colours	Weight	Use	Care
Sanforized cotton	Woven	Pre-shrunk	White	Light (stiff)	Linen or cotton dresses	Washable
Permastiff cotton	Woven	Coarse weave	White	Medium	Linen, heavy cottons	Washable
Colinta cotton	Woven	Permanent finish	White	Light (stiff)	Shirt collars and and cuffs	Washable
Rayon Canvas	Woven	Stiffened spun	Black White	Light (stiff)	Lightweight suits and coats	Washable
Leno Muslin	Woven	Very coarse	Black White	Medium (stiff)	Millinery and fancy dress	Dry-clean
Organdie	Woven	Cotton	White	Light	Cotton dresses and blouses	Washable
Organza	Woven	Silk	All colours	Very light	Silks, chiffons, all sheer fabrics	Dry-clean
Marquisette	Woven	Nylon mesh	White	Light	To add body to delicate fabrics	Washable
Moyceel	Woven	Iron-on cotton	Black White Natural	Light	Small areas only	Washable
Book Muslin	Woven	Coarse	Black White	Medium (stiff)	Handicrafts	Dry-clean
Tarlatan	Woven	Coarse	Various	Light (stiff)	Fancy dress	Cannot be washed or dry-cleaned
Buckram	Woven	Very coarse	Natural	Very heavy	Pelmets, handi-crafts, etc.	Cannot be washed or dry-cleaned

Fabric	Type	Description	Colours	Weight	Use	Care
Vilene A40	Non-woven	Has no grain line	White	Light	Cotton and rayon dresses	All Vilene: washable and dry-cleanable, so can be used with any fabric if correct quality is used
Vilene A50	Non-woven	Has no grain line	White	Medium	General purpose	
Vilene S50	Non-woven	Has no grain line	Black	Medium	General purpose	
Vilene A65	Non-woven	Has no grain line	White	Medium	Satins, tweeds and brocades	
Vilene A80	Non-woven	Has no grain line	White	Heavy	For heavy satin and brocade	
Vilene F2	Non-woven	Iron-on, has no grain line	White	Light	For soft finish small areas only	
Vilene F3	Non-woven	Iron-on has no grain line	White	Light	For crisp finish small areas only	
Vilene O34	Non-woven	Has no grain line	White	Very light	For voile, silk taffeta	
Vilene O32	Non-woven	Has no grain line	White	Light	Light woollens and jersey	
Vilene 244	Non-woven	Terylene, no grain line	White	Light	General purpose synthetics	
Vilene 255	Non-woven	Terylene, no grain line	White	Medium	Coats	
Vilene 237	Non-woven	Has no grain line	Cream	Heavy	Pelmets, home furnishings	

Mounting and Lining

Mounting and lining are a second thickness of fabric that supports the garment fabric and gives it extra resistance to strain. Both help to hold the shape of dresses, suits, coats, shorts and at-home wear. *Mounting and Lining*, beginning on page 95, describes how to mount or line dresses of various styles and fabrics.

Mounting and lining should be selected with care. The fibre content need not be the same as that in the dress fabric, except in sheer fabrics; however, the colours should match.

Fabrics that are appropriate for mounting and lining – or are made expressly for them – are: silk organza, Jap silk, taffeta (silk, nylon or rayon), batiste, voile, peau de soie, silk crêpe, Bemberg, all of which are available in colours. Bemburg resembles Jap silk but is less expensive. Nylon tricot can be used for jersey fabrics to keep a fluid line.

The table below suggests types of fabrics that can be used for mounting and lining different dress and suit fabrics.

DRESS OR SUIT FABRICS	SUGGESTED MOUNTING AND LINING FABRICS
Soft silks and lightweight rayons to be dry-cleaned	Silk organza, Jap silk, Bemberg – all available in colours.
Heavy- and medium-weight silks, wools and rayons	Silk organza, Jap silk, Bemberg, taffeta – all available in colours.
Cottons to be dry-cleaned	Batiste, voile, Jap silk, organza – all available in colours. (Shrink batiste and voile.)
Sheer wools and chiffons	Taffeta, peau de soie, silk crêpe, satin – all available in colours.
Lightweight wools	Jap silk, organza, Bemberg – all available in colours.
Jersey and loosely woven fabrics	Jap silk, Bemberg, nylon tricot, voile, batiste – all available in colours. (Shrink batiste and voile.) If skirt is full use taffeta.
Wool suit skirts	Jap silk, taffeta, Bemberg, crêpe with which jacket is lined – all available in colours.
Linens to be dry-cleaned	Voile, batiste, lawn, Jap silk or Bemberg – all available in colours. (Shrink voile and batiste.)
Lace	Taffeta, satin, peau de soie, lawn, silk organza, net, marquisette, chiffon – all available in colours.

Some of the fabrics suggested for interfacing are also used for mounting and lining, particularly for gored and circular skirts and suits and coats that are bouffant – for example, hair canvas, Vilene, Victoria lawn, Mullo.

Beginning to Sew

If you are a novice dressmaker, you may sometimes think that your sewing machine was built only to outwit you. But be patient. This carefully constructed piece of equipment requires some understanding. Those of you who have been sewing for a while know that if you take a little time to master your machine, you will have a versatile and willing partner in creativity.

Getting to Know Your Machine

The operation of any sewing machine is simple if you understand the function of the principal parts and know how to thread the machine and regulate the three elementary controls: tension, pressure and stitch length.

Your instruction book contains information on these essential points. Do not hesitate to refer to it frequently.

The principal parts of a *Touch & Sew** sewing machine by Singer are illustrated below. Although your machine may be of a different model or make, it has many features in common with all machines, and the explanations that follow will be applicable to it.

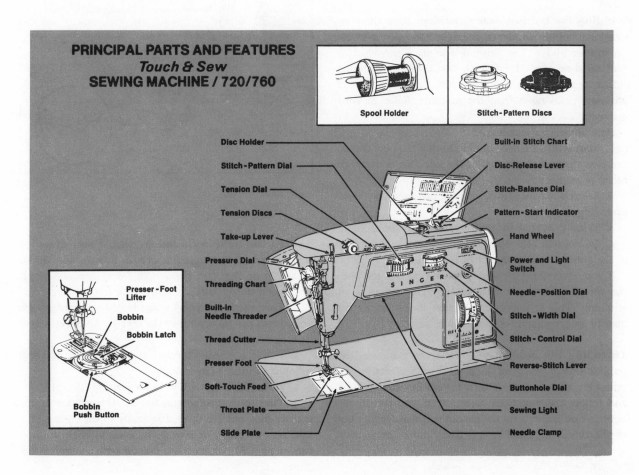

PRINCIPAL PARTS AND FEATURES
Touch & Sew
SEWING MACHINE / 720/760

Spool Holder

Stitch-Pattern Discs

Disc Holder

Stitch-Pattern Dial

Tension Dial

Tension Discs

Take-up Lever

Pressure Dial

Threading Chart

Built-in Needle Threader

Thread Cutter

Presser Foot

Soft-Touch Feed

Throat Plate

Slide Plate

Built-in Stitch Chart

Disc-Release Lever

Stitch-Balance Dial

Pattern-Start Indicator

Hand Wheel

Power and Light Switch

Needle-Position Dial

Stitch-Width Dial

Stitch-Control Dial

Reverse-Stitch Lever

Buttonhole Dial

Sewing Light

Needle Clamp

Presser-Foot Lifter

Bobbin

Bobbin Latch

Bobbin Push Button

Threading the Machine

In threading the machine, you are concerned with four operations: (1) winding the bobbin, (2) threading the bobbin case, (3) threading the needle (or upper threading), and (4) raising the bobbin thread. Always follow the diagram shown in the instruction book given with your machine.

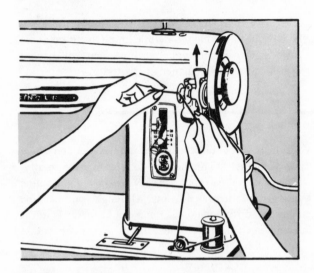

Winding the bobbin. Many machines have the conventional bobbin winder on the right-hand side as in the illustration above. The *Touch & Sew* machine, which is illustrated on page 21, has push-button bobbin winding – that is, you wind the bobbin with the needle thread without removing it from the machine. Refer to your instruction book.

Here are the basic rules:

1. Start with an empty bobbin so that the new thread can pass through the eyelet on the side. *Never wind one colour over another.*

2. Select a thread identical to the one used for upper threading.

3. Wind it evenly in level layers across the bobbin.

4. Do not wind the bobbin so full that it will be tight in the bobbin case; it should fit in easily.

If you observe these rules, you will find that the bobbin thread will feed evenly to the very end of your stitching. This is important because it influences the quality and regularity of your stitch.

Threading the bobbin case. On some machines the bobbin thread leads off in a clockwise direction; in others it is anti-clockwise. Refer to your instruction book and follow the directions carefully. If you thread the bobbin case incorrectly the thread will usually slip out of the threading notches and from under the tension spring.

Threading the needle. Upper threading is simple if you follow this sequence:

1. Raise the take-up lever to its highest point.

2. Lead the thread from the spool pin through the threading points as shown in diagram – (1) thread guide, (2) needle-thread tension discs, (3) thread guide, (4) take-up lever, (5) thread guides and (6) needle. The direction for threading the needle varies. Some machines are threaded from left to right, others from right to left, and others from front to back.

3. Draw enough thread through the eye of the needle to start sewing.

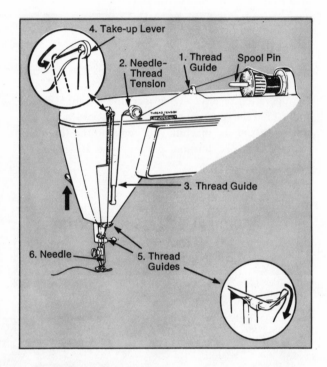

Raising the bobbin thread. You must now draw the bobbin thread through the needle hole in the throat plate. To do that (*see sketches at top of opposite page*):

1. Hold needle thread lightly with left hand.

2. Turn the hand wheel towards you until the needle goes down and up again and the take-up lever returns to its highest point.

3. Pull the needle thread; the bobbin thread will follow and form a large loop.

4. Undo the loop with your finger.

5. Place both needle and bobbin threads under the presser foot and lay them diagonally to the right.

You are now ready to sew. If you want to begin at once, turn to page 27, which starts you off with a simple seam.

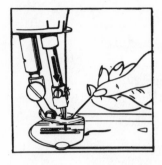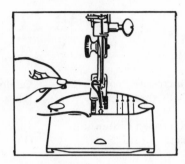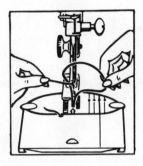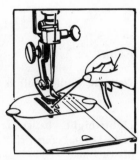

Regulating Stitch Length

The length of your stitch depends on the weight and texture of the fabric you are sewing as well as the type of sewing you are doing. Make it a habit to test the stitch length on a scrap of the fabric.

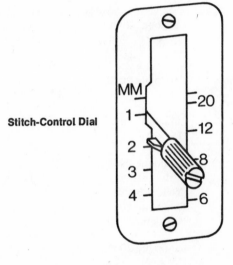

Stitch-Control Dial

Delicate fabrics require a *short, fine stitch.*

Heavy fabrics require a *long, heavy stitch.*

For top stitching, the stitch length should be shorter than inside stitching when fine thread is used, longer when heavy thread is used.

Curved seams require a shorter stitch than that used for straight stitching. If you are using a 2 mm (12) stitch length for straight stitching, you will need a 1·5 mm (15) stitch for curves to give the seams greater elasticity and strength.

Bias and *semi-bias cut seams* also require a short stitch since they must have more elasticity than seams following the lengthwise or crosswise grain of the fabric.

Scallops require a shorter stitch than curves to maintain a smooth rounded contour and close layering of seams.

Bound buttonholes and *pockets* are made with a short stitch to ensure strength and durability – generally a 1·5 to 1 mm (20) stitch length.

When stitching is used to *control fullness* at the sleeve head, at the elbow of long sleeves, at the top of a hem, or at a point where one seam edge is eased to another, a slightly longer stitch is required than the one used for straight stitching.

The three types of *temporary stitching* require different stitch lengths. For regular machine tacking, use a 4 to 3 mm (6 to 8) stitch length. For chain stitching, which is available on some sewing machines, use a 2·5 to 2 mm (10 to 12) stitch length. For speed tacking, which is also available on some models, you have a wide choice. You can choose any length from 6 to 'fine' and produce a tacking stitch up to 5 cm (2 inches) long.

In some *zig-zag sewing,* such as decorative satin stitching and buttonholes, use a 'fine' stitch setting. For other zig-zag sewing, use longer stitches.

If you compare different grades of clothing, you will notice that good quality garments are stitched with a short stitch and appropriate weights and types of thread, and that less expensive clothing is stitched with a longer stitch and weaker thread.

To determine the stitch length appropriate for your fabric, test the stitch on a scrap of fabric.

For directions on setting the stitch length selector on your machine, check your machine instruction book as well as the diagram shown here. A stitch length selector that is clearly marked is easy to set.

Selecting the Thread

The rules that guide thread selection are easy to observe:

Select a thread two shades darker than the fabric. Since thread on the spool appears to be darker than it actually is, draw a strand over the fabric to make sure you have the right colour.

Select the proper thread for your fabric. There are two types of general-purpose thread: mercerised cotton and spun polyester. When fine thread is appropriate choose silk, nylon twist or fine spun polyester for lingerie.

When stitched, the thread must set into the weave of the fabric. A thread that is too heavy will remain on the surface and give shorter service and less strength than a fine thread that imbeds itself in the texture of the fabric.

Consult the chart on page 24 for further suggestions on thread selection.

FABRIC, THREAD AND NEEDLE CHART†

FABRIC	THREAD	NEEDLES	
		TYPE	SIZE
Delicate – tulle, chiffon, fine lace, organza	Fine mercerised cotton, fine synthetic thread, silk	Catalogue 2020 (15 × 1)	9††
Lightweight – batiste, organdie, jersey, voile, taffeta, crêpe, chiffon, velvet, plastic film	50 mercerised cotton, silk, synthetic thread	Catalogue 2020 (15 × 1)	11
Medium-weight – gingham, percale, piqué, linen, chintz, faille, satin, fine corduroy, velvet, suiting, knits, deep-pile fabrics, vinyl	50 mercerised cotton, 60 cotton, silk, synthetic thread	Catalogue 2020 (15 × 1)	14
Medium-heavy – gaberdine, tweed, sailcloth, denim, coatings, furnishing fabrics, vinyl, deep-pile fabrics	Heavy-duty mercerised cotton, 40–60 cotton, synthetic thread	Catalogue 2020 (15 × 1)	16
Heavy – overcoatings, dungaree, upholstery fabrics, canvas	Heavy-duty mercerised cotton, 24–40 cotton, synthetic thread	Catalogue 2020 (15 × 1)	18
All weights – decorative top stitching	Silk or polyester buttonhole twist, boldstitch	Catalogue 2020 (15 × 1)	16 †††
All weights – decorative hemstitching	50 mercerised cotton, silk, synthetic thread	Catalogue 2020 (15 × 1)	18
Synthetic knits and stretch fabrics – polyester double knit, nylon tricot, jersey, ciré tricot, panné velvet	Nylon, 50 mercerised cotton, silk	Catalogue 2045 Perfect stitch (Yellow Band)	14
		Catalogue 2021 Ball Point	11
Leather – suede, kidskin, capeskin, lambskin, lined leathers	36 mercerised cotton, synthetic thread, silk	Catalogue 2032 (15 × 2)	11 14 16
Light- and medium-weights – decorative twin-needle stitching	50 mercerised cotton	Catalogue 2028 (twin)	14

† does not apply to chainstitching.
†† Size 9 needle recommended for sewing only. For bobbin winding, use larger size needle.

††† Use with 50 mercerised cotton or silk in bobbin.

Selecting the Sewing Machine Needle

In selecting the needle, remember that: (1) You must consider both the thread and the fabric. (2) The eye of the needle must be large enough for the thread to pass through freely; a needle too fine for the thread will cause the thread to fray. (3) The needle blade must be fine enough to enter the fabric without spoiling it with a large puncture, yet heavy enough to pierce the fabric without being bent or deflected. (4) A needle too fine for the fabric may break.

Regular, general-purpose needles are available in sizes 9, 11, 14, 16 and 18. Ball-point needles, which separate the yarns rather than piercing them when penetrating the fabric, are recommended for knitted fabrics, see pages 421–422 for further information. A special wedge-point needle is available for sewing real and fake leather fabric.

Always have a supply of all sizes on hand to meet your

needs. A bent needle causes the fabric to draw to one side, feeding in a curve rather than a straight line. A blunt needle can cause snags in the fabric.

Also take care to position the needle properly in the needle clamp. If you do not, your machine will skip stitches or not stitch at all.

Refer again to the chart for further information on needle selection.

Regulating the Pressure

Pressure is the force the presser foot exerts on the fabric when it is being stitched. Pressure is important because it influences the straightness of your seams, the uniformity of stitch length, and the even handling of both layers of fabric. The pressure should be heavy enough to prevent side creeping and light enough to carry the fabric without marking it. *Too light a pressure* will cause irregular feeding, which affects the quality of the stitch and evenness of seams. *Too heavy a pressure* will affect the stitch length and seam quality and mar a smooth surface or pile fabric.

Regulate the pressure according to the fabric. Generally, heavy fabrics require heavy pressure; medium-weight fabrics require pressure midway between light and heavy; and lightweight fabrics require light pressure. Surface finish and texture must also be considered; soft fabrics, for example, require less pressure than crisp. **To test for pressure,** take two layers of fabric cut on the lengthwise grain and stitch without thread. If all seam edges are handled evenly, the pressure is correct; if they are not, turn the pressure dial or thumb screw until they are and until the fabric moves easily under the presser foot without showing feed marks.

To decrease pressure, turn the thumb screw anti-clockwise.

To increase pressure, turn the thumb screw clockwise.

If you have a Singer machine with a pressure dial inside:

To decrease pressure, turn the dial to a lower number.

To increase pressure, turn the dial to a higher number.

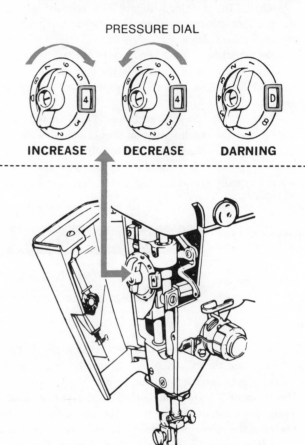

PRESSURE DIAL

INCREASE   DECREASE   DARNING

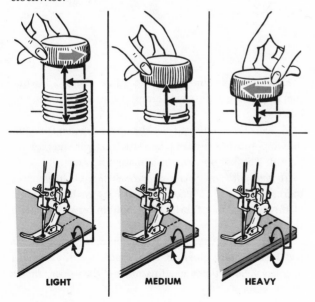

LIGHT   MEDIUM   HEAVY

Regulating the Tension

Tension controls the threads as they interlock to form a stitch on the sewing machine. There are two tensions – the upper, which controls the needle thread, and the lower, which controls the thread from the bobbin case or shuttle. A perfectly locked stitch can be formed only when the two tensions are in balance and the two threads are drawn into the fabric to the same degree. The tensions should be heavy enough to pull the threads to the centre of the fabric and form a good stitch.

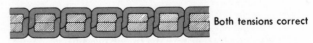

Both tensions correct

To determine whether your tension adjustment is correct, test the stitch on a scrap of your fabric with the needle and thread you are going to use. You will find that a seam stitched with balanced tensions is twice as strong as one stitched with unbalanced tensions. Test this for yourself by making the following *strength-of-seam test:*

– Use a size 14 needle.

– Thread the machine with size 50 mercerised thread, using a light colour for the upper threading and another colour for the bobbin.

– Set a stitch length at 2·5 or 2mm (10 or 12).

– On a square of fine muslin or the equivalent, stitch on the bias and on both the lengthwise and crosswise grains.

– Inspect the lines of stitching. They should not pucker and the stitch formation should appear well set on the top and underside of the muslin. If the lines of stitching pucker, you are likely to find also that they are not equally set on the top and underside and look like this:

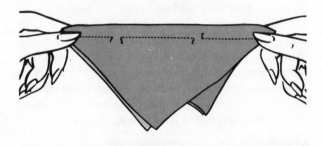

Loose upper tension
Tight lower tension

Tight upper tension
Loose lower tension

– *To determine whether the upper tension is too tight or too loose,* use the following test. Grasp the bias line of stitching between the thumb and index finger. Space the hands about 7·5 cm (3 inches) apart and pull with an even, quick force until one thread breaks. If the broken thread is the colour of the needle thread, you know that the upper tension is too tight. If the broken thread is the colour of the bobbin thread, you know that the upper tension is too loose. If both threads break together and require more force to break, you know the tensions are balanced.

To decrease tension, turn the thumb nut anti-clockwise. Each lower number denotes less tension.

To increase tension, turn the thumb nut clockwise. Each higher number denotes increased tension.

TENSION DIAL

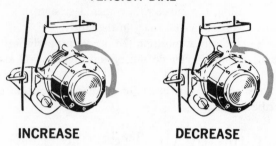

INCREASE   DECREASE

– Repeat the test until both threads break together.

Bobbin-thread tension. The tension on the bobbin thread is regulated by the small screw on the bobbin case or shuttle. It is seldom necessary for you to change it since you can usually obtain a balanced stitch by varying the tension on the needle thread.

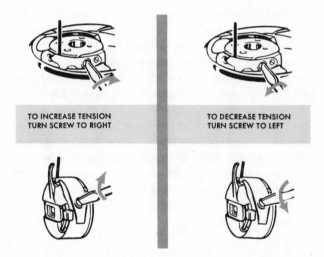

TO INCREASE TENSION TURN SCREW TO RIGHT   TO DECREASE TENSION TURN SCREW TO LEFT

Here are some simple rules to guide you in adjusting the upper tension for different types of threads and fabrics:

To sew with silk thread. Set the upper tension from one to two points lower than when stitching with mercerised thread. The bobbin tension remains the same.

To sew with heavy cotton or linen thread. In general, increase the upper tension when sewing with this weight of thread on dense fabrics. The bobbin tension remains the same.

To sew with certain sewing machine accessories. Follow the instructions given in this book for the specific accessory. Sometimes an adjustment of the upper tension is necessary.

To sew on zig-zag machines. Loosen the upper tension when doing decorative, closely spaced satin stitches. Wide, closed stitching requires a lighter needle-thread tension than narrow stitching. See page 266.

To stitch special fabrics. Nylons, dense fabrics, polished cottons, some resin-treated drip-dry fabrics, and others of similar close weave usually require tension adjustment. Always test your stitch on a scrap of your fabric.

Your First Steps in Sewing

Your machine is threaded and ready to go. If this is your first venture into serious, creative sewing, you should allow yourself a period of practice before you try a pattern.

First, familiarise yourself with simple stitching. Work carefully and correctly from the start. The good habits you form now will make all your later work easier and more professional-looking. Proof of your efficient handling of the sewing machine will be found not only in an evenly controlled acceleration of the machine and a perfectly formed and positioned first stitch in a seam, but in the exact assembling of seams, collars, facings and pockets, and a competence in all the intricate details of sewing.

Begin your practice period with the 'exercises' described here.

Posture and Speed Control

Correct posture at the machine enables you to work comfortably and well. Follow these rules:

1. Sit back on the chair or stool squarely in front of the needle. Do not lean against the chair back; instead, bring your body forward slightly.

2. Place both feet flat on the floor, with one foot forward. If your machine has a knee control, place the left foot forward and press the right knee against the control. If your machine has a foot control, place the right foot forward and press on the control.

3. Position the bulk of the fabric to the left of the needle and the seam edge to the right.

4. Place the left hand lightly on top of the fabric so that your fingers can control it. Make sure that the weight of your left arm is not resting on the fabric since this will cause uneven feeding.

5. Place the right hand about 10 cm (4 inches) in front of the needle so that your fingers can guide the edge.

6. Gradually press on the foot or knee control until you reach a slow, even speed. Never try to sew too fast. Skilful machine operation depends on your ability to

sew easily, rhythmically. You can work up to a high speed later when you are stitching long, straight seams.

How to Start and End a Seam

To start and end a seam, take these steps in sequence:

1. Raise the take-up lever to its highest point by turning the hand wheel towards you.

2. Place both needle and bobbin threads under the presser foot and lay them diagonally to the right.

3. Place the fabric under the presser foot with the bulk of the fabric to the left and the seam edge to the right.

4. Lower the needle into the fabric where the first stitch is to begin. Hold the thread ends and lower the presser foot.

5. Stitch with a slow, rhythmic speed.

6. When you reach the end of the seam, turn the hand wheel to raise the take-up lever to its highest point.

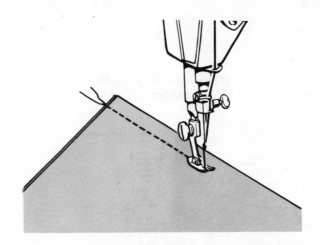

7. Raise the presser foot and removed the fabric by drawing it to the back and left.

8. Snip the thread ends on the thread cutter.

The Seam Guide and throat plate guidelines will help you keep the stitching parallel to the seam edge. See page 81.

How to Reinforce a Seam with Backstitching

Follow the procedure described on previous page. At step 4, lower the needle into the fabric about 1·2 cm (½ inch) from the seam end and back-stitch to the end of the fabric. Then stitch forward to end of the seam and finish with backstitching to reinforce the end.

How to Guide and Support the Fabric

Most fabrics need to be guided only in front of the presser foot. Exceptions are fabrics of unusual texture and weave, filmy sheers, crêpes, knits, tricots and the

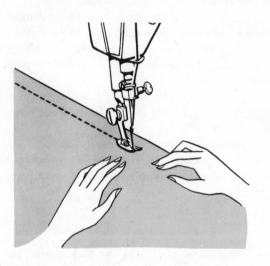

like. For them, gently apply tension to the seam by holding the fabric in front and in back of the presser foot as

illustrated at bottom of previous column. Never pull the fabric when sewing. If you are sewing fabric of unusual texture on a zig-zag machine, use the straight-stitch throat plate and presser foot for close control.

How to Pivot

You need to 'pivot' when stitching corners on collars, lapels, shaped necklines, bound buttonholes and pockets. Here is what you do:

1. Stitch to the intersecting seamline at the corner.
2. With the needle in the fabric, turn the hand wheel forward to bring the needle to its upward stroke. Just before the needle leaves the fabric, raise the presser foot and turn the fabric, pivoting on the needle.
3. Lower the presser foot and stitch.
4. To avoid bulk at the point of a collar or lapel, take from one to three stitches diagonally between the intersecting lines of stitching. See page 91. Practise pivoting a few times. You will find that it is easy.

How to Stitch Curved Seams

Curved seams should be stitched slowly. To guide the fabric on small curves, such as scallops, stop the machine with the needle in the fabric, lift the presser foot slightly, and turn the fabric just enough to follow the seamline.

Practise stitching and guiding straight seams, curved seams and corners until you have mastered them.

The chapter beginning on page 81 tells you how to make many different kinds of seams.

Basic Techniques for Hand Sewing

Some hand sewing is required in almost all the work you will be doing. If you already know how to sew by hand, check yourself against the guides given here. You may find some suggestions which will improve your technique.

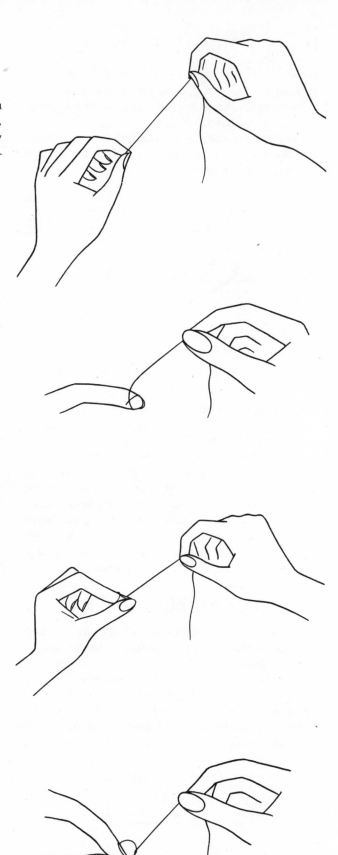

Threading the Hand Needle

1. With sharp scissors, cut the thread end on an angle. Avoid breaking, biting or tearing the thread, for then you will have trouble threading it through the needle eye.

2. Hold the needle in the left hand and the thread end tightly in the right hand between the thumb and index finger. Then pass the thread through the needle eye, and with the same motion, transfer the needle into the grip of the right thumb and index finger. With the left hand, draw the thread end from the eye about halfway down the remaining supply of thread.

3. Always sew with a short thread. For finishing stitches, use less than a 60-cm (24-inch) length; for tacking, use a slightly longer thread. A thread that is too long will tangle and weaken from being pulled through the fabric repeatedly; also, it requires tiring arm motions to draw each stitch in place. With the exception of sewing on buttons, press-fasteners and hooks and eyes, you will seldom need to use a double thread in hand sewing. Some prefer a single thread for all operations.

Tying a Knot

To prevent the longer thread end from pulling through at the beginning of tacking, form a secure knot as follows (*shown in sketches*):

1. Hold the thread end between the thumb and first finger of the left hand.

2. Use the right hand to bring the thread over and around the finger tip of the left hand, crossing it over the thread end.

3. Hold the longer thread taut while pushing the thumb towards the finger tip. This causes the thread to roll around the loop.

4. Slip the loop off the finger tip and at the same time pull against the longer thread held in the right hand to set the knot.

Using a Thimble

Do not allow yourself to develop the habit of sewing without a thimble. A thimble will prevent your finger from being roughened and sore, and will enable you to sew better and faster.

Thimbles are available in sizes 0 to 6 in both metal and plastic. It is easy to select an inexpensive one that fits your finger snugly.

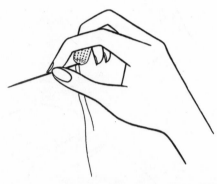

The thimble is worn on the second finger of the right hand and is used to direct and force the needle through the fabric. At first it may seem to be awkward and uncomfortable. If so, make hand stitches on a heavy, dense fabric such as drill cloth. You immediately will feel the need for the protection a thimble gives. If you continue to find sewing with a thimble awkward, make sure you are using a needle of correct length for the work you are doing. In general, use a long needle for long stitches or running stitches and a short needle for short, single stitches. Check the description of needles on page 2 to determine the best size and style for your work.

Fastening Stitches

The fastening stitch is used at the end of a line of tacking to hold the stitches in place. To fasten a line of tacking, take one short backstitch. This is easy to remove when the permanent stitching has been completed.

To fasten a line of fine hand stitching, bring the needle through to the underside. Take one backstitch, catching only a single thread in the fabric; pull the needle through, leaving a small loop in the thread. Take another

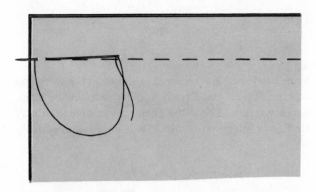

small backstitch, then pass the needle through the thread loop of the first stitch and set the knot close to the fabric. Repeat if greater security is needed.

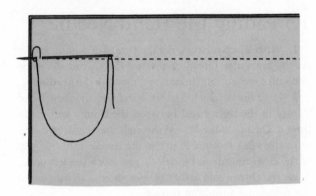

Removing Kinks and Twists

The simple process of pulling thread through fabric often causes the remaining supply of thread to twist. Some threads twist more readily than others – for example, buttonhole twist. And some hand sewing operations, such as fine over-sewing, tend to cause greater twisting and kinking than straight running stitches.

To remove the excessive twist without unthreading the needle, merely hold the thread end in the left hand while sliding the needle down against the fabric. Then without holding the thread end, slide the needle upward on the thread to a sewing position. This motion pushes the extra twist to the end of the thread and the remaining work can be completed without troublesome knotting and kinking.

Pattern Preliminaries

Buying the right pattern is a challenge, for it requires that you reconcile the often conflicting demands of fashion, figure, practicability and purse. Selecting the correct size may pose a problem too, especially if you are buying a pattern for the first time.

Read carefully the suggestions given here. They offer practical guides to keep you out of trouble.

Selecting a Pattern Style

Whatever you make should reflect current style and fashion. With that in mind:

Study the fashions in magazines, newspapers and shop windows as well as in the pattern catalogues. Choose a pattern from the latest fashions *but do not follow fashion blindly*. The extremes in high fashion are to focus your attention but are quickly out-dated.

Look for lines and styles that dramatise your best points. Do not be misled by an attractive style modelled by a 20-year-old if you are twice that age, or by a style that emphasises all the wrong proportions of your figure. Remember that vertical lines give an illusion of tallness, a full skirt draws attention to large hips, a bloused bodice makes a full bust look larger and a 'V' neckline makes a pointed chin more pronounced.

Consider suitability and purpose. Can the garment be worn all the year round? Will it be fashionable for more than one season? Will it require special accessories? Does it suit the occasion?

If you already have the fabric, be careful to choose a pattern that suits its texture and weight.

Determining the Correct Pattern Size

Clothes that look well, fit well. And proper fit begins with the selection of the correct pattern size. To determine that, take body measurements accurately. Wear a good foundation garment, the lingerie you normally wear, and the same style of shoes you will wear with the finished garment.

Taking Your Measurements

Measurements must be taken with the correct position of these seams in mind:

The *shoulder seam* begins at the neckline, 2·5 cm (1 inch) behind the earlobe, and extends across the top of the shoulder to the arm joint.

Side seams are perpendicular to the floor, hanging straight from underarm to lower edge. Locating this seam is known as 'forming a plumb line' from the underarm.

The natural armhole seam falls straight down from the arm joint for 6 to 7·5 cm (2½ to 3 inches), depending on size, then curves under the arm about 2·5 cm (1 inch) below the armpit.

The natural neckline or beadline hugs the base of the neck closely, crossing just above the pit of the throat and the prominent vertebra at the back of the neck.

The waistline is the smallest part of the torso. To find it easily when taking your measurements, pin a ·6-cm (¼-inch) tape or elastic around your waist before you start. Always measure *to* the lower edge of tape for bodice length and *from* the lower edge for skirt length.

The bustline measurement is taken across the fullest part of the bust and from the back, with the tape very slightly raised.

The bodice length is measured from the shoulder seam at the neckline, over the fullest part of the bust, to the waistline.

The hipline measurement is taken over the fullest part of the hips and from the front. If the distance from waistline to hipline (measure at side seam) varies from the standard 18 cm (7 inches), show the correct figure on your measurement chart.

Recording Your Measurements

The illustrations below show you exactly where to take the measurement for each part of your body. *Measure from the right side, unless otherwise indicated,* and enter each measurement in the space provided on the Measurement Chart. As your figure changes with time, correct the recorded measurements.

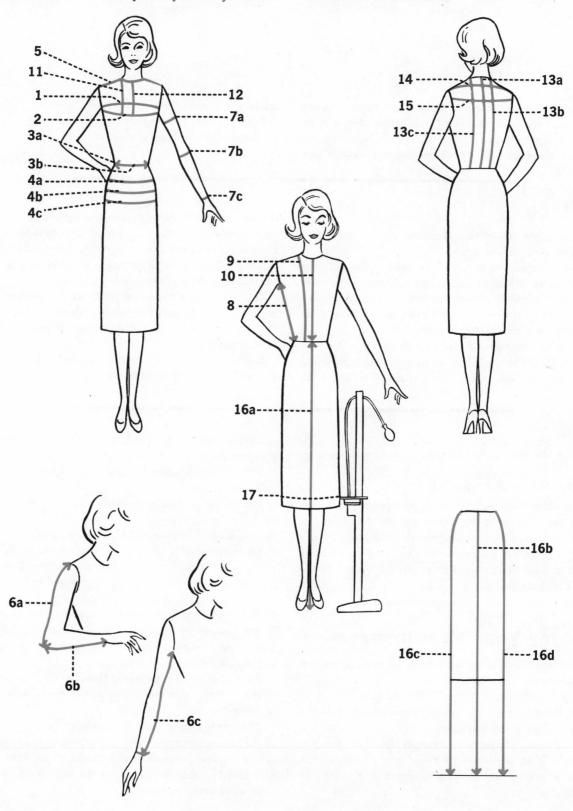

MEASUREMENT CHART

	Your Own Measurement (cm) (inches)	Usual Allowance for Ease (cm) (inches)	Pattern† Measurement (cm) (inches)
1. **CHEST** – Tape straight across back	_____	_____	_____
2. **BUST** – Fullest part; tape slightly higher in back	_____	7·5 cm (3 in)	_____
3. **WAISTLINE** –			
a – Find natural waistline. Place tape or elastic band around waist	_____	2·5 cm (1 in)	_____
b – Across front, side seam to side seam	_____		_____
4. **HIPLINE** –			
a – 7·5 cm (3 inches) below waist; mark with pins	_____		_____
b – 18 cm (7 inches) below waist	_____	5 cm (2 in)	_____
c – 23 cm (9 inches) below waist	_____	5 cm (2 in)	_____
5. **SHOULDER LENGTH** –			
Neck to seam line – Right	_____	_____	_____
Neck to seam line – Left	_____	_____	_____
6. **SLEEVE LENGTH** –			
a – Shoulder to elbow	_____	_____	_____
b – Elbow to wrist	_____	_____	_____
c – Inside from underarm seam to wrist	_____	_____	_____
7. **SLEEVE WIDTH** –			
a – Upper arm	_____	5–7·5 cm (2–3 in)	_____
b – Lower arm (below elbow)	_____		_____
c – Wrist	_____		_____
8. **UNDERARM TO WAISTLINE** –			
2·5 cm (1 inch) below armpit – Right	_____	_____	_____
2·5 cm (1 inch) below armpit – Left	_____	_____	_____
9. **SHOULDER TO WAISTLINE** – H.P.††	_____	1–2·5 cm (½–1 in)	_____
10. **CENTRE FRONT** – Neck to waistline	_____	_____	_____
11. **SHOULDER TO BUSTLINE** – H.P.††	_____	_____	_____
12. **CENTRE FRONT TO BUSTLINE**	_____	_____	_____
13. **BACK LENGTH** –			
a – Neckline to waistline	_____	1–2·5 cm (½–1 in)	_____
b – Shoulder (H.P.††) to waistline – Right	_____		_____
c – Shoulder (H.P.††) to waistline – Left	_____		_____
14. **SHOULDER TO SHOULDER**	_____	_____	_____
15. **BACK WIDTH** – 10 cm (4 inches) below neckline with arms forward and raised slightly	_____	1–2·5 cm (½–1 in)	_____
16. **FULL LENGTH** – Waistline to floor			
a – Centre front	_____	_____	_____
b – Centre back	_____	_____	_____
c – Left side	_____	_____	_____
d – Right side	_____	_____	_____
17. **SKIRT LENGTH PLUS HEM ALLOWANCE**	_____	_____	_____

† Remember seam allowance in checking with pattern.   †† Highest point.

Basic Rules for Pattern Size

Pattern sizes are based on actual body measurements and allow enough ease for comfort and proper fit. The amount of ease will vary with the style and with the manufacturer. Some pattern companies may allow more ease than others; however, this does not mean that you cannot use all makes of patterns.

Pattern sizing has recently been changed to correspond more closely to standard ready-to-wear sizing. However, patterns with former sizing may be available for some time. All patterns using the new sizing will be clearly indicated on the envelope.

Generally you will take the same size in a pattern as in ready-to-wear. Check your measurements with those on the back of the pattern envelope, and *select your pattern by bust measurement* and make any needed adjustments in other places. It is easier to adjust the waist and hip than the shoulder and bust. (Remember that an 'up-lift' bra will very often raise the bustline enough to measure a size larger.)

If, however, the bust is larger in proportion to the other measurements, take a chest measurement. If the difference between bust and chest is 10 cm (4 inches) or more, buy your pattern one size smaller than the bust measurement and enlarge it through the bust. The smaller size is recommended for this reason: it is important that your pattern fits well through the shoulders and armholes; therefore, to retain shape and fit, that area should be changed as little as possible. If you buy a pattern by the larger (bust) measurement, you will also have to cope with a longer shoulder line and deeper armholes than you may need. The smaller size pattern, however, will probably match your measurements more closely.

If only the bust is large in proportion to the rest of your body, and if you prefer not to alter the bustline, buy two patterns, one by bust measurement, the other a size smaller. Use only the front bodice of the larger pattern and all other pattern pieces of the smaller pattern. Increase the darts at underarm, shoulders and waistline so that the front and back sections are equal at the seams.

For skirts. In general, select the pattern by hip measurement, especially if hips are full, as it is easier to adjust the waistline than the hipline.

For trousers. Buy the pattern according to hip measurement.

Always buy the same pattern size for dresses, suits and coats.

TYPES OF PATTERNS AVAILABLE TO YOU

Girls'	*Size 7 to 14*	Designed for under-developed figures. *Not an age.*
Young Junior/Teen	*Size 5/6 to 15/16*	Designed for the developed pre-teen and teen figures; about 1·55 m to 1·60 m (5 ft 1 in to 5 ft 5 in) without shoes.
Junior Petite	*Size 3JP to 13JP*	Designed for the well-proportioned, petite figure with shorter waist and larger bust than the Junior pattern; about 1·525 m to 1·55 m (5 ft to 5 ft 1 in) without shoes.
Miss Petite	*Size 6mp to 16 mp*	Designed for the shorter Miss figure; about 1·575 m to 1·625 m (5 ft 2 in to 5 ft 4 in) without shoes.
Misses'	*Size 6 to 20*	Designed for the well-proportioned, developed figure with normal waist length; about 1·65 m to 1·675 m (5 ft 5 in to 5 ft 6 in) without shoes.
Women's	*Size 38 to 46 (sometimes to 48 and 50)*	Designed for the larger, more fully mature figure; about 1·65 m to 1·675 m (5 ft 5 in to 5 ft 6 in) without shoes.
Half-size	*Size 10½ to 20½ (sometimes to 24½)*	Designed for the shorter woman with fully developed figure and a short backwaist length. Waist and hips are larger in proportion to bust than the Misses' and Women's patterns. About 1·575 m to 1·60 m (5 ft 2 in to 5 ft 3 in) without shoes.

Types of Patterns Available to You

To lessen the need for pattern adjustment, pattern companies have designed patterns *proportioned to fit many figure types.*

The table on the opposite page, which was made up from information found on the last pages of pattern catalogues, calls your attention to what is available. This is a general summary; not all companies show these exact proportions for each figure type. The illustration below shows the difference in pattern proportion.

Pattern companies have also developed *patterns that combine two sizes in one pattern.* This should make it easier for certain figure types to obtain the right fit.

Two of these improvements are discussed here.

The standard size pattern with cutting guidelines for two sizes of patterns (your size and the size smaller or larger). If the measurements require the smaller size bodice and the larger size waistline and hipline, you can use the cutting guidelines that agree with your figure proportions. This is only one example of the possible combinations you may select from the two sizes.

The standard size pattern with additional cutting guidelines for a smaller and a larger size at waistline and hipline. You can use the cutting guidelines that conform to your measurements.

Each of these pattern innovations also has complete instructions for other combinations of bust, waist and hip measurements.

The difference in pattern proportions is illustrated below in five front-bodice patterns for different figure types. Size 12 is used for each except the 'Miss Petite', which is size 11, and the 'Half-Size', which is size 12½.

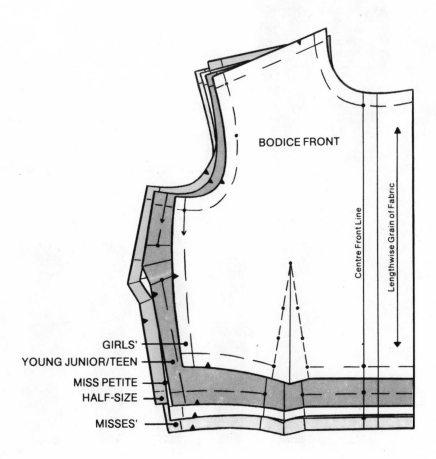

Recognising Your Figure Type

It is important that you recognise your figure type before selecting your pattern size. Each figure illustrated in the two groups here measures the same in the bustline; however, height, width of shoulders, hips and height of bustline differ. It can readily be seen that certain pattern adjustments will be necessary. If the proper pattern is selected, however, those adjustments can be kept to a minimum.

Study the illustrations and find the figure type nearest your own. Use the size and adjustment suggestions as a guide.

In the first group shown, each figure type is Size 12, but figure proportions are quite dissimilar.

Average figure should select Size 12 Misses' pattern since she has no figure problem.

Short figure with small waistline and high bust should select the Miss Petite pattern Size 11.

Tall figure should select Size 12 Misses' pattern and lengthen both bodice and skirt.

Figure with wide shoulders and narrow hips should select Size 12 Misses' pattern and widen the bodice through the shoulders and take in the skirt.

Figure with large hips and narrow shoulders will probably obtain a better fit by selecting Size 10 Misses' pattern and enlarging the hips.

Figure with narrow hips and average shoulders should select Size 12 Misses' pattern and take in the skirt.

Each figure type illustrated in the group at the bottom of the page is Size 40. The pattern size is proportioned for the more mature figure.

Average figure should select Size 40 Women's pattern since she has no figure problem.

Short figure with narrow shoulders and large waistline should consider the Half-Size pattern, Size 20½.

Tall figure should select Size 40 Women's pattern and lengthen both bodice and skirt.

Figure with a high, large bust should select Size 38 Women's pattern and adjust the bustline in both width and length.

Figure with a low bust and large waistline and hips should select Size 40 Women's pattern and lower the dart at underarm and enlarge the waistline and hips.

Figure with narrow hips and broad shoulders should select Size 40 Women's pattern and widen the bodice through the shoulders and take in the skirt.

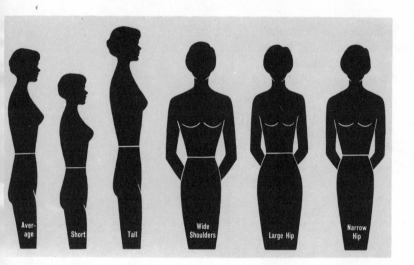

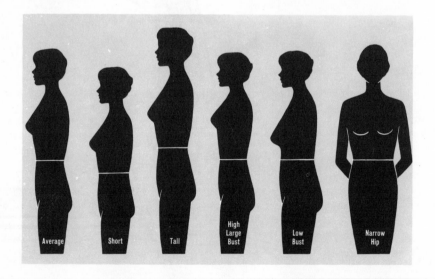

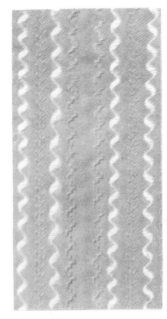

Plate 1
BANDS OF FASHION

LEFT: Bold fashion stitching, in bright coloured bands, adds charm to this young style dress.

ABOVE AND LEFT: The classic look is achieved in this long skirt with rows of fashion stitching, each row of a different stitch.

LEFT: Delicate rows of Flexi-stitching on the yoke and cuffs, give a feminine touch to this elegant blouse.

Patterns by courtesy of Butterick

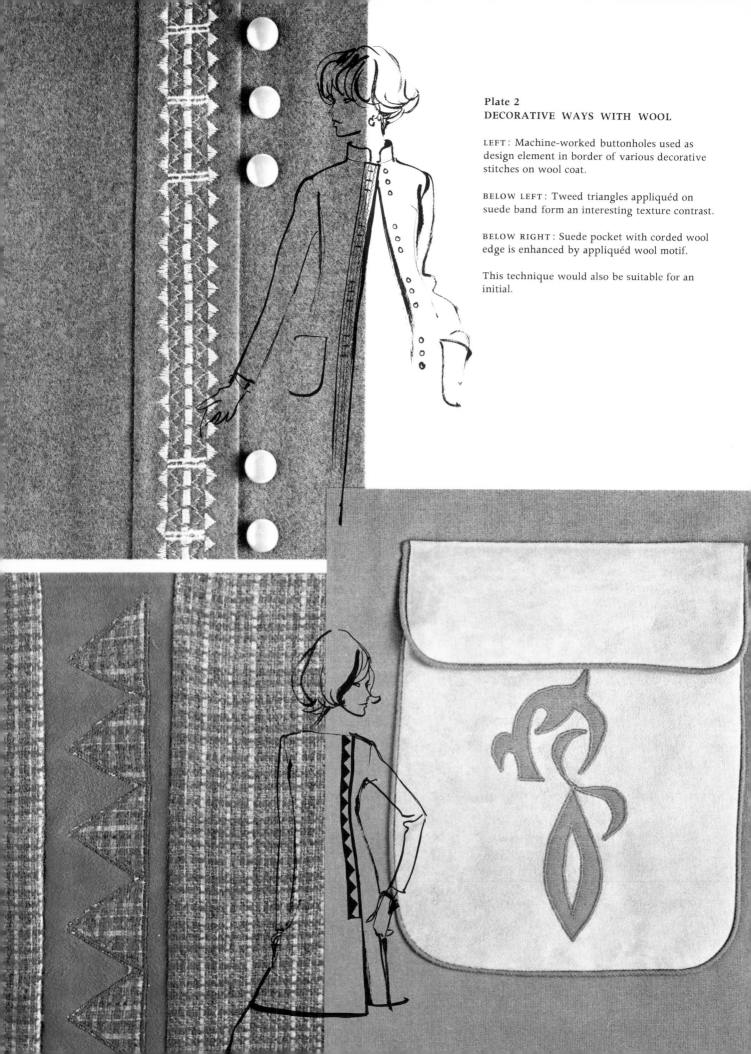

Plate 2
DECORATIVE WAYS WITH WOOL

LEFT: Machine-worked buttonholes used as design element in border of various decorative stitches on wool coat.

BELOW LEFT: Tweed triangles appliquéd on suede band form an interesting texture contrast.

BELOW RIGHT: Suede pocket with corded wool edge is enhanced by appliquéd wool motif.

This technique would also be suitable for an initial.

Fitting the Pattern to Your Figure

All the work you have done so far has been a build-up to the steps you are about to take. For now you are ready to open the pattern envelope and begin.

To make sure the pattern will fit your figure:

1. Check the pattern against the measurements you recorded on your chart.
2. Try on the tissue pattern.
3. Adjust the pattern where necessary.

Checking the Pattern Against Your Measurements

The pattern envelope shows different versions of the pattern. Choose the one you prefer, and then read carefully the pattern guide inside the envelope. Select the pattern pieces you need for the version you have chosen and replace the others in the envelope.

Press all pattern pieces with a lukewarm iron to remove the creases. Be careful not to use too hot an iron as it will make the tissue patterns curl up.

Measure the pattern from seam allowance to seam allowance in the same places that body measurements were taken. When there is no centre seam or opening, measure from seam allowance to centre line. *Never include seam allowances in pattern measurements.*

When comparing the pattern measurements with your body measurements, do not expect them all to match exactly. All pattern companies allow ease for comfort and body movement, and some allow more than others. In addition, some styles call for more ease than others. To make sure that you retain the style of the design, as well as the necessary ease, *do not over-fit*.

The check list below indicates where pattern measurements should be the same as body measurements and where you should allow for ease. Compare the pattern measurements with your own – allowing for ease where required – and note any necessary adjustments on the pattern. In noting your adjustments, remember that only half the pattern is given. In all measurements round the body make *one-quarter* the amount of the adjustment in the front section and *one-quarter* in the back section. If only the front or back section requires changing, make *one-half* the amount of the adjustment in the one pattern section.

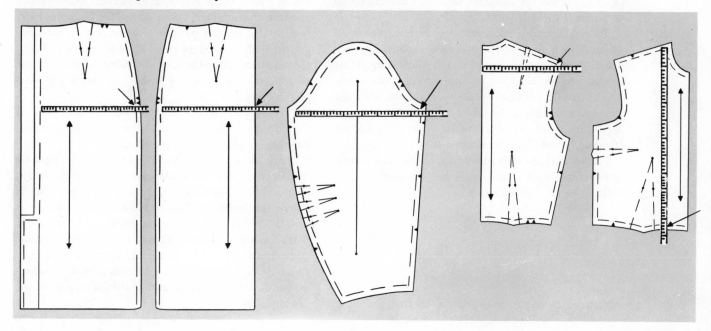

Shoulder length must be identical to your body measurement. Measure length of shoulders on the pattern front, not on the back, as the back shoulder seam has ease or a dart.

Across the back, from armhole to armhole, allow ease for freedom of arm movement.

On the bustline, allow between 5 and 7·5 cm (2 and 3 inches) for ease, depending on the style of the pattern. A smoothly fitted garment will require 7·5 cm (3 inches) of ease; a loosely fitted one, a little more. For a strapless evening dress or sun dress, where you need just enough ease to breathe freely, 5 cm (2 inches) should be sufficient. In these dresses the pattern is cut to give ease on the bust line but a tight fit at the upper edge.

The waistline should fit snugly. Add about 2·5 cm (1 inch) to your total measurement. However, this may be adjusted according to individual preference.

The length of the pattern from shoulder to waistline must be from 1·2 to 2 cm ($\frac{1}{2}$ to $\frac{3}{4}$ inch) longer than the body measurement. Some designs need as much as 5 cm (2 inches) for ease.

Darts must follow the contour of your figure. If they are poorly fitted, your dress will be uncomfortable and will not look well made. For specific instruction on the correct position of darts, see page 100.

Buttons and buttonholes should be spaced to suit the individual figure. If you lengthen or shorten the pattern, or change the bustline, change the spacing of buttonholes. If you plan to use buttons larger than the size suggested on the pattern, make proper allowance in the measurement between the centre line and the finished edge. This is fully explained under *Position of Buttonhole*, page 107.

The high hipline measurement which is about 7·5 cm (3 inches) below the waistline, requires a minimum ease of 2·5 cm (1 inch).

The regular hipline measurement which is usually about 18 cm (7 inches) below the waistline, requires between 5 and 10 cm (2 and 4 inches) for ease. Allow enough ease so that you can sit down without straining the seams. A skirt that fits too tightly will split at the seam or cause the woven threads in the fabric to separate. When you are sitting, it will crease across the front; when you are standing, it will cling under the seat.

The length of the skirt pattern should be the measurement from centre back waistline to hemline plus sufficient allowance for the hem.

Trying on the Tissue Pattern

Although a tissue pattern fits differently from the fabric,

this fitting will show you if the pattern adjustments you planned are necessary. It will also help you decide if the style is suitable for your figure type.

In every step of fitting, wear a good foundation garment, the lingerie you normally wear and shoes with the correct heel height.

To prepare the tissue pattern for fitting, trim the pattern margins from the armhole and neckline seams. Pin in darts, tucks and ease allowance. Pin shoulder seams, side seams and seams within the bodice or skirt sections by placing pattern sections, wrong sides together, with seam edges even. Place the pins parallel to the seamline, taking the seam allowance indicated on the pattern, usually 1·5 cm ($\frac{5}{8}$ inch). Pin bodice and skirt sections together.

Try the pattern on the right side of the figure. If shoulder pads or shapes will be worn in the garment, slip them in place under the tissue pattern.

Check the fit. The shoulder seam should be right on top of the shoulder, and side seams should hang straight from armpit to lower edge. If the pattern has a set-in sleeve, the underarm seam of the armhole should be at least 2·5 cm (1 inch) below the armpit. If this seam is fitted too high, it is uncomfortable; if too low, it causes strain across the sleeve. A round high neckline should fit snugly. The pattern includes a seam allowance, which makes the neckline seem smaller than it will be in the finished dress.

Adjusting the Pattern

RULES TO REMEMBER

1. When you need to lengthen or widen a pattern, use tissue paper for the adjustment. Cut it 2·5 cm (1 inch) wider than the adjustment so that the pattern will overlap the tissue 1·2 cm (½ inch) on each side of the adjustment.

2. Pin the pattern to the tissue, placing the pins parallel to the adjustment. If the pattern is one you may use more than once, machine-tack after pinning, or stick with sellotape.

3. When making a pattern piece smaller with the use of tucks or darts, remember that the width of the tuck or dart should be only half the amount to be removed.

4. When making pattern pieces wider or narrower, and only half the pattern is given, divide the amount of adjustment into quarters, and add or subtract one-quarter in both the front and the back of the pattern. If only a front or back section requires adjustment, add or subtract one-half the amount of the adjustment in the section that needs it.

5. Always measure the pattern again after making adjustments.

To Lengthen the Pattern

Slash across the pattern on the printed lengthening line. Place a piece of tissue underneath. Spread the pattern the necessary amount and pin it to the tissue. Keep the grain line straight. If the grain line does not extend as far as the lengthening line, extend it the full length of the pattern before slashing. Adjust the facing by the same amount.

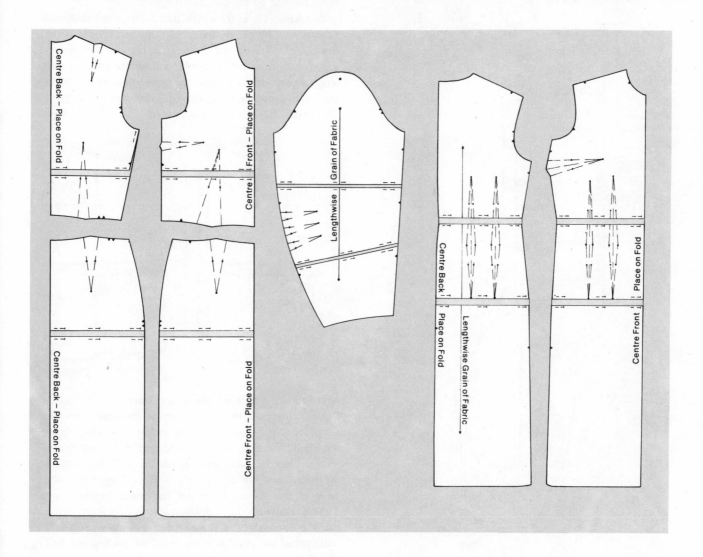

To Shorten the Pattern

Fold the pattern on the printed shortening line and pin in a tuck, even in width, of the necessary amount. Remember that the width of the tuck should be only half the amount to be removed. For example, to shorten a pattern 1·2 cm (½ inch), make a ·6-cm (¼-inch) tuck. Keep the grain line straight. Adjust the facing by the same amount.

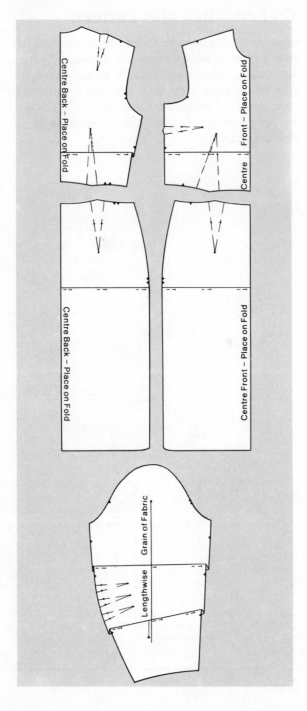

Full Bust

When a pattern fits everywhere except over a very full bust, buy the pattern by hip measurement and adjust the bustline. You may need extra length and width. Two methods are shown:

Method 1: With shoulder dart (*Below left*). Draw a line from the centre of the waistline dart to the fullest part of the bust and another from the shoulder to the fullest part of the bust. Then draw a horizontal line across the fullest part of the bust. Place a large piece of tissue underneath and slash the pattern on these lines. Pin the upper centre section to the tissue and spread the pattern, using the point where the lines cross as a pivot. Add the necessary amount on the horizontal line and one-half the amount needed on the vertical line. Pin the remaining three sections in position. Keep the grain line straight and the pattern flat. Adjust the facing by the same amount on the horizontal line.

To take up the extra width, add a dart at the shoulder as indicated by the dotted lines. The dart should point towards the fullest part of the bust. Increase the under-arm dart so that the front and back bodice are the same length; keep waistline darts the same length but increase the width (note the dotted lines). Trim the outer edge of the tissue.

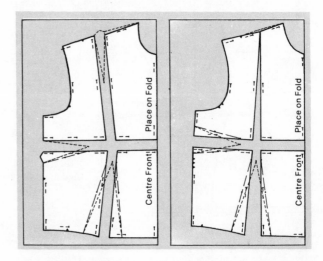

Method 2: Without shoulder dart (*Above right*). Draw a line over the fullest part of the bust from the shoulder to the centre of the waistline dart. Then draw a horizontal line across the fullest part of the bust. Place a large piece of tissue underneath and slash the pattern on these lines. Pin the upper centre front section to the edge of the tissue. Then pin the lower centre front section, allowing the additional length necessary. Bring the shoulder edges of the two upper sections together and spread the pattern at the bustline, adding one-half the width necessary. Pin to tissue. Spread the lower side

section and pin to tissue. Keep the grain line straight and the pattern flat. Adjust the facing by the same amount on the horizontal line.

Keep underarm and waistline darts the same length but increase them the necessary amount in width, as shown by the dotted lines. Straighten the shoulder line. Trim off the outer edges of the tissue.

Flat Bust

Adjust the necessary amount by folding a tuck across the chest, decreasing in width at the armhole. Pin in place. Make a corresponding dart in front of the sleeve so that the armhole and sleeve will fit correctly. Remember, the width of the dart and tuck are only half the amount to be removed.

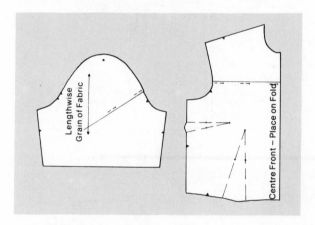

Hollow Chest

Fold a dart across the chest, tapering towards the armhole. Pin in place. Remember, the width of the dart is only half the amount to be removed. Straighten the centre front as shown by the dotted lines. No sleeve adjustment is necessary as the point of the dart ends at the armhole.

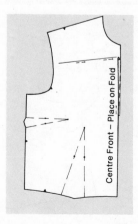

Low Bust

A low bust needs the dart lowered at the underarm. Slash across the pattern the length of the dart, about 2·5 cm (1 inch) below the armhole; then slash down towards the waistline. Place the tissue underneath and pin it to the pattern at the upper edge of the slash. Slide the dart section down until the point of the dart is in line with the fullest part of the bust. Pin to tissue. Form a tuck in the pattern below the dart so that the pattern will lie flat.

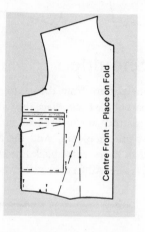

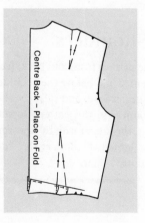

Erect Back (*Above*)

Slash across the pattern just above the waistline. Lap and pin the slashed edges the necessary amount, tapering to a point at the side seam. Straighten the centre back and dart as illustrated by the dotted lines.

If the pattern is too long from shoulder to armpit, pin a tuck across the back. Dart the back of the sleeve to correspond with the bodice so that the sleeve and arm-

hole will fit correctly. Straighten the grain line on the
sleeve as indicated by the dotted lines.

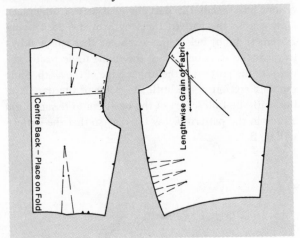

Round Shoulders

Slash across the pattern from the centre to the armhole
at the fullest part of the back. Place the tissue underneath
and raise the pattern at the neck to add the necessary
amount across the shoulders. Add the amount needed
at centre back to keep centre back line straight. Pin the
pattern to the tissue. Add a dart at the neckline to regain
original neck size.

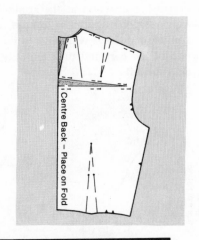

Square Shoulders

Slash across the pattern front and back, from the armhole
towards the centre just below the shoulder line. Place a
piece of tissue underneath and raise the shoulder line the
necessary amount. Pin the pattern to the tissue. Raise
the armhole at the underarm by the same amount to
retain size. Straighten the dart at the shoulder as illustrated by the dotted lines.

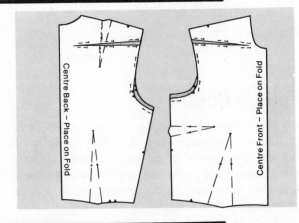

Sloping Shoulders

Slash across the pattern front and back, from the armhole
towards the centre, just below the shoulder line. Lap
and pin the slashed edges the necessary amount at the
armhole, tapering to a point. Lower the armhole by the
same amount at underarm to retain the shape and size of
the armhole as illustrated by the dotted lines. Straighten
the shoulder dart.

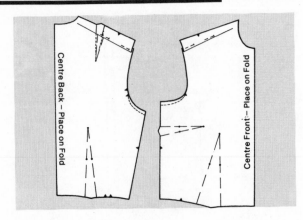

Broad Shoulders

Slash the pattern front and back, from the centre shoulder down as far as the armhole notches. Then slash across almost to the armhole edge. Place the tissue underneath and spread the outer edge of the shoulder the necessary width. Pin the pattern to the tissue. Straighten the shoulder line as illustrated by the dotted lines.

For Magyar sleeves, place a large piece of tissue under pattern front and back, and cut it the same shape as the shoulder and sleeve of the pattern. Slash the pattern from shoulder to waistline. Spread the pattern and add the necessary amount at the shoulder. Bring the slashed edges together at the waistline. Pin the pattern to the tissue. Adjust the sleeve edges as illustrated by the dotted lines and the tissue to retain the original line.

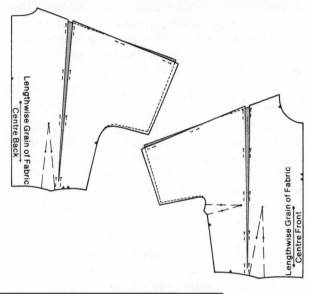

Narrow Shoulders

Slash the pattern front and back from the centre shoulder line diagonally to the notches in the armhole. Lap and pin the slashed edges the necessary amount at the shoulder. Adjust the shoulder seam as illustrated.

For Magyar sleeves, place the tissue under the pattern front and back and cut it to the same shape as the shoulder and sleeve of the pattern. Fold and pin a dart at the shoulder to take up the necessary amount. Adjust the edges to retain the original shape, as illustrated by the dotted lines.

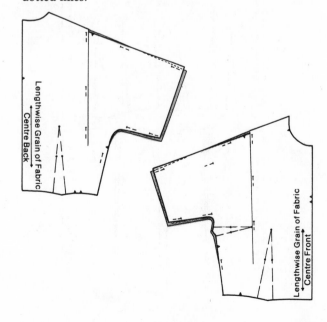

43

To Lengthen Back Bodice (*Right*)

If you need extra length in the back and underarm but not in the front below the bust, slash across the back bodice on the lengthening line. Place the tissue underneath and spread the pattern the necessary amount. Pin it to the tissue. Slash across the front bodice almost to the centre line. Place the tissue underneath and spread the pattern at the underarm seam the same amount as the back bodice, tapering to a point at the centre front. Pin the pattern to the tissue. Straighten the centre front, front darts and side seams, as illustrated by the dotted lines.

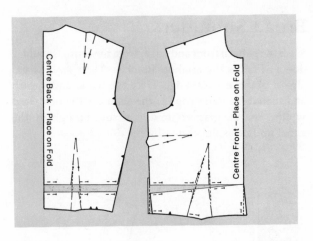

Large Waistline

For this you must adjust both the bodice and the skirt. To adjust the bodice, slash the pattern front and back from the waistline towards the shoulder. Place the tissue underneath. Spread both front and back bodices to add the necessary width. Divide the required amount into quarters and add one-quarter to each section. Pin the pattern to the tissue.

To adjust the skirt, slash the pattern front and back from the waistline down towards the hipline. Place the tissue underneath and spread the pattern to correspond with the bodice section. Pin the pattern to the tissue.

When the extra is only needed at the front or back, add one-half the amount of the adjustment to that section only.

Small Waistline

Take in the same amount in both the bodice and the skirt in the front and back of the pattern by increasing the size of each waistline dart or tuck. To decrease the waistline 2·5 cm (1 inch), for example, increase the two darts in the front and the two in the back ·3 cm ($\frac{1}{8}$ inch) in depth.

If you need an even smaller size either take in the side seams, or slash the pattern, both bodice and skirt, from the waistline and lap the slashed edges the necessary amount. A seam allowance ·6 cm ($\frac{1}{4}$ inch) deeper at the sides, or a ·6-cm ($\frac{1}{4}$-inch) lapped slash will decrease the waistline 2·5 cm (1 inch).

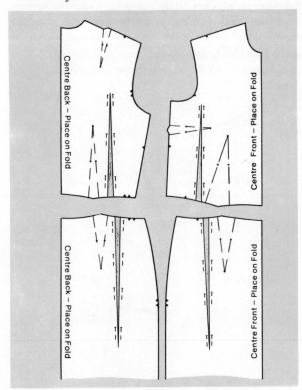

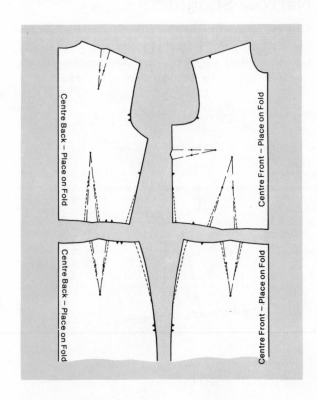

Large Arm

On each side of the sleeve, draw a horizontal line about 7·5 cm (3 inches) long, beginning at the underarm; from this, draw a vertical line to the lower edge on each side. (If the sleeve is short, carry the vertical slash to the end of the sleeve.) Slash on these lines and place the tissue underneath. Spread the pattern, adding one-half the necessary amount on each side. Pin the pattern to the tissue.

To adjust the armhole seam, slash from the armhole almost to the waistline on the front and back bodice. Place the tissue underneath and spread the pattern sections to correspond with the sleeve adjustment. Adjust the armhole seam as illustrated.

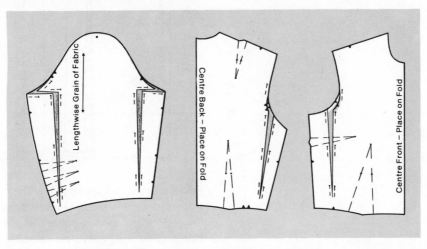

Large Upper Arm

To enlarge the upper part of the sleeve, use either of these methods:

Method 1: Place the sleeve over tissue of the same size and trim the tissue to match the head of the sleeve. Slash the pattern from the shoulder line to the lower edge. Then spread each side of the pattern to gain the additional width. Pin the lower sections of the pattern to the tissue. Bring the slashed edges of the head together at the top, folding a dart on each side so that the pattern will lie flat. Pin the pattern to the tissue. Keep the grain line straight. Lower the armhole in the bodice at the underarm to fit the adjusted sleeve.

Method 2: Slash the sleeve from the shoulder line to the lower edge. Place the tissue underneath and spread the pattern to add the necessary width. Pin the pattern to the tissue. Lower the armhole in the bodice at the underarm to fit the adjusted sleeve.

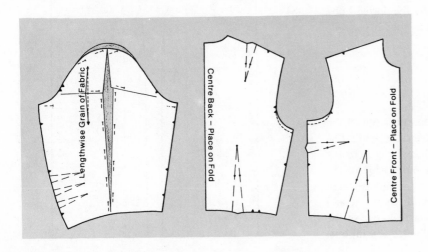

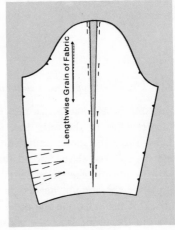

Small Arm (*Below left*)

Fold a small tuck, lengthwise, through the centre of the sleeve and increase the underarm seam by the remaining amount necessary. Raise the armhole at the underarm the same amount so that the sleeve and armhole will fit correctly, as illustrated for 'Square Shoulders', but omit the slash to raise the shoulder line.

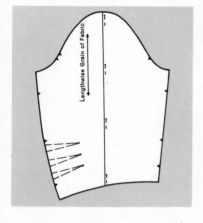

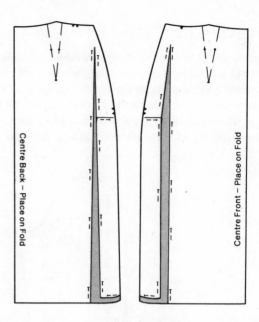

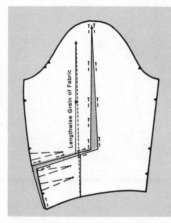

Fullness at Elbow (*Above right*)

Extend the grain line the full length of the sleeve. Slash the sleeve across the elbow to the centre; then slash up to the top of the sleeve. Place the tissue underneath and spread the pattern the necessary width. Pin the pattern to the tissue. Increase each dart by dividing the number of darts into the amount of the increase.

Straighten the grain line by drawing a straight line between the two ends as illustrated by the dotted lines. Increase the outer edge at the elbow as shown.

Full Hips (*Top of next column*)

Slash the front and back skirt, near the side seams, from the lower edge to the waistline. Keep the grain line straight. Place the tissue underneath and pin it to the inside edge of the slash. Spread the outer edge of the pattern to add the necessary width at the hipline. Add one-quarter the amount needed to both the front and the back of the skirt. Pin the other slashed edge of the pattern to the tissue from the waistline to the hipline.

Fold a dart in the pattern below the hip, tapering to the side seam, as illustrated, to remove excess fullness at the lower edge. Add the necessary length to the lower outside edge to compensate for the dart. Make exactly the same adjustments to back and front.

Narrow Hips

To remove excess width from the skirt front and back, divide the amount into quarters. At the hipline, form a lengthwise tuck in the skirt front and back to take up one-quarter the amount in each section. Taper the tuck to a point at the waistline but keep it the same width from hipline to lower edge. Make the adjustment near the side seam to avoid crossing darts and grain line.

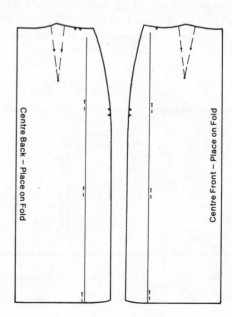

Large Seat

Extend the grain line the full length of the pattern. To add width across the hips and length at the centre back, draw a line through the centre of the waistline dart to the hemline. Draw another line from the centre back to the side seam at the fullest part of the hips. Place the tissue underneath. Slash the pattern on the drawn lines. Spread the upper sections of the pattern to add one-half the necessary width across the hips. Pin the edges to the tissue.

Spread the lower centre section to add the necessary length to the centre back. Pin it to the tissue. Spread the lower outside section to add length and width; join the upper and lower sections at the seam edge. Pin to the tissue. Fold a dart below the hipline to avoid excess fullness at the hem edge. Pin lower section to tissue. Add length to the lower outside edge as illustrated, to keep the pattern even.

Adjust darts to fit the waistline, and straighten the seamline at the point of adjustment, as illustrated by the dotted lines.

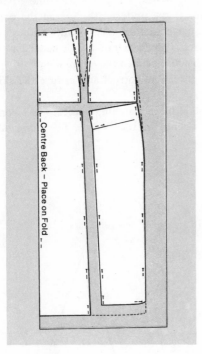

Hollow Back

Use either of these methods:

Method 1: Slash across the skirt from the centre back to the seam edge about 5 cm (2 inches) below the waistline. Lap and pin the slashed edges at the centre back usually about 1·2 cm ($\frac{1}{2}$ inch), tapering to a point at the seamline. Use sellotape to hold the point in place. Add, as illustrated, to the centre back to keep it straight. Straighten darts as shown by the dotted lines.

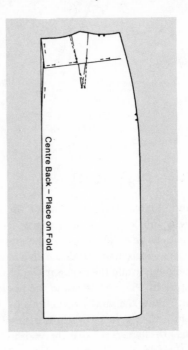

Method 2: You can also adjust for a hollow back after you have cut the skirt. To do this, measure 1·2 cm ($\frac{1}{2}$ inch) down from the waistline edge of the fabric at the centre back and mark with a pin. Then make a line with pins, gradually tapering to the seam edge at each side, as illustrated. Tack along this line. Do not trim away any surplus fabric yet. When fitting and joining the skirt to the bodice, stitch 1·5 cm ($\frac{5}{8}$ inch) below the tacked line. Trim away the extra seam allowance after you have made the permanent line of stitching.

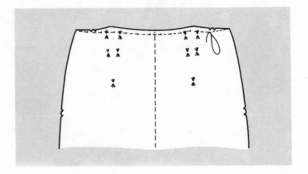

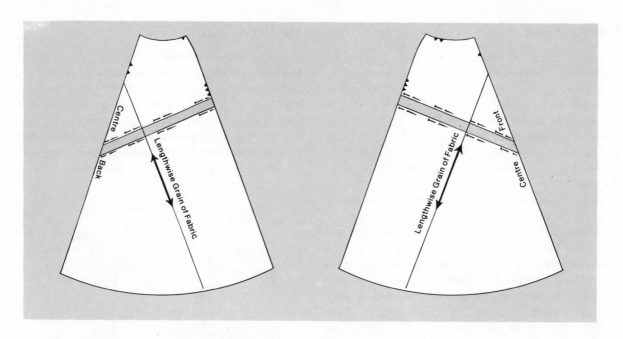

Gored or Flared Skirt

To lengthen. Extend the grain line of the front and back skirt the full length of the pattern. Draw a line across the pattern at a right angle to the grain line and slash on this line. Place tissue underneath and spread the pattern far enough to add the necessary length. Keep the grain line straight. Pin the pattern to the tissue.

To shorten. Follow the same instructions for lengthening, but fold a tuck across the pattern to take up the necessary length. Remember that the width of the tuck is just half the amount to be removed. Or adjust length at lower edge.

To enlarge waistline. Slash the front and back pattern sections lengthwise, from the waistline to the lower edge. Place tissue underneath. Spread the pattern and add one-quarter the necessary width to both the front and the back. (When extra width is needed at the waistline, it is usually needed the entire length of the skirt to keep the grain line correct and ensure the skirt hangs properly.)

If the skirt has a matching bodice, make corresponding adjustments in the bodice. See *Large Waistline*, page 44.

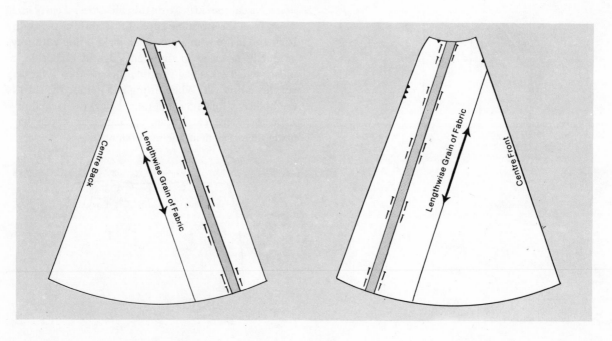

Shorts and Trousers

Buy the pattern by the hip measurement and make adjustments in the crutch and waist as illustrated below. **Method 1, Model seated:** Measure at the side seam from the waistline to the chair seat. (Chair seat should be firm.) Add 1·2 cm (½ inch) for ease on small sizes and 2·5 cm (1 inch) on large sizes. *Recommended for the average figure.*

To measure the pattern, extend the grain line on the front and back sections the full length of the pattern. Draw a line at a right angle to the grain line, from the point where the seams join at the crutch to the side seam, as illustrated. Measure the pattern from the waistline to the drawn line as shown. If there is a difference in pattern and body measurements, adjust both the front and the back pieces. Pin the pattern pieces together and try on.

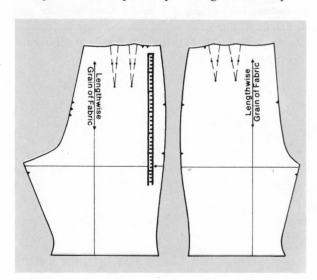

Method 2, Model standing: Measure the crutch from the front waistline, between the legs to the back waistline. Add 7·5 cm (3 inches) for ease. *Recommended for the rounded figure.*

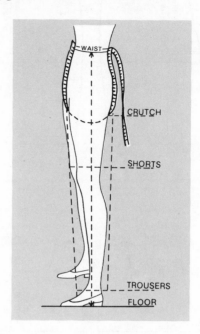

To measure the pattern, pin the front and back sections together at the crutch. (Fold under the seam allowance on one side and lap over the seam allowance on the other.) Measure around the crutch from the back waistline to the front waistline *at the seamline* not the seam edge. (Stand the tape on edge to get an accurate measurement of the curve of the crutch.) If there is a difference between body measurement and pattern measurement, adjust as follows:

If the figure is equally proportioned, adjust both front and back equally. If the figure is large in the back, add

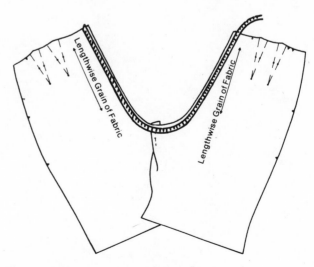

49

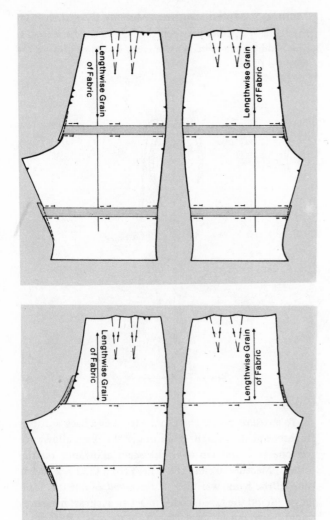

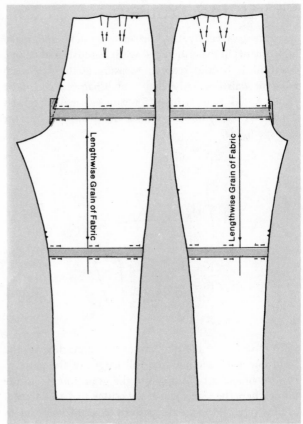

For length of trousers measure from waistline to floor at inside leg and side seams. Then measure the number of centimetres (inches) you prefer from the floor and subtract the total length. Add the necessary amount for hem or turn-up. The waistband is not included in full-length measurements.

only to the back section. Pin the pattern pieces together and try on. Lengthen or shorten the pattern as illustrated.

Laying Out the Pattern and Cutting

Before laying the pattern pieces on the fabric, you should have completed the following steps:
1. Pressed your pattern and made all necessary pattern adjustments. See page 37.
2. Shrunk the fabric, if necessary, and straightened the fabric ends. See page 14.
3. Pressed out all creases and wrinkles in the fabric. See pressing instructions, page 64.

The guides given here cover the three steps you will take now:
1. Working with your pattern layout.
2. Cutting the fabric.
3. Transferring notches and markings to the fabric sections.

Pattern Layout

RULES TO REMEMBER

1. Clear a large, flat surface to accommodate your work. A dining-room table (protected with brown paper), a cutting board, a bedboard placed on the bed, or a ping-pong table, makes an excellent cutting surface.

2. Study the cutting layouts shown in the instruction guide included with your pattern. Select and circle the layout for the view you have chosen as well as for your pattern size and for the width and type of fabric you are using.

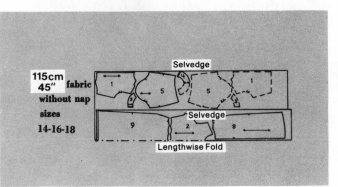

3. Consider the type of fabric you will be working with. Some checks and florals have an 'up' and 'down' to the design and must be matched. Napped and pile fabrics have the nap or pile running in one direction and therefore must be cut with all pattern pieces laid in the same direction. Satin, wool broadcloth, and similar weaves often show a varied degree of sheen in different directions; when in doubt, stay on the safe side by laying all pattern pieces in one direction.

4. Lay the pattern pieces printed side up unless otherwise instructed.

Solid Colours or Small Prints

When the cutting layout shows a *double thickness*, fold the fabric right sides together. Pin edges together along the ends and selvedges. Slash the selvedge edges if they draw.

When the cutting layout shows a *single thickness*, lay the fabric right side up and the pattern printed side up. When right and left sides are cut separately, be sure to *turn the pattern pieces over to cut the second half of the garment*; otherwise you will have two bodice or skirt sections for the same side, or two sleeves for one arm.

When the layout shows a combination of *single and double layers of fabric*, make sure that you lay the correct

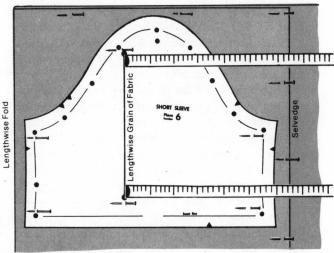

pattern pieces on the single or double layer and that they face the direction shown in the layout.

Some layouts show the fabric opened to its full width and folded on the crosswise grain, right sides together. Napped, pile, check and floral fabrics cannot be cut by this layout. See page 53.

The lengthwise grain line printed on the pattern must always be parallel to the fabric selvedge. Place each pattern piece accurately on the fabric and pin at one end of the grain line marking. Use a tape measure or yardstick to measure, and adjust the pattern position so that the distance from grain line marking to selvedge is the same at both ends. Then complete pinning along the grain line.

For pattern pieces marked 'place on lengthwise fold of fabric', place the fold line *exactly* on the lengthwise fold of the fabric, and pin along the fold. (This marking appears when there is no centre or back seam or opening in a bodice or skirt section.)

After you have accurately located the grain line, smooth out the pattern so that it will lie flat on the fabric. Pin pattern sections to the fabric along the edges, using plenty of fine, sharp pins to keep the fabric from slipping. Pin with the grain of the fabric and within the seam allowance. Re-check each grain line position.

Lay and pin all pattern pieces before you start cutting.

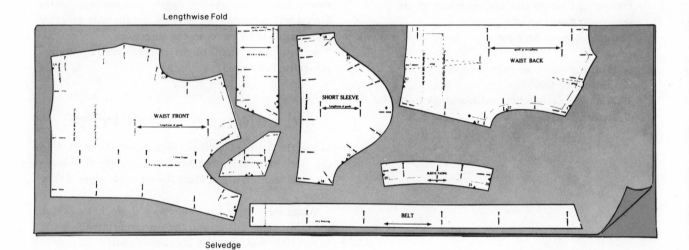

Lengthwise Fold

Selvedge

Cutting the Fabric

RULES TO REMEMBER

1. Use bent-handle dressmaker's shears with 15- to 18-cm (6- or 7-inch) blades. *Do not use pinking shears*; they are for seam finishing only.

2. Keep the fabric flat on the table and cut along the 'cutting line' or edge of the pattern. Cut with long smooth strokes but do not close the shears to the point. Doing that will produce irregular edges. Leave pattern pieces pinned to the fabric until all markings have been made.

3. Cut the notches after cutting each garment section except when they are cut outward. See *Notches*, page 56.

4. Cut out the entire garment at one time. Also, cut the interfacing and mounting before beginning to sew. The mounting is usually cut by the same pattern as the garment after all markings have been made on the fabric.

Plate 3
SIMPLY SEAMED

Flattering seam lines, give this Trevira dress a classical look.
The seams are top-stitched using a buttonhole twist thread.

Plate 4
TOWN AND COUNTRY

A trouser suit, particularly a boldly checked jacket teamed with plain camel pants, is a most useful outfit for any wardrobe. Fabric – Trevira

This swing-style coat, in a fleecy Courtelle fabric, is cosy and comfortable for the cold weather. Fabrics – Epatra

Patterns by courtesy of Butterick and Vogue

Working with Different Fabrics
Checks

If the pattern is suitable for checks, the pattern envelope will usually indicate how many yards of fabric you need. If it does not, buy an extra ¼ to ½ metre (¼ to ½ yard) of fabric, depending on the size of the check.

A word about your pattern: to work successfully with checks, avoid selecting a pattern with diagonal bustline darts, shoulder darts, or seams within a bodice or skirt. Too many seams will break the continuity of the check. If the pattern shows darts at the waistline, convert them to tucks or gathers so that the checks will match.

The check must match exactly in colour and stripe at side seams, centre seams or openings, shoulder seams, waistline, armholes and sleeves. Therefore, during dress construction, slip-tack all seams following the instructions on page 62. This will enable you to match the checks successfully and will prevent the fabric from slipping during the stitching.

Checks may be even or uneven. Your pattern layout will depend on the type of check you have chosen.

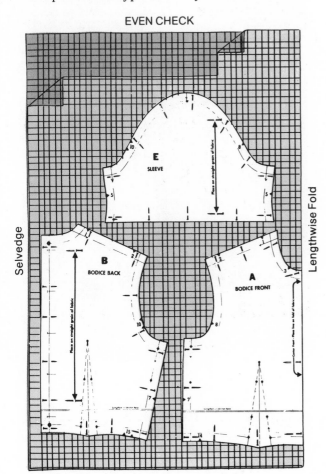

EVEN CHECK

EVEN CHECKS

Even checks repeat their design on *both the lengthwise and the crosswise stripes*. They are identical in colour, right and left and up and down. To work with them, follow these rules:

1. Fold the fabric, right sides together, so that the centre of the check or the centre of a bold lengthwise stripe falls on the centre back and centre front of the bodice and skirt. The upper and lower layers of the folded fabric must match exactly in colour and stripe; pin them together along the stripe lines to prevent slipping during cutting.

2. Lay the pattern pieces on the fabric in either direction. Notches that will be joined together must be placed on the same colour stripe. Matching notches occur at side seams, shoulder seams, armholes, sleeves and waistline. Be careful to match at the *seamline*, not the seam edge. Match crosswise stripes of the sleeves and bodice.

UNEVEN CHECKS

Checks may be *uneven in lengthwise or crosswise* directions or in both.

When *only the crosswise stripes* of the plaid are *uneven*, follow these rules:

1. Fold the fabric lengthwise, right sides together, so that the centre of the check or the centre of a bold lengthwise stripe falls on the centre back and centre front of the bodice and skirt. The upper and lower layers of the folded fabric must match exactly in colour and stripe; pin them together along the stripe lines to prevent slipping during cutting.

2. Lay all pattern pieces on the fabric in *one direction*. Notches that will be joined together must be placed on the same colour stripe. Match at the *seamline*, not the seam edge. Match crosswise stripes of the sleeves and bodice.

When *only the lengthwise stripes* of the check are

53

uneven, they can be matched only when the pattern has a centre seam or opening in the front and back of both bodice and skirt.

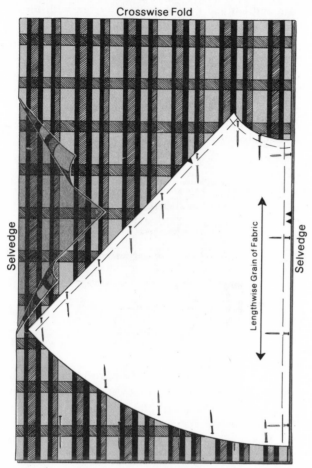

Crosswise Fold

Selvedge

Lengthwise Grain of Fabric

Selvedge

1. Open the fabric its full width and fold on the crosswise grain, right sides together. Match the identical stripes in the upper and lower layers of the folded fabric and pin them together along the stripe lines to prevent slipping during cutting.

2. Lay the pattern pieces on the fabric in *one direction* with the centre of the check or the centre of a bold lengthwise stripe falling on the centre back and centre front of the bodice and skirt. Notches that will be joined together must be placed on the same colour stripe. Match the *seamline*, not the seam edge. Match the crosswise stripes of the sleeves and bodice.

When both *lengthwise and crosswise stripes* are *uneven*, they can be matched only when the fabric has no right or wrong side and when the pattern has a centre seam or opening in the front and back of both bodice and skirt.

1. Use the pattern layout 'with nap'; lay the fabric right side up.

2. Lay all pattern pieces in *one direction* on *a single thickness of fabric*, with the centre seam on a prominent lengthwise stripe. Notches that will be joined together must be placed on the same colour stripe. Match at the *seamline*, not the seam edge. Match the crosswise stripes of the sleeves and bodice. Cut this half of the garment.

3. For the second half, lay the pattern on the fabric with the first half still pinned to it, matching identical lengthwise and crosswise stripes. Cut the second half of the garment. Cut notches and make markings through the two layers of fabric.

4. Reverse one side of each garment section when joining seams because there is no right or wrong side to the fabric.

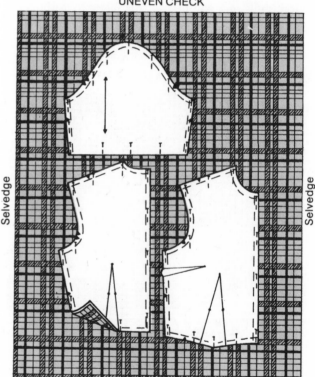

UNEVEN CHECK

Selvedge

Selvedge

Stripes

Stripes may be *even* or *uneven*. They are cut in the same way as checks. In placing the pattern on the fabric, be sure that notches that will be joined together fall on the same stripe.

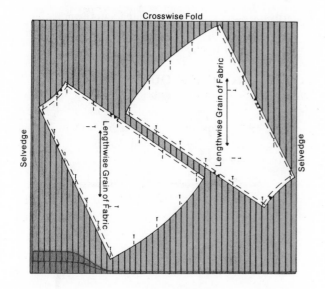

If the garment is cut on the bias, choose a pattern with a centre seam or opening in the front and back and follow these rules:

1. Fold the full width of the fabric on the crosswise grain, right sides together.

2. Lay the pattern with the grain line parallel to the selvedge. Notches that are to be joined together must be on the same stripe. Stripes must be matched at side seams and centre seams or centre openings. Match at the *seamline*, not the seam edge.

3. During dress construction, slip-tack all seams.

When the stripes are *uneven*, lay the pattern pieces on the fabric in *one direction*.

Small checks

Checks ·6 cm (¼ inch) or more in size *must* be matched; smaller checks are more attractive when matched.

Florals, Prints and Jacquards

Many floral fabrics have an 'up' and 'down' to the motif, and when they do, you must lay all pattern pieces in *one direction*.

To achieve a pleasing effect with medium or large motifs, make sure that they fall above the bustline instead of directly over it, approximately in the same position in the front as in the back, and in the same place on each sleeve. Match at the seamline whenever possible.

As with checks, avoid patterns that require many seams within the bodice and skirt. Simple lines are most suitable for prints, both large and small.

Incorrect   Correct

Pile Fabrics

Pile fabrics such as velvet, velveteen and corduroy should be cut with the pile standing up to emphasise the rich dark tone. To determine the direction of the pile, brush the fabric with the fingers. If the surface is smooth, you are brushing with the pile; if rough, you are brushing against the pile. Use the 'rough' direction for the top of your pattern layout; and lay all pieces in the *same direction*, following the 'with nap' instruction guide with the pattern. Use fine needles to pin the pattern to the fabric.

Incorrect   Correct

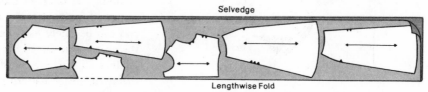

55

Napped Fabrics

Napped fabrics such as wool broadcloth, face-cloth, vicuna and cashmere, have surface fibres running in *one direction*. Often the direction is visible to the eye. If it is not, brush the fabric with your fingers as for velvet.

Cut napped fabrics with the *nap running down*. Lay all pattern pieces in *one direction*. Use fine needles to pin the pattern to the fabric.

Transferring Notches and Markings

The notches and markings on the pattern are your key to successful dress construction. Each has a special meaning and each must be transferred to the fabric while it is still pinned to the pattern.

Notches

Notches are guides for joining the garment sections. They indicate which edges are seamed together and where the ease is located. On some patterns they are numbered to indicate the sequence in which the seams are sewn. Like notches are always joined.

Notches may be cut *inwards* or *outwards* depending on the fabric you are using and your personal preference. Fabrics which fray easily or seams needing an untrimmed, smooth seam edge, such as a French seam or a flat felled seam, should be cut with notches outwards. Some beginners prefer to cut notches outwards as a precaution against cutting too deeply into the seam allowance. Patterns may have either method marked.

TO CUT NOTCHES INWARDS
After cutting the pattern piece, lift the fabric and fold it in the centre of the notch. With the scissor points

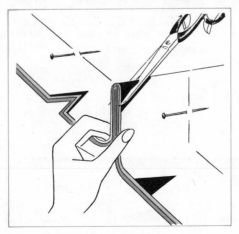

towards the outer edge, as illustrated, cut the notch only ·3 cm ($\frac{1}{8}$ inch) deep. Be careful not to cut too deeply because this will weaken the seam allowance.

TO CUT NOTCHES OUTWARDS
Notches are cut outwards as the garment is cut, following the markings that project beyond the seam edge. Cut them the exact shape of the pattern or you will not get an accurate joining. Use outward notches on chiffons and other sheer fabrics.

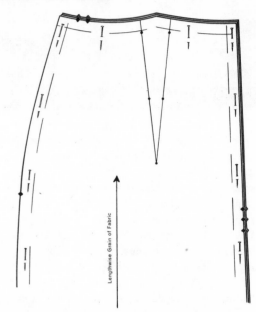

OTHER METHODS FOR MARKING NOTCHES
If the fabric frays easily, make a tailor's tack (see next page) at the point of each notch. Or, if you are an experienced dressmaker, snip or clip in ·3 cm ($\frac{1}{8}$ inch) from the edge of the fabric at the point of each notch, using scissors that cut sharply at the point. This is a time-saving method. Watch closely for these clipped edges when assembling the garment.

Markings

Dots, squares, triangles or crosses on the pattern indicate the position for darts, buttonholes, tucks and pleats, seam allowances, joining points for gussets and yokes and other construction details. To transfer these markings from the pattern to the fabric, use tailor's tacks, chalk, chalked thread, tracing wheel and tracing paper, or pins. The safest of these is tailor's tacks, which are preferred for fine fabrics. The other methods are quicker and can be safely used on many fabrics if you observe the precautions noted here.

Since all markings must be accurately made, transfer them while each pattern piece is pinned in position.

TAILOR'S TACKS

Tailor's tacks are markings that will not rub off, press off or damage the fabric. To make them, use a double thread about 60 cm (24 inches) in length and in a contrasting colour to the fabric. Do not knot the end. Use a different colour for each symbol, then it is simple to join like colours. Although mercerised thread is suitable, some dressmakers prefer embroidery or darning thread because it is soft and clings to the fabric. Follow these rules:

1. At the point to be marked, take a small stitch through the pattern and double thickness of fabric, leaving about a 2-cm ($\frac{3}{4}$-inch) thread end.

2. Take a backstitch in the same place and leave a loop a little shorter than the thread end. Cut the thread, leaving a 2-cm ($\frac{3}{4}$-inch) thread end. Continue in this manner until all markings have been finished.

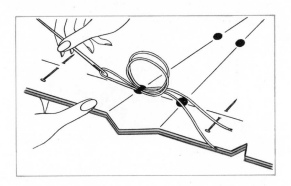

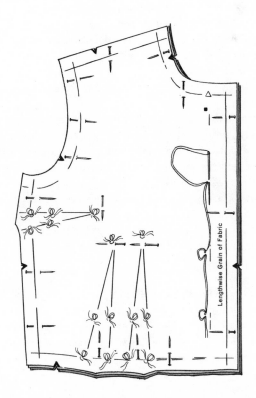

If a group of tailor's tacks are made close together, such as in darts, move from one marking to another without cutting the thread between the marks.

Before removing the pattern, cut the threads between the tacks. Remove pins, and carefully remove the pattern by pulling the threads through the tissue so that the tailor's tacks are not disturbed.

3. Raise the upper layer of fabric slightly, and cut the threads between it and the bottom layer, leaving thread tufts in both layers of fabric.

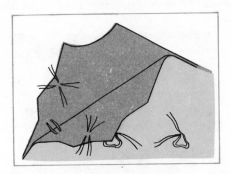

CHALK

Tailor's chalk may be used when there is no danger of damaging the fabric. As it rubs off easily, use it only when the construction will be done immediately. (Always mark the wrong side of the fabric.) Chalk is available in several colours, with or without a wax base.

1. Place a pin through the pattern and double thickness of fabric at the point of the marking. Carefully slip the tissue pattern over the heads, then the points of the pins.

2. With tailor's chalk, mark the fabric over the pins on one side. Turn the section over and chalk the other side in the same place.

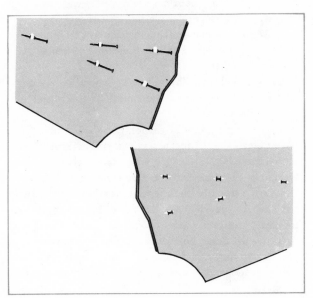

CHALKED THREAD

Chalked thread is thread that has been coated with tailor's chalk. Use it as you would tailor's chalk above.

Thread a needle, using a double thread about 30 cm (12 inches) long. Do not knot the end.

1. Pull the thread around the square of tailor's chalk several times until it is well coated, right to the end.

2. Take a stitch in each marking through the pattern and double thickness of fabric. As the chalked thread is pulled out, it leaves a tiny chalked marking in each thickness of fabric. Re-chalk the thread frequently.

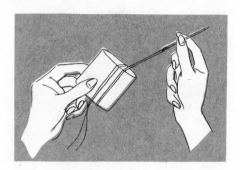

TRACING WHEEL AND TRACING PAPER

Dressmaker's carbon paper is available in white, blue, red, yellow and orange. Several colours are combined in one package. If you plan to use it, remember to:

1. Use a white tracing paper whenever possible. If you need a colour, choose one near the colour of the fabric with just sufficient contrast to make visible marks.

2. *Always mark the wrong side of the fabric* since the marks remain on the fabric until it is washed or cleaned. Although they can be removed from almost any fabric with a household dry cleaner such as carbon tetra-chloride or petrol (benzine), on many delicate fabrics it is wiser to choose a safer method of marking.

3. Work on a flat surface. If you use a table, cover it with heavy cardboard so that it will not be damaged by the tracing wheel.

4. Mark lightly with the tracing wheel. Do not press down too hard because the points of the wheel will damage the fabric.

5. Use small pieces of carbon paper and move them from one section to another as you are marking.

Practise using the tracing wheel and carbon paper on a scrap of the same fabric before marking the garment. **To mark a double thickness of fabric,** which you will have when you cut with the fabric folded right sides together, use two pieces of carbon paper. Place one, right side up, under both layers of fabric. Remove enough pins to slip the second piece of tracing paper, right side down, between the pattern and top layer of fabric. (See illustration).

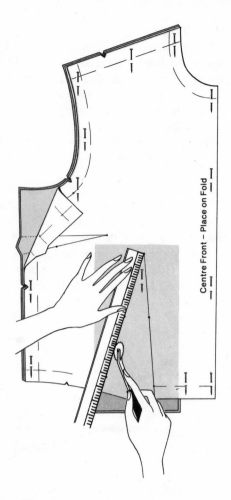

Centre Front – Place on Fold

Use a ruler to keep the lines straight as you mark with the tracing wheel. Move the tracing wheel along the exact line of the darts or other details with one smooth, even stroke so that you do not change their shape. *Do not 'saw' back and forth.*

If the fabric is heavy, you may have to mark one layer at a time.

To mark the right side of the fabric, as you must for pockets, buttonholes and similar details, mark the wrong side with the tracing wheel and carbon paper and then tack along the marked line to transfer the markings to the right side.

To mark a single thickness of fabric, which you will have when you cut with the right side of the fabric up, place a piece of carbon paper, right side up, under the fabric and mark.

MARKING WITH PINS

Pin markings are not suitable for fine fabrics or patterns with intricate details. Use this method only when the darts, tucks or other details will be tacked immediately after each section is marked. Do not pin and set aside and later expect to find the pins still in place.

58

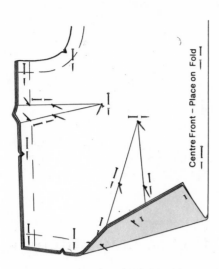

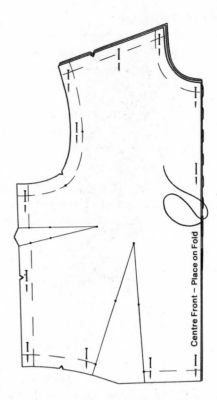

From the pattern side, stick a pin through the pattern markings and two layers of fabric. Push the pins down so that the heads are tightly against the pattern.

Turn the section over and place a second pin through in the same point as the first pin.

Remove the pattern, carefully pulling the pinhead through the pattern.

When the two layers are separated, the fabric is pin-marked on both the left and the right sides.

Raise the upper layer of fabric and cut the thread between the two layers. Fold on the line of the tailor tacks and pin. Make long tacking stitches in the fold, following the instructions above. Remove the tailor tacks.

CENTRE LINE MARKINGS

The centre line of both front and back sections of the skirt and bodice is a guide for fitting as well as for joining facing and collars at the neck, lapping two sections when there is an opening, positioning buttonholes, joining the bodice and skirt, and folding the hem smoothly. Mark the centre line after you have completed *all* other markings. Use a thread of contrasting colour to the fabric and the other markings.

On folds, make long tacking stitches in the fold, using a single thread. Knot the end of the thread at the beginning and take one backstitch at the end (See top right.)

For openings, tack through the pattern and two layers of fabric along the centre line, using a double thread. Make the stitches small and about 5 cm (2 inches) apart, leaving a loop between the stitches. Cut the looped thread between the stitches and carefully lift the pattern from the fabric, leaving the thread markings in the fabric.

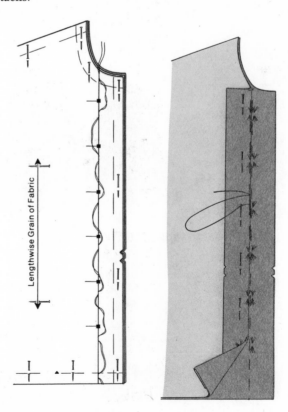

Assembling Your Work

With the fabric cut out, pins ready, and with a threaded needle and a threaded machine waiting to be used, the moment has come to put your creation together. Your next steps will be:

1. Stay stitching.
2. Tacking.

Stay Stitching

Stay stitching is a line of machine stitching, placed through a single thickness of the seam allowance, 1·2 cm (½ inch) from the seam edge. It is used to hold the original shape of necklines, shoulder lines, waistline and hip-lines, and to prevent them from stretching when fitting and handling the garment. Stay stitching is not always a necessary step in dress construction. Some dress-makers like to stay-stitch fabrics which stretch easily or are to be pinned together.

For your stitching, use matching thread and the correct stitch length for stitching seams in your fabric. Chain stitching can also be used to stay-stitch seams. See page 63.

Direction of Stay Stitching

NECKLINE – from shoulder to centre

SHOULDER LINE – from neckline to armhole

WAISTLINE (skirt and blouse) – from side seams to centre

HIPLINE and bias skirt seams – from lower edge to waistline

'V' NECKLINE – from point of 'v' to shoulder line

Tacking

Tacking is a temporary stitch made to hold two or more pieces of fabric together before final stitching. It makes it easier to fit and stitch so that a good finish is achieved. Tacking may be done by hand, or by machine. A very simple garment may be pinned together. It is removed after each seam is stitched.

Hand Tacking

Use a long, slender needle and a single strand of thread not more than 75 cm (30 inches) in length and in a contrasting colour so that it can easily be seen in the fabric. You may use 'tacking' thread, which is soft and lightly twisted, or mercerised thread. Use silk thread for fine fabrics when tacking on the right side to hold two or more layers in position during final pressing – for example, along the finished edge of a facing, the fold for a hem and similar details. In these cases silk is better because it does not leave a mark after pressing and will not mark fine fabrics at the needle puncture.

When tacking sections of a garment, work on a flat surface such as a table or lap board. Place the seam edges together; pin at each end, at notches and at the centre. Then space the pins at equal intervals, working outwards. Place the pins at right angles to the seamline, with heads to seam edge. Do not ease or stretch seam.

Knot the longer end of the thread at the beginning of the tacking line and fasten the line with a short back-stitch at the end. Tack by hand, using one of the methods illustrated.

UNEVEN TACKING

Uneven tacking may be used to tack any seam and *should* be used to mark the stitching line for top-stitching zips, seams and facings.

Working from right to left, make a short stitch on the underside of the fabric and a long stitch on the top side. To remove, clip every 7·5 to 12·5 cm (3 to 5 inches) and pull out.

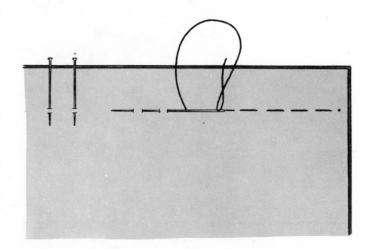

EVEN TACKING

Even tacking may also be used to join the side seams on any fabric. It is a better method for fabrics with a smooth finish and for areas that require close control – for example, set-in sleeves.

Working from right to left, take several long running stitches on the needle before pulling it through. To remove, clip every 7·5 to 12·5 cm (3 to 5 inches) and pull out.

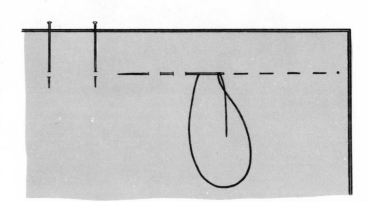

DIAGONAL TACKING

After the facing edges of collars, lapels, cuffs, scallops and similar design details have been stitched, layered and turned, they are held in place for pressing with *diagonal tacking*. This is usually done with silk thread. Diagonal tacking is not used to mark a stitching line or to hold a seam when fitting.

Working from right to left and with the needle pointed towards you, take a short stitch at a right angle to the edge through all layers of fabric. The stitch length should be from ·6 to ·9 cm ($\frac{1}{4}$ to $\frac{3}{8}$ inch), depending on the thickness of fabric. Place succeeding stitches in the same way, spacing them ·3 to ·6 cm ($\frac{1}{8}$ to $\frac{1}{4}$ inch) apart. A diagonal stitch will appear on the upper side and a straight stitch, at a right angle to the edge, on the underside.

Diagonal tacking is also used to hold interfacings and mountings firmly against the fabric during assembly steps. In this application, the spacing between the short stitches may be as much as 2·5 cm (1 inch).

To remove diagonal tacking, cut the diagonal thread every 3 or 4 stitches, and pull out.

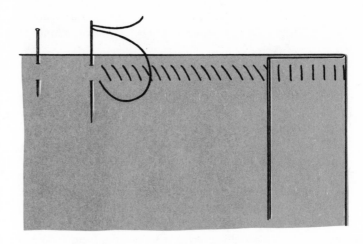

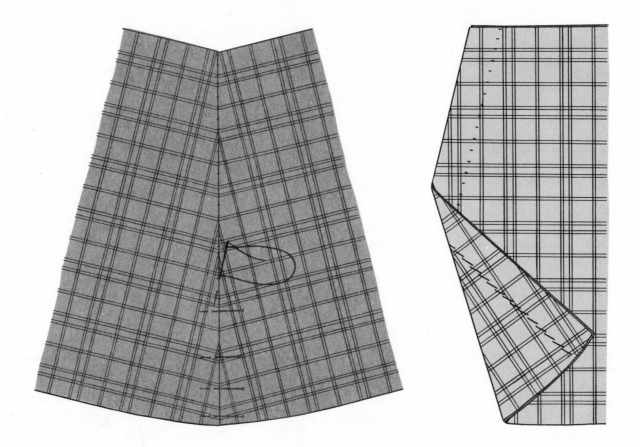

SLIP TACKING

Use slip tacking to match stripes or checks and to join intricate curved sections.

Work from the right side of the garment; fold under the seam allowance on one edge and pin. (Tack if necessary.) Lap the folded edge over the seam allowance of the adjoining section, being careful to match each stripe or check. Place pins at right angles to the folded edge, with heads towards the seam edge. Space the pins about 1·2 cm ($\frac{1}{2}$ inch) apart, depending on the size of the stripe or check.

Insert the needle, from the wrong side, up through the three thicknesses of fabric near the folded edge, and pull through. Then from the top side, directly opposite the previous stitch, insert the needle through the single thickness and bring it up through the three thicknesses and near the folded edge. A long stitch appears on the underside and a short stitch appears under the folded edge. The long stitch is usually from ·6 to 1·5 cm ($\frac{1}{4}$ to $\frac{5}{8}$ inch) in length but may vary with the angle or curve of the seam, or the stripe, check or texture of the fabric.

If you used a tacking thread to retain the fold, remove it before stitching. Machine-stitch the seam from the wrong side through the centre of the short tacking stitches.

To remove the tacking, clip the longer tacking threads every two or three stitches and use tweezers to pull out the threads.

Machine Tacking

Machine tacking is quick and easy, but it should be used only on fabrics where the needle puncture will not show.

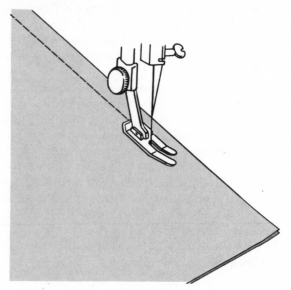

Pin the seam edges together as instructed for hand tacking. Adjust the stitch length selector on the machine for a 4 to 3 mm (6 to 8) stitch length and stitch on the seamline. To remove, clip the top thread at intervals of four or five stitches, then pull the under thread.

Pin Tacking

Pin tacking may be used on straight seams in fabrics that are easy to handle.

Place pins at right angles to the seamline, with the heads towards the edge; if you are going to use the Seam Guide, place the points towards the seam edge. The pins should just nip into the fabric at the stitching line; they should not extend under both sides of the presser foot and should never be placed on the underside of the fabric in contact with the feed of your machine. Machine-stitch on the seamline, using a hinged presser foot.

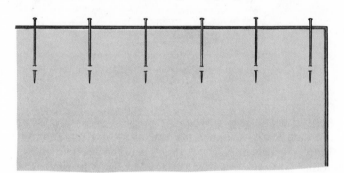

Chain Stitching

The chain stitch is made by the needle thread alone. On top it looks like straight machine stitching, on the underside you can see that it is a series of interlocking loops that can be removed by pulling a thread. This makes chain stitching a convenient method of tacking seams for fitting, marking construction guidelines, inserting 'growth tucks' in children's clothes and applying removable trimming.

Chain Stitch Accessories are provided with some machines by Singer. Check your instruction book for the many sewing jobs you can do with chain stitching.

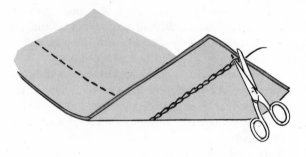

Pressing as You Sew

Pressing often seems to be an unnecessary interruption to your work. But it is very important to remember that *pressing is an integral part of dressmaking*.

After stitching seams, darts, tucks, facings and hems, you must press them. You must also press garment sections before joining them. If you do this faithfully as you sew, only a finishing touch with the iron will be needed when you have finished your work.

Get into the habit of pressing correctly and at the proper time, as explained in this chapter, and you will have the perfect finish of professional tailormade clothes.

The instructions that follow explain what you should know about:

1. Pressing equipment.
2. Fundamentals of pressing.
3. Pressing different kinds of fabrics.
4. Pressing various construction details.

Pressing Equipment

Begin with proper pressing equipment conveniently arranged near the sewing machine. This will encourage you to use the methods professionals use. Once you have established a routine, you will find these methods valuable time-savers. They produce good results immediately and eliminate the re-pressing that is discouraging to the experienced dressmaker as well as to the beginner.

The following equipment is basic and essential for good pressing:

Iron. The undisputed 'first' of good pressing tools is your iron. Choose one with a dependable fabric dial so that you are always sure of using the degree of heat appropriate for your fabric.

A steam iron is a good investment and may be used for both pressing and ironing. On some fabrics and in some areas of pressing, steam from the iron may supply enough moisture; generally, however, you will need additional moisture for an expert pressing job.

Ironing board. A sturdy board that you can easily adjust to several heights is the next requirement. Make sure that your board has a smooth, padded surface.

Sleeveboard. This small ironing board, which is used on your ironing board, is used for pressing sleeves, seams and all fine details. The ironing board supports the weight of the garment and prevents unfinished areas from stretching or wrinkling.

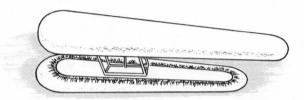

Seamboard. This board, which is also placed on the ironing board, is used for pressing seams open on facings and especially at points. It is excellent for worsteds and other fabrics with a hard finish which must be pressed on a firm surface if you want to get a flat, sharply pressed seam.

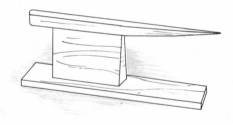

Pressing mitt. This is essential for pressing darts, the top of set-in sleeves and curved seams where the contour and fit of the garment must be preserved. Place the pressing mitt on the narrower end of the sleeveboard.

Tailor's ham. The tailor's ham is used on the ironing board for pressing and shaping curved seams, darts, collars and lapels on suits, coats and other tailored garments. It can be bought at a haberdashery counter and where tailors' equipment is sold.

You can also make one quickly, easily and inexpensively. Buy about ½ metre (½ yard) of cotton drill and

shrink it before cutting. Make a paper pattern, egg-shaped, about 35 cm (14 inches) long and 25 cm (10 inches) in width at the wide end. Then cut two pieces of drill by the pattern. Pin them together and stitch 1·2 cm (½ inch) from the edge, leaving a 12·5-cm (5-inch) opening. Back-stitch at each end of the stitching. Press, then turn to the right side. Fill with clean, sifted sand or sawdust, packing the filling firmly into the cover. Turn the raw edge under on one side and lap the folded edge over the opposite edge; close the opening with hand stitching.

Pressing cloths. You will need three kinds of pressing cloths to properly press the range of fabrics mostly used; (a) if available, a chemically treated pressing cloth is useful for pressing heavy fabrics, or use a firm woven starch-free cloth; (b) a double thickness of soft muslin or cheesecloth or a thin, starch-free cloth, for pressing medium and lightweight fabrics; and (c) wool woven interlining fabric for top pressing on all fabrics.

You will also need a metre (yard) of good quality soft muslin. Use it, moistened, when pressing cottons and linens; place it over the dry pressing cloth to provide uniform moisture when pressing silks, woollens and many construction details. To moisten the muslin, dip it in water, then wring as dry as possible.

Wooden pounding block. Use this to flatten the edges of faced lapels and collars, hems, facings and pleats on tailored garments made of heavy or bulky fabrics. Steam the area first, then quickly apply the pounding block. After a little practice you will be able to determine the amount of pressure needed.

Sponge and small camelhair paintbrush. Use these to moisten the seams of woollens.

Clothes-brush. Use this for brushing napped fabrics after pressing.

Pressing pad. You will need a pressing pad when pressing monograms, lace and construction details such as zips, corded buttonholes and pockets in napped fabrics.

To make a pad, take three or four thicknesses of wool interlining (domette) about 50 cm (20 inches) long and 35 cm (14 inches) wide, and stitch them to a backing of drill. Place the pressing pad on the ironing board with the layers of wool interlining right side up.

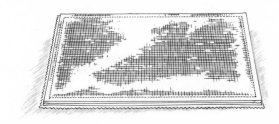

Fundamentals of Pressing

Pressing demands a different technique from ironing. In pressing there is little motion of the iron when it is in contact with the fabric. In ironing, you slide the iron over the fabric in the direction of the fabric grain to remove creases and to restore the shape of a garment or fabric that has been laundered. The amount of heat, moisture and pressure required will vary with the fibre content. Here are the rules to follow in pressing:

1. Always test the fabric for pressing. If necessary, make a seam or dart in a scrap of the same fabric and press it to see how much heat and moisture the fabric

requires. Labels are not always available and some fabrics are difficult to classify.

2. Place the garment in position for pressing, making sure that the fabric is straight and smooth. Lift the fabric with both hands when it is necessary to move it.

3. Always press on the wrong side to guard against shine.

4. Use a pressing cloth on all fabrics, except cottons and linens; place it between the iron and the fabric. The kind of pressing cloth you use and the amount of moisture required will depend on the fabric.

5. Place the iron lightly over the section to be pressed and allow the steam to enter the fabric. Use minimum pressure on the iron and press in the direction of the fabric grain. This helps to retain the shape. Lift the iron to move to another section.

Do not over-press. It will take the life out of the fabric and cause shine. Over-pressing results when you use too hot an iron, leave the iron in one place too long, use an inadequate pressing cloth, apply too much moisture or press too frequently.

How to Press Different Kinds of Fabrics

Fibre texture and thickness determine how a fabric is pressed. Fibre content dictates the temperature of the iron, texture dictates the method of handling the fabric.
Nylon, Terylene, Dacron and similar fabrics require little heat. Set the heat control to the lowest temperature. Press the fabric on the wrong side, using a thin pressing cloth. The iron will not steam at this low setting. If moisture is required, place a single thickness of moist soft muslin over the dry pressing cloth.
Rayon requires a low heat, slightly more than nylon. Set the heat control on 'Rayon'. Press the fabric on the wrong side using a thin pressing cloth. Generally, steam from the iron will supply sufficient moisture. For heavy seams on which you will need more moisture, place a single thickness of moist soft muslin over the thin, dry pressing cloth.
Silk requires slightly more heat than rayon. But guard against too hot an iron, for it will weaken the fibre and discolour pastels and white. Set the heat control on 'Silk'. Press the fabric on the wrong side. For lightweight silk, use a thin pressing cloth. The steam iron should give sufficient moisture. For added moisture on thick seams, place a single thickness of moist soft muslin over the thin, dry pressing cloth. On medium- and heavy-weight

silks, use a double thickness of moist muslin over the thin, dry pressing cloth for extra moisture.
Lightweight cotton requires slightly more heat than silk. Set the heat control on 'Cotton'. Press on the wrong side. You may place the iron directly on the fabric unless you are using a dark colour. To provide uniform moisture on seams, facings and similar construction, cover with moist soft muslin; press dry.
Wool requires more heat than lightweight cotton. Turn the heat control to 'Wool'. Press on the wrong side using a heavy pressing cloth or a double thickness of muslin, covered with moist muslin. Do not press dry. (Over-drying will produce a shine.) If you are working with a napped fabric, brush it with a clothes-brush, while there is still a moist steam, to raise the nap after pressing.
Linen and heavy cotton require a very hot iron. Set the heat control on 'Linen'. Press on the wrong side. You may place the iron directly on linen except when the fabric is of a dark colour. To prevent shine on thick seams and dark colours, use a thin pressing cloth covered with damp soft muslin for added moisture. Press dry.
Velvet and velveteen are steamed. *Do not bring the iron in contact with the fabric or you will flatten the pile.* Stand the iron on its heel and place a damp turkish towel over the soleplate. Hold the wrong side of the velvet close to the towel and move it back and forth to allow the steam to penetrate the fabric.

You can also steam velvet and velveteen on a velvet board, which has fine fibre needles, or you can use a wool-faced pressing pad for steaming. Place the velvet face down over the velvetboard or pressing pad. Hold the steam iron close to the fabric – not on it – and brush the fabric lightly to distribute the steam. Press the seam

open with the finger tips, and steam it by holding the iron close to it. Keep your fingers dry; to avoid finger marks, lift the velvet only when it is dry.

Blended fabrics require varying degrees of heat, depending on the fibre content. The fibe requiring the lowest heat determines the proper temperature for the fabric. Press blends on the wrong side, using a thin pressing cloth. For a blend of Dacron and cotton, steam from the iron should supply sufficient moisture. For a blend of Dacron and silk, you will need additional moisture; use a single thickness of moist soft muslin over a thin pressing cloth. For a blend of silk and wool, which requires more steam than silk and Dacron, use a heavy pressing cloth covered with moist muslin.

Crêpe weaves may present a problem since they tend to shrink in when damp and stretch when under pressure. Place the pressing pad *under* the crêpe, and the soft muslin or wool pressing cloth *over* the fabric to retain the crinkle in pressing. The iron temperature is governed by the fibre content.

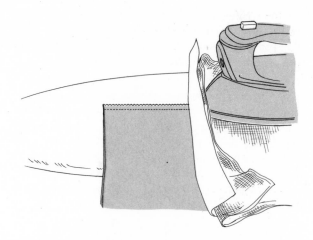

Step 2: Place the seam over the sleeveboard so that you can see the detail clearly and the bulk of the garment can rest on the ironing board. Use your fingers and the *point of the iron* to open the seam. The fingers should work about 5 cm (2 inches) ahead of the iron. Use a moist sponge or camelhair paintbrush to apply moisture in seams of woollens before pressing them open.

How to Press Various Construction Details

RULES TO REMEMBER

1. Remove pins and tacking stitches before pressing. Pins damage the fabric and the soleplate of the iron; tacking stitches leave an imprint. If you need tacking to hold two or more layers of fabric together during pressing (for example, facings), use silk thread and diagonal tacking as instructed on page 61.

2. When pressing the first detail of a garment, press the entire section and not just the area around the seam or dart. In many cases, there is a slight shrinkage of the fabric even though it has been pre-shrunk.

Seams

Always use a sleeveboard when pressing seams, or a seamboard if you have one.

PLAIN SEAM

A plain seam should be pressed as follows:

Step 1: Press the seam in the same position as it was stitched. This will give you a smooth seam and imbed the stitching. To prevent shine, place the correct pressing cloth over all fabrics except light-coloured cottons, which need no protection.

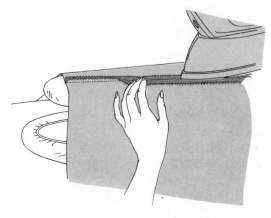

Step 3: Press the seam open, using a pressing cloth between the iron and fabric. See page 66, *How to Press Different Kinds of Fabrics*, for the amount of moisture

and the weight of pressing cloth you need. For heavy fabrics, place a strip of brown paper under the seam allowance to prevent the imprint of the seam edge from appearing on the right side of the fabric.

CURVED SEAM

A curved seam must be layered before it is pressed. See *Seam Layering*, page 89. For the first pressing, follow Step 1, page 67. Then place the curved seam over the curve of a pressing mitt (which has been placed on the end of a sleeveboard) or over the curve of a tailor's ham. Follow the pressing instructions in the second and third steps for the *Plain Seam*.

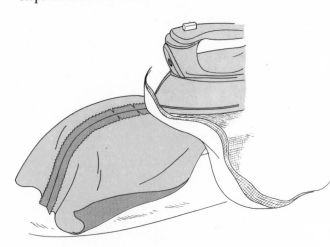

FRENCH SEAM

The French seam is first pressed in the same position as it was stitched, then pressed open with the *point of an iron*. Remember, this seam is on the right side of the fabric and must be protected with a pressing cloth to guard against shine. After trimming the seam allowance and turning to the wrong side, fold sharply on the first line of stitching and press again. The final pressing is done

after you have made the second line of stitching; press the same as in the first step. Use a pressing cloth and moisture required by the fabric.

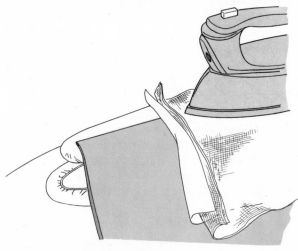

FLAT FELLED SEAM

The flat felled seam is usually formed on the right side of the fabric and must be pressed with a pressing cloth between the iron and fabric. Trim off the edge of one

seam allowance, then press the seam open the same as the French seam. Fold on the seamline and press both seam edges in the same direction, with the longer edge on top. After turning the edge under and stitching a second time, press again from the wrong side, covering with a pressing cloth. (*See the two illustrations at bottom of previous page.*)

Darts

Darts should be pressed with care, for pressing further moulds the dart to bring shape and roundness to the garment.

1. Press the dart flat, as it was stitched, *carrying the crease only as far as the stitching.* Protect the fabric with the proper pressing cloth and use the sleeveboard.

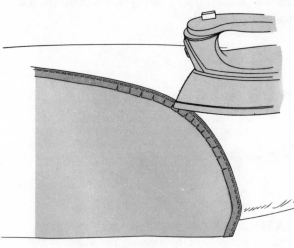

LAPPED SEAM

A lapped seam is pressed on the wrong side after the edge on one side has been folded under and tacked. Press only the very edge on curved seams. Cover the fabric with the proper pressing cloth and use moisture. Press

again on the wrong side after the seam is lapped and stitched. If top pressing is required, place the wool pressing cloth over the fabric.

2. Place the dart over the curve of a pressing mitt, which has been placed on the small end of a sleeveboard, or over the curve of a tailor's ham. Darts are pressed *towards the centre* of skirt front and back, blouse front and back and shoulders; they are pressed downwards at the underarm and elbow. Turn your dart in the proper direction and if the fabric is heavy, slip a strip of brown paper under the dart to prevent the imprint of the dart from appearing on the right side of the fabric. Cover the dart with the correct pressing cloth and use the amount of moisture required by the fabric. Press towards the point of the dart. Then press the entire section of the garment, using a pressing cloth.

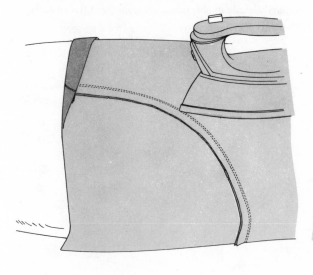

DARTS IN HEAVY FABRICS

Darts in heavy fabrics are slashed and pressed open. After pressing the dart flat, as stitched, place the dart over the curve of a pressing mitt or tailor's ham. Open the dart with the *point of the iron*. Place a strip of brown

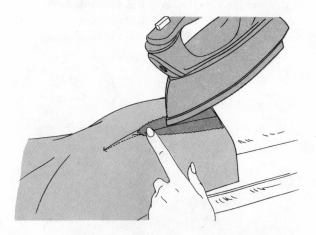

paper under each side of the dart, cover with the correct pressing cloth and use the proper amount of moisture. Press the dart open.

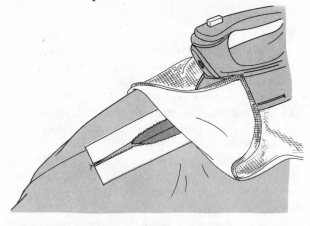

CURVED DARTS

Curved darts are slashed at the waistline to within ·6 cm ($\frac{1}{4}$ inch) of the stitching to relieve strain. Press them in

two operations: (1) press one-half the dart over the curve of a pressing mitt or tailor's ham the same as the conventional dart above; (2) reverse the garment and press the other half. Protect the fabric with a pressing cloth and use the moisture required by the fabric.

Tucks and Gathers

TUCKS

Tucks are first pressed in the same position as they were stitched. Do not allow the point of the iron to go beyond the stitching. Then press the tucks in the proper direction, which is usually towards the centre. When tucks are formed on the outside, the pattern may show them pressed either towards or away from centre. Protect the fabric with the correct pressing cloth and use the proper moisture for the fabric.

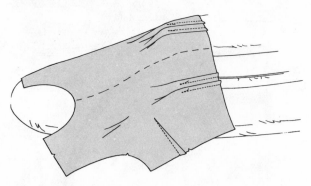

GATHERS

Gathers are pressed by moving the point of the iron upwards to the stitching. Lift the iron and repeat. The pressing can be done best with the iron directly against the wrong side of the fabric; for that reason, control of the iron's heat is very important. Since gathers are customarily made in soft fabrics, steam from the iron should give sufficient moisture.

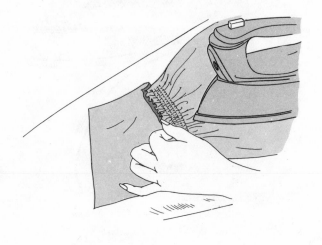

Buttonholes and Pockets

To achieve professional-looking buttonholes and pockets, you must not only follow the sewing instructions exactly but press at every step of construction. There are several excellent methods of making bound buttonholes and pockets. (Refer to 'Buttonholes' or 'Pockets'.) The pressing technique illustrated here is one you should master since it is basic to most buttonholes and also applies to pockets, which follow a construction sequence similar to that of buttonholes.

The first pressing is done after the fabric patch is stitched in place for the buttonhole or pocket. Place the work, wrong side up, over the sleeveboard. Cover with the proper pressing cloth and press, using moisture appropriate for the fabric.

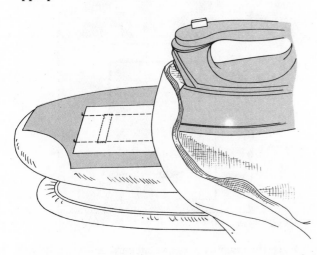

After slashing through the centre and to each corner, turn the facing to the wrong side. Place the work, wrong side up, over the sleeveboard. Fold back the facing and pull the triangular ends away from the opening to square the corners. Apply moisture with a moist soft muslin cloth, and press away from the opening with the *point of the iron*. If the corners are slashed deeply enough, they will be square.

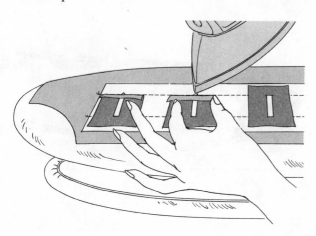

On each side of the buttonhole, fold the patch back, apply moisture with a moist muslin cloth, and press the seam allowances away from the opening, with the point of the iron touching the stitching. Press the entire length of the patch to crease the fold beyond each end of the stitching.

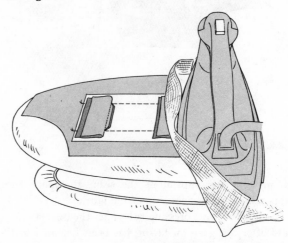

After tacking the folds in place to fill the opening, press on the wrong side, using the correct pressing cloth and the appropriate amount of steam. Slip brown paper between the buttonhole seam allowances and garment

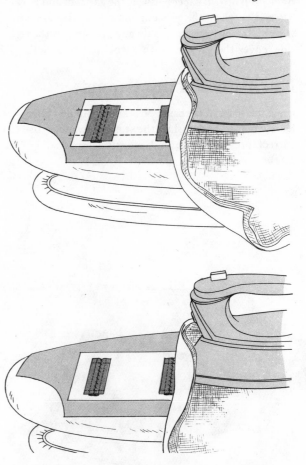

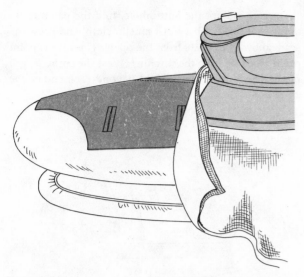

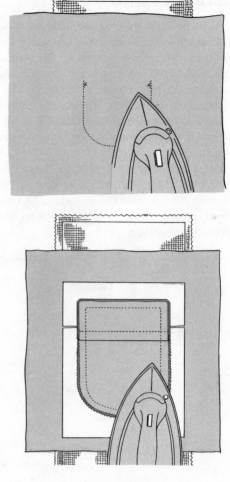

to prevent the imprint of the seam allowance from appearing on the right side of the fabric.

Follow the same pressing rules after the final stitching and after the garment facing has been hemmed to the buttonhole as illustrated above.

For the final pressing of corded buttonholes, corded pockets, patch pockets and pockets with a flap, place the wool-faced pressing pad on the ironing board. (See above right.) Slip brown paper between the garment and pocket bag and between the garment and pocket flap as shown at right. If it is necessary to do any pressing on the right side, cover the garment with a wool pressing cloth.

Neckline Facing Seams

Press the seam in the same position as stitched after you have trimmed and slashed the seam allowances. Use the correct pressing cloth and moisture required by the fabric.

Place the seam over the seamboard and open it with the *point of the iron*. Apply moisture with a moist sponge or paintbrush. Carefully control the heat of the iron so that you can press without a pressing cloth in this step.

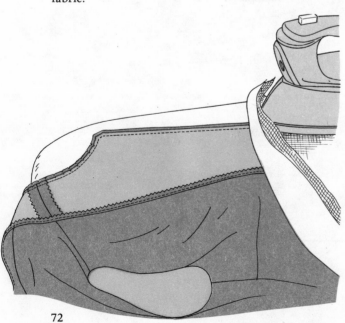

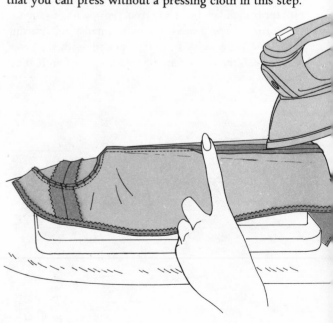

On the curve of the neckline, press just a small portion at a time. Lift the garment with both hands to move it.

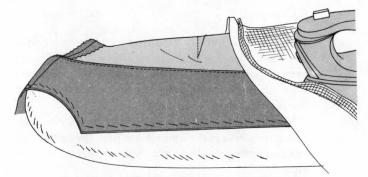

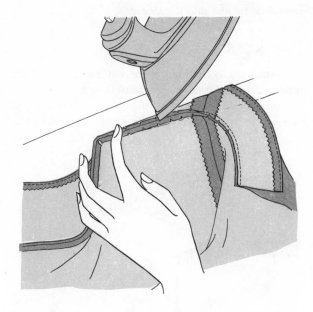

Turn the facing to the underside, then ease it under slightly at the stitching line and tack. Use silk thread and diagonal tacking to hold the facing securely in place on silks and woollens. Silk thread will not leave an imprint on the fabric. Press on the underside; cover with a wool pressing cloth and use the amount of moisture appropriate for the fabric.

Outside curved seams, as in collars and cuffs, are pressed open over the heel of the seamboard.

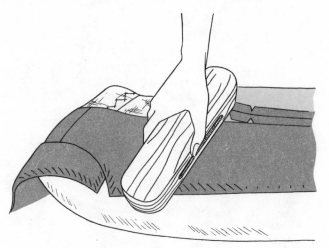

To press faced lapels and collars on tailored suits and coats that are made of heavy or bulky fabrics, steam the area until you have plenty of live steam, then quickly pound the finished edge of the garment with a wooden pounding block. This will force out the steam and leave a flat edge without shine. (See above.)

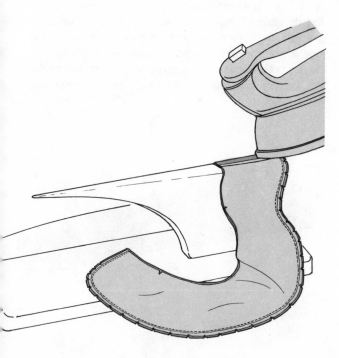

73

Sleeves

Correct pressing makes the difference between a home-made and a professional-looking sleeve. The underarm seam is pressed as it was stitched, the same as a plain seam; then the sleeve is placed over a sleeveboard, and the seam is pressed open.

Your first pressing of a set-in sleeve comes after pin-fitting the sleeve in the armhole. See page 159 for instructions on setting the sleeve into the armhole. Follow these rules:

1. Remove the sleeve from the armhole. Use a pressing mitt on the narrow end of the sleeveboard. Place the sleeve head over the pressing mitt and secure it with pins. Cover the seamline with a dry pressing cloth and moist muslin. Move the *point of the iron* over the seam allowance to shrink out the fullness. Be careful not to press beyond the stitching as you will flatten the head of the sleeve.

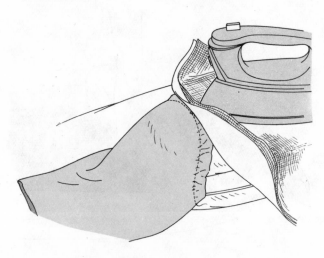

2. After you have stitched the sleeve into the armhole, press the armhole seam allowances over the narrow end

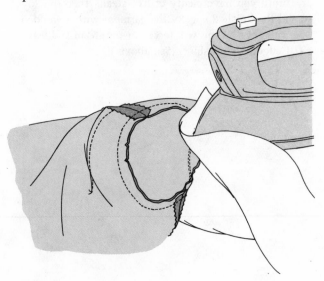

of the sleeveboard. Use the *point of the iron* and press into the sleeve *only as far as the stitching*, never beyond it. Turn the seam allowance into the sleeve without further pressing.

In heavy fabrics, such as coating, press the seam open. In a puffed sleeve, as in children's clothes, the seam should be turned into the sleeve.

Plackets

The usual placket closing is the zip. See page 176 for instructions on various ways of inserting zips. Your first pressing comes after closing the opening with machine tacking. Press the curved seam open in the machine-

tacked area; place it over the curve of a pressing mitt, which has been placed on the narrow end of the sleeve-board or over the curve of a tailor's ham.

Your second pressing step comes after the final hand or machine stitching. Place the wool-faced pressing pad on the ironing board with the wool interlining upwards. Lay the garment, right side down, on the pad. Place a dry pressing cloth, then a moist muslin cloth, on the wrong side of the garment and press along the stitching line. Do not press over the metal teeth or synthetic coil of the zip, for you may damage the fabric, zip and soleplate of the iron.

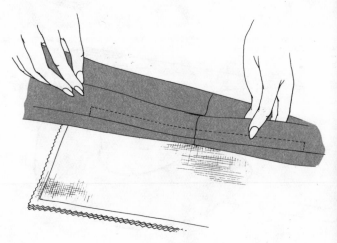

After you have removed the machine tacking, you may need a final press. Place a strip of brown paper between the placket opening and the metal chain or synthetic coil of the zip. Protect the fabric with a wool pressing cloth and press only the stitching line.

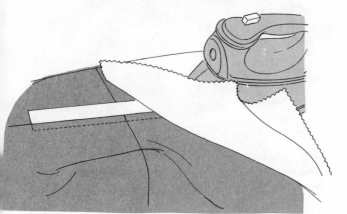

Hems

Hems should not be visible in the finished garment. To achieve this, you must not only mark, fold and finish the hem properly (see page 187), but *press* it carefully.

The first pressing step occurs after you have folded the hem and tacked ·6 cm (¼ inch) from the fold. Place the garment, wrong side up, over the end of the ironing board; cover with the correct pressing cloth and apply the moisture required by the fabric. Do not slide the iron; lift it from one section to the other, pressing lightly and forcing steam through the pressing cloth to form a sharp crease at the fold.

If the fabric is heavy or bulky, steam the hem edge; then use the wooden pounding block, following the

directions for *Faced Lapels and Collars*, on page 73.

Fashion may dictate a **soft hem fold** for fabrics such as double knits, loosely woven woollens, raw silks and bonded fabrics. In such cases, press the hem *very lightly* so that you do not flatten the fold.

HEMS IN GORED AND FLARED SKIRTS

Gored and flared skirts have fullness at the top of the hem which is controlled with machine stitching. To shrink out any excess fullness before applying seam binding, place the free edge of the hem over the curve of a pressing mitt (which has been placed over the narrow end of the sleeveboard) or over the curve of a tailor's ham. Cover with the same pressing cloth and use the same amount of moisture required in the first step. Press to shrink out the fullness.

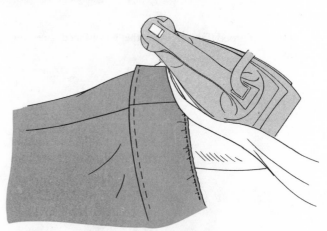

After you have stitched the seam binding in place or completed the appropriate finish, press the hem on the wrong side in the position it will be hand-stitched, using a pressing cloth. Move the iron upwards from the fold of the hem to the top of the seam binding.

When the garment is of a heavy fabric, slip a strip of

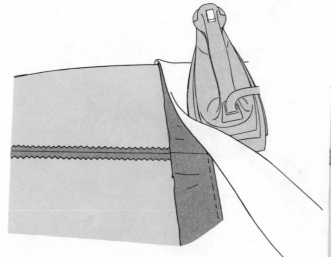

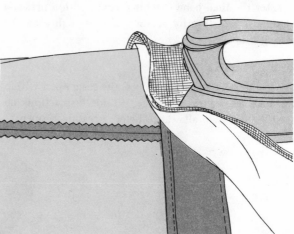

brown paper between the skirt and hem before pressing. This prevents the imprint of the hem edge from appearing on the right side of the garment.

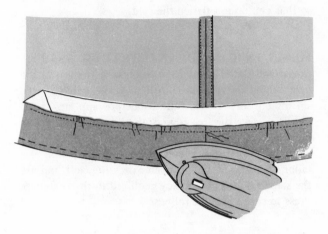

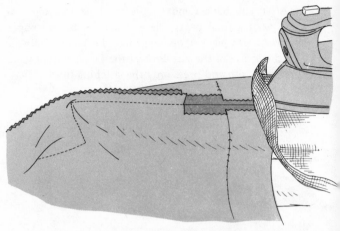

Press napped fabrics over the wool-faced pressing pad.

After you have finished the hem, turn the skirt to the wrong side, turn the pleat away from the skirt and press.

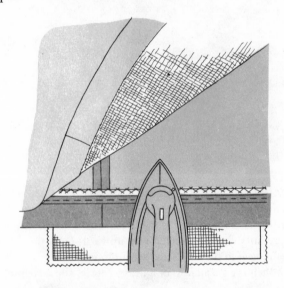

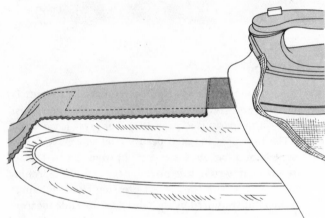

After the final hand stitching, cover with a pressing cloth, use moisture for steam and press lighly on the wrong side.

To sharpen the edge of a pleat, turn the garment to the right side. Place the pleat section over the sleeveboard with the underfold of the pleat up. Cover with the wool pressing cloth and press the length of the pleat. For instructions on pressing pleated skirts, see page 211.

PLEAT HEM
When the skirt has a pleat, press the seam open within the hem allowance. See page 191 for instructions on slashing the seam allowance before pressing it open.

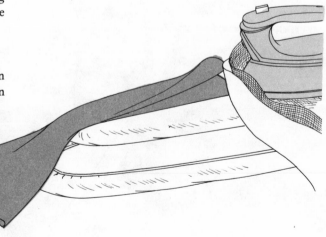

Fitting as you Sew

Fittings are pleasant steps in sewing that show you how your work is progressing. Even though you adjusted the tissue pattern to your measurements before cutting the fabric, you may find that minor changes are required when you fit the fabric.

Be critical. The success of your garment depends as much on its fit as on the suitability of the pattern design and fabric. Fashions can be copied, but the garment becomes individually yours when it fits your figure properly. For a good fit, the fabric grain lines must fall correctly in the proper places on your figure. This is explained below in *Understanding Balance Lines*.

In addition to explaining balance lines, this chapter also takes you through the basic fittings. A word of advice: do not feel bound to fit your dress only at the intervals given here. You may want to fit it more often – especially if the pattern is intricate or you are not sure of an adjustment or are a beginner. Sometimes it is necessary to try on only the bodice or skirt section to test the fit. Fit as often as you feel you should before making the permanent line of stitching. Remember, changes made at the proper time are easier and quicker, and your dress is sure to be a success. If you have a Dress Form (shape), follow a similar procedure.

Understanding Balance Lines

The lengthwise and crosswise grains of the fabric must be in proper relation to the individual figure for any garment to fit well. The positions of the key grain lines are known as 'balance lines'.

The grain lines are in the correct positions on the tissue pattern. However, if your figure does not conform to standard measurements, adjustments are necessary. In adjusting the pattern and in fitting your dress, you must retain the correct position of the balance grain lines on your figure so that your dress will fit as it should.

The illustrations and text here point out the correct position of balance lines on a sheath dress.

Bodice Front

CHEST – about 10 cm (4 inches) below the base of the neck, on the *crosswise grain*.

BUST – across the fullest part of the bust, on the *crosswise grain*.

WAIST – about 4 cm (1½ inches) above the waistline, on the *crosswise grain*.

CENTRE FRONT – centre of body, from base of neck to waistline, on the *lengthwise grain*.

Bodice Back

SHOULDER – about 10 cm (4 inches) below the prominent vertebra, on the *crosswise grain*. (This corresponds with the chest on the bodice front.)

UNDERARM – about 4 cm (1½ inches) below the armhole,

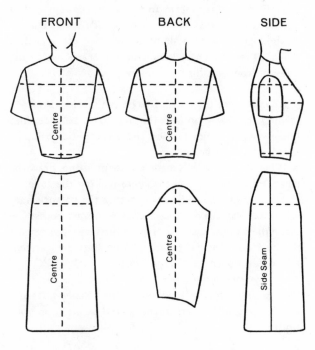

77

across the shoulder blades, corresponding with the bustline, on the *crosswise grain*.

WAIST – about 4 cm (1½ inches) above the waistline, corresponding with the front grain line, on the *crosswise grain*.

CENTRE BACK – centre of body, from prominent vertebra at neck to waistline, on the *lengthwise grain*.

Sleeves

CENTRE – from shoulder line marking to centre of wrist, on the *lengthwise grain*.

SLEEVE HEAD – about 7·5 cm (3 inches) below the shoulder line, across the sleeve head at a right angle to the lengthwise grain. This line is on the crosswise grain and corresponds with the chest and shoulder grain line of the bodice.

Skirt – Front and Back

CENTRE FRONT AND BACK – centre of body from waistline to hemline, on the *lengthwise grain*.

HIPS – across the fullest part of the hips, usually about 18 cm (7 inches) below the waistline, parallel to the floor, on the *crosswise grain*.

The *side seams* of bodice and skirt must hang perpendicular to the floor although they are seldom cut on the straight grain of the fabric. In full skirts, the centre front and back seams may be bias and the side seams may be straight grain, with a slight curve from the waistline about 10 cm (4 inches) down. All four seams must hang straight from waistline to hemline.

Always mark the centre line on the fabric with hand tacking. It is wise to tack the horizontal balance lines when sewing on fine fabrics, and it is especially important if you are a beginner.

When a calico toile is made for use in fitting, draw the balance lines on the calico before making the toile. In this way, you can easily see whether the balance lines are in the correct position. If adjustments are necessary, make them in the toile. Then make the same adjustments to the tissue pattern before cutting into the garment fabric. See *Calico Toile*, page 315.

As you and your dress proceed through the basic fittings described, keep an eye on the balance lines and make sure that they are in the correct position on your figure.

Pin Fitting

Assembling Your Dress

Before pin-fitting your dress, you should have completed these steps:

1. Transferred all markings from pattern to fabric.
2. Stay-stitched if necessary.
3. Tacked darts and tucks.
4. Machine-stitched where needed to control any gathered fullness.
5. Tacked sectional seams together so that you have four pieces: upper front, upper back, skirt front and skirt back.

Work on a flat surface. Pin bodice sections together at the shoulder line and underarm seams and skirt sections together at the side seams. Place pins parallel to the seamline with the fabric right side out and seam edges extended. Leave an opening on the left side of both bodice and skirt for the zip. Turn under the waistline seam allowance of the skirt, and pin.

Fitting Your Dress

Try on the garment, right side out, in front of a full-length mirror if possible. Wear the lingerie and shoes you will wear with the finished garment. And don't forget make-up. It will help you visualise how the dress will look on you. If you plan to wear shoulder pads, insert them (and use them in every step of fitting).

If there is a centre opening, lap the opening (with centre lines together) and pin together at buttonhole markings. Pin seams together in the opening for the zip. Pin the bodice and skirt together at waistline, with the skirt seam allowance overlapping the bodice seam allowance; be sure to match centre lines, darts and side seams. Adjust the shoulder line to your figure and make certain that the tacked centre lines of the garment coincide with the centre of your figure.

If you are a newcomer to dressmaking, you will probably be carried away by the fact that 'it' actually looks like a dress. But let your eye roam critically over the several parts of the work. You will observe that the fabric fits a little differently from the tissue pattern. The need for minor adjustments, which you could not easily detect in fitting the tissue pattern, will become apparent now. As you make them, note them for future reference, for you will want to incorporate them in patterns you use later.

In studying your pin-fitted garment in front of the mirror, remember these points and consider them in your fitting:

1. The neckline has an extended seam allowance, which makes it seem smaller than it will be when the neckline is finished.

2. All ease allowances must be correct as outlined in checking and fitting the pattern. See page 37. Do not over-fit the garment. The amount of fullness allowed in the pattern will differ with the style.

Fit the fabric for right- and left-figure differences, which occur most frequently at shoulders, waistline and hipline. The paragraphs below explain how to make some of the most usual adjustments.

BODICE ADJUSTMENTS

Observe and change when necessary the position of the waistline, side seams and shoulder line and the alignment of buttonholes.

Check the length of the shoulder seam. Bring the arms forward to test the ease across the back, from armhole to armhole.

Sloping shoulders will cause the balance line to drop at the armholes and form wrinkles. To correct, re-pin the shoulder seams, making them slightly deeper as you approach the shoulder points. This means lowering the armhole so that the sleeve will fit as it should. Tack the position of the new seamline. Lay the pattern on the fabric with the shoulder seamline of the pattern on the tacked line of the fabric, and re-cut the armhole. Both shoulders are seldom identical and it may be necessary to change only one.

If **square shoulders** are the problem, the balance line swings up at the armholes and causes wrinkles to form diagonally towards the bustline and below the back neckline. Re-pin the shoulder seams, making them deeper at the neckline and tapering the seam allowance at the shoulder points.

Bustline darts may need adjustment. Check the length and angle of the darts. If there is fullness below the bustline and the balance line seems to drop below the fullest part of the bust, raise the underarm darts enough to bring the points in line with the fullest part of the bust; if there is fullness above the bustline and the balance line is above the fullest part of the bust, lower the underarm darts.

A small, flat bust will cause the balance line to sag at the centre front. Decrease the underarm darts enough to correct the balance line position and achieve a smooth effect. Now the bodice front will be longer than the bodice back at the underarm seams. *It is a common mistake for a beginner to make the bodice too short;* therefore, try on the dress again to prove the adjustment is correct. Then make a tuck across the tissue pattern, decreasing the length of the bodice front the same amount as you decreased the darts. Lay the pattern on the bodice front, and re-cut the lower edge of the fabric.

SKIRT ADJUSTMENTS

Difference in hips. It is not unusual for the side seams to fit differently on the right and left sides of the skirt because one hip is higher or larger than the other. Be sure that the side seams hang straight from waistline to lower edge. The skirt should have enough ease at the hipline for you to sit comfortably and enough ease below the hipline so the skirt will not cling under the seat.

A hollow back will make the grain line sag at the centre back and cause wrinkles below the waistline. To correct, raise the waistline of the skirt in the centre back from 1·2 to 1·5 cm ($\frac{1}{2}$ to $\frac{5}{8}$ inch). Mark the adjusted seamline with tacking, gradually tapering to the waistline seam allowance as you approach the side seams. Sometimes it is necessary to lift the skirt on only one side of the waistline.

If the skirt lifts in the front and the side seams jut forward, raise the back and sides of the skirt at the waistline just enough to bring the balance line in correct position and the side seams in a straight line to achieve a smooth effect.

Skirt darts should extend to the fullest part of the hips. It may be necessary to lengthen or shorten the darts to follow the curve of your figure.

Check the length of the skirt and the amount allowed for the hem.

Pin-mark any adjustments. Remove the garment and mark the adjustments with tacking.

You are now ready for some serious stitching. Before you begin, it may be wise to re-read the pressing advice given in *Pressing As You Sew*, page 64.

Tacked Fitting

Garment Construction to be Completed

The steps in construction to complete before this fitting are as follows:

1. Stitch and press all darts.
2. Make bound buttonholes if your pattern calls for them.
3. Tack, stitch and press seams in the front and back sections.
4. If mounting is used, stitch and press the darts, then tack the mounting to the wrong sides of the garment sections.
5. Stitch and press shoulder seams.
6. Apply the interfacing, and finish the neckline and front or back opening.
7. If your dress has sleeves, tack the darts or control any fullness at the elbow. Tack the sleeve underarm seam.
8. Try the sleeve on the right arm, right side out, with the arm flexed to allow for muscle expansion. If there is a marked difference between the right and left arms, fit both sleeves.
9. Tack any adjustments and re-fit the sleeve. Stitch and press sleeve underarm seams.
10. Tack the side seams in the bodice and in the skirt, right sides together, noting the adjustments made in the pin fitting.
11. Pin and tack the sleeves into the armholes.
12. Tack bodice and skirt together at the waistline, right sides together, noting any changes made in the pin fitting.

Fitting Your Dress

Try on the dress, right side out, to confirm the adjustments made in the pin fitting before stitching the side seams.

1. Lap and pin the opening. Check that the seams and centre lines are in the right places.

2. Tie a tape measure or a strip of fabric, about 2·5 cm (1 inch) wide, around your waist to find the normal waistline. The seam should be below the tape. Check the waist length, the ease allowances in all round measurements, the position of side seams and shoulder line and the hang and fit of the sleeves. The balance lines in the sleeves and bodice should correspond.

3. Bring the arm forward to test the ease across the back, from armhole to armhole, for freedom of arm movement. Insufficient ease will cause strain across the sleeve and be uncomfortable, and the sleeves will pull out at the seamline after you have worn the garment a few times. If shoulder seams are too long, the sleeves will drop off the shoulders and be uncomfortable. Bend the arms to be sure you have allowed enough ease in the sleeves for comfort. Pin-mark any adjustments. Tack the new adjustments and try on the garment again to prove them.

Subsequent Fittings

Fitting to Check Sleeve and Waistline

Before this fitting, remove the waistline and sleeve tacking. Stitch and press the side seams in the bodice and skirt. Tack sleeves into the armholes again and tack bodice to skirt, right sides together, checking any changes made in the earlier fitting.

Now, try on the dress; lap and pin the opening. Check the bodice length, the fit in the waistline, the position of the ease in the sleeves; decide the sleeve length. If you are satisfied, complete the final stitching.

Your Final Fitting

Before the final fitting, stitch sleeves into armholes, join skirt and bodice at the waistline and insert the zip.

Try on the dress and test the fit. If you are satisfied, mark the hemline.

Seams, Seams, Seams

Seams do more than hold your dress together. Plain seams give the line of your dress through subtle shaping. Correctly put together, they are almost invisible. Decorative seams can emphasise line in the dress design.

This chapter explains what you should know about seams to achieve the effect you want. The material is grouped in five sections:

1. General rules and helps in seaming.
2. Different kinds of seams.
3. Seam layering.
4. Seam finishes.
5. Understitching.

General Rules and Helps in Seaming

A seam is when one or more lines of stitching are used to join two or more pieces of fabric. The steps in forming a seam are these:

1. Pin the seam edges together at ends, at notches and at centre, finally working between centre and ends.

2. Hand-tack the seam. If your fabric is easy to handle and if you are sufficiently skilled in stitching, you can pin it together instead of tacking it.

3. Stitch the seam with thread the exact colour of the fabric. Set the stitch selector for the stitch length appropriate for your fabric (refer to the *Fabric, Thread and Needle Chart* on page 24) and then test the stitch on a scrap of the fabric. Stitch along one side of the tacking thread, close to it but not through it. Back-stitch at each end of the seam to secure the threads. Remove the tacking thread.

4. Finish the seam edges. See page 91.

5. Press the seam in the same position as it was stitched and then press it open unless the pattern instructs otherwise.

Seam Guidelines

The Seam Guide and throat-plate guidelines help you guide the stitching straight and parallel to the seam edge. The Seam Guide is adjustable for spacing stitching between ·3 and 3·1 cm ($\frac{1}{8}$ and $1\frac{1}{4}$ inches) from the edge of the fabric. The throat-plate markings progress at ·3-cm ($\frac{1}{8}$-inch) intervals, starting at ·9 cm ($\frac{3}{8}$ inch) and extending to 2 cm ($\frac{3}{4}$ inch) from the needle at the right. Since most patterns have a 1·5-cm ($\frac{5}{8}$-inch) seam allowance, the 1·5-cm ($\frac{5}{8}$-inch) line is more prominent than the other markings on the throat-plate.

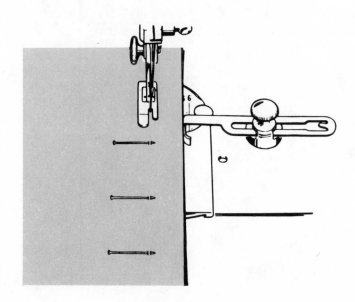

Directional Stitching

There are also rules on the direction you should follow in stitching seams. In general, shoulder seams are stitched from the neckline to the armhole; bodice seams from underarm to waistline; sleeve seams from underarm to wrist; skirt seams from hem to waistline. There are exceptions, however; for example: pile fabrics such as velvet, velveteen and corduroy are cut with the pile standing up, and all seams should be stitched upwards with the pile (from lower edge to top edge).

Different Kinds of Seams

Your pattern will indicate the types of seams you are to use, and below you will find instructions for stitching them. Unless otherwise stated, all seams are stitched from the wrong side of the fabric.

Plain Seam – Straight

The plain seam is stitched with the right sides of fabric together. Place the seam under the needle, with the edges to the right. Position the needle about 1·2 cm (½ inch) from the back edge and lower the presser foot. Back-stitch to the edge of the fabric for reinforcement; then stitch forwards to the end of the seam and back-stitch to reinforce it. Raise the presser foot and remove the fabric. Get into the habit of using the Thread Cutter behind the presser bar assembly and just above the presser foot.

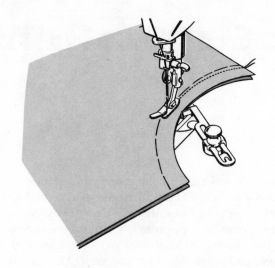

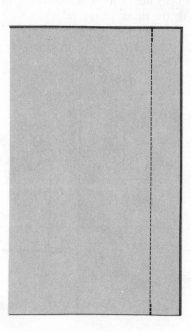

Plain Seam – Curved (*Top right*)

Curved seams require special attention in handling and shaping. Use a shorter stitch than for a straight seam. If you used a 2 mm (12) stitch length for straight seams, use a 1·5 mm (15) stitch length for curved seams to ensure extra elasticity and strength and to prevent seam failure under strain. Position the Seam Guide at an angle so that you get a uniform seam edge.

Curved seams must be layered so that they will lie flat. See instructions on page 89.

Bias Seam

Hand-tack bias seams, leaving the threads loose at the ends. Allow your work to hang overnight before stitching. Always use a shorter stitch length for a bias seam. Fabric requiring a 2 mm (12) stitch length on a straight seam requires a 1·5 mm (15) stitch length on a bias seam to increase the elasticity of the seam. Stitch with the grain.

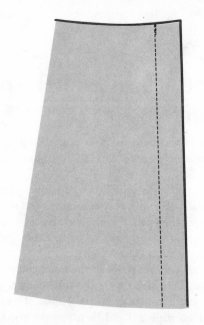

Seam with Bias Edge and Straight Edge

To join a bias edge to a straight edge, pin and tack with the bias section on top. Stitch with the bias edge against the feed to ensure a smooth, even joining. (*See illustration at top of next page.*)

Double-Stitched Seam

Use this seam in sheer fabrics and lace for curved as well as straight seams.

Place the first row of stitching on the seamline. Press. Place the second row of stitching within the seam allowance, about ·6 cm ($\frac{1}{4}$ inch) from the first row, using a fine multi-stitch zig-zag. Straight stitching may also be used. Trim the seam allowance close to the outside row of stitching.

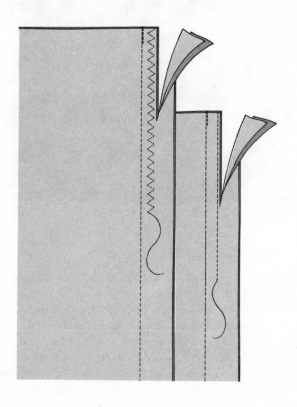

Lapped Seam

Use lapped seams when joining sections of interfacing and interlining to eliminate bulk.

Lap one edge over the other, with the seamlines meeting in the centre. Stitch through the centre, using a multi-stitch zig-zag or straight stitching. If the seam edges are too wide, trim after stitching.

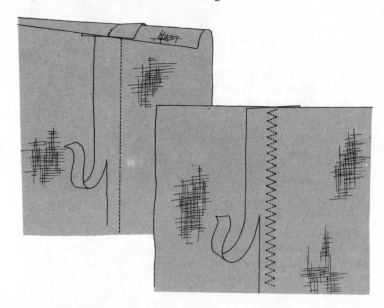

Abutted Seam

Use an abutted seam for non-woven interfacings and interfacings of hair canvas, lawn and similar fabrics.

Trim away the seam allowance on both sections. Bring the two edges together and pin over an underlay of a lightweight fabric. The underlay should be 2·5 cm (1 inch) wide and slightly longer than the seam. Stitch

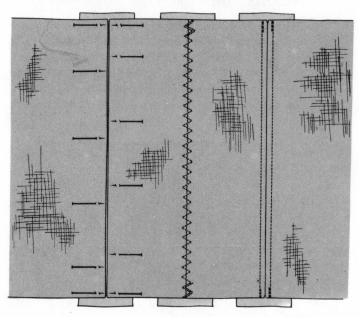

83

from the right side, using the multi-stitch zig-zag, widest stitch width and 1·5–1 mm (20) stitch length. Back-stitch at each end. The abutted line should be aligned with the centre of the presser foot. Straight stitching may also be used on each side of the abutment.

Ease in a Seam

A seam with slight ease often occurs at the shoulder or elbow where a long seam edge joins a shorter one.

Working from the long side, pin the edges together, matching at the ends of the seam and at the notches. Between the notches, ease the long side to the short side by inserting pins at frequent intervals, distributing the fullness evenly. Hand-tack, then stitch with the full side against the feed.

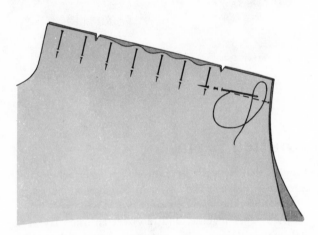

Seams that Cross

Seams that cross occur at the shoulder line, waistline and underarm and where darts join a seam or tuck.

Press the seams open and finish the edges as required by the fabric. To ensure accurately matched seams that cross, pin with a fine needle, with only the point nipped into the fabric at the stitching line; then pin on each side

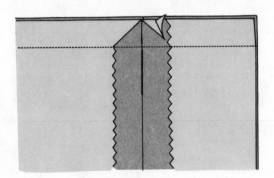

on the seamline. The needle prevents one seam from slipping beyond the other during stitching and will not mark delicate fabrics. Trim away the excess seam allowance at the point where the seams cross.

Top-Stitched Seam

Top stitching is used as a styling point along the finished edge of a garment or along the seam within a garment.

When preparing a curved, top-stitched seam, stay-stitch near the seamline on both the overlap and the underlap. Fold under the seam allowance on the overlap and pin, tack, trim and press. Lap the folded edge a full seam's width over the underlap, then pin and tack. Remove the first tacking. Top-stitch from the right side, close to the folded edge. If the stitching is ·6 cm (¼ inch) or more from the edge, mark the stitching line with tacking as instructed for *Top Stitching*, page 335.

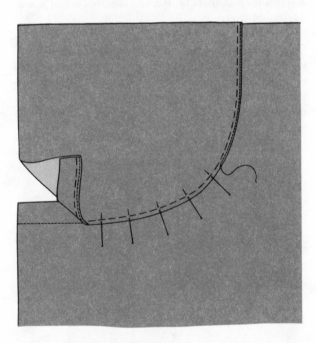

Tucked Seam

Use tucked seams as a design detail in blouses, dresses, skirts and other garments.

Working from the right side, fold under the seam allowance on one side and pin; tack, if necessary. Lay the folded edge on the seamline of the second section and pin, keeping the raw edges even on the underside. Tack the tuck, keeping an even distance between the folded edge and the tacking line. Then stitch, following the even tacked line. Trim off the seam edge on the undersection. On older model machines the Quilter is an aid when stitching this seam because the guide keeps your stitching straight and parallel to the folded edge.

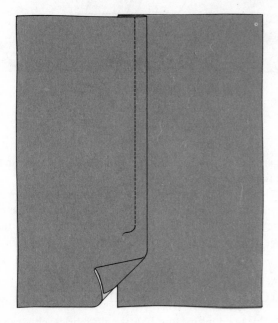

Self-Bound Seam

Use self-bound seams in net curtains, children's clothes, blouses and similar articles.

Make a plain seam and press it as stitched. Trim one edge to within ·3 cm ($\frac{1}{8}$ inch) of the stitching. Turn under the other edge and pin it to the seam at the line of stitching, enclosing the first edge. Stitch near the folded edge.

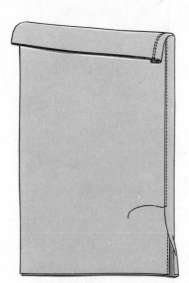

Hemmed Seam

A hemmed seam is appropriate when a fine, narrow seam is required, such as in net curtains and children's clothes.

When using this seam in a garment, the fitting must be done first and seam edges trimmed to ·6 cm ($\frac{1}{4}$ inch). Attach the Hemmer Foot to the machine in place of the regular Presser Foot. With right sides of the fabric together, place the upper layer ·3 cm ($\frac{1}{8}$ inch) to the left of the lower layer. Insert the edge into the scroll of the Hemmer and stitch so that the wide edge is hemmed over the narrow edge. See *Hemmer Foot*, page 283.

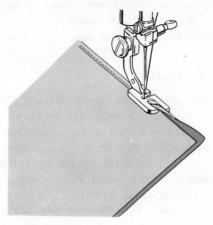

Lingerie Seam

With zig-zag stitching, you can make very fine lingerie seams. This method is particularly good where flat bias seams are needed.

After straight-stitching the bias seam on the wrong side, press as stitched. Pink, and then press both seam allowances in the same direction. From the right side, stitch with a fine zig-zag stitch, allowing the needle to enter the seamline, then the seam thickness.

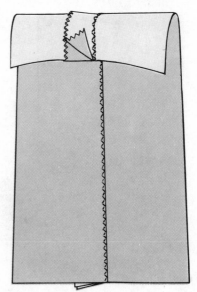

Herringbone Seam (*Right*)

A herringbone seam is used where the garment is interfaced or mounted. This is an excellent means of preventing seam edges from rolling when the garment is dry-cleaned. Use it in shoulder seams and notched collars and where collar and facings join.

Trim the interfacing or mounting seam allowance close to the stitching. Press the plain seam open, then herringbone the seam edges by hand. Working from left to right, with the needle pointed to the left, catch only one or two threads in the seam allowance, then only a single thread outside the seam allowance and in the interfacing or mounting. Alternate the stitches along the seamline. The stitches will not show from the right side.

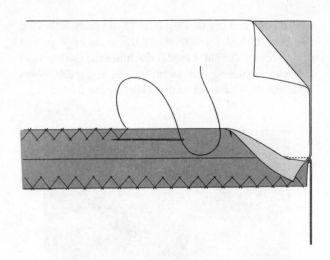

French Seam

Use a French seam in fine fabrics, blouses, children's clothes and lingerie. It is not suitable for curved seams.

A French seam is a seam within a seam and, when finished, is usually ·6 cm ($\frac{1}{4}$ inch) or less in width. Place the wrong sides of the fabric together and stitch about ·6 cm ($\frac{1}{4}$ inch) from the seamline. Press as stitched. Trim seam allowances to within ·3 cm ($\frac{1}{8}$ inch) of stitching and press the seam open. Turn the right sides of the fabric

together; fold on the stitching line and press. Then stitch on the seamline.

The Edge Stitcher may be used in making a French seam. The slot in the accessory assures a straight line of stitching. See page 284 for instructions on using the *Edge Stitcher*.

Mock French Seam

Use this seam in fine and lightweight fabrics, children's clothes and blouses, in place of the conventional French seam. Both straight and curved seams may be finished in this way.

Stitch along the seamline with right sides of the fabric together. Press as stitched. Trim the seam edges slightly if they are too wide. Fold both seam edges to the inside and stitch them together.

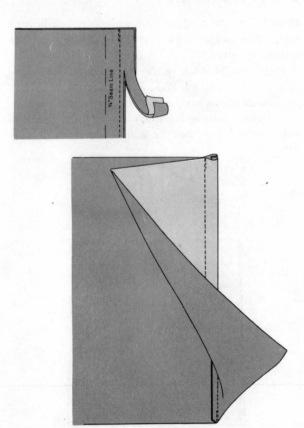

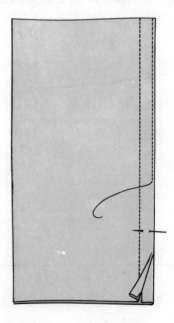

Flat Felled Seam

Men's and boys' wear usually call for flat felled seams. They are also used to give a tailored appearance to women's sportswear. It is a matter of preference which side of the seam is made on the right side. One side shows an inside seam with parallel stitching, and the reverse side shows a top-stitched seam with a parallel row of stitching.

With wrong sides of the fabric together, take the full seam allowance with the first row of stitching. Press the seam open, then press both seam allowances to one side, keeping the right side of the stitching on top. Trim the under seam allowance to one-half its width. Turn the upper seam allowance edge evenly over the trimmed edge; then top-stitch.

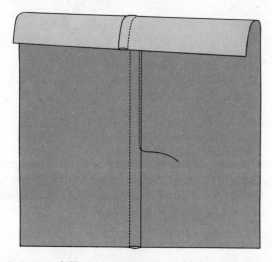

Opinions differ on the handling of flat felled seams. On men's wear, the seam edges that are layered are usually: (1) the back seams on side seams and sleeve seams, (2) the sleeve seam edge on shoulder seams, (3) the garment section on yoke seams, and (4) the front seam on shoulder seams.

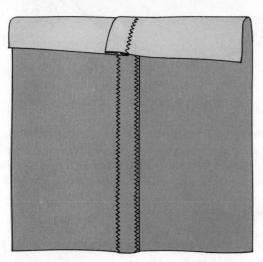

Zig-zag stitching gives strength and durability to flat felled seams. You can substitute it for straight stitching, following the directions given above. Use a 1·5 mm (15) stitch length and a medium-width zig-zag stitch.

Channel Seam

Channel seams are used as decorative seams in skirts, blouses, dresses, suits, coats and children's clothes made of heavy- or medium-weight fabrics.

Pin and machine-tack on the seamline, leaving one long thread at each end. Press as stitched, then press the seam open. Clip the machine tacking on one side at four or five stitch intervals. Cut an underlay of the same or contrasting fabric 2·5 cm (1 inch) wider than the two seam edges. Working from the wrong side, centre the underlay over the seam and pin in position. Tack from the right side. Then from the right side, stitch along each side an equal distance from the seam depression. The distance may be from ·6 to 1·2 cm ($\frac{1}{4}$ to $\frac{1}{2}$ inch), depending on the fabric. If less than ·6 cm ($\frac{1}{4}$ inch), gauge the distance with the presser foot; if more than ·6 cm ($\frac{1}{4}$ inch),

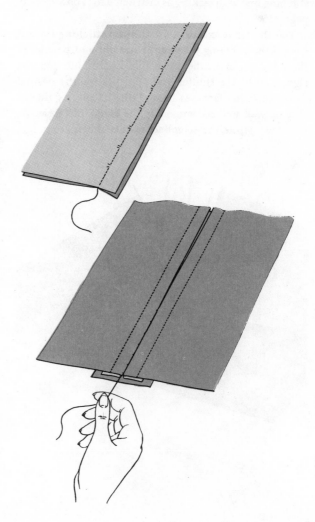

mark both stitching lines with tacking as instructed for *Top Stitching*, page 335. Remove the machine tacking by pulling the long thread, and remove any short threads that are visible with tweezers.

The Quilter is convenient for top stitching. The space guide on the Quilter is guided into the line of the machine-tacked seam, ensuring an accurate stitching line parallel to the fold. See the instructions below for *Welt Seam*.

Welt Seam

Welt seams are style seams that are often found in suits and coats made of firm fabrics.

Stitch a plain seam on the wrong side, using the stitch length appropriate for the fabric. Press first as stitched; then press the seam open. Trim ·5 cm ($\frac{3}{16}$ inch) from one seam edge and press both seam edges to one side so that the wide edge covers the narrow edge. Tack flat. From the right side, stitch an even distance from the seamline. If the distance is greater than ·6 cm ($\frac{1}{4}$ inch), mark the stitching line with tacking as instructed for *Top Stitching*, page 335.

The Quilter is excellent for this top stitching since it gauges the stitching, keeping it straight and parallel to the seamline. Insert the removable space guide from the right side of the Quilter and adjust it for the desired distance. If the fabric is heavy, tilt the space guide so that its wall will accommodate the layers of fabric. As you sew, guide the seamline against the space guide.

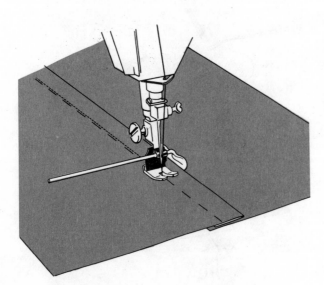

Hairline Seam

A hairline seam makes a perfect finish for enclosed seams of fine collars and facings. Set your zig-zag machine for a short stitch length and a narrow stitch width, and use a filler cord of either heavy-duty thread or buttonhole twist. Unwind a sufficient amount of the filler cord to prevent strain or tension on the cord. Lead the end of the cord through the right eyelet on the Special Purpose Foot. Draw the cord under and in back of the foot. Stitch

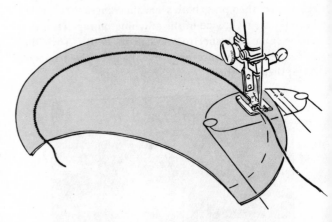

on the seamline, covering the filler cord. Press, and trim away the seam allowance close to the stitching. Turn to the right side and press. Seam allowances that would ordinarily show through are eliminated.

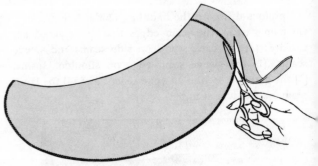

Seams in Chiffon

Carefully hand-tack seams in chiffon. Using a 1·5 to 1 mm (15 to 20) stitch length, test the stitching on a scrap of the chiffon. The quality of the stitching depends on the machine and the softness of the fabric. Stitch slowly, and apply gentle tension on the seam by holding it both in front and in back of the presser foot.

If your machine does not stitch chiffon satisfactorily with the above method, place tissue paper under the seam before stitching. Remove the tissue paper by gently pulling it away from one side of the stitching, then from the other.

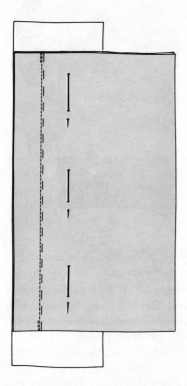

Seams in Knitted Fabrics

Because of their loop construction, knitted fabrics are not always seamed and finished in the same way as woven fabrics. The kind of seam that is most appropriate for a specific knitted fabric will depend on the amount of stretch in the fabric, the weight or thickness of the fabric, the kind of garment it will be used for and the position of the seam within the garment. The technique for easing one seam to another is quite different from that for woven fabrics. Also, the kind of seam finish, if one is required and the seam width will be different from those for woven fabrics. See section beginning on page 417.

Seams in Magyar Sleeves

To make seams in magyar sleeves, see *Magyar Sleeve – without Gusset*, page 162; or *Magyar Sleeve – with Gusset*, page 164.

Seam Layering

To 'layer' a seam means to remove the bulk so that the seam will lie flat. The procedure varies depending on whether the seam is enclosed or fitted and whether it is an inside curve, an outside curve, a straight seam or square corner or point. Seams that require layering are stitched and then layered according to the methods described here.

Fitted Seams

Fitted seams are found at the shoulder line where the neck is built up, in a princess-line bodice, at the waistline in suit jackets, in yokes and in seams extending over the bust and hipline. These seams are usually pressed open and the edges are finished as required by the fabric.

Fitted seams may be inside or outside curves. Do not trim them, but layer them as follows:

Inside curves. Slash into the seam allowance far enough to relieve the strain imposed by the seam edge so that it will lie flat. The depth of the slash and the number of slashes will vary with the degree of the curve and texture of the fabric; however, the slashes usually extend to within ·6 cm ($\frac{1}{4}$ inch) of the stitching and are made at evenly space intervals. Sometimes only one slash is necessary.

Outside curves. Cut narrow notches or wedges out of the seam allowance, sufficient in depth to remove only

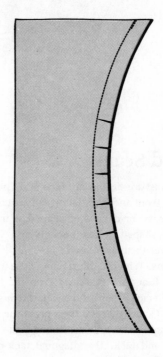

the portion of the seam edge that may overlap when the seam is pressed open. Avoid cutting out a wedge so large that it will produce a saw-tooth effect in the seam edge that will press through and mark the right side of the fabric. Cut the notches at evenly spaced intervals. The frequency and spacing depend on the degree of the curve and the texture of the fabric. When the curve is slight and the fabric flexible, it may not be necessary to slash the seam.

Often an inside curve is seamed to an outside curve. This requires slashing the inside curved edge and notching the outside curved edge.

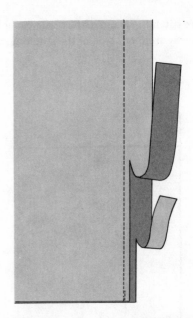

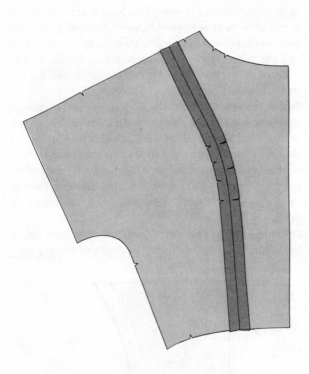

Enclosed Seams

Enclosed seams are found in facings. They may be straight, as in front and back facings of blouses, dresses, jackets and coats; or curved or shaped as in necklines, collars, cuffs, shaped yokes, pockets and similar construction. Layer them as follows:

Straight seams. Trim the interfacing close to the stitching if it is included in the seam. Trim the facing seam allowance to ·3 cm ($\frac{1}{8}$ inch) and the garment seam allowance to ·6 cm ($\frac{1}{4}$ inch). Press, then press the seam open. Turn to the right side; ease the facing under slightly at the seamline and tack. Use diagonal tacking and silk thread. Press flat. (*See illustration at top of next column.*)

Inside curves. If interfacing is included in the seam, trim it close to the stitching. Trim the facing seam allowance of ·3 cm ($\frac{1}{8}$ inch) and the garment seam allowance to ·6 cm ($\frac{1}{4}$ inch). Slash these layered seam edges to within ·3cm ($\frac{1}{8}$ inch) of the seamline at evenly spaced intervals. This relieves the strain imposed by the seam edge and prevents pulling. Press the seam open. Then, turn to the right side; ease the facing under slightly at the seamline and tack. Use silk thread and diagonal tacking. Press flat.

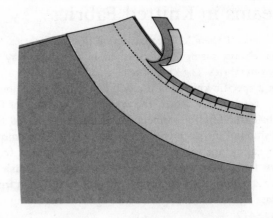

Outside curves. If interfacing is included in the seam, trim it close to the stitching. Trim the facing seam allowance to ·3 cm ($\frac{1}{8}$ inch) and the garment seam allowance to ·6 cm ($\frac{1}{4}$ inch). Cut notches in the seam allowance at evenly spaced intervals to remove the bulk. Cut away only enough to allow the seam to lie flat so that you do not have a saw-tooth effect in the seam edge. Press, then

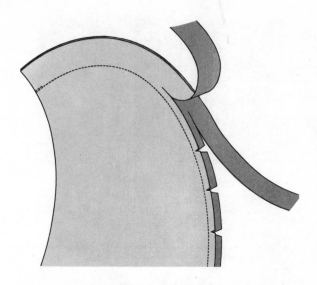

upward stroke, and turn the fabric so the stitching is directed diagonally across the corner; then take one, two or three stitches. Pivot again, turn the fabric and stitch, following the seamline.

If interfacing is included in the seam, trim it close to the stitching. Trim the seam allowance on the facing to ·3 cm ($\frac{1}{8}$ inch) and on the garment to ·6 cm ($\frac{1}{4}$ inch). Trim away the seam allowance diagonally across the point and very close to the stitching; then trim away the seam allowance diagonally at the sides of the point. Press the seam open before turning to the right side. Ease the facing under slightly at the seamline and tack. Use silk thread and diagonal tacking. Press.

press the seam open over the curved edge of a seamboard or a pressing mitt. Turn to the right side; ease the facing under slightly at the seamline and tack. Use silk thread and diagonal tacking. Press flat.

Square corners and points. Square corners and points need diagonal stitching across the point to allow enough space to smoothly enclose the seam edge when turned to the inside. The number of diagonal stitches varies with the weight of the fabric. Lightweight, crisp fabrics will need only one stitch across the point and heavy fabrics may need as many as three.

Stitch to within one or two stitches of the intersecting seamline. Pivot with the needle in the fabric, but on its

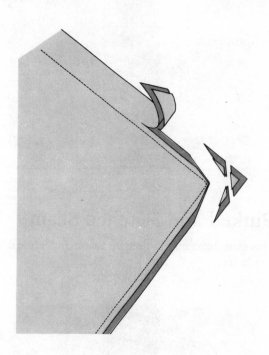

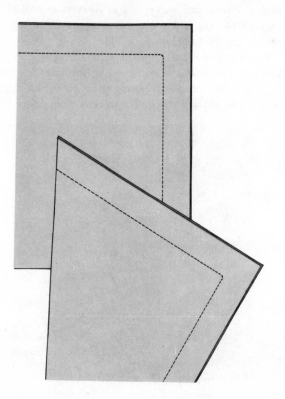

Seam Finishes

Seam edges are 'finished' to prevent them fraying in use and during washing or dry cleaning; to improve the appearance of the inside of your garment; and to strengthen the seam itself.

Seams in a garment should be finished as the garment is made and before being crossed by another seam. The seam finish must be without bulk so that it is not visible when the garment is worn and does not form a ridge on the right side when the garment is pressed.

There are many methods of seam finishing you can use, choose the most suitable one for each garment you make. When in doubt, try several different methods on test seams before making up your mind.

Pinked Seam

Use a pinked seam only on fabrics which will not fray.

After stitching a plain seam, pink the seam edges with pinking shears. Remove only the seam edge. Cut with a medium stroke; do not fully open the shears or cut right to the point. Press the seam in the same position as it was stitched, and then press it open.

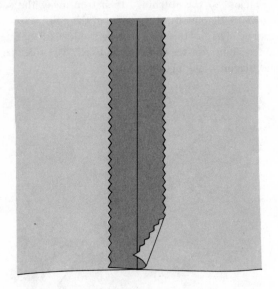

Pinked and Stitched Seam

This seam finish may be used on almost any fabric which would fray.

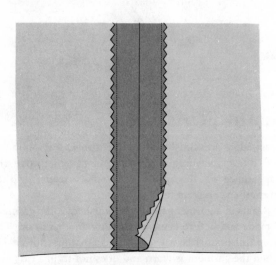

Stitch a plain seam. Place a line of stitching about ·6 cm (¼ inch) from the seam edge, using a 1–1·5 mm (20) stitch length. Pink the edges. The stitching will prevent the seam from fraying and curling.

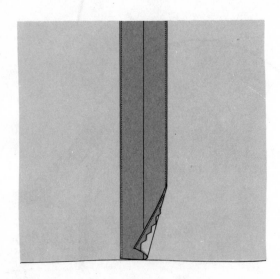

Edge-Stitched Seam (*Above*)

Use this finish on lightweight and medium-weight fabrics as well as on unlined jackets and boleros.

Stitch a plain seam. Press the seam flat, then press it open. Pink the edges; then fold them under ·3 to ·6 cm (⅛ to ¼ inch) and stitch on the folded edge. The *Edge Stitcher* will help you keep this stitching straight and parallel to the edge. For instructions on using it, see page 284.

Open Bound Seam (*Below*)

Binding is an excellent finish for fabrics that tend to fray, such as tweed and heavy, coarse weaves, as well as for unlined jackets and coats. Instructions for using the *Binder* may be found on page 282.

Stitch a plain seam. Press the seam, then press it open. With the Binder on the machine and fine bias seam binding, bind each seam edge, using either straight stitching or an open zig-zag stitch. To prevent seam edges from

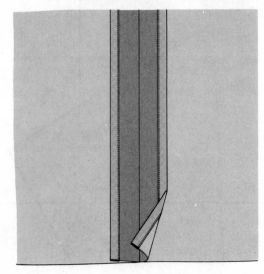

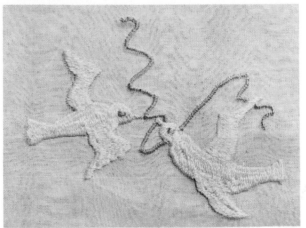

Plate 5
WHAT THE BRIDE WEARS

Dreamy voile embroidered with doves makes this
romantic dress. Rippling frills form the sleeves and add a
graceful line to the skirt.

LEFT: The dove motif is shown worked on voile, using free
motion embroidery with Sylko 50 thread.

Dress by courtesy of Pronuptia

Plates 6 and 7
VARIED TABLE FARE

ABOVE LEFT: Diamond stitch pattern motifs arranged in flower-like design.

ABOVE RIGHT: Shadow appliqué of white and a single shade of green organdie: various layers are cut away to obtain two shades of green.

BELOW LEFT: Linen appliquéd on organdie.

BELOW RIGHT: Linen appliquéd band. First a band of background colour is appliquéd in the centre of a dark green band and the arrowhead stitch pattern is stitched. The decorative band is then appliquéd across the ends of the place mat.

Plate 8
AFTER EIGHT

Patterns by courtesy of McCalls

This soft, flowing evening dress, left, in a printed polyester twill, features long full sleeves which gather into a buttoning cuff. A tie belt is optional.

A versatile halter dress, right, in a shimmer crêpe which can be worn the year round; here a detachable gold lurex collar is added and a matching bag.

stretching or fraying in loosely woven fabrics, place a row of stitching ·3 cm (⅛ inch) from the seam edge before applying the binding.

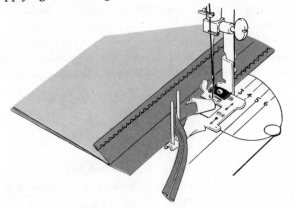

Net Bound Seam

Delicate fabrics that fray easily, such as chiffon velvet and sheer metallic, may have seam edges bound with nylon net, which prevents fraying without adding bulk.

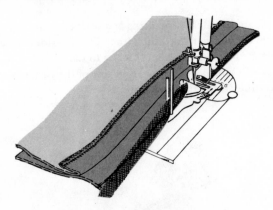

Cut the net into 1·2-cm (½-inch) strips and insert, unfolded, into the Binder. Feed seam edges into the Binder with napped or right side up. Stitch, using a medium-width zig-zag stitch.

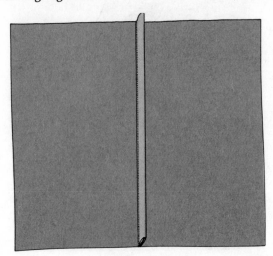

Plain Bound Seam (*Bottom, previous column*)

This seam is practical for household items such as cushions, simple loose covers and articles made of plastic.

After stitching a plain seam, trim the seam edges to ·6 cm (¼ inch). Press. Insert both edges into the Binder and stitch, keeping the seam edges well into the scroll as you sew.

Machine Over-Edged Seam

The blindstitch zig-zag provides an excellent finish for tweed, raw silk, double knit and heavy woollens.

Stitch a plain seam. Press the seam as stitched, then press it open. Use the blindstitch zig-zag, and form the stitches over the edge of the seam. Both the stitch length and the stitch width settings vary with the fabric.

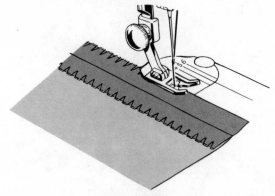

When both seam edges are turned in the same direction as in a sleeve armhole and pocket bag, press the plain seam as stitched. Trim the seam allowance to about ·6 cm (¼ inch). Then stitch the edges together, using the blindstitch zig-zag.

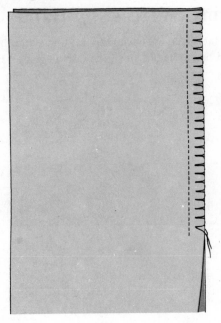

Zig-Zag Seam

Zig-zag stitching is an ideal seam finish for jersey, double knit and other fabrics with 'give' because the stitch is as flexible as the fabric. Either the plain or multi-stitch zig-zag may be used.

After stitching a plain seam, press it open. Select a plain zig-zag stitch, medium stitch width and between 1·5 and 1 mm (15 and 20) stitch length. Stitch near the seam edge but not over it. Press. Trim off the seam edge close to the stitching.

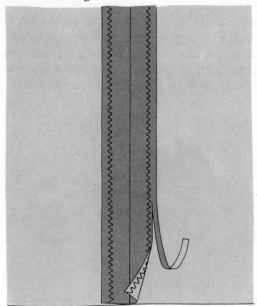

For the multi-stitch zig-zag, select a wide stitch width and a short stitch length (in the 'fine' area), and stitch close to the seam edge. Press.

Seams Overcast by Hand

If the fabric has a tendency to fray and a machine finish would be too harsh, finish the seam edge by hand.

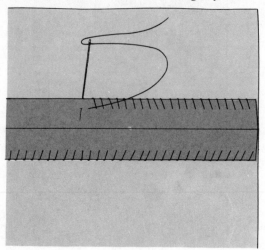

Stitch a plain seam and press it open. By hand, make slanting stitches over the seam edge, about ·6 cm ($\frac{1}{4}$ inch) apart and about ·3 cm ($\frac{1}{8}$ inch) in depth, depending on the weight of the fabric. Do not pull the threads too tightly.

When the seam is pressed open, overcast the edges separately. When both seam edges are pressed in the same direction (sleeve and waistline seams are examples), overcast the two edges together.

Understitching

To prevent a facing edge from rolling beyond the garment edge, you must stitch the seam allowances to the facing on the underside.

Before doing this you will have completed a certain amount of garment construction – namely: the facing will be stitched in place and the seam layered and pressed; then the facing will be turned to the underside and eased under slightly at the seamline before pressing again.

To understitch, turn facing and seam allowances away from the garment and stitch from the right side, through facing and seam allowances, close to the seamline. Since this stitching is not on the right side of the garment, it is invisible in the finished work.

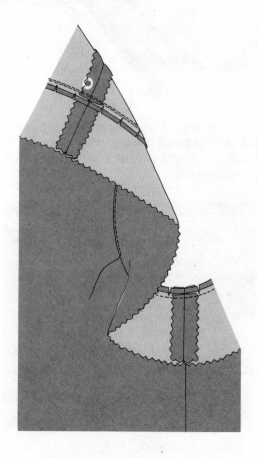

Mounting and Lining

Adding a mounting or lining to your dress is one way of achieving a professional tailor-made look. Many fabrics and fashion styles require either one or the other to retain the shape and add body to the garment.

Simply defined, mounting and lining are a second thickness of carefully selected fabric that is used to support the garment fabric and add resistance to strain. *Mounting* is included in the seams with the garment fabric. Hand stitches, which hold down facings and hems, are made in the mounting instead of the garment fabric. *Lining* is constructed separately and attached to the skirt at the waistline seam or to the dress at the neckline, armhole and waistline seams.

Do not confuse mounting and lining with interfacing. See page 134. When a garment is mounted or lined, interfacing is still included in facings, lapels, collars and cuffs.

Whether to mount or line a garment is a decision you

should make when you are planning your dress and choosing a pattern. The type of mounting or lining you select depends on the fabric you are using as well as the effect you wish to achieve. For example, a sheer fabric such as organza makes an ideal mounting for soft silks and woollens, peau de soie and imported cottons which will be dry-cleaned. It allows them to retain their naturally soft, luxurious feeling, which would be lost if a bulky or heavy mounting were used. For a closely woven wool or raw silk, a heavier fabric such as Jap silk or Bemberg may be a good choice – and lining rather than mounting may be preferable. Lay your dress fabric over the mounting or lining fabric so that you can judge the final effect.

Almost any fabric may be mounted; generally, however, only firm and opaque fabrics are lined. For guides on fabrics to use as mounting or lining, see page 20.

How to Mount Dresses and Skirts

You may mount the entire dress or just a section of it. The mounting in skirts may extend to the fold of the hem, to the top of the hem or to about 30 cm (12 inches) below the hipline.

Mounting a Dress

Cut the mounting by the same pattern pieces and on the same grain as the garment. Notch and mark each section the same as the dress fabric, and place the corresponding pieces together.

Stitch the darts and seams within the bodice and skirt sections separately in the dress fabric and mounting unless the fabric is sheer. See page 97. Finish seam edges, and press.

Place the fabric, wrong side up, on a flat surface; lay the mounting over it. Both pieces must be smooth and wrinkle-free. Pin them together along the centre line,

side seams and waistline. Place several rows of diagonal tacking within each section, as illustrated below and on the following page, to hold the two layers of fabric together. Use silk thread and make the stitches from

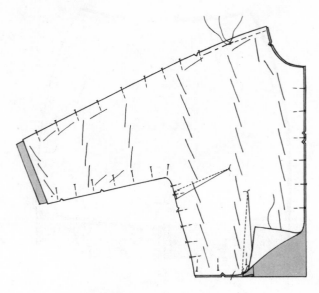

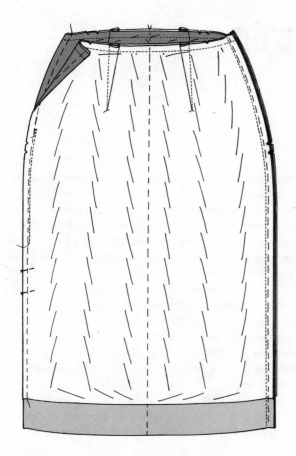

of the skirt and bodice, machine-stitch the mounting to the dress fabric 1·2 cm (½ inch) from the seam edge. Make up the fabric and mounting as one piece of fabric in assembling the garment.

Hemming Mounted Garments

When the mounting extends to the top of the hem, pink the lower edge of the mounting; then fold it under ·6 cm (¼ inch) and stitch near the folded edge, using the multi-stitch zig-zag.

When the mounting extends to the fold of the hem, fold the hem over the mounting and stitch by hand, taking the stitches through only the mounting and hem.

Hem the skirt, using the method suitable for the fabric. See *Hems and Hem Finishes* page 187.

Mounting a Skirt with a Pleat

When there is a pleat in the skirt, you should extend the mounting to the top of the hem.

In the skirt fabric, stitch the darts and seam for the pleat, following the instructions accompanying the pattern.

In the mounting, stitch the seam above the pleat from the waistline to the top of the pleat. Trim off excess fabric, allowing 1·5-cm (⅝-inch) seam allowance. Pink

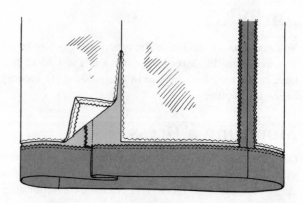

·9 to 1·2 cm (⅜ to ½ inch) in length and about 5 cm (2 inches) apart. Do not draw the thread tightly. *Do not remove these tackings until the hem is finished.* (If the two fabrics are of different lengths, the skirt will not hang evenly.) Hand-tack 1·5 cm (⅝ inch) from all seam edges in the bodice and side seams of the skirt. At the waistline

the seam edges and lower edge of the mounting back and front. Fold the pinked edges under 1·5 cm (⅝ inch) and stitch around the lower edge and both sides of the slit, using the multi-stitch zig-zag for added strength. Stitch the darts. Tack the fabric and mounting together, following the instructions for *Mounting a Dress,* above, and make up as one in assembling the garment.

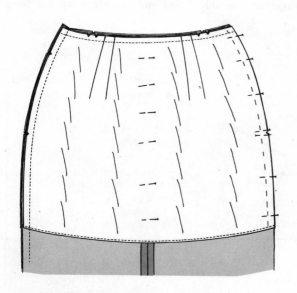

Mounting Fine (Sheer) Fabrics

Fabrics such as chiffon and lace should be mounted on a smooth, firm, opaque fabric of a similar fibre content. Colours should match or complement each other to create an illusion of colour intensity or variation. Two mounting methods are given here; choose the one suitable for the design of your dress and the effect you wish to achieve.

Method 1: A complete mounting, stitched as one with the garment fabric, allows you to treat a sheer fabric as a heavier fabric and to use patterns with darts and styling seams, as the mounting conceals them in the finished dress.

Place mounting sections, right side up, on a flat surface and the sheer dress fabric, right side up, over them. Tack together following the directions for *Mounting a Dress*, page 95. Hand-tack through the centre of darts to hold the two layers of fabric together. Pin, tack, then stitch the darts through the two layers. Make up the fabric and mounting as one in assembling the garment.

To create the illusion of a sheer yoke and sleeves or of strapless, bare shoulders, mount the upper part of the bodice with net or chiffon and the lower part of the bodice with a firm, opaque fabric. Join the two fabrics above the bustline.

Method 2: If the dress has a full skirt, the bodice section may be mounted and the skirt section lined – that is, the two fabrics in the skirt can be seamed and hemmed separately and joined only at the waistline.

Treat the bodice section as instructed above. For the skirt, follow the instructions given on page 99, *Lining a Sheer Skirt*.

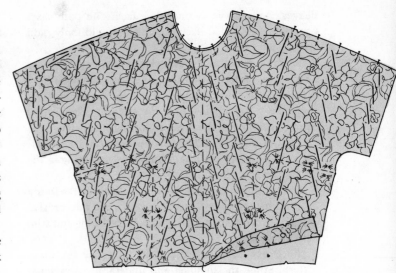

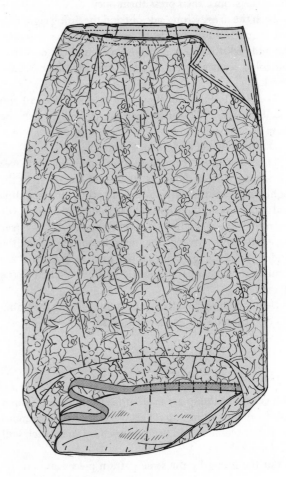

How to Line Dresses and Skirts

When dresses or skirts are lined the top fabric and lining are made up separately and are placed wrong sides together so that the seam allowances are hidden. In dresses, the lining is joined to the top fabric at the neckline, armhole, or waistline seams; in skirts it is joined to the top fabric at the waistline. Do not confuse these lining methods with those used in tailored coats and suits which are covered in *Tailoring*, pages 325 and 329.

Lining a Dress

In a blouse or sheath dress which is collarless and sleeveless, the lining can serve as a one-piece neckline and armhole facing. In a collarless garment with set-in sleeves, it can serve as a neckline facing. In both cases you omit an added facing, which would only add unnecessary bulk.

If the dress is collarless and sleeveless, cut the lining by the dress pattern. Stitch the underarm seam separately in the dress and in the lining. Neaten the seam edges and press the seams open. *Leave the shoulder seams open.* Apply the lining to the dress, following the instructions for the *One-piece Neckline and Armhole Facing,* page 141. But substitute the full-length lining for the facing in the instructions.

Hem the lining and dress separately, making the lining 2·5 cm (1 inch) shorter than the dress. To add a decorative touch, you can make a narrow hem in the lining and trim with lace edging.

If the dress has sleeves, cut the lining by the dress pattern. Stitch the shoulder and underarm seams separately in the dress and in the lining. Neaten seam edges. Press the seams, then press them open.

Turn the dress wrong side out and the lining right side out. Place the lining inside the dress, right sides together. Pin and tack the lining to the dress around the neckline, matching centre lines, notches and shoulder seams. Stitch.

Trim the lining seam allowance to ·3 cm ($\frac{1}{8}$ inch) and the dress seam allowance to ·6 cm ($\frac{1}{4}$ inch). Slash the seam allowances on curves and trim off corners where seams cross at the underarm. Press.

Turn the lining through the neck opening and over the wrong side of the dress; then turn the dress to the right side. Ease the lining under slightly at the seamline and tack. Press, then remove tacking. Understitch the seam to prevent the lining from rolling out of place (see page 94). Press. Arrange the lining smoothly against the underside of the garment fabric, then tack around the armholes. Make up as one fabric when you stitch in the sleeves.

Hem the lining and dress separately, making the lining 2·5 cm (1 inch) shorter than the dress.

Lining a Skirt

The skirt and lining are made up separately and joined only at the waistline seam. This is an excellent treatment for heavy woollens and firmly woven cottons which will be dry-cleaned.

Cut the lining by the same pattern pieces and on the same grain as the skirt. Notch and mark each section the same as the skirt fabric.

Stitch and press the darts and all seams in the skirt and sew in the zip. Then stitch and press the darts and all seams in the lining. Make the opening for the zip the same length in the lining as in the skirt fabric.

Place the lining inside the skirt, wrong sides together, and pin together at the waistline, matching seams, darts and markings. Turn the skirt to the wrong side with the lining on the top side. At the end of the placket opening in the lining, slash diagonally on each side ·6 cm ($\frac{1}{4}$ inch) beyond the seamline. Fold under the edges and pin them to the tape of the zip, as illustrated. Slip-stitch in place. Stitch the skirt and lining together at the waistline, 1·2 cm ($\frac{1}{2}$ inch) from seam edge. Add the waistband.

Hem the skirt and lining separately, making the lining 2·5 cm (1 inch) shorter than the skirt.

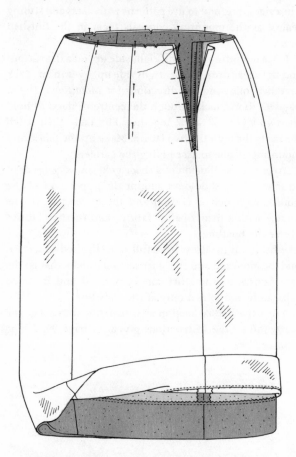

Lining a Slit Skirt

In the method explained here, the slits in the lining do not correspond with those in the skirt. If the skirt is slit in the back, as in the illustration, the lining is slit at each side seam; if the skirt is slit at the side seams, the lining is slit in the centre front or centre back. Then a facing is stitched to the lining, behind the slits of the skirt.

Cut the lining by the same pattern pieces and on the same grain as the skirt. Notch and mark each section the same as the skirt fabric.

Make up the skirt, leaving the seams open the depth of the slits plus hem. Reinforce with backstitching. Machine-tack the seams together in the slits.

Make up the lining so that the seams will face the seams in the skirt. Stitch darts and the full length of the seams that correspond with the slits in the skirt.

Cut a facing of the skirt fabric 12·5 cm (5 inches) longer than the slit plus hem and seam allowance, and 20 cm (8 inches) wide so that it will extend 10 cm (4 inches) on each side of the slit. (The skirt illustrated has two slits in the back and required only one piece of the fabric for the facing. It was cut 20 cm (8 inches) wider than the distance between the two slits.) Fold under the seam allowance at the top and each side of the facing. Press.

Place the facing right side up centrally over the outside of the lining, keeping the lower edges even; pin. Tack, then stitch near the folded edges. (If the slits in the skirt are at the side seams, place the facings centrally over the side seams of the lining.)

Pin the front and back lining sections together at the side seams. Stitch, leaving the seams open the depth of the slits. Reinforce with backstitching. Machine-tack the seams together in the slits. Neaten the seam edges. Press, then press the seams open.

Turn the lining to the right side. Place it inside the skirt, with the faced side of the lining to wrong side of the skirt. Pin together at the waistline, matching seams and markings. Finish, following the instructions above under *Lining a Skirt*.

Hem the skirt and lining separately, keeping them the same length. See *Hem in Slit Skirt*, page 191.

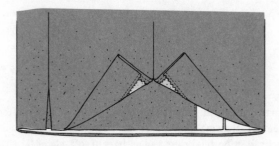

Lining a Sheer Skirt

To create an interesting variation, the lining is sometimes fitted closely to the figure and the sheer top skirt is allowed to flow freely creating a misty effect.

Seam the sheer fabric and lining separately; use a fine French seam in the sheer fabric. Place the lining inside the sheer skirt, with the right side of lining next to the wrong side of the skirt. Join them at the waistline (see page 98), then join the skirt to the mounted bodice. Hem the two fabrics separately. A narrow hem is essential for the sheer full skirt – make either a hand-rolled hem or a hem with horsehair braid (crin). See pages 197 and 192. Make a 5- or 7-cm (2- or 3-inch) hem in the fitted lining.

If both the sheer and the lining are circular or flared, they must also be hemmed separately to prevent the sheer from 'blousing' over the lining. Make a narrow hem in each.

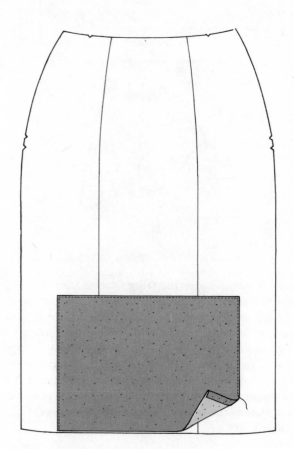

Darts, Tucks and Gathers

Darts, tucks and gathers are three friends you will often meet in dressmaking. Darts are better in firm fabrics; tucks in smooth fabrics; and gathers in soft, sheer fabrics. All three have a functional and decorative use in sewing; each in its own way gives fit and shape to a garment. For purely decorative applications of tucks and shirring, see pages 235 and 243.

Darts

First Tips

Darts provide fullness at the bust, hip, shoulder and elbow. They must point towards the fullest curve of the figure but must not extend as far as the curve.

It may be necessary to change the position of darts to follow your figure. Darts extending from waistline to bustline are sometimes moved closer to the centre or further apart to bring them directly under the fullest part of the bustline. To accommodate a lower bustline, darts extending from underarm towards the bustline should be placed lower than those marked on the pattern.

The length of dart in a skirt may also have to be adjusted for a better fit. A short figure may require shorter darts, and a very tall figure longer darts. If darts in the bodice are moved closer to the centre or further apart, then the darts in the skirt must be moved to correspond with them.

Darts are usually made on the wrong side of the garment. They are stitched on the right side only when they are styling points and the continuous-thread dart is used. See page 101.

Stitching a Dart

Darts should be barely visible when completed, they must be tapered gradually to the point so that there is no bulge where the dart ends.

Fold the dart and match markings; start pinning at the seam edge, then at the point, and at intervals between. Place the pins at right angles to the seamline, with the heads towards the folded edge. Tack from the seam edge

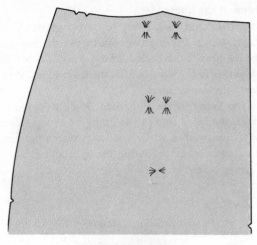

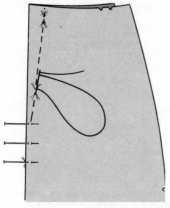

to the point. Remove the tailor's tacks. Start stitching near the seam edge and reinforce with backstitching, tapering gradually to the point; the last three or four stitches should be parallel to the fold of the dart, *just a thread's width from the fold.* Continue stitching to form a chain about 1·2 cm ($\frac{1}{2}$ inch) beyond the point. Cut the thread ends about 5 cm (2 inches) from the point. Tie the thread chain into a single knot, using a pin to set the knot close to the fabric. (*Illustrated at the top of the next column.*)

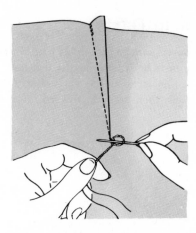

In heavy fabrics such as tweed and flannel, darts are frequently slashed and pressed open. If the fabric is one that frays easily, overcast the slashed edges. On firm fabrics which do not fray easily, finish with pinking shears.

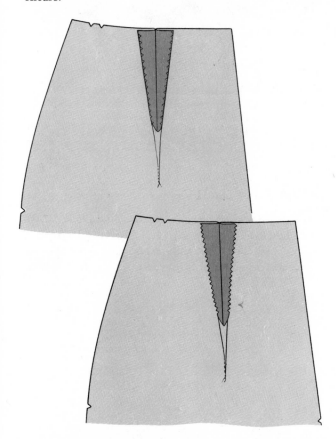

Pressing Darts

Pressing further shapes and moulds the dart after stitching. Darts are pressed towards the centre in skirt back, blouse front and back, and shoulder; and downwards at the underarm and elbow. Use the curved surface of a pressing mitt or tailor's ham.

First press the dart flat as it was stitched, carrying the crease only as far as the stitching. Protect the fabric with a pressing cloth. Then place the dart over the tailor's ham or pressing mitt. Turn the dart in the correct direction. Cover it with a pressing cloth, and use the amount of steam required by the fabric. Press towards the point of the dart.

Continuous-Thread Darts

The continuous-thread dart is used (1) on 'outside' darts, that is, when the fold of the dart is on the outside of the garment; and (2) on inside darts when the fabric is sheer. The stitching begins *at the point* rather than the seam edge as in the conventional dart, and no thread ends are left to be tied in a kot at the point.

Thread the bobbin thread through the needle in the opposite direction from the usual threading, and tie it to the upper thread in a single knot. Re-wind the spool until the knot has passed all threading points and is a sufficient distance from the last thread guide nearest the spool to provide enough thread to stitch the full length of the dart.

Position the tip of the needle into the point of the dart,

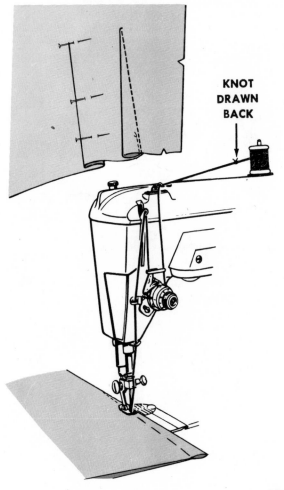

KNOT DRAWN BACK

101

just a thread's width from the fold. Pull the slack out of the thread by turning the spool. Lower the presser foot and stitch, carefully shaping the point while stitching towards the seam edge. Reinforce the seam edges with backstitching. Re-thread the machine for each dart.

The *Touch & Sew** machine has push-button bobbin winding, which simplifies threading for continuous-thread darts. The bobbin stays in the machine and is wound with thread directly from the needle, which gives a continuous thread. If you have a *Touch & Sew* machine, wind an empty bobbin with enough thread to make a single dart (usually about 1 metre (1 yard)). Stitch as instructed above. Wind an empty bobbin for each dart.

Skirt Darts

Darts in the back skirt extend to the fullest part of the hips and are pressed towards the centre. Darts in the front skirt are smaller and may be in groups of two. Skirt and bodice darts must meet at the waistline.

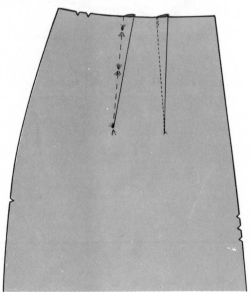

Underarm Darts

Underarm darts point to the fullest part of the bustline and may be on a horizontal or diagonal line. They are made in the same way as the conventional dart. Press flat as stitched; then press downwards over a pressing mitt.

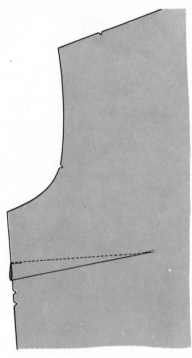

Shoulder Darts

Shoulder darts are usually narrow and about 10 cm (4 inches) in length, depending on the size of the pattern. They are stitched in the same manner as the conventional dart and pressed towards the centre over a pressing mitt.

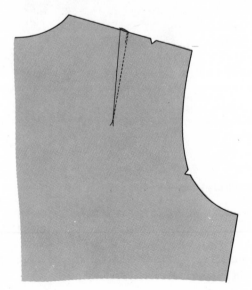

Elbow Darts

Long close-fitting sleeves are usually darted at the elbow. The darts are stitched in the same manner as the conventional dart. Press flat as stitched; then press downwards over a pressing mitt.

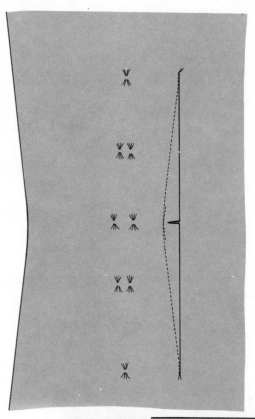

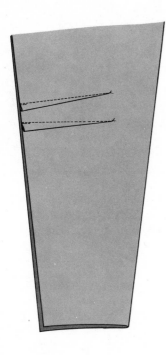

Contour Darts

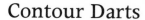 Darts that fit the waistline and taper to a point at each end are sometimes known as 'contour' or 'fish' darts. They are used in suits, princess-line coats and dresses and overblouses or tunic tops.

To form the dart, fold the fabric and match markings; pin at the waistline, at each point and at intervals between. Tack.

Stitch the dart in two steps, beginning at the waistline and stitching to the point each time. Overlap the stitching about 2 cm ($\frac{3}{4}$ inch) at the waistline. Tie the thread ends at each point. Slash to within ·6 cm ($\frac{1}{4}$ inch) of the stitching at the waistline. Press flat as stitched; then press each end over a pressing mitt.

The continuous-thread method may be used when stitching the contour dart. Follow the instructions for *Continuous-Thread Darts*. Start stitching from one of the points to ·9 cm ($\frac{3}{8}$ inch) beyond the waistline. Re-thread the machine (or, on a *Touch & Sew* machine, re-wind the bobbin). Repeat the operation from the other point, overlapping the stitch about 2 cm ($\frac{3}{4}$ inch) at the waistline. Slash and press the same as above.

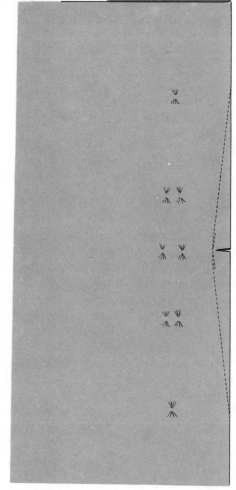

Diagonal Bust Darts

Diagonal darts may originate at the underarm seam or at the waistline, and they always point diagonally towards the fullest part of the bust. They may have the conventional fold or a cut out section where seam edges are joined.

Interfacing Darts

To make darts in interfacing and eliminate bulk, cut out the dart allowance on the stitching line. Bring the two cut edges together and pin over an underlay of a lightweight fabric such as organza. Cut the underlay 2·5 cm (1 inch) wide and slightly longer than the dart. Stitch from the right side.

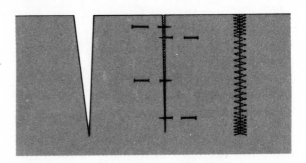

When using a zig-zag machine, select the multi-stitch zig-zag, widest stitch width and 1–1·5 mm (20) stitch length. Align the abutted line with the centre of the presser foot.

If you are using straight stitching, stitch on each side of the abutted line. Reinforce with backstitching at each end. Press over the curved surface of a pressing mitt.

Tucks

Tucks for Shaping

Tucks are found at the front shoulder line, front and back waistline of the bodice and the front section of the skirt. They are used to provide fullness and are usually formed on the wrong side of the garment. (They may, however, be formed on the right side as a styling point. See *Continuous-Thread Tucks* below.)

Tucks extending down from the shoulder seam and

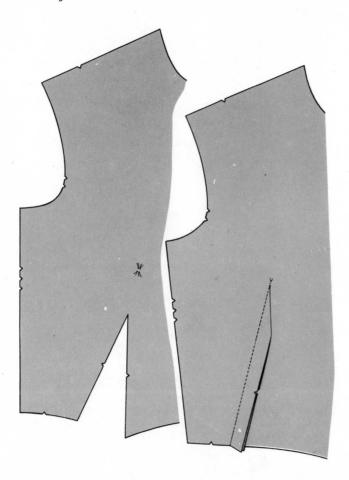

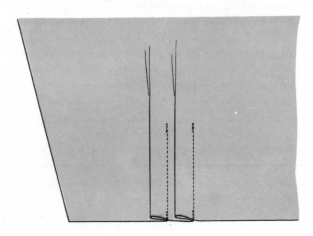

To make the diagonal dart, begin at the waistline or underarm seam and place the seam edges of the dart together, matching markings. Pin at the wide end, at the point and at intervals between, easing the seam on the long side. Tack. Begin stitching from the wide end; reinforce with backstitching, and gradually taper the stitching to the point; the last three or four stitches should be parallel to the fold and a *thread's width from it*. Tie the thread ends into a single knot, using a pin to set the knot close to the fabric.

Press flat as stitched; then press both edges towards the centre over a pressing mitt. The seam in the dart may be pressed open if the fabric is heavy.

up from the front waistline should be directly in line with the fullest part of the bust. Tucks in the front skirt section should match the tucks in the bodice section when joined.

Fold the tuck, match the markings and keep the seam edges even. Pin and tack.

Start stitching at the seam edge and reinforce with backstitching. Continue stitching to the end of the tuck, then back-stitch again for reinforcement.

Continuous-Thread Tucks

When the fold of the tuck is on the right side of the garment as a design feature, the continuous-thread tuck is used so that no backstitching shows. (Threads may be drawn to the underside and tied, but the continuous-thread method lasts longer and looks better.)

Pin and tack the tuck, keeping the seam edges even. Begin the continuous-thread stitching at the end of the tucks farthest from the seam edge (below the bustline) and finish it at the seam edge with backstitching.

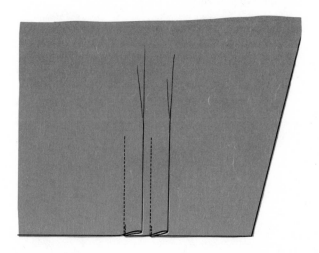

Place the tuck under the needle and lower the presser foot. Hold the needle thread loosely with the left hand while turning the hand wheel with the right hand to form a stitch. Draw the bobbin thread up through the fabric. Thread the bobbin thread through the needle in the opposite direction, following the instructions for *Continuous-Thread Darts* on page 101. Then, position the point of the needle in the fabric and pull the slack out of the thread by turning the spool. Stitch slowly to the seam edge and reinforce with backstitching.

For instructions on pressing tucks, see page 70.

Gathers

Gathering to Control Fullness

Patterns for soft or sheer fabrics may have gathering to control fullness at the shoulder, at the waistline of the bodice or skirt, at yoke joinings in a bodice or skirt, at the shoulder or cuff of sleeves and at other styling points. The pattern should indicate the number of rows of stitching.

Use a 3 to 2·5 mm (8 to 10) stitch length in medium-weight fabrics and a 2 to 1·5 mm (12 to 15) stitch length in soft or filmy fabrics. Loosen the upper tension enough to draw the bobbin thread. (Do not forget to return the tension to its previous setting.)

Place the first row of stitching in the seam allowance 1·5 cm ($\frac{5}{8}$ inch) from the seam edge; place the second row in the seam allowance about 1·2 cm ($\frac{1}{2}$ inch) from the seam edge. Neither of these rows will show in the finished garment. Additional lines of gathering, which will show in the finished garment, may be placed ·3 to ·6 cm ($\frac{1}{8}$ to $\frac{1}{4}$ inch) apart. Work the first additional row the chosen distance from the first row of stitching at the 1·5-cm ($\frac{5}{8}$-inch) position.

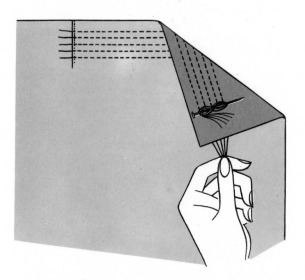

At one end, draw the threads through to the under-side. Tie by forming a single knot in the two strands of thread and set the knot tightly against the fabric. Hold these thread ends and fold the fabric at the end of the rows of stitching. Stitch close to the fold, forming a pin tuck across the end, extending it from the seam edge to the last row of stitching. Cut off the ends of the gathering threads 1·2 cm ($\frac{1}{2}$ inch) from the stitching.

At the other end of the stitching, anchor the threads on the right side of the garment by forming a figure eight

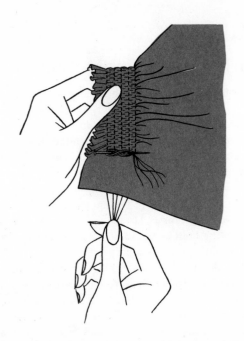

gathers. Finish the second end by drawing threads to the underside and tying. Make a pin tuck across.

Gathered Skirts

In gathered skirts, use mercerised or polyester thread on the bobbin so that it will not break while you are easing the fullness across the width of the skirt.

First stitch the side seams and put in the zip. Pin-mark the waistline at the zip opening and at the right side seam. Then place the stitching for the gathers as instructed above; however, stitch the front and back sections separately. Extend the stitching from the right side seam to the zip opening in each section, and leave 7·5-cm (3-inch) thread ends. (The pin tuck is eliminated in this method.)

Match markings on the skirt with those on the waistband or bodice, and pin. To gather each skirt section between the markings, pull the bobbin thread at each end of a section and ease the fullness towards the centre. Pull threads to the underside and join the broken lines of stitching by tying the four threads together into a single knot close to the stitching. See illustration on page 306. Pin the skirt to the waistband or bodice at close intervals, then stitch.

around a pin. One thread for each row of stitching remains on the wrong side of the garment. Tightly twist these threads together and pull, and at the same time ease the fabric back on the stitches to form uniform

Buttonholes without Tears

The thought of making buttonholes has been known to throw the budding dressmaker into a panic. It need not. What may seem like the bane of dressmaking will soon become a pleasant routine if you approach the task cautiously but courageously.

Remember first that buttonholes may be decorative as well as functional. Properly positioned, they contribute to the fit and comfort of your garment.

This chapter tells you about the preparatory steps and explains how to make the several kinds of buttonholes –

fabric bound, piped, machine-worked (using either the zig-zag machine or the Buttonholer) and hand-worked. The type of buttonhole you make depends on the fabric, the style of the garment and your preference and skill. Piped and bound buttonholes are usually preferred in women's dresses, suits and coats; machine-worked buttonholes are used in sportswear and children's clothes as well as men's and boy's wear; hand-worked buttonholes are found in babies' clothes and blouses of soft, fine silk, linen or cotton.

Preparatory Steps

Position of Buttonhole

The rules for the position of buttons and buttonholes apply to all types of buttonholes:

– Buttonholes in women's and girls' clothes are placed on the right side of the garment; in men's and boys' wear, on the left side.

– *Horizontal* buttonholes are placed to extend ·3 cm ($\frac{1}{8}$ inch) beyond the centre line tacking; *vertical* buttonholes are placed so that the centre line tacking falls in the centre of the buttonhole.

– Buttons are stitched on the opposite side of the garment with the centre of the button positioned exactly on the centre line tacking. When the garment is buttoned, the centre lines on the right and left sides match. If the centres are overlapped more or less than the pattern, the fit of the garment is altered.

– The pattern usually gives the button size the garment is designed to carry. The space from the centre line tacking to the finished facing edge must be at least three-quarters the diameter of the button. With this spacing, the button will not extend beyond the facing edge when the garment is buttoned. If you plan to use a button size different from that indicated on the pattern, take this into account when cutting the garment so that you allow

the proper distance between the centre line and finished edge. Adjust facing width by the same amount.

– Spaces between buttonholes should generally be equal, although fashion may show a different arrangement, especially in loosely fitted garments. Your pattern will have the spacing marked. However, if you have had to adjust the pattern – that is, lengthen or shorten the bodice or skirt, or alter the bustline – or if you use a button larger or smaller than the size indicated on the pattern, you will have to modify the buttonhole spaces accordingly.

Buttonholes should be spaced to suit the figure. When they are incorrectly spaced, there will be gaps which will give the appearance of a poorly fitted garment.

– *The three key points for the positioning of buttonholes* are: at the fullest part of the bust, the neckline and the waistline.

Mark the position of the buttonhole at the fullest part of the bust, then at the neckline (and then at the waistline if you are making a coat, jacket, tunic top or overblouse or princess-line dress).

After marking these key points, space additional buttonholes evenly between them.

If the pattern has buttons all the way down the front, place the last buttonhole about 10 cm (4 inches) from the hem edge.

Decide the positions of the buttonholes and mark the fabric while the pattern is still pinned to it. During the first fitting, check the positions to prove that they are accurate.

Length of Buttonhole

Since the length of the buttonhole depends on the size of the button, *select buttons before making buttonholes.* To determine the length, measure the diameter plus the thickness of the button. To test the length, cut a slash in a double thickness of a scrap of fabric. If the button slips through the slash easily, the size is correct.

Always make a test buttonhole in a scrap of the fabric you are working with. Fold the fabric, duplicating a facing, and include the same type of interfacing you will use in the garment. Buttonholes should be long enough so that the button slips through easily, yet snug enough so that the garment stays buttoned.

Bound and Piped Buttonholes

In making bound buttonholes, you have a range of methods from which to choose: the patch, one-piece, two-piece piped, and corded. All produce attractive durable buttonholes. The two-piece piped method is recommended for loosely woven fabrics; for all other fabrics, the choice is up to you.

Bound buttonholes are not difficult when you follow the directions given here. They are made through the garment fabric and either a stay or lightweight inter-facing before the facing is attached.

Use a stay of a lightweight fabric such as batiste, lawn or silk organza to reinforce the stitching around the buttonhole when you are using a *heavy-weight* inter-facing. *Never make bound buttonholes through hair canvas or heavy interfacing.*

When the interfacing is of a *lightweight* fabric such as batiste, lawn, organdie, it may serve as a stay as well as an interfacing.

Place the stay or lightweight interfacing on the wrong side of the garment, and pin. Then tack guidelines for the position and size of the buttonholes as instructed below.

When making a series of bound buttonholes, always carry through the same step for each buttonhole before proceeding to the next step. Press carefully after completing each step.

Always make a test buttonhole in a scrap of the same fabric you are using in the garment regardless of how many buttonholes you have made previously.

Guidelines for Bound Buttonholes

Study the lines **A, B** and **C** on the diagram. These lines of tacking are made on the true grain of the fabric and are your guidelines for stitching the buttonholes. For tacking, use thread contrasting in colour to that of the fabric so that it can be easily seen and removed.

On the right side of the garment, place a vertical line of machine tacking ·3 cm (⅛ inch) outside the centre line as at **A**. (The centre line should have been tacked before the pattern was removed from the fabric.) Measure the length of the buttonholes and place the second vertical line of machine tacking the measured distance from **A** – as at **B**. Machine-tack the position of each buttonhole on a horizontal line, extending each end of the stitching about 2 cm (¾ inch) beyond the vertical markings – as at **C**. Tack by hand if machine tacking will mark the fabric.

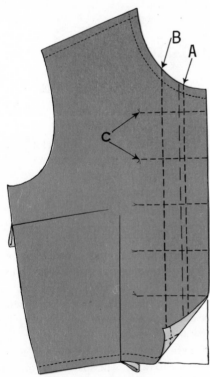

Patch Method

The patch method requires additional markings for accurately stitched buttonholes. First, machine-tack the vertical and horizontal guidelines, **A, B** and **C**, as in-

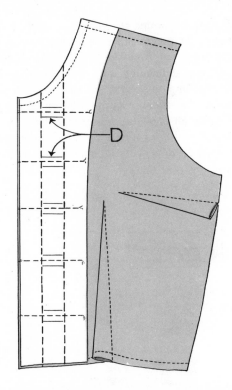

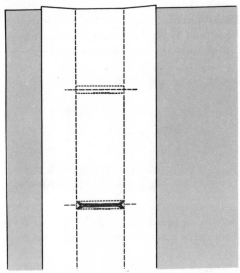

2. On the right side of the garment, place a patch centrally over each buttonhole marking, right sides together. Pin in position; tack if necessary. (*See illustration below end of previous column*)

3. On the wrong side, stitch round the buttonhole, following the markings. Use a 1 mm (20) stitch length. Begin at the centre of one side and stitch to the end; leave the needle in the fabric, raise the presser bar and turn the fabric on the needle. Lower the presser bar and stitch across the end, taking four or five stitches. Continue stitching round the buttonhole, turning each corner in the same way; make the same number of stitches at each end and overlap about four stitches at the starting point. Press.

structed above. Then on the stay or lightweight interfacing on the underside, draw a pencil line on each side of and ·3 cm ($\frac{1}{8}$ inch) from the horizontal tacking as at **D**. This is the stitching line. If the fabric is bulky, draw the lines farther from the tacking but not more than ·6 cm ($\frac{1}{4}$ inch).

1. For each buttonhole, cut a patch of fabric on the crosswise grain or on the true bias, 5 cm (2 inches) wide and 2·5 cm (1 inch) longer than the finished buttonhole. Crease lightly through the centre following the crosswise grain (or true bias) of the fabric.

If you have a Singer Buttonholer for your zig-zag machine, it will perform this basic stitching. It controls the buttonhole length and width and eliminates turning the fabric.

4. Remove tacking threads across each end of the buttonhole. Carefully cut through the centre of the buttonhole to within ·6 cm ($\frac{1}{4}$ inch) of each end; then cut diagonally to each corner. Do not cut through the stitching.

5. Draw the patch through the opening to the underside.

6. Carefully pull out the triangular ends to square the

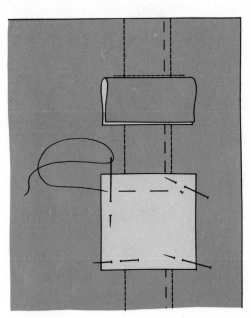

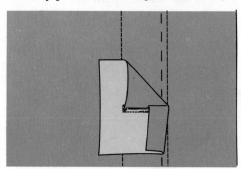

corners. If the slashes are made deep enough into the corners, the opening will be smooth. Press the triangular ends and side seam allowances away from the opening. See *Pressing as You Sew*, page 71.

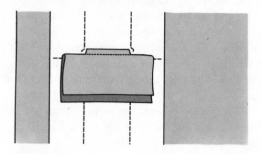

7. Fold each side of the patch to form pleats that meet at the centre of the buttonhole and cover the opening. Carry the folds to the edge of the patch. From the right

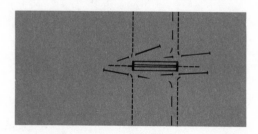

side, tack along the centre of each fold, then overcast the folds together. Remove tacked guidelines. Press.

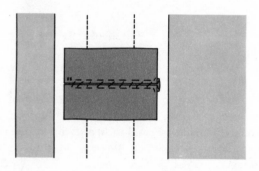

8. Place the garment right side up on the machine, fold it back and stitch the pleats to the seam allowances. First stitch across the triangular ends on the original

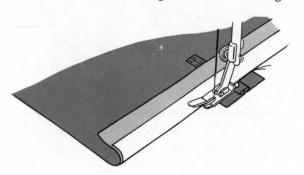

stitching line, beginning and ending the stitching at the raw edge of the patch. Then stitch along the seams on each side, *just a hair's breadth from the original stitching line*, beginning and ending at the raw edge of the patch. The side stitching crosses the end stitching and squares the corners. The stitching is not visible on the right side.

9. Remove all hand tacking except the overcasting holding the pleats together. Press. Trim the patch to within ·6 cm ($\frac{1}{4}$ inch) of the stitching.

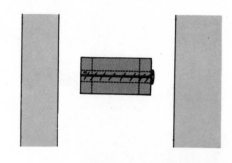

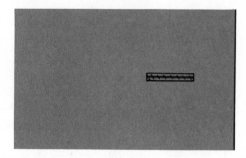

TREATING HEAVY INTERFACING

If the garment is interfaced with a heavy-weight or hair canvas, use a stay of lightweight fabric under the buttonholes. Attach the interfacing to the garment after the buttonholes have been made. Make sure the interfacing

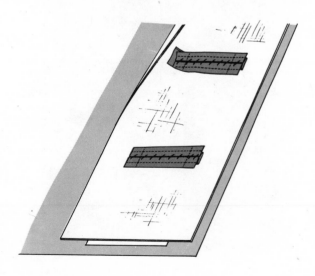

lies smoothly against the fabric. Pin round each buttonhole. From the right side, insert pins straight through each of the four corners to mark the position of the buttonhole on the interfacing. Using the pins as a guide, cut out a piece from the interfacing, barely outside the pin mark, which is slightly longer and wider than the buttonhole. Pull the seam edges of the buttonhole through the opening in the interfacing.

FINISHING THE BACK OF BUTTONHOLES

Finish the back of buttonholes *after you have attached the facing* to the garment. Tack the facing to the garment round each buttonhole, then finish it using one of the three methods illustrated below.

Method 1: Use this method if the fabric does not fray easily and if the facing side of the buttonhole will not be visible when the garment is open. From the right side, insert pins straight through each of the four corners to mark the position of the buttonhole on the facing. On the underside, cut the facing between the pins to within ·6 cm (¼ inch) of the ends; then cut diagonally to the corners. Use the point of the needle to turn under the edges, and slip-stitch the facing in place. The facing side has the same rectangular shape as the front of the buttonhole.

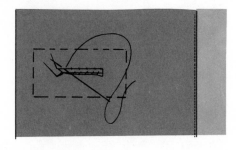

Method 2: This method is preferred for tweeds and fabrics that fray easily. From the right side, insert a pin straight through each end of the buttonhole. Cut the facing between the pins. Turn under the edges with the point of the needle and slip-stitch the facing in place, forming an oval shape.

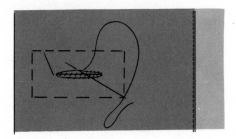

Method 3: If the facing side of the buttonhole will be visible at times (as in coats or suits that may be worn closed at the neckline or open with lapels), it must be as neat as the outside.

After you have attached the facing (see pages 134 and 135), pin it in place around the buttonhole. Mark the buttonhole position on it by inserting pins straight through the four corners from the right side of the garment. Then from the facing side, insert pins straight through the facing in the same places. Remove pins on the top side and round the buttonhole. Carefully separate the facing from the garment, leaving the facing pin-marked. Hand-tack the outline of the buttonhole, using the pins as a guide.

Finish with a faced rectangular opening. Select organza the exact colour of the garment fabric. To cut, stitch and turn the organza patch to form the opening, follow *Steps 2 to 5* on page 113 for the *Two-Piece Piped Method*. Then trim off the edges of the organza ·9 cm (⅜ inch) from the opening.

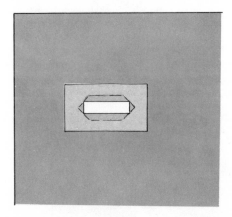

Pin, then tack the facing in place again. The opening in the facing should be the exact size of the finished buttonhole in the garment, and the buttonhole stitching should not be visible. Be sure the organza does not show on the right side of the facing. Slip-stitch in place, making invisible stitches.

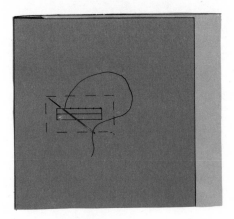

One-Piece Method

Place the stay or lightweight interfacing on the underside, then tack guidelines to mark buttonhole positions as described on page 108.

1. For each buttonhole, cut a strip of fabric on the crosswise grain, 2·5 cm (1 inch) wide and 2·5 cm (1 inch) longer than the finished buttonhole.

2. Make the buttonhole strip by accurately folding the cut edges to the centre, wrong side together, and tack along each fold. This will form a folded strip 1·2 cm (½ inch) in width. Cover with a pressing cloth, and press. Remove tacking.

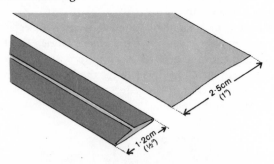

3. On the right side of the garment, place a buttonhole strip centrally over each buttonhole marking and pin at each end. Tack through the centre of each fold to hold the strip in place.

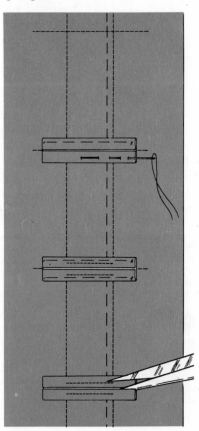

4. Stitch on each side of the buttonhole, using a short stitch. Stitch in the exact centre between the fold and the cut edge on each side. Begin and end the stitching exactly on the tacked lines marking the buttonhole length. Remove tacking. Draw the threads through to the underside and tie. Press. See *Pressing as You Sew*, page 71.

5. Remove the horizontal tacking, marking the buttonhole position. Cut through the centre of the *buttonhole strip only*.

6. Working from the underside, carefully cut between the two lines of stitching, through the garment and stay, to within ·6 cm (¼ inch) of the ends of the buttonhole; then cut diagonally to each corner. The tacked guidelines across the ends will prevent fraying at the corners until the ends are stitched to the strip.

7. Draw the strip through the opening to the underside, with the folded edges meeting at the centre of the opening. Carefully pull the triangular ends away from the opening to square the corners. Press. Overcast the folded edges together.

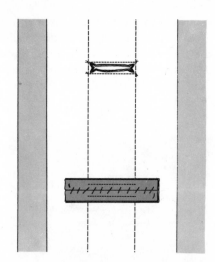

8. Place the garment right side up on the machine; fold it back and stitch the triangular ends to the strip at each end of the buttonhole. Remove the vertical tacked guidelines. Trim ends of the buttonhole strip to within ·6 cm (¼ inch) of the stitching. Press.

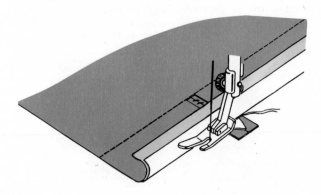

Treat the interfacing as described on page 110. Finish the back of the buttonhole after the facing is attached, as instructed on page 111.

A corded effect may be given to buttonholes by cutting the strip on the true bias. Follow the same procedure given above for the *One-Piece Method* up to *Step 8*. From the underside, draw wool yarn through the pleats; a single or double strand may be used. Then stitch across the ends.

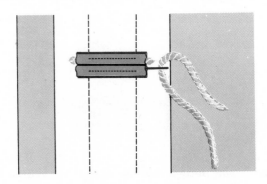

Two-Piece Piped Method

Use this method when the fabric is heavy, bulky or loosely woven. Since such fabrics require heavy interfacing, always apply the interfacing *after* making the buttonholes to eliminate bulk.

1. Place a stay of lightweight fabric on the underside, and tack guidelines to mark buttonhole positions as described on page 108. Then on the stay on the underside, draw a pencil line on each side of and about ·5 cm ($\frac{3}{16}$ inch) from the horizontal tacked line. This marks the stitching line.

2. Cut a patch of organza 5 cm (2 inches) wide and 2·5 cm (1 inch) longer than the finished buttonhole. (The organza must match the fabric exactly in colour.) Place the patch centrally over the buttonhole marking on the right side of the fabric. Pin; tack if necessary.

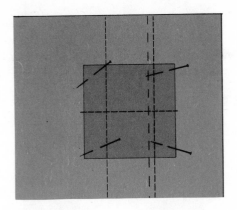

3. Turn the garment to the wrong side and stitch round the buttonhole, following the markings and using a 1 mm (20) stitch length. Begin the stitching at the centre of one side; at the corners, pivot the fabric on the needle; make the same number of stitches (four or five) across the ends; and overlap about four stitches at the starting point. Press. Carefully remove the tacked guidelines through the centre and across the ends of the buttonhole.

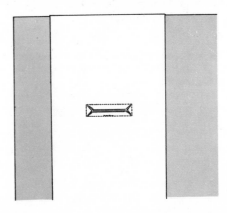

4. Cut through the centre of the buttonhole to within ·6 cm ($\frac{1}{4}$ inch) of each end; then cut diagonally to each corner.

5. Turn the organza patch through the opening to the underside. Carefully pull out the triangular ends to square the corners and press them away from the open-

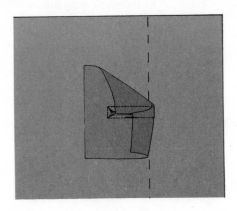

ing. Turn the seam allowances and organza patch away from the opening along the sides, fold on the stitching line, and press flat against the fabric. You now have a faced rectangular opening.

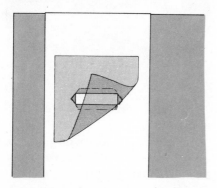

6. *For the piping*, cut two strips of garment fabric on the crosswise grain, 4 cm (1½ inches) wider and 2·5 cm (1 inch) longer than the finished buttonhole. Place them right sides together and tack through the centre following the fabric grain line. Leave threads at each end so the tacking can be easily removed.

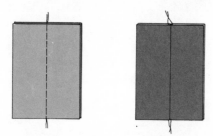

7. Press, then press the tacked seam open. Place a pressing cloth between the fabric and iron because you are pressing on the right side of the fabric. (You should now have each strip folded, wrong sides together, and the two strips temporarily tacked together along the folds.)

8. With the garment right side up, place the strip over the wrong side of the opening with the tacked seam in the centre and the ends extending 1·2 cm (½ inch) beyond the opening. Pin the strip in place with fine needles close to the ends of the opening.

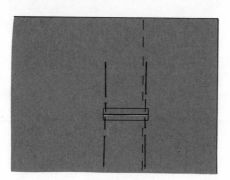

9. Place the garment right side up on the machine; turn back the edge and stitch the seam allowances and organza patch to the strip. Use a 1 mm (20) stitch length and place the stitching barely beyond the previous stitching so that the organza patch will not be visible on the top side of the garment. First pin the triangular ends to the strip with fine needles and stitch across the ends;

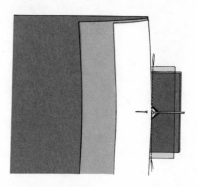

then, just before stitching along each side, remove the needles on the top side and pin the seam allowances and organza to the strip on the underside to prevent them

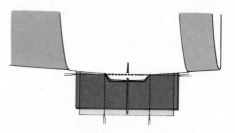

from slipping during the stitching. Trim the ends of the strip to within ·6 cm (¼ inch) of stitching; along the sides, trim the seam allowance on the top layer of the strip to ·6 cm (¼ inch) and on the under layer to ·9 cm (⅜ inch). Before pressing, slip brown paper between the garment and seam allowance to prevent the outline of the seam allowance from pressing on to the fabric.

Treat the interfacing as described on page 110. Finish the back of the buttonhole after the facing is attached, following the directions on page 111. Remove the tacking joining the buttonhole strips.

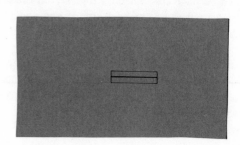

Corded Buttonholes

Additional markings are required for accurate corded buttonholes. First tack the vertical and horizontal guidelines, as instructed on page 108. Then on the stay or lightweight interfacing on the underside, draw a pencil line on each side and ·5 or ·6 cm ($\frac{3}{16}$ or $\frac{1}{4}$ inch) from the

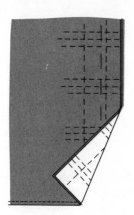

buttonhole marking. Tack on these lines to transfer the markings to the right side. The spacing of these lines from the buttonhole marking will vary, depending upon the size of the cord and the weight of the fabric used.

Prepare the corded strips from a true bias cut 2·5 cm (1 inch) wide and long enough to make all the buttonholes. To work out the length of the corded strip needed, allow twice the length plus 5 cm (2 inches) for each buttonhole.

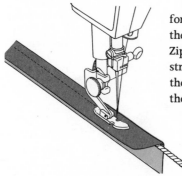

Use No. 00 piping cord for the cording. Replace the Presser Foot with the Zipper Foot. Fold the bias strip, right side out, round the cording. Stitch close to the piping cord. Press.

1. For each buttonhole, cut two corded strips 2·5 cm (1 inch) longer than the buttonhole. Place two strips over

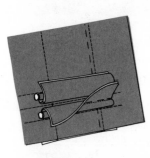

each buttonhole marking, aligning the corded edges with the outside markings and keeping the raw edges towards the centre. Tack in position.

2. Stitch on each side of the buttonhole, stitching between the cord and previous line of stitching. Use a short stitch, and adjust the Zipper Foot to the left of the needle. Begin and end the stitching exactly on the guidelines marking the buttonhole length. Remove hand tackings. Pull the threads through to the underside and tie. Remove all horizontal tacking lines. Press. See *Pressing as You Sew*, page 71.

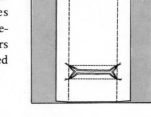

3. From the underside, carefully cut between the two lines of stitching, through the garment and stay, to within ·6 cm ($\frac{1}{4}$ inch) of the ends of the buttonhole; then cut diagonally to each corner. The tacked guidelines across the ends will prevent fraying at the corners until the ends are stitched in place.

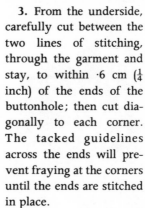

4. Draw the strip through the opening to the underside, with the corded edges meeting at the centre of the opening. Carefully pull the triangular ends away from the opening to square the corners. Press. Overcast the corded edges together.

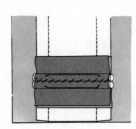

5. Place the garment right side up on the machine; fold it back and stitch the triangular ends to the corded strip at each end of the buttonhole. Replace the Zipper Foot with the Presser Foot for this operation. Remove the vertical guidelines. Trim the ends and sides of the corded strip to within ·6 cm ($\frac{1}{4}$ inch) of the stitching. Press. Treat the interfacing as described on page 110. Finish the back of the buttonhole after the facing is attached as described on page 111.

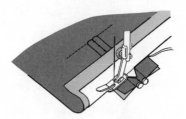

115

Buttonholes in a Seam

Buttonholes in a seam are often found on a horizontal line at the waistline of a jacket, where the peplum joins the bodice, and in yoke seams across the bodice; and on a vertical line where a binding or an extended facing is used. Where there is no seam, additional buttonholes are made, using one of the conventional methods shown earlier in this chapter.

1. Carefully mark the position of the buttonhole in the seam. With right sides of fabric together, pin and tack a 1·5-cm ($\frac{5}{8}$-inch) seam in the garment.

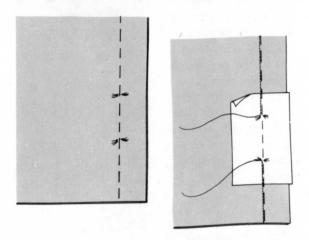

2. Cut two stays for each buttonhole 2·5 cm (1 inch) longer than the buttonhole and 3 cm (1$\frac{1}{4}$ inches) wide for reinforcement. Use batiste, organza or a similar fabric, and cut the stays on the same grain as the garment. Place one on each side of the seam over the buttonhole marking, keeping seam edges even. Pin.

3. Beginning at the end of the seam, stitch to the buttonhole marking. Leave thread ends long enough to tie. Then from the opposite end of the buttonhole, stitch the entire length of the seam or to the marking for the

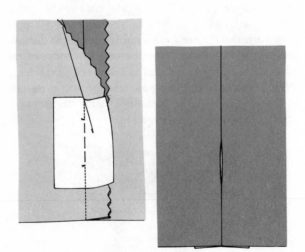

next buttonhole. At each end of the buttonhole, pull the threads to one side and tie. Remove tailor's tacks, if used, and tacking, except across the buttonhole opening.

4. Press the seam, then press it open. Trim the stay on each side of the buttonhole to within ·9 cm ($\frac{3}{8}$ inch) of opening.

5. Treat the interfacing as instructed on page 110. Finish the back of the buttonhole *after the facing is attached*, as described on page 111.

Worked Buttonholes

Machine-worked and hand-worked buttonholes are made after the garment is finished. For machine-worked buttonholes you may use either the zig-zag machine or a straight stitch machine with a Buttonholer.

Use interfacing in the buttonhole area for reinforcement. It is essential if the fabric is loosely woven or is one that stretches easily (for example, a knitted fabric such as jersey), it holds the fabric firmly so that you can make a neat buttonhole; it also keeps the finished buttonhole in shape.

Decide the buttonhole position and length as described on pages 107 and 108.

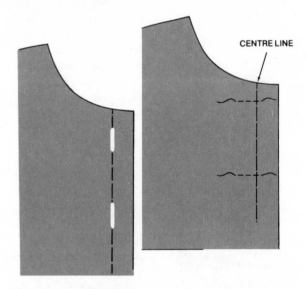

CENTRE LINE

With Zig-Zag Machine

Worked buttonholes of any length and varying widths can be made quickly and easily on a zig-zag machine.

To work out the length of the cutting space (the opening through which the button passes), refer to page 108. The length of the finished buttonhole is the cutting space plus ·3 cm ($\frac{1}{8}$ inch) at each end for bar tacks. After

116

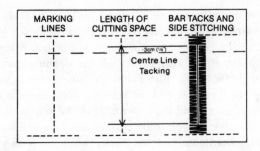

MARKING LINES	LENGTH OF CUTTING SPACE	BAR TACKS AND SIDE STITCHING

Centre Line
Tacking

·3cm (⅛")

determining the size of the buttonhole, mark the button-hole size with either chalk or hand tacking along the thread of the fabric.

Set the selectors on the machine for a plain zig-zag stitch, and set the stitch length selector for satin stitch-ing. Work a sample buttonhole in a scrap of the same fabric used in the garment. Fold the fabric, duplicating the facing, and include the same type of interfacing used in the garment. Follow the instructions for making buttonholes in the instruction book accompanying the machine.

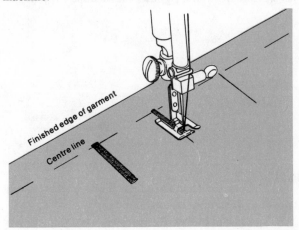

Finished edge of garment

Centre line

Corded buttonholes. Both gimp and buttonhole twist make suitable filler cords for corded buttonholes.

Unwind a sufficient amount of the filler cord to pre-vent tension or strain on the cord. Lead the end of the cord through the left eyelet of the Special Purpose Foot. Draw the cord under and in back of the foot. Proceed with stitching as for regular buttonholes. The zig-zag stitches are made over the filler cord.

With the Buttonholer

Mark the end position as well as the line of the button-hole along the thread of the fabric. Use chalk or hand-tack. To determine the buttonhole position and length, see pages 107 and 108.

Select the size template required for the buttonhole and insert it in the Buttonholer. Regulate the stitch width and cutting space required according to the fabric.

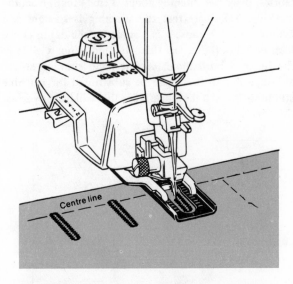

Centre line

Then make a test buttonhole in a scrap of the same fabric used in the garment. Fold the fabric, duplicating the facing, and include the same type of interfacing used in the garment. Follow the directions given in the instruc-tion book accompanying the Buttonholer. See also *Buttonholer*, page 287.

Hand-Worked Buttonholes

Hand-worked buttonholes may be made on a horizontal or vertical line. If horizontal, they have a fan at the out-side end near the edge of the garment, which carries the strain, and a bar tack at the inside end. If vertical, they have a bar tack at each end.

Use the buttonhole stitch and thread that matches the fabric exactly in colour. Work with a thread about 46 cm (18 inches) in length and re-thread the needle for each buttonhole because the thread will fray when repeatedly pulled through the fabric.

Determine the buttonhole position and length as described on pages 107 and 108. Then follow the instruc-tions below, beginning with a practice buttonhole in a scrap of your fabric.

117

HORIZONTAL BUTTONHOLE

1. Carefully mark the length and line of the buttonhole with chalk or hand tacking along the true grain of the fabric. Pin the layers of fabric together to prevent them from slipping.

2. Machine-stitch around the buttonhole for reinforcement. Use a 1 mm (20) stitch length and place the stitching ·2 cm ($\frac{1}{16}$ inch) from the buttonhole marking; take two or three stitches across the ends. In heavy fabrics, place the stitching about ·3 cm ($\frac{1}{8}$ inch) from the marking. Take care that the stitching is straight and evenly spaced because it is a guide for the depth of the hand stitches (however, this stitching is not visible in the finished buttonhole). A fine hand running stitch, although not so firm, may be substituted for machine stitching. Press. If the fabric is one that will fray, overcast the edges.

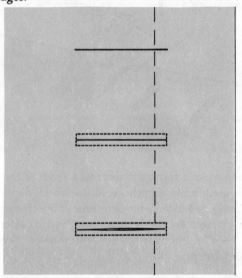

3. Cut the buttonhole between the two lines of stitching, using sharp, pointed scissors.

4. Buttonholes may be worked from right to left, or left to right. The illustrations show working from *right to left*. Hold the fabric, needle and thread in the position shown in the illustrations. With the right side of the garment up, *start working at the inside end*. Bring the cut buttonhole over the first finger of the left hand.

Do not knot the end of the thread. Take two small backstitches at the end to fasten the thread. Cut off the thread end after several stitches have been made. Bring the thread to the left, then to the right, to form a loop around the point where the stitch will be made. Insert the point of the needle through the opening and up through the fabric just below the machine stitching. Keep the thread at back of both the point and the eye of the needle. Hold the lower edge of the loop with the left thumb until you draw up the thread for the stitch. Pull the needle through the fabric, then away from you, to place the purl of the stitch on the cut edge of the buttonhole. Pull the thread gently yet firmly enough to make smooth, flat stitches. Continue making buttonhole stitches until you reach the outside end. Keep the spacing between the stitches uniform and the depth as even as possible.

5. Fan the stitches at the outside end. Place about five or seven stitches in the fan and make them slightly longer than the side stitches so that they will appear to be the same length.

Work down the opposite side to the inside end. Turn the buttonhole to the right as you work around it.

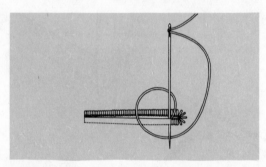

6. Make a bar tack across the inside end by taking two straight stitches through the fabric.

7. Complete the bar by working over the stitches, using a blanket stitch. Make the stitches through the fabric and under the bar. Fasten the thread on the underside with two backstitches.

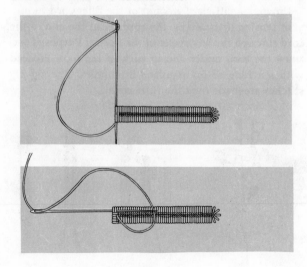

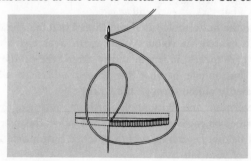

VERTICAL BUTTONHOLE

Vertical buttonholes are set so that the centre line tacking is in the centre of the buttonhole.

1. Mark the length and line of the buttonhole on the true lengthwise grain of the fabric.

2. Machine-stitch around the buttonhole for reinforcement. Use a 1 mm (20) stitch length and place the stitching ·2 cm ($\frac{1}{16}$ inch) from the buttonhole marking; take two or three stitches across the ends.

3. Cut the buttonhole between the two lines of stitching.

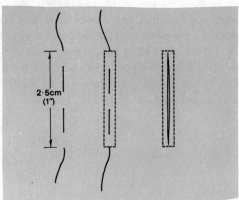

4. Place the garment right side up. Start working at the lower end, using the buttonhole stitch as described in *Step 4*, page 118. Make a bar tack across the upper end by taking two straight stitches through the fabric. Complete the bar by working across the stitches, using the blanket stitch. Make the stitches through the fabric and under the bar.

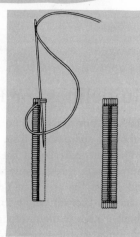

5. Work down the opposite side and finish the lower end with a bar tack. Fasten the thread on the underside with two backstitches.

TAILORED BUTTONHOLE

Tailored buttonholes have an eyelet at the outside end near the edge of the garment. The shank of the button fits into the eyelet opening. This prevents the wrap from bulging when the garment is buttoned.

1. Mark the position of the buttonhole with hand tacking, chalk or pencil on the crosswise grain of the fabric.

2. Cut the buttonhole on the marked line. At the outside end, near the edge of the garment, make two small slashes about ·3 cm ($\frac{1}{8}$ inch) in depth or punch a small hole, using a stiletto.

3. Overcast round the cut edges to prevent them fraying and to hold the layers of fabric together. Make the stitches about ·3 cm ($\frac{1}{8}$ inch) in depth.

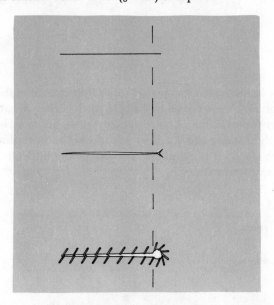

4. Start at the inside end, and thread a strand of buttonhole twist along the edges of the buttonhole through the overcasting. Fasten the ends by forming a figure eight round a pin.

Take one backstitch at the inside end to tie the thread. Follow the instructions on page 118 for *Steps 4 and 5*, and make buttonhole stitches over the twist. Fan the stitches at the eyelet end.

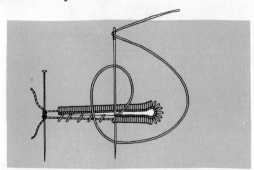

5. Make a bar tack across the inside end by taking two straight stitches through the fabric. Complete the bar by working over the stitches, using a blanket stitch. Make the stitches through the fabric and under the bar. Fasten the thread on the underside with two backstitches.

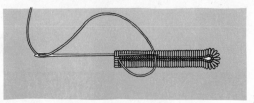

Pick a Pretty Pocket

The fashion interest in pocket styles fluctuates from the concealed set-in pocket to the bold patch pocket. Whatever the style, the secret of pocket making lies in accurately marking and stitching your pocket and pressing each step as it is completed. Pockets are not difficult if you remember this.

The pattern usually marks the position of pockets in a garment; however, if you decide to add them, do so in the planning stage so that you can measure and mark their position on the pattern. Make the pockets after the pin fitting, before assembling the garment pieces.

Always make a practice pocket in a scrap of the garment fabric before working on the garment itself. For instructions on pressing, see page 71.

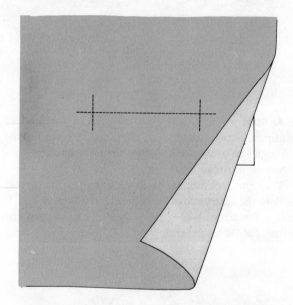

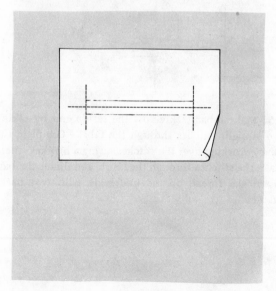

Set-in Pockets

Guidelines for Pockets

Mark the position of the pocket with tailor's tacks before removing the pattern from the garment section.

Place an underlay of batiste, muslin, lawn or similar fabric under the stitching line to reinforce the opening and retain the shape of the pocket. Cut the underlay 4 cm (1½ inches) wider than the pocket opening and about 7·5 cm (3 inches) long. Place it centrally over the markings on the wrong side of the garment, and pin.

From the right side, machine-tack across the ends of the pocket to mark the width. Then machine-tack through the centre, extending the stitching about 2 cm (¾ inch) beyond the ends, to form guidelines. Follow the grain of the fabric unless the pocket is on a diagonal line. Use thread contrasting in colour so that it can easily be seen and removed. Hand-tack if machine will mark the fabric.

On the wrong side, draw pencil lines on each side of and ·6 cm (¼ inch) from the centre tacking to mark the stitching line. This distance may vary depending on the style of the pocket.

(Additional markings are required for a *corded pocket* and are illustrated under the instructions for making the pocket.)

120

Stand Pocket

Mark the guidelines of the pocket as instructed on opposite page.

Cut a piece of fabric on the lengthwise grain twice the pocket depth plus twice the depth of the stand, and 2·5 cm (1 inch) wider than the opening. Crease the pocket section crosswise, 2·5 cm (1 inch) above the centre.

1. On the right side of the garment, place the pocket section, right sides together. Align the crease with the marking on the garment, extending the long end of the pocket below the marking. Pin. Tack if necessary.

2. On the wrong side, stitch round the pocket opening, following the guidelines. Use a short stitch and begin the stitching at the centre of one side; pivot the fabric on the needle at the corners and take the same number of stitches across each end. Overlap about six stitches at the starting point. Do not stitch on the tackings. Remove the tacked guidelines, and press.

3. Cut between the two lines of stitching, through all thicknesses, to within 1·2 cm ($\frac{1}{2}$ inch) of the ends; then cut diagonally to each of the four corners. Do not cut through the stitching.

4. Draw the pocket through the opening to the wrong side. Pull out the triangles at the ends to square the corners. Press the triangular ends and seam allowances along the side away from the opening.

5. Fold the lower section of the pocket to form a pleat to cover the opening. Check both the right and wrong sides to be sure that the pleat is even and covers the opening. Hand-tack on the folded edge, carrying the tacking to each end of the pocket. Press the folded edge. Overcast the fold to the top edge of the opening. (Pin the upper section of the pocket to the garment to keep it out of the way for the next step.)

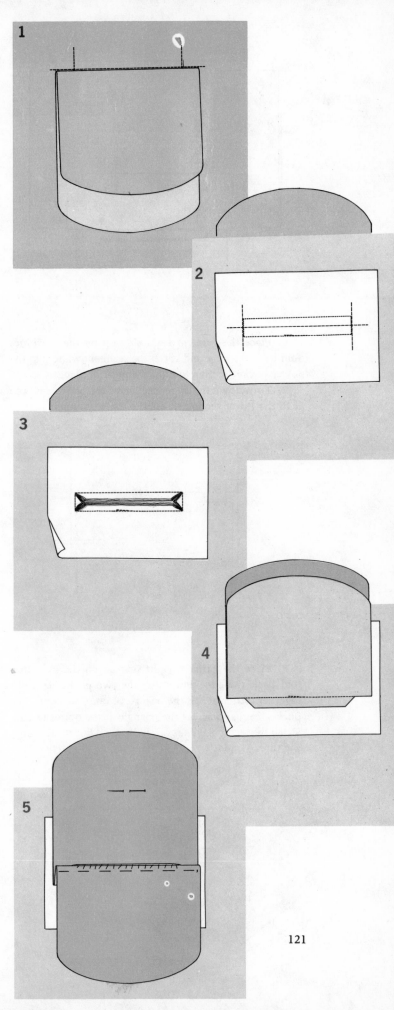

121

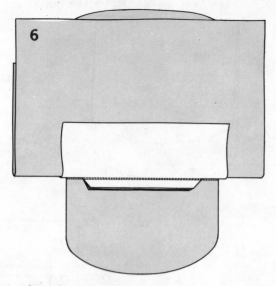

6. Place the garment right side up on the machine; fold back the edge and stitch the seam allowances to the lower pocket section to hold the pleat in place.

7. Turn down the upper section of the pocket and pin it to the lower section. Press the top seam open.

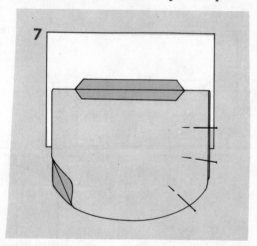

8. Place the garment right side up on the machine; fold back the edge and stitch the two pocket sections together. Stitch across the triangle at one end, round the pocket bag, and across the triangle at the opposite end. Stitch the triangular ends on the original line of stitching. Tie thread ends.

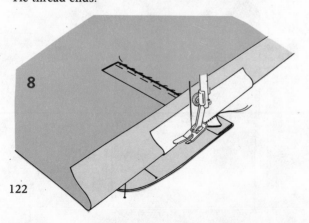

Trim seam allowances evenly and neaten the edges according to the fabric. Remove all tackings and press. Trim underlay to within 1·2 cm (½ inch) of stitching.

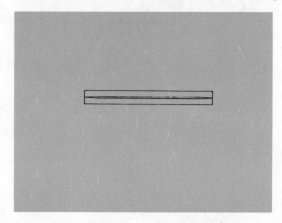

Bound Pocket – Two-Piece

The bound pocket is often called a buttonhole pocket because it is made exactly like a buttonhole.

Mark the guidelines of the pocket as instructed on page 120.

Cut one pocket section the depth of the pocket plus 5 cm (2 inches) and 2·5 cm (1 inch) wider than the opening. Cut another section the depth of the pocket plus the seam allowance, and 2·5 cm (1 inch) wider than the opening. (To avoid bulk in suits, coats and garments of heavy fabric, you may cut the lower section [the short one] from the lining fabric or a lightweight fabric matching in colour.)

1. On the right side of the garment, place the long section of the pocket, right side down, extending the edge 4 cm (1½ inches) below the marking. Pin. Tack if necessary.

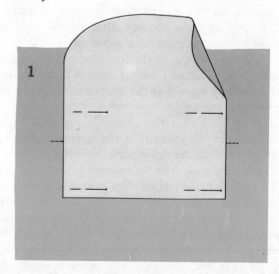

2. On the wrong side, stitch round the pocket opening, following the guidelines. Use a short stitch and

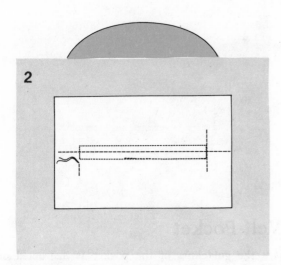

5. Fold the pocket section to form a pleat on each side which meets at the centre and covers the opening. Check both the right and wrong sides to be sure that the pleats are even in width. Tack along the centre of each fold, then overcast the folded edges together. Tack to the raw edge of the pocket section. Remove the centre tacked guidelines, and press.

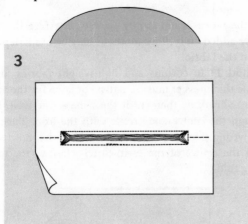

begin stitching at the centre of one side; pivot the fabric on the needle at the corners and take the same number of stitches across each end. Overlap about six stitches at the starting point. Remove the tacked guidelines at the ends, and press.

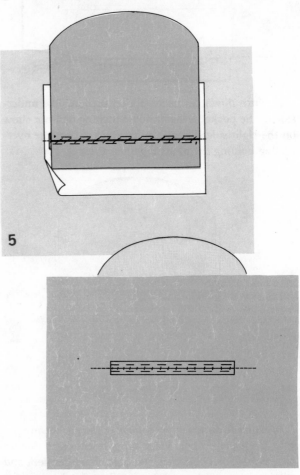

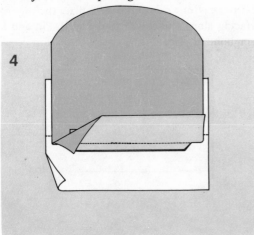

3. Cut between the two lines of stitching, through all thicknesses to within 1·2 cm (½ inch) of the ends; then cut diagonally to each of the four corners. Do not cut through the stitching.

4. Draw the pocket through the opening to the underside. Pull out the triangular ends to square the corners. Press the triangular ends and seam allowances along the sides away from the opening.

6. Place the garment right side up on the machine; fold back the edge and stitch the seam allowances to the pleats. First stitch across the triangular ends on the original stitching line; then stitch across the seam at the top, *just a hair's breadth from the original stitching line*. The side stitching crosses the end stitching and squares the corners.

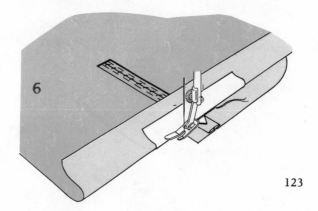

7. Place the second pocket section under the bottom seam, right side up; then stitch the seam allowance to the pleat and the lower pocket section in one operation.

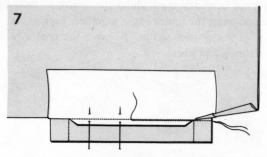

8. Turn down the lower pocket section. The underside of the pocket is illustrated. Stitching will not show on the right side. Remove all tackings except the overcasting holding the pleats together. Press.

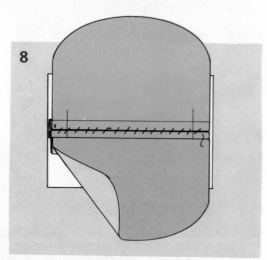

9. Turn down the upper section of the pocket and pin it to the lower section. Place the garment right side up on the machine. Fold back the edge of the garment and stitch the two pocket sections together. Stitch across the triangle at one end, round the pocket bag and across the triangle at the opposite end. Stitch the triangular ends on the original line of stitching. Tie thread ends.

Trim seam allowances evenly and finish the edges according to the fabric. Remove all tackings and press. Trim underlay to within 1·2 cm (½ inch) of the stitching.

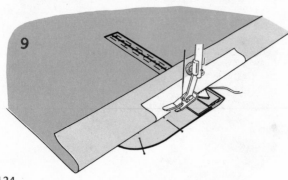

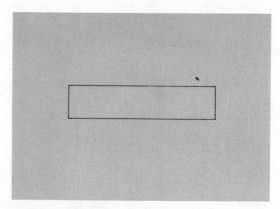

Welt Pocket

Mark the guidelines of the pocket as instructed on page 120.

Welt. If a pattern for the welt is not included, cut one on the crosswise grain the width of the pocket opening plus seam allowances, and twice the depth of the finished welt plus seam allowances. (Allow ·6 cm (¼ inch) for each seam.)

If the fabric is not firmly woven, interface the welt to give added body. Two methods may be used, depending on the fabric.

Method 1: In cottons and lightweight fabrics, use a double thickness of muslin, batiste or lawn for the interfacing. Shrink it; then cut it the same as the welt. Fold through the centre and crease with the iron. Turn the welt wrong side up and place the fold of the interfacing along the centre of the welt. Stitch close to the interfacing fold.

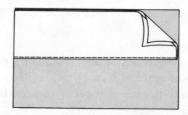

Method 2: In coats, suits and garments of heavy fabric, interface with hair canvas. Shrink the interfacing; then cut it the width of the welt and one-half the depth. Trim off the seam allowance on each end and along the lower edge. On the wrong side of the welt, place the edge of the interfacing along the centre of the welt. Pin and tack. Herringbone in place.

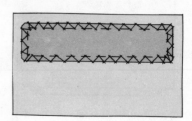

For Methods 1 and 2, fold the welt in half on the crosswise grain, right sides together. Stitch across the ends. Back-stitch at each end for reinforcement. Cut diagonally across corners at the top edge. Trim the facing seam allowance to ·3 cm (⅛ inch). If *Method 1* is used, trim the interfacing seam allowance close to the stitching. Press.

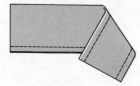

Turn the welt right side out. Fold on the stitching line; pull out the corners and press. Machine-stitch ·6 cm (¼ inch) from the lower edge to hold the layers of fabric together.

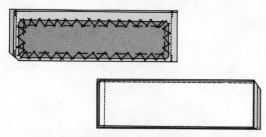

Pocket. Cut one pocket section the depth of the pocket plus 5 cm (2 inches) and 2·5 cm (1 inch) wider than the opening. Cut another section the depth of pocket plus seam allowance, and 2·5 cm (1 inch) wider than the opening. (To avoid bulk in suits, coats and garments of heavy fabric, you may cut the lower section [the short one] from the lining fabric or a lightweight fabric matching in colour.)

To make the welt pocket, proceed as follows:

1. Turn garment right side up. Place the welt below the pocket marking, right side down, with the raw edge on the centre line. (The ends must be even with the guidelines. Adjust if necessary.) Pin and hand-tack. On the underside, pin at each corner, using fine needles to prevent the welt from slipping as you stitch in *Step 3*.

2. On the right side of the garment, place the upper pocket section (the long one) over the marking, right sides together, extending the edge 2·5 cm (1 inch) below the centre marking. Pin. Tack if necessary.

3. On the wrong side of the garment, stitch round the pocket opening, following the guidelines. Use a short stitch and begin stitching at the centre of the upper side; pivot the fabric on the needle at the corners and take the same number of stitches across each end. Overlap about six stitches at the starting point. Check the right side to be sure the end stitching does not extend beyond the welt. Remove all tackings and press.

4. From the underside, cut between the two lines of stitching, through all thicknesses, to within 1·2 cm (½

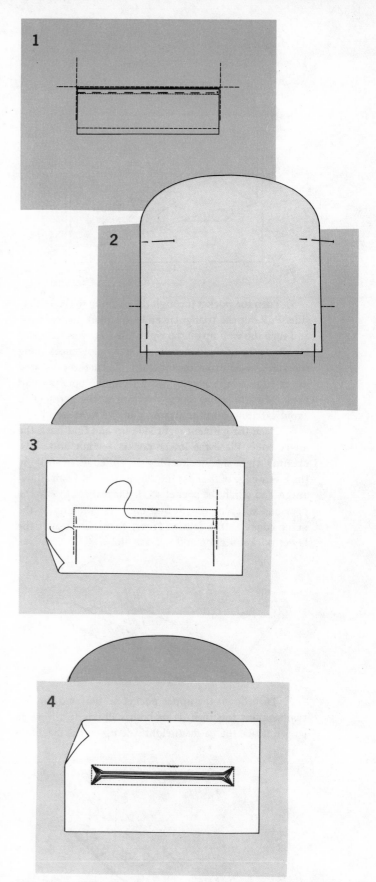

inch) of the ends. Slash diagonally to each corner. Do not cut through the stitching.

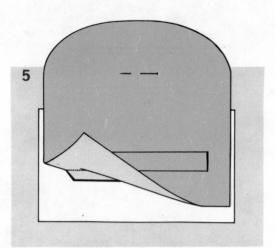

Fold back the edge and stitch the pocket sections together. Stitch across the triangle at one end, round the pocket bag and across the triangle at the opposite end. Stitch the triangular ends on the original line of stitching. Tie the threads. Remove all tacking and press.

Neaten seams as required by the fabric. Trim underlay to within 1·2 cm (½ inch) of the stitching.

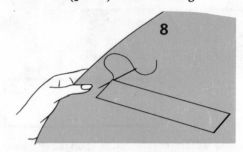

5. Turn the pocket through the opening to the underside. Pull out the triangular ends to square the corners, and turn the welt up on the right side to cover the opening. Press the triangular ends and seam allowances along the sides away from the opening. Turn the extended lower edge of the pocket away from the opening and press. (Pin the upper pocket section to the garment to avoid catching it in the stitching of the next step.)

6. Place the garment right side up and fold back the lower edge. Place the lower pocket section under the opening, right side up, keeping the cut edges even along the lower edge of the opening. Turn back the seam allowances, and stitch the pocket section together close to the previous stitching. Begin and end the stitching at the outer edges of the fabric. Press; then turn down the lower pocket section and press again.

8. On the right side, slip-stitch the ends of the welt to the garment.

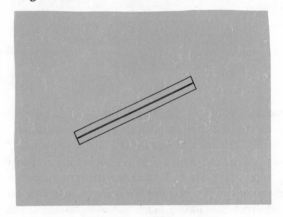

Corded or Piped Pocket

Mark the guidelines of the pocket as instructed on page 120. Then mark additional lines for the position of the cording. The position of these lines is determined by the size of the cord; take twice the width of the cord plus ·2 cm ($\frac{1}{16}$ inch). (You may have to make an extra allowance for very thick fabric.) On the underside, draw a pencil line on each side of and ·8 cm ($\frac{5}{16}$ inch) (or the necessary distance) from the centre tacking. This marks

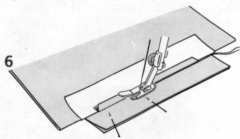

7. Turn down the upper pocket section and pin the two sections together. Trim both sections to the same length. Place the garment right side up on the machine.

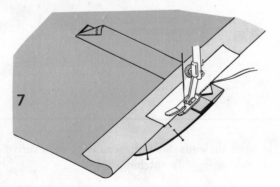

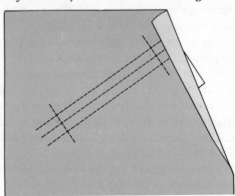

the position of the corded strip. Machine-tack on these lines to transfer the markings to the right side.

Cording (Piping). Refer to page 244, for instructions on cutting the bias strip and covering the cord. For each pocket, mark two corded strips the width of the pocket plus 2·5 cm (1 inch); avoid seams within the strips.

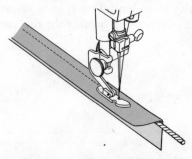

Pocket. Cut two pocket sections the depth of the pocket plus 2·5 cm (1 inch) and 2·5 cm (1 inch) wider than the opening. (You will use them in *Steps 6 and 8*.)

To make the corded pocket, proceed as follows:

1. On the right side of the garment, place a corded strip on each side of the pocket markings. Align the corded edges with the outside markings, keeping the cut edges towards the centre. Pin close to the cord. Check the underside to make sure that the pins are midway between the outside and centre markings. (Use fine needles to pin heavy fabric.) Hand-tack, close to the cord, the entire length of the corded strip.

2. Using a short stitch, stitch the cording in place, stitching between the cord and previous line of tacking. Begin and end the stitching exactly on the end guidelines. Adjust the Zipper Foot to the left of the needle for this operation.

Check the underside to make sure the line of stitching on each side is midway between the centre and outer guidelines. Pull the threads through to the underside and tie. Remove all tackings except those across the ends. Press.

3. From the underside, cut between the two lines of stitching through the garment and underlay, to within 1·2 cm ($\frac{1}{2}$ inch) of the ends; then cut diagonally to each of the four corners. Do not cut through the stitching, and hold the corded strips out of the way to avoid cutting into them.

4. Turn the cut edges of the corded strips through the opening to the underside, with the corded edges meeting at the centre to cover the opening. Pull out the triangular ends to square the corners. Press the triangular ends and seam allowances along the sides away from the opening. Overcast the corded edges together.

5. Place the garment right side up on the machine; fold back the edge and stitch the triangular ends to the cording. Remove machine tacking across the ends, and press.

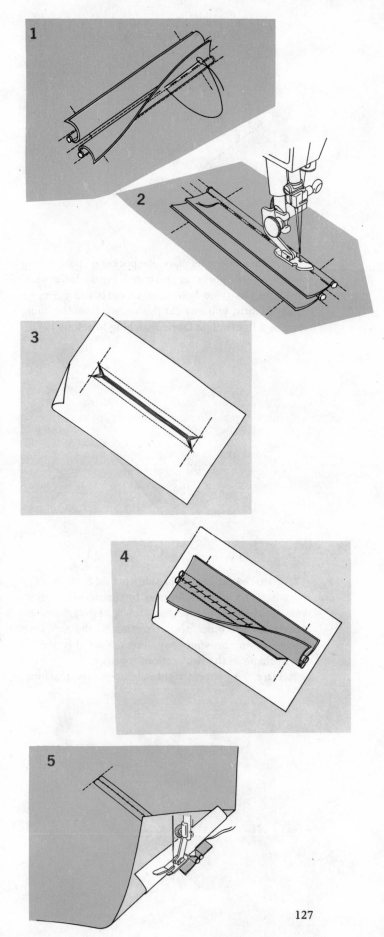

127

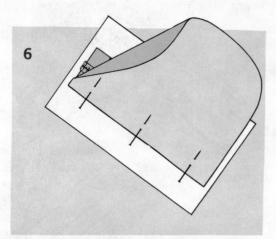

6. On the underside, place one pocket section, wrong side up, over the pocket as illustrated. Pin the lower seam allowance. (To avoid bulk in suits, coats and garments of heavy fabric, you may cut this section from the lining fabric or a lightweight fabric matching in colour.)

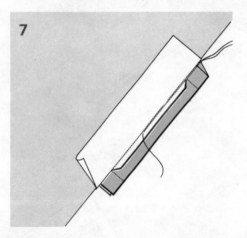

7. With the garment right side up, fold back the edge and stitch the seam allowances to the pocket section. Press. Fold the pocket section down, and again press.

8. Stitch the other pocket section to the top seam allowances in the same way. Press. Fold this section down; then pin the two sections together.

9. Place the garment right side up on the machine;

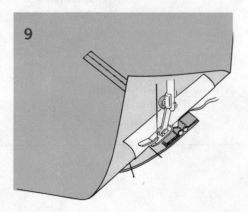

fold back the edge and stitch the two pocket sections together. Begin stitching at the edge above the triangular point, round the pocket bag and across the triangle at the opposite end. Stitch the triangular ends on the original line of stitching. Press.

Neaten the seam edges according to the fabric. Trim the underlay to within 1·2 cm (½ inch) of the stitching. Remove the overcasting holding the two corded edges together.

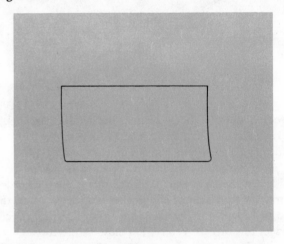

Pocket with Flap

Mark guidelines of the pocket as instructed on page 120.
Flap. Cut the flap and the facing the width of the opening plus seam allowances and the depth desired plus seam allowances (·6-cm (¼-inch) seam allowances are sufficient in most fabrics). Curve the lower corners, if desired.

Interface the flap to give the added body necessary. Two methods are given below. Select the one most suitable for your fabric.

Method 1: In cottons and lightweight fabrics, interface with muslin, batiste or lawn. Shrink, then cut a double thickness of interfacing the same size as the flap. Pin the interfacing to the wrong side of the flap. Tack, if necessary.

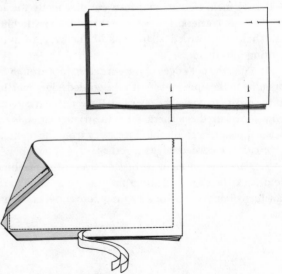

Method 2: Interface woollens, heavy silks and similar fabrics with pre-shrunk hair canvas. Cut the interfacing the same size as the flap. Trim away the seam allowance plus ·3 cm (⅛ inch). Tack the interfacing to the wrong side of the flap as shown. Herringbone in place round the edges. Press.

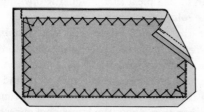

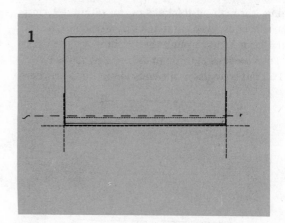

For Methods 1 and 2, pin the facing to the flap, right sides together. Stitch on the seamline, leaving the upper edge open. Backstitch at each end. Cut off corners at the lower edge. Trim the facing seam allowance to ·3 cm (⅛ inch) and the flap seam allowance to ·6 cm (¼ inch). If *Method 1* is used, trim the interfacing seam allowance close to the stitching. Turn the flap right side out. Pull out the corners. Ease the facing under slightly at the seamline and tack. Press. Top-stitch if desired. Stitch across the cut edges ·6 cm (¼ inch) from the edge to hold the layers of fabric together. Remove tackings.

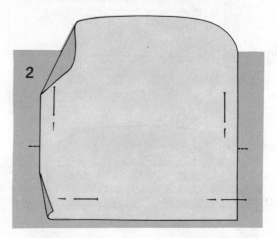

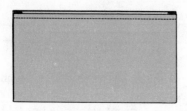

Pocket. Cut one pocket section the depth of the pocket plus 5 cm (2 inches), and 2·5 cm (1 inch) wider than the opening. Cut another section the depth of the pocket plus seam allowance, and 2·5 cm (1 inch) wider than the opening. (To avoid bulk in suits, coats and garments of heavy fabric, you may cut the lower section [the short one] from the lining fabric or a lightweight fabric matching in colour.)

To make the pocket, proceed as follows:

1. Turn the garment right side up. Place the flap above the pocket marking, right side down, with the raw edge on the centre tacking line. The flap should just touch the end tackings. Tack. On the underside, use fine needles to pin each corner to prevent the flap from slipping as you stitch in *Step 3*.

2. On the right side, place the long pocket section, right sides together, over the opening, extending the lower edge 5 cm (2 inches) below the centre tacking. Pin in place.

3. From the wrong side, stitch round the pocket opening; use a short stitch and follow the guidelines. Start stitching at the centre of the lower side; pivot the fabric on the needle at the corners and make the same number of stitches at each end. Overlap about six stitches at the starting point. Check to be sure the end stitching does not extend beyond the ends of the flap. Remove all tackings and press.

4. From the underside, cut between the two lines of

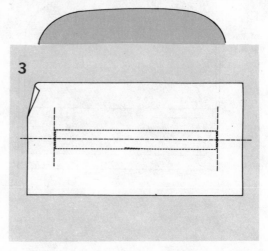

stitching, through all thicknesses, to within 1·2 cm (½ inch) of the ends; then cut diagonally to each of the four corners. Do not cut through the stitching.

5. Turn the pocket through the opening to the underside. Pull out triangles at the ends to square the corners.

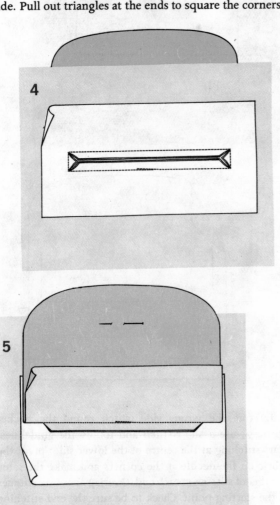

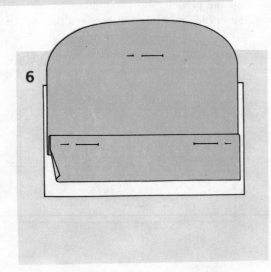

Press triangular ends and seam allowances along the sides away from the opening. Turn down the flap before pressing the seam across the top. Pin the upper pocket section to the garment to avoid catching it while stitching *Step* 7.

6. Fold the pocket extension, which is below the opening, to form a pleat that covers the opening. Hand-tack on the fold. Press.

7. Place the garment right side up; fold back the lower edge and pin the free edge of the pleat to the seam allowance. Place the lower pocket section underneath, right side up, and pin. Stitch the pleat and pocket section to the seam allowance at the same time. Press the seam; then turn down the lower pocket section and press. Trim the seam allowances to different widths to avoid forming a ridge on the right side when pressing.

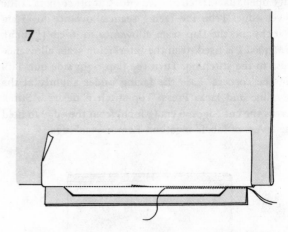

8. Turn the upper pocket section down and pin the two sections together. Trim both sections to the same length. Place the garment right side up; fold back the edge and stitch the two pocket sections together. Stitch across the triangle at one end, round the pocket bag and across the triangle at the opposite end. Stitch the triangular ends on the original line of stitching. Tie thread ends and press.

Neaten seam edges as required by the fabric. Trim underlay to within 1·2 cm (½ inch) of the stitching.

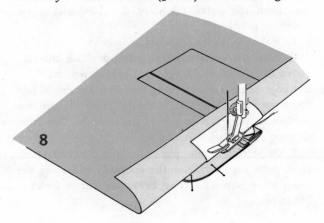

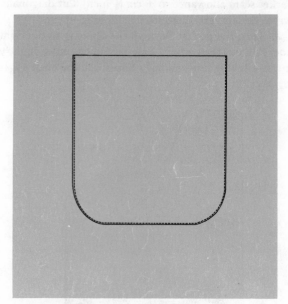

ing line, pull out corners and press. Draw up bobbin thread, easing the fabric back on the stitches round the curved edge. Adjust the fullness for a smooth curve.

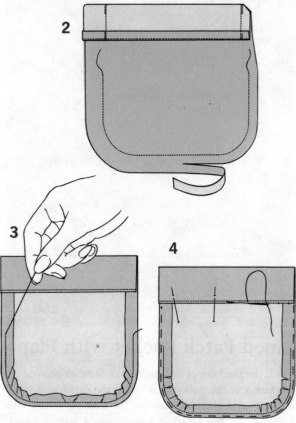

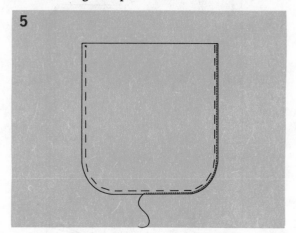

Unlined Patch Pocket

Mark the position of the pocket with tailor's tacks before removing the pattern from the garment. If the addition of pockets is your idea, mark their position on the pattern; then mark the garment. Follow the fabric grain unless the pocket is on a diagonal line.

Cut the pocket the width and depth desired plus seam allowances and a hem at the top. Curve the lower corners.

1. Fold under the top edge of the pocket ·6 cm (¼ inch) and stitch near the fold. Press. Fold the top hem to the right side. Pin and stitch across the ends on the seamline. Back-stitch at each end. Press. Stitch round the curve of the pocket, 1·2 cm (½ inch) from the edge, to control the fullness of the seam allowance. Leave thread ends long enough to draw up. (Loosen the upper tension. Do not forget to return the tension to its previous setting.)

4. Turn the edges under on the seamline and tack. Notch the seam allowance on the curve to remove bulk so that the seam will lie flat. Press. Pin the hem in place at the top and slip-stitch.

5. Pin and tack the pocket over the markings on the right side of the garment. Stitch close to the edge or slip-stitch in place. Pull threads to the underside and tie. Remove tackings and press.

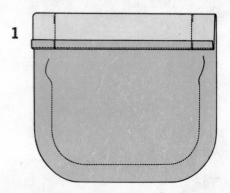

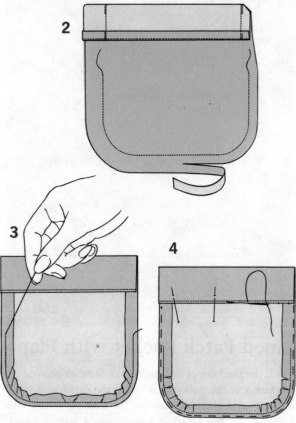

2. Trim the seam allowance to within ·6 cm (¼ inch) of the stitching and cut diagonally across corners at the top of the hem.

3. Turn the hem to the wrong side. Fold on the stitch-

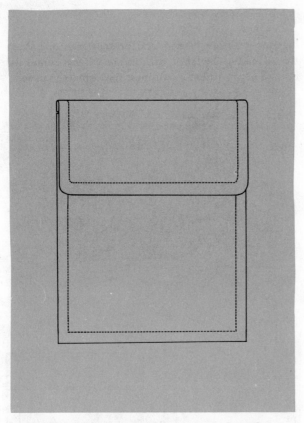

Trim lining seam allowance to ·3 cm ($\frac{1}{8}$ inch) and pocket seam allowance to ·6 cm ($\frac{1}{4}$ inch). Cut diagonally across the corners, close to the stitching. Press.

2. Turn the pocket through the opening to the right side. Pull out the corners. Ease the lining under slightly at the stitching line and tack. Slip-stitch the open edges together. Press.

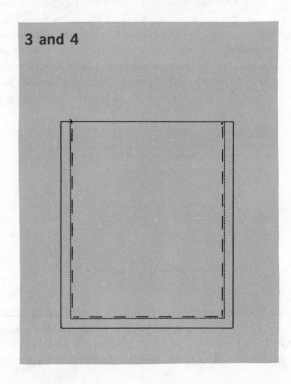

3. Pin and hand-tack the pocket over the markings on the right side of the garment. Tack a second line exactly ·9 cm ($\frac{3}{8}$ inch) from the edge to mark the stitching line. Use a seam gauge to keep the line even. The Quilter may also be used to gauge the stitching line. See *Top Stitching*, page 335, and *Welt Seam*, page 88.

Lined Patch Pocket with Flap

Mark the position of the pocket the same as above.
Pocket. Cut the pocket and lining the depth and width desired, plus seam allowances. Use a lining of the same fabric or, if the fabric is heavy, use a lighter weight lining, matching in colour.

1. Pin the lining to the pocket, right sides together. Stitch round the pocket, leaving 6 cm (2$\frac{1}{2}$ inches) to turn through. Back-stitch at the beginning and ending of the seam and take one stitch across each corner. Press.

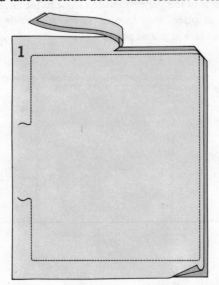

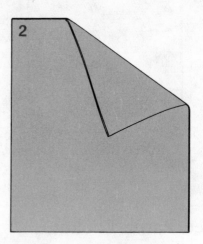

4. Stitch the pocket to the garment along the ·9-cm (⅜-inch) line; pivot the fabric on the needle at the corners. Draw threads to the underside and tie. Remove tackings and press.

If top stitching is not used, slip-stitch the pocket to the garment.

Flap. Cut the flap and facing the width of the pocket and depth required, plus seam allowances. Curve the lower corners, if desired.

5. Interface the flap to give the added body necessary. See *Pocket with a Flap*, page 128, and use either *Method 1* or *2*, depending on the weight of the interfacing and the fabric used.

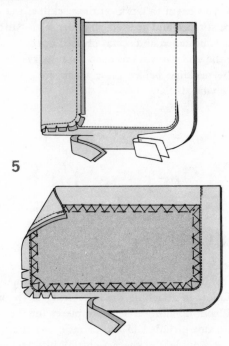

5

For **Methods 1 and 2**, pin the facing to the flap, right sides together. Stitch on the seamline, leaving the upper edge open. Back-stitch at each end. Press.

Trim the lining seam allowance to ·3 cm (⅛ inch) and the flap seam allowance to ·6 cm (¼ inch). If *Method 1* is used, trim the interfacing seam allowance close to the stitching. Notch the curved edges. Press.

6. Turn the flap to the right side. Ease the lining under slightly at the stitching line and tack. Press. Pin the cut edges together and tack 1·5 cm (⅝ inch) from the edge. Top-stitch the flap ·9 cm (⅜ inch) from the edge, following the direction of the pocket.

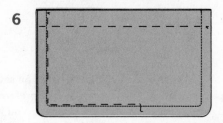

6

7. Pin and tack the flap to the garment, right sides together, placing the seamline 1·2 cm (½ inch) above the pocket. Stitch. Pull threads to the underside and tie. Press the seam. Turn under the cut edge and slip-stitch in place. Turn the flap down over the pocket. Press.

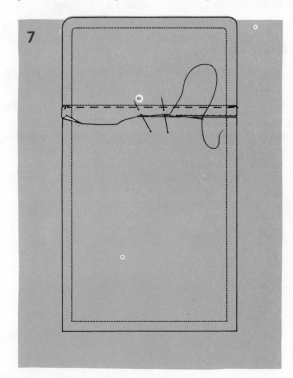

7

Neckline Finishes

How you should complete a neckline depends on several things – pattern design, fabric and personal preference. Many different types of finishes are possible. You may, for example, face the neckline (and the front opening, too, if you have one); you may bind or pipe it; or you may add a collar.

Interfacing

Almost every neckline will need interfacing. Interfacing is a third layer of fabric placed between the facing and garment section. It gives added body to the neckline, the front or back opening and to collars and around buttonholes. In selecting interfacing, choose one appropriate

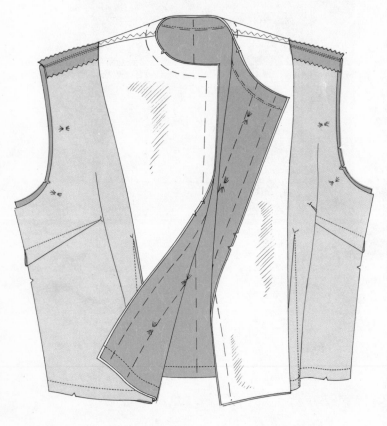

in type and weight for your fabric, and style, and shrink it before cutting it out. See page 16 for guidance on the kind of interfacing to use.

Before you begin to work on the neckline, the darts should be stitched and pressed, shoulder seams stitched, seam edges neatened and seams pressed open.

Leave the underarm seams open because it is easier to finish the neckline before these seams are joined and while the work is flat.

Faced Neckline Finishes

Faced Neckline and Front Opening

The type of interfacing you are using – whether lightweight or heavy-weight – governs the method you should follow in attaching the interfacing to the neckline and front opening. If separate pieces for the interfacing are not included in the pattern, use the facing patterns as a guide. Cut the pre-shrunk interfacing and follow the appropriate instructions below.

FACING WITH LIGHTWEIGHT INTERFACING
Interfacing. Join the interfacing pieces for the back and front sections at the shoulder line with a lapped seam, using the multi-stitch zig-zag to eliminate bulk. See *Lapped Seam*, page 83.

Pin and tack the interfacing to the wrong side of the garment, keeping the seam edges even. (Bound buttonholes may be made through the garment and lightweight interfacing before the facing is stitched in place.)
Facing. Join facings for the back and front sections at the shoulder seams. Stitch, then press. Neaten seam edges and press seams open.

Pin and tack the facing to the garment, right sides together, matching markings and shoulder seams. Stitch on the seamline, taking one stitch diagonally across the corners.

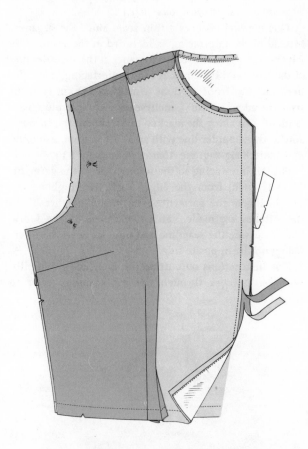

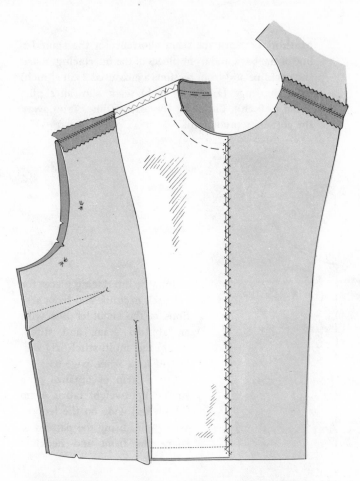

Trim the interfacing seam allowance close to the stitching; then trim the facing seam allowance to ·3 cm (⅛ inch) and the garment seam allowance to ·6 cm (¼ inch). Cut diagonally across the corners close to the stitching. Slash the seam allowance on the neckline curve at even intervals and cut off corners where seams cross at the shoulder line. Press, then press seams open.

Turn the facing to the underside. Pull out the corners to square them; ease the facing under slightly at the seamline and tack with silk thread. Use diagonal tacking on woollens and silks. Press.

Neaten the free edge of the facing. For lightweight fabrics, pink the edge, then fold under ·6 cm (¼ inch) and edge-stitch. For heavy fabrics, pink the edge, then stitch ·3 cm (⅛ inch) from the edge, or stitch seam binding over the right side of the edge. The multi-stitch zig-zag is ideal for finishing jersey, double knit and similar fabrics. If bound buttonholes are used, you must finish the back of the buttonholes. See page 111. Tack the facing to the garment shoulder seam allowances.

When the front facing and bodice are cut in one, turn the facing to the underside and press. Then turn the facing away from the garment. Trim off the front seam allowance on the interfacing. Pin the interfacing to the wrong side of the garment, aligning the front edge with the crease for the facing. Tack the interfacing in place at the neckline and front opening; herringbone it in place along the front opening and machine-stitch it to the waistline 1·2 cm (½ inch) from the seam edge.

On washable blouses and children's clothes you may omit the herringbone. Buttons and buttonholes will hold the interfacing in place along the front opening; remove the tacking holding the interfacing after sewing on the buttons and making the buttonholes.

Finish the neckline, following the instructions given above.

FACING WITH HEAVY-WEIGHT INTERFACING

Interfacing. Heavy-weight interfacing such as hair canvas or Vilene is used in dresses of heavy fabric and in suits and coats to give extra body to certain areas. Bound buttonholes are made *before* the heavy interfacing is attached to the garment.

To eliminate bulk, do not sew the interfacing in with the seam but attach it by one of the following methods:

135

Method 1: Mark the seam allowance at the shoulder line of the back and front pieces of the interfacing; mark the neckline and front sections a measured 2 cm ($\frac{3}{4}$ inch) from the edge (1·5-cm ($\frac{5}{8}$-inch) seam allowance plus ·3 cm ($\frac{1}{8}$ inch)). Cut along the marked line. Trim away the corners to avoid bulk.

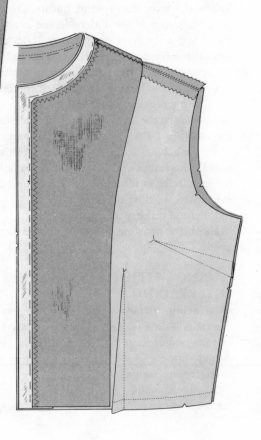

Join the interfacing pieces for the back neckline and front sections at the shoulder line with an abutted seam, and stitch, using the multi-stitch zig-zag. See *Abutted Seam*, page 83.

Cut a strip of organza or a similar lightweight fabric 4 cm (1$\frac{1}{2}$ inches) wide on the lengthwise grain, using the pattern to shape the front and neckline edges.

Pin the organza strip over the interfacing, extending the edge 2 cm ($\frac{3}{4}$ inch) beyond the interfacing. Then stitch in place, using the multi-stitch zig-zag or two lines of straight stitching. Press.

Pin, then tack, the interfacing to the wrong side of the garment, keeping the organza strip and garment edges even. (*Illustrated lower left.*)

This method ensures a thin seam since the organza, instead of the interfacing, is included in the seam.

Method 2: Mark the seam allowance at the shoulder line of the front and back pieces of the interfacing; mark the neckline and front sections a measured 2 cm ($\frac{3}{4}$ inch) from the edge (1·5-cm ($\frac{5}{8}$-inch) seam allowance plus ·3 cm ($\frac{1}{8}$ inch)). Cut along the marked line; trim off the corners. Join at the shoulder line with an abutted seam, using the multi-stitch zig-zag. See *Abutted Seam*, page 83.

Pin the interfacing to the wrong side of the garment, 2 cm ($\frac{3}{4}$ inch) from the edge. Tack. Herringbone the interfacing to the garment, using matching thread. As the stitches are made, catch one thread in the fabric barely outside the seamline and only through the interfacing on the opposite side.

(For instructions on cutting the interfacing and slipping buttonholes through the cut opening, refer to page 110.)

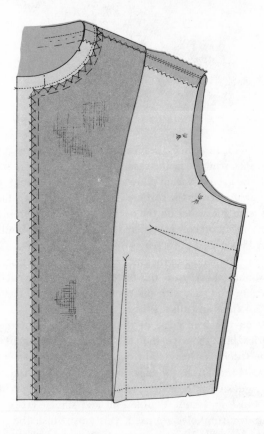

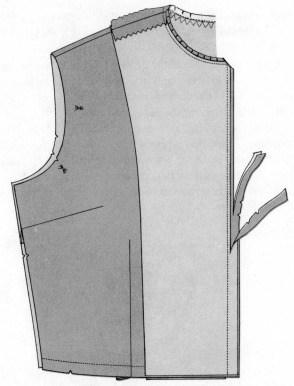

Trim the facing seam allowance to ·3 cm (⅛ inch) and the garment seam allowance (and organza in *Method 1*) to ·6 cm (¼ inch). Cut diagonally across the corners close to the stitching. Slash the seam allowance on the neckline curve at even intervals and cut off the corners where seams cross at the shoulder line. Press, then press the seam open. On soft woollens and fabrics which fray easily, press before layering the seam.

Turn the facing to the underside. Pull out the corners to square them; ease the facing under slightly at the seamline and tack with silk thread. Use diagonal tacking on woollens and silks. Press.

Neaten the free edge of the facing, following the directions on page 135.

If your garment is lined, you will not need to neaten the facing edge. If bound buttonholes are used, you must finish the back of the buttonholes. See page 111.

Slip-Stitched Facing

When a narrow facing is turned to the right side of the garment, use a slip stitch rather than top stitching to hold it in place.

For added body, place the interfacing between the top facing and garment. Use self fabric or a lightweight fabric such as organza or batiste, depending on the fabric in the garment. Cut the interfacing by the facing pattern.

SELF-FABRIC INTERFACING

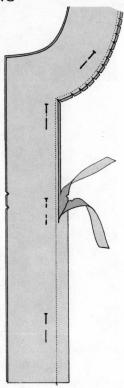

Place the facing and interfacing, wrong sides together, and pin along the inside edge as illustrated. Tack if necessary. Stitch on the seamline; pivot the fabric on the needle at the inside corners.

Trim the interfacing seam allowance to ·3 cm (⅛ inch) and the facing seam allowance to ·6 cm (¼ inch). Cut into the corner almost to the stitching and notch the seam on the outside curve. Press, then press seam open.

Turn the facing and interfacing to the right side of the garment. Ease the facing under slightly at the seamline and tack, using diagonal tacking and silk thread. Press.

Facing. For *Methods 1* and *2*, join the facing for the back neckline and front sections at the shoulder line. Stitch. Finish the seam edges, then press the seam open.

Pin and tack the facing to the garment, right sides together; match markings and shoulder seams. Stitch, taking one stitch diagonally across the corners.

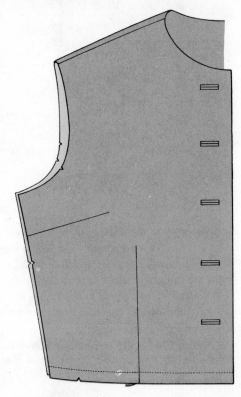

On the wrong side, place the facing with the right side next to the garment and pin *only* the outer edge of the facing in place. Stitch on the seamline, taking one or two stitches diagonally across the point.

Trim the interfacing edge to a generous ·3 cm ($\frac{1}{8}$ inch) outside the stitching of the facing seam. Carefully tack the interfacing to the facing. Leave this tacking in until the facing is turned on the top side.

Lightweight interfacing. Pin the interfacing to the wrong side of the facing. Stitch a scant 1·5 cm ($\frac{5}{8}$ inch) from the edge of the facing, as illustrated. Press.

On the wrong side of the garment, position the facing, to which the interfacing is attached, with the right side next to the garment, and pin along the outside edge. Tack, then stitch on the seamline.

Trim the interfacing seam allowance close to the stitching. Trim the garment seam allowance to ·3 cm ($\frac{1}{8}$ inch) and the facing seam allowance to ·6 cm ($\frac{1}{4}$ inch). Clip diagonally across the corners close to the stitching, and slash the seam on the inside curve. Press, then press the seam open.

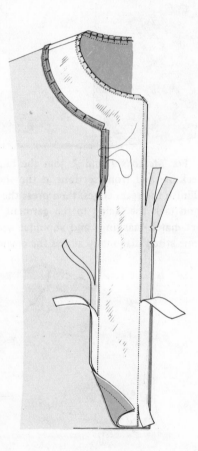

Trim the garment seam allowance to ·3 cm ($\frac{1}{8}$ inch) and the facing seam allowance to ·6 cm ($\frac{1}{4}$ inch). Cut diagonally across the corners close to the stitching. Slash the neckline seam allowance on the inside curve. Press, then press the seam open.

Turn the facing to the outside of the garment. Ease the garment side under slightly at the stitching line and tack. Pin and tack the free edge of the facing to the garment. Slip-stitch in place. Remove all tackings and press.

On the free edge of the facing, trim the interfacing edge close to the stitching and trim the facing edge to within ·6 cm ($\frac{1}{4}$ inch) of the stitching. Clip into the corner almost to the stitching. Turn free edge to the wrong side, barely beyond the stitching and tack. Notch the seam allowances on the outside curve so that they will lie flat. Press.

Turn the facing to the top side of the garment and finish, following the procedure given for self-fabric interfacing.

Faced Scallops

You may use scalloped facings in both heavy and light-weight fabrics, but avoid them in sheers because of the shadow effect in the seams. Faced scallops accent the edges of front and back openings, sleeves and hemlines of jackets and skirts. They can give a feminine look to your outfit.

Interface shaped and bias edges with a lightweight fabric. Tack the interfacing to the wrong side of the fabric.

Lightly draw the scallops on the wrong side of the facing. Don't forget a seam allowance. *Do not cut the scallops.* Pin and tack the facing to the garment, right sides together.

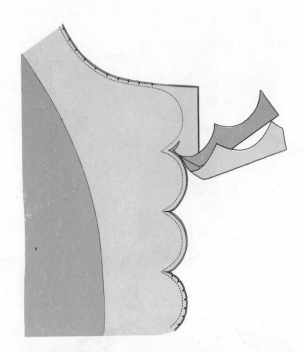

If the interfacing is included in the seam, trim it close to the stitching. Trim the garment and facing seam allowances to a bare ·3 cm (⅛ inch) on small scallops and to a generous ·3 cm (⅛ inch) on large scallops. Trim one edge shorter than the other except on small scallops. Slash at the point, almost to the stitching. Cut notches from the seam allowances at evenly spaced intervals. Press.

Turn the facing to the underside, gently working the seam edges between the thumb and finger to bring the stitching line to the very edge. Tack the edges with silk thread to retain the shape of the scallops until after pressing.

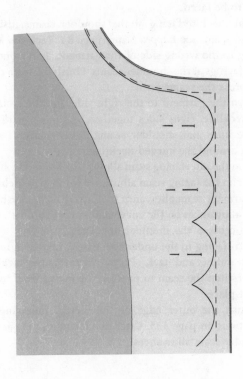

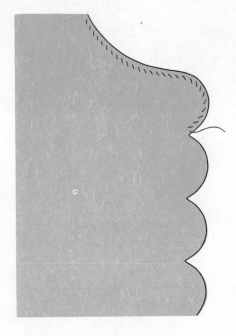

Use a short stitch and a lighter than regular pressure adjustment so that you can turn the fabric freely. Stitch on the traced outline of the scallops, taking one stitch across the point between each scallop. This space provides width when you are cutting and prevents the point between the scallops from pulling in the finished work. Remember that accurate stitching is essential. The Quilter makes it easier to stitch small scallops because of its open, short toe.

139

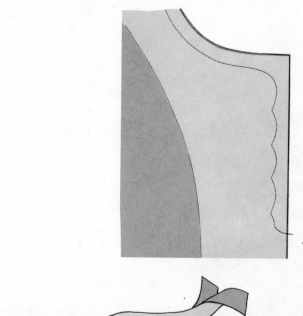

If you have a zig-zag machine, you will find that it greatly simplifies the stitching of small scallops. Set the selectors for the scallop pattern and adjust the stitch length and stitch width, which vary the length and depth of the scallop. Always start stitching at the beginning of a scallop unit. See page 266. As you sew, the fabric passes straight under the Presser Foot and the needle follows a scallop pattern. Press, layer the seams and turn the facing as instructed on previous page.

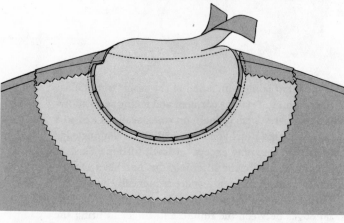

Round Neckline with a Facing

Cut the facing and pre-shrunk interfacing to match the edge to be faced.

Join the interfacing at the shoulder seams, using a lapped seam. See *Lapped Seam*, page 83. Tack the interfacing to the wrong side of the garment. Join front and back facings at the shoulder seams. Finish the seam edges and press the seams open.

Turn the garment to the right side. Pin the facing to the neckline, right sides together, matching markings, centre lines and shoulder seams. Stitch, using a short stitch around the curved neckline.

Trim the interfacing seam allowance close to the stitching; trim the facing seam allowance to ·3 cm ($\frac{1}{8}$ inch) and the garment seam allowance to ·6 cm ($\frac{1}{4}$ inch). Slash into seam allowances on the curve and cut off corners where seams cross at the shoulder line. Press.

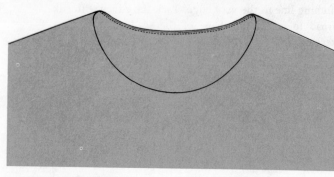

Turn facing to the underside, ease it under slightly at the seamline and tack. Press, then remove tackings. Understitch the seam to prevent the facing from rolling out of place.

Finish the outer edge of the facing, following the directions on page 135. Catch the facing to the garment shoulder seam allowances.

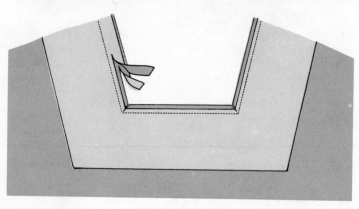

Square or V-Neckline with a Facing

Follow the instructions for a round neckline, but pivot the fabric on the needle at the corners to square them, and slash diagonally into the seam allowances at the corners so that the facing will turn smoothly.

One-Piece Neckline and Armhole Facing

If a one-piece facing is not included with your pattern, cut one using the bodice pattern as a guide. Lay the front and the back pattern pieces over paper as wide as the pattern and long enough to extend 10 cm (4 inches) below the armhole at the underarm seam. Cut round the neckline, shoulder, armhole and underarm to 10 cm (4 inches) below the armhole. Remove the pattern pieces. Trim off the lower edge of the facing pattern about 10 cm (4 inches) from the armhole and neckline edges. Cut the facing by this pattern.

Stay-stitch the neckline and armholes if you are not using interfacing. If you are using interfacing, you can omit stay stitching because the interfacing, which is cut the same shape as the neckline and armholes, is sufficient support.

Cut the interfacing by the facing pattern, and tack it to the underside of the garment with the cut edges even at the neckline and armholes. Stitch the underarm seams of the garment, right sides together, and include the interfacing. Finish the seam edges and press the seams open. *Leave shoulder seams open.*

Pin and stitch the underarm seams of the facing, right sides together. Trim the seam allowances to one-half their width and press the seams open. Leave shoulder seams open. Trim ·3 cm (⅛ inch) off the armhole edges from the shoulder to the notches of the facing only. This will permit the neckline and armhole edges to roll under slightly at the seamline after the facing is turned. The result will be a neat, smooth finish because the facing will not be visible along the edges. To neaten the outer edge of the facing, pink it, then turn it under ·6 cm (¼ inch) and edge-stitch. For heavy fabrics, pink, then stitch near the edge, using a short stitch.

Two methods of applying a one-piece facing are illustrated. Select the one you prefer and feel competent to do. Use the same method when mounting a *collarless and sleeveless blouse or dress.*

Method 1: Fold under the seam allowance on the shoulder seam of the facing. Tack.

Turn the garment to the right side. Pin the facing to the front and back neckline and each armhole, right sides together. Match notches, centre lines and underarm seams, and keep the cut edges even. Tack if necessary. Turn garment to the wrong side and stitch from the facing side. Begin and end the stitching 1·5 cm (⅝ inch)

(seam allowance) from the shoulder edge and backstitch at each end. Compare front and back shoulder to check that the distance between the neckline and armhole stitching is the same. Remove tackings.

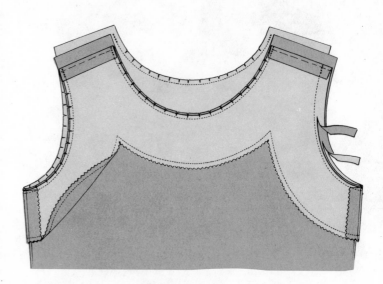

Trim the interfacing seam allowance close to the stitching. Trim the facing seam allowance to ·3 cm (⅛ inch) and the garment seam allowance to ·6 cm (¼ inch). Slash the seam allowances on curves and cut off corners diagonally where seams cross at the underarm. Press.

Turn the facing to the wrong side, ease it under slightly at the seamline and tack. Press. Remove tackings.

Understitch the neckline and armhole seams to prevent the facing from rolling out of place. Begin and end the stitching about 6 cm (2½ inches) from the shoulder line.

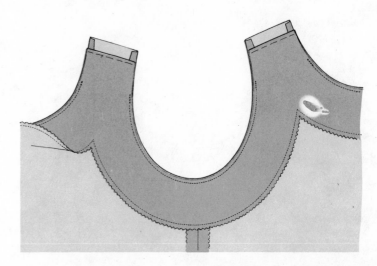

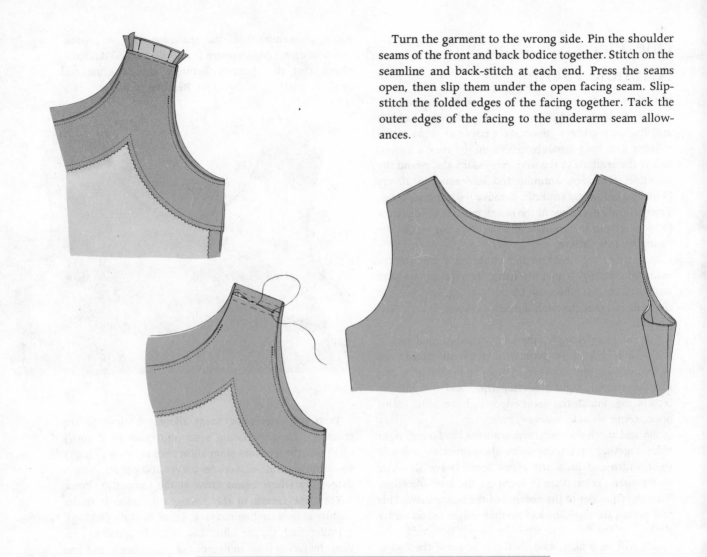

Turn the garment to the wrong side. Pin the shoulder seams of the front and back bodice together. Stitch on the seamline and back-stitch at each end. Press the seams open, then slip them under the open facing seam. Slip-stitch the folded edges of the facing together. Tack the outer edges of the facing to the underarm seam allowances.

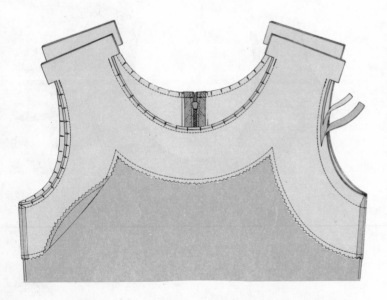

Method 2: Prepare the dress and facing, following the directions beginning on page 141. If there is a neckline opening, insert the zip before attaching the facing.

Turn the dress to the right side. Place the facing over the dress, right sides together, and pin along the seamline of the neck and each armhole. Match centre lines, underarm seams and notches; keep the cut edges even. Tack if necessary.

Turn the dress to the wrong side. Stitch round the front and back neckline and armholes from the facing side, beginning and ending the stitching 4 cm ($1\frac{1}{2}$ inches) from the shoulder edge. Back-stitch at each end. Compare front and back shoulders to be sure that the distance between the neckline and armhole stitching is the same.

Trim the interfacing seam allowance close to the stitching. Trim the facing seam allowance to ·3 cm ($\frac{1}{8}$ inch) and the garment seam allowance to ·6 cm ($\frac{1}{4}$ inch) where stitched. (Leave the full seam allowance above the stitching until you have stitched the shoulder openings.) Slash the seam allowances almost to the stitching and at frequent intervals. Cut diagonally across corners where seams cross at the underarm. Press seams.

Turn the facing to the inside. Ease it under slightly at the seamline and tack. Press, then remove the tacking.

Turn the dress to the wrong side so that right sides of the dress are together. Pin the front and back shoulder seams of the dress together. (They are the two inside edges.) With the front of the dress towards you, slip your fingers up between the facing and the garment. Grasp the shoulder seam edges of both facing and garment (four of them); pull down on the edges and at the same time turn the front facing back to bring the shoulder seam into view. This procedure turns the front shoulder of the garment and facing right sides together, and pulls the back shoulder and facing into the front one. The two shoulder seam edges that were previously pinned together are on the bottom, and the two facing edges are above, right sides together.

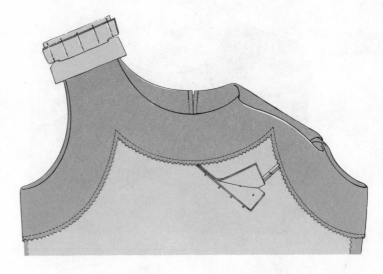

Stitch the shoulder seam of the garment, taking 1·5-cm ($\frac{5}{8}$-inch) seam allowance. Then, pin and stitch the facing shoulder seam. Press seams.

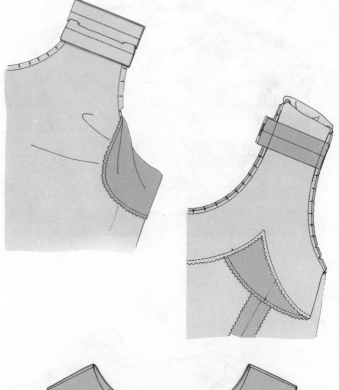

Pull the back part of the shoulder seam farther into the front one so that the shoulder seam allowances are in full view and the unstitched portion of the neckline and armhole seams can be stitched. Press the shoulder seams open. Use a seamboard, and slip the pointed end through the open seam on each side of the garment. Press.

Pin the neckline edges together and the armhole edges together; then stitch across the openings, overlapping the previous stitching on each side of the shoulder seam. Trim seam allowances and press.

Turn the front facing to the wrong side of the dress, then pull the back shoulder into position. Press. Stitch the opposite shoulder.

Understitch the neckline and armhole, following the directions given for *Method 1*. Catch the outer edges of the facing to the underarm seam allowances.

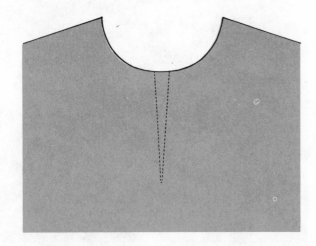

Faced Slash Opening

Mark the position of the slash. *Do not cut.* Stitch round the opening for the slash, using a short stitch. Begin at the neckline, ·6 cm ($\frac{1}{4}$ inch) from the centre, and gradually taper to ·2 cm ($\frac{1}{16}$ inch) at the point; take one stitch across the point. Continue stitching up the opposite side, gradually tapering to ·6 cm ($\frac{1}{4}$ inch) from the centre at the neckline. This stitching will not show in the finished work.

Cut the facing the same as the edge to be faced and about 5 cm (2 inches) longer than the front opening. Join the seams at the shoulder line. Neaten the seams and press them open.

Turn the garment to the right side. Pin and tack the facing to the neckline, right sides together. Match markings, shoulder seams and centre lines.

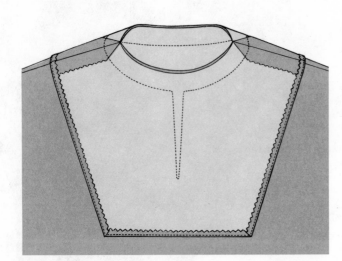

Place the work under the needle with the facing next to the feed. Stitch the neckline seam from one shoulder line to within ·6 cm ($\frac{1}{4}$ inch) of the centre front marking. Take one stitch diagonally, then stitch down one side of the centre front marking, gradually tapering to ·2 cm ($\frac{1}{16}$ inch) at the point. Take one stitch across the point, then continue up the opposite side in the same manner and round the neckline, overlapping a few stitches at the starting point. The width at the point provides space for cutting and prevents pulling at the point in the finished work.

Trim the facing seam allowance to ·3 cm ($\frac{1}{8}$ inch) and the garment seam allowance to ·6 cm ($\frac{1}{4}$ inch). Snip into the seam allowance on the curve and cut off corners where seams cross at the shoulder line. Cut between the two rows of stitching, almost to the point of the slash, then cut off corners at the top of the slash, close to the stitching.

Turn facing to the wrong side. Pull out the corners to square them. Fold on the seamline and tack. Press. Remove tackings.

Understitch the neckline seam to prevent the facing

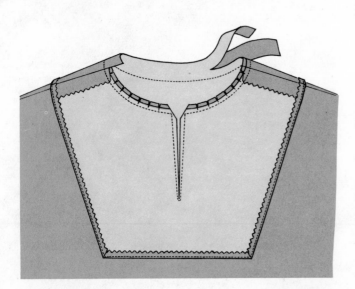

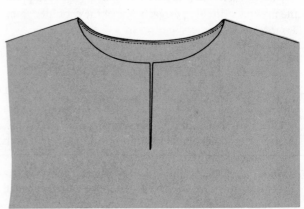

144

from rolling out of place. Do not understitch round the slash.

To re-inforce the point of the slash, fold a 4-cm (1½-inch) length of straight seam binding through the centre and press. Pin it to the underside of the facing with the upper edge exactly at the point of the slash. Stitch near the top edge of the seam binding.

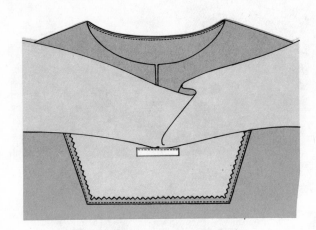

Bound and Corded or Piped Neckline Finishes

Double-Fold Bias Binding

A double-fold bias binding is used as a neckline finish on blouses, dresses and children's clothes. It is also applied to the edge of sleeves and at the waistline of a garment. The bias binding may be of self or contrasting fabric. The finished width is usually about ·6 cm (¼ inch).

If binding is not specified on the pattern, cut away the neckline seam allowance. Stay-stitch ·5 cm ($\frac{3}{16}$ inch) from the edge. (This stitching will not show in the finished work.)

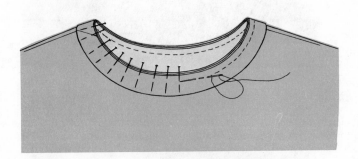

Cut a strip on the true bias, six times the width of the finished binding. See *Cutting Bias Strips*, page 244. Fold it through the centre, wrong sides together, and finger-press lightly.

On the right side of the garment, pin the double bias strip round the neckline, matching seam edges. Stretch the binding slightly on this inside curve. Join the bias on the lengthwise grain at the shoulder line. See *Joining Bias Strips*, page 244. Tack. Stitch a ·6 cm (¼ inch) from the edge, using a short stitch, and overlap a few stitches at the starting point. Press the seam only.

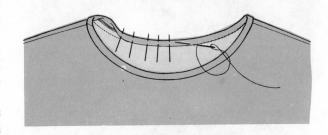

Fold the binding over the seam edge to the stitching line on the underside, enclosing the cut edges. Pin. Finish by hand, using a slip stitch.

WHEN THERE IS AN OPENING AT THE NECKLINE

Fold the facing for the opening to the underside and press. Pin and tack it to the neckline of the garment.

Turn under the end of the binding ·6 cm (¼ inch) before folding it through the centre. Align the folded end with the folded edge of the opening. Treat the neckline and facing as one, and pin the double bias strip round the

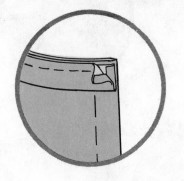

neckline, matching seam edges. Fold the binding under ·6 cm (¼ inch) at the other end. Then finish, following the procedure given above. Slip-stitch the folded edges of the binding together at each end.

145

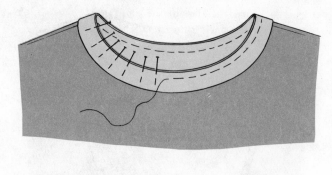

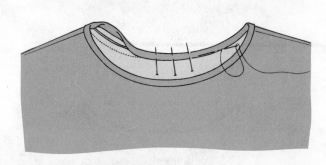

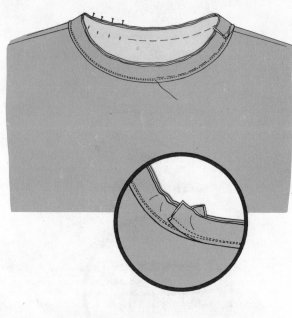

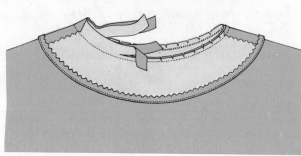

Single-Fold Bias Binding

The single-fold bias binding may be used in place of the double-fold. The finished width is usually about ·6 cm (¼ inch).

Trim off the neckline seam allowance if binding is not specified on the pattern. Stay-stitch ·5 cm ($\frac{3}{16}$ inch) from the edge. (This stitching will not show in the finished work.)

Cut a strip on the true bias four times the finished width. See *Cutting Bias Strips*, page 244.

On the right side of the garment, pin one edge of the bias strip to the neckline, right sides together. Match the seam edges, and stretch the binding slightly along the edge when the seam is on inside curve. Join the bias on the lengthwise grain at the shoulder line. Tack. Stitch ·6 cm (¼ inch) from the edge, using a short stitch, and overlap a few stitches at the starting point. Press.

Turn under the cut edge of the binding ·6 cm (¼ inch) and finger-press. Fold the binding over the seam edge to the stitching line on the underside, enclosing the cut edges. Pin. Finish by hand, using a slip stitch.

WHEN THERE IS AN OPENING AT THE NECKLINE

Follow instructions given under *Double-Fold Bias Binding* on page 145.

Corded or Piped Neckline

A corded or piped neckline is an excellent finish for blouses, dresses and children's clothes. It is a detail that is often found on expensive ready-to-wear garments. The covered cord may be made of self or contrasting fabric.

Follow instructions on page 245 for preparing the cording.

Pin the cording to the right side of the neckline, keeping the stitching of the cording on the seamline. The seam allowance on the cording is full and requires easing so that the cord will lie smoothly along the curve. Allow 1·5 cm ($\frac{5}{8}$ inch) at each end of the cording for joining at the shoulder line. Pull the cord from its bias cover and cut off 1·5 cm ($\frac{5}{8}$ inch) at each end so the cord will just meet at the joining. Ease the two ends of the bias slightly towards the seam as illustrated. Adjust the Zipper Foot to the right of the needle. Stitch, using a stitch shorter than for straight stitching. *Do not stitch too close to the cord.* Press the seam.

Pin and tack the facing over the neckline, right sides together, matching the shoulder seams and centre lines. Place the work under the needle with the first row of stitching uppermost so you can use it as a guide. Stitch between the cord and the previous stitching; overlap a few stitches at the starting point.

Trim the corded seam allowance to ·3 cm ($\frac{1}{8}$ inch) and the garment and facing seam allowances to ·6 cm ($\frac{1}{4}$ inch). Snip into the seam edge on the inside curves at even intervals. Cut off corners where seams cross at the shoulder line. Press.

Turn the facing to the underside. Fold on the seamline and press. Neaten the outer edge of the facing and catch it to the shoulder seam allowance.

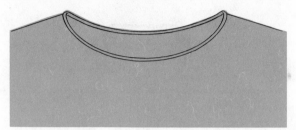

To eliminate bulk, the facing is often omitted, especially if the fabric is double knit or heavy, and the garment is mounted. The cording is stitched to the neckline between the cord and previous line of stitching. Trim the neckline seam allowance to ·6 cm ($\frac{1}{4}$ inch) and slash it at even intervals. Trim the cording seam allowance which will be next to the garment to ·3 cm ($\frac{1}{8}$ inch). Press, then turn the seam allowances to the inside and press. Pin the wide seam allowance to the garment; then herringbone, taking stitches through the seam allowance and the mounting. (These stitches will not show on the outside.)

WHEN THERE IS AN OPENING AT THE NECKLINE

Stitch the facing to opening, layer seams, then press. Pin cording to the neckline, extending the end 1·5 cm ($\frac{5}{8}$ inch) beyond the facing seam on each side. Start stitching at the facing seam and continue round the neckline to the opposite facing seam. Tie the threads. (*Below*)

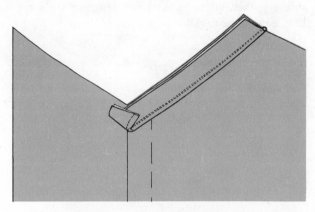

Pull out the cord at each end and clip off 1·5 cm ($\frac{5}{8}$ inch). Then fold the bias ends diagonally towards the neckline seam and stitch in place, as illustrated. Press.

Pin and tack the facing to the neckline, right sides together. Stitch, layer the seams and press, following the procedure given above.

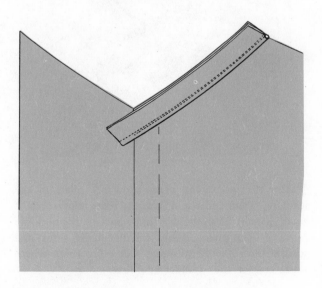

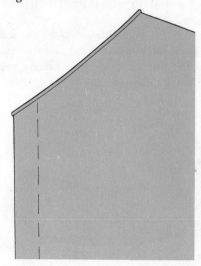

147

Collars

Before attaching a collar, make sure that you have: (1) stay-stitched the neckline of the garment; (2) stitched, finished and pressed the shoulder seams and darts; (3) attached the facing and interfacing to the front opening, leaving the neckline edge free. Refer to *Faced Neckline and Front Opening*, page 134. Leave the underarm seams open to make it easier to complete the neckline. Several methods of constructing and attaching a collar are described below. Choose the one most suitable for your garment and fabric.

Collar with Bias Facing

This method may be used for cotton fabrics and children's clothes.

Cut pre-shrunk interfacing by the same pattern as the undercollar, and tack it to the wrong side of the undercollar, matching markings.

Pin and tack the top collar to the undercollar, right sides together, matching markings. Stitch on the seamline, leaving the neckline edge open.

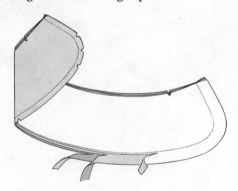

Trim interfacing seam allowance close to the stitching. Trim seam allowance on the undercollar to ·3 cm ($\frac{1}{8}$ inch) and on the top collar to ·6 cm ($\frac{1}{4}$ inch). Notch the outside curved edges. Press.

Turn the collar to the right side. Work the seam edges between the thumb and finger and ease the undercollar slightly to the underside at the seamline; then tack. Press. Top-stitch if desired.

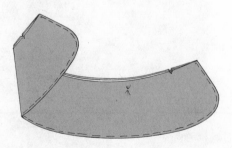

ATTACHING THE COLLAR

Turn the garment to the right side. Pin the interfaced collar to the neckline edge, matching markings, shoulder line and centre lines and tack by hand. Roll the collar as it will be worn, allowing sufficient ease in the top collar for it to fit smoothly over the roll. Fold the front facing back over the right side of the collar and pin.

Cut a true bias strip 3·2 cm ($1\frac{1}{4}$ inches) wide and long enough to extend round the neckline. Pin it over the collar at the neckline, allowing ·6-cm ($\frac{1}{4}$-inch) seam on the bias and extending the ends of bias strip ·9 cm ($\frac{3}{8}$ inch) over the front facings. Stitch round the neckline in one continuous line from one front edge to the other. Backstitch at each end for reinforcement.

Trim the interfacing seam allowance close to the stitching. Trim collar and garment seam allowances to ·6 cm ($\frac{1}{4}$ inch). Slash the seam allowance on the neckline curve at even intervals and cut diagonally across the corners close to the stitching. Cut off corners where seams cross at the shoulder line. Press.

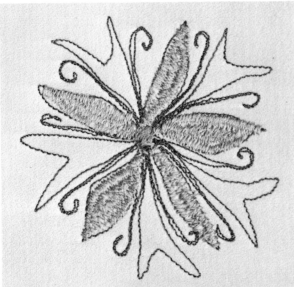

Plate 9
FREE AND EASY

This housecoat features free motion embroidery, in shades of chocolate, coffee and salmon pink. Straight stitch forms the outline and the filling in is worked with a zig-zag stitch, shown at left. The main body of fabric is polyester crêpe.

Pattern by courtesy of Vogue

Plate 10
BEADING ADDS GLITTER TO GALA EVENINGS

RIGHT: Peau de soie leaves and bands in warm golden tones appliquéd on peau de soie obi. Hand-sewn bugle beads.

BELOW LEFT: Beading applied with open-spaced zig-zag stitching in a design that explodes with the gaiety of a sparkling fountain. Clusters of round beads sewn by hand.

BELOW RIGHT: Muted glimmer on a short evening dress. Satin band is decorated with zig-zag stitching, appliqué, and hand-sewn beads; then slip-stitched on dress and edged with beading.

Turn the front facings and the bias strip to the underside. Fold the bias under ·6 cm (¼ inch) and pin it to the garment across the back of the neckline. Finish by hand, using a hemming stitch. Tack the front facings to the shoulder seam allowance. Press.

Collar and Revers with Back Facing

Use this method for a smooth finish and for fabrics that will require dry-cleaning.

The collar may be cut in one or two pieces.

One-piece collar. Press a crease crosswise through the centre. Cut pre-shrunk interfacing half the width of the collar; cut off the corners. Pin the interfacing to the wrong side of the collar just below the crease. Fold the collar in half, right sides together, and stitch across the ends. Trim the interfacing seam allowance close to the stitching. Trim the seam allowance on the undercollar to ·3 cm (⅛ inch) and on the top collar to ·6 cm (¼ inch). Cut diagonally across the corners close to the stitching.

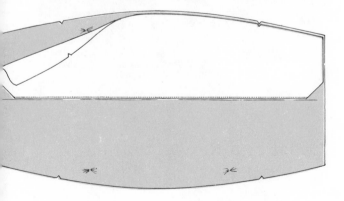

Turn collar to the right side. Pull out the corners and ease the undercollar slightly to the underside at the seamline; tack. Press.

Two-piece collar. Cut pre-shrunk interfacing the same as the collar. Pin and tack it to the wrong side of the undercollar. Cut off the corners of the interfacing to avoid bulk when the collar is turned through.

Lay the top collar over the undercollar, right sides together, matching markings. Pin and tack. Stitch on the seamline, leaving the neckline edge free. Take one stitch diagonally across the corners. Trim the interfacing seam allowance close to the stitching. Trim the seam allowance on the undercollar to ·3 cm (⅛ inch) and on the top collar to ·6 cm (¼ inch). Cut diagonally across the corners close to the stitching. Turn the collar to the right side. Pull out corners and ease the undercollar slightly to the underside at the seamline. Tack and press.

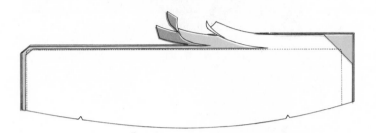

ATTACHING THE COLLAR

After joining the front and back facings at the shoulder seams, stitch the facing to the garment, right sides together, along the front seams, leaving the neckline edges free. Press. Trim the seams and press them open. Slash into the neckline seam allowance almost to the stay stitching.

Pin and tack the undercollar and the interfacing to the

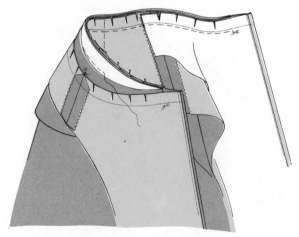

neckline, matching markings, shoulder line and centre lines. Stitch in a continuous line, beginning ·3 cm (⅛ inch) from one collar edge and stitching to within ·3 cm ($\frac{1}{8}$ inch) of the opposite collar edge.

Turn the facing over the right side of the garment and pin it to the neckline from the front edge to the collar edge. Pin and tack the neckline facing to the top collar, matching markings and centre lines. Stitch in a continuous line, beginning ·3 cm ($\frac{1}{8}$ inch) from one collar edge and stitching to within ·3 cm ($\frac{1}{8}$ inch) of the opposite collar edge.

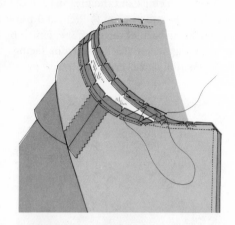

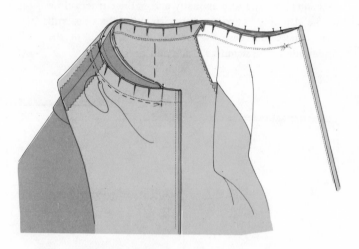

Stitch the facing to the neckline from the front edge into the collar ·3 cm ($\frac{1}{8}$ inch), joining the previous line of stitching. Trim the interfacing seam allowance close to the stitching. Trim the facing seam allowance to ·3 cm ($\frac{1}{8}$ inch) and the garment and the collar seam allowances to ·6 cm ($\frac{1}{4}$ inch). Slash the seam allowances on the neckline curve at even intervals and cut diagonally across the corners close to the stitching. Cut off corners where seams cross at the shoulder line. Press, then press seams open.

Roll the collar over the left hand, shaping it as it will be worn, and pin through all thicknesses at the roll line. Allow sufficient ease for the top collar to fit smoothly over the undercollar. Bring the top and undercollar seams together, matching shoulder seams and centre lines. Pin, then catch-stitch together by hand.

Turn the facing to the underside. Finish the free edge of the facing and tack it to the shoulder seam allowances.

Collar and Revers without Back Facing

Clip into the garment neckline seam allowance almost to the stay stitching.

Make up the collar as explained on page 149.

Pin the undercollar and the interfacing to the neckline

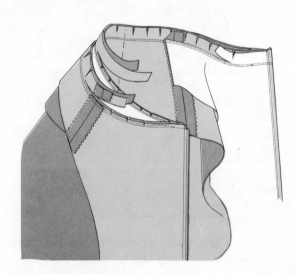

150

across the back from shoulder seam to shoulder seam, leaving the top collar free. Match markings and centre lines. Then pin the undercollar, top collar and interfacing to the neckline from shoulder to centre front on each side, matching markings.

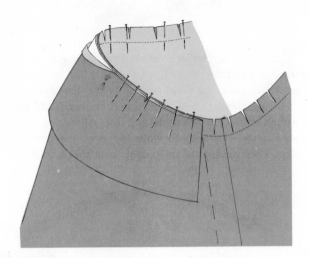

Turn the front facing over the collar, right sides together, and pin, matching markings. Tack from front edge to shoulder seam. Slash the top collar the depth of the seam allowance at each shoulder line, then tack the undercollar and interfacing to the neckline across the back. Continue tacking to the opposite edge.

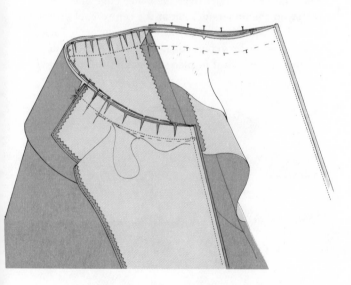

Stitch in a continuous line from one front edge to the other, leaving the top collar free across the back. Trim the interfacing seam allowance close to the stitching. Trim the garment and collar seam allowances to ·6 cm

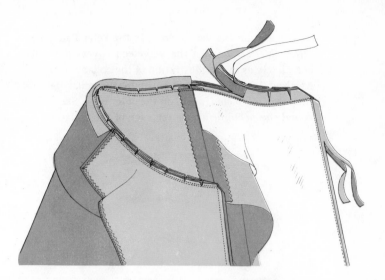

($\frac{1}{4}$ inch). Slash the seam allowance on the neckline curve at even intervals and cut diagonally across the corners close to the stitching. Cut off corners where seams cross at the shoulder line. Press. Turn the facing to the underside.

Turn the seam allowance into the collar across the back neckline. Roll the collar over the left hand, shaping it as it will be worn, and pin through all thicknesses at the roll line. Allow sufficient ease for the top collar to fit smoothly over the undercollar. Turn under the free edge of the top collar and pin it to the stitching line across the back. Slip-stitch in place. Catch the front facings to the shoulder seam edges.

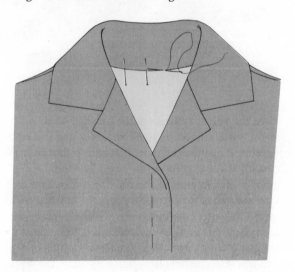

Velvet Overcollar

An overcollar of velvet or velveteen can be added to coats, suits and dresses for women and children.

A velvet collar covers the finished collar and the garment should be completed before applying it.

Follow *Method 1* when the edge of the collar forms a

151

border around the velveteen as in the Peter Pan collar; follow *Method 2* when the velveteen covers the collar completely as in the illustration of the collar and revers.

Method 1: Cut the velvet collar by the collar pattern, then trim off ·6 cm (¼ inch) on the outer edge. Stay-stitch round the neckline and outer edge of the collar 1·2 cm

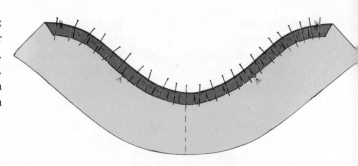

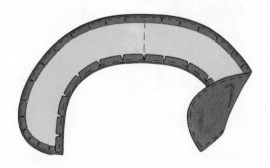

(½ inch) from the edge. Fold under the 1·5-cm (⅝-inch) seam allowance and tack ·6 cm (¼ inch) from the folded edge. Notch the seam allowance on the outside curve and slash it on the neckline curve so that the seams will lie flat.

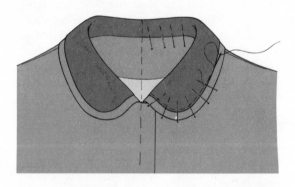

Place the velvet collar over the finished collar on the garment, matching centre lines, shoulder line and neckline seams. Pin at the neckline. Roll both collars over the left hand, shaping them as they will be worn, and pin through all thicknesses at the roll line. Allow sufficient ease for the velvet to fit smoothly over the finished collar. Then pin the outer edge of the velvet collar in place ·6 cm (¼ inch) from the edge of the finished collar. Pin at the centre back, front edges, then at intervals between. Slip-stitch velvet collar in place, catching only the upper layer of the finished collar.

Method 2: Cut the velvet collar by the pattern used for the garment collar. Stay-stitch round the neckline, 1·2 cm (½ inch) from the edge. Fold under the 1·5-cm (⅝-inch) seam allowance and tack ·6 cm (¼ inch) from the folded edge. Slash the seam allowance on the inside curve of the neckline and notch it on the outside curve so that the seams will lie flat.

Place the velvet collar over the finished collar on the garment, matching centre lines, shoulder line and neckline seams. Pin at the neckline. Roll both collars over the left hand, shaping them as they will be worn, and pin through all thicknesses at the roll line. Allow sufficient ease for the velvet to fit smoothly over the finished collar. Then pin the collars together near the outer edge.

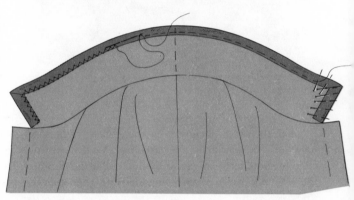

Fold the velvet collar over the collar edge and pin it in place on the underside. Pin at the centre back, front edges, then at intervals between. Mitre corners. Tack.

Herringbone the velvet collar in place on the underside, then slip-stitch it in place at neckline on the right side.

Waistline Seams and Waistbands

Before you join the bodice and skirt, you should have completed these steps:

    1. Stay-stitched the waistline of both the bodice and the skirt.

    2. Stitched the bodice underarm seams and the skirt side seams, neatened the seam edges and pressed the seams open.

    The opening for the placket may be on the left side, as illustrated, or in the centre back.

To Join Bodice to Plain or Gored Skirt

Turn the skirt to the wrong side and the bodice to the right side. Place bodice inside the skirt, right sides together, and pin at the waistline, matching centre lines, seams, darts and notches. Tack.

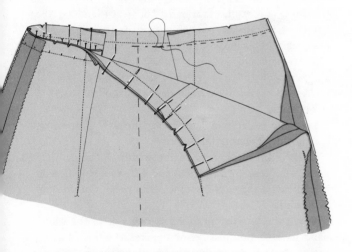

    Stitch round the waistline from one edge of the placket opening to the other. Reinforce with backstitching at each end. Press.

    Turn the seam allowances away from the garment. On the bodice side, stitch pre-shrunk straight seam binding to the seam allowance barely below the first line of stitching. Begin and end the stitching about 3·2 cm (1¼

inches) from each side of the opening. Press. (The seam binding prevents the seam from stretching.) Cut off corners where seams cross on the right side and at darts. Press. Turn the seam allowance down towards the skirt.

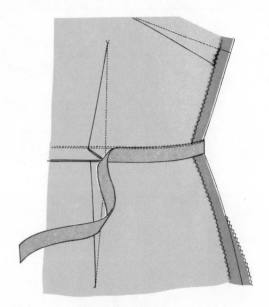

    After the zip is inserted, turn under the ends of the seam binding and catch them to the zip tape.

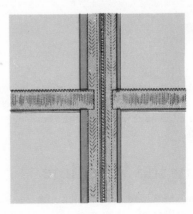

To Join Bodice to Gathered Skirt

Turn the skirt to the wrong side and the bodice to the right side. Place the bodice inside the skirt, right sides together. Pin the bodice and skirt together at the waistline, matching centre lines, side seams and markings. Adjust the gathers to fit the waistline and pin. Tack. Turn to page 106 for instructions on *Gathered Skirts*.

Stitch the seam with the bodice next to the feed. Place a second row of stitching in the seam allowance ·6 cm ($\frac{1}{4}$ inch) from the first line of stitching. Pink the edges.

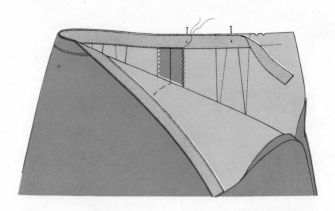

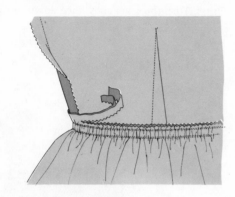

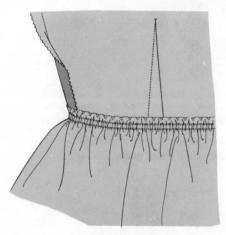

If the fabric is loosely woven, overcast the edges either by hand or by machine, using the blindstitch zig-zag. Turn seam allowance up against the bodice.

To Stay the Waistline

To prevent stretching and to allow for ease in fitting, stay the waistline of a skirt with seam binding.

Cut pre-shrunk straight seam binding to the waistline measurement plus seam allowances. Pin it to the wrong side of the skirt waistline, keeping edges even and the seam binding within the seam allowance so that the

stitching will not show in the finished garment. Evenly distribute the slight ease in the skirt. Stitch the binding to the skirt. Press.

To Attach Waistband to Skirt

Before attaching a waistband to the skirt, the waistline of the skirt should be stay-stitched; darts and seams stitched, finished and pressed; and the zip inserted in the placket on the left side or centre back. See *Skirt Placket Zip* in *Lapped Seam*, page 179.

The method used in joining a waistband to a skirt will vary, depending on the style of the garment, weight of the fabric and personal preference. The band should be interfaced for added body. The band extension may either wrap over on the front, wrap under on the back or wrap on both sides. The width of the finished band is usually 2·5 to 3·2 cm (1 to $1\frac{1}{4}$ inches).

Method 1: Cut the fabric for the waistband on the lengthwise grain as follows: twice the finished width plus seam allowances, and the length of the waistline measurement plus 5 cm (2 inches) for seam allowance and wrap on the front of the opening and 6·3 cm ($2\frac{1}{2}$ inches) for seam allowance and wrap on the back of the opening.

Fold the waistband lengthwise through the centre, wrong sides together, and crease.

Cut the interfacing twice the width of the finished waistband, less ·6 cm ($\frac{1}{4}$ inch) and the same length. Fold it lengthwise through the centre and press. Cut one end to a point.

Stitch the interfacing to the wrong side of the waistband back section just below the crease and then along the opposite edge, leaving a seam allowance in the band at the pointed end.

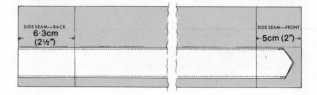

Mark the wrong side of the waistband 5 cm (2 inches) from the pointed edge for the wrap over, and 6·3 cm (2½ inches) from the opposite end for the underwrap. The length between the two markings should be the waist measurement.

Open the zip. Place the waistband over the waistline of the skirt, right sides together, extending the pointed end 5 cm (2 inches) beyond front edge of the placket, and pin. Extend the opposite end 6·3 cm (2½ inches) beyond the back seam of the placket opening, and pin. (This end should extend the width of the zip underlay.) Pin waistband to waistline at the right side seam, allowing an equal amount of ease in front and back of skirt.

Match the front seamline of the placket opening with the right side seam, and pin. Fold the front section of the waistband and pin mark the centre. Match the back seamline of the opening with the right side seam, and pin. Pin-mark the centre back of the waistband in the same way as the front. Pin the band to the skirt at centre front and back. Evenly distribute the ease in the skirt between the markings, and pin. Tack. Stitch on the seamline, and back-stitch at each end. Cut off corners where seams cross at the right side and at darts. On firmly woven fabrics, trim the waistline seam allowance to ·6 cm (¼ inch).

Remove tackings, and press. Turn the waistband away from the skirt and press the seam allowances towards the waistband.

Fold the pointed end of the waistband in half, right sides together, and pin across the end and along the lower edge as far as the placket opening. Stitch just outside the interfacing, taking one stitch across the point. Reinforce each end of the seam with backstitching. Fold the opposite end, right sides together, and pin; stitch across the end. Trim the seam allowances to ·6 cm (¼ inch) and press. Turn the waistband to the right side and press the ends.

Fold the waistband in half and pin along the fold. Turn under the seam allowance on the free edge of the waistband and pin to the seam at the waistline, enclosing the seam allowances. Finish by hand, using a hemming stitch. Take the stitching through the waistband and seam allowance only, so that it will not show on the outside. Press. If top stitching is desired, stitch round the waistband from the outside.

Sew on hooks and eyes, as illustrated. Take the stitches through the underside of the waistband and interfacing. If you want a button instead of hooks and eyes to fasten the waistband, work a buttonhole near the point and sew the button in position at the opposite end. If a bound buttonhole is used, make it before attaching the interfacing to the waistband. However, sew on hooks and eyes at the end of the underwrap to hold it in position on the inside.

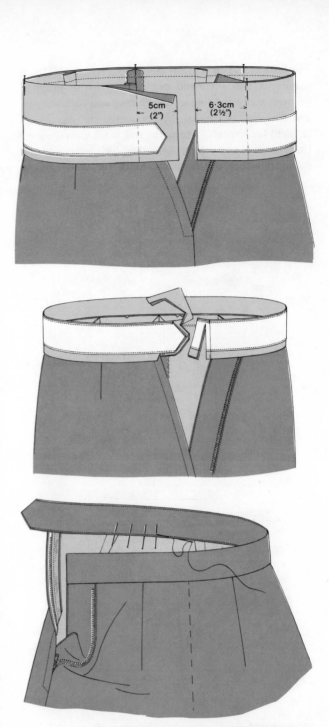

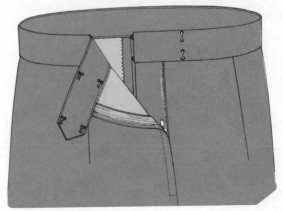

Method 2: When there is no wrap over on the front seam, cut the waistband on the lengthwise grain as follows: twice the *finished width* plus seam allowances, and the *length* of the waistline measurement plus 2·5 cm (1 inch) for depth of the point and seam allowance on the front side and 6·3 cm (2½ inches) for underwrap and seam allowance on the back. Mark the waistband at

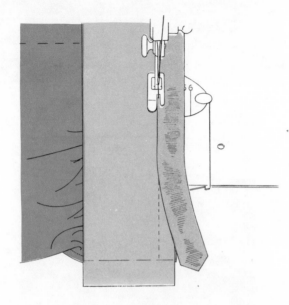

these intervals. The length between the two markings should be the waistline measurement.

Open the zip. Place the waistband (without interfacing) over the waistline of the skirt, right sides together, extending the end 2·5 cm (1 inch) beyond the front edge of the placket opening, and pin. Extend the opposite end 6·3 cm (2½ inches) beyond the back edge of the placket opening, and pin. (This end should extend the width of the zip underlay.)

Finish pinning the waistband in place as instructed in *Method 1*. Tack.

For the interfacing, use 2·5 cm (1 inch) wide petersham belting. Cut it the same length as the waistband and cut one end to a point.

Lap the petersham belting over the waistband side of the seam allowances, keeping the edge even with the seamline. Pin. Stitch on the edge of the interfacing with the skirt next to the feed. Back-stitch at each end. Remove tackings and press.

Turn the waistband away from the skirt and press the seam allowances and interfacing towards the waistband. Trim seam allowances under the interfacing to ·6 cm (¼ inch) and cut off corners where seams cross at the right side and at darts.

Pink the free edge of the waistband, then stitch ·6 cm (¼ inch) from the edge, using a 1 mm (20) stitch.

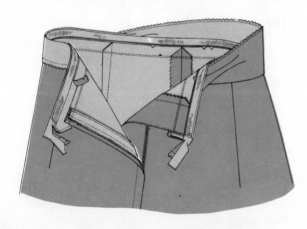

Fold the pointed end of the waistband, right sides together, and pin across the end. Stitch barely outside the interfacing. Take one stitch across the point. Reinforce the ends with backstitching. Fold the opposite end, right sides together, and pin. Trim the end of the interfacing to the seamline of the waistband. Stitch across the end of the waistband. Trim the seam allowances to ·6 cm (¼ inch) and press. Turn the ends to the right side, ease out the corners, and press.

Turn the free edge of the waistband over the interfacing and pin to the seam at the stitching line on the underside, enclosing the seam allowances. At the front seam, fold under the raw edges of the waistband as far as the zip tape. Finish by hand with a backstitch, stitching through the seam allowance and waistband only, so that the stitches will not show on the right side. Sew on hooks and eyes as illustrated in *Method 1*.

To Attach Waistband to Knitted Fabric

To ensure a good fit in knitted fabrics and still allow as much 'give' in the waistband as in the fabric, use 2·5-cm (1-inch) elastic inside the waistband instead of petersham. Use zig-zag stitching for flexibility.

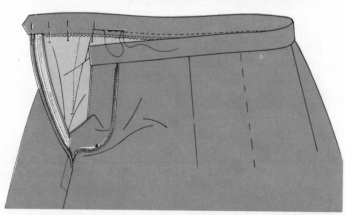

156

Follow the instructions in *Method 2* on cutting the waistband and pinning it to the skirt. Cut the elastic 2·5 cm (1 inch) shorter than the waistband and cut one end to a point. Lap the elastic over the waistband side of the waistline seam allowance, keeping the edge even with the seamline, and pin. Distribute the ease evenly in front and back skirt section. Stitch near the edge of the elastic, stretching the elastic between the pins as you sew. Use a medium-width plain zig-zag stitch and 2 mm (12) stitch length. Back-stitch at each end for reinforcement.

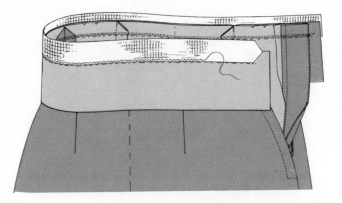

Trim the seam allowance under the elastic to ·6 cm (¼ inch) and cut off corners where seams cross at darts and at the right side seam. Turn the waistband away from the garment and press the seam allowance and elastic towards the waistband. Finish the free edge of the waistband with the multi-stitch zig-zag.

Fold the pointed end of the waistband, right sides together, and pin. Stitch across the point, just outside the elastic. Fold the opposite end, right sides together, and pin. Trim elastic end even with the seamline of the waistband. Stitch across the end of the band just outside the elastic. Trim seam allowances to ·6 cm (¼ inch) and press. Turn ends to the right side and press.

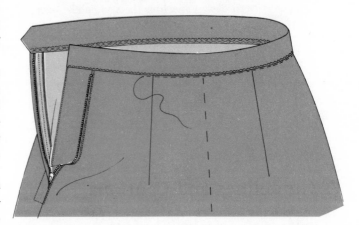

Fold the waistband smoothly over the elastic and pin to the seam at the stitching line on the underside, enclosing the seam allowances. Tack. Stitch from the outside, stretching the elastic as you stitch so that it will retain its stretch after the stitching is complete. Use a medium-width plain zig-zag stitch and a 2 mm (12) stitch length. Sew on hooks and eyes as illustrated in *Method 1*. Take the stitches through the underside of the waistband and elastic. Or, work a buttonhole and sew on a button.

Pin the elastic to the inside of the garment waistline at the marked intervals; fold ends of the elastic under 1·2 cm (½ inch) and pin to facing or zip tape on each side of the opening. Stretch the elastic between the pins as you stitch so that it will retain its strength after the stitching is completed. A narrow multi-stitch zig-zag or two rows of straight stitching may be used. Fasten the ends of the elastic securely with hand stitches.

To Attach Elastic at the Waistline

Your pattern design may show the bodice and skirt of a dress, or the bodice and peplum of a jacket, cut in one and belted at the waistline to form soft gathers. To ensure that the gathers are evenly distributed, stitch narrow elastic to the inside of the waistline.

Mark the waistline of the garment. Fit the elastic comfortably at the waistline, allowing 2·5 cm (1 inch) for finishing at the opening.

Divide the garment waistline and elastic into quarters, allowing 1·2 cm (½ inch) at each end of the elastic for finishing.

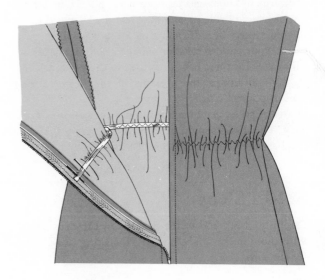

Sleeve Styles and Finishes

Look to the sleeve for fashion. Construct it with care. It makes all the difference between a home-made and a professional-looking garment.

Your pattern design specifies the style and finish of your sleeve and gives you clear directions to follow. The paragraphs below will help you work carefully and confidently.

Constructing Different Sleeve Styles

Guidelines and Cautions

– Transfer accurately from pattern to fabric all *markings in the sleeve and armhole*.

– Never omit pinning and tacking.

– The shoulder length of the bodice is important to the fit of the sleeve, especially the plain, set-in sleeve.

The fashion of the pattern may show the garment shoulder line extending beyond the natural shoulder line. Do not fit the fashion out of this sleeve. If the natural shoulder line is the fashion of your pattern, make sure that it is the correct length for your figure. If it is too wide, the sleeve will hang off the shoulder, giving the garment a home-made appearance; if it is too narrow, the sleeve will ride up and may tear at the seam. There should always be sufficient ease for movement.

– If your pattern calls for shoulder pads or shapes, an allowance for them has been made in the pattern.

– Do not forget the pressing of the sleeve during construction.

Sleeve styles are numerous and many are illustrated here. Variations should be constructed along the same lines as those described below.

Set-in Sleeve

Carefully check and match notches in the sleeve head with those in the armhole to avoid making two sleeves for the same arm.

Three-quarter and full-length sleeves have fullness at the elbow, which is controlled with darts or gathers. Stitch darts and press them downwards over a pressing mitt. See *Elbow Darts*, page 103.

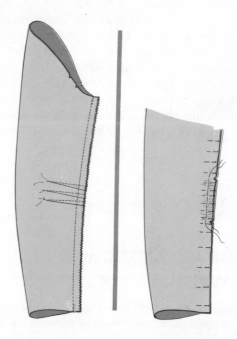

If gathers are marked, control the fullness with a row of stitching between the notches, just outside the seamline. Fold the sleeve, right sides together, and pin on the seamline, matching markings. Draw the thread to ease in the fullness at the elbow; distribute the fullness evenly between the notches. Tack, then stitch underarm seams and neaten seam edges. Press the seam; then slip the sleeve over a sleeveboard, and press the seam open.

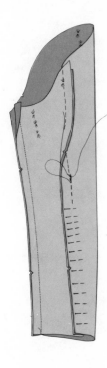

The two-piece sleeve is generally used in suits and coats. There is a slight ease in the upper sleeve section at the elbow. When joining sleeve sections, control the ease by pinning the seam at ·6-cm (¼-inch) intervals between the notches. After the seam is tacked and stitched, shrink the fullness by pressing.

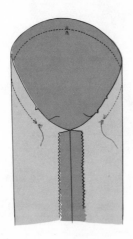

Turn the garment to the right side and lay the shoulder over the hand to check the 'hang' of the sleeve. Check that the ease is in the correct place. The centre lengthwise grain of the sleeve should fall in a straight line and the crosswise grain should fall at right angles to it. See *Understanding Balance Lines*, page 77.

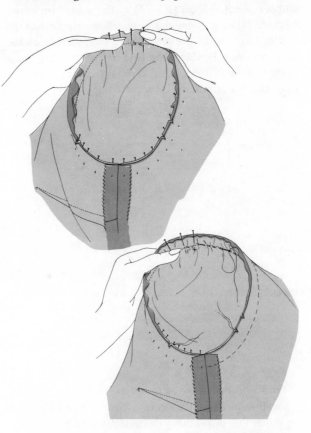

SETTING SLEEVE INTO ARMHOLE (*Above*)

Turn the sleeve to the wrong side and, from the inside, place one or two lines of stitching round the head of the sleeve between the notches to control the ease. Place the first line just outside the seamline, in the seam allowance. Use the same length stitch as used in stitching the garment and leave thread ends long enough to draw up. (Loosen the upper tension enough to draw the bobbin thread to ease the fullness. Do not forget to return the tension to its previous setting.) If two lines of stitching are used, place the second line in the seam allowance, ·5 cm (3/16 inch) from the first line of stitching.

Turn the sleeve to the right side. With the wrong side of the garment towards you, slip the sleeve into the armhole, right sides together. Pin, matching underarm seams, notches and shoulder line. Working with the sleeve towards you, pull the bobbin threads at each end of the stitching, easing in the fullness from the notches to within 1·2 cm (½ inch) of the shoulder line. Ease the threads enough to fit the sleeve head to the armhole. (The 1·2 cm (½ inch) at the shoulder line is on the straight grain of the fabric and should not be eased.) *Roll the seamline of the sleeve and armhole over the fingers and distribute the sleeve ease evenly.* Pin the sleeve in the armhole at close intervals, picking up only a few threads at the seamline.

With the sleeve towards you, tack, using a short stitch.

If you are working with wool, it may be necessary to shrink the fullness at the sleeve head before tacking. See *Pressing*, page 74. Re-pin the sleeve in the armhole the same as before, then tack.

Try on the garment before stitching in the sleeve. Pin

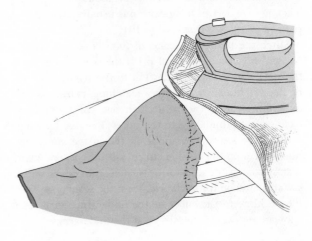

the bodice and skirt sections together so that the bodice will not slip out of place. Check the true fit of the sleeve. Make any necessary adjustments.

Stitch from the sleeve side, just beyond the stitching used to control the ease. Begin the stitching at the underarm seam and continue round the sleeve, overlapping stitches about 2·5 cm (1 inch) at the underarm seam. Remove tacking. Trim the seam allowance to half its width. Cut off the corners where seams cross at the underarm and shoulder. The first row of stitching, used to control the fullness, can also be taken out. See *Sleeves*, page 323, for additional information.

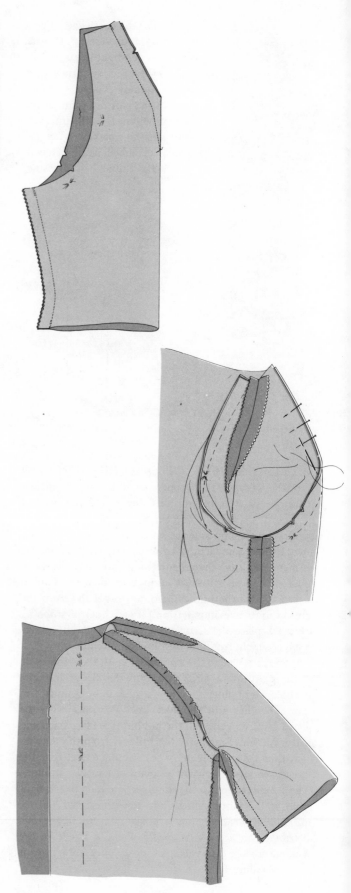

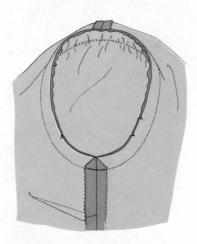

Press into the sleeve as far as the stitching. Turn the seam allowance into the sleeve. In heavy coat fabric, use only one line of stitching to control the ease. Press the seam, then press it open. See *Pressing*, page 74.

Raglan Sleeve

Pin, tack and stitch the dart at the shoulder, matching markings. A dart in this position is usually slashed and pressed open. See *Darts*, page 101.

Stitch the underarm seams of the sleeve and bodice. Neaten the seam edges and press the seam open. Turn the sleeve to the right side. Pin to the front and back bodice, right sides together, matching markings and underarm seams. Tack. Stitch in one continuous line from one neckline edge to the other. Remove tackings.

Slash the seam allowances on the inside curve and notch them on the outside curve. Cut off corners where seams cross at the underarm. Neaten seam edges with a suitable method for the fabric. Press the seam open from the neckline to the curve at the underarm. Turn seam allowances towards the sleeve at the underarm.

Epaulette Sleeve

The epaulette sleeve has a yoke extending over the shoulder from the top of the sleeve head to the neckline.

At the head of the sleeve, where the epaulette begins, stay-stitch the point where the seam allowance will be slashed. Use a short stitch and take one stitch across the point. Press. Stitch the underarm seams of the sleeve and bodice. Finish the seam edges and press the seam open.

Turn the sleeve to the right side. With the wrong side of the bodice towards you, place the sleeve into the armhole, right sides together. Pin, matching underarm seams, shoulder markings and notches. Then with the sleeve towards you, pin at close intervals. Tack in one continuous line from one side of the shoulder to the other.

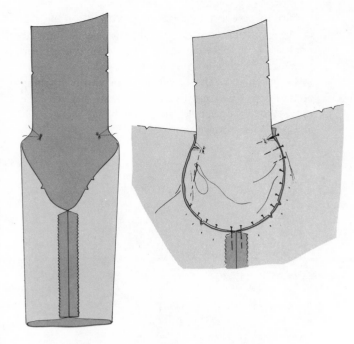

At the shoulder line of the sleeve, slash almost to the stay-stitched point. Pin the epaulette to the shoulder line of the bodice on each side, matching markings. Check that the corners do not pucker. Tack with a short stitch. Check the right side to make sure that the corners are square.

Stitch from the sleeve side in a continuous line from one neckline edge to the other. Pivot the fabric on the needle at the corners; take one stitch across the point; pivot again and continue stitching. Smooth out the fabric at the point so that a pleat is not formed. Remove tackings. Cut off the corners where seams cross at the underarm. Press the seam as stitched, then press the seam edges towards the epaulette. In the sleeve section, turn seam allowances towards the sleeve.

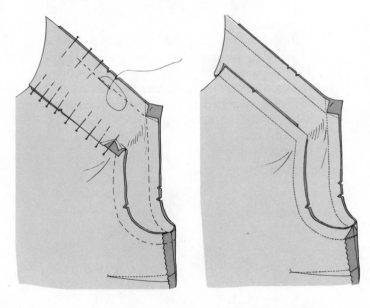

Puff Sleeve

Puff sleeves are found in children's clothes, blouses, many shirt dresses and lingerie.

Stitch underarm seams. (A French seam is frequently used in children's clothes and garments made of sheer fabric.)

Turn the sleeve to the wrong side and, from the inside, stitch two lines of gathering round the head of the sleeve between the notches. Place the first line of stitching just outside the seamline in the seam allowance and the second line in the seam allowance, about ·5 cm ($\frac{3}{16}$ inch) from the first.

At the lower edge of the sleeve, stitch a line of gathering between the markings. Gather and finish the lower edge.

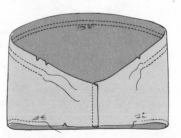

161

Turn the sleeve to the right side. With the wrong side of the garment towards you, slip the sleeve into the armhole, right sides together. Pin, matching underarm seams, notches and shoulder lines. With the sleeve towards you, draw the threads for both rows of stitching at the same time, and gather the sleeve between the notches to fit the armhole. Distribute the fullness evenly, and pin. Tack, using a short stitch.

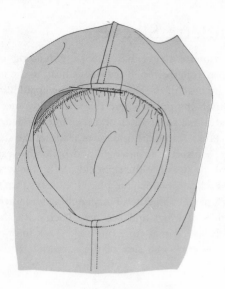

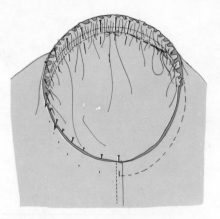

Stitch from the sleeve side, just beyond the first line of gathering stitches and overlap the stitching about 2·5 cm (1 inch) at the underarm. Stitch again on the second line of gathering stitches. Trim the seam allowance close to the second line of stitching. Press. Neaten the seam edges with binding or overcast them together, using the blindstitch zig-zag. Turn the seam allowances towards the sleeve.

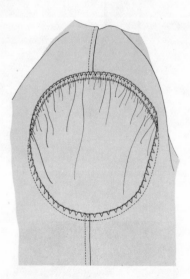

In sheer fabrics, place the second line of stitching round the head of the sleeve, ·3 cm ($\frac{1}{8}$ inch) from the first line, and use only one line of stitching to sew in the sleeve. Trim the seam allowance on the sleeve side to ·6 cm ($\frac{1}{4}$ inch). Turn the cut edge under ·3 cm ($\frac{1}{8}$ inch) on

the bodice side; fold this seam allowance over the sleeve seam allowance to the stitching line, enclosing the cut edge. Pin. Slip-stitch to the sleeve seam barely above the stitching. This seam finish is barely visible through sheer fabric.

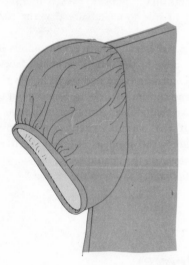

Magyar Sleeve – Without Gusset

To prevent the seam from splitting under strain, use a stay, following one of the methods given here.

Method 1: Pin, tack and stitch the seam, using a shorter stitch on the curved section. Slash the seam allowances almost to the stitching line on the curve to relieve the strain. Press the seam, then press it open.

Use straight seam binding over the open seam from the hem fold in the sleeve to the lower edge of the bodice. Turn the seam allowance away from the garment and stitch the binding to each side of the seam allowance.

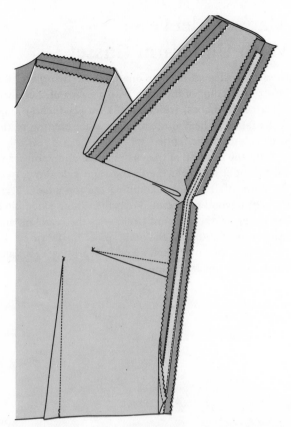

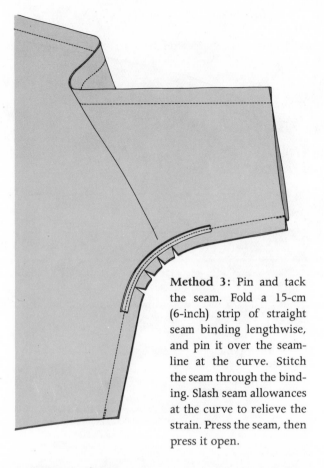

Stitch again through the curve on one side, close to the seamline. The binding is stitched only to the single seam allowance and will not show from the right side. Press seam open.

Method 3: Pin and tack the seam. Fold a 15-cm (6-inch) strip of straight seam binding lengthwise, and pin it over the seamline at the curve. Stitch the seam through the binding. Slash seam allowances at the curve to relieve the strain. Press the seam, then press it open.

Method 4: On *knitted fabrics*, after stitching underarm seam, tack straight seam binding over curved section of the open seam. Then, from the right side, stitch the binding to the curved section of the seam, using a narrow zig-zag stitch (generally, a 1·5 to 1 mm (12 to 15) stitch length and medium stitch width).

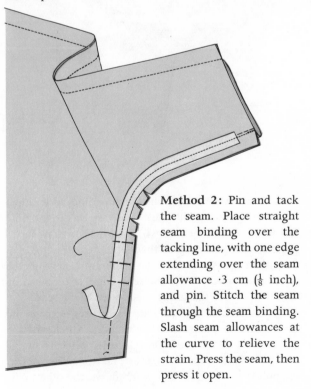

Method 2: Pin and tack the seam. Place straight seam binding over the tacking line, with one edge extending over the seam allowance ·3 cm ($\frac{1}{8}$ inch), and pin. Stitch the seam through the seam binding. Slash seam allowances at the curve to relieve the strain. Press the seam, then press it open.

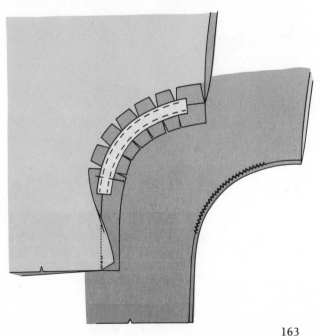

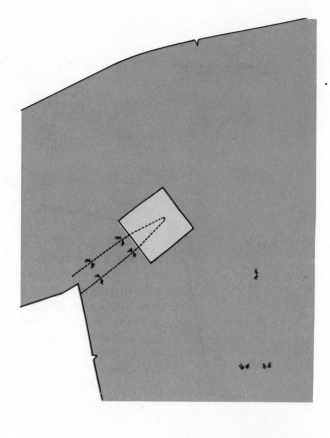

Magyar Sleeve – With Underarm Gusset

Gussets in sleeves may be one-piece or two-piece. Reinforce the point of the slash with a facing of the fabric cut 5 cm (2 inches) wide and 6·3 cm (2½ inches) long. If the fabric is heavy, use straight seam binding of the same colour as the fabric.

Mark the position of the gusset at the underarm seam. On the right side, pin the facing right side down over the point of the slash, extending the top edge 1·2 cm (½ inch) beyond the point. From the wrong side, stitch the facing to the garment, following the seamline and using a short stitch. At the point, pivot the fabric on the needle and take one stitch across; then pivot again and stitch down the other side. Press.

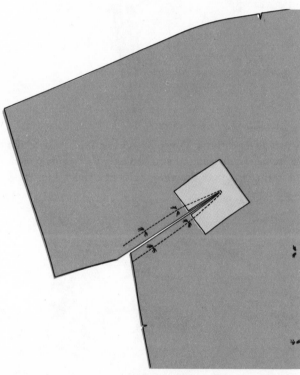

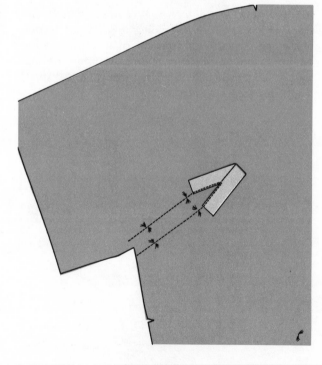

Slash halfway between the stitching lines to within a few threads of the point. Turn the facing on the stitching line to the wrong side. Press. The reinforcement forms a wider seam allowance at the point.

One-piece gusset. Stitch the underarm seams of the sleeve and bodice. Finish the seam edges as required by the fabric. Press the seams, then press them open.

Pin and tack the gusset to the slashed edges, matching markings at the point and at the seamline. Stitch with the gusset next to the feed. On one side, stitch from the underarm seam to the sleeve seam; take one stitch across the point; pivot again and stitch down the other side.

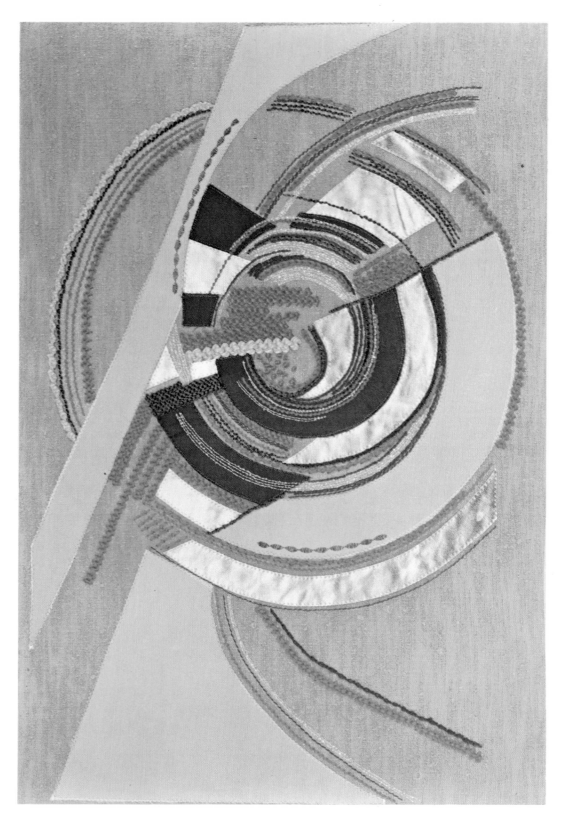

Plate 11
AN IMAGINATIVE AND SUNNY COLLAGE

Furnishing fabric in a warm colour forms the background of this creative work. Various shaped pieces of fabric are incorporated in the design, which uses a variety of coloured threads and different stitches – both hand and machine.

Plate 12
GIFTS TO MAKE

The elephant – one of the most attractive soft toys – is from a Simplicity pattern, and shown here made up in grey felt with decorative fashion stitching in silver, white, burgundy and turquoise.

The apron is made from diamond patchwork pieces formed into a chevron pattern and stitched together with a three-step zig-zag stitch – a floral print in two colours was used with the addition of a plain cotton fabric for the waistband and pocket.

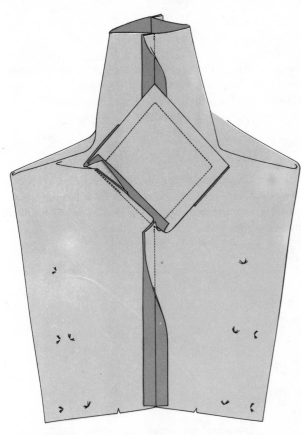

Stitch with the gusset next to the feed. Follow the seamline to the point; pivot the fabric on the needle and take one stitch across the point; then pivot again and stitch down the other side. Press the seams, then press the seam allowance away from the gusset. Stitch the underarm seam in a continuous line from the sleeve edge to the waistline. Back-stitch at both ends. Neaten the seam edges with a suitable method. Press the seam, then press it open.

To prevent pulling. To prevent the gusset from being pulled out at the point of the slash, which can happen with frequent wearings, use straight seam binding over the shoulder from one point of the gusset to the other.

Turn one end of the straight seam binding under ·6 cm ($\frac{1}{4}$ inch) and pin it to the gusset seam allowance and re-inforced facing, near the stitching line. Bring the binding over the shoulder and down to the same point on the

On the other side, stitch from the sleeve seam to the underarm seam. Pull threads through to the underside and tie. Press seam allowances away from the gusset.
Two-piece gusset. Pin and tack one gusset section to the slashed edges of the front bodice and the second gusset section to the back bodice, matching markings at the point and at the seamline.

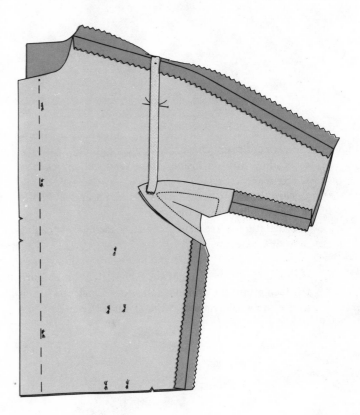

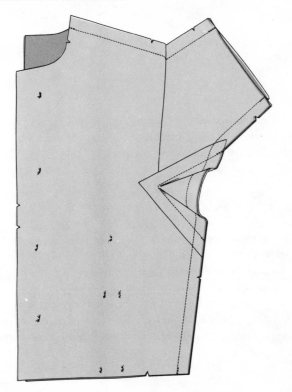

opposite side, and pin. Pin a ·2-cm ($\frac{1}{16}$-inch) tuck, under the binding, in both the front and the back of the bodice. Then adjust the length of the binding to fit smoothly over the shoulder line. Pin the binding to the shoulder seam allowance, then tack it in place at each point and at each side of the shoulder seam allowance. Remove the pin tucks, which will allow just enough ease in the garment to prevent pulling.

Armhole with Fitted Facing

Cut the facing the same as the edge to be faced. Join seams at the shoulder and at the underarm. Finish seam edges, and press seams open.

Turn the garment to the right side. Pin the facing to the armhole, right sides together, matching notches and seams at the shoulder and underarm. Tack. Stitch round the armhole on the seamline, overlapping a few stitches at the starting point. Press.

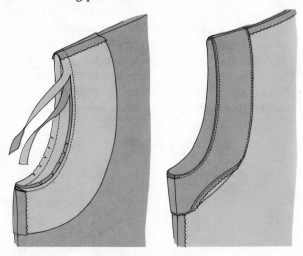

Trim the facing seam allowance to ·3 cm (⅛ inch) and the garment seam allowance to ·6 cm (¼ inch). Slash the seam allowance on inside curves and cut off corners where seams cross.

Turn the facing to the inside and ease it under slightly at the seamline. Tack, then press.

Understitch the seam to prevent the facing from rolling out of place. Press.

Neaten the free edge of the facing by pinking; then turn it under ·6 cm (¼ inch) and edge-stitch. Press. Turn the facing into the armhole and press. Catch the facing to the seam allowances at the shoulder seam and the underarm seam.

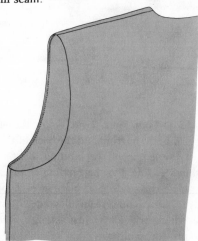

Finishing the Sleeve

To ensure that a sleeve is the correct length, most sleeves are finished at the lower edge after the sleeve is sewn into the armhole. Short sleeves may be finished before they are sewn into the armhole.

Hemmed Edge – Short Sleeve

Fold the hem evenly to the inside and tack ·6 cm (¼ inch) from the fold. Press. Pin, then stitch seam binding ·6 cm (¼ inch) from the free edge of the hem. Join the binding by folding the end under ·6 cm (¼ inch) and overlapping 1·2 cm (½ inch) at the seam. Press.

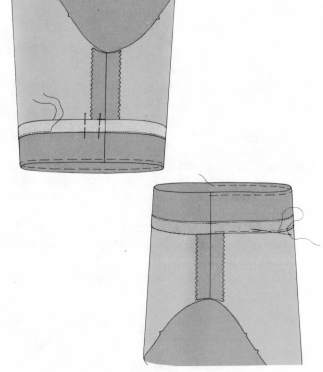

Pin the free edge of the binding to the sleeve. Tack. Slip-stitch in place, catching only a single thread of the fabric. Remove tackings, and press.

Wrist Opening

Turn the sleeve to the wrong side. Pin, then stitch, straight seam binding to the front edge of the wrist opening ·3 cm (⅛ inch) from the seamline, extending it 1·2 cm (½ inch) above the opening.

Pin, then stitch binding to the back edge of the wrist opening, ·3 cm (⅛ inch) from the seam edge, extending it 1·2 cm (½ inch) above opening. Slash diagonally into

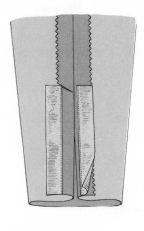

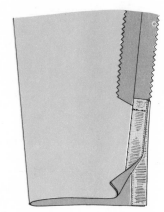

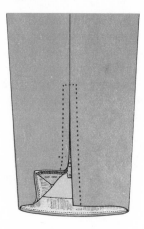

Zip Opening

Choose a fine neckline zip, about 10 to 15 cm (4 to 6 inches) long, for a wrist opening. Insert the zip following the instructions for the *Neckline or Sleeve Zip in Channel Seam* on page 181. Then open the zip and finish the lower edge of the sleeve with straight seam binding, following the method described above.

this seam allowance from the top of the binding to the opening. Press.

At the back edge of the opening, fold the binding to the underside and pin the free edge to the sleeve. Finish by hand, using a hemming stitch. At the top of the opening, stitch the front and back seam edges together the depth of the seam allowance.

At the front edge of the opening, fold the binding to the underside and pin the free edge to the sleeve. Finish by hand, using a hemming stitch.

At the lower edge of the sleeve, pin, then stitch, binding ·6 cm (¼ inch) from edge, extending the ends ·6 cm (¼ inch) beyond the edges of the opening. Press. Cut diagonally across corners of the sleeve seam allowance

Vent Opening

The vent opening is frequently used in the back seam of two-piece tailored sleeves. It is also used in jackets at centre back or side seams.

SLEEVE SEAMS

Mark the line of the fold for the vent opening and for the hem at the lower edge of the sleeve. If a bound buttonhole is used in a three-quarter length sleeve, make the buttonhole before seaming the sleeve.

Join the seams of the upper and lower sleeve sections, leaving the back seam open below the marking for the vent. Reinforce seam ends with backstitching. Slash

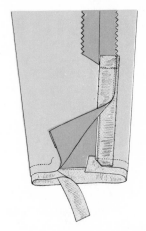

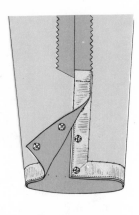

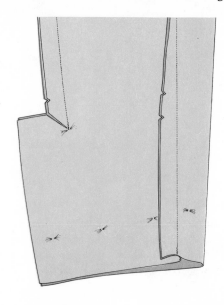

close to the stitching. Fold the binding to the underside, mitre the corners, and tack the free edge to the sleeve. Press. Finish by hand, using a hemming stitch. Remove tackings and press. Sew on small press fasteners.

diagonally into the seam allowance of the under section from the cut edge to the top of the opening. (This wide seam allowance in the opening will extend under the front seam allowance when the vent is finished.) Press seams, then press them open, carrying the crease in the back seam of the upper section to the lower edge of the opening. Fold the hem to the underside, and press.

THE INTERFACING

Cut pre-shrunk muslin interfacing on the true bias, 1·2 cm (½ inch) wider than the hem and long enough to extend round the sleeve; extend one end the depth of the opening. Place the interfacing on the wrong side of the sleeve with the lower edge along the hem fold and the extended edge along the lengthwise fold of the opening on the upper section. Pin, then tack. Herringbone each edge of the interfacing along the hem; make a tiny stitch barely outside the interfacing, catching only a single thread in the fabric; then make a stitch on the opposite side through the interfacing only. Space the stitches about 1·5 cm (⅝ inch) apart. Do not pull the threads too tightly. Remove tackings. The interfacing along the fold of the opening will be held in place when the buttons are sewn on; you may herringbone it if you wish, however, and you should herringbone it if you do not plan to use buttons on the opening.

in the opening on the upper section, taking the stitches through the hem and interfacing only. The stitches will not show on the right side, and the interfacing above the hem will not be visible when the lining is in place.

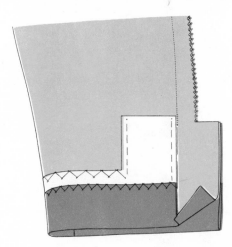

Side hem and opening. On the upper section, trim the hem to ·6 cm (¼ inch) from the cut edge to the lengthwise fold in the opening. Mitre the corner to the point where the lining will overlap the hem. Press. Fold the seam allowance in the opening to the underside and pin in place. Slip-stitch the mitred corner in place, then herringbone the free edge of the seam allowance to the interfacing the depth of the opening.

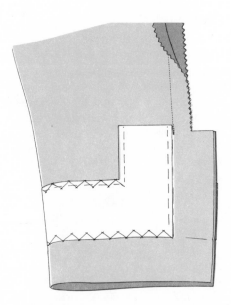

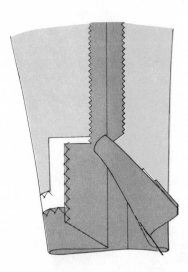

Turn the sleeve to the right side. Wrap the upper section over the under section the depth of the seam allowance in the opening and pin. Take care the lower edges are even.

Work from the wrong side and herringbone the edge of the back seam allowance in place from the lower edge to the top of the interfacing. Take fine stitches through

THE HEMS

Hem at lower edge. Fold the hem over the interfacing and tack ·6 cm (¼ inch) from the fold. Press. Pin, then tack the free edge of the hem to the interfacing. Herringbone in place from the back edge to the lengthwise fold the seam allowance and interfacing only. Tack the seam edges to the interfacing at the top of the opening. Remove all tackings and press.

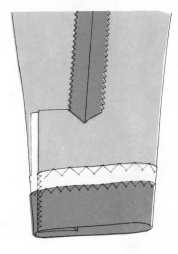

After you have stitched the underarm seam, fold the cuff hem to the underside and press. Tack before pressing if necessary. Fold the free edge of the hem under ·6 cm (¼ inch), and finger-press. Pin the free edge to the sleeve, matching seams. Stitch near edge. (In the illustration the sleeve is turned to the wrong side so that the work may be easily seen.)

Turn the sleeve to the right side. Fold the cuff back over the sleeve, 1·2 cm (½ inch) below the stitching.

Turn the sleeve to the right side and sew on buttons through all thicknesses of fabric. The interfacing above the hem will not show when the lining is in place.

Hemmed Cuff

The hemmed cuff is an excellent finish for blouses and children's clothes. The cuff and sleeve are cut in one, with the cuff section shaped to turn back smoothly over the sleeve.

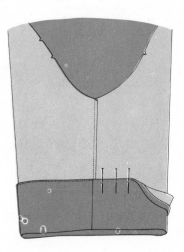

Turn-Back Cuff

The ends of the cuff may be stitched together, as illustrated here, or left open. When the ends are left open, make the cuff in the same way as a collar and attach it to the sleeve, following the instructions given below.

Stitch the ends of the cuff together on the under cuff and on the upper cuff. Reinforce with backstitching. Press, then press seam open.

Cut pre-shrunk interfacing by the cuff pattern. The instructions for attaching it to the cuff vary, depending on the weight of the interfacing and the fabric in the garment. Follow the appropriate method as given overleaf.

With lightweight interfacing. Join interfacing ends

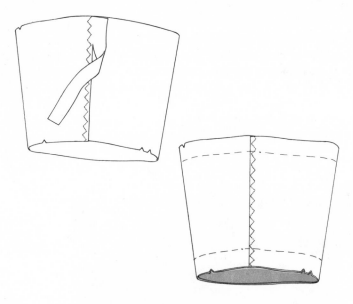

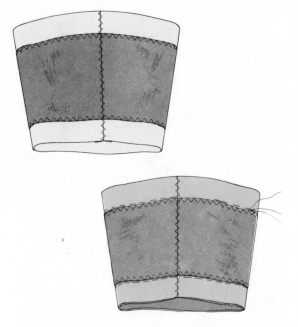

edges of the interfacing, and trim off the seam allowance at each end.

Cut two strips of organza 4 cm (1½ inches) wide – one the shape of the top of the cuff and the other the shape of the lower edge. Lay the organza strip over the upper edge of the interfacing, extending it 2 cm (¾ inch) beyond the interfacing edge. Pin. Follow the same procedure at the lower edge. Then stitch, using the multi-stitch zig-zag. Press. Join ends with an abutted seam. See *Abutted Seam*, page 83.

with a lapped seam, using the multi-stitch zig-zag to eliminate bulk. See *Lapped Seam*, page 83.

Turn the under cuff to the wrong side and slip interfacing over it, matching seams. The interfacing should fit smoothly over the cuff. Pin, then tack each edge of the interfacing to the cuff.

Turn the under cuff right side out with the interfacing to the inside. Slip the upper cuff over the under cuff, right sides together, matching markings and seams. Pin along the top edge, easing the upper cuff between the markings. Tack, then stitch, overlapping a few stitches at the starting point.

Turn the under cuff to the inside and slip the interfacing over it, matching seams. The interfacing should fit smoothly over the cuff. Pin, then tack each edge of the interfacing to the cuff.

Turn the under cuff right side out with the interfacing to the inside. Slip the upper cuff over the under cuff, right sides together, matching markings and seams. Pin along the top edge, easing the upper cuff between the markings. Tack, then stitch, overlapping a few stitches at the starting point.

Trim the interfacing seam edge close to the stitching; then trim the seam allowance of the under cuff to ·3 cm (⅛ inch) and of the upper cuff to ·6 cm (¼ inch). Notch the seam edges on the outside curve and cut off corners where seams cross. Press.

Turn the cuff to the right side with the upper cuff to the top. Ease the under cuff slightly to the underside at the seamline and tack. Press.

With heavy-weight interfacing. Trim off the seam allowance plus ·3 cm (⅛ inch) on the upper and lower

Trim the under cuff seam allowance and organza strip to ·3 cm (⅛ inch) and the upper cuff seam allowance to

·6 cm (¼ inch). Notch seam allowance on the curve and cut off corners where seams cross. Press.

Turn the cuff to the right side with the upper cuff to the top. Ease the under cuff slightly to the underside at the seamline, and tack, using diagonal tacking and silk thread. Press.

ATTACHING CUFF TO THE SLEEVE

Turn the sleeve and cuff to the right side. Slip the cuff over the sleeve. Pin, then tack the under cuff and interfacing to the lower edge of the sleeve, matching markings and seams. (Fold back the upper cuff to keep it out of the way for the next step.) Stitch from the sleeve side, overlapping a few stitches at the starting point.

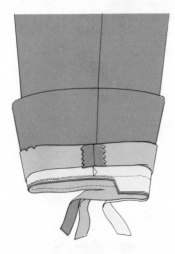

Trim the interfacing seam allowance close to the stitching; trim the under cuff seam allowance to ·3 cm (⅛ inch) and the sleeve seam allowance to ·6 cm (¼ inch). Cut off corners where seams cross and slash the curved seam allowance of the cuff. Press, then press the seam open.

If a sleeve facing is not included in the pattern, cut one about 7·5 cm (3 inches) deep, using the sleeve pattern as a guide. (The facing must not be deeper than the cuff.) Stitch the ends together, then press the seam open. Pin and tack the facing to the free edge of the upper cuff,

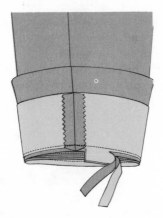

matching markings and seams. Stitch, overlapping a few stitches at the starting point.

Trim seam allowance to ·6 cm (¼ inch). Cut off corners where seams cross and slash the curved seam allowance at evenly spaced intervals. Press, then press the seam open.

Slip the fingers of the left hand between the sleeve and cuff and pin the cuff sections together about 1·2 cm (½ inch) above the lower edge. Slip-stitch the open seams of the two cuffs together, allowing sufficient ease in the upper cuff for it to fit smoothly over the fold of the interfacing and under cuff. This prevents the under cuff from slipping out of place at the top.

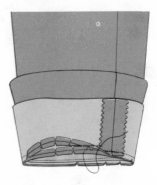

If the garment is unlined, neaten the free edge of the facing, then turn the facing into the sleeve, and pin the free edge to the sleeve. Finish by hand, spacing the stitches about 2·5 cm (1 inch) apart.

When a facing is not used, follow the above method up to instructions for cutting the facing. Turn the cuff away from the sleeve and press the seam allowances towards the cuff. Turn the cuff back over the sleeve. Slip the fingers of the left hand between the sleeve and cuff and pin the cuff sections together about 1·2 cm (½ inch) above the lower edge. Fold under the seam edge on the upper cuff and pin it to the sleeve at the stitching line, enclosing the seam allowances inside the cuff. Allow sufficient ease in the upper cuff for it to fit smoothly over the fold for the interfacing and under cuff. Finish by hand, using a hemming stitch. (Work inside the sleeve.)

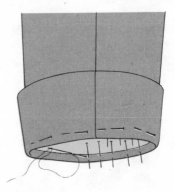

French Cuff

The French cuff is a popular sleeve finish for tailored dresses, blouses and shirts. It is cut twice the finished width and is folded crosswise through the centre to form a double cuff open at the ends. It has four buttonholes, for cuff links, or for buttons joined with French tacks.

If bound buttonholes are used, make them before stitching the cuff.

Cuff. Cut pre-shrunk interfacing by the cuff pattern. Tack it to the wrong side of the upper cuff. Cut off the four corners of the interfacing to eliminate bulk when the cuff is turned through.

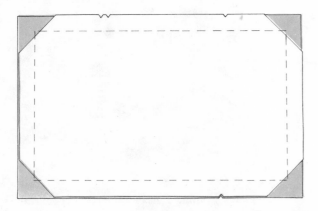

Pin the upper cuff over the under cuff, right sides together, matching markings. Tack if necessary. Stitch round three sides, leaving open the edge that will join the sleeve. Take one stitch across the corners and back-stitch at each end of the seam. Remember to make one cuff for the left sleeve and one for the right. Remove all tackings and press.

Trim the interfacing seam edge close to the stitching. Trim the under cuff seam edge to ·3 cm (⅛ inch) and

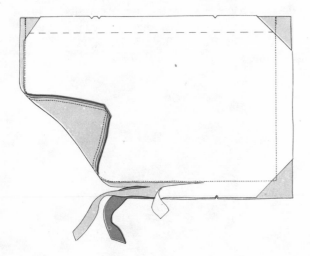

the upper cuff seam edge to ·6 cm (¼ inch). Cut diagonally across corners, close to the stitching. Press. Turn the cuff to the right side. Pull out corners to square them. Ease the under cuff slightly to the underside at the seamline and tack. Press.

Sleeve. Mark the position for the opening in the sleeve and finish it with a continuous bound placket before stitching the underarm seams. See page 185.

Turn the sleeve to the wrong side and, from the inside, place two lines of stitching around the lower edge to gather the fullness. Place the first line of stitching 1·5 cm (⅝ inch) from the seam edge and the second line in the seam allowance, ·6 cm (¼ inch) from the first line. Use the same stitch length you used in stitching the garment and loosen the upper tension slightly. (Do not forget to return the tension to its previous setting.) Leave thread ends long enough to draw up.

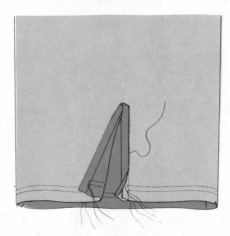

ATTACHING CUFF TO SLEEVE

Turn the sleeve to the right side. On the right side, wind the thread ends around a pin, forming a figure eight at each end of the stitching. Place the cuff over the sleeve, with the upper cuff and right side of the sleeve together. Pin the upper cuff and interfacing to the sleeve, matching markings and extending the placket binding beyond each end of the cuff.

Working with the wrong side of the sleeve towards you, draw both threads at the same time and gather the sleeve to fit the cuff. Distribute the fullness evenly, then pin the sleeve to the cuff at close intervals. Pull the gathering threads to the underside and tie.

Fold the placket binding back over the gathers, and pin. Tack the cuff to the sleeve. Stitch from the sleeve side, just beyond the first line of gathering stitches. Back-stitch at each end. (Do not catch the under cuff on the stitching.)

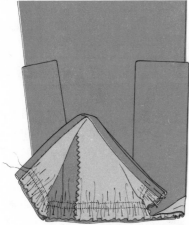

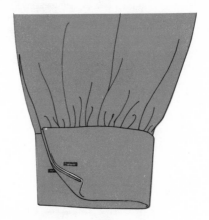

buttonholes in fine cottons or woollens. Cut buttonholes and insert cuff links.

Trim the interfacing seam edge close to the stitching. Trim the cuff seam edge to ·3 cm (⅛ inch) and the sleeve seam edge to ·6 cm (¼ inch). Press the seam, then turn the cuff away from the sleeve and press the seam edges towards the cuff.

Fold the cuff smoothly through the centre. Slip the fingers of the left hand between the fold to be certain there is enough ease in the upper cuff for it to fit smoothly over the fold of the interfacing and under cuff. Pin through all thicknesses, about 1·2 cm (½ inch) above the fold. Fold the free edge of the cuff under ·6 cm (¼ inch) and pin it to the sleeve at the stitching line, enclosing the gathered seam allowance inside the cuff. Slip-stitch in place.

Cuff Cut in One with the Sleeve

The cuff cut in one with the two-piece sleeve is generally found in suits and coats. Since it is most often a soft cuff, it requires a light- or medium-weight interfacing. The cuff opening is in the back seam of the sleeve.

Mark the fold line of the cuff on the sleeve.

Join the upper and lower sleeve sections at the front seam, right sides together. Press the seam open.

Cut pre-shrunk interfacing by the cuff pattern. Trim off the seam allowance plus ·3 cm (⅛ inch) on the top edge and at each end. Cut a strip of organza 4 cm (1½ inches) wide to fit across the top edge and the ends of the cuff, using the pattern to shape the outer edges. Pin the organza strip over the interfacing, extending the edges 2 cm (¾ inch) beyond the interfacing. Cut off the corners of the interfacing to eliminate bulk when the cuff is turned. Stitch, using the multi-stitch zig-zag. Press.

Pin the interfacing over the wrong side of the under cuff, which is cut in one with the sleeve. Tack in place along the lower edge and each end of the cuff.

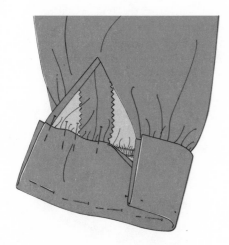

Check the position of buttonholes on both cuff layers to be sure that they coincide and then work a buttonhole at each end of both the cuff sections, using hand-worked buttonholes in soft, silk fabrics and machine-worked

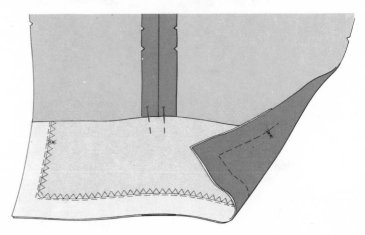

173

Join the upper and lower sleeve sections at the back seam, leaving the seam open below the marking for the cuff. Back-stitch at each end of the seam. Press, then press the seam open.

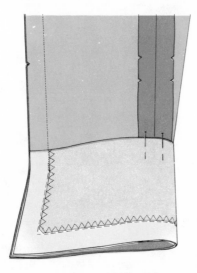

Turn the sleeve to the right side. Place the upper cuff over the under cuff, right sides together. Pin in place along the edge and ends, matching markings. Pin at the points and markings, then at intervals between, easing the upper cuff between the markings.

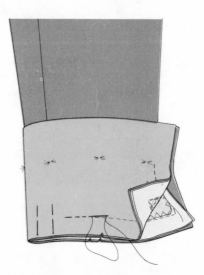

Stitch from the interfacing side, beginning at one end of the cuff opening and continuing around the cuff to the opposite end. Take one stitch across the corners. Pull the threads to the underside and tie. Remove tackings.

Pin the upper cuff seams together above the opening, then stitch. Press the seam open. Trim the under cuff

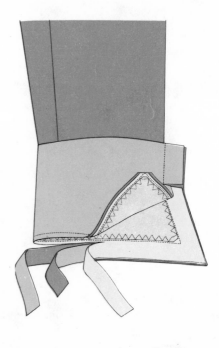

seam edge and organza strip to ·3 cm (⅛ inch) and the upper cuff seam edge to ·6 cm (¼ inch). Cut diagonally across corners, close to the stitching. Press.

Turn the cuff to the right side. Pull out the corners to square them. Ease the under cuff to the underside slightly at the seamline, and tack, using diagonal tacking and silk thread. Press.

With the sleeve right side out, turn the cuff back over the sleeve. Slip the fingers of the left hand between the sleeve and cuff and pin through all thicknesses, 1·2 cm (½ inch) above fold. Turn the free edge of the cuff into the sleeve, allowing sufficient ease in the upper cuff for it to fit smoothly over the fold of the interfacing and under cuff. Tack the free edge to the sleeve seam allowances. Remove all tackings. The lining, when it is attached, will hold the cut edge of the cuff in place.

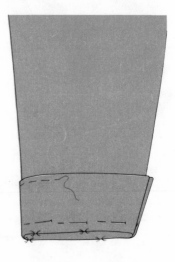

Double-Fold Bias Binding

A double-fold bias is used as a sleeve finish in blouses, dresses and children's clothes. The same type of finish is also used at the neckline. The finished width of the binding is usually ·6 cm ($\frac{1}{4}$ inch); the sleeve edge may be straight or gathered as in the puff sleeve.

Trim the seam allowance on the lower edge of the sleeve to ·6 cm ($\frac{1}{4}$ inch). Gather the lower edge of the sleeve as indicated on the pattern.

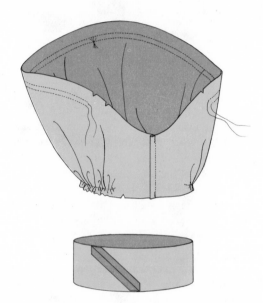

Cut a strip on the true bias six times the width of the finished binding. See *Cutting Bias Strips*, page 244.

Join the bias strip on the lengthwise grain to fit the sleeve edge, taking a ·6-cm ($\frac{1}{4}$-inch) seam. Press the seam open.

Fold the bias through the centre, wrong sides together, and finger-press lightly. Pin the double bias over the right side of the sleeve, keeping the cut edges even. Tack. Stitch from the sleeve side ·6 cm ($\frac{1}{4}$ inch) from the edge, using a short stitch and overlapping a few stitches at the starting point. Press.

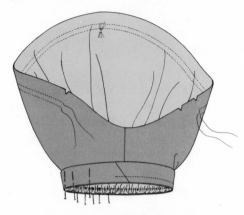

Turn the sleeve to the wrong side. Fold binding over the seam edge to the stitching line on the underside, enclosing the cut edges. Pin. Finish by hand, using a slip stitch.

Homeward Bound: Zips, Hems, Belts and Buttons

Your dress at last looks almost ready to wear. The adjustments and fittings and the tacking and stitching are over. All that is lacking now are the final details – a zip, a hem, maybe a belt and some buttons.

Zips and Plackets

There are several ways of inserting zips; the one you select depends on the position of the zip in the garment and the type of garment. Generally zips are either concealed in a lapped seam with only one line of stitching visible or are central under a channel seam with two lines of stitching showing. The lapped seam method is used in side seam openings for dresses, skirts and shorts.

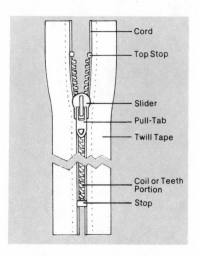

Cord
Top Stop
Slider
Pull-Tab
Twill Tape
Coil or Teeth Portion
Stop

It is also popular for centre back openings when long zips are used. The channel seam method is used in neckline, sleeve and centre back or front openings. It is sometimes used for side openings instead of a lapped seam.

The pattern envelope will state the length and type of zip to buy. To ensure a neat, professional zip insertion, follow the step-by-step methods given.

Dress Placket Zip in Lapped Seam

Before you put in the zip, the bodice and skirt sections should be joined at the waistline. The left side seam should be open above and below the waistline. The placket opening should be 1·2 cm ($\frac{1}{2}$ inch) longer than the metal or synthetic portion of the zip. Check that the ends of the permanent stitching on both the skirt and bodice are reinforced with backstitching.

Inspect the fit of the dress; the side seams should hang straight from underarm to hemline.

If the waistline is small and the hips rounded, the seam below the waistline will be curved and inserting the zip will require a little extra care. If the waistline is comparatively large and the hips flat, the seam will be fairly straight, and the zip insertion will be simpler. Compare the front and back seams of the opening to make sure they are the same length. Chalk or tack exactly on the seamline on each side of the opening. Choose a dress placket zip of the correct length 25 or 30 cm (10 or 12 inches).

1. Turn the dress to the wrong side. Pin the seams

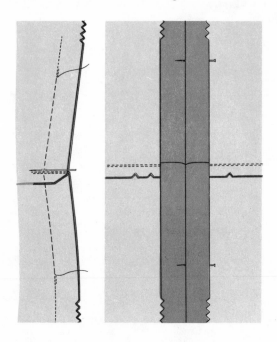

together, carefully matching the waistline seams. Tack on the seamline the exact length of the opening. Cut off corners where seams cross at the waistline.

If the placket seam allowance is less than 2 cm ($\frac{3}{4}$ inch), stitch seam binding to the seam edge on the front side.

2. Press the seam open over the curve of a pressing mitt to retain the shape of the hipline. Press the zip tape.

Mark the ends of the permanent stitching by placing pins across the seam but not through the dress.

3. Fold under the back seam allowance ·3 cm ($\frac{1}{8}$ inch) from the tacked seam and place the fold over the right side of the zip tape, with the top end ·3 cm ($\frac{1}{8}$ inch) below the top of the opening; pin. Roll the zip and folded edge over the fingers of the left hand to ease the seam, then pin the folded edge to the zip tape. The end stop should be ·3 cm ($\frac{1}{8}$ inch) above the opening in the skirt. This allows ·6 cm ($\frac{1}{4}$ inch) for ease throughout the length of the zip. Pin the seam allowance to the tape above and below the opening. Tack.

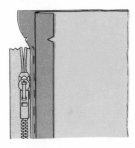

4. Replace the Presser Foot with the Zipper Foot and adjust the foot to the left of the needle. Turn the *pull-tab up* to lessen bulk in stitching. Stitch from the lower end to the top near the edge of the fold. *Remove tacking and turn the pull-tab down.*

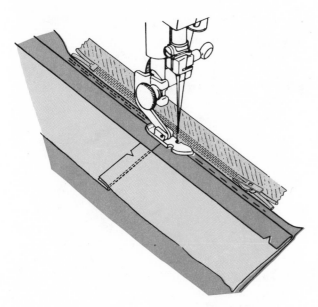

5. Turn the dress to the right side. Turn the zip and back seam allowance flat against front seam allowance. Place the fingers of the left hand under the zip; press the zip in position. Work from the right side and roll the zip and seam over the fingers of the left hand to ease the fabric. Pin through all thicknesses, placing pins at right angles to the seam, through the fabric, and under the teeth or coil of the zip. Alternate the direction of the pins to distribute the slight ease evenly.

Tack a measured distance of ·9 to 1·2 cm ($\frac{3}{8}$ to $\frac{1}{2}$ inch) from the tacked seam, using a long and short tacking stitch. Use the tacking as a guide in stitching.

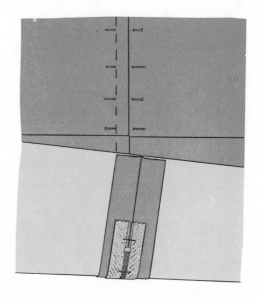

6. Adjust the Zipper Foot to the right of the needle. From the right side of the garment, stitch across the lower end, up along the zip, following the even line of tacking, and across the top end. Pull the thread ends to the underside and tie.

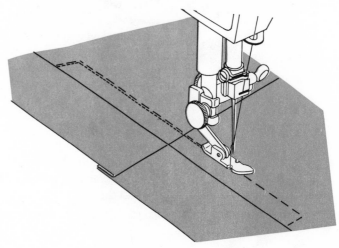

7. Remove the tacking. Turn the dress to the wrong side and remove the tacking under the back seam allowance by clipping every four or five stitches, then pulling the long thread. Press the work over the curve of a pressing mitt to retain the shape of the hipline. Cover it with a woollen pressing cloth to protect the fabric from shine.

A dress placket made in this way is almost invisible because the front seam overlaps the zip ·3 cm ($\frac{1}{8}$ inch) and the placket has been shaped to fit the curve of the hip.

HAND-FINISHED ZIP INSERTION

To add a professional touch, you can back-stitch the zip in by hand at the final step instead of top stitching by machine. If you are working with chiffons, sheers, velvets, or any other delicate fabrics, you must back-stitch because machine stitching is too harsh.

1. To finish by hand, follow the instructions given above up to *Step 6*, which is top stitching.

2. With a fine needle and matching thread, start working at the lower end of the zip. Fasten the thread end with two backstitches on the underside of the zip tape. Bring the needle through from the underside at the seamline. Take

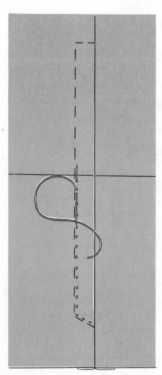

a backstitch across only one or two fabric threads; then bring the needle up through all thicknesses ·3 cm ($\frac{1}{8}$ inch) from the backstitch. Begin each additional backstitch just outside the preceding stitch. The stitches on the underside will be twice as long as those on the right side. Continue the stitches across the end, up the side along the tacked line, then across the top end. Push the needle through to the underside, and fasten the thread with two backstitches in the tape.

3. Turn the dress to the wrong side and machine-stitch the edge of the front

seam allowance to the zip tape for added support.

Remove the tacking. Press.

BLINDSTITCHED ZIP INSERTION

Blindstitching the final step of a zip insertion gives a finish which is almost invisible. The placket seam allowance should be 2 cm ($\frac{7}{8}$ inch) and extra should be allowed when the garment is cut.

1. Follow the instructions beginning on page 176, up to *Step 6*, which is top stitching.

Select the blindstitch zig-zag on the zig-zag machine, 1·5 mm (15) stitch length, and narrow stitch width. Adjust the Zipper Foot to the right of the needle.

2. Turn the dress to the wrong side. Place the lower end of the zip tape over the feed of the machine and turn back the front section of the dress to the tacking line, creating a soft fold. Place the work so that the straight

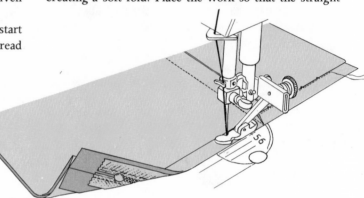

line of stitching is made through the seam allowance and zip tape, and the sidewards stitch pierces only a few threads of the soft fold. Stitch slowly. Pull the thread ends to the underside and tie.

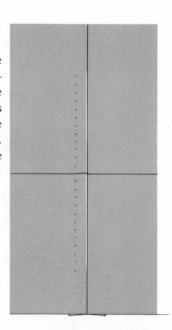

Sew the front seam allowance to the zip tape at both ends. Remove tackings. Press.

NO-PIN, NO-TACK METHOD

To use this method of inserting a zip, follow the rules below:

1. Turn the dress to the wrong side. Pin, then tack the side seams together the exact length of the opening. Press the seam open over the curve of a pressing mitt to retain the shape of the hipline. Stay-stitch ·9 cm ($\frac{3}{8}$ inch) from the seam edge on each side of the placket opening. Mark the length of the opening with pins.

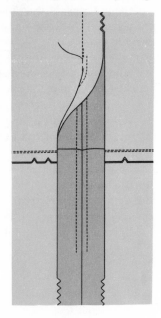

2. Adjust the Zipper Foot to the right of the needle. Open the zip and place it face down over the back seam allowance, with the edge of the teeth at the seamline and the end stop at the end of the opening. Stitch the tape to the seam allowance from bottom to top alongside the zip.

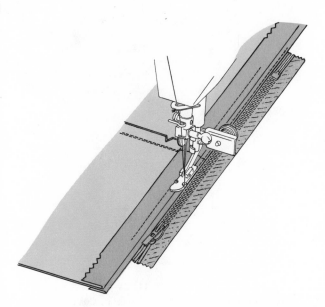

3. Adjust the Zipper Foot to the left of the needle.

Close the zip and turn it face up. Smooth back the seam allowance at the edge of the zip and stitch it to the tape.

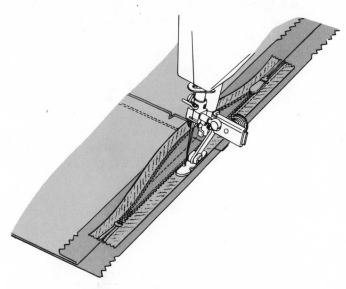

4. Turn the dress to the right side and work on the underside. Turn the zip face down, flat over the front seam allowance. Stitch across the lower end, up the front along the zip tape guideline, then across the top end. Pull the thread ends to the underside and tie. Remove tacking under the back seam allowance. Press.

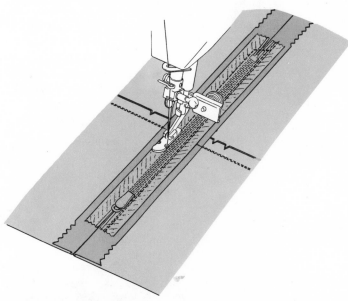

Skirt Placket Zip in Lapped Seam

A skirt-weight zip is used in shorts and slacks as well as skirts. It is a heavier zip designed to withstand strain and is inserted before the waistband is attached.

A skirt must be fitted in the same careful way as a dress. The opening in the left seam should be 2·5 cm (1 inch) longer than the teeth or coil of the zip. Compare the front and back seams of the opening to be sure they are the same length. Check the end of the permanent stitching to make certain that it is reinforced with back-stitching. Chalk or tack exactly on the seamline on each side of the opening.

1. Turn the skirt to the wrong side. Pin the seams together and tack on the seamline the exact length of the opening.

2. Press the seam open over a pressing mitt to retain the shape of the hipline. Mark the end of the opening by placing a pin through the seam only.

3. Fold under the back seam allowance ·3 cm ($\frac{1}{8}$ inch) from the tacked seam and place the folded edge over the right side of the zip tape with the pull-tab 2 cm ($\frac{3}{4}$ inch) (1·5 cm ($\frac{5}{8}$ inch) seam allowance plus ·3 cm ($\frac{1}{8}$ inch)) below the seam edge at the top, and the end stop ·3 cm ($\frac{1}{8}$ inch)

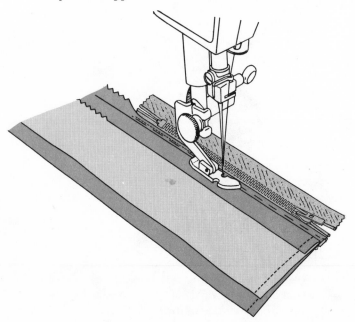

above the lower end of the opening; pin. This allows ·3 cm ($\frac{1}{8}$ inch) for ease throughout the length of the zip. Roll the zip and folded edge over the fingers of the left hand and pin the folded edge to the zip tape. Tack.

4. Replace the Presser Foot with the Zipper Foot, and adjust the Zipper Foot to the left of the needle. *Turn the*

pull-tab up to lessen bulk when stitching. Stitch from the lower end to the top near the edge of the fold. Remove tacking.

5. Turn the skirt to the right side. Turn the zip and back seam allowance flat against the front seam allowance with the *pull-tab still turned towards the top.* From the right side, roll the zip and seam over the fingers of the left hand to ease the fabric. Pin through all thicknesses, placing pins at right angles to the seam, through the fabric, and under the teeth portion of the zip. Alternate the direction of the pins to distribute the slight ease evenly. See illustration on page 177, *Step 5.*

Tack a measured 1·2 cm ($\frac{1}{2}$ inch) from the tacked seam, using a long and short tacking stitch. Use the tacking as a stitching guide.

6. Adjust the Zipper Foot to the right of the needle. Stitch across the lower end, then up along the zip, following the even line of tacking, to the waistline. Pull the thread ends to the underside and tie. (If hand sewing is used instead of machine stitching, follow the directions on page 178.)

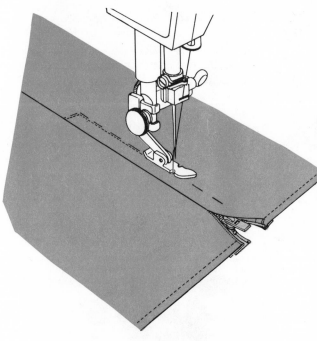

7. Remove the tacking. Press the work over a pressing mitt to retain the curve of the hipline. Cover it with a woollen press cloth to protect the fabric from shine. Trim the tape in line with the waistline seam edge.

TO ATTACH UNDERLAY

An underlay is usually placed under the zip to improve the fit of the skirt. It supports the underwrap of the waistband and the zip is less likely to stick.

The underlay may be either a double or a single lengthwise strip of the same fabric cut the length of the zip tape. If single, cut it 6 cm (2½ inches) wide, using the selvedge of the fabric for the finished edge. If double, cut it 13 cm (5 inches) wide, and fold it lengthwise through the centre; stitch near the fold and cut edge. Pink the edge.

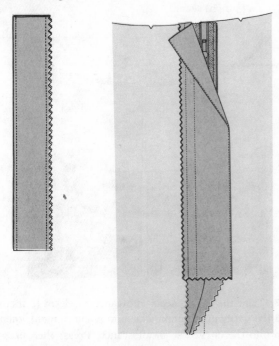

Turn the skirt to the wrong side. Place the underlay over the zip tape, keeping the cut edges even with the back seam edge. Pin only to the seam allowance. Turn the seam allowance and underlay away from the skirt and stitch the underlay to the seam allowance. Tack the lower end of the underlay to the front seam allowance. The skirt is now ready for the waistband.

Neckline or Sleeve Zip in Channel Seam

A neckline zip is usually inserted in a centre front or back seam at the neckline of a dress, kaftan or blouse, or in a sleeve seam at the wrist. An extra fine neckline zip is available for this purpose.

Insert a neckline zip before joining the front and back bodice at the shoulders and underarms since it is easier to work on a flat section than a partially assembled garment.

The length of the opening should be 2·5 cm (1 inch) longer than the metal or synthetic part of the zip. (The seam allowance at the neckline is 1·5 cm ($\frac{5}{8}$ inch), and ·9 cm ($\frac{3}{8}$ inch) provides space for crosswise stitching at each end of the zip.) You will not have to allow for ease since the zip is usually set into a straight grain seam. The seam below the opening should be permanently stitched and the end reinforced with backstitching.

1. Turn the garment to the wrong side. Pin the seams together and machine-tack the exact length of the opening.

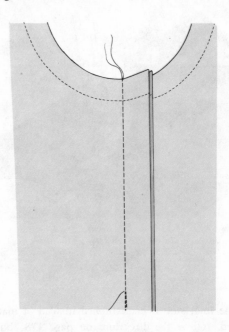

2. Press the seam, then press it open. Mark the end of the opening with a pin on the right side.

3. Turn the garment to the right side. Turn the zip *pull-tab up to lessen bulk when stitching.* Pin the zip in position, with the machine-tacked seam to the centre of the teeth or coil. Place the pull-tab at the top, ·6 cm (¼ inch) below the 1·5 cm ($\frac{5}{8}$ inch) seam allowance at the neckline, and the stop ·3 cm ($\frac{1}{8}$ inch) above the lower end of the opening. Place pins at right angles to the seam, through all thicknesses, and under the teeth or coil of the zip. Alternate the direction of

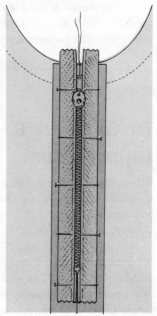

the pins. Tack by hand, a measured ·6 cm ($\frac{1}{4}$ inch) each side of the centre seam. Use the tacks as a guide in stitching.

4. Replace the Presser Foot with the Zipper Foot, and adjust the foot to the left of the needle. On the right side of the garment, stitch around the zip ·6 cm ($\frac{1}{4}$ inch) to the left of the centre seam, using the measured tacking as a guide. Pivot the fabric on the needle at the corners and take the same number of stitches on each side of the centre seam.

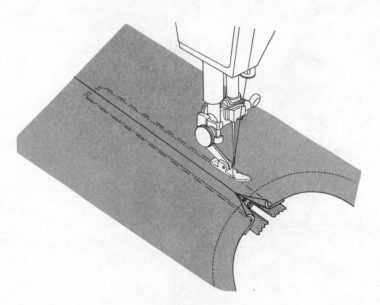

If the final step is backstitched instead of machine-stitched, follow the directions on page 178; but also machine-stitch the edge of the seam allowance to the zip tape on each side for added support.

5. Remove both hand and machine tackings. Press carefully. Trim the zip tape in line with the neckline seam edge. The garment is ready for the neckline finish.

Zip in Centre Back Lapped Seam

Before inserting the zip in a centre back opening, join the dress sections at the shoulder line, underarm and waistline seams.

Leave an opening 2·5 cm (1 inch) longer than the metal or synthetic part of the zip. (The neckline seam allowance is 1·5 cm ($\frac{5}{8}$ inch) and ·9 cm ($\frac{3}{8}$ inch) provides space above and below the zip.) You will not need to allow for ease as a centre seam is usually on the straight grain of the fabric. Check that the end of the permanent stitching in

the skirt is reinforced with backstitching. Compare the right and left seams of the opening; they must be the same length.

TO FINISH NECKLINE

Before inserting the zip, finish the neckline as explained here to eliminate bulk across the top of the zip.

1. Pin the facing to the neckline. Start stitching 2 cm ($\frac{3}{4}$ inch) from the seam edge that is on the right-hand side when the dress is worn, and continue to within 3·2 cm (1$\frac{1}{4}$ inches) of the seam edge on the left-hand side, taking a 1·5 cm ($\frac{5}{8}$ inch) seam.

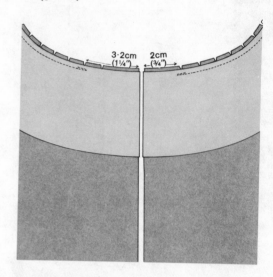

2. Trim the facing seam allowance to ·3 cm ($\frac{1}{8}$ inch) and the garment seam allowance to ·6 cm ($\frac{1}{4}$ inch); then clip into the curved seam allowance. Press; then press the seam open. Turn the facing to the underside, ease it under slightly at the seamline, and tack. Press. Under-stitch the seam to prevent the facing from rolling out of place. Fold and press the garment and facing on the seamline, from the stitching to the centre opening.

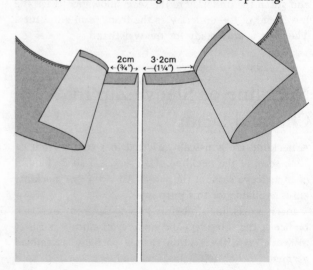

TO INSERT THE ZIP

Trim the waistline seam allowance on the right-hand side when the dress is worn, to ·6 cm (¼ inch) from the centre seam edge to a depth of 2 cm (¾ inch) and trim the seam allowance on the opposite side to ·6 cm (¼ inch) from the centre seam edge to a depth of 3·2 cm (1¼ inches). This removes bulk under the zip seam.

1. Turn the dress to the wrong side. Turn the neckline facing away from the garment. Pin the centre seams together, carefully matching waistline seams and folded seams at the neckline. (Check the seam edges of the opening are the same length.) Machine-tack the exact length of the opening. If the seam allowance that is on the left-hand side when the dress is worn is less than 1·5 cm (⅝ inch), stitch seam binding to the edge.

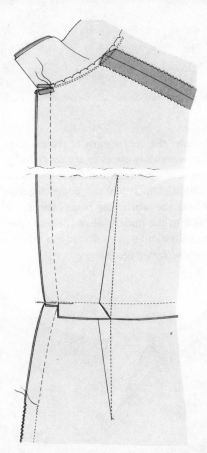

2. Press, then press the seam open. Mark the end of the opening by placing a pin through the seamline only.

3. On the right-hand side when the dress is worn, fold the seam allowance under ·3 cm (⅛ inch) from the machine-tacked seam. Pin the folded edge over the right side of the zip tape, with the pull-tab at the top, ·6 cm (¼ inch) below the folded neckline seam, and the stop ·3 cm (⅛ inch) above the end of the opening. Pin the seam allowance to the zip tape below the opening. Tack by hand.

4. Adjust the Zipper Foot to the left of the needle. *Turn the pull-tab up* to lessen bulk when stitching. Stitch from the lower end of the zip up to the neck-line, close to the folded edge. Tie thread ends at the neckline. Remove hand tacking.

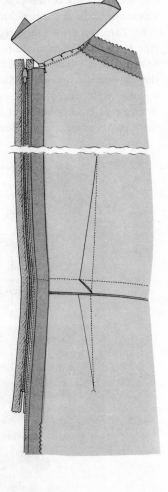

5. Snip into the zip tape on each side of the neckline, almost to the cord; then trim close to the cord up to the end of the tape.

Turn ends of the tape away from the pull-tab and tack them to the seam allowance, using matching thread.

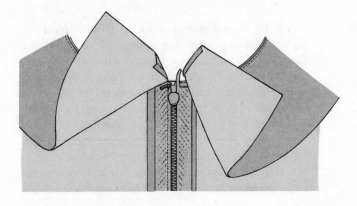

Cut off the ends of the tape to 1·2 cm (½ inch). This eliminates bulk at the neckline.

6. Turn the dress to the right side. With the *pull-tab still turned up*, turn the zip and seam allowance flat against the left-hand side of the seam allowance. Press the zip against the seam with the left hand. Working from the right side, place pins at right angles to the seam, through all thicknesses, and under the teeth or coil of the zip. Alternate the direction of the pins.

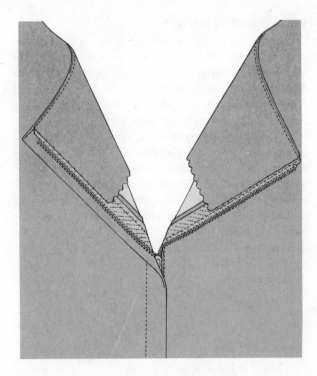

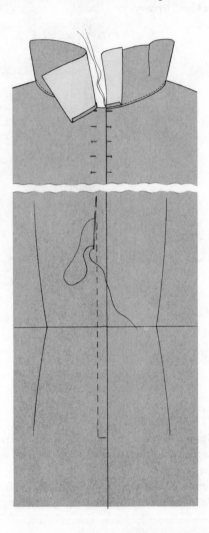

Tack by hand a measured 1·2 cm (½ inch) from the machine-tacked seam, using a long and short tacking stitch. Use the tacking as a guide in stitching.

7. Adjust the Zipper Foot to the right of the needle. On the right side of the dress, stitch across the lower end and up the side to the neckline, following the evenly tacked line. Pull threads to the underside and tie. (When backstitching is used instead of machine stitching, follow the directions on page 178.) Remove hand tacking, then turn the dress to the wrong side and remove the machine tacking under the seam allowance.

8. Fold under the centre ends of the neckline facing, and trim the seam allowances to 1·2 cm (½ inch). Pin the folded edges to the zip tape and finish by hand, using a hemming stitch. Slip-stitch the edges together at the neckline where the fabric fold covers the zip. Press.

Sew a hook to the underside of the fold covering the zip at the neckline and make a thread eye on the opposite side. See *Thread Eye*, page 207.

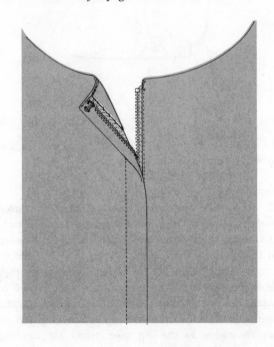

Continuous Bound Placket

The continuous bound placket may be in a seam or slash. It is found in sleeve openings where a cuff or band is used and in children's dresses.

PLACKET IN A SLASH

1. Mark the position for the slash, and stay-stitch round the point, using a 1·5 mm (20) stitch length. Take one stitch across the point to allow it to turn through smoothly. Press. Slash the opening to within about two threads of the point.

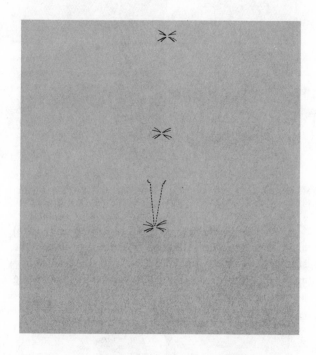

stitching line on the underside, enclosing the seam allowances. Pin. Either machine-stitch or finish by hand, using a short hemming stitch. Press.

Fold the strip under on the side which will overlap,

2. Cut a strip of fabric on the lengthwise grain, 3·2 cm (1¼ inches) wide and twice the length of the opening. If the fabric is heavy, cut the strip 4 cm (1½ inches) wide.

At one end, pin the strip to the opening, right sides together, keeping the cut edges even. *Draw the point of the slash back ·5 cm ($\frac{3}{16}$ inch) from the edge of the strip* and pin at the point; then pin at the opposite end, keeping the cut edges even. Pin at intervals between. Tack.

3. From the garment side, stitch ·6 cm (¼ inch) from the *edge of the strip*, beginning at the end and stitching to the point. With the needle in the fabric, raise the presser foot and fold the garment back, forming a 'V' at the point; then lower the foot and stitch to the opposite end of the opening. Reinforce the ends with back-stitching. Press, then turn the strip away from the garment and press the seam allowance over the strip.

4. Fold under the free edge of the strip ·6 cm (¼ inch) and crease. Then fold the strip over the seam edge to the

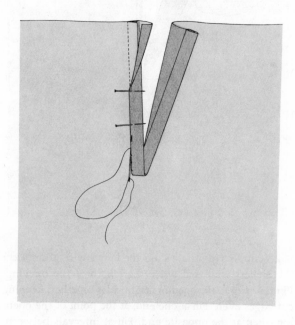

as illustrated. Press. The fabric strip will not show in the opening.

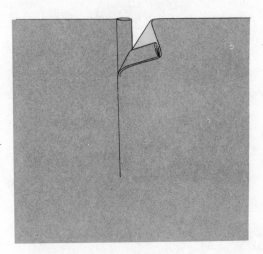

PLACKET IN A SEAM

1. Stitch the seam below the opening. Reinforce the end with backstitching. Snip into the seam allowances at the end of the opening, then trim the seam allowances to ·6 cm (¼ inch) from this point to the end of the opening. Press the seam open below the placket opening.

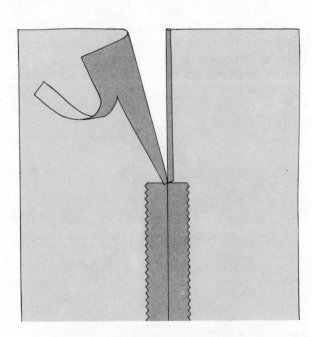

2. Cut a strip of fabric on the lengthwise grain 4 cm (1½ inches) wide and twice the length of the opening. Pin the strip to the opening, right sides together, keeping cut edges even. Pin at one end, at the point of the opening, then at the opposite end. Pin at intervals between.

3. Stitch from the garment side, taking a ·6-cm (¼-inch) seam. Reinforce the ends with backstitching. Press, then turn the strip away from the garment and press the seam allowance over the strip.

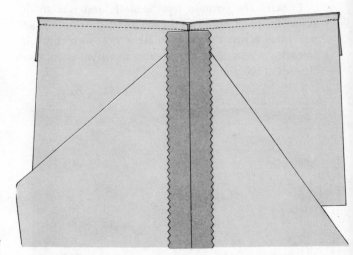

4. Fold under the free edge of the strip ·6 cm (¼ inch) and crease. Then turn the strip over the seam edge to the stitching line on the underside, enclosing the seam allowances. Pin. Either machine-stitch or finish by hand, using a short hemming stitch.

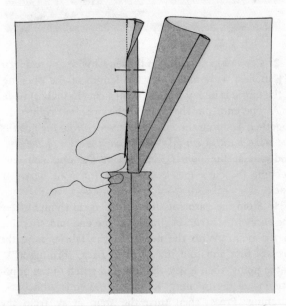

Fold the strip under on the side which will overlap, as illustrated in the slash above. Press. The fabric strip will not show in the opening.

Hems and Hem Finishes

The hem is your last step in finishing the garment. It is usually finished by hand and the stitches should be invisible on the right side. However, a narrow hem, which is used for frills and sashes, may be finished either by machine or by hand. Correct pressing is essential in making a smooth hem; do not forget it.

The hem in a skirt should never be obvious but should be wide enough to hang in smooth, graceful lines. A slim skirt usually needs a deeper hem than a full skirt. The hem depth marked on the pattern is generally the depth you should use, since it is appropriate for the style of the garment and the fabric recommended. If you want a deeper hem than that shown on the pattern – for example, to create a shadow effect in a full-skirted dress made of sheer fabric – allow for the extra depth when cutting the garment.

Although fashion dictates to some extent the length of skirts, take into consideration your figure proportions as well.

Checking the Fit of the Dress

Try on the dress for the final inspection, wearing the foundation garment, slip and shoes you will wear with the dress. Review the general fitting. Check that the front and back centre line tackings are in place and hang perpendicularly to the floor; that the waist seam is in the right place. If any adjustment in fit is necessary, make it before marking the skirt length. A skirt that hangs well is the result of correct pattern adjustments, careful cutting with the grain of the fabric, and proper pressing.

If your dress has a bias or semi-bias skirt, always allow it to hang overnight with the side seams hand tacked, threads loose at the ends, before stitching any seams. Then, after the skirt is stitched, hang it again overnight before marking the skirt length so that the true bias will drop.

Preparing the Hem

To ensure a smooth and inconspicuous hemline, follow closely the steps given below. They are basic for all hems. *Step 4*, however, will vary with the fabric, the style of the skirt and individual preference.

STEP 1: MARK THE HEMLINE
Mark the skirt an even distance from the floor. Use chalk skirt marker on a stand. To avoid any unnecessary movement of posture or position, the person taking the skirt

length should move round the model. If the lining is attached to the waistline only, mark the hemline in the skirt and in the lining separately.

For full-length evening dresses, the model should stand on a stool or platform which will allow the dress to hang freely over the edge.

STEP 2: FOLD THE HEM
Turn the hem on the chalk line and place pins at right angles to the folded edge. The fold of the hem should follow an even line. Should slight irregularities occur, owing to the sway of the body or the unevenness of the floor, adjust the hem fold accordingly. However, *do not make radical adjustments*. Ease the hem down slightly at the seams to allow for the fold over the seam allowances.

Tack with silk thread ·6 cm (¼ inch) from the folded edge. Press to sharpen the crease, sliding the iron along the lengthwise grain of the fabric. See *Hems*, page 75.

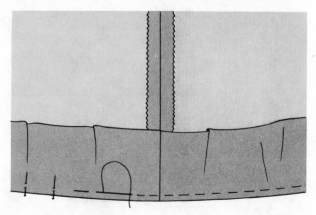

STEP 3: MAKE THE HEM AN EVEN DEPTH

Lay the skirt on a flat surface with the right side down and work from the hem side. Measure and chalk-mark the desired hem depth. Then cut away the surplus fabric. Trim all seam allowances to half their depth from fold to hem edge.

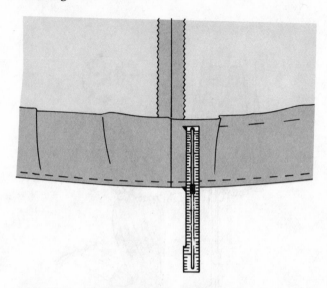

STEP 4: FINISH THE HEM

A variety of methods for finishing hems are given below. Choose the one you prefer, keeping in mind the fabric you are working with and the shape of the skirt at the hemline.

Finishes for Skirt Hems

EDGE-STITCHED HEM

Edge-stitching provides a sturdy hem finish for cottons which must withstand repeated laundering and for linings and mountings which are hemmed separately from the skirt.

1. Prepare the hem for the finish, following the three steps outlined above.

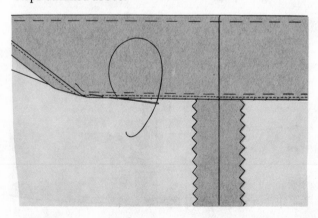

2. Fold the free edge of the hem under ·6 cm (¼ inch) and stitch near the edge of the fold. Press. Pin the hem to the skirt, matching seams and centre lines. Tack by hand. Finish using a slip stitch. See page 228. Remove tackings and press.

PINKED HEM – BLIND HERRINGBONE

The pinked hem is suitable for fabrics that do not fray easily and are likely to show a line on the outside of the skirt if other hem finishes are used – for example, silk, crêpe, jersey, double knit, and firmly woven woollens. The blind herringbone is invisible and holds the hem securely without strain. This is also known as a *French hem*.

1. Prepare the hem for the finish, following the three steps outlined on page 187.

2. Pink the free edge of the hem, then stitch ·6 cm (¼ inch) from the edge, using a 1 mm (20) stitch length.

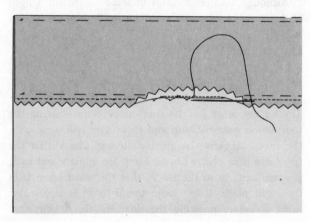

3. Pin, then hand-tack the hem to the skirt just below the stitching line, matching seams and centre lines. With the left hand, fold back the pinked edge along the tacking and herringbone below the hem edge and between the hem and skirt. Work from left to right with the needle pointed to the left. Hold the hem edge between the thumb and index finger. Take a stitch in the underside of the hem edge, then take a stitch in the skirt, catching only a single thread of the fabric. Alternate the stitches in a zig-zag fashion. Do not tighten this hand stitch, but knot the stitches frequently. Remove tackings, and press.

BOUND HEM

Hems in heavy or napped woollens and fabrics that fray easily are often finished with a bound edge of rayon or silk bias binding. They do not show when the garment is worn.

1. Prepare the hem for the finish, following the three steps outlined on page 187.

2. Bind the free edge of the hem, using the Binder and a medium-width open zig-zag stitch. Press.

3. Pin the free edge of the hem to the skirt, matching centre lines and seams; then, tack just below the binding. Herringbone between the hem and skirt, as instructed for a *Pinked Hem – Blind Herringbone*, above. Knot the stitch at frequent intervals. Never pull the thread tight enough to show on the right side of the fabric. Remove tackings, and press over a pressing pad.

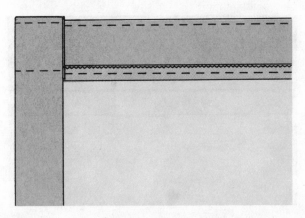

a soft fold. Place the work so that the straight stitches are made on the hem edge and the side stitches pierce only one or two threads of the soft fold.

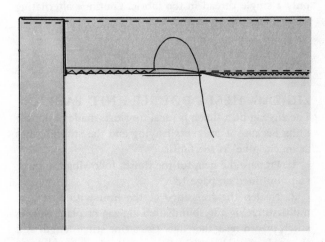

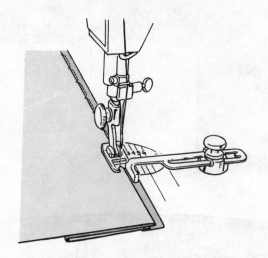

BLINDSTITCHED HEM

Blindstitching provides a durable hem finish that is almost invisible on the right side of the garment. It is especially suited to children's clothes, straight and full skirts and curtains. Taped, bound, edge-stitched or unfinished hem edges may be blindstitched by machine with equal ease.

1. Prepare the hem for the finish, following the three steps outlined on page 187.

2. When straight or bias seam binding is used, pin the binding to the hem ·6 cm ($\frac{1}{4}$ inch) from the free edge. Stitch, using a narrow zig-zag stitch and 2 to 1·5 mm (12 to 15) stitch length. Press.

3. Tack the hem to the skirt ·6 cm ($\frac{1}{4}$ inch) from the free edge.

4. Use the blindstitch zig-zag; select a narrow to medium stitch width and 1·5 to 1 mm (12/15 to 20) stitch length. (The selection is determined by the weight and texture of your fabric.) The blindstitch zig-zag produces four straight stitches separated by a single side stitch to the left.

Place the hem edge over the feed of the machine; turn back the bulk of the fabric to the tacking line, creating

Attach the Seam Guide to the machine and adjust it over the right toe of the Presser Foot so that it rests next to the soft fold. When stitching, feed the fold against the edge of the guide. When you have finished, swing the Seam Guide out of position before raising the Presser Foot. Remove tackings, and press.

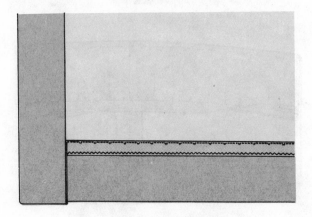

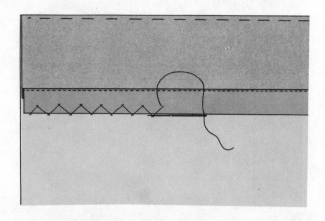

HERRINGBONE HEM

The herringbone hem is suitable for loosely woven woollens and raw silk. The hem edge may be finished with pinking as described on page 188, or with straight or bias seam binding and then herringboned in place.

1. Prepare the hem for the finish, following the steps outlined on page 187.

2. Neaten the free edge of the hem.

3. Pin, then tack the hem to the skirt ·3 cm ($\frac{1}{8}$ inch) from the finished edge, matching centre lines and seams. Herringbone in place. Work from left to right with the needle pointed to the left. Take a stitch in the binding, then one in the skirt over the edge of the hem, catching only a single thread in the fabric. Continue alternating the stitches. Press.

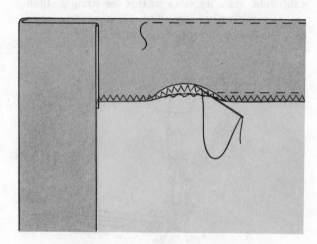

ZIG-ZAG HEM – DOUBLE-KNIT FABRIC

The zig-zag hem finish is ideal for skirts made of double knits because it prevents fraying and the stitching has as much 'give' as the fabric.

1. Prepare the hem for the finish, following the three steps outlined on page 187.

2. Neaten the free edge of the hem with a row of multi-stitch zig-zag, blindstitch zig-zag or plain zig-zag stitch placed near the edge. Use a fine stitch length and the widest stitch width. Press. Trim the edge close to the stitching.

3. Pin, then tack the free edge of hem to the skirt just below the zig-zag stitching, matching seams and centre lines. Finish with a blind herringbone between the hem and skirt, as instructed for the *Pinked Hem – Blind Herringbone*, page 188.

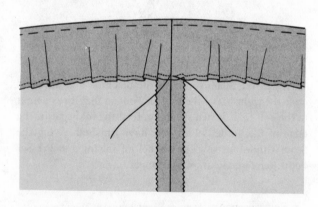

GORED AND SLIGHTLY FLARED SKIRTS

1. Prepare the hem for the finish, following the three steps outlined on page 187.

2. Control the fullness that exists with a line of stitching placed exactly ·6 cm ($\frac{1}{4}$ inch) from the free edge of the hem and extending from seam to seam. Pin the hem to the skirt, matching seams and centre lines. Draw the bobbin thread and ease the fullness between the seams. Be careful not to draw in the top of the hem too much. The hem must conform exactly to the body of the skirt.

3. Place the hem over the curve of a pressing mitt and shrink out the fullness by pressing with steam.

4. Bias seam binding is often used on a hem with fullness. For silk and synthetic fabrics, use rayon or silk bias binding. Pre-shape the seam binding by steam press-

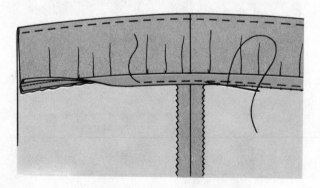

ing; pin, then stitch it to the hem edge, barely covering the control line of stitching. At the joining, fold under the end and overlap the binding about ·9 cm ($\frac{3}{8}$ inch). Press. (Binding may be applied as an inside seam, as illustrated, or it may be top-stitched.)

5. Pin the free edge of the hem to the skirt, matching seams and centre lines. Tack ·3 cm ($\frac{1}{8}$ inch) from the edge. Finish by hand, using a blind hemming stitch. See page 228. When finished, fasten the threads with two tiny backstitches in the hem edge. Remove tackings and press.

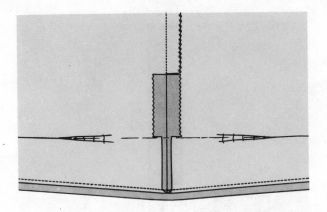

HEM ACROSS PLEAT IN SKIRT (*Upper right*)

Seams on the inside fold of a pleat must be layered and pressed open in the hem area to eliminate bulk.

1. After you have marked the hem, press the seam open to the point where the hem will be sewn to the skirt. Trim the seam edges within the hem area to half their width. Slash seam allowances to within a few threads of the stitching at the top of the hem.

2. Tack the hem, and finish according to the method best suited to the fabric.

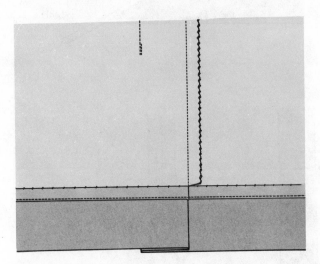

HEM IN SLIT SKIRT

The pencil-slim skirt, without a pleat, is often slit at the seams to allow for greater freedom of movement. (For instructions on lining the skirt, see page 98.) To hem the skirt, proceed as follows:

1. Check that the end of the seam above the slit is reinforced with backstitching. Pin, then machine-tack the seams together in the slit, beginning exactly at the top of the slit.

Stay-stitch 1·2 cm ($\frac{1}{2}$ inch) from the seam edge on each side of the slit. Press, then press the seam open.

(*Continued on following page*)

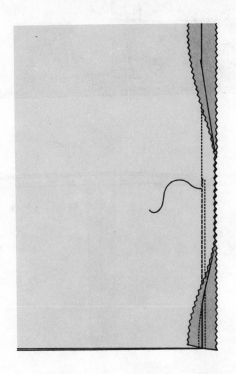

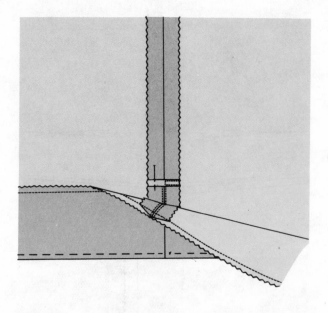

2. Cut a strip of pre-shrunk straight seam binding to fit the width of the open seam allowance. Fold through the centre and press. Pin the binding to the seam allowance, keeping the lower edge even with the top edge of the machine-tacked opening. Turn the seam allowance away from the skirt, and stitch the binding to one side of the seam allowance, as illustrated; then stitch the opposite side the same way. Follow this procedure for slits in the lining. The stay tape reinforces the ends in the slits and prevents splitting.

3. Prepare the hem for the finish, following the steps outlined on page 187.

4. Remove the machine tacking in the slit. Finish the hems in the skirt and lining separately, following the method best suited to the fabric. Ease the hem under slightly on each side of the slit, and pin. Slip-stitch in place.

HEM IN CIRCULAR SKIRT

To ensure a smooth hemline, the hem in a circular skirt should be narrow. A wide hem is bulky. Use rayon or silk bias binding for the finish. Before marking the hem, hang the skirt for 24 hours to allow for any 'dropping'.

1. Mark the hem as instructed in *Step 1*, page 187. Trim away the excess fabric ·9 cm ($\frac{3}{8}$ inch) below the marking.

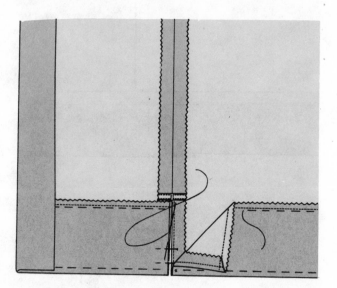

2. Pin bias seam binding ·6 cm ($\frac{1}{4}$ inch) from the edge of the skirt, right sides together. Apply seam binding as an inside seam, as illustrated. Stitch, guiding the fabric in both the front and the back of the needle to prevent puckering or stretching. Cut off corners where seams cross. Press.

3. Turn the binding to the underside, then fold the skirt ·3 cm ($\frac{1}{8}$ inch) beyond the binding and tack by hand. Press.

4. Tack the hem to the skirt near the edge of the binding. Finish by hand, using a blind hemming stitch or slip stitch. Remove tackings and press.

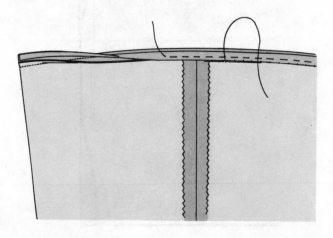

Horsehair braid is often used to give stiffness to circular hems in evening, cocktail and wedding dresses. Prepare the hem the same as above.

1. Tack 2·5-cm (1-inch) horsehair braid to the right side of the hem, edges even. Stitch ·3 cm ($\frac{1}{8}$ inch) from the edge. Press. (*Illustrated at top of next page*)

2. Turn the horsehair braid to the underside; fold the hem ·3 cm ($\frac{1}{8}$ inch) beyond the stitching line, and pin.

The lower edge of the horsehair will extend to the hem fold.

3. Work on the right side, and hand-sew the horsehair to the skirt, just above the ·3-cm (⅛-inch) hem, using a fine backstitch. See page 230.

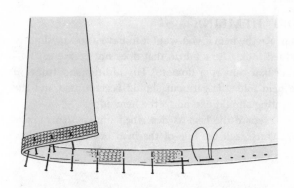

SPLICED HEM

Heavy woollens sometimes resist the shaping and easing required to make a smooth circular hem. Should this be the case, use the following method. (This type of skirt usually has a lining that extends nearly to the hem fold.)

1. Prepare the hem for the finish, following the three steps outlined on page 187.

2. Cut narrow wedges in the hem at regular intervals, several inches apart. Do not cut deeper than 2·5 cm (1 inch) from the hem fold.

Bring the cut edges together with a line of machine stitching ·6 cm (¼ inch) from the free edge. Darn the slashes together with matching silk thread or a thread drawn from the weave of the fabric.

3. Pink the free edge. Finish with a herringbone stitch between the hem and skirt as instructed on page 188.

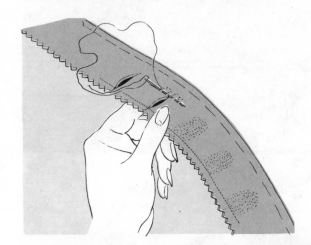

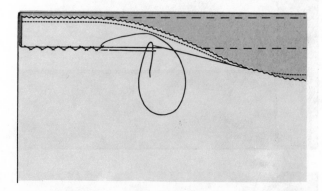

DOUBLE-STITCHED HEM

Wide hems, or hems in heavy fabrics, sometimes tend to sag because one line of stitching is insufficient for the weight of the hem. To prevent this, stitch the hem twice – once through the centre and again at the free edge. The two rows of stitches distribute the weight of the hem, and the hem is not visible in the finished skirt.

1. Prepare the hem for the finish, following the three steps outlined on page 187.

2. Finish the hem edge, using the method best suited to the fabric. Pin, then hand-tack the centre of the hem to the skirt, matching centre lines and seams. Fold back the hem on the tacking line, and herringbone between the hem and the skirt as instructed for a *Pinked Hem – Blind Herringbone*, page 188. Be careful not to pull the stitches too tight or they will show on the right side of the garment.

3. Pin, then tack the free edge of the hem to the skirt, matching centre lines and seams. Finish by hand, using a herringbone stitch between the hem and the skirt.

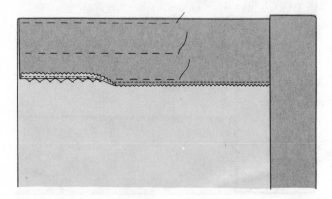

SOFT HEMLINE

Interface the hem if you want it to have a soft or slightly padded look. Use a fabric that does not crease easily – either hair canvas or domette. For additional softness in the hem fold, the garment should be mounted and the mounting should extend to the hem edge.

1. Prepare the hem as described under *Step 1*, page 187. Trace tack the line of the hem but do not fold or

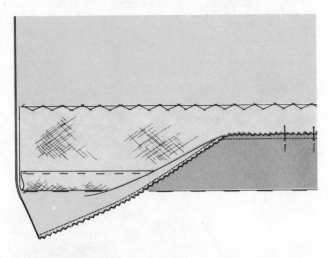

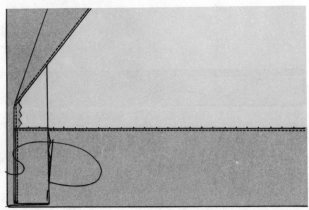

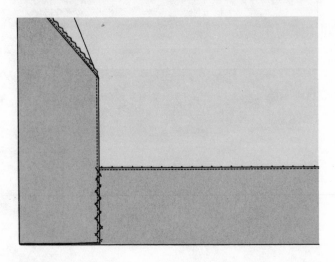

crease it. Mark the hem depth as described under *Step 3*, page 188, and finish the free edge as required by the fabric.

2. Cut interfacing on the true bias 5 cm (2 inches) wider than the hem and the length required plus 2·5 cm (1 inch) for seam allowances. Allow extra length so you can join the bias on straight grain. See *Joining Bias Strips*, page 244. Turn the interfacing up 2·5 cm (1 inch) along one edge, creating a soft fold. Pin, then tack 2 cm (¾ inch) from the soft fold. Take small stitches, spacing them about ·6 cm (¼ inch) apart, secure the thread because this is permanent tacking which will prevent the interfacing from slipping at the hemline.

Place the interfacing over the underside of the garment and align the soft fold with hemline tacking. Join ends on straight grain by lapping 2·5 cm (1 inch) and tacking together. Pin the interfacing in place along top edge and herringbone. Take a stitch through interfacing and mounting, then a stitch in only the mounting over the interfacing edge so that stitches will not show on the right side. Continue alternating the stitches. Press.

3. Turn the hem over the interfacing and hand-tack in place, using silk thread. (The interfacing is 2·5 cm (1 inch) wider than the hem.) Finish by hand, using herringbone stitch. Take the stitches through only the hem and interfacing. To keep the hem fold soft, do not press it, but do press along the line of the hand stitches. Remove all tackings.

A garment with this type of hem is generally lined, and the lining extends nearly to the hem fold, covering the interfacing.

HEMS AT CORNERS

When the skirt of a garment is open all the way down the front or back, the opening is faced and you have a corner to deal with.

1. Prepare the hem for the finish, following the three steps outlined on page 187. However, extend the hem across the facing at the opening.

2. Finish the hem, using the method best suited to the fabric. (The edge-stitched finish is shown in the illustration.) Remove tackings and press.

3. Fold the facing to the underside and press. Pin through the centre of the facing, catching the hem beneath. Place the pins parallel to the facing edge. Fold the facing back on the pinned line and catch it to the hem by hand to prevent it slipping out of place. Turn the free edge against the hem and pin; then herringbone it to the hem.

If the hem is not cut out under the facing, the skirt can be lengthened later if necessary.

HEM WITH MITRED CORNER

Hems in linens are usually mitred at the corners to remove bulk.

1. Fold the hem along all edges, measuring the width evenly. Press. Fold under ·6 cm ($\frac{1}{4}$ inch) on the free edge and press.

2. Turn the hem away from the fabric. Turn the corner towards the inside, folding the lengthwise grain to the crosswise grain with the diagonal fold crossing exactly at the junction of the lengthwise and crosswise folds of the hem. Press. The diagonal fold indicates the exact position for stitching the mitre.

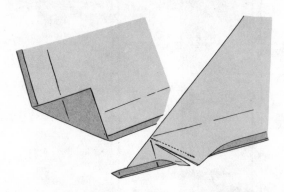

3. Fold the lengthwise hem over the crosswise hem, right sides together, matching the crease on the diagonal line. Pin, then stitch, extending the stitching as far as the first fold of the hem. Back-stitch at each end.

4. Trim the seam to ·6 cm ($\frac{1}{4}$ inch) and cut off the corner at the hem fold. Press, then press the seam open over the pointed end of a seamboard.

5. Turn the hem to the underside and carefully tack the free edge in place. Linens may be finished with hem-stitching, a decorative zig-zag stitch, machine stitching or hand stitching.

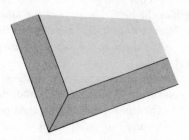

Narrow Hem Finishes

A narrow hem is used on frills, ties, scarves, lingerie, aprons, blouses, sashes in children's clothes and circular skirts of evening and cocktail dresses. The hem may be finished by hand or by machine, depending on where it is used and the type of fabric.

MACHINE-STITCHED HEM

A machine-stitched hem is used to finish the edges of lingerie, frills and sashes in children's clothes and aprons, and frills on curtains. The Hemmer Foot is a must for this, for it makes a perfectly turned narrow hem without any tacking or pressing on your part. See *Hemmer Foot*, page 283.

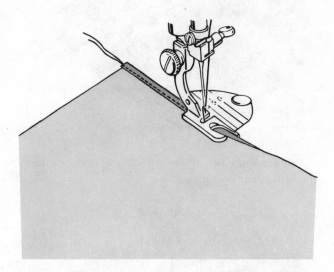

Cut the edge of the fabric evenly on the lengthwise or crosswise grain or on a true bias. To prevent the fabric from stretching when it is cut on the bias, place a row of stitching near the edge, using a short stitch. Press, then trim as close to the stitching as possible before placing the fabric in the Hemmer Foot.

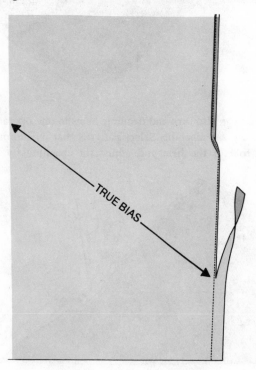

TRUE BIAS

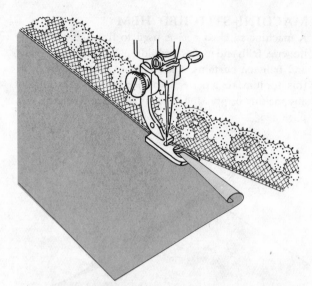

appropriate stitch length and stitch width; then hem from the right side of the fabric.

A soft shell edge makes an attractive finish for lingerie and many delicate fabrics. To obtain this effect, set the selectors on the machine for either the blindstitch or the multi-stitch zig-zag; then hem with the fabric right side up.

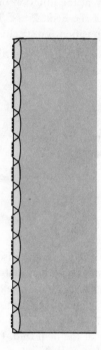

You can apply lace, if you are using it, over or under the hem in one operation.

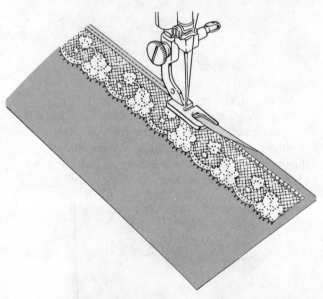

You can also turn and decorate hems in one operation on a zig-zag machine. Select patterns that will form on the fold of the hem and adjust the machine for the

To make a ·6-cm (¼-inch) hem or one slightly wider, use the Presser Foot and turn the fabric by hand the entire length of the hem. The edge of the fabric must be cut evenly. Make a double-fold hem so that the cut edge will not be visible through the fabric. (*Illustrated at top of next page*)

You can turn the hem easily if you work on an ironing board. As you turn and measure each fold, pin through the fabric into the ironing board pad, then press.

1. Turn a measured ·6 cm (¼ inch) to the underside and pin along the cut edge. Press the fold. Then make the second turn a measured ·6 cm (¼ inch) from the fold and pin along the first fold; press the second fold.

2. Stitch near the folded edge, using a shorter stitch than that used to stitch the garment. If the hem is slightly wider than ·6 cm (¼ inch), tack before stitching.

If you plan to finish the hem with decorative zig-zag stitching, tack the hemline to form a guide for the top stitching (except on sheer fabrics where the hem edge is

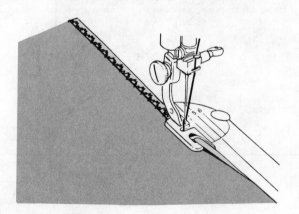

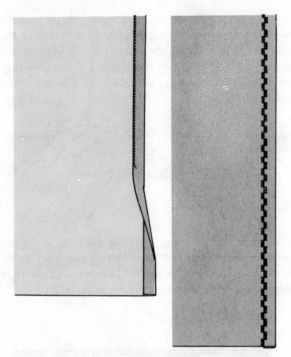

visible through the fabric). Select the stitch pattern desired, set the stitch length selector for satin stitching, and stitch from the right side of the fabric.

HAND-ROLLED HEM

A hand-rolled hem is a delicate finish, suitable for chiffon, crêpe, velvet, lace, wool and many other fabrics. It is the usual hem for scarves and full-skirted sheer evening, cocktail and wedding dresses.

1. Mark the hem as instructed under *Step 1* on page 187.

2. Machine-stitch ·3 cm (⅛ inch) below the marking for the hem, using a short stitch. Trim off the seam allowance ·3 cm (⅛ inch) below the stitching. Press.

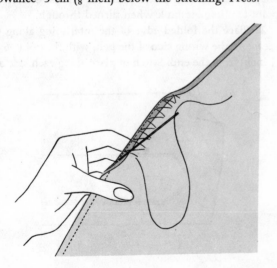

3. Fold the edge to the wrong side, barely beyond the stitching. Use a fine needle and matching thread. Working from right to left, or towards you, take a stitch through the fold; then, ·3 cm (⅛ inch) from the fold, take a stitch diagonally in the fabric, catching only a single thread. Continue, alternating the stitches and spacing them about ·3 cm (⅛ inch) apart. After making about six stitches, pull the thread to draw the fold down and form a neatly rolled hem.

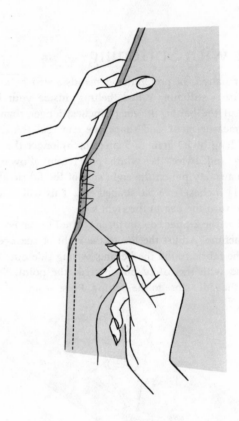

BLOUSE HEMS

A tuck-in blouse should have an unobtrusive finish at the lower edge so it will lie smoothly under the skirt. Two excellent methods are suggested.

1. For lightweight fabrics or those which fray easily, pink the lower edge of the blouse and fold it under ·6 cm (¼ inch). Stitch near the fold; then stitch again ·3 cm (⅛ inch) from the hem fold.

2. For fabrics that will not fray, pink the edge and stitch ·3 cm (⅛ inch) from the pinked edge, using a 1 mm (20) stitch length.

Overblouses or tunic tops should be finished with a hem 1·2 to 5 cm (½ to 2 inches) deep. Either machine or hand stitching may be used.

Belts and Belt Carriers

Belts can be a focal point in your outfit, providing a contrast in colour and texture, or they can be an integral part of the design made of matching fabric. Often you can alter the appearance of your dress by merely changing the belt.

The paragraphs below explain how to make several different kinds of belts and the carriers that hold your belt in place.

Belt with Stiffening

If your pattern or preference demands a stiff belt, you must use a stiffening called 'belting' inside your belt.

1. Cut the belting 10 cm (4 inches) longer than the waist measurement, and shape one end. Cut the fabric on the lengthwise grain, 2·5 cm (1 inch) longer than the belting and twice the width plus seam allowances. Fasten a safety pin on the right side of the fabric about 4 cm (1½ inches) from the shaped end. This will be used later to turn the belt to the right side.

2. Use the Zipper Foot in place of the Presser Foot on the machine. Adjust the toe to the right of the needle. Fold the fabric round the belting, wrong side out; turn the end with the safety pin towards the point. Stitch along the side, close to the belting. Press seam.

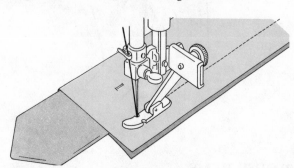

3. Move the fabric round the belting, bringing the seam to the centre. Press the seam open, then trim the seam allowances to ·6 cm (¼ inch). Stitch the point barely outside the edge of the belting. Back-stitch at each end. Trim the seam edges to ·6 cm (¼ inch). Withdraw the belting.

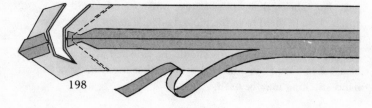

4. Turn the belt fabric to the right side by pushing the safety pin towards the open end and working the belt back over it. Work the end of the belt between the thumb and finger to bring the stitching to the very edge for a smooth point. Make sure the seam is in the centre and press the belt.

5. Insert the belting, cupping the edges slightly between the thumb and forefinger to ease your work. Press. If top stitching is desired, stitch round the right side of belt, close to the edge. Sew on the buckle.

Lined Soft Belt

1. Cut the fabric on the lengthwise grain 10 cm (4 inches) longer than the waist measurement and twice the width of the finished belt plus seam allowances. Fold lengthwise, wrong sides together, and crease.

Cut the interlining of lawn, lining or organdie on the lengthwise grain, the length of the fabric and twice the finished width. Crease lengthwise through the centre. Shape one end to a point, then cut off the end of the point to eliminate bulk when turned through.

2. Place the folded edge of the interlining along the crease on the wrong side of the belt, with the point ·6 cm (¼ inch) from the end. Stitch in place along each side and

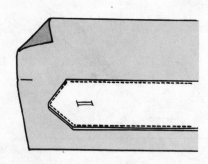

198

round the point. Press. Fasten a safety pin through the lining and fabric near the shaped end. This will be used later to turn the belt to the right side.

3. Fold the belt, right sides together, and pin the seam

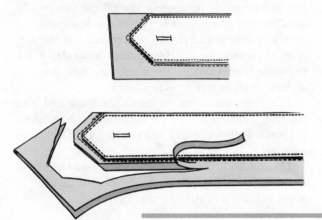

edges together. Stitch just outside the edge of the interlining along the side and shaped end, taking one stitch across the point. Back-stitch at each end. Trim seam edges. Press seam.

4. Turn the belt to the right side by pushing the safety pin towards the open end and working the belt back over it.

Carefully fold on the stitching line and press. If top stitching is desired, stitch round the right side of belt, close to the edge.

Contour Belt

Keeping the shape of the belt is your primary concern here. If you need to adjust the length of the belt, measure your waist and add 13 cm (5 inches). Measure the pattern and note the difference between the measurements. **To shorten,** take half the amount to be shortened from each end. **To lengthen,** add half the amount to be lengthened to each end. Make the belt as follows:

1. Cut the belt and lining of the same fabric, using the pattern as a guide. Stay-stitch the top section of the belt ·6 cm (¼ inch) from the seamline, in the seam allowance. Stay-stitch the lining barely outside the seamline in the seam allowance.

2. Use a double thickness of heavy Vilene for the interfacing. Pin the pattern over the Vilene and trace the outline of the pattern along the *seamline*. Machine several lines of stitching across the two layers of Vilene to hold

them together, using the multi-stitch zig-zag or straight stitching. Press. Cut out the Vilene interfacing, following the drawn lines.

3. Work on a flat surface with the wrong side of the top belt fabric up, and the pointed end to the left. Place the interfacing over the belt fabric and pin through the centre. Fold the seam edge of the fabric over the interfacing and pin, working from the centre to the outer edges. Snip into the seam edges on the inside curve almost to the stay stitching, and cut notches in the seam edges on the outside curve so that the seams will lie flat. Mitre the corners at the pointed end. Tack.

4. Herringbone the fabric seam allowance to the interfacing, taking the stitches through the seam allowance and interfacing only so that they are not visible on the right side. Press. (*Continued on following page*)

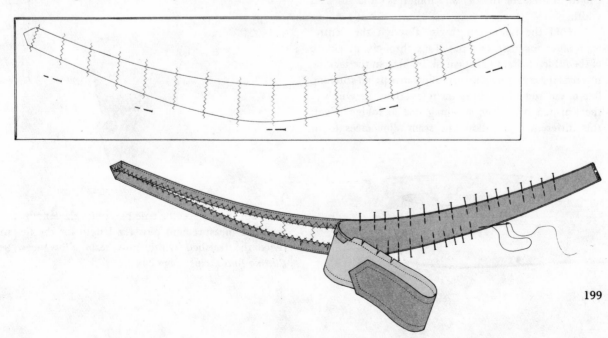

199

5. Trim the seam allowance to ·9 cm (⅜ inch) on all edges of the belt lining except the straight end which will be sewn to the buckle. Clip into the seam allowance on the inside curve and notch the seam allowance on the outside curve. Place the lining over the belt, wrong sides together, and pin through the centre for the length of the belt. Fold under the cut edge of the lining and pin just below the belt edge. Slip-stitch in place.

If top stitching is desired, stitch round the right side of the belt, close to the edge.

Narrow Tie Belt

The narrow tie belt may be from 2·5 to 4 cm (1 to 1½ inches) wide when cut on the lengthwise grain and about 1·2 cm (½ inch) when cut on the true bias. The ends should be long enough to wrap or tie in a knot or bow. A wide seam allowance is used as an interlining in the instructions below.

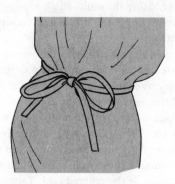

1. Cut the belt on the lengthwise grain or on the true bias, the length of the waistline measurement plus the length desired for the tie, and four times the finished width.

2. Fold the fabric lengthwise through the centre, right sides together, and pin. Tack through the centre of the folded belt. Stitch ·2 cm (1/16 inch) from the tacking towards the cut edge. The seam allowance (from stitching line to cut edge) is ·3 cm (⅛ inch) less than the width of the finished belt (from stitching line to folded edge); this difference will allow the seam allowances to fit

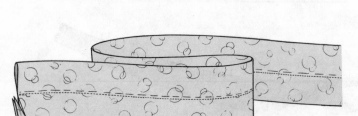

smoothly inside the finished belt. (The Seam Guide adjusted to the desired distance from the needle will help you guide and stitch the fabric evenly.)

3. Press, then fold one cut edge back on the stitching line and press the seam open. Cut off the corners diagonally from stitching to cut edge. If you are working with a lightweight fabric, leave both edges of the wide seam allowance for the interlining; however, if less thickness is required for the interlining, trim one edge of the seam allowance to ·6 cm (¼ inch).

4. Fasten a safety pin on the inside of one end, near the fold. Turn the belt to the right side by pushing the pin towards the open end and working the fabric back over it.

5. Carefully fold on the stitching line, and tack. Press. Turn the open ends into the belt ·6 cm (¼ inch) and pin. Slip-stitch the folded edges together.

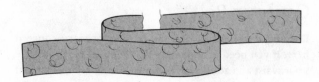

Sash Belt

The illustrated sash belt fits round the waistline, is crossed in the back and tied in the front. It is suitable for taffeta, satin and many cottons. The sash is made of a double thickness of fabric cut on the true bias. Widths may vary, but to make a 23-cm (9-inch) finished sash requires 105 cm (1⅛ yards) of 115-cm (45-inch) fabric so that only one join is necessary.

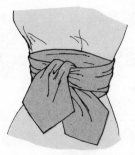

1. Cut the sash on the true bias twice the length of the waistline measurement plus the length for the tie, and twice the finished width plus seam allowances. See *Cutting Bias Strips*, page 244.

200

2. Fold the sash through the centre, right sides together, and pin. Shape the ends, and pin. Tack. Stitch, leaving an opening near the centre for turning the belt to the right side. Take one stitch across the points and back-stitch at each end of the seam. Trim one seam edge to ·3 cm ($\frac{1}{8}$ inch) and the other to ·6 cm ($\frac{1}{4}$ inch). Cut off the corners at the points, close to the stitching.

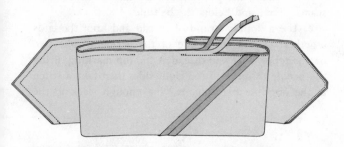

3. Turn the sash to the right side through the opening in the seam. Fold on the stitching line, and tack. Press. Slip-stitch the edges of the opening together. Remove tackings.

Corded Belt

Cording of various sizes may be used in belts. A single large cord or a plait of several cords is equally attractive. The cord is covered with a bias strip of soft satin or crêpe. See *Tubular Cording or Piping*, page 247.

1. When plaiting the cords, leave an unplaited length at each end for a tassel effect. At the end of the plait, tie one cord in a knot round the remaining cords. Tack the knot in place on the underside to prevent it coming loose.

2. Trim the ends evenly. Pull out 1·2 cm ($\frac{1}{2}$ inch) of the cord and cut it off. Turn the ends of the fabric to the

inside and slip-stitch them together, or knot each end. Ease the knot down to within 1·2 cm ($\frac{1}{2}$ inch) of the end. Tuck the ends under the knot with a heavy needle, and tack in place, taking care that the stitches are not visible.

Cummerbund with Featherboning

1. Cut the fabric for the cummerbund on the true bias the length of the waistline measurement plus 5 cm (2 inches) for seam allowances and overlap, and about 23 cm (9 inches) in width. See *Cutting Bias Strips*, page 244. Cut the lining of the same fabric, the length and width of the cummerbund. If the fabric is heavy, cut the lining of soft silk of the same colour.

2. Fold the cummerbund, with the front section 2·5 cm (1 inch) longer than the back (the front of the waistline is always larger than the back); and pin near the fold. Tack along the fold to mark the position of the seam on the right side.

3. Place the lining over the top fabric, right sides together, and pin on the seamline. Tack across the left front end and along each side. (Leave the opposite end open for turning the cummerbund to the right side.) Stitch the tacked edges, taking a 1·2-cm ($\frac{1}{2}$-inch) seam;

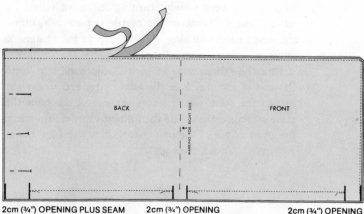

2cm (¾") OPENING PLUS SEAM   2cm (¾") OPENING   2cm (¾") OPENING

at the lower edge leave an opening of 2 cm ($\frac{3}{4}$ inch) at the closed end and at the marking for the right side seam, and 2 cm ($\frac{3}{4}$ inch) plus 1·2-cm ($\frac{1}{2}$-inch) seam allowance at the open end as illustrated. Reinforce each seam end with backstitching. (These three openings are for the bones, which you will insert between the two layers of fabric.)

4. Trim lining seam to ·3 cm ($\frac{1}{8}$ inch), fabric seams to ·6 cm ($\frac{1}{4}$ inch) and trim both seam edges across the openings to ·6 cm ($\frac{1}{4}$ inch). Press. Turn the cummerbund to

201

the right side. Fold on the stitching line and tack. Press.

5. At the open end, turn the seam edges to the inside 1·2 cm (½ inch), and pin together. Tack and press. Stitch from the right side, close to the edge. Stitch again ·9 cm (⅜ inch) from the first row of stitching to form the casing for the stay. Pull threads to the underside and tie. Stitch the opposite end in the same way to form the casing there.

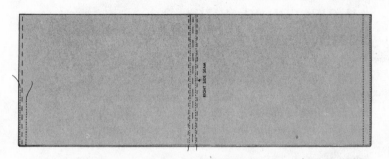

6. At the right side seam, pin and tack on each side of the marking to keep the bias from stretching while stitching. Space the tackings about 1·2 cm (½ inch) apart. Stitch on each side of the marking, spacing the lines of stitching ·9 cm (⅜ inch) apart. Pull threads to the underside and tie. Press. Remove tackings.

7. Cut three lengths of featherboning 9 cm (3½ inches) long. At the lower edge of the cummerbund, slip a featherbone into each opening between the rows of stitching and work it up to the top edge. Stitch the featherboning in place about ·3 cm (⅛ inch) from the top edge. Stitch very slowly, turning the hand wheel by hand. Turn the fabric on the needle and stitch again on the first line of stitching. Pull threads to the underside and tie.

Ease the fabric back on each featherbone stay until the end of the stay is at the lower edge and under the fold of the seam. Stitch across the end of the bone the same as before. Distribute the fullness evenly. Slip-stitch the open edges of the casing together. Use four hooks and eyes to fasten the ends.

Belt Carriers

Belt carriers are used to hold a belt in position. They may be hand-worked with a blanket stitch or chain stitch, or they may be made of fabric.

BLANKET-STITCH CARRIERS

1. Pin-mark the position for the carriers at the side seams, above and below the beltline.

2. Use a double strand of thread and knot the ends together. On the underside of the garment, take two backstitches to tie the thread at the top marking. Bring the needle through to the right side, then take a stitch at the opposite marking, leaving enough slack in the

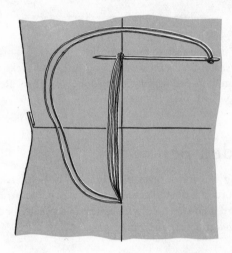

thread to fit over the belt. Work back and forth two or three times, always allowing the same amount of slack. Blanket-stitch over the strands of thread, drawing the stitches firmly. Fasten the thread securely on the underside with two backstitches.

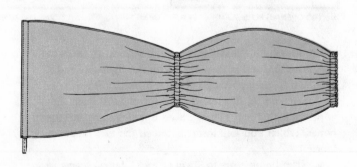

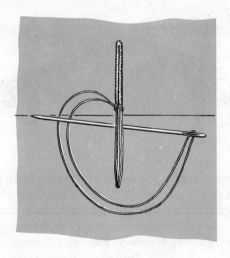

CHAIN-STITCH CARRIERS

1. Mark the position for the carrier the same as above.
2. Use a double thread and knot the ends together. On the underside, take two backstitches in the seam at the top marking. Bring the needle through to the right side, then take a small stitch and draw the thread part way through, leaving a 5-cm (2-inch) loop. Hold the loop open with the needle. Reach through the loop with the

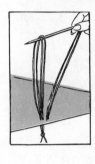

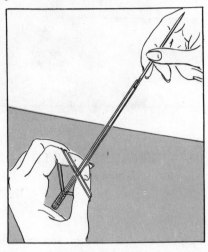

thumb and one finger of the left hand and grasp the needle thread, pulling it through to form a new loop. Draw the released loop down to the fabric. Make the chain the length required. Pass the needle through the last loop to lock the chain. Stitch through the fabric and fasten the thread with two back-stitches on the underside.

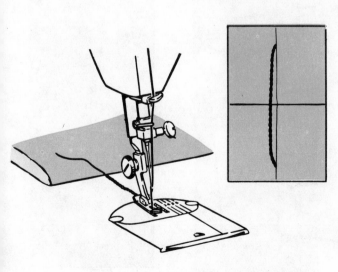

You can make chain-stitch carriers quickly by machine if you have the Chain Stitch Accessories. Refer to the instruction book accompanying the machine and to page 63.

FABRIC CARRIERS

Fabric carriers can be a useful design feature. They are found on the waistbands of skirts, shorts and slacks and in side seams of dresses. Generally, four to six carriers are used around the waistline. They vary from ·6 to 1·2 cm ($\frac{1}{4}$ to $\frac{1}{2}$ inch) in width, depending on the fabric and garment.

1. Cut a strip of fabric on the lengthwise grain, twice the finished width plus 1·2 cm ($\frac{1}{2}$ inch) for seam allowances, and long enough to make the number of carriers required.
2. Fold the strip lengthwise, right sides together, and stitch ·6 cm ($\frac{1}{4}$ inch) from the edge. Trim the seam edges to ·3 cm ($\frac{1}{8}$ inch). Ease the seam to the centre of the strip and press open with the fingers. Stitch across one end.
3. Turn the strip right side out. (Use an orange stick or toothpick with a straight end.) Turn the stitched end to the inside, then ease the strip back over the orange stick. Cut off the stitched end. Ease the seam to the centre and press.
4. Cut each carrier long enough to fit over the belt with ease plus 2·5 cm (1 inch) for seam allowances. Fold under 1·2 cm ($\frac{1}{2}$ inch) at each end and press.

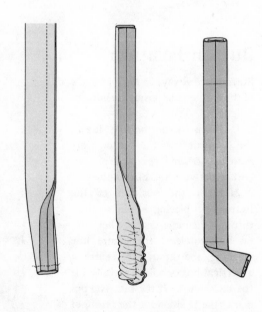

5. Mark the position for the finished end of the carrier on the garment. Place the carrier right side up, with the cut end ·3 cm ($\frac{1}{8}$ inch) inside the marking. Stitch ·3 cm ($\frac{1}{8}$ inch) from the edge. Back-stitch at each end; do not

stitch beyond the edges of the carrier. Trim the end close to the stitching and press.

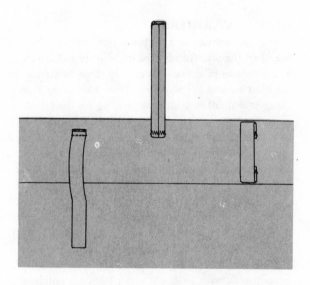

6. Fold the carrier back on the stitching line and press. Stitch ·3 cm ($\frac{1}{8}$ inch) from the fold, using a closely spaced zig-zag stitch. Finish the opposite end in the same manner.

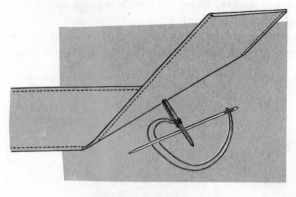

BELT ATTACHED WITH FRENCH TACKS
A French tack may also be used to hold a belt in place. See *French Tacks*, page 208 for instructions.

Buttons and Fastenings

Button Position

Buttons are always *on the centre line* of the garment, opposite the button-holes.

1. Wrap the buttonhole side of the garment over the button side, *matching centre lines*, and pin to-gether between the buttonholes.

2. Mark the position of the button by placing a pin straight through the outer end of a horizon-tal buttonhole at the centre line marking, and through the centre of a vertical buttonhole. Carefully lift the buttonhole off the pin. The pin marks the position for the centre of the button.

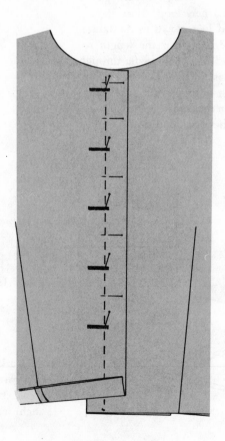
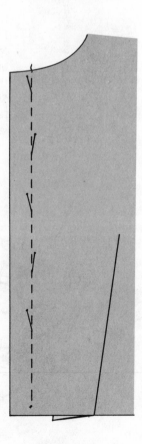

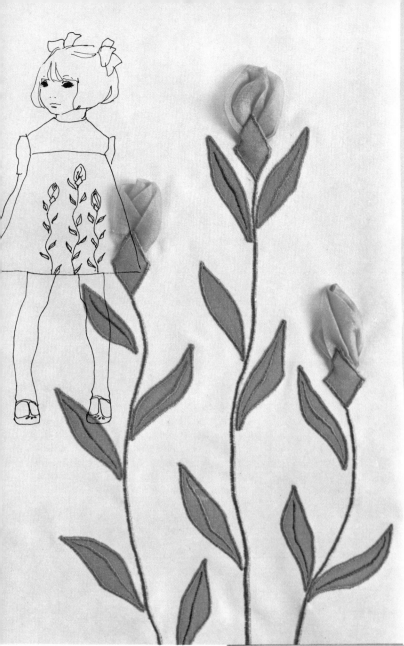

Plate 13
A GIRL'S GARDEN OF ROSES

ABOVE: Roses cut out of a printed linen handkerchief, appliquéd to sheer fabric.

BELOW: Flowered ribbon slotted through two rows of buttonholes.

ABOVE: Folded sheer fabric forms rosebuds, which are held in place by appliquéd leaves.

Plates 14 and 15
FASHION FOR THE UNDER FIVES

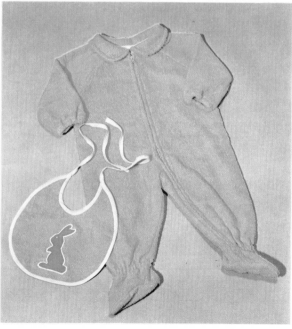

ABOVE: The dress was made up in a striped cotton polyester fabric. A lacy cotton trim finishes all edges. Cotton poplin was used for the underslip.

LEFT: A brightly coloured towelling is ideal for a baby, and the style allows plenty of ease for movement.

RIGHT: A warm garment in a quilted cotton. Features include a lacy trim and easy popper closing.

Pattern by courtesy of Butterick

Plate 15

Plate 16
FRAGILE FEMININITY

ABOVE: Rows of lace
edging applied with
scallop stitch pattern
form the yoke of an
organdie party dress.

ABOVE RIGHT: Gingham
trimmed with bias strips and
lace edging, applied with
scallop stitch pattern.

LEFT: On organdie, open-spaced
plain zig-zag stitching forms
floral outline with lace flower
tacked in centre. Rows of
decorative stitching trim
double-fold hem.

Sewing on Buttons

Buttons may be sewn on by hand or with a zig-zag sewing machine. Whether or not you make a thread shank depends on the garment and the thickness of the fabric. A shank is not necessary on skirts, blouses, washable dresses and pyjamas; it is necessary on suits, coats and garments of heavy fabric. The shank raises the button from the surface of the garment, allowing space for the layers of fabric on the buttonhole side to fit smoothly under the button. Mercerised cotton thread is generally used on lightweight and washable fabrics; buttonhole twist is preferred for suits, coats and garments made of suede.

BUTTONS WITHOUT A SHANK

Use thread matching the button in colour. Knot the long end of the thread. Place the button over the marking and *on the centre line* of garment.

Bring the needle through the fabric from the underside and up through one eye of the button. Place a pin across the button between the eyes, then bring the needle down through the second eye and back into the fabric. Take about six stitches; then fasten the thread with two or three overcast stitches around the threads on the underside.

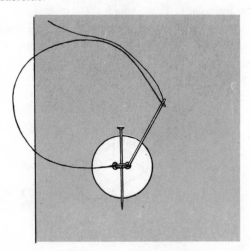

Buttons with four eyes may be sewn in various ways for decorative effects.

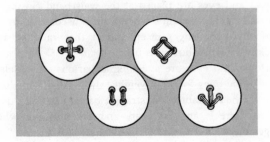

BUTTONS WITH THREAD SHANK

For coats, suits and garments which may be worn open, make the stitches through the garment and interfacing, but not through the facing. Knot the long end of the thread.

1. On the right side of the garment, take a stitch through the top layer of fabric and interfacing at the position for the button and on the centre line of the garment. Bring the needle up through one eye of the button. Place a bodkin or matchstick across the button between the eyes, then bring the needle down through the second eye. Take a stitch through the top layer of fabric and interfacing. Make about six stitches the same way. On the last stitch, bring the thread down through the eye.

2. Remove the bodkin, then pull the button away from the fabric and wind the needle thread evenly round the threads between the fabric and button to form the thread shank. Fasten the thread securely with two overcast stitches.

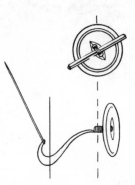

REINFORCED BUTTON

On garments made of suede, leather or heavy coating, where the underside must be as neat as the top side, sew a small button on the underside so that the stitches will be inconspicuous. This gives added strength and prevents the thread from cutting the suede or leather.

Use buttonhole twist and knot the end of the thread.

1. Position the top button. Bring the needle through the fabric from the underside and up through one eye of the button. Place a bodkin across the button between the eyes. Then bring the needle down through the second eye and fabric, and through the eye of the bottom button. Make about six stitches through the eyes of the top and bottom buttons at the same time. On the last stitch, bring the thread down through the eye of the top button.

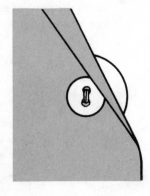

2. Remove the bodkin, pull the top button away from the fabric and finish the thread shank between the top button and fabric as described above.

205

MACHINE-STITCHED BUTTONS

A zig-zag machine may be used to stitch buttons with or without a thread shank. Refer to the instruction book accompanying your machine for directions.

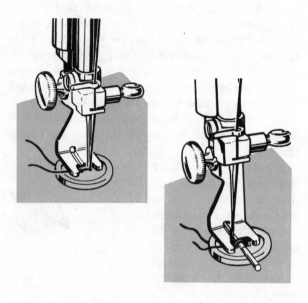

Press Fasteners

Press fasteners are usually placed at the neckline and waistline to hold the facing edge flat when buttons are used; at the pointed end of the waistband with hooks and eyes; and at the waistline of blouses and the opening for long, closely fitted sleeves. They are seldom used alone.

Press fasteners are available in various sizes. Select a size that is not too heavy for the fabric. A small size is usual in dressmaking.

1. Mark the position on the wrap about ·3 cm ($\frac{1}{8}$ inch) from the finished edge so that it is not visible when the garment is worn.

2. Sew the ball part of the fastener to the underside of the wrap. Take about six stitches through one hole, then carry the thread under to the next hole. Alternatively use blanket stitch. Take the stitches through the facing and interfacing only so that they will not show on the right side of the garment. Fasten the thread securely with two overcast stitches round the threads.

3. Chalk the ball and press it against the underwrap to mark the position of the socket. (On some fabrics, pressing the ball against the underwrap will mark the position.) Or use a needle through guide hole to align the two parts. Sew the socket to the underwrap.

Lingerie Strap Holder

Strap holders are used at the shoulder seam to hold lingerie straps in position.

Use straight seam binding about 4 cm ($1\frac{1}{2}$ inches) long. Fold under the ends and press, then fold through the centre and press. Stitch on each side. Mark the position for each end of the strap at the shoulder seam. Hand-stitch one end to the seam allowance at the marking near the armhole.

Sew one part of the press fastener to the free end of the strap and the other part to the seam allowance.

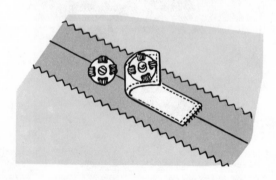

Hooks and Eyes

Hooks and eyes are placed at the waistband closing of the skirt, at the neckline when a zip is used, at an opening where the edges meet, and at the waistline and neckline when a button is used.

Hooks and eyes are available in various sizes. Select small, fine ones for lightweight fabrics, and a medium size for heavy fabrics. A straight bar is generally used when there is an overwrap, and a round eye when edges meet.

OVERWRAP IN A WAISTBAND

1. Sew the hook to the underside of the overwrap of the waistband, placing the end far enough from the edge so that it will not show when the garment is worn. Take about six stitches through each loop, then carry the thread under the hook and take several stitches through the end to hold it flat. Alternatively use blanket stitch. Do not stitch through to the right side of the garment. Fasten the thread securely.

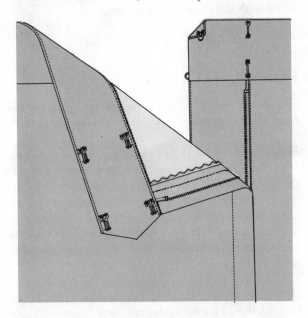

2. To mark the position for the bar, wrap the opening and pin-mark the underwrap directly opposite the end of the hook. Place the straight bar over the marking and sew through each loop.

3. On the underwrap, sew a round eye at the end of the band. Fasten the hook in the eye, then sew it in place on the underside of the front band section.

WHEN EDGES MEET

1. When the edges of an opening meet, mark the position for the hook and eye on each side of the closing. Sew a round eye on one side, extending the edge slightly, or make a thread eye, following the instructions given below.

2. Fasten the hook in the eye, then bring the garment edges together to determine exactly where you should sew the hook on the opposite edge. Sew the hook in place. Be sure the stitches do not show through on the right side of the garment.

Thread Eye or Bar

A thread eye is generally used at a neckline opening with a zip and at a waistline opening with a button.

1. Sew the hook to the underside of the overwrap, placing the end far enough from the edge so that it will not be visible when the garment is worn.

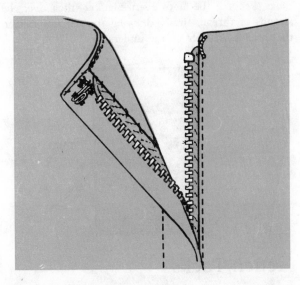

2. To mark the position for the eye, wrap the opening and pin-mark the underwrap directly opposite each side of the hook end.

3. **To make a thread eye,** use thread matching the fabric in colour. Knot the long end of the thread. Bring the needle through from the underside at one end of the marking for the eye. Then take a stitch at the opposite end. Work back and forth two or three times, then blanket-stitch over the strands of thread, firmly drawing the stitches. Fasten the last stitch securely on the underside.

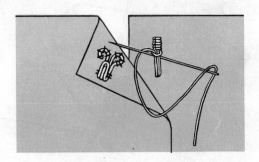

Thread Loops

Thread loops are often used with buttons at a neckline opening in a dress or blouse.

1. Decide the spacing for the buttons and mark the edge of the garment. Stitch the buttons to the centre line of the left side. Pin-mark the position for the loop on each side of the button, on the opposite marked edge of the garment.

2. Use a single strand of matching thread and knot the long end of the thread. At the top marking, bring the needle through the fabric from the underside near the edge of the opening; then take a stitch in the edge at the bottom marking, leaving a loop large enough to slip easily over the button. Work back and forth two or three times, keeping the loops even. Blanket-stitch over the strands of thread, firmly drawing the stitches. Fasten the threads securely on the underside.

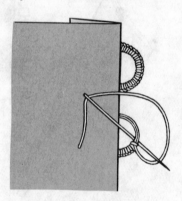

French Tacks

French tacks are used when two fabric surfaces are caught together with some allowance for ease – for example, linings in coats or curtains, or the lower edge of facings in coats. They are placed at the seams and intervals between. French tacks may also be used in attaching a belt to a garment or joining buttons to form cuff links.

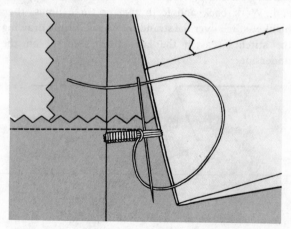

1. Use a double strand of silk or mercerised thread or a single strand of buttonhole twist. Knot the end of the thread. Take a stitch near the top of the garment hem (through the hem and seam allowance), then a stitch directly opposite in the lining, leaving a ·6- to 2·5-cm (¼- to 1-inch) slack in the thread. Work back and forth two or three times, allowing the same amount of slack.

2. Blanket-stitch over the strands of thread, very firmly. When finished, fasten stitches securely in the fabric with one or two overcast stitches.

Eyelets

Eyelets are used in belts and for lacings. They may be hand-worked or machine-worked with the Buttonholer.

HAND-WORKED EYELETS

1. Mark the position for the eyelets. Punch a hole in the fabric with a stiletto. (It may be necessary to cut out the excess fabric with sharp, pointed scissors. Do not make the hole too large.)

2. Use a single strand of silk or mercerised thread, or buttonhole twist. Bring the needle up through the fabric from the underside ·3 cm (⅛ inch) from the edge of the hole, leaving about 2·5 cm (1 inch) of the thread on the underside. Work round the hole and over the 2·5-cm (1-inch) thread on the underside with blanket stitches, forming the purl on the outer edge. Keep the stitches as even as possible. When finished, fasten the thread securely on the underside with one or two overcast stitches.

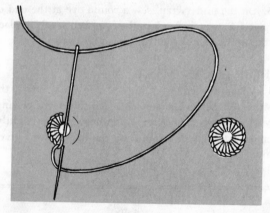

Pleats and Godets

Pleats and godets are design details that appear and disappear at intervals, depending on the whim of fashion. Both add fullness and interest to a skirt.

Pleats

In your sewing you will come across many kinds of pleats. This chapter deals with the four most common ones: wrap pleats, inverted pleats, box pleats and pleated skirts.

Knife or Wrap Pleats

Knife or wrap pleats fold in one direction – from right to left. They are often used to provide fullness at the lower edge of a pencil-slim skirt.

If the pattern you are using does not extend the pleat allowance the entire length of the skirt, do so by marking the fabric with chalk before cutting.

1. Mark the position of the pleat and the seamline above the pleat with tailor's tacks. Pin and tack the seamline and the extension for the pleat. Then stitch close to the tacking. Remove tackings and press.

Tack the fold line for the pleat and remove tailor's tacks.

2. Working from the wrong side, turn the pleat and seam allowance to the left side. Cut out the top layer of fabric above the pleat, leaving a 1·5-cm ($\frac{5}{8}$-inch) seam allowance. This eliminates bulk. The second layer of fabric will hold the pleat in position so that you do not need to stitch across the top of the pleat on the right side.

3. Press the seam open above the pleat. Turn the pleat and seam allowance to the left side and press. Press lightly in the hem area since the crease is reversed in the hem when it is folded.

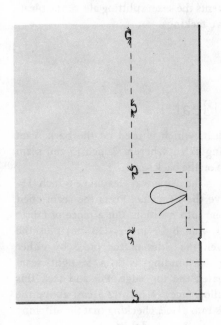
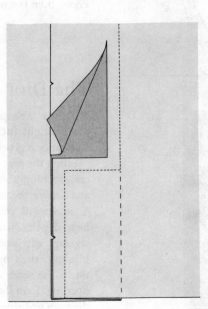
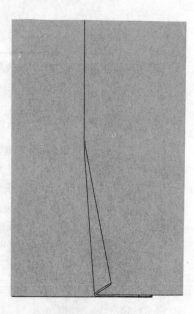

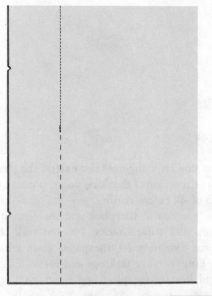

Inverted Pleat with Underlay

An inverted pleat is formed by folding two pleats towards each other. When an underlay is used on the underside of an inverted pleat, there is a seam instead of a fold on each side of the pleat which is concealed by the depth of the pleat.

If the pattern does not extend the pleat allowance the entire length of the skirt, do so by marking the fabric with chalk before cutting.

1. Mark the position of the pleat and the seamline above the pleat with tailor's tacks.

Pin and tack the entire length of the seam and pleat. Then stitch the seam from the waistline to the top of the pleat, reinforcing the ends with backstitching. Remove tackings along the stitching line, but not in the pleat. Press. Then press the wide seam open the entire length of the seam and pleat. Press lightly in the hem area.

2. Place an underlay over the pleat section, right side down, extending the edge 1·5 cm ($\frac{5}{8}$ inch) above the top of the pleat. Pin and tack the underlay to each side of the pleat section. Stitch seams, and press.

3. To reinforce the top of the pleat, cut straight seam binding the width of the pleat. Fold it lengthwise through the centre, and press. Turn the pleat away from the skirt. Pin the stay across the pleat with the lower edge exactly at the top of the pleat. Stitch the underlay and stay to the pleat from seam edge to centre. Make the opposite side in the same way. This eliminates the need to stitch across the top of the pleat on the right side and also prevents the seam splitting above the pleat. Press, then remove tackings.

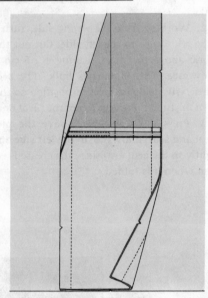

The Dior Pleat

This is a false pleat, which is used on the back seam of a straight fitting skirt, where a 2-inch (5-cm) seam allowance is given on the back seam.

Stitch the seam in the usual way, leaving a 6-inch (15-cm) opening above the hem line. Press the seam open and secure the hem into position. Cut a piece of fabric 4 inches (10 cm) wide by 7 inches (18 cm) plus the hem depth. Neaten the sides of the piece by either zig-zag stitching or binding with a straight seam binding, then neaten the top edge. Pin and tack this on to the seam allowances, 1 inch (2·5 cm) above the opening. Hem this into place, checking that the stitching does not go through to the actual skirt.

Turn up the hem on the false hem piece, making the piece $\frac{1}{4}$ inch (·6 cm) shorter than the skirt, to allow for the false hem settling into position in wear.

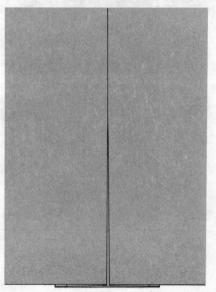

Box Pleats

A box pleat is formed by folding two wrap pleats in opposite directions to make a panel. Transfer the markings for the pleats, following the instructions given for a *Pleated Skirt*; then make the pleats.

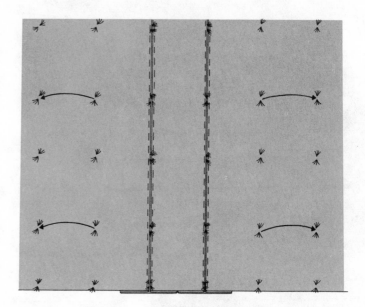

Pleated Skirt

When the entire skirt is pleated, each pleat in the pattern is marked with two vertical lines from the waistline to the lower edge. One line marks the top fold for the pleat, the other the position of the fold that forms the pleat. Each pleat is made proportionately deeper at the waistline. The depth of the pleats conceals the seams within the skirt.

1. Transfer the markings to the fabric with tailor's tacks, using contrasting colours of thread to mark the two lines that form the pleat. This will simplify your work later when you begin to fold the pleats, for you can fold one colour to the other. *Take care to use the correct marking on the pattern to form the top fold for each pleat.*

2. Before forming the pleats, stitch the seams within the skirt, and press. Check the skirt length and finish the hem at the lower edge.

Three methods are suggested for making the pleats. Use the one best suited to your fabric. Always work on a flat surface, and remember to press. See page 66 for information on pressing various types of fabric.

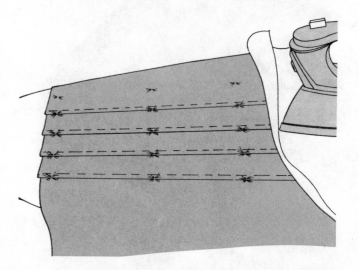

Method 1: Use this method of pleating for any medium-weight fabric with body that creases easily.

Work on the right side of the fabric. Fold the pleats, matching markings. Place pins at right angles to the pleats. Tack near the fold, using silk thread. Press from the wrong side. Use the appropriate pressing cloth and moisture, and slide the iron the length of the pleat.

Method 2: Use this method on woollens which are crease-resistant and heavy fabrics where pressing the fold of the pleat against the fabric would form a ridge under the fold.

Work on the right side of the fabric. Pin, then tack the top fold for each pleat, using silk thread. Press from the underside of the fold to form a sharp crease. Since this step requires pressing on the right side of the fabric, use a woollen pressing cloth and moist muslin as protection.

Fold the pleats, matching markings. Pin, then tack, using silk thread. Press from the wrong side, as instructed in *Method 1*, and crease the underfold for the pleat.

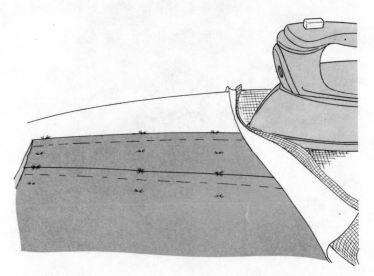

211

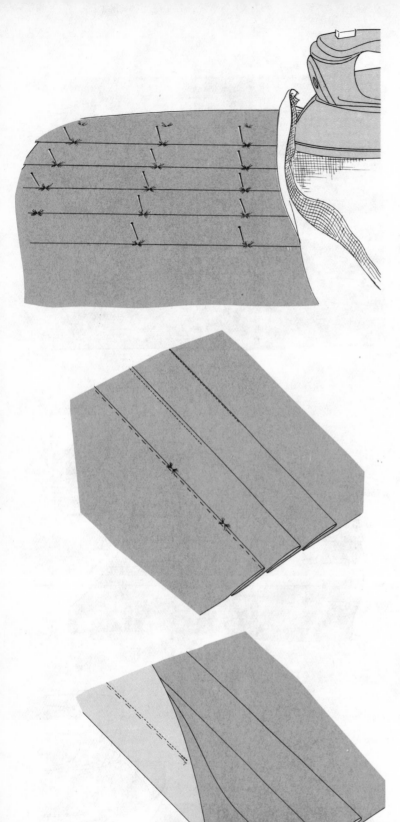

Method 3: Use this quick and easy method for cottons and similar fabrics.

Work on the ironing board. Turn the fabric right side up and fold each pleat, matching markings. Pin straight through the fabric into the ironing board. Press between pins. Since the pressing is done from the right side, use the appropriate pressing cloth and moisture required by the fabric. Remove pins, and press again.

Stitching Pleats

Pleats may hang freely from the waistline or may be stitched from waistline to hipline. They may be top-stitched or stitched from the underside. Stitch after you have inserted the zip and before you attach the waist-band.

After you have tacked and pressed your pleats as described in any one of the methods above, follow the instructions given here.

TOP-STITCHED PLEATS

Pleats may be either edge-stitched or stitched about ·6 cm ($\frac{1}{4}$ inch) from the edge. As they are made proportionately deeper at the waistline, they overlap in this area.

Pin-mark the length to be stitched on each pleat. On the underside, fold back the pleat that precedes the line of stitching; then on the right side, stitch the pleat in place from the marking up to the waistline. Stitch each pleat in the same way. Pull threads to the underside and tie. Press. Attach the waistband; then remove all tackings for the pleats.

PLEATS STITCHED ON UNDERSIDE

Remove the tacking from the waistline to about 7·5 cm (3 inches) below the hipline. Turn the skirt to the inside. Then turn the pleat away from the skirt and mark the length for the stitching with chalk. Pin and tack in the crease of the top fold of the pleat. Then stitch in the crease from the marking up to the waistline. Reinforce each end with backstitching.

Turn the pleats in the direction they were pressed. Then press from the inside.

Attach the waistband before you remove the tackings.

Pleated Ruffles

The small pleats required for ruffles can easily be made with the Ruffler. See page 281 for instructions.

As the Ruffler forms each pleat at the seamline, finger-press the entire length of the pleat. Then press with an

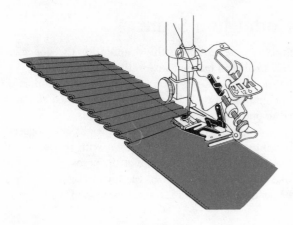

iron. For fabrics that you cannot finger-press satis-factorily, use an iron after pleating the ruffle. Work on the ironing board and fold the pleat from the stitching line to the outer edge; then place a pin straight through the outer edge and into the ironing board. Pin each pleat in the same way. Press.

Inserting Godets

Godets may be set in to a shape cut out of the skirt or in a seam. They should be stitched in place before you stitch the side seams as it is easier to work with a flat piece of fabric.

Godet in a Cut Out

When inserting a godet, you will be working with two curves – an outside curve, which is on the godet, and an inside curve, which is in the cut out of the skirt.

1. Stay-stitch 1·5 cm ($\frac{5}{8}$ inch) from the seam edge of the cut out for the godet. Press. Slash the seam allowance on the curve almost to the stitching.

2. On the underside, pin the centre of the godet to the centre of the cut out, right sides together. Then, on each side, pin from the centre to the lower edge. Care-fully shape the inside curve of the cut out round the outside curve of the godet and ease the godet slightly round the curve, keeping seam edges even. Tack by hand with small stitches on each side from centre to lower edge. Check the right side to be certain that the curve is maintained on both pieces of fabric. Hang the garment overnight to allow for any stretching on the bias.

3. Place the godet next to the feed and stitch slowly in a continuous line from one edge to the other. Neaten seam edges as required by the fabric. Press the seam, then press it away from the opening.

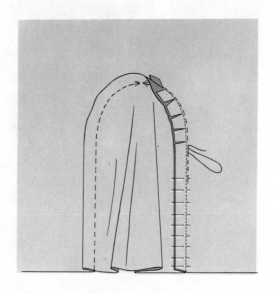

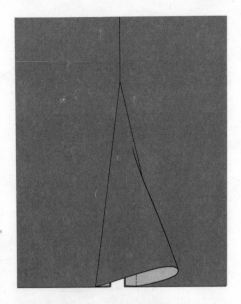

Godet in a Seam

Stitch the seam above the opening for the godet and reinforce each end with backstitching. Neaten the seam edges. Snip into the seam allowances at the top of the opening, almost to the stitching. Press; then press the seam open.

1. Place the godet in the opening, right sides together, matching the marking at the point with the end of the seam above the opening; pin at the point. Pin and tack one side from the point to the lower edge; keep seam edges even. Do not stretch the bias seam in the godet.

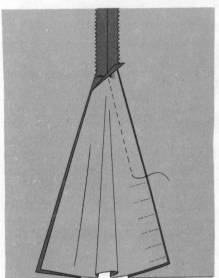

2. Stitch on the garment side, from the lower edge to the point, joining the stitching in the seamline above the godet. Pin, tack and stitch the opposite side in the same way.

At the point of the godet, pull all threads to the underside and tie them together in a single knot. Remove tackings and press. Neaten seam edges.

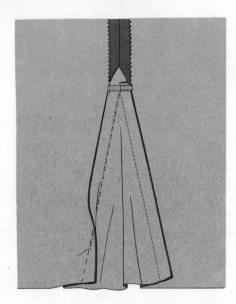

3. To reinforce the seam at the point, cut straight seam binding the width of the open seam edges. Fold the binding lengthwise through the centre and press. Pin the stay across the godet and garment seam allowances, keeping the lower edge of the stay exactly at the top of the stitched point. Turn the seam allowances away from the garment and stitch from seam edge to seamline; treat the opposite side in the same manner. Cut off seam allowances at the point ·6 cm ($\frac{1}{4}$ inch) from the stitching.

Fabrics that Require Special Handling

There is a wide array of fabrics that demand special attention in sewing. To mention a few – knitted fabrics, silks, sheers, leathers and fur fabrics. Techniques used in stitching and handling vary with the fabric. Although these fabrics require a little more time and patience, if you follow the suggestions given here as well as the usual methods of good dressmaking, your finished garment is certain to be a success.

Instructions for the various sewing techniques referred to in this chapter can be found in other parts of this book. Check the alphabetical index.

Silk Fabrics

Silk can go anywhere. Ranging in weight from sheer chiffon to heavy tweed, it is suitable for all types of garments. 'Light and gentle' describes the hand for working with silk.

Preparing to Sew

Pattern. You can select almost any pattern for silk provided you also select the correct weight of silk for the garment. Heavy silks are suitable for tailored dresses, suits and coats; soft silks for blouses and dresses; and sheer silks, such as chiffon, or lace, for softly draped styles and full skirts. Unless completely mounted, however, sheer silks will not be pleasing to the eye if neckline and sleeve facings are used, or if styling seams and darts are obvious.

Cutting. Do not try to cut silk on a highly polished surface and certainly not on the carpet or floor. A cork or felt surface is best, but cotton sheeting pinned tightly over your usual cutting table or board will make a good substitute.

Use fine pins or, better still, needles, when pinning the pattern to the fabric. Place them close together and within the seam or dart allowance. Use sharp scissors of medium length. Careful cutting will give accurate seam width and maintain garment proportions. On sheer silk, cut notches outwards so that they will not interfere with the seam construction or final finishing.

Markings. Use tailor's tacks only.

Mounting and lining. For the professional look, you should either mount or line silk fabric. The chapter on mounting and lining contains comprehensive instructions. See page 95. Select such fabrics as Jap silk, silk organza, silk crêpe, silk taffeta, or a suitable synthetic.

Interfacing. Select the interfacing with care. If the silk is sheer, use self-fabric or silk organza; match the fabric colour as closely as possible.

Stitching and Handling

Tacking. Hand-tack the seams and darts. Avoid temporary machine stitching that must later be removed since many silks will show needle marks. Tack with silk thread in a contrasting colour, and use a size 8 or 9 hand-sewing needle of appropriate length.

Thread and needle. Machine-stitch silk fabric with silk thread as the expert always does. Use a size 11 machine needle in lightweight silks and a size 14 on heavy or rough-surfaced silks. In most cases, the needle thread tension must be lessened one to two points or until the stitching looks the same on the top and underside and does not pucker.

Stitch length and pressure. Use a 1·5 to 1 mm (15 to 20) stitch length for sheer and soft silks and a 2 mm (12) stitch length for medium and heavy silks.

The pressure exerted by the Presser Foot on the fabric should be light, no heavier than needed to carry the fabric gently and evenly under the foot.

Stitching. Medium and heavy silks require guiding only in front of the needle during the machine stitching. Crêpe weaves and chiffon require gentle support; when stitching them, hold the seam in back of the Presser Foot as well as in front of the needle. Do not pull the fabric under the foot; merely place it under slight tension. When stitching with a zig-zag machine, use the straight-stitch throat plate and Presser Foot for best results.

Darts. If the silk is mounted, stitch the darts in the silk and mounting separately unless the fabric is sheer. On sheer fabrics, make the darts through both layers together so that they will not show through on the right side. Unstitched darts, gathers and shirring are better in a sheer fabric than the stitched dart.

Seams and seam finishes. Select a finish that will give the seam as little bulk as possible. Some closely woven silks require no seam finish; others you may prefer to pink. Neaten rough, open weaves that tend to fray with either the blindstitch zig-zag or the multi-stitch zig-zag.

Sheer silks, such as chiffon, need narrow French seams. The hairline seam is a neat finish for enclosed seams in facings and collars, and fine double-fold bias binding makes a more pleasing neckline and sleeve finish than a shaped facing.

Zip opening. Follow the conventional method of inserting the zip until the final step. Then, instead of top-stitching, hand-sew, using a fine, short backstitch, or machine-stitch using the blindstitch zig-zag. The method you choose is a matter of personal preference.

Buttonholes. Machine-worked, hand-worked or bound buttonholes are appropriate for all silks except sheers, where buttonholes should be avoided. Always use an underlay of a firmly woven lawn or muslin to reinforce the stitching round the buttonholes.

Hems. Seam tape is acceptable for the hem edge finish, but a pinked edge with a line of machine-stitching ·6 cm ($\frac{1}{4}$ inch) from the edge is preferred. Rough, open weaves that tend to fray may be finished with the blindstitch zig-zag or multi-stitch zig-zag.

Always hand-sew the hem with silk thread, using the French method, which places the stitches between the hem and garment and not over the hem edge.

If the silk is sheer and the lining is joined only at the waistline, hem the silk and lining separately. A double-fold hem is ideal. It adds weight to and so improves the hang of the skirt, it eliminates the turned, raw edge which would otherwise show through. However, it can be used only if the hemline is straight, not flared. Double the hem allowance, if you want a 10-cm (4-inch) hem, allow 20 cm (8 inches). Turn 10 cm (4 inches) and press, then turn 10 cm (4 inches) again. Slip-stitch the hem in place, catching only one thread of the skirt in each stitch and slipping the needle inside the fold between the stitches to conceal the thread. When the hemline is circular or flared, make a narrow machine-stitched or hand-rolled hem. Hem the sheer silk and mounting separately to prevent the sheer from 'blousing' over the mounting.

Pressing. Follow the instructions given for pressing silk on page 66.

Lining. Coats and jackets should be lined in the usual way. Choose a lining of crêpe or taffeta.

Knitted Fabrics

Knitted fabrics have as many different faces and characteristics as woven fabrics, and for that reason no single set of sewing guidelines can be applied to them all. *The Many Faces of Knitted Fabrics*, page 417, describes their construction and the uses and characteristics of the various types. It includes guidelines for stitching and suggestions for many different seams and constructions appropriate for the fabrics in each group.

Firm, stable knitted fabrics – such as double knits and warp knits of polyester, wool or blends of polyester and wool or cotton – are the most popular. They are the easiest to sew, and they react more like woven fabrics than some others. For a brief guide as to how to sew them, read the suggestions below.

Preparing to Sew

Pattern. Many styles of suits, dresses and coats make up well in knitted fabrics. In selecting your pattern, pick one with simple, uncluttered lines. Some patterns are designated 'suitable for knits'; other patterns include jersey or double knits in the list of suitable fabrics on the pattern envelope. Do not choose a pattern designated 'stretchable knits only' if you are working with a firm knitted fabric. Smart ways to accent double knits and firm warp knits include matching fabric, braid or satin binding; top stitching; and welt seams.

Shrinking. Washable knitted fabrics, such as polyester and polyester-and-cotton blends, should be laundered before cutting to remove the excess finishing solution. Bonded knits do not need shrinking. Wool double knits should be sent to the dry-cleaner for shrinking unless labelled washable. Prepare them for shrinking by folding on a lengthwise rib, right side out, squaring the ends with a table, and tacking the ends and edges. (Knitted fabrics that are finished out-of-square can seldom be straightened by pulling diagonally.)

Cutting. Lay out the pattern following a 'with nap' pattern layout. Knitted fabrics have an up-and-down direction because of their loop construction and will reflect light differently in the crosswise and lengthwise directions. If the fabric has a deep centre crease, it can seldom be pressed out, so avoid including the crease in the garment. If the crosswise courses of the knit do not run at right angles to the lengthwise rib, or if a design

in one direction is not at right angles to one in the other direction, make all half pattern pieces into whole pattern pieces by re-cutting in tissue paper; cut the fabric singly, using the most prominent direction of a fabric as the 'grain line'.

Use fine pins, preferably within dart and seam allowances. To avoid stretching, do not let the fabric hang over the edge of the cutting table. Cut with sharp, heavy-blade shears. Cut notches outwards.

Markings. Use hand tacking for centre lines and tailor's tacks for internal markings. Tracing paper and a tracing wheel do not give a good result on most firm knitted fabrics.

Mounting and lining. Both are optional and impart different characteristics to a garment. Mounting and lining cancel the comfort of a knitted fabric. They increase the stability of the fabric and cause the garment to hang free of the figure just like a woven fabric. Select a thin, soft, supple fabric for a softly draped look or a thin, crisp fabric for a mounted look. Suit jackets may be lined with a synthetic tricot to preserve the give of knit.

Interfacing. Collars, cuffs, pockets flaps and front facing areas should be interfaced. Select a thin, supple woven interfacing or terylene non-woven interfacing; a lightweight hair canvas for a tailor-made design; or a suitable iron-on interfacing (fused to the underside of the outside section) for a crisp effect.

Stitching and Handling

Tacking. Hand tacking ensures a smooth seam and enables you to test the fit of the garment before machine stitching the seams. Machine tacking with the Even Feed Foot, or 'speed basting' (of your sewing machine has this feature), will give you the same advantages as hand tacking.

Thread and needle. Select strong thread for machine stitching. Silk, nylon, spun polyester and mercerised cotton threads are suitable. They provide both stretch and strength. Use a size 14 ball-point needle (Singer* No. 2021 or Perfect Stitch No. 2045). Regulate tensions to produce a balanced stitch.

Kind of stitch. For plain seams in firm knits, a 2 mm (12) length straight stitch made with a strong thread is suitable. For seams that will be subjected to strain, the straight stretch stitch is recommended. Use one of the over-edge stitches for finishing hem and facing edges.

Presser-foot pressure. Use medium or normal presser-foot pressure.

Stitching. For straight stitching, use the straight-stitch Presser Foot and throat plate. Guide and support the fabric while stitching by holding the seam under tension in back of the Presser Foot and in front of the needle. Or use the Even Feed Foot instead to ensure that the seam ends come out even without tacking or guiding and supporting the seam.

Strengthen seams that must not stretch, such as shoulder, neckline and waistline seams, with woven-edge seam binding.

Armhole seams for set-in sleeves should be double-stitched, first on the seamline with a straight or straight stretch stitch, then ·6 cm ($\frac{1}{4}$ inch) outside the seamline with a straight stitch or a zig-zag over-edge stitch. Trim seam allowance outside second stitching.

Top stitching with buttonhole twist is a decorative detail often used on knitted fabrics. Use a size 16 or 18 needle to carry the buttonhole twist, and thread the bobbin with either silk or mercerised thread. Increase the needle-thread tension slightly to set the stitch firmly. The Even Feed Foot will improve the feeding of the fabric layers for all top-stitched detail. Top stitching may also

be done with the same thread used for stitching the garment.

Darts. To eliminate bulk in small darts, slash through centre and press open. Trim the inside layer of slanted bustline darts to 1·2 cm ($\frac{1}{2}$ inch) and press downwards.

Seam layering. Layer, trim and clip seam allowances inside collars, cuffs and similar constructions in the same way as on woven fabrics.

Seam finishes. Press plain seams open. Edges do not fray and do not require a seam finish.

Buttonholes. Bound or machine-worked buttonholes are suitable. Always make buttonholes through firm woven or terylene non-woven interfacing.

Hems. To ensure an even and accurate hemline, allow the garment to hang at least 24 hours before hemming. Mark, fold and tack the hem in the same way as on woven fabrics. Finish the hem edge with a zig-zag over-edge stitch or a straight stitch ·6 cm ($\frac{1}{4}$ inch) from edge. Blind-stitch hem by hand. For deep hems, place the first row of blind hemming stitches at the centre of the hem width and the second row ·6 cm ($\frac{1}{4}$ inch) from the hem edge.

Pressing. Always use a thin pressing cloth between the iron and the fabric. A slightly dampened muslin cloth will produce sufficient steam with the iron on the silk setting. Steam-press polyester thoroughly as you sew. Little or no pressing is required after laundering if thorough pressing is done during the construction of the garment.

Stretch Fabrics

Since the stretch characteristic has been added to fabrics primarily for comfort in wear plus smoothness of fit, the direction in which the stretch is used in a garment is important. Stretch should run across the shoulders in blouses, shirts, dresses and jackets; from waistline to ankle in trousers; and from side to side in skirts and shorts. Examine the fabric carefully *to be sure that the stretch goes in the right direction* for your garment.

Some fabrics are woven to look the same lengthwise as crosswise even though they stretch in only one direction. They can be used for any garment, but you must cut the fabric with the stretch running in the proper direction, as stated above. For a description of stretch fabrics, see page 11.

Preparing to Sew

Pattern. Select a pattern in your usual size, with slim, simple styling. In adjusting the pattern to your fitting requirements, remember that you may not need quite so much ease allowance as you do when using a firm fabric.

Shrinking. It is advisable to shrink the fabric before cutting since laundering may cause it to shrink more in the stretch direction than a firm fabric.

Cutting. Lay the pattern pieces on the fabric in the direction of the desired stretch. Use fine pins with sharp points, and place them at right angles to the direction of the stretch. Cut, following the same procedure you use for conventional fabrics. A 2·5-cm (1-inch) seam allowance is recommended for lightweight or medium-weight twill weaves and heavy stretch fabrics. Simply cut 2·5 cm (1 inch) from the seamline marking on the pattern.

Markings. Use either tailor's tacks or tracing wheel and dressmaker's carbon paper. Tailor's tacks are recommended for heavy fabrics since the tracing wheel may not mark the under layer.

Interfacing. Choose a suitable weight of woven or non-woven interfacing. Do not use 'iron on' interfacing.

Stitching and Handling

Tacking. Hand tacking is recommended for stretch fabrics. It saves time in the long run because it enables you to test the fit of the garment before machine stitching; also, it ensures an even seam width when stitching. Tack darts towards the point, leaving a 10-cm (4-inch) thread end at the point. After fitting the garment, clip the seamline tacking at intervals to allow for stretching the fabric during the machine stitching.

Thread and needle. Select strong thread for machine stitching. Trylko and Drima are excellent because they provide strength plus give to seams. Silk threads may also be used. Select size 14 machine needle.

Regulate the tension to produce a balanced stitch, otherwise strength is sacrificed.

Stitch length and pressure. Use 2 mm (12) stitch length. The pressure exerted by the Presser Foot on the fabric should be medium.

Stitching. Seams on the stretch grain require special handling. Make a test sample on your fabric before actually stitching on the garment. Do not forget to clip seamline tackings at 10-cm (4-inch) intervals. As you sew, stretch the fabric by holding it in front and in back of the Presser Foot; in other words, keep the fabric under tension while stitching. If you are using Trylko or Drima thread, both of which have a certain amount of elasticity, stretch the fabric slightly during the stitching. If you are using silk thread, stretch the fabric the full amount of the built-in stretch. Use medium to slow speed. Back-stitch at each end of the seam for reinforcement. After stitching a seam, stretch it the full amount to be sure that the thread will not break under strain. If you have a slant-needle zig-zag machine, you can use the Over-edge Foot and *Fashion* disc, which will produce a flexible stitch that will stretch with the fabric.

In some seams stretch is undesirable, such as those at the neckline, waistline and shoulders. Stay them with straight seam binding.

Seam finishes. Press the seam open and finish the edges with a plain zig-zag stitch, wide stitch width, and 2 mm (12) stitch length; or with a multi-stitch zig-zag, wide stitch width, and 'fine' stitch length. Pink the seam edges if the fabric is firmly woven. Layer seams inside collars, cuffs, facings and similar construction in the usual way.

Waistband on skirt and trousers. Cut the band on the lengthwise grain of the fabric and interface it with petersham. If you want stretch in the band, cut the band on the stretch grain and interface it with elastic that has been fitted for the desired snugness. (Remember, the waistline of the garment must also be on the stretch grain.) Stretch both the elastic and fabric as you sew, using a medium width zig-zag stitch.

Zip opening. Insert the zip in the conventional way. Do not stretch the fabric since the zip tape will not stretch. A side opening or fly front is usual for skirts, shorts or trousers.

Buttonholes. Machine-worked or bound buttonholes are suitable. Always stay buttonholes with a backing of firmly woven fabric.

Hems. Finish the hem edge the same way as the seam edges. Then blind-stitch the hem in place, using the machine. If the hem is along the stretch grain, use a plain zig-zag stitch, medium stitch width, and 2 mm (12) stitch length instead of the blindstitch.

Pressing. Press carefully to avoid stretching the fabric. Use the regular steam setting on the iron. Place the iron lightly over the section to be pressed and allow the steam to enter; lift the iron and move to another section. Do not slide the iron in the direction of the stretch grain. To avoid the imprint of the seam edge on the fabric, slip a strip of brown paper under the seam allowance.

Lining. Select a stretch fabric for the lining, if you are using one; otherwise you will lose the 'stretch' advantages of your garment.

Bonded Fabrics

In bonded fabrics (see description on page 12), the face fabric and lining are bonded together. This means that you can make a garment in less time than with other fabrics because only a single cutting and sewing operation is required.

Preparing to Sew

Pattern. Bonded fabrics are appropriate for dresses, suits and coats with tailored lines. Avoid circular skirts and softly draped styles. Top stitching is a smart way to accentuate the lines of the garment.

Cutting. A fabric that has an 'up' and 'down' to the design should be treated the same way as any one-way fabric. If the face fabric is knitted, treat the rib as the true lengthwise grain and follow the directions for knitted fabric. When you are unable to straighten the fabric because of the bonded lining, square off the crosswise grain with a ruler and use only the lengthwise grain as a guide in cutting. See page 15. These fabrics are quite satisfactory because the bonded lining retains the shape of the fabric.

Always fold the fabric wrong sides together, and lay the pattern on the right side. Use plenty of fine pins.

Markings. Mark with tailor's tacks or chalk pencil.

Interfacing. Pre-shrunk muslin and batiste are used for tailored dresses. Hair canvas may be used for suits and coats.

Stitching and Handling

Tacking. Pin or hand-tack all seams, darts and the hem to ensure an even seam. Tacking will also allow you to test the fit before stitching.

Needle and thread. Silk, mercerised cotton or synthetic thread may be used for the machine stitching depending upon the face fabric. Use a size 14 needle. Regulate the tension to produce a balanced stitch.

Stitch length and pressure. Select a 2 mm (12) stitch length. The fabric requires medium pressure.

Stitching. Guide and support the fabric in front and in back of the foot. Do not pull the fabric as it passes under the foot; merely place it under slight tension. This will allow give in the seam and prevent puckering. Where sleeve and bodice are cut in one, stitch underarm seams with a narrow, open zig-zag stitch to allow for greater ease in the seam.

To emphasise the seamline, make channel seams or press seams open and top-stitch on each side 1·2 cm ($\frac{1}{2}$ inch) from the seamline. Strengthen seams at shoulders, neckline and waistline with straight seam binding to prevent stretching. If set-in sleeves are chosen, strengthen the armhole seams; pre-shape the binding by steam pressing and pin it over the seamline. After setting the sleeve into the armhole, finish the seam allowance with zig-zag stitching as described on page 323. Corners should be blunt. Either curve the corners slightly, or take two or three stitches across the point to allow sufficient width for turning.

Darts. Slash through the centre of darts and press them open to eliminate bulk.

Seam layering. Layer seams inside collars, facings and pockets in the usual way to eliminate bulk.

Seam finishes. Seam edges require no neatening as the cut edges will not fray.

Finishing the edges. Tailored binding (see page 334) or braid is a good finish for neckline, sleeves and outside edges of dresses, jackets and coats.

Buttonholes. You may use machine-worked or bound buttonholes. Always use an underlay such as batiste or muslin to reinforce the stitching round the buttonholes.

Hems. Finish the free edge of the hem with pinking, then stitch close to the edge, using a 1 mm (20) stitch length. Make a French hem – that is, a herringbone below the hem edge and between the hem and garment.

Pressing. Use the regular steam setting on the iron. Cover the fabric with a lightweight pressing cloth, and press from the wrong side. For extra moisture on seams, use a moist muslin cloth over the press cloth. Faced edges may be tapped gently with a wooden pounding block to flatten them. Press the hem lightly so that the fold will not be sharply creased.

Laminated Fabrics

Laminates are relatively easy for the home dressmaker to handle. For a description of them, see page 12.

Preparing to Sew

Pattern. Choose a simple, smooth style with a minimum of darts and seam details. Designs with centre front and back seams or openings are best. Adjust the pattern margin on the cutting line before placing the pattern on the fabric.

Cutting. Lay the pattern pieces on the right side of the fabric so that the fabric grain line is always visible. For accuracy in cutting, cut only a single layer of fabric at a time. When the fabric is folded with wrong sides together, the foam sticks together. (A lightweight fabric, however, can be cut double.) Place pins parallel to the seamline. Follow the same cutting procedure used for conventional fabrics. Large, bent-handled cutting shears give a cleaner edge to seams than smaller scissors. Cut all notches outwards.

Markings. Use tailor's tacks only.

Interfacing. Laminated fabrics do not require interfacing.

Stitching and Handling

Tacking. Seams, darts and hems should be hand-tacked to prevent the fabric from slipping during machine stitching. Tacking also allows you to test the fit of the garment before stitching.

Thread and needle. You may use silk or mercerised cotton thread for machine stitching. Trylko or Drima threads are also satisfactory and stronger than mercerised thread. Usually, a size 14 machine needle produces the best results. Regulate the tension to produce a balanced stitch.

Stitch length and pressure. Select 2·5 to 2 mm (10 to 12) stitch length. The pressure on the fabric should be medium.

Stitching. Before machine stitching, tack straight seam binding or a strip of lawn about 1·5 cm ($\frac{5}{8}$ inch) wide over the foam sides so that both the Presser Foot and feed dog are in contact with the lawn or seam binding and not with the foam. This prevents the foam from sticking to the Presser Foot and feed and produces a smooth seam. After the stitching is completed, trim lawn to ·6 cm ($\frac{1}{4}$ inch) to eliminate bulk yet strengthen the seam.

Corners must be blunt, not pointed. Either curve corners slightly, or place two or three stitches across the point to allow sufficient width at the point for a smooth turning.

Darts. Slash through the centre of darts, and press them open to eliminate bulk.

Seams. Press the seam open. Top-stitch on each side of, and about ·6 cm ($\frac{1}{4}$ inch) from, the seamline. Trim the seam allowance on the underside to ·6 cm ($\frac{1}{4}$ inch). This will produce a tailored finish as well as strengthen the seam. A welt seam is also appropriate. See pages 335 and 88.

If the fabric is heavy, stitch the top collar and facing to the undercollar and garment with the foam sides together. Trim the seam allowance to 1·2 cm ($\frac{1}{2}$ inch), and bind the edges with a bias strip or braid. See *Tailored Binding*, page 334.

Seam layering. Layer seams inside collars, cuffs, facings and pockets in the usual way to eliminate bulk.

Buttonholes. Always stay buttonholes with a backing of a firmly woven muslin or lawn. Machine-worked or bound buttonholes are suitable.

Hems. You may sew the hem in place by machine or by hand. Fold and tack the hem in the conventional manner. Place several parallel rows of top stitching in the hemline, spacing them about ·6 cm ($\frac{1}{4}$ inch) apart.

If a hand finish is desirable, finish the hem edge by stitching seam binding over the cut edge. Then finish by hand, using a blind hemming stitch. Make the stitches through the entire fabric, catching only one thread on the right side of the fabric. Stitches made through foam alone will not hold.

Pressing. Laminates require little pressing. Finger pressing is effective. Light steam pressing, with a pressing cloth between the fabric and iron, helps to sharpen seams.

Lining. Garments made of laminated fabrics should be lined to protect the foam backing. Follow the method used in lining a jacket or coat.

Drip-dry Fabrics

The term 'drip-dry' as used here means any fabric that is washable and requires little or no ironing after washing. It can be of cotton, nylon, polyester, Orlon, Acrilan, Terylene and other fibres, or a blend of synthetic and natural fibres.

When selecting a drip-dry fabric, bear this in mind: the fabric must be finished *straight on grain* – that is, the crosswise threads must be at right angles with the lengthwise threads (or selvedge edge). If they are not, it means that the fabric has been finished off grain and cannot be straightened, therefore, it must be squared off with a ruler and cut with only the lengthwise grain as a guide. See page 15. Obviously, this fabric fault impairs the quality of the garment.

Preparing to Sew

Pattern. A wide variety of styles are appropriate for drip-dry fabrics. Avoid those with seam details; select a design that calls for single seam construction rather than multiple thickness.

Cutting. If the manufacturer folded the fabric through the centre, press out the crease before cutting. If the crease cannot be pressed out, arrange the pattern pieces to avoid the crease so that it does not appear in the finished garment. Pin the pattern to the fabric with fine, sharp-pointed pins. (Blunt pins may mark some fabrics permanently.) Cut with sharp scissors.

Markings. Use either tailor's tacks or a tracing wheel and dressmaker's tracing paper. Do not use a wax chalk since the marking cannot be removed from drip-dry fabrics.

Interfacing. Choose a suitable weight of non-woven interfacing.

Stitching and Handling

Thread and needle. On cotton fabrics with a drip-dry finish, mercerised cotton is best. Drip-dry blends of natural and synthetic fibres may be stitched with mercerised cotton, Trylko or Drima thread, depending on the fibre make-up of the blend. (Check the fabric label for fibre content.) The size of the needle is determined by the thread: size 14 for mercerised cotton; size 11 for Trylko or Drima.

Stitch length and pressure. As a rule a 2 mm (12) stitch length is preferred. Pressure should be heavy enough to carry the fabric without showing the print of the feed.

Stitching. Since many drip-dry fabrics are blends of two or more fibres, it is wise to test your stitching on a scrap of your fabric. If the seams pucker after being stitched with one of the synthetic threads, you must adjust the tension. Begin by changing the upper tension to a lower number; then if the stitch is not locked in the centre of the fabric, it may be necessary to loosen the lower tension slightly. (A dense or tightly woven fabric usually requires a heavier upper tension.)

Stitch slowly. Check seams immediately after stitching and then a few hours later. Synthetic threads have a 'recovery' factor. Although the seam may appear to be smooth and without pucker immediately following stitching, a few hours later the thread may recover its set dimension and cause a pucker. Seams that are smooth after stitching and before pressing will remain smooth through many washings. This is the secret of sewing drip-dry fabrics successfully.

Velvet, Velveteen, and Corduroy

Velveteen is fashionable for daytime, sports and formal wear; velvet is used primarily for evening wear. Corduroy, which is generally less expensive than the other two, is practical for sportswear and children's clothes. These pile fabrics are also used for bedspreads, curtains and loose covers.

Pile fabrics have an 'up' and 'down'. To determine the direction of the pile, follow the instructions on page 55.

Preparing to Sew

Pattern. Many pattern designs are suitable for velvet, velveteen and corduroy. The most effective, however, are those with simple lines that show off the rich tone of the fabric. Avoid too many styling seams within the garment. Unpressed pleats are suitable. Always cut off the pattern margin on the cutting line before placing the pattern on the fabric.

Fitting. It is important to fit and adjust the pattern exactly to your requirements before you cut pile fabrics. Any alterations after cutting affect the pile and are noticeable. If your pattern design is intricate, cut, stitch and fit a calico toile (see page 315) to which you can make adjustments before cutting the fabric.

Cutting. Lay the fabric on a smooth, flat surface with the pile side (right side) up. For sections where you must lay the pattern on a fold, be sure to fold the fabric lengthwise with the pile side on the outside. You must lay all pattern pieces in one direction with the pile running up. To avoid marking the pile, pin the pattern to the fabric with long, fine needles instead of pins.

Markings. Make tailor's tacks only, with silk thread.

Interfacing. Use pre-shrunk muslin, batiste or a similar fabric for interfacing, silk organza is excellent for a soft velvet. Interface suits and coats with a fine hair canvas, following *Method 1*, on page 136.

Mounting and lining. You may mount or line the entire garment or just a portion of it. Cut the mounting or lining by the same pattern pieces and on the same grain as the garment. Select such fabrics as silk crêpe, Jap silk or a suitable synthetic lining to match the fabric.

Stitching and Handling

Tacking. Always tack with silk thread. Fit the garment and make all necessary adjustments before machine stitching. Avoid temporary machine stitching that must later be removed, it will mark the pile.

Thread and needle. Stitch velvet with silk thread and velveteen and corduroy with silk or mercerised cotton thread. Use a synthetic thread for nylon velvet. If corduroy or velveteen is washable use mercerised cotton thread. Most pile fabrics require a size 14 needle; however a size 11 can be used to stitch velvet. When stitching with silk thread adjust the tension until the stitching looks the same on the top and underside.

Stitch length and pressure. A 2 mm (12) stitch length is correct. The pressure exerted by the Presser Foot should be somewhat lighter for pile than for a flat woven fabric of the same thickness – just heavy enough to carry the fabric without showing the print of the feed.

Stitching. The rule is to stitch with the pile. Since the pile runs up, this means that seams are stitched from the lower edge to the top. A plain seam, pressed open, is best.

Seam finishes. Several methods of neatening the seam edges are appropriate. They are pinking; binding with nylon net; overcasting by hand; or over-edging by machine, using the blindstitch zig-zag. Do not allow edges of the fabric to pucker.

Darts. Slash through the centre of darts and press them open to eliminate bulk.

Mounting and lining. A pencil-slim skirt should be completely lined to retain its shape. Page 95 describes how to use mounting and lining. Use the method where mounting and skirt are joined only at the waistline.

To eliminate bulk in velvet, velveteen and corduroy, omit the facing at the neckline and at the lower edge of short sleeves and let the lining serve in its place.

Line the bodice from the neckline to about 5 cm (2 inches) below the armhole. First stitch and press the shoulder seams separately in the velveteen and lining. Place velveteen and lining sections right sides together. Pin, tack and stitch round the neckline, following the seamline. Layer the seams and press. Turn the lining to the underside and ease it under slightly at the seamline; tack flat against the velveteen. Press. Handle as one fabric throughout the rest of the construction.

To line short sleeves, stitch underarm seams separately in the velveteen and lining; then, at the lower edge of the sleeve, stitch the velveteen to the lining, right sides together. Layer seams and press. Turn the sleeve to the right side, with the lining on the underside. Ease the lining under slightly at the seamline; tack and press. Tack the two fabrics together at the sleeve head and handle as one throughout the rest of the construction.

Zip opening. Hand-sew the zip to give your dress the couturier touch. Follow the conventional method of inserting the zip up to the final step. Then, finish by hand, using a short backstitch. See page 178.

Hems. The edge of the hem may be finished with silk or rayon seam binding or bound with nylon net. Always hand-stitch the hem with silk thread. Place the stitches between the hem and garment and not over the hem edge. On a circular skirt, where a narrow hem is essential, use a hand-rolled hem.

Pressing. Follow the instructions given on page 66.

Lace Fabrics

Lace fabrics may be made of cotton, rayon, wool, linen, silk or other fibres. They may be expensive or inexpensive, depending on what fibres they contain and whether they are made by hand or by machine.

Fashion dictates the uses of lace. It may advocate lace fabrics for wedding and evening dresses, for day dresses, blouses, stoles, jackets and evening coats; for tailored suits and beach wraps. The lace must, of course, be appropriate for the occasion. Silk laces are used primarily for formal wear; most of the other lace fabrics may be used for other occasions as well as for formal wear.

make a special underslip of opaque fabric to wear with the dress. In a dress-and-jacket ensemble, the dress may be mounted with an opaque fabric and the jacket with fine net or organza. Wool crêpe is an appropriate mounting for wool lace.

Generally, the mounting should match the lace exactly in colour, although a subtle contrast may occasionally be used effectively – for example, off-white with white, écru with white, or a shade darker than the colour.

Mounting and Lining beginning on page 95, describes the techniques you should follow.

Preparing to Sew

Pattern. To emphasise the design of the lace, choose a simple style. The pattern should have a minimum of darts and seam details; too many break the continuity of the design of the lace. Designs with bodice and sleeve cut in one are excellent. Avoid neckline and sleeve facings unless you plan to mount the lace with an opaque fabric; cut the facings of matching fine net or tulle to eliminate bulk. Do not use styles requiring faced front and back openings unless the facing and bodice are cut in one, which will eliminate the seam. Avoid shoulder pads or shapes, even when in fashion, if you are using a sheer lining.

Cutting. The design of the lace must be matched. Some laces have an 'up' and 'down' to the design and must be cut with all pattern pieces laid in the same direction. See the directions for *Florals, Prints and Jacquards*, page 55. Always fold the lace wrong sides together. Use sharp pins. (Some dressmakers prefer needles to avoid damaging the lace.) As a further precaution, pin within the seam allowances and gathered areas. Cut all notches outwards so that they will not interfere with seam construction or final finishing. Shears should be sharp and lightweight.

Markings. Use tailor's tacks only.

Mounting and lining. Mounting is necessary to support the delicate network of threads in lace fabrics. Lining, however, is sometimes used in full skirts if there is little openwork in the lace and the texture is firm. Select a smooth, firm fabric. Opaque fabrics such as taffeta, satin, peau de soie, polished cotton or wool crêpe will place the lace in the category of a heavy fabric. If you wish to maintain the sheerness of the lace, mount with silk organza, fine net, marquisette or chiffon, and

Stitching and Handling

Tacking. Use a size 8 or 9 hand-sewing needle and tack all seams to prevent the lace from slipping during machine stitching. If there is a design to be matched at the seamline, slip-tack.

Thread and needle. Select silk thread for the machine stitching on silk, wool or synthetic lace, and mercerised cotton for cotton and linen. These threads require a size 14 needle; however, use a size 11 if you can do so without the thread breaking. Stitching synthetic laces with synthetic thread you will be able to use a size 11 needle.

Stitch length and pressure. In stitching the fine openwork of lace, use a 1·5 mm (15) stitch length and light pressure – no heavier than needed to carry the fabric evenly under the Presser Foot without marking the lace.

Stitching. Medium-weight laces require guiding only in front of the needle during machine stitching; soft and silk laces require a little more support. Gently control the fabric both in front and at the back of the foot, taking care not to pull or stretch the lace.

Darts. Use darts only if your mounting is opaque; it will conceal the darts in the finished garment. If your mounting is sheer, change darts to soft gathers.

Seams and seam finishes. An opaque mounting will prevent the seam allowances from showing through the lace, so you may use a plain seam in your dress. Pink the seam edges and press the seam open. If you are using a sheer lining, however, or are attaching the skirt and lining at the waistline only, you must use a fine, narrow seam and conceal the seam edges. Use a French seam or, to eliminate bulk, a double-stitched seam.

Seam layering. Layer curved seams in the usual way to eliminate bulk.

Finishing the edges. A fine double-fold bias binding makes a pleasing finish for the neckline, sleeves and front or back opening. Use it rather than shaped facings. Satin, taffeta and organza, matching the lace exactly in colour, are all excellent fabrics for the binding.

Zip opening. Insert the zip by hand to give the couturier touch. Buy a fine zip and follow the conventional method of inserting it up to the final step. Then, instead of top stitching, hand-sew, using a short backstitch. To vary the conventional zip insertion, use the channel seam method. Place the zip under the machine-tacked seam; hand-sew ·6 cm ($\frac{1}{4}$ inch) from the centre seam.

Fastenings. Do not make buttonholes in lace; thread loops are better suited to the fabric. Choose small buttons; large buttons are too heavy for lace.

Hems. If the lace has a border or scalloped edge, use that as the finish. In circular skirts, where a lining is used, hem the two fabrics separately. A narrow hem is essential; make a hand-rolled hem. If the lace is mounted with an opaque fabric, form a hem of average width. Finish the edge with a multi-stitch zig-zag, or pink it and stitch ·6 cm ($\frac{1}{4}$ inch) from the edge, using 1 mm (20) stitch length. Then make a French hem by herringboning below the hem edge and between the hem and the garment.

Pressing. Use the steam setting on the iron. Place a wool-faced pressing pad on the ironing board with the wool-facing side up. Lay the lace, right side down, on the pad. (A turkish towel may be substituted for a pressing pad.) Cover the lace with a thin pressing cloth; if additional moisture is required for seams, place a moist muslin cloth over the thin pressing cloth before pressing. If you follow these suggestions, you will not flatten the raised design of the lace during the pressing.

Soft Leather and Suede

Find out all you can about the size and shape of the skins you want to use. Remember that many skins have thin areas and you must avoid placing them in garment sections subject to strain. Unless you are experienced in selecting and handling skins, limit your sewing to accessories and trimmings. It takes experience and sound judgment to select skins of the correct weight and texture for large garments.

Preparing to Sew

Pattern. Select a design with seams which will fit into the size and dimension limitations of your skins. Any other seaming, unless it contributes to styling, is to be avoided.

Fitting. You must do all fitting *before* you cut the suede or leather. Adjust the pattern; cut, stitch and fit a calico toile; then make all corrective fitting adjustments to the *toile*. Trim seam allowances to ·9 cm ($\frac{3}{8}$ inch) for economy *unless* you plan to place top stitching more than ·6 cm ($\frac{1}{4}$ inch) from the edge, or to use a welt seam. The narrow seam allowance will also eliminate bulk in the finished garment.

Cutting. Lay the calico pattern pieces on the wrong side of a *single layer* of suede or leather. Do not fold the skins or cut two pieces at one time. Turn the pattern pieces over to cut the second half so that you will have a right and left side. Since leather has no grain, the pattern pieces may be laid either lengthwise or crosswise on the skins, depending on which direction gives you the most even distribution of thickness. Note, however, that *all pieces must be laid in the same direction*. Since suede has an up and down, you must lay all pattern pieces lengthwise on the skins and in one direction with the nap running down. To determine the direction of the nap, brush the suede with your fingers as you would velvet and napped fabrics. See pages 55 and 56. Do not pin into the body of the garment since punctures will permanently damage the leather. Either pin within the seam allowance or use sellotape to hold the calico pattern in position. Use sharp scissors. Cut all notches outwards or mark them with chalk on the underside of the leather.

Markings. Mark darts, buttonholes, centre lines and styling points with chalk on the wrong side of the skin.

Do not use a tracing wheel; it will damage the leather. To transfer markings, turn back a portion of the pattern and fold along the line of the dart, buttonhole or other marking; chalk-mark the skin along the line of the fold. Use a ruler to keep lines straight. Reinforce thin spots with Moyceel iron-on interfacing on the wrong side of the skin.

Lining. Suede and leather garments should be lined. Synthetic linings such as Tricel, rayon taffeta and Bemberg are suitable.

Interfacing. Interface collars, cuffs and front facing areas with lightweight hair canvas, or non-woven interfacing. Follow directions given for *Method 1* on page 136. For additional shape retention, extend the front section of the interfacing to the armhole.

Stitching and Handling

Tacking. Although seams may be pinned or tacked, be careful to make the pin or needle punctures within the seam allowance. Paper clips are a safe substitute. Or, you may find that you can handle the seaming without pinning or tacking, depending upon your sewing skill.

Thread and needle. Use either silk or heavy-duty mercerised cotton for machine stitching. Select size 14 machine needle for medium-weight skins, size 11 needle for fine leather and thread, and size 16 for heavier leather and thread. A wedge-point needle, designed expressly for stitching leather, is available at your Singer Centre in the sizes mentioned. The narrow wedge point pierces the leather cleanly, ensuring a neat, uniform stitch.

Regulate the tension to produce a balanced stitch. In most cases the upper tension should be slightly higher for leather than for medium-weight woven fabrics.

Stitch length and pressure. Regulate the stitch length to 2 mm (12) for lightweight and medium-weight leathers, and to 2·5 mm (10) for heavier weights. The pressure should fall within the medium range and carry the leather without showing the print of the feed.

Stitching. Pre-shrink straight seam binding and use it for staying seams and points of strain. Hold the tape gently against the upper side of the leather and against the Presser Foot as you sew the seam. The tape will strengthen the seam and prevent the leather from sticking to the Presser Foot. Stitch slowly and handle the leather lightly. Do not pull the leather as it passes under the Presser Foot, for this may stretch it. After the seams are stitched, slash the edges of the tape at even intervals to prevent them from pulling. Make sure your garment fits correctly before you begin stitching because un-picked seams have needle holes that will permanently mark the skins.

Corners must be blunt, not pointed. Either curve the corners slightly or place two or three stitches across the point to allow sufficient width for turning.

Seams and seam layering. To emphasise centre front and back seams and yoke seams, use welt seams, or press the seam open and top-stitch on each side an equal distance from the seamline.

Layer seams inside collars, cuffs, facings and pockets in the usual way. To prevent facings and seams from rolling out of place, stick the seam allowances in place. Use rubber solution, Copydex or a similar liquid adhesive suitable for leather, fabric, or a combination of two materials. Spread the adhesive on the underside of the seam allowance; then finger-press the seam allowance against the garment.

Darts. Slash through the centre of darts, and press them open to eliminate bulk.

Lining. Line the skirt, following the method given on page 98 where lining and skirt are joined only at the waistline.

Avoid facings and hems in a waistcoat or tank-top. The lining can serve as facing as well as support the suede. See *One-Piece Neckline and Armhole Facing*, page 141. Before joining shoulder and underarm seams, place the suede and lining sections right sides together. Stitch round the neckline, front opening, lower edge and armholes, following the seamline. Trim seams, turn to right side, ease lining under slightly at the stitching line, and press. Join shoulder and underarm seams of suede with machine stitching, and press seams open. Then, on the lining, fold under the seam allowance on one side and lap it over the opposite seam allowance, and pin. Slip-stitch in place. Top-stitch round the neckline, front opening, lower edge and armholes, stitching either ·6 or 1·5 cm ($\frac{1}{4}$ or $\frac{5}{8}$ inch) from the finished edge.

Buttonholes. Machine-worked, hand-worked or bound buttonholes are suitable. Stay them with a backing of firmly woven muslin or lawn between the facing and top fabric.

If you are making bound buttonholes, follow the *One-Piece Method*. See page 112. Instead of tacking the buttonhole strip in place, place sellotape across the ends, and use a 2 mm (12) stitch length in the stitching.

The facing treatment is different from the method used for woven fabrics. Stitch the facing in place in the usual way. Then, from the right side of the garment, machine-stitch round the buttonhole just inside the seam on the buttonhole strip and across the ends through the facing. Slash the facing and trim away the suede or leather inside the stitching line.

Hems. The depth of the hem should be no greater than 4 cm (1½ inches) and the hem must conform exactly to the body of the skirt. Use chalk to mark the hemline on the wrong side of the leather. For an invisible finish, stick the hem in place. See *Seams and Seam Layering* above. Lay the skirt right side down on a flat surface and work from the hem side. Spread the adhesive along the underside of the hem as far as the fold line. Turn the hem; then finger-press it against the skirt. Begin at the centre front or back and work towards the side seams, matching seams and centre lines.

Pressing. Seams in leather and suede should be pressed with a warm, not hot, iron (do not use steam). Cover the area with brown paper, and press on the wrong side. Seams may also be tapped lightly with a wooden pounding block to compress them.

Lining. Stitch straight seam binding to the free edge of jacket front facings and slip-stitch the lining to this binding. This is easier than hand stitching lining to leather.

Glass Fibre Fabrics

Glass fibre is a synthetic fabric that is ideal for curtains and bedspreads. It is available in a variety of weaves, either translucent or opaque. It will not shrink, stretch or sag, and needs no ironing. There is no problem in stitching it when a few simple rules are followed.

Instructions for making home furnishings begin on page 338 of this book.

Preparing to Sew

Cutting. To cut a plain fabric, always draw a thread from the fabric to indicate the cutting line. Cut printed designs on the patterns. If the fabric is cut off grain, curtains and draperies will not hang well.

Lining. Glass fibre curtains are seldom lined. The translucent beauty of the unlined fabric is preferred by many people. If a lining is used, however, it should also be of glass fibre, so that it will not shrink, stretch or sag. When extra opaqueness is desired, make an under-drapery instead of a lining, and hang it from a separate rod so that it can be drawn and closed independently.

Be sure to use washable, pre-shrunk stiffening in the heading.

Stitching and Handling

Thread and needle. Select mercerised cotton or Drima thread for the machine stitching. Use a new, sharp machine needle, size 11 for translucent glass fibre and size 14 for heavy or rough-surfaced glass fibre.

Regulate tensions to produce a balanced stitch. If the seam puckers, it may be necessary to loosen the upper tension.

Stitch length and pressure. A 2·5 to 2 mm (10 to 12) stitch length is satisfactory for sheer as well as opaque glass fibre. The pressure must be light – no heavier than required to carry the fabric gently and evenly under the Presser Foot. If the pressure is too heavy, the print of the feed shows on the fabric and the feed may cut the threads of the glass fibre.

Stitching. Pin the seam edges together. Stitch slowly and guide the fabric gently behind the Presser Foot and in front of the needle. Let the machine do the work. When using a straight stitch on a zig-zag machine, use the straight stitch throat plate and Presser Foot for best results.

To prevent the edges from fraying and to achieve a finished underside, make French seams on all glass fibre fabrics.

It is wise to experiment with stitch length, tension and pressure, and with guiding the fabric on a swatch of the glass fibre before you begin your work. You will find that with a little practice you can handle the fabric expertly.

Seam finishes. Seam edges in net curtains and draperies should be enclosed and do not require finishing. Finish the seam edges of bedspreads with the blindstitch zig-zag.

Hems. Make a double-fold hem in sheer fabrics to eliminate the turned raw edge that would normally show through. Pin hems in sheer fabrics with a straight stitch and hems in heavier and rough-surfaced fabric with either a straight stitch or the blindstitch zig-zag.

Hand Sewing-Plain and Fancy

Hand sewing is still an essential part of dressmaking. In professional, well-made clothes, hems are finished by hand. In children's clothes and table linens, decorative fashion details are added by hand to provide an attractive accent. To achieve the made-to-measure look in home decoration, hand sewing is best in many areas.

This chapter tells you how to make many of the basic hand stitches. If any of them are unfamiliar to you, practise making them on a scrap of fabric before you attempt to use them in your work. All the decorative or embroidery stitches described here may be used individually or in various combinations to produce a design; they may be worked in matching or contrasting thread, or in two or more colours of thread.

A Word about Thread

Hems should be finished with mercerised cotton, silk or synthetic thread, depending on the fabric; the thread should match the fabric exactly in colour.

Hand embroidery stitches may be made with single or multiple strands of sewing thread, stranded cotton, silk floss, pearl cotton, buttonhole twist, and wool or synthetic yarn. The selection depends on the fabric, the size of the stitch and the effect desired. Choose colourfast threads to stitch children's clothes and household linens which will be laundered.

Slip Stitch

The slip stitch is almost invisible. It is used when one edge is turned under as in hems, bias binding, curved seams, top facings, coat or suit linings and similar places.

Tack the folded edge in position. For stitching, use mercerised cotton, silk or synthetic thread to match the fabric.

Work from right to left, with the hem fold between the thumb and index finger of the left hand. Bring the needle up through the fold. Directly opposite and barely outside the fold, take a stitch, catching only one thread of the fabric; then slip the needle through the fold a stitch length. Continue making the stitches, spacing them from ·6 to ·9 cm ($\frac{1}{4}$ to $\frac{3}{8}$ inch) apart. In seams that may be subject to strain, space the stitches only ·3 cm ($\frac{1}{8}$ inch) apart. Do not pull the threads taut. When completed, fasten the thread with two tiny backstitches in the hem edge or seam.

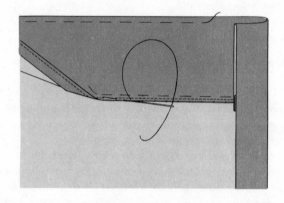

Blind Hemming (Invisible) Stitch

This is the stitch most frequently used for hemming. The edge may be finished with seam binding or edge stitching.

Tack the hem in place. For stitching, use mercerised cotton, silk or synthetic thread matching the fabric.

Work towards you, or from right to left, with the hem fold between the thumb and index finger of the left hand. Bring the needle up through the hem edge. Directly opposite and barely outside the hem, take a stitch,

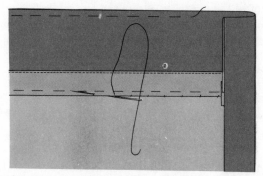

For stitching, use a short, fine needle and fine thread.

Place the lace or ribbon right sides together. Pin or tack the edges to prevent them from slipping. Make small over-and-over stitches along the edge of the seam. Space the stitches about ·2 cm ($\frac{1}{16}$ inch) apart.

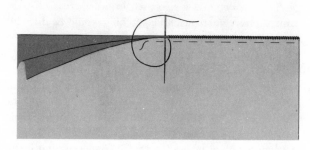

catching only one thread of the fabric; then direct the needle diagonally up through the hem edge. Continue making the stitches, spacing them from ·6 to ·9 cm ($\frac{1}{4}$ to $\frac{3}{8}$ inch) apart, depending on the fabric. Do not pull the thread taut. When completed, fasten the thread with two tiny backstitches in the hem edge. The stitches are invisible on the right side.

Hemming Stitch

The hemming stitch is another popular stitch for hemming. The edge may be finished with bias seam binding, edge stitching or straight seam binding.

Tack the hem in place. For stitching, use mercerised cotton, silk or synthetic thread matching the fabric.

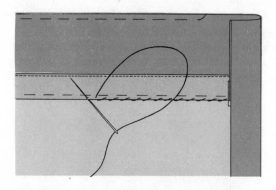

Work towards you, or from right to left, with the hem edge between the thumb and index finger of the left hand. Bring the needle up through the edge of the hem and take a stitch in the fabric over the hem edge, catching only a single thread of the fabric; then bring the needle out through the hem edge. When completed, fasten the thread with two tiny backstitches in the hem edge. The stitch is invisible on the right side and long slanting stitches are visible on the wrong side.

Whipping Stitch

The whipping stitch is a tiny stitch used to join lace, insertion and ribbon.

Herringbone Stitch

The herringbone stitch is used in hemming, in seaming lapped seams on the underside, in attaching interfacings to garments and in hand sewing darts and tucks in suit and coat linings.

Tack the hem, facing, tuck, dart or edge in place. For stitching, use mercerised cotton, silk or synthetic thread.

Work from left to right, with the needle pointed to the left. Hold the hem edge between the thumb and index finger of the left hand. Make a stitch in the hem or facing, catching one or two threads in the top layer of fabric; then make a stitch barely outside the hem edge, catching only a single thread of the under layer of fabric. Alternate the stitches along the edge in a zig-zag fashion. The threads will cross between the stitches. When finished, fasten the thread with tiny backstitches in the hem.

When using a herringbone stitch to sew darts and tucks in coat and suit linings, work on the right side of the fabric and make the stitches through all thickness of fabric, near the top fold for the tuck or dart.

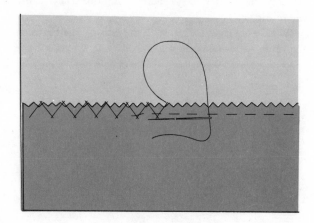

Backstitch

The backstitch is a small stitch that is used when top stitching by machine would be too harsh – for example, in the final stitching of the zip in sheer, delicate fabrics or fine woollens. It is also used in other areas of dress construction where machine stitching would be difficult (for example, in lapped seams in interfacings) and in the repairing of split seams.

For stitching, use the same kind of thread you used for the machine stitching. Fasten the thread with two backstitches on the underside. Work towards you, or from right to left. Bring the needle up through the fabric to the right side. Insert it one or two fabric threads behind the place where the thread came out, and bring the needle forward and out ·3 cm ($\frac{1}{8}$ inch) from the backstitch. Begin each additional stitch just outside the preceding stitch. (The stitches on the underside will be twice as long as those on the top side.) Make the stitches through all layers of fabric. When completed, fasten the thread on the underside with two tiny backstitches.

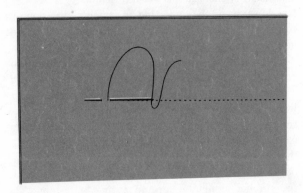

Running Stitch

The running stitch is used for seaming, tucking, mending, gathering and other kinds of delicate sewing.

For stitching, use a long, slender needle, size 7 or 8, and mercerised cotton, synthetic or silk thread matching the fabric.

Work from right to left, with the fabric edge between the thumb and index finger of the left hand. Weave the

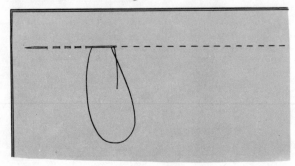

point of the needle in and out of the fabric five or six times before pulling the thread through. Make small, even stitches. When finished, fasten the thread with one or two tiny backstitches.

Handpicked Stitch

Handpicked stitching adds a tailored look to collars, cuffs, lapels, pockets and fashion seams of coats, suits and tailored dresses. The garment should be completed before you add this fashion detail.

On the right side, tack the line for the stitches ·9 to 2·5 cm ($\frac{3}{8}$ to 1 inch) from the finished edge, depending on the fabric, the design of the garment and personal preference. Use a gauge to measure the distance as you tack.

For stitching, use buttonhole twist matching the fabric.

Work towards you with the needle pointed in the same direction. Bring the needle up through the interfacing and top layer of fabric. Insert it ·2 cm ($\frac{1}{16}$ inch) behind the place where the thread came out, through the top layer of fabric and interfacing; then bring it out ·9 cm ($\frac{3}{8}$ inch) from the backstitch. (With this spacing, the finished stitches should be about ·6 cm ($\frac{1}{4}$ inch) apart.) Do not draw the threads taut; the backstitch should lie beadlike on the fabric surface. Remove the tackings as you work. When completed, fasten the thread between the layers of fabric with two tiny backstitches. The stitches are not visible on the underside.

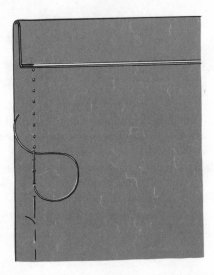

If your costume has lapels, you must transfer the stitches to the opposite side of the seam at the turn of the lapel. At this point, and on the backstitch, bring the needle through all layers of fabric to the opposite side of the seamline and continue making the same stitches.

Padding Stitch

The padding stitch is used primarily in tailoring to hold two layers of fabric together to prevent slipping – for example, to hold the interfacing in place along the roll line of lapels and collars.

Tack the interfacing in place. Work towards you and on the wrong side, with the needle pointed to the left. For stitching, use thread to match the fabric colour. Hold the work between the thumb and fingers of the left hand and take a short stitch from right to left through the

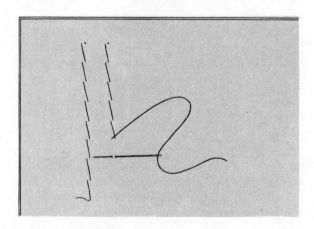

interfacing and fabric, catching only one thread in the fabric. Space the stitches about ·9 cm (⅜ inch) apart. The long slanting stitches on the wrong side are visible but the short crosswise stitches on the right side are not.

Buttonhole Stitch

The buttonhole stitch is used for a decorative finish on edges as well as for hand-worked buttonholes. As a decorative finish, the stitches may be almost any depth; in buttonholes, however, they should be from ·2 to ·3 cm (1/16 to ⅛ inch) in depth and closely spaced.

For the stitching, see *A Word about Thread*, page 228. Work from right to left. Hold fabric, needle and thread in the position shown in the illustration.

With the right side of the fabric up, bring the edge over the first finger of the left hand. Take two backstitches at the edge to fasten the thread. Bring the thread to the left and then to the right to form a loop round the edge where the stitch will be made. Insert the point of the needle from the underside up through the fabric, keeping the thread behind both the point and the eye of the needle. Hold the loop with the left thumb and pull the needle up through the fabric, then away from you to place the purl of the stitch on the edge of the fabric. Keep the stitches as even as possible.

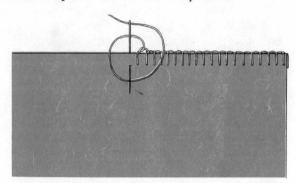

Blanket Stitch

The blanket stitch is often used to decorate children's clothes, lingerie and household linens. It is an excellent edge finish for babies' blankets, matinée jackets and night gowns. It is also used for hand appliqué.

Fold and tack the hem.

For stitching, select thread appropriate for the fabric. Take two backstitches on the underside in the hem fold

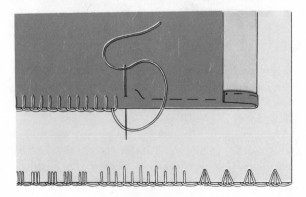

to fasten the thread. Work from left to right, with the right side of the edge towards you. Hold the thread down with the thumb and insert the needle from the right side, barely catching the top edge of the hem; then bring it out from under the edge and over the thread. Draw the thread through by pulling it towards you, forming the blanket stitch. Do not pull the thread taut. When completed, fasten the thread on the underside with two tiny backstitches in the lower edge of the hem. The stitches may be evenly spaced, closely spaced in groups of three or varied in length to form a pattern or a fan-shape design.

Chain Stitch

The chain stitch is an outline stitch used in children's and babies' clothes as well as in linens and lingerie.

Knot the long end of the thread. Work from right to left. Bring the needle up through the fabric to the right side. Hold the thread against the fabric with the left thumb. Insert the needle close to the point where the thread came out and bring it out over the thread just a stitch length to form a loop. Keep the thread to the left of the needle. Begin each successive stitch inside the loop to form a chain. The length of the stitch will depend on the fabric. Do not pull the thread taut. When finished, fasten the thread on the underside with two tiny backstitches.

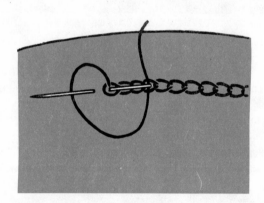

Cross Stitch

The cross stitch is one of the oldest decorative stitches. It may be used on household linens, blouses, children's clothes and collar and cuff sets as well as on canvas in needle-tapestry work.

The cross stitch is usually made over an iron-on transfer design; however, if the design of the fabric is a small ·6-cm (¼-inch) check, you may use it as a pattern. If you are working with hopsacking or a similar coarse

weave, you can make even cross stitches by counting the fabric threads for each stitch.

Work from left to right with the needle pointed towards you. Bring the needle up through the fabric to the right side of the lower left corner of the cross, leaving a thread about 1·2 cm (½ inch) long; catch that thread under the stitches as they are made to fasten it. Carry the thread diagonally to the right, insert the needle in the upper right corner, and bring it out at the lower left corner of the next cross. A diagonal stitch will appear on the right side and a straight stitch on the underside. Continue making the same stitches across the work. Then work back over the stitches in the opposite direction to form the crosses. Be sure that the crosses touch. The stitches should be firm so that the threads lie smooth on the surface.

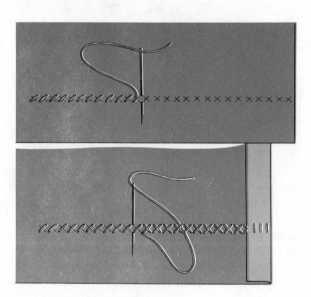

Featherstitch

The featherstitch is appropriate for decorating household linens, children's and babies' clothes and is used in stitching darts and tucks in suit and coat linings.

Tack or chalk the line of the stitch on the right side of the fabric. Work towards you and bring the needle up through the fabric to the right side where the stitch is to begin. Hold the thread down with the thumb and take a small stitch on the right side of the line, slanting the needle towards the line and passing the thread under the needle. Make the same kind of stitch on the left side of the line, slanting the needle towards the line. Continue alternating the stitches on the right and left, keeping the stitch length, spacing and slant of the needle the same in each stitch. Draw the thread firmly enough to keep it flat, yet loosely enough to curve it slightly. When completed, fasten the thread on the underside with two tiny backstitches.

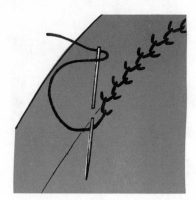

French Knot

The French knot is a familiar embroidery stitch in the centre of flowers. Groups of knots are also used to form designs. They are generally placed close together and combined with other stitches.

Knot the long end of the thread. Bring the needle up through the fabric at the point where the knot is to be made. Hold the needle close to the fabric and wind the thread two or three times round the point. Hold the thread taut round the needle and insert the needle through the fabric close to the point where the thread

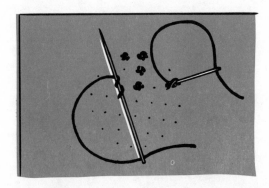

came out. Place your thumb over the knot to hold the twist in place and pull the thread through to the underside, bringing the knot snugly against the fabric. Then bring the needle up through the fabric for the next French knot. When the work is finished, fasten the thread on the underside with two tiny backstitches.

Lazy Daisy or Detached Chain Stitch

The lazy daisy is a loop stitch used to form a daisy petal.

For stitching, select a thread size that is appropriate for the size of the petal.

Bring the needle up through the fabric at the centre end of the petal. Loop the thread to the left. Insert the needle close to the point where the thread came out, and then bring it out over the thread at the opposite end of the petal. Insert the needle barely outside the petal loop and bring it out again at the centre where the next petal begins. Do not draw the thread taut. When the daisy is finished, fasten the thread on the underside with two tiny backstitches. French knots are usually placed in the centre of the design.

Outline or Stem Stitch

This stitch may be used to form a border, to make flower stems and leaf veins, or to outline a design.

Lightly mark or transfer the design to the fabric. Knot the long end of the thread.

Work from left to right with the needle pointed to the left. Bring the needle up through the fabric from the underside. Make small backstitches, lapping each stitch

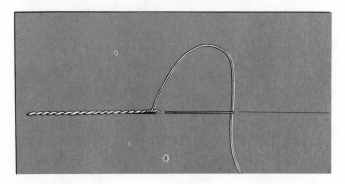

slightly by bringing the needle out about ·2 cm ($\frac{1}{16}$ inch) behind the previous stitch. Hold the thread down with the thumb as you pull the threads through. Keep the thread above the needle; insert the needle and bring it out on the line of the design. When completed, fasten the thread on the underside with two backstitches.

For double hemstitching, turn the work and make the same kinds of stitches on the opposite edge, picking up the same threads in the fabric to form a bar. Fasten the thread on the underside with two small fastening stitches.

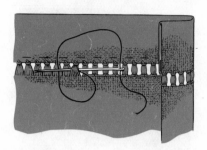

Hand Hemstitching

Hemstitching is used in table linens, lingerie and babies' clothes.

Measure the hem allowance and draw about three or four threads from the fabric parallel to the hem. The number of threads drawn will depend on the weave of the fabric and the width desired for the hemstitching. Fold the fabric edge under ·6 cm ($\frac{1}{4}$ inch); then fold and tack the hem, keeping the folded edge just below the drawn work.

For stitching, use a fine mercerised thread. Knot the long end of the thread. Work from right to left on the wrong side. Bring the needle up through the hem edge so that the knot will be between the hem and top fabric. Slide the needle under several threads of the fabric; loop the thread to the left under the point of the needle. Pull

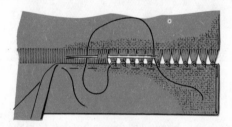

the thread through and draw up the stitch tightly by pulling the thread towards you. Then take a stitch in the edge of the hem fold, catching only a single thread of the fabric. Repeat the stitch until one edge is finished. Keep the same number of fabric threads in each group.

Faggoting

Faggoting is a decorative stitch used to join sections in blouses, dresses, lingerie, collars and cuffs.

Fold under the seam allowance on the cut edges, press and hem. Tack the edges to heavy paper for support. The distance between the edges is the width of the faggoting.

For stitching, use pearl cotton, buttonhole twist or a similar thread. Knot the long end of the thread. Bring the needle up through the fabric fold. Carry the thread diagonally across the opening, and insert the needle up through the fabric fold on the opposite side; pull the thread through. Pass the needle under the thread, diagonally across the opening, and up through the fabric on the opposite side. Continue alternating the stitches across the opening. Evenly spaced stitches are essential. When finished, fasten the thread on the underside. Remove the tacked paper, and press.

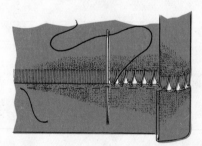

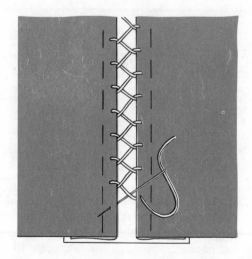

Decorative Touches

A decorative touch which adds interest and individuality to your dress marks you as a competent, creative dressmaker. It transforms a simple dress into a special dress, a plain-looking blouse into an elegant one.

The many fashion 'extras' you can add by sewing are described in this chapter. They include tucks, frills, shirring, cording, appliqué, smocking, quilting, beads and sequins, lace edging and insertion, and braid. Some of them can be used in home decorating as well as in clothing.

Tucks

Tucks are always in fashion in dresses, blouses, children's clothes and lingerie. They are equally at home in sheer and heavy fabrics. They may be very narrow, as a dainty 'pin tuck', or 2·5 cm (1 inch) or more wide. They may be machine-stitched or hand-stitched.

Since the beauty of a tuck depends on its absolute accuracy, you must stitch exactly along the woven thread of the fabric. The Edge Stitcher guides the width for tucks from 'pin' width to ·6 cm ($\frac{1}{4}$ inch). See page 284. This is a time-saver and contributes a great deal to the attractiveness of your work.

To Estimate Fabric Width Requirements

If the pattern calls for tucks, it will allow sufficient width for the size of the tuck specified. If you decide to add tucks to the dress as a point of interest, you will need extra fabric as follows:

When the tucks and spaces are equal, fabric twice the finished width is required. When the fold of the tuck touches the stitching of the previous tuck, as in a blind tuck, three times the finished width is required.

If an entire section such as a pocket, yoke or collar, is to be pin-tucked, you should *tuck the fabric first and then cut out the section according to the pattern.*

To Mark the Position of Tucks

Tucks are usually made on the lengthwise grain of the fabric as it is always firmer than the crosswise grain and gives a better finish. Occasionally, however, a design calls for crosswise tucking to emphasise style lines.

Draw a single thread from the fabric to mark the position for each tuck. Fold and press the fabric on the drawn thread the entire length of the tuck. If tucks are ·6 cm ($\frac{1}{4}$ inch) or wider, tack along the line of each tuck to prevent the layers of fabric from slipping during the stitching.

To Stitch Tucks
RULES TO REMEMBER
Always stitch tucks so that the stitching uppermost under the needle is visible when the garment is worn (unless you are applying lace in the tucking operation as on page 237). When tucks are used on both sides of the garment, they are turned in opposite directions from the centre, and you must alternate the direction of the stitching on the right and left sides.

Be sure that tensions are balanced. As tucks are topstitched, they require a shorter stitch than that used for inside, straight seams. See the *Fabric, Thread and Needle Chart*, page 24. The thread should either blend perfectly with the fabric in colour and texture or be a definite contrast.

Always make a few practice tucks in a scrap of your fabric to be certain that the stitch length, tuck size and spacing are satisfactory.

235

PIN TUCKS

Pin tucks, as their name implies, are only as wide as a pin. They are generally spaced about ·5 cm ($\frac{3}{16}$ inch) apart in groups of three or five, with a wider space between each group. Lace is often inserted between the groups.

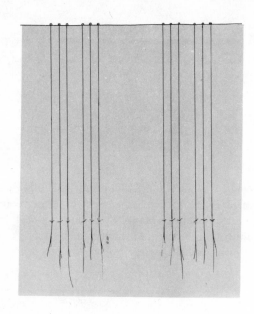

HAND-STITCHED TUCKS

Hand-stitched tucks are found in babies' clothes and sheer blouses.

Mark the position for each tuck, following the instructions given on page 235. Stitch, using a long, slender needle, fine thread and a very small running stitch. When finished, fasten the thread on the underside of the fabric. Press.

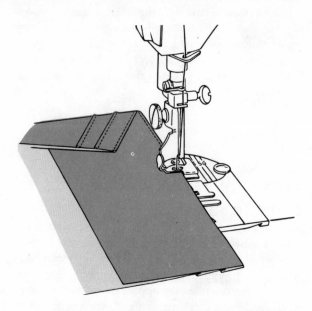

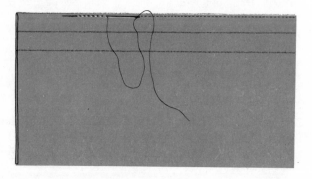

Mark the position for each tuck, following the instructions given above. Adjust the Edge Stitcher, see page 285, so that the stitching is very close to the folded edge of the fabric. Stitch slowly, guiding the fabric. Press.

When the tucks extend only a few cm (inches) into the garment section, as in the yoke of a baby's dress or shoulder of a blouse or dress, pull the threads through to the underside and tie the two threads together at the end of each tuck.

TUCKS AND SPACE OF EQUAL WIDTH

When spacing and tucks are equal, you will need twice the finished width in the fabric. The space between the markings for each tuck is four times the width of the finished tuck, or 2·5 cm for a ·6-cm tuck (1 inch for a $\frac{1}{4}$-inch tuck).

Mark the position for the tucks, following the instruc-

236

tions on page 235. Stitch, using the *Edge Stitcher*. See page 285. Press.

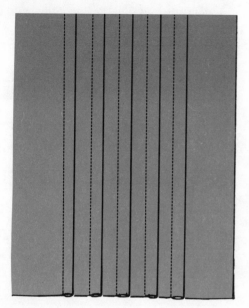

BLIND TUCKS

In blind tucking, the fold for the tuck touches the stitching of the previous tuck. The tucks may be of almost any width; the 2·5-cm (1-inch) tuck is illustrated. The space between the markings for each tuck is three times the width of the finished tuck.

Mark the position for the first tuck, following the instructions given on page 235.

The position of the second and succeeding tucks must be marked before you begin to stitch. Stitch slowly, guiding the fabric. Press.

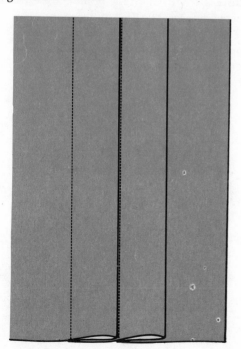

DECORATIVE TUCKS

Decorative tucks are made by using a zig-zag machine.

Mark the position for the first tuck, following the instructions given on page 235. Mark the position of the other tucks. Select a stitch pattern appropriate for tucks and stitch slowly, guiding the fabric. Press.

TUCKS WITH LACE

You can make ·6-cm (¼-inch) tucks and apply lace underneath with a single line of stitching when you use the Edge Stitcher.

Select lace wide enough to extend beyond the tuck

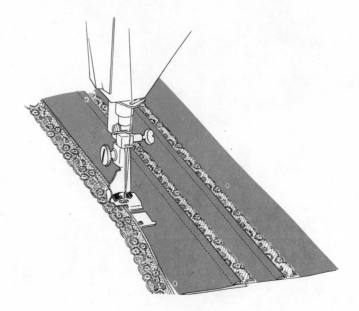

237

but not overshadow it. Mark the position for each tuck, following the instructions on page 235.

Use the Edge Stitcher with the lug adjusted far enough to the left to place the stitching on the selvedge of the lace. Insert the folded edge from the right in slot 5, and the lace edge from the left in slot 1. Stitch slowly, guiding the fabric and the lace. Press the tuck over the lace.

SMOCKED TUCKING

Smocked tucking, a variation of straight tucking, provides a texture contrast on the yoke or pockets of a dress or blouse made of plain fabric.

Tuck the fabric on the lengthwise grain, making ·3- or ·6-cm ($\frac{1}{8}$- or $\frac{1}{4}$-inch) tucks spaced ·6 cm ($\frac{1}{4}$ inch) apart, using the Edge Stitcher. See page 284.

For the crosswise stitching, use the Edge Stitcher. Adjust it so that each side is the same distance from the needle. Alternate the direction of each row of stitching, keeping the rows the same distance apart. The Edge Stitcher turns the tucks in the same direction of the stitching, creating a smocked effect.

When the stitching is completed, press. Cut the tucked section by the plain pattern piece.

SHELL TUCKS

Shell tucks are an attractive treatment for babies' dresses and blouses. Usually ·3 to ·6 cm ($\frac{1}{8}$ to $\frac{1}{4}$ inch) in width, they can be stitched by hand or by machine. Use silk, batiste or a similar soft fabric.

Hand-stitched. Mark the position for the tucks as instructed on page 235. Machine-stitch the tucks, using a line of straight stitching and the Edge Stitcher to keep the stitching an even distance from the edge.

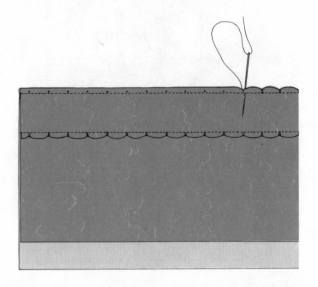

Lightly mark the size of each shell or scallop at equal intervals – usually ·6 to ·9 cm ($\frac{1}{4}$ to $\frac{3}{8}$ inch) apart. Use a fine needle and knot the end of the thread. Bring the needle up through the tuck at the first marking; take two stitches across the tuck, drawing the thread tightly to form a scallop. Slip the needle between the two layers of fabric in the tuck and bring it out at the marking for the next stitch. When finished, fasten the thread on the underside of the fabric. Press.

Machine-stitched. Mark the position for each tuck as instructed on page 235. Tack if necessary. Set selectors on the machine for the blindstitch zig-zag. Make a test on a sample of your fabric to find the right needle thread tension, stitch length and stitch width.

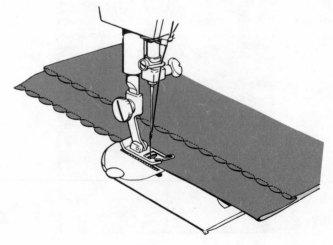

Place the folded tuck under the Presser Foot, with the fold towards the left. Stitch slowly, guiding the fabric by hand so that the sidewards stitches do not pierce the folded edge. Press.

SCALLOPED TUCKS

Dainty, scalloped tucks are used as self-trimming on blouses, dresses, lingerie and children's clothes.

Allow sufficient width in the fabric for the tucks, as instructed on page 235, plus an additional 1·2 cm ($\frac{1}{2}$ inch) for seam allowances on the edge of the scallops.

Fold and crease the fabric on the line for the tuck, with right sides together. Trace the scallop on the fabric, placing the edge of the scallop ·6 cm ($\frac{1}{4}$ inch) from the fold to allow for stitching.

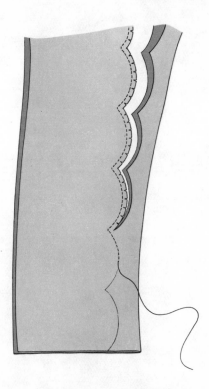

Use a short stitch and the Quilter if you have one. (The open construction and short toe of the Quilter makes it easier to stitch small scallops.)

Stitch round the scallops exactly on the traced line, taking one stitch across the point between each scallop. This extra stitch gives you width when cutting and prevents pulling at the point between the scallops in the finished work.

On small scallops, trim the seam allowances to a bare ·3 cm ($\frac{1}{8}$ inch); but on large scallops, trim them a generous ·3 cm ($\frac{1}{8}$ inch), and trim one edge shorter than the other. Slash at the point almost to the stitching. Cut notches in the seam edges at evenly spaced intervals. Press.

Turn the scallops to the right side. Gently work the seam edges between the thumb and finger to bring the stitching to the very edge. Tack the edges with silk thread to retain the shape of the scallop until after pressing.

Using the desired width, stitch the tucks an even distance from the edge with a line of straight stitching. Press.

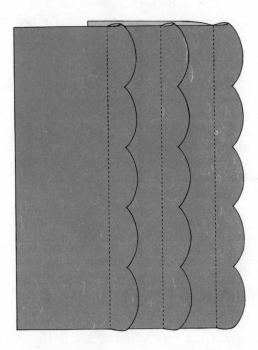

You can also stitch small scallops easily on the zig-zag machine. Set the selectors for the scallop pattern. The stitch length and stitch width vary the length and depth of the scallop; select the length and width you want. As you stitch, the fabric passes straight under the Presser Foot, and the needle follows a scallop pattern. Always start each row of stitching at the beginning of a scallop unit. See page 266 for instructions. Press, layer seams and turn the scallops as instructed above.

To Press Tucks

Press the underside of each tuck in the same position as it was stitched. Then on the wrong side, press the tucks to one side, flat against the fabric. (Usually, tucks are turned away from the centre of the garment.) Cover the fabric with the appropriate pressing cloth and use the amount of moisture required.

239

Frills

Frills add a feminine touch to blouses and dresses. They are also a pleasing trimming on lingerie and children's clothes, and on curtains and bedspreads.

To Prepare the Fabric

Frills on garments are usually cut on the crosswise grain or true bias. Frills on sheer curtains are cut on the lengthwise grain to keep seams to a minimum. The texture of the fabric makes a difference in the fullness – soft and medium-weight fabrics are most suitable for frills than firm fabrics.

Double or triple fullness may be required for the frill depending on the width of the frill as well as the texture of the fabric. Wide frills require more fullness than narrow frills. It is always wise to cut and gather up more than the estimated requirement.

Cut the fabric two to three times longer than the length of the finished frill.

Before gathering the frill, finish the outer edge either by machine, using the Hemmer Foot; by hand; or by one of the pattern stitches on the zig-zag machine that is suitable for an edge finish. You may apply lace at the same time you machine-stitch the hem.

To Gather the Frill

The Ruffler enables you to gather the fabric quickly, easily and evenly. See *Ruffler*, page 280, for instructions.

After you have adjusted the setting of the Ruffler, test the fullness on a scrap of the same fabric you are working with.

To ruffle organdie or chintz, dampen the fabric along the seamline with a small, moist sponge and gather while damp.

To Apply the Frill

TO AN EDGE

Pin the frill to the edge, right sides together, extending the straight edge 1·2 cm (½ inch) beyond the gathering stitches of the frill. Pin at close intervals. Tack if necessary. Stitch with the frill-side up, just beyond the gathering stitches.

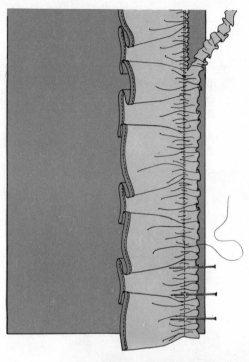

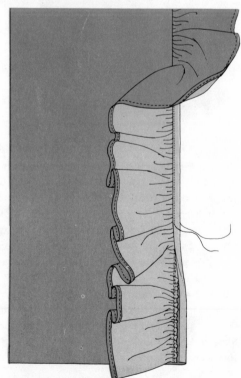

Trim the seam allowance on the frill to ·3 cm (⅛ inch). Fold the straight edge under ·3 cm (⅛ inch), then fold it over the seam edges to the stitching line on the underside, enclosing the cut edge. Pin. Stitch near the first fold. Press. Turn the frill away from the garment and press the seam towards the garment.

The fabric may be gathered and stitched to a straight edge in one operation. See page 281.

FOR A LINGERIE EDGE

Pin the frill to the edge, right sides together, keeping the edges even. Stitch with the frill uppermost under the needle.

Trim the seam allowance to ·6 cm (¼ inch). Overcast the cut edges together, using the blindstitch zig-zag. Use a fine stitch length and medium stitch width.

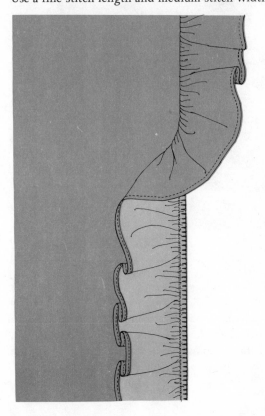

IN A STRAIGHT SEAM

Pin the frill to the seam edge, right sides together, extending the straight edge 1·2 cm (½ inch) beyond the gathering stitches of the frill. Stitch from the frill-side on the gathering stitches. Press the seam.

Place the attached frill over the second seam edge, right sides together. Pin at close intervals. Tack if necessary.

Place the work under the needle with the first line of stitching uppermost so that you can use it as a guide. Stitch barely beyond the previous line of stitching. Press. The stitching is not visible on the right side.

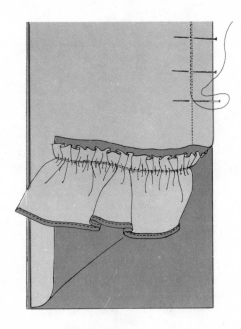

TO A FACED EDGE

When a frill is added as a decorative trimming to the edge of a collar or cuff, it is set between two layers of fabric and often must be eased round a corner.

Pin the frill to the outer edge of the top collar or cuff, right sides together. From 1·2 cm (½ inch) on each side of the corner, ease the gathers closer together with the thumb as you pin. This will give the extra fullness needed round the corner. Tack if necessary. With the frill side up, stitch on the gathering stitches. Press the seam.

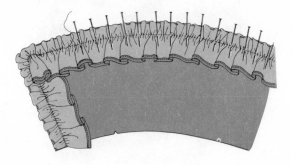

Place the edge of the attached frill over the under-collar or cuff, right sides together, matching markings. Pin and tack, leaving the neckline edge, or lower edge of the cuff, open. Smooth out the frill so that only the seam allowance is caught in the stitching.

Place the first line of stitching uppermost under the needle; stitch barely beyond it. Press the seam.

Trim the seam allowances on the undercollar and frill to ·3 cm (⅛ inch) and the seam allowance on the top collar to ·6 cm (¼ inch). Cut off the corners and notch into the seam allowances on the outside curve. Turn the collar to the right side, and press.

be gathered to fit the bodice length. You will often find it necessary to adjust the fullness of the frill after you have gathered it. Loosen the upper tension slightly on your machine and use the Ruffler to gather the fabric. See page 280 for instructions on using the Ruffler. Leave long threads at each end of the seam. (Do not forget to return the tension to its previous setting.)

Pin the frill to the pinafore, matching markings. Work from the centre to the outer edges, and adjust the frill to fit the pinafore by easing the fabric back on the bobbin thread.

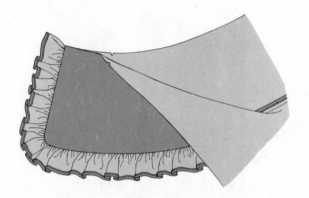

To Attach Frill with Heading

Finish both edges before gathering the frill. See *Frill with Heading*, page 281 for instructions.

Turn the straight edge of the garment to the underside and make a ·3-cm (⅛-inch) double fold. Press. Pin the frill to the right side of the edge at closely spaced intervals, with the gathering stitches over the double fold. Stitch from the frill side on the previous line of stitching. The folded edge and frill are held in place with one line of stitching.

To Attach Pinafore Frills

Shoulder frills in the bodice of a pinafore are shaped at each end; that is, they are wider through the centre and taper almost to a point at each end. Therefore, they must

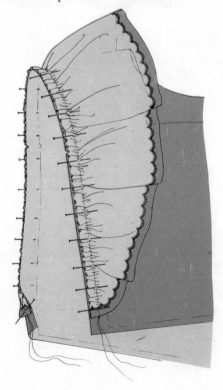

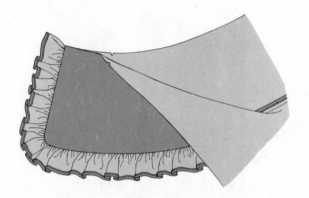

Shirring

Rows of shirring are often a styling point at the shoulder line, waistline and lower edge of sleeves. Sometimes an entire section, such as a yoke or pocket, may be shirred for a rouched or decorative effect.

Soft fabrics – batiste, voile, silk, net and fabrics of similar textures – lend themselves better to shirring than firm fabrics. Crisp sheers, however, can be shirred if they are steam pressed to soften the finish and stitched while damp. The true bias or crosswise grain of the fabric is more easily shirred than the lengthwise grain. Shirring by machine is quick and produces strong, even stitches.

Shirring with the Gathering Foot

You can achieve many lovely effects with simple rows of evenly spaced shirring made with the Gathering Foot. For instructions on how to use foot and the stitch length required, see page 285.

Draw a single thread or crease the fabric on the crosswise grain at selected intervals for the spacing desired. Stitch on each of these lines, using the Gathering Foot. If you are spacing your rows 1·2 cm ($\frac{1}{2}$ inch) apart, you can gauge the distance by the edge of the foot.

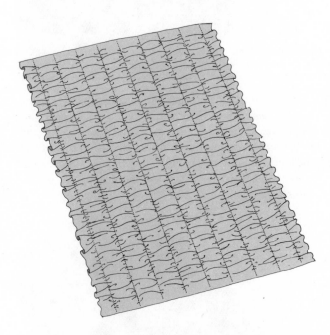

When you are shirring an entire section such as a yoke or pocket, shirr the fabric, then cut the section according to the pattern. Always test the fullness on a scrap of your fabric before working on the garment.

WAFFLE SHIRRING

Waffle shirring gives texture interest to smooth-surfaced fabrics. It can be used on cottons, silks, woollens and rayons, and is particularly interesting for details on children's dresses, blouses and lingerie.

With the Gathering Foot, stitch on the crosswise grain of the fabric and then on the lengthwise grain. Use a stitch length short enough to produce only a slight fullness.

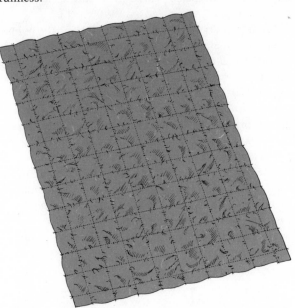

Controlled Shirring

When a section of a seam is to be shirred and stitched to a straight seam, the shirring must be controlled so that the seams, when joined, are of the same length. See *Gathering to Control Fullness*, page 105.

Use a stay of the same fabric to prevent strain on the shirring. Cut the stay 1·2 cm ($\frac{1}{2}$ inch) deeper than the rows of shirring and wide enough to fit across the entire garment section when shirred.

Place the stay over the wrong side of the shirred section, keeping the seam edges even. Pin and tack in position. Include the stay in the seam when the garment sections are joined.

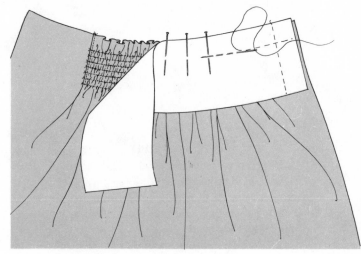

Shirring with Elastic Thread

Elastic shirring is appropriate for lingerie, children's clothes and washable skirts. It requires no special machine accessory.

Wind the bobbin with elastic thread, using the bobbin winder on the machine. The elastic thread will stretch slightly as it is wound on the bobbin. If you have a *Touch & Sew** machine, wind the bobbin by hand, stretching the elastic thread slightly. For a heavy fabric where greater strength is required, wind double strands of elastic thread on the bobbin. Use mercerised cotton thread for the top threading of the machine.

Select a 2·5 to 2 mm (10 to 12) stitch length, depending on the fabric. Always test the fullness on a scrap of the same fabric used in the garment. When stitching the second and subsequent rows, stretch the elastic in the previous rows as you sew so that the shirring will be even. Rows spaced ·6 cm ($\frac{1}{4}$ inch) apart may be gauged by the edge of the Presser Foot.

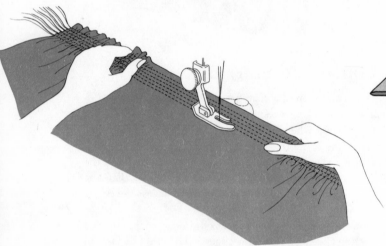

At each end of the stitching, tie the elastic and needle threads together by forming a single knot in the two strands of thread; use a pin to set the knot tightly against the fabric.

Cording or Piping

Cording is a versatile and handsome detail in dressmaking and an excellent finish for loose covers, bedspreads and cushions. It is made by covering a length of cord with a bias strip of either the same colour as your work or a contrasting colour.

Corded seams may be either delicate or bold, depending on the size of the cord. If you are going to use corded seams, make a corded piping, which can be stitched into the seam or on to an edge. If you are going to use the cording for button loops, trimming or frogs, you will make what is called 'rouleau' cording. Instructions for both are given here. But first you must cut and join your bias strips.

Cutting Bias Strips

The true bias is the diagonal line of a square of fabric. Fold the crosswise grain of the fabric to the lengthwise grain; this forms a true bias. Cut along the fold.

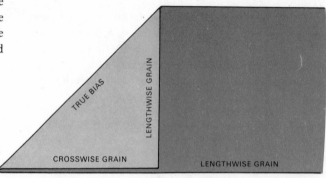

How wide to make your bias strips depends on the size of the cord. Cut the strips 3·1 cm ($1\frac{1}{4}$ inches) plus three times the width of the cord. Use a ruler and measure the required width from the true bias edge of the fabric. Mark the line with tailor's chalk. Measure and mark as many strips as you will need, then cut on the markings.

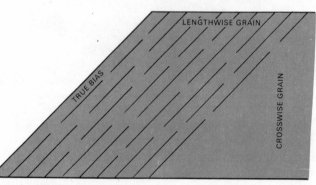

Joining Bias Strips

If you need only a short length of cording, avoid piecing it; however, if you need a long, continuous length, you will have to join bias strips.

All bias strips are joined on the lengthwise grain so that the seams will be less noticeable. If one end of your bias strip is on the crosswise grain, fold this fabric end on the lengthwise grain and cut.

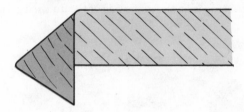

Join the lengthwise ends; offset the width of the joining seam and stitch, taking a ·6-cm (¼-inch) seam. Be careful to match any prominent weave, stripe or design of the fabric. Press the seams open.

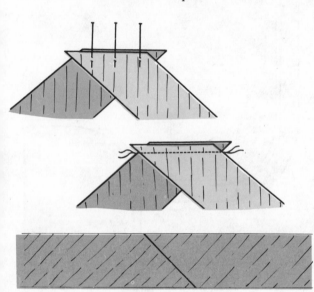

Corded or Piped Seams

COVERING THE CORD

Replace the Presser Foot with the Zipper Foot and adjust it to the left of the needle.

Bring the bias strip round the cord, right side out,

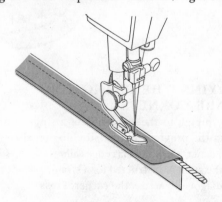

keeping the seam edges even. Use a slightly longer stitch than that ordinarily used for seaming the fabric. Stitch close to the cord, but not too close. You have now made a 'piping'. Press the stitching.

A chain stitch is an ideal stitch for fabrics that are cut on the bias since the loop formation of the stitches makes them less taut than regular straight stitches. If your machine has Chain Stitch Accessories, refer to the instruction book of the machine and to page 63.

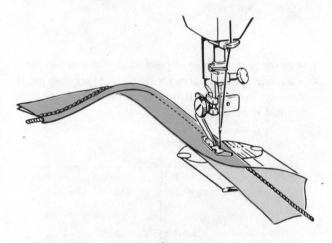

If sheer fabric is used to cover the cord, underline the bias strip with an opaque fabric, such as taffeta or polished cotton, which matches the sheer fabric in colour. Cut bias strips of the underlining. Place the sheer bias strip, right side up, over the right side of the underlining and handle the two as one in covering the cord. Follow the above procedure.

APPLYING THE CORDING TO A STRAIGHT SEAM

Pin the cording to the right side of the single seam edge, keeping the previous line of stitching over the seamline. Adjust the Zipper Foot to the right of the needle. Stitch with the same stitch length used when covering the cord. Press the stitching.

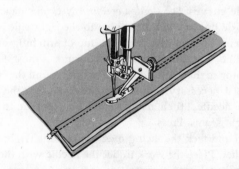

Pin and tack the second seam edge over the cording, right sides together. Place the work under the needle

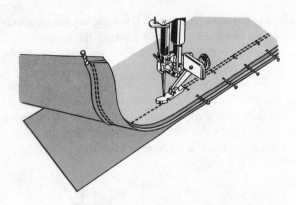

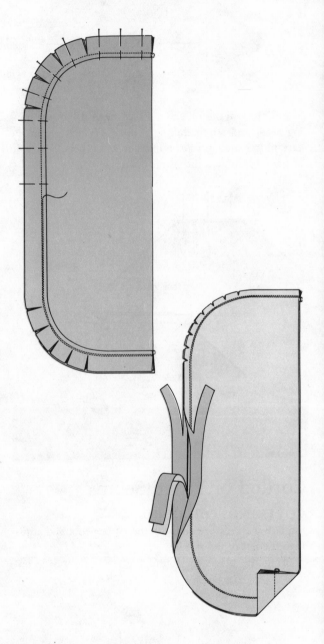

Trim the piping seam allowance to ·3 cm (⅛ inch) and the garment and facing seam allowances to ·6 cm (¼ inch). Notch the seam allowance on the curve at regular intervals. Press. Turn the facing to the underside. Fold on the seamline and press. Finish the free edge of the facing. All stitching is on the underside of the finished garment.

with the first stitching uppermost so that you can use it as a guide. Stitch *between the cord and the previous line of stitching*. Press. All stitching is on the underside of the finished garment.

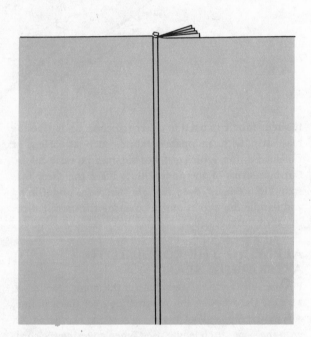

APPLYING THE CORDING TO CURVES

Inside curves. See *Corded or Piped Neckline*, page 146.
Outside curves. Pin the piping to the right side of the garment, keeping the previous line of stitching on the seamline. Cut into the seam allowance almost to the stitching so that the cord will lie smooth round the curve. Tack, if necessary. Adjust the Zipper Foot to the right of the needle. Stitch, using a stitch shorter than that for straight seams. Press.

Pin and tack the facing over the cording, right sides together. Place the work under the needle with the first line of stitching uppermost so that you can use it as a guide. Stitch between the cord and the previous line of stitching. Press.

APPLYING THE PIPING TO SQUARE CORNERS

Pin the piping to the right side of a single seam edge, keeping the previous line of stitching on the seamline. At the corner, slash the bias edges almost to the stitching. Stitch the seam as instructed for a straight seam; take one stitch diagonally across the corner. Press.

246

Lay the facing over the piping with the right sides together, and pin.

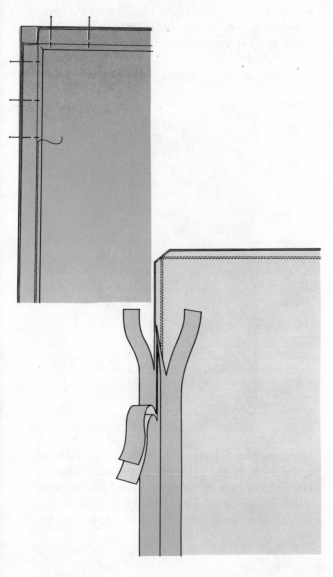

Stitch between the cord and the previous line of stitching. Press.

Cut diagonally across the corner close to the stitching. Trim the piping seam allowance to ·3 cm (⅛ inch) and the garment and facing seam allowances to ·6 cm (¼ inch). Press then turn to the right side and press.

Rouleau

To Make Rouleau

Cut a true bias strip 2·5 cm (1 inch) wide plus three times the width of the cord. Cut one end to a point.

Use a cord twice the length of the bias strip. Machine-stitch the centre of the cord to the wrong side of the pointed end. Stitch from the point to about ·9 cm (⅜ inch) from it.

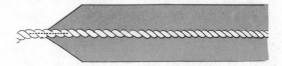

Turn about ·9 cm (⅜ inch) of the pointed end and the cord to the right side of the bias, then fold the bias in half round the cord. The remaining half of the cord extends from the point.

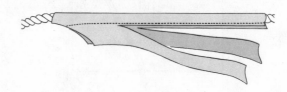

Adjust the Zipper Foot to the right of the needle. Use a short stitch. To avoid stitching the turned-under point, form a funnel at the point and taper it for about 2·5 cm (1 inch); then stitch close to the cord and, at the same time, stretch the bias slightly. Half the cord is covered and half extends beyond the funnel end. Press, then trim the seam allowances to ·3 cm (⅛ inch).

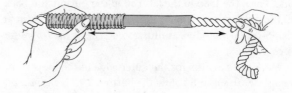

(If your machine has Chain Stitch Accessories, use them for stitching fabrics that are cut on the bias. See page 63.)

Work the bias back over the extended cord while pulling the encased cord. *Do not twist.* The stitches will

not break if you have used a short stitch and have stretched the bias in the stitching.

Button Loops

Button loops are in and out of fashion. When they are 'in' they may be found at openings in the neckline, sleeves and front bodice; in jackets and in lingerie. Ball and half-ball buttons are appropriate for this type of fastening.

Always make a test button loop in a scrap of your fabric before working on the garment.

LENGTH AND SPACING OF BUTTON LOOPS

To work out the length and spacing of button loops, make a paper diagram. Draw a straight line 1·5 cm ($\frac{5}{8}$ inch) from the edge to represent the seamline. Draw a second line in the seam allowance, ·6 cm ($\frac{1}{4}$ inch) from the first line and parallel to it to represent the position of the loop ends.

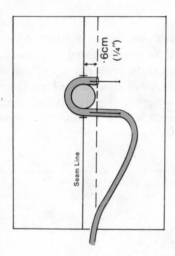

Place the exact centre of the button on the seamline. Bring the rouleau round the top edge of the button *with the seam to the inside of the loop.* Pin the end of the cording on the marking you made ·6 cm ($\frac{1}{4}$ inch) from the seamline. Form the loop to the left round the button and back to the seam ·6-cm ($\frac{1}{4}$-inch) line. Pin. Mark the rouleau at the ·6-cm ($\frac{1}{4}$-inch) line as illustrated. *This is the length for each button loop.*

Mark the position for the outer edge of the loop at the seamline, above and below the button. *This is the spacing required by each loop.*

Measure the space and mark the fabric at these intervals. Measure the determined amount for each loop and mark the rouleau at these intervals. Cut through the seam allowance and into the cord at each marking, but not far enough to separate the loops.

STITCHING OF BUTTON LOOPS

Turn the garment to the right side. Tack or draw a line in the seam allowance, ·6 cm ($\frac{1}{4}$ inch) from the seamline (·9 cm ($\frac{3}{8}$ inch) from seam edge). Lightly mark the spacing for the button loop as determined on the paper diagram. Be sure to make your marks within the seam allowance so that you do not mark the garment. If interfacing is used, tack it to the wrong side of the garment.

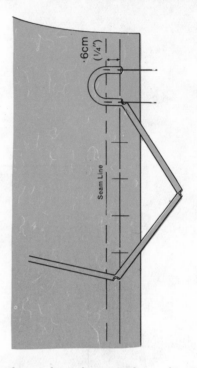

Form the button loops between the markings, extending the ends to the guideline in the seam allowance, ·6 cm ($\frac{1}{4}$ inch) from the seamline. (The loops are formed away from the opening.) Pin the loops in place at the seamline with fine needles. The outer edges of the loops

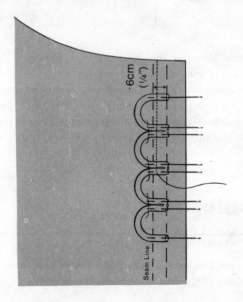

should touch. Tack the loops together so that they hold their shape until the stitching is completed. Stitch the loops to the garment ·2 cm ($\frac{1}{16}$ inch) outside the seamline. This stitching is not visible in the finished work.

Pin and tack the facing over the garment, right sides together. Place the work under the needle with the previous stitching uppermost so that you can use it as a guide. Stitch on the 1·5 cm ($\frac{5}{8}$ inch) seamline to conceal the previous line of stitching.

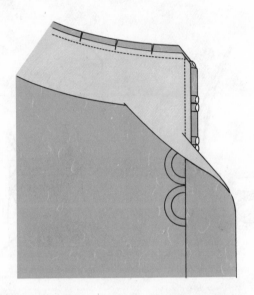

Trim the facing seam allowance to ·3 cm ($\frac{1}{8}$ inch) and the garment seam allowance to ·6 cm ($\frac{1}{4}$ inch). Press.

Turn the facing to the underside. Fold on the seamline, and press. When the facing is turned, the loops will extend beyond the opening edge.

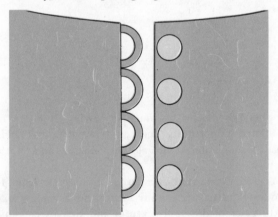

Frogs

Rouleau may be looped into many interesting designs to form 'frogs'.

Loop rouleau into the desired design, keeping the seam on the underside. Decide the length needed for each loop and pin-mark the cording at these intervals.

Do not cut. Allow a ·6-cm ($\frac{1}{4}$-inch) seam allowance at each end. Pull out the cord at the ends and cut off ·6 cm ($\frac{1}{4}$ inch).

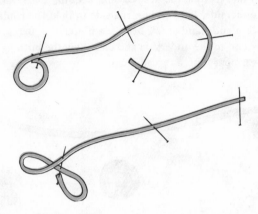

Form the first loop and insert a pin up from the underside to hold the loop in place. Then slip each consecutive loop over the end of the pin as illustrated. Leave the last loop free to slip over the button.

Catch the loops together where they cross on the underside, concealing the end. Catch through the first two loops but only the underside of the third loop. Work out the length required to slip over the button, then form the last loop and catch it to the underside, concealing the end.

Make a frog for each side of the opening. Pin them on the right side of the garment, then stitch them in place on the underside. Use half-ball, full-ball and shank buttons with frogs.

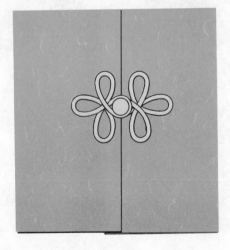

Buttons

To make buttons from rouleau, fold under the end, then wind into a circle the desired size, keeping the seam on the underside. Pin through the side to hold the rouleau in place and hand-stitch it on the underside. Bring the outer end to the underside and tack. Sew the buttons on the garment with a thread shank.

Other Rouleau Trimming

You can make rouleau scrolls. Follow the instructions for the button; however, allow enough for two buttons. Begin at the centre of the rouleau; at one end wind it clockwise and at the other end wind it anti-clockwise.

You can loop rouleau into a graceful design and apply it to your dress as you would braid. You can also use it for 'spaghetti' trimming in belts and bows.

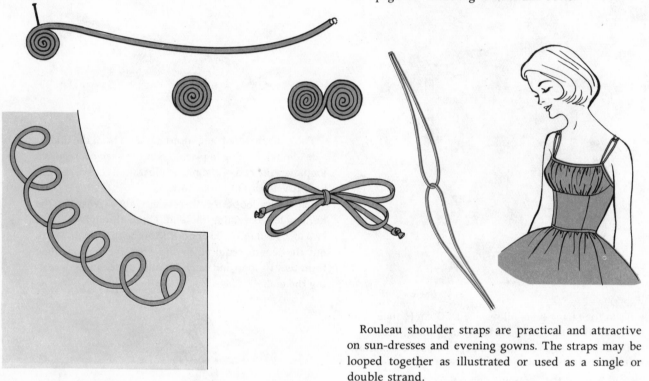

Rouleau shoulder straps are practical and attractive on sun-dresses and evening gowns. The straps may be looped together as illustrated or used as a single or double strand.

Appliqué

Appliqué is the loving touch in sewing. It offers an unlimited opportunity for self-expression and adds beauty and interest to clothes, linens, and fabric furnishings.

You can create your own design or buy pattern motifs and appliqué transfers ready for tracing. Fabrics of like textures or of different textures and weaves combine equally well.

Printed linen handkerchiefs or furnishing fabric, chintz and other fabrics with a definite design make interesting appliqués.

Appliqué may be done by machine or by hand. Machine appliqué, however, is often better, as the work may be accomplished with greater ease and accuracy.

250

The zig-zag machine ensures close evenly-spaced stitches and enables you to stitch many intricate designs, too difficult for hand work.

Transferring the Design

Transfer the design on a piece of fabric slightly larger than the design, using one of the methods given below:

1. If you are using an iron-on transfer, carefully follow the instructions given.

2. If you are not using the hot-iron method, trace the design on stiff paper or lightweight cardboard, and cut it out. Place the template on a piece of fabric slightly larger than the design. Mark lightly round it with pencil or chalk.

3. If the fabric is not too heavy, place the pattern for the design over a windowpane and secure it with sello-tape. Hold the fabric over the design and trace lightly around it.

4. On heavy fabrics, place dressmaker's tracing paper between the design and the fabric. Then trace lightly round the design.

5. Place sheer fabrics such as organdie over the design, then lightly trace the design on the fabric with pencil or chalk.

Do not cut out the fabric after tracing the design.

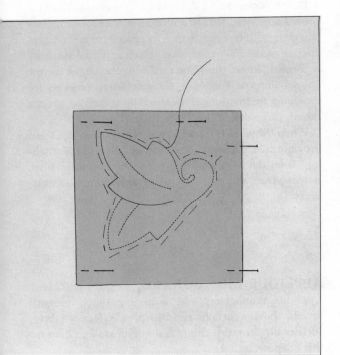

Machine Appliqué

A closely spaced zig-zag stitch is the most versatile in appliqué work. Although you may vary the width of this stitch to accommodate fabric weaves and textures, never allow the stitch to be too wide.

PREPARATION (*Lower left*)

Carefully place the fabric design on the article to be decorated and pin it in place. Hand-tack near the design outline.

Outline the design with straight stitching; use a short stitch. Stitch any lines shown within the design. Remove tackings and press.

Replace the Presser Foot on the machine with the Special Purpose Foot designed for use in appliqué work. Set the selectors for a narrow zig-zag stitch and shorten the stitch length for satin stitching. See *Satin Stitching*, page 266.

Before starting to work, study the design to determine which section you should complete first. Avoid crossing the lines of stitching whenever possible since this may break the continuity of the design.

SIMPLE APPLIQUÉ

Two methods may be used in the appliqué stitching. Choose the one appropriate for your fabric. Remember a test sample is always advisable.

Method 1: Use a closely spaced zig-zag stitch. Stitch over the straight stitch outline. Stitch any lines shown within the design first. Pull the threads to the underside and tie. Press. Cut away the fabric on the outer edge close to the stitching, using embroidery scissors.

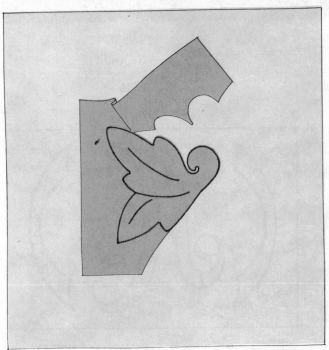

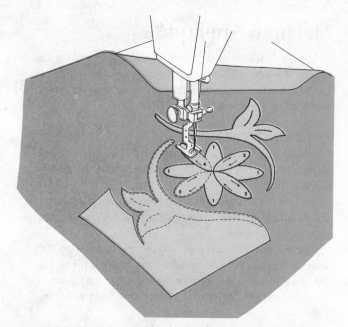

Method 2: Trim the outside edge of the fabric close to the straight stitching. For added body, tack an underlay of lawn on the wrong side of the fabric, under the design.

Stitch over the edge of the design with a closely spaced zig-zag stitch. A smooth, lustrous finish results, which requires no additional trimming. Pull the threads through to the underside and tie. Press. Trim the underlay on the wrong side close to the stitching, using embroidery scissors.

To make smooth, rounded corners, stop the machine with the needle in the outside edge of the fabric; lift the foot, turn the fabric slightly, and take two stitches, turning the hand wheel by hand. Repeat several times. To make square, open corners, pivot the fabric on the needle when the needle is on the inside edge.

CORDED APPLIQUÉ

Corded appliqué is an ideal finish for a motif of lace. Use gimp, fine crochet thread, buttonhole twist or heavy-duty thread for the filler cord.

Select wide lace edging with a definite floral design. If you are applying the lace to an edge, extend the fabric edge at least 2·5 cm (1 inch) beyond the line of the appliqué stitch. Choose a motif from the lace and place it separately above the edging; tack in place.

Either *Method 1* or *2* described above may be used for corded appliqué. *Method 1* is recommended for intricate lace designs. The only change in procedure is the introduction of the filler cord, over which appliqué stitching is formed. Insert the filler cord into the eyelet on the Special Purpose Foot. See *Hairline Seam*, page 88 for threading instructions. This stitching technique gives a raised, three-dimensional effect.

When the work is finished, remove the tackings. From the right side, cut away the excess lace close to the stitching; from the wrong side, trim the excess fabric ·6 cm ($\frac{1}{4}$ inch) from the stitching, using embroidery scissors. Press.

APPLIQUÉ MONOGRAMS

Appliqué monograms add a luxury touch to bath towels, shower curtains and bedspreads. Heavy fabrics such as slipper satin, chintz and taffeta are excellent for this purpose.

Use *Method 1* for monogramming bath towels, and either method for bedspreads and shower curtains. Corded appliqué is also an effective finish.

SHADOW APPLIQUÉ

Shadow hems and designs are lovely for table linens and children's clothes of crisp organdie or fine linen.

Tack the hem the full depth of the design and mitre all corners. Lightly trace the design for the hem and motif on the right side of the article to be appliquéd. See page 251.

Cut a piece of the same fabric slightly larger than the motif. Pin it over the wrong side of the motif. Tack ·6 cm ($\frac{1}{4}$ inch) from the lines of the motif and the hem.

Follow the instructions for *Corded Appliqué* and stitch round the design, using a fine filler cord; remove tacking and press.

Cut away the outer edges of the fabric on the underside close to the stitching, using embroidery scissors. Press.

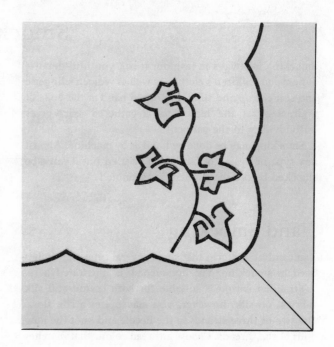

Hand Appliqué

The cut edges of the design are folded to the underside in hand appliqué.

Trace the design to be appliquéd on a piece of fabric slightly larger than the motif. See page 251.

Cut out the design ·6 cm ($\frac{1}{4}$ inch) from the marking. Fold the cut edges to the underside ·6 cm ($\frac{1}{4}$ inch) and tack. Mitre the corners; notch the seam edges on outside curves, and clip into them on inside curves so that the seams will lie flat. Steam-press.

For stitching use one or two strands of stranded cotton and a fine needle, and blanket-stitch over the edge of the design. Uneven as well as even stitches may be used. Fasten the threads on the underside. Remove tacking and press. Stems and lines within the design may be embroidered.

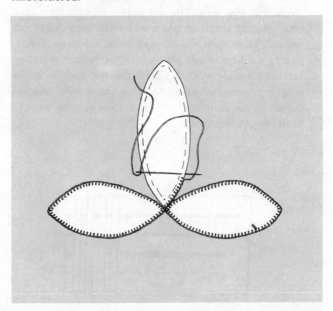

Carefully place the fabric design on the article to be decorated and pin. Tack about ·6 cm ($\frac{1}{4}$ inch) from the edge. Remove the first tacking on the folded edge.

If you prefer an invisible finish, slip-stitch the design in place instead of using the blanket stitch.

253

Smocking

Smocking is always in fashion. It is a youthful detail – at home on children's clothes as well as women's lingerie and soft cotton and silk. A smocked band at the yoke of a dress or at the hipline of a gathered skirt gives individuality to the garment.

Smocking may be done by hand or by machine. Almost any type or design of fabric can be used but it must be smocked before the garment is assembled.

Hand Smocking

You can buy patterns that show several types of stitches used in smocking. The honeycomb is illustrated here.

Stranded cotton is suitable for both cotton and silk fabrics; on silk, however, you may prefer a silk floss. Use two or three strands in the needle and knot the long ends of the threads. Choose a thread colour that matches your fabric or, for a change and decorative effect, one that contrasts with it.

When smocking by hand the smocking transfer, which consists of evenly spaced dots, is usually pressed on to the wrong side of the fabric, and then rows of gathering threads are run through the dots and drawn up to form evenly-spaced pleats. The depth of the pleat depends on the distance between the dots. (A child's garment does not need such deep pleats as an adult's.) The decorative smocking stitches are worked on the right side of the fabric, picking up the top of the pleats.

In honeycomb smocking two rows of stitching are worked at one time. The decorative thread, after each small joining stitch, is taken under the pleat fold from one row to the next row, up and down, across the fabric, joining the tops of two pleats, alternately, and then two further rows are worked, alternating the position of the stitching over the pleats to form the honeycomb, as shown in the illustration. Further rows may be worked to the depth required.

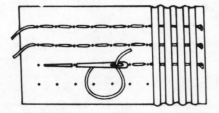

Chain stitch, outline stitch and cable stitch (alternately one stitch above and one below) may also be used to form decorative bands across the pleats.

The gathering threads are removed when the decorative stitching is finished.

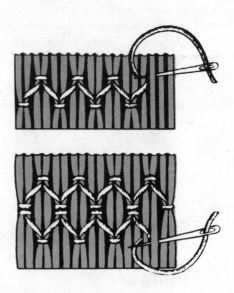

To press with a steam iron, pin the top row of the smocking securely to the ironing board; place a pin above each stitch. Hold the iron about 2·5 cm (1 inch) above the smocking and allow the steam to penetrate the fabric while you gently pull the smocking from the bottom.

To press with a dry iron, follow the instructions for velvet, page 66.

Machine Smocking

Machine smocking resembles hand smocking when the rows are accurately stitched. It is quick and easy and any one of the three methods given below may be used.

Method 1: Use matching thread and loosen the upper tension slightly so that the bobbin thread may be drawn later to gather the fabric.

From the right side of the fabric, place a row of stitching in the seam allowance, 1·2 cm ($\frac{1}{2}$ inch) from the edge. This stitching is not visible in the finished work. Place a second row of stitching barely beyond the 1·5 cm ($\frac{5}{8}$ inch) seam allowance, and a third row ·3 cm ($\frac{1}{8}$ inch) from the second row. Place additional rows in groups of two, spaced ·3 cm ($\frac{1}{8}$ inch) apart, and allow 1·2 cm ($\frac{1}{2}$ inch) between each group.

Gather the fabric to the desired width. See *Gathering to Control Fullness*, page 105.

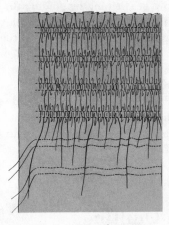

Cut an underlay of lawn or organdie the length and width of the shirring. Place it on the underside, over the shirring. Pin it in place from the right side.

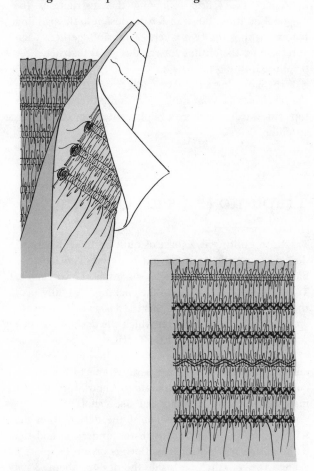

Select one of the zig-zag stitch patterns and stitch between the rows that you spaced ·3 cm ($\frac{1}{8}$ inch) apart, using thread in a contrasting colour. For an interesting effect, select two stitch patterns and alternate them in stitching the rows.

Method 2: Use the Gathering Foot and heavy-duty thread for both the bobbin and the upper threading. Stitch, following a design. See *Gathering Foot*, page 285 for instructions on its use.

Method 3: Use heavy-duty thread for both the bobbin and the upper threading and about 2·5 mm (10) stitch length. Stitch from the right side, following a design similar to the one illustrated. You may use different colours of thread in stitching alternate rows. (If you are using a heavy thread only on the bobbin, stitch from the wrong side of the fabric.)

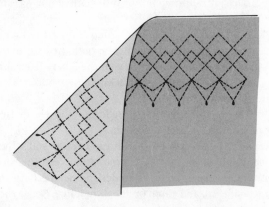

After you have stitched the design, wind the bobbin with elastic thread and place several rows of stitching across the work, spacing them in harmony with the design. See *Shirring with Elastic Thread*, page 244.

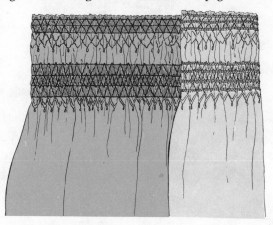

Quilting is the art of stitching two or more thicknesses of fabric together in a planned design. A light padding is stitched to the underside of the fabric to produce a soft, puffed effect that enhances some clothing and many fabric furnishings.

Your sewing machine enables you to quilt quickly and easily and to achieve a variety of effects. The Quilter Foot, which has an open construction and short toe, simplifies the stitching of padded fabrics. Its adjustable and removable space guide may be placed to the right or left of the needle. This makes it especially adaptable to diagonal quilting.

Select the thread, needle and stitch length appropriate for your fabric. (Do not use a long stitch.) The pressure should be slightly heavier than that for medium-weight fabrics.

Diagonal Quilting

Cotton or wool domette, terylene wadding or lightweight interlining make practical padding. If you choose wadding, back it with voile or soft batiste for greater durability.

Place the padding over the wrong side of the fabric. Tack the layers of fabric together on both the lengthwise and the crosswise grains to prevent the layers from slipping as you sew. Space the tacking rows about 5 cm (2 inches) apart.

Draw a diagonal line on the padding to mark the first line of stitching in each direction.

Replace the Presser Foot with the Quilter and adjust the space guide for the width desired between the rows of stitching. Place the work under the needle with the padded side up, and stitch on the drawn line. Space each

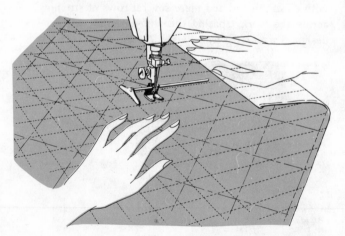

successive row of stitching by guiding the edge of the space guide along the previous row, as illustrated.

If you are quilting a large piece, work from the centre to the edge of the fabric. After you have completed the stitching in one direction, stitch the lines in the opposite direction to form squares or triangles.

Guide the work with both hands placed on the fabric so that the lengthwise grain forms a straight line between the hands. This ensures even quilting, with a characteristic soft puff.

Pattern Quilting

Floral and scroll designs may also be stitched with the Quilter. The space guide is removed, however.

Prepare the fabric following the instructions for diagonal quilting, but transfer the design to the padding before tacking the two layers of fabric together. Then stitch round the outline for the design as instructed for trapunto quilting below.

If the fabric has a floral or scroll design, the pattern in the fabric can be your quilting design. Stitch it from the top side, using either straight stitching or zig-zag stitching.

Trapunto (Raised) Quilting

(Illustrated on next page)

Trapunto quilting is a form of quilting in which small designs are made to stand out in relief. The fabric is backed with soft batiste, voile, silk organza or organdie. Trace the motif on a piece of the backing. Carefully plan the position of each motif so that the design is attractively spaced. Tack the backing on which the design has been traced to the wrong side of the fabric.

Raise the space guide of the Quilter or remove it entirely. The short open toe permits you to follow the curved lines easily and accurately. Choose thread that matches the fabric in colour, and use a short stitch.

After stitching each portion of the design from the wrong side, pull the threads to the underside and tie. If the design has large leaves, flowers or scrolls, place a second row of stitching inside the design, about ·3 cm ($\frac{1}{8}$ inch) from the first row.

When the stitching is completed, pad the design with strands of wool yarn carried by a tapestry needle or darning needle. (Wool yarn should be used because of its resiliency.) Pass the needle through the backing from

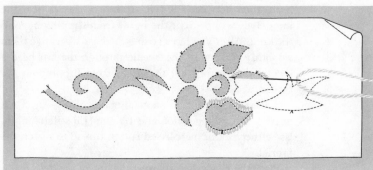

one stitching line to the other. Often it is necessary to use several strands of yarn to fill a section of the motif.

Clip both ends of the yarn close to the stitching. Gently stretch each portion of the design on the bias to conceal the ends of the yarn on the inside of the backing.

Lace and other transparent fabrics are often backed with satin or taffeta and the design padded with silk yarn to produce a delicately tinted pattern.

Beads and Sequins

Beads and sequins are glamorous accents on cocktail and evening dresses, sweaters, blouses, scarves and evening bags. They may be used alone or combined with decorative zig-zag stitching as illustrated on page 276. A variety of fabrics may be used for this work.

design. Use matching thread and machine-stitch on the lines of the design to transfer it to the right side of the fabric.

Thread the beads on a double strand of matching mercerised cotton or silk thread, using a fine needle. Knot the ends together. Pass the needle through the first

Beading by Machine

Small beads may be stitched in place by machine. Use a medium-width, open-spaced zig-zag stitch and the Zipper Foot. Stitch the beads in place before you assemble the garment sections so that you have only a small section to deal with.

The spaces between the sections within the design must be far enough apart for the Zipper Foot to work between them. In straight or block designs, however, several rows may be stitched close together. (For small, intricate designs, bead by hand.)

Transfer the motif for the beading to a backing of organdie, voile or lawn. If the garment is mounted, transfer the design to the mounting. Carefully place the backing on the wrong side of the fabric and pin near the

bead, then between the two strands of thread near the knot. This will prevent the beads from slipping beyond the knot. After you have strung the beads, arrange them smoothly; then pass the needle through the last bead a second time to prevent the beads from slipping on the thread.

Adjust the machine for a medium-width zig-zag stitch in central needle position and 1·5 mm (15) stitch length. Use either silk or mercerised cotton thread to match the fabric.

Place the beads directly over the line of the design and adjust the Zipper Foot far enough to the left or right to ride against the beads. This adjustment enables you to position the zig-zag stitching over the beading thread. As you sew, hold the beads in place with the index finger, close to the needle. The threads are drawn between the beads, making the stitching invisible.

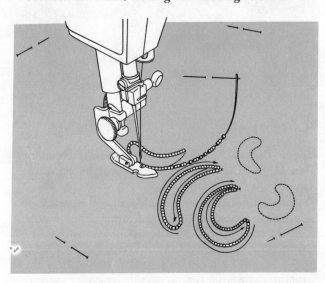

On scroll designs, start the stitching on the inside curve with the Zipper Foot adjusted to work inside the design; stitch to the beginning of the outside curve. Stop the machine *with the needle in the fabric*, adjust the Zipper Foot to the opposite side, then work outside the design, as illustrated. (It is necessary to remove the foot to make this adjustment since the needle is in the fabric.) In the illustration, dotted lines and arrows indicate the direction of the stitching and the position of the Zipper Foot in relation to the beads.

After stitching each portion of the design, draw the thread ends to the underside and tie them together in a single knot set close to the fabric. Cut the bead threads about 10 cm (4 inches) from the design and remove all beads on them except one to cover the knot. With a needle, bring the thread ends through the first bead at the beginning for a smooth join; then bring the needle through to the underside of the fabric and fasten the threads with several backstitches.

Beading by Hand

Round beads, pearls and bugle beads can be sewn in place by hand. Tack or lightly trace the design on the right side of the fabric, then follow one of the methods described below.

Method 1: Use a needle fine enough to slide through the beads without splitting them and select thread matching the fabric in colour.

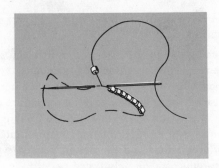

Fasten the thread on the underside of the fabric with two tiny backstitches. Bring the needle up through the fabric. Pass the needle through a bead; take a backstitch and bring the needle out exactly a bead length from where the thread came out. Start each successive backstitch against the previous bead to place the beads close together. Draw up the thread tightly enough for the beads to lie flat against the fabric. When completed, fasten the thread on the underside with tiny backstitches.

Method 2: Thread the beads on mercerised cotton or nylon thread, leaving a 10-cm (4-inch) thread end to fasten on the underside.

Use a second thread, matching the fabric exactly in colour, and a fine, short needle to 'couch' on the beads. Fasten the thread on the underside of the fabric with two tiny backstitches. Hold the beads in position and

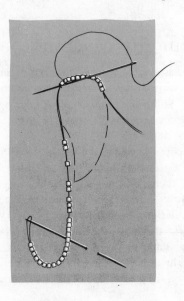

bring the needle up through the fabric on the left side of the beading thread. Bring the thread to the right, between the beads, and take a slanting stitch over the beading thread, bringing the needle out on the left side of the beading thread at the end of the next bead.

When completed, fasten the needle thread on the underside with tiny backstitches. Cut the beading thread about 10 cm (4 inches) from the design and remove the excess beads. Use a needle to bring the end threads to the underside. Tie them in a single knot set close to the fabric.

Sewing on Sequins

Outline the design, then fill in the centre. Use a fine needle and a thread matching the sequins exactly in colour.

Fasten the thread on the underside of the fabric with tiny backstitches. Bring the needle up through the fabric

and through a sequin. Hold the sequin flat against the fabric, right side up, and take a stitch in front of it. Pass the needle through a sequin from the right side and take a backstitch as illustrated. Draw up the thread and at the same time turn the sequin right side up. The sequins will overlap and the stitches will be hidden. The stitch length on the underside must be the same size as the sequin. When finished, fasten the threads on the underside with tiny backstitches.

TO ADD A BEAD TO THE CENTRE OF A SEQUIN

Bring the needle up through the fabric and through a sequin. Pass the needle through a bead, then down through the sequin and fabric. Draw up the thread and take a tiny backstitch to fasten it. (The bead acts as an anchor, holding the sequin in place.) Bring the needle up through the fabric at the point where the next sequin will be sewn on. This method is excellent when sequins are not stitched close together.

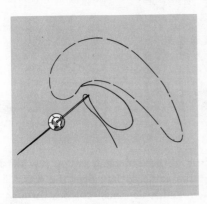
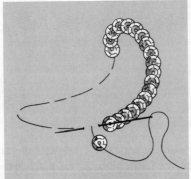
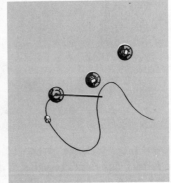

Lace Edging and Insertion

Lace adds a delicate trimming to blouses, women's and children's dresses, babies' clothes, lingerie and household linens.

You may apply lace to the edge of the fabric or set it into the fabric. Lace edging and insertion of cotton, silk, linen, rayon, nylon, wool and other fibres are available in a variety of widths, patterns and types.

The delicate network of threads in lace requires special sewing techniques. Whether you stitch the lace by hand or by machine depends on your fabric, the position of the lace on the garment, and personal preference. In all cases, use a short stitch and fine needle and thread. In handwork, the needle should be short as well as fine. *Always press the lace before applying it to the fabric.*

Gathering Lace

To gather lace, gently draw the top thread of the selvedge and ease the lace back on the thread to the desired fullness. Be careful to distribute the fullness evenly.

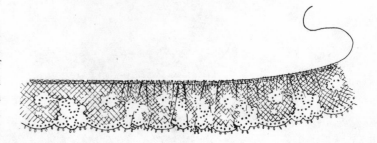

259

Applying Lace Edging

LACE OVER ROLLED EDGE

Straight lace. Tack the lace over the seam allowance of the fabric; both lace and fabric should be right side up. Trim the seam allowances under the lace to ·6 cm (¼ inch). On the underside, roll the edge of the fabric and make small stitches through the rolled hem and lace. On the right side, the lace covers the hem.

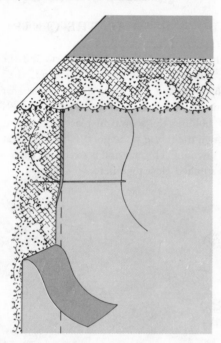

Gathered lace. Tack the gathered lace on the seamline of the fabric, right sides together. Trim the fabric seam allowance to ·6 cm (¼ inch). Roll the fabric edge over the stitching line, and make small stitches through the rolled hem and lace. When finished, turn the lace over the rolled hem.

If you want the rolled hem on the right side in the finished work, tack the gathered lace on the seamline of the fabric, *wrong sides together* instead of right.

GATHERED LACE UNDER ROLLED EDGE

Place a line of stitching ·3 cm (⅛ inch) from the seamline, using a short stitch. Press. Trim off the edge close to the stitching.

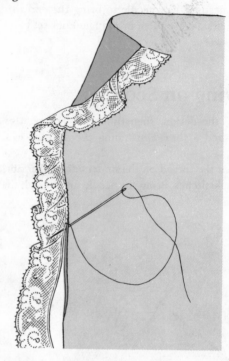

Roll the fabric to the underside as you sew the lace in place. Place the gathered lace over the rolled hem, right side down, and make small stitches through the lace and rolled hem. On the right side, the lace is under the hem.

LACE ON FINISHED EDGE

By hand. The fabric edge may be finished with a hem

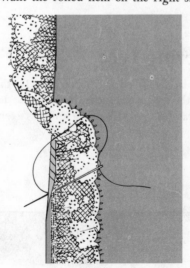

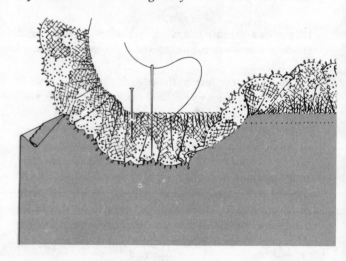

or facing. Lay the lace over the finished edge, right sides together, keeping the edges even. Pin. Working from the lace side, make very small whipping stitches over the edge. The stitches should be loose enough so that the seam may be spread open when it is finished.

By machine. Lace edging and a narrow hem may be stitched in place with one line of machine stitching when the Hemmer Foot is used. The lace may be stitched over or under the fold for the hem. See *Hemmer Foot*, page 283.

Joining Lace Edging and Lace Insertion

By hand. The lace edging may be straight or gathered. Match the lace patterns when cutting the lace into lengths. Lay the right sides of the lace together, keeping the edges even, and pin. Work from the gathered side and make small whipping stitches over the edge. The stitches should be loose enough so that the lace and insertion may be spread open when the stitching is finished. Two rows of insertion may be joined in the same way.

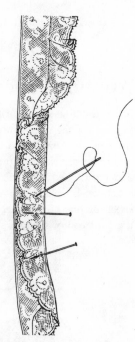

By machine. Match the lace patterns when cutting the lace into lengths. Replace the Presser Foot with the Edge

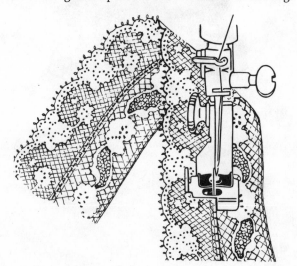

Stitcher. Place one piece of lace in slot 1 and the other in slot 4. (The edges will barely overlap.) Adjust the lug to position the stitching close to the lace edge, and guide the lace against the slots as you sew. See *Edge Stitcher*, page 284.

Joining Lace Insertion and Fabric Bands

Fold the edge of the fabric under 1·2 cm ($\frac{1}{2}$ inch), and press. Replace the Presser Foot with the Edge Stitcher. Place the fabric band in slot 1. Adjust the lug to position the stitching close to the folded edge. Insert the lace in slot 4 with the fabric band overlapping it slightly. Stitch, guiding the band and lace against the edges of the slots as instructed above. See *Edge Stitcher*, page 284.

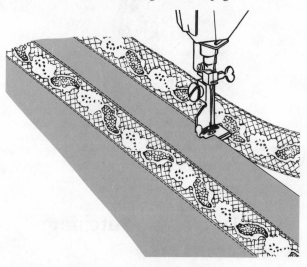

Inserting Lace

Pin each edge of the lace insertion in place; both lace and fabric must be right side up. Machine-stitch on each

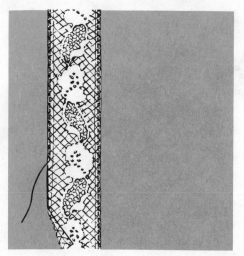

side of the insertion close to the edge. Press. If the fabric is to remain under the lace the work is finished.

If desired, trim the fabric under the lace to within ·3 cm (⅛ inch) of the stitching. Turn the fabric edges away from the lace, and press.

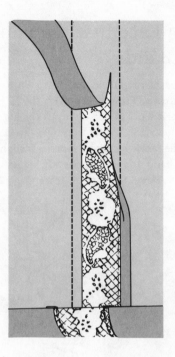

Tack the lace edging over the fabric about 1·2 cm (½ inch) from the edge; tack the insertion in place on the garment. Select one of the decorative zig-zag stitches and set the stitch length for satin stitching. Place the work under the needle so that when the needle is on the extreme right stroke, it catches the selvedge of the lace edging. Stitch. Then stitch down one edge of the insertion in the same way. Turn the fabric and stitch the other edge of the insertion from the opposite end. This procedure places the points of the design in opposite directions. Press. Trim the fabric under the lace close to the stitching.

Applying Lace to Curved Area

Mark the line on the right side of the fabric for the position of the lace. Draw the thread on the top edge of the lace and shape it to fit the curve. With both fabric and lace right side up, pin and tack in position. The lace may be stitched in place by hand, using a short whipping stitch or by machine. A narrow open-spaced zig-zag stitch or one of the decorative zig-zag stitches may be used instead of straight stitching.

Using Decorative Stitching with Lace

Many of the decorative zig-zag stitch patterns can be used effectively as both a finished and a trimming for lace edging and insertion.

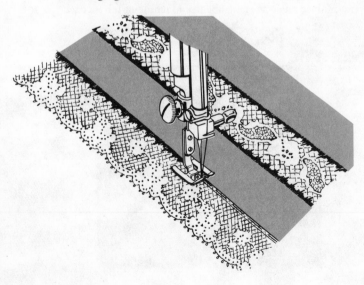

Applying Lace to Square Corner

Mitre the lace insertion at the corner and press. Join with whipping stitches across the mitre. On the underside, cut away the excess at the corner.

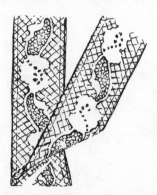

Stitch the lace edging and insertion together. The lace edging is generally gathered round the corner. About 1·2 cm (½ inch) from the corner, draw the top thread of the lace edging and gather it just enough so that it will lie flat when turned down. Catch the loop of the drawn thread under the whipping stitches as the lace and insertion are joined.

If lace edging is used alone, you may mitre it at the corner instead of gathering it.

Insertion Braid and Edging Braid

Insertion Braid

Insertion braid, sometimes called beading, is a narrow insertion of open embroidered design. It is used between fabric edges in blouses, lingerie and babies' and children's clothes. The wider width can be slotted with ribbon.

Place the insertion over the fabric, right sides together, with the embroidered edge on the seamline. Stitch close to the embroidery. Press; then press the seam edge away from the insertion. On the underside, trim seam edges to ·3 cm (⅛ inch) and overcast them together.

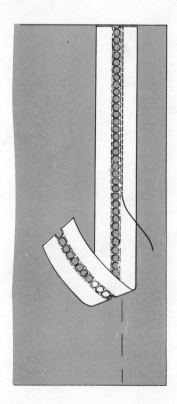

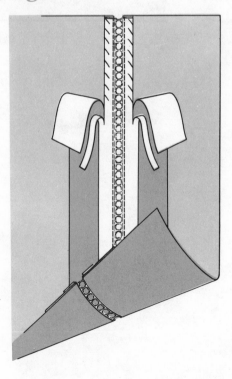

(*Continued on next page*)

If top stitching is desired, fold the seam allowance to the underside and press. Lap the fabric over the insertion, keeping the fold close to the embroidered edge. Stitch close to the fold. Trim, and then overcast the seam edges on the underside.

Braid

Braid is then used to edge collars, cuffs, lapels and pockets and to accent other parts of a dress. Finish the edges in the usual way before applying the braid. Carefully pin the braid over the finished edge; shape it to conform to curved edges, and mitre square corners. Tack. Slip-stitch each edge of the braid in place.

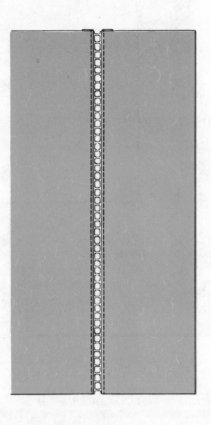

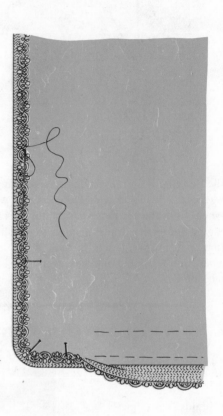

Zig-Zag Sewing

Zig-zag sewing has found a permanent place in dress-making and household mending. That is not the end of the story, however. To stimulate your creative imagination, this chapter explains how you can also use your zig-zag machine for decorative sewing and fashion detailing. The opportunities for self-expression and originality are almost unlimited. You can enhance the appearance of clothing, household linens and fabric furnishings without adding to their cost; you can achieve lovely effects in a formal evening dress or a simple apron.

Most women are probably more creative than they realise. Learn to look for suggestions in ready-to-wear and in newspaper and magazine fashions; learn to use as design sources such unlikely material as wallpaper, children's colouring books and printed fabrics. Decorative zig-zag sewing is easy, but do not make the mistake of over-decorating. Plan your stitch patterns carefully, considering the fabric and the age of the person for whom the garment is intended or the type of household article you are making. If you do, your results will be pleasing and rewarding.

Many of the machine accessories may be used in zig-zag sewing. Check the instructions for accessories, beginning on page 280. For guides on how to use the zig-zag stitch in dressmaking and mending, consult the alphabetical listing under *Zig-Zag Sewing* in the index.

Planning Preliminaries

The decision to use decorative zig-zag stitching must be made when the garment or article is in the planning stage. Often the stitching will extend through a seam allowance and must, therefore, be applied before the seam is stitched. Or the decorative stitching may be confined to a small section of the garment as for a motif or monogram; then it is easier to handle the small section under the needle than the finished garment.

Mercerised cotton or silk sewing thread may be used in decorative stitching. It may blend with the fabric in colour or be a contrast in shade or colour. Subtle colour contrasts give a more expensive look to your dressmaking. Do not hesitate to experiment, however. Even the experts find that they can always learn something new about colour combinations.

To Prepare the Work for Stitching

You can do decorative zig-zag stitching on almost any fabric. On soft fabrics you must add a backing to ensure firm satin stitching, and on many other fabrics you will achieve better results when a backing is used. Crisp lawn, organdie or organza is suitable for this purpose. When the work is completed, the backing is cut away close to the stitching with small, sharp scissors.

To prepare your work for stitching, take these steps:

1. Steam-press the fabric so that it is smooth.

2. Transfer the design to the fabric.

3. Cut the backing on the same grain as the fabric and at least 10 cm (4 inches) wider than the decorative stitching that will be applied.

4. Press the backing and place it carefully on the wrong side of the fabric, where the stitching will be worked. Pin, then tack in place.

5. After you complete each line of decorative stitching, press the work on the wrong side before doing any additional stitching.

To Prepare the Machine

Some zig-zag machines have built-in discs and one or two selectors that may be set for any stitch pattern you want. Others have an assortment of discs (or cams), and you insert one for each stitch pattern.

The *stitch length selector* regulates the space between the stitches. The *stitch width selector* regulates the width of some stitch patterns and completely changes the pattern of others. The instruction book accompanying the machine explains how to select the stitch patterns as well as how to adjust the stitch length, stitch width and tension.

SATIN STITCHING

For decorative zig-zag stitching the stitch length should be very short so that the zig-zag stitches are placed close together. A series of closely spaced zig-zag stitches that form a smooth, satinlike surface is known as 'satin stitching'. It is used for almost all the decorative work described in this chapter.

A Special Purpose Foot, designed for use in satin stitching, is generally provided with the machine. The foot has a raised centre section that allows mounds of satin stitches to move freely under it. It also has an eyelet through which a filler cord or decorative thread may be inserted. Use this foot in your decorative stitching.

TO ADJUST THE STITCH LENGTH FOR SATIN STITCHING

Move the stitch length selector to a close zig-zag. Then run the machine at slow speed and gradually tighten the thumb nut until the stitches are closely spaced and form a smooth surface on your fabric.

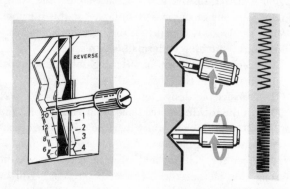

TO ADJUST THE TENSION FOR SATIN STITCHING

Satin stitching requires a lighter needle-thread tension than straight stitching or open-spaced designs. The wider the satin stitch, the lighter the tension required. A properly balanced satin stitch should lie flat across the fabric. Any tightness or puckering usually indicates too high a needle thread tension.

TEST STITCHING

To be sure that you have the correct tension setting, stitch length and stitch width, test your stitching on a piece of the same fabric you are using in your work. Use a backing if your fabric requires one.

On the same piece, make a stitching test to determine

which stitch pattern you wish to use. If you are planning to use two or more patterns, decide which ones may be combined attractively and how they should be spaced.

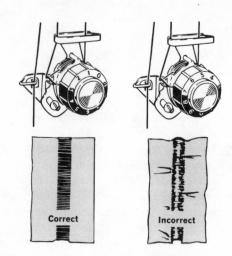

To Find the Beginning of a Pattern Unit

When you use a decorative stitch pattern in a motif or monogram, you must always start stitching at the beginning of a pattern unit. To do this, stitch on a scrap of fabric until you come to the end of a complete pattern unit – that is, to the end of the diamond, arrowhead or

whatever pattern you are using. Now you are ready to start stitching at the beginning of the next unit. Remove the scrap of fabric from under the Presser Foot and position the motif or monogram under the needle, aligning the marking with the centre of the Presser Foot. Lower the foot, and stitch. After you have stitched one portion of the design, pull the threads through to the underside and tie them. This sequence of working is recommended for all accurate design positioning.

Decorative Zig-zag Stitching

The stitch patterns may be applied in a simple or an elaborate way. Either is attractive. It would be impossible to illustrate all of the many interesting, pleasing and practical applications you can devise. The suggestions that follow give you an idea of what you can do. They also give instructions that are basic to the positioning of *all* stitch patterns.

Applying a Trimming
BRAID, RIBBON AND RIC-RAC

Metallic braid or narrow velvet ribbon adds an unusual and dramatic touch when combined with one of the decorative stitch patterns as a trimming. If a backing is required, tack it to the wrong side of the fabric. Then tack the braid or ribbon in position. Select one of the decorative stitch patterns, and set the stitch length selector for satin stitching. Stitch down one side of the braid or ribbon; then turn the fabric and stitch down the other side from the opposite end. This procedure places the points of the stitch pattern in opposite directions. In the illustrations, only the points of the stitching catch into the metallic braid, and the satin stitches are on the edge of the velvet ribbon with the points extending into the fabric. When finished, remove tacking and press. Trim the backing close to each side of the stitching.

Braid and decorative stitching are an effective trimming on hand towels, pillows and other household articles. For a stitch pattern such as the one illustrated, position the work under the needle with the edge of the braid aligned with the centre of the Presser Foot. Stitch as instructed above. Press.

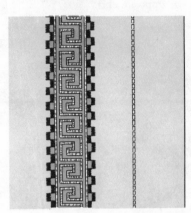

For a simple treatment on children's clothes, aprons and curtains, add ric-rac braid – either a single row or two colours twisted together. Tack the ric-rac in position. Align the centre of the ric-rac with the centre of the Presser Foot, and stitch in place using a decorative stitch pattern or an open zig-zag stitch. Press.

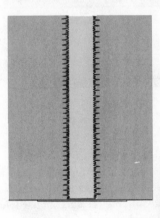

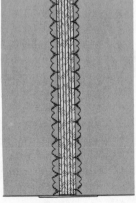

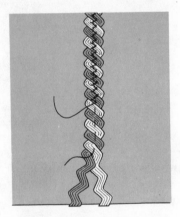

BIAS BINDING WITH LACE OR RIC-RAC BRAID
(*Illustrated on next page*)

Decorative stitching combined with bias binding and lace or bias binding and ric-rac is an interesting treatment for little girls' dresses, blouses and lingerie.

Open out the binding and stitch the ric-rac or lace to each side of the cut edge. Extend the edge of the ric-rac about ·3 cm ($\frac{1}{8}$ inch) beyond the binding edge; keep the edges of the binding and lace even, and match the patterns in the lace. Fold the binding edge back in place; the lace or ric-rac will extend beyond it. Press.

Tack the binding in position on the garment. Select a stitch pattern, and set the stitch length selector for satin stitching. To place the stitching on each edge of the binding, as illustrated with ric-rac, position the work under the needle so that when the needle is on the extreme left stroke it catches the left edge of the binding; then turn the work and stitch down the other side of the binding from the opposite end.

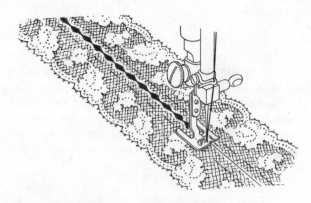

BIAS BINDING WITH NET FRILLS
Bias binding applied with decorative stitching adds a finishing touch to net frills on petticoats.

Replace the Presser Foot with the Binder and insert in it either nylon or rayon bias binding. Carefully select a stitch pattern that complements the binding. Set the stitch length selector for satin stitching, and bind the edge. Press. See page 282 for instructions on using the *Binder*.

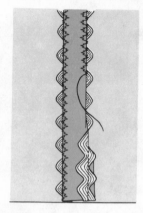

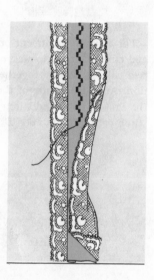

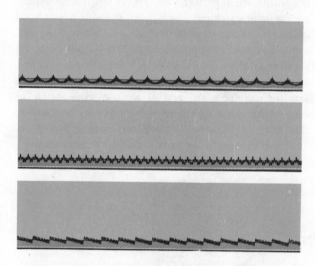

To place one row of stitching through the centre, as illustrated with lace, align the centre of the binding with the centre of the Presser Foot, and stitch. Remove tacking, and press.

LACE WITH DECORATIVE STITCHING
Tack two strips of lace in position on the garment with the inside edges of the lace touching. Match the patterns in the lace. Tack a backing of crisp lawn to the underside. Select the stitch pattern, and set the stitch length selector for satin stitching. Align the centre of lace with the centre of the Presser Foot, and stitch. Remove tacking and press. Trim the backing close to the stitching.

(Illustrated at top of next column)

Stitching Designs
GEOMETRIC DESIGN
A geometric design with an interlaced effect will enhance the appearance of a full-skirted dress made of organdie, organza or linen. It is also suitable for such household articles as place mats and hand towels.

Trace the design lightly on the right side of the fabric. See page 251. Tack a backing of crisp organdie or lawn on the underside of the design for added body. Study the design to determine which sections you should stitch first. Select a narrow, plain zig-zag stitch, and set the stitch length selector for satin stitching. Align the markings of the design with the centre of the Presser Foot, and stitch round each edge. Press.

Next, select an open-spaced stitch pattern, and stitch midway between the two previous lines of stitching. Pull the threads through to the underside and tie. Remove tacking; press. Trim the backing close to the stitching. To add glitter to glamour on a cocktail dress, sew on a few sequins or beads by hand.

OUTLINE DESIGN

An outline design may be used in the same places as the geometric one. Prepare the work as described above. Select one of the open-spaced stitch patterns, and set the stitch length selector for satin stitching. Align the marking for the design with the centre of the Presser Foot, and stitch. Guide the fabric with both hands, turning it as you sew. At the corners, stop with the needle in the fabric, raise the presser bar, and turn the fabric, pivoting on the needle. Lower the presser bar and continue the stitching. (On sharp curves, you may need to raise the presser bar slightly when the needle is in the fabric, and ease the fabric to the right or left.) When completed, pull the threads through to the underside and tie. Press. Either stitch the lines within the design, using a narrow, plain zig-zag stitch, or sew on beads. Trim the backing on the underside close to the stitching.

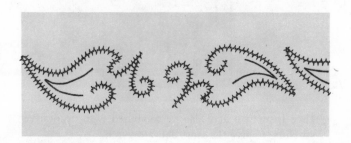

SCALLOPED HEMS

Scalloped hems add interest to babies' and children's clothes, cotton dresses for adults and household linens.

Fold and press the hem. Mark a 5-cm (2-inch) scallop about 2·5 cm (1 inch) below the top of the hem. Tack close to the marking to prevent the two layers of fabric from slipping.

Select an open-spaced stitch pattern, and set the stitch length selector for satin stitching. Position the work under the needle with the scallops to the right, and align the marking with the centre of the Presser Foot. Stitch round the scallops, using both hands to guide the work and turning the fabric gradually as you sew. At the point of the scallop, and on the left swing of the needle, stop with the needle in the fabric. Raise the presser bar and turn the fabric, pivoting on the needle, then lower the presser bar and stitch the next scallop. (On sharp curves, it is sometimes necessary to raise the presser bar slightly when the needle is in the fabric and ease the fabric slightly to the right or left.) When completed, press. Trim the upper edge of the hem on the underside, close to the stitching.

Many of the decorative stitch patterns are adaptable to scallops that have a curve instead of a point between the scallops.

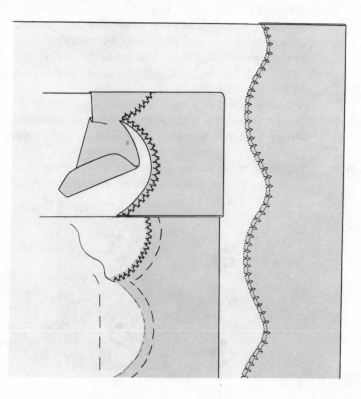

PIN TUCKS, LACE AND STITCH PATTERNS

Groups of pin tucks combined with pattern stitching add a fashionable and delicate touch to blouses, babies' clothes and children's dresses made of soft fabrics.

Pin-tuck the fabric as instructed on page 236. Then lightly mark the position for the decorative stitching midway between the groups of tucks. Select one of the open-spaced stitch patterns, and set the stitch length selector for satin stitching. Align the marking for the pattern with the centre of the Presser Foot and stitch. Press.

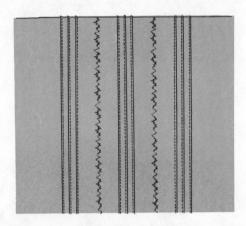

Lace insertion may also be combined with decorative stitching to give the same delicate touch.

INDIVIDUAL MOTIFS

You can give individuality to blouses, summer dresses, children's clothes and place mats by grouping small designs made of such stitch patterns as the solid scallop or pyramid. The designs may form a border or they may be placed asymmetrically on the garment.

Dot the fabric with chalk to mark the position of the design. Prepare the work as described under *Geometric Design*, page 268. Select the stitch pattern, and set the stitch length selector for satin stitching. Start at the beginning of the pattern unit as instructed on page 266. Stitch, completing only one pattern. With the needle in

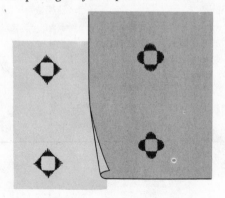

the fabric, pivot, turning the fabric left 90 degrees (quarter circle). Stitch, completing another stitch pattern, then pivot again. Continue in the same manner until the four sides are finished. Pull threads through to the underside and tie. Press.

ARROWHEADS AS A FINISH

The arrowhead provides a decorative and secure finish on fashion seams or darts that end within the garment, at the top of pleats, and at the ends of pockets in tailored clothes.

Start at the beginning of the arrowhead pattern. See page 266. Begin the stitching at the very end of the seam, dart or pocket. When finished, pull threads to the underside and tie. Press.

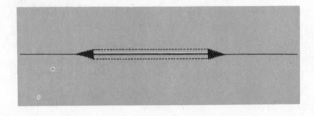

FLOWER-LIKE DESIGN

Bar tacks may be placed in sequence to form flower-like points – an exquisite touch in babies' and children's clothes, blouses and summer dresses. The design may be used round the neckline, in a yoke, above the hem or along each side of a front fastening.

Dot the fabric with a pencil to mark the position of each flower. When the design borders a curved edge, such as a neckline, mark the cutting line instead of cutting the fabric. By not cutting the edge, you can prevent it from stretching as you stitch and guide the fabric.

Adjust the machine for a wide zig-zag stitch. Make the feed inoperative so that it will not move the fabric as you sew. (This is done by either raising the throat plate or lowering the feed. Check the instruction book accompanying your machine.)

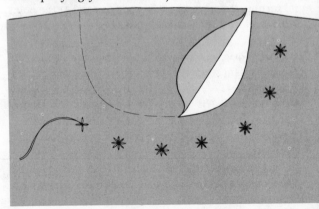

When the needle is on the left stroke, position it in the fabric at the marking for the design. Lower the Presser Foot and make four stitches, stopping with the left stroke of the needle in the fabric (centre of the design). Raise the Presser Foot and turn the fabric left 180 degrees (half circle), pivoting on the needle. Lower the Presser Foot and make four stitches, again stopping with the needle in the fabric on the left stroke (centre). Pivot again, turn the fabric left 90 degrees (quarter circle), and make four more stitches; then pivot, turn the fabric left 180 degrees (half circle), and make four stitches. You have now finished the first four points.

To make the remaining four points, pivot and turn the fabric on the needle far enough each time to place stitches midway between each of the four finished points. Take four stitches each time, stopping with the needle in the centre of the design. When finished, use a needle to bring the thread through to the underside; then tie it with a bobbin thread. Press.

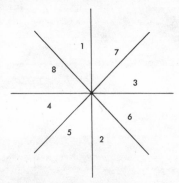

'TWIN-NEEDLE' SCALLOPS

Scallops stitched with a twin needle add a delicate touch to dresses, blouses and children's clothes.

Select the scallop pattern. The stitch length and stitch width vary the length and depth of the scallop; make the appropriate selection. If you are making several rows, start each row at the beginning of a scallop unit. See page 266. Press.

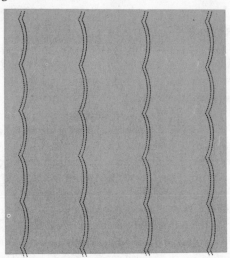

APPLIQUÉD DESIGNS

Interesting block designs lend distinction to curtains, place mats and dresses. For a vivid note you can combine blocks contrasting in colour with the fabric. Or you may appliqué a striped fabric to a plain-coloured fabric for a simple trimming on blouses, dresses and informal table linens. See *Appliqué*, page 250.

For the block design, first appliqué the blocks in position. Then lightly mark the lines for the crossbar stitching. Align the marking with the centre of the Presser Foot and stitch, using a narrow, closely spaced zig-zag stitch. Press.

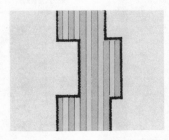

To appliqué a stripe to a plain colour, mark a geometric or irregular design on the striped fabric and appliqué the striped fabric in place.

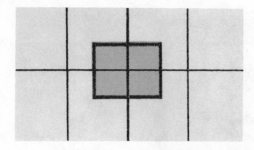

BORDER DESIGNS

Border designs of unlimited variety can be created by combining several stitch patterns. Simple or elaborate, delicate or bold, they can be varied to suit the application. And they have many applications on dresses, blouses, children's clothes, men's or boys' sports shirts, curtains or linens. Use a border design as you would a braid – at the top of a hem, through the bodice and sleeve sections, in a yoke, and on collars, cuffs, belts and pockets. The stitching may be placed on the horizontal, vertical or bias line.

Preparation. Mark the centre line for the first row of stitching with a light mark of pencil or chalk, using a ruler to keep the line straight. If the spacing between rows is no greater than 1·2 cm ($\frac{1}{2}$ inch), you can gauge additional rows with the Presser Foot. If the spacing is wider, mark each line for the stitching. Use a backing of crisp lawn, organdie or organza. See page 265. Make a

271

test sample on a piece of your fabric before proceeding with the actual work.

Stitching. Select the stitch pattern and set the stitch length selector for satin stitching. Stitch the centre row, aligning the marking with the centre of the Presser Foot. Select the pattern for the next row and stitch down one side of the centre row; then turn the fabric and stitch down the other side from the opposite end. This procedure places the points of the stitching in opposite directions. Repeat it for each additional row of stitching used in the border.

Borders may be made more glamorous by 'couching' metallic thread or bouclé yarn with one of the open-spaced stitch patterns or by using the twin needle, as illustrated below. When finished, press. Trim the backing on the underside close to the stitching.

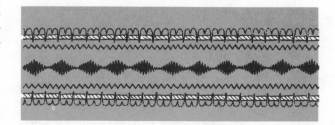

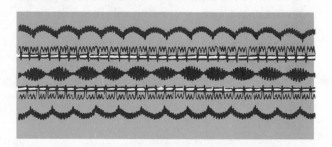

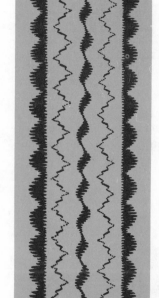

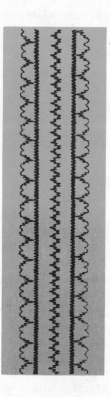

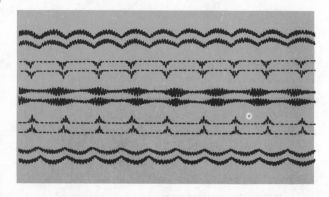

FAGGOTING

Seam edges joined with faggoting are a delicate addition to blouses, dresses, lingerie and children's clothes. Two strips of bias binding joined with faggoting make an unusual yoke treatment.

Fold under the seam allowance and press. Tack the folded edges to tissue paper or tracing paper, allowing ·3 cm ($\frac{1}{8}$ inch) between the edges.

Select either the multi-stitch zig-zag or the faggoting stitch pattern. Use the widest stitch width and close stitch length. Align the centre of the work with the centre of the Presser Foot. As you sew, the stitches will catch into the fabric fold on alternate sides.

When completed, remove the tackings and gently pull

272

the paper away from one side of the stitching, then from the other. Press.

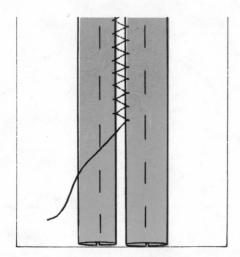

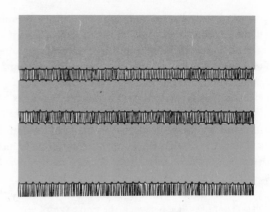

BUTTONHOLES FOR SLOTTING

Buttonholes, accented with decorative stitching, can be used for decorative slotting on clothing for children and teenage girls as well as for adults.

Mark the position of each buttonhole. Use a backing of crisp lawn or organdie. Refer to the instruction book accompanying the machine, and work the buttonholes. Press. Add a row of decorative stitching above and below the buttonholes. Velvet ribbon, grosgrain ribbon or braid may be slotted through the buttonholes.

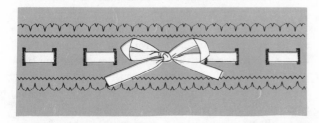

DRAWN WORK

Fabrics with a balanced weave are suitable for this decorative treatment, which may be used on informal table linens and scarves.

Draw a thread from the fabric to mark each edge of the drawn work. Select the blindstitch zig-zag pattern, a close stitch length and medium stitch width. Stitch down the left side of the drawn work, then turn the fabric and stitch down the other side from the opposite end. This procedure places the point of the stitching in the solid fabric. Draw the remaining threads from the fabric to form the openwork between the rows of stitching.

To fringe the edge, draw a thread from the fabric to mark the depth of the fringe. Stitch with this edge to the right. Draw the threads below the stitching to make the fringe. Press.

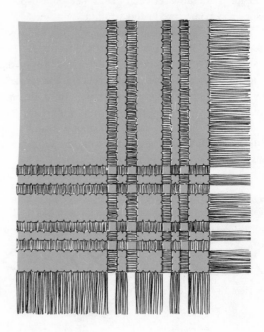

SHADOW DESIGN

A shadow effect is an interesting finish for collars and cuffs, facings and yokes. It can be created easily on a double thickness of sheer fabric such as organdie, organza, voile and sheer woven nylon *when a closely spaced stitch pattern is used. Open-spaced stitch patterns are not suitable for this work.*

Cut the garment section by the pattern and construct

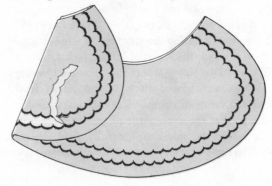

it, using a hairline seam. See page 88 for instructions. Turn the section to the right side and press it, forming a sharp crease on the stitching line. Tack the two layers of fabric together just outside the line for the decorative stitching.

Select a closely spaced stitch pattern, such as the scallop in the illustration, and set the stitch length selector for satin stitching. Place two rows of stitches on the right side of the fabric – the first row about ·9 cm ($\frac{3}{8}$ inch) from the edge, the second about ·9 cm ($\frac{3}{8}$ inch) from the first. Carefully guide the fabric with both hands, turning it as you sew. Remove tackings and press. Cut away the undersection of fabric between the two rows of stitching to create a shadow effect. Use small, sharp-pointed scissors and trim close to the stitching.

A narrow plain zig-zag stitch may also be used to obtain shadow effects. Set the stitch length selector for satin stitching. For the design illustrated, lightly draw the scallops on the fabric. Then reverse the work and draw the scallops facing the opposite direction, over-lapping the first scallops about 2 cm ($\frac{3}{4}$ inch).

Prepare the work as described above. Stitch round the design. When completed, cut away the fabric on the underside between the rows of stitching.

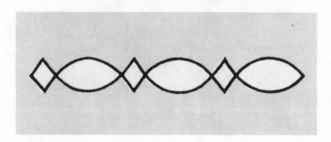

EDGE-STITCHED FINISH

Edge-stitching is a delicate finish for babies' clothes, children's dresses, frills and lingerie *when a closely spaced zig-zag stitch pattern is used. Open-spaced patterns are not suitable for this work.* Edge-stitching may be used on many types of fabrics.

Mark the seamline, but instead of cutting on the seam edge, cut at least 2·5 cm (1 inch) from the seamline. When curved edges are not cut, the fabric is easier to guide and will not stretch during the stitching. If edge-stitching is used on a single thickness of fabric, tack a backing of crisp lawn to the wrong side of the fabric for added body.

Select a closely spaced stitch pattern, and set the stitch length for satin stitching. Place the work under the needle so that the outer edge of the stitching will fall barely inside the seamline. Carefully guide the fabric with both hands, turning it as you sew. Remove tackings and press.

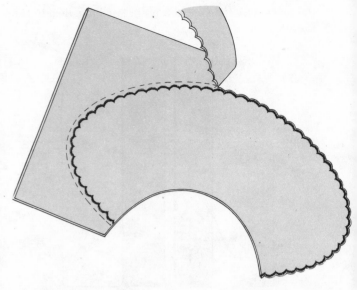

Trim the outer edge of fabric and backing close to the stitching, using embroidery scissors. Then trim the backing close to the inside edge of the stitching.

Frills. Edge-stitching is a simple finish for frills. If the frill has a heading, finish each edge. After stitching the first edge, turn the fabric and stitch down the other side from the opposite end.

Large scallops. An edging of large scallops can be very attractive when it is made with a narrow, plain, zig-zag stitch.

Lightly mark the scallops 5 cm (2 inches) from the edge of the fabric. *Do not cut.* For added body, tack a backing of crisp lawn on the underside of the scallops.

Select the plain zig-zag stitch, narrow stitch width; set the stitch length selector for satin stitching. Use a filler cord to prevent the scallops from stretching. Replace the Presser Foot with the Special Purpose Foot, and insert the filler cord into the eyelet. See *Hairline Seam*, page 88 for threading instructions. Position the work under the needle with the scallops to the right; align the marking with the centre of the Presser Foot. Guide the fabric with both hands as you sew, turning it gradually, following the scallops. At the point of the scallop, and when the needle is in left position, raise the presser bar

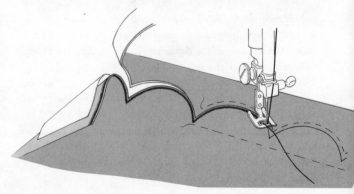

and turn the fabric, pivoting on the needle. Then lower the presser bar and stitch the next scallop. When finished, press. Trim surplus border and backing close to the stitching. Then trim the backing close to the inside of the scallops.

COUCHING

You can achieve novel effects by couching gimp, yarn or braid with zig-zag stitch patterns. Spaced patterns, such as the blindstitch zig-zag or narrow, open-spaced zig-zag, are most appropriate since they allow the decorative cord to show as part of the work. You may use either a single or twin needle in the machine.

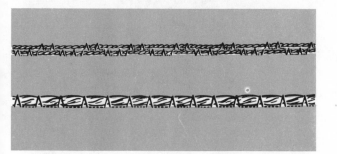

Lightly mark the position for the couching. Place the cord over the marking, and align it with the centre of the Presser Foot. Stitch, allowing the stitches to form over the cord. Press.

Patchwork

The zig-zag machine makes very attractively finished patchwork, which in turn can be used to produce colourful bedspreads, cushion covers, skirts or capes and other items. There are many shapes that can be used and the patches may be diamonds, triangles, squares or hexagons.

It is advisable not to mix fabrics of different weights: that is, keep similar weaves of cottons together, or use all nylons and terylenes together, and in all cases be sure to use pre-shrunk fabrics. If using patterned fabrics remember that a plain colour here and there gives a fascinating contrast. Scraps of fabric can be used for the irregular shapes at the edges when finishing.

You can buy a master pattern piece – a template (made of metal or plastic). Or, you can make your own from thin cardboard, but accuracy is essential as all the shapes must fit together and lie flat.

Using the template, first cut out the shapes in paper (which can be removed later after sewing) or Vilene (which can remain as it gives body to the finished article).

To cut the top fabric pieces, place the Vilene or paper pattern on the fabric and allow ¼ inch (·6 cm) turning

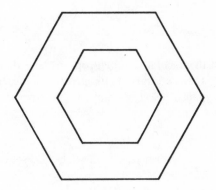

all round. If making a hexagon patch a 'window' hexagon template can be used to mark the fabric in pencil round the shape. You then cut on the pencil line. (Inside the 'window' will give the Vilene or paper size, and outside the 'window' the fabric size.)

Tack each fabric shape, using a fine thread and stitch, over a Vilene or paper shape, and mitre the corners or points neatly. The patches are then usually sewn into large or small units (rough squares) and these are then joined to other units until you have the size and shape required. To join the tacked patches together using a fine mercerised cotton (60), sewing silk or Drima thread, and a 15 to 20 (1·5 to 1 mm) stitch length, if using dress weight fabric, and satin stitch zig-zag.

Lay two patches together with one side edge of each touching, and stitch together. Match the sides carefully so that it is not necessary to ease the joins. Place the next patch in position and continue.

After stitching the whole area the tackings should be removed and the work pressed. Then make up as an ordinary length of fabric. Bedspreads should be lined and cushions need a piped edge.

You can also use a faggot stitch to join the patches together, see page 273.

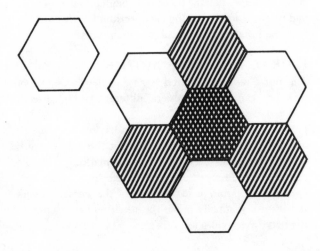

Many of the decorative stitch patterns lend themselves perfectly to the creation of attractive and unusual motifs or monograms. Select a simple design from the many transfer patterns available, or sketch one to suit your purpose.

Motifs

IMITATION APPLIQUÉ
A design for children's clothes similar to the one illustrated in a special decorative touch that looks like appliqué.

Trace the design lightly on the right side of the fabric. See page 251 for instructions. Tack a backing of crisp organdie or lawn on the underside for added body. Set the stitch length selector for satin stitching and use the following stitches: (1) A narrow, plain zig-zag stitch to outline the design; (2) the scallop stitch pattern for the eyebrows, hair and lines within; (3) the ball stitch pattern for the eye and nose; and (4) the arrowhead for the bow at the neckline. Pull the threads through to the underside and tie them after stitching each section. When finished, trim the backing close to the stitching. Press.

FLORAL AND LEAF MOTIFS
The floral motif illustrated is an excellent example of how you can combine several different stitch patterns and achieve pleasing results.

Prepare the work as described under *Imitation Appliqué*. Select the stitch pattern, and set the stitch length selector for satin stitching. Align the marking with the centre of the Presser Foot, and stitch. To bring a stitch pattern to a point, as in the ends of the stems, flowers and leaves, gradually move the stitch width selector to the narrowest width as you sew.

The leaf-like motif is appropriate for dresses and table linens where a small design is required for the accent desired. Prepare the work and stitch as instructed in *Imitation Appliqué*.

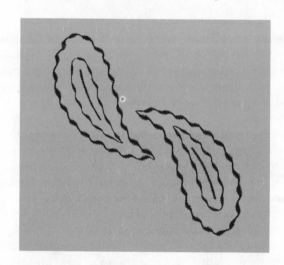

BEADS WITH STITCH PATTERNS
Beads combined with decorative stitches are an elegant way of embroidering cocktail and evening dresses, jackets and stoles.

Prepare the work as described under *Imitation Appliqué* above. Set the stitch length selector for satin stitching. Select a closely-spaced and an open-spaced stitch

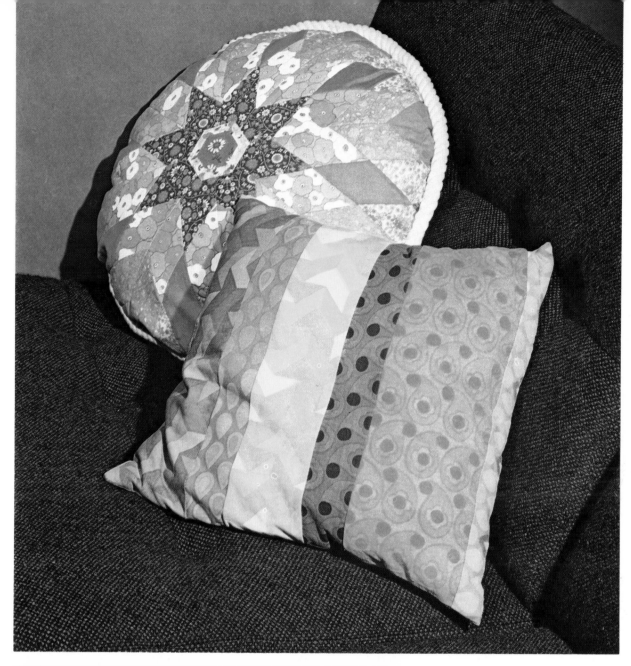

Plate 17
CUSHIONS AND WALLHANGING

ABOVE: Printed and plain fabrics make
the diamond shapes round the centre
hexagon of this colourful circular cushion
edged with cord. The eight central
diamonds are first joined with a point of
each meeting in the middle – then further
rounds of diamonds are added to the size
required. The two hexagonal patches in
the centre are finally stitched over the
diamond points.
The striped cushion shows another
patchwork technique using strips of
scrap fabrics of varying widths.

LEFT: This mounted panel is worked on a
hessian background and features unusual
drawn-thread work. The use of gold
threads, wools, and bugle beads gives a
rich textured finish.

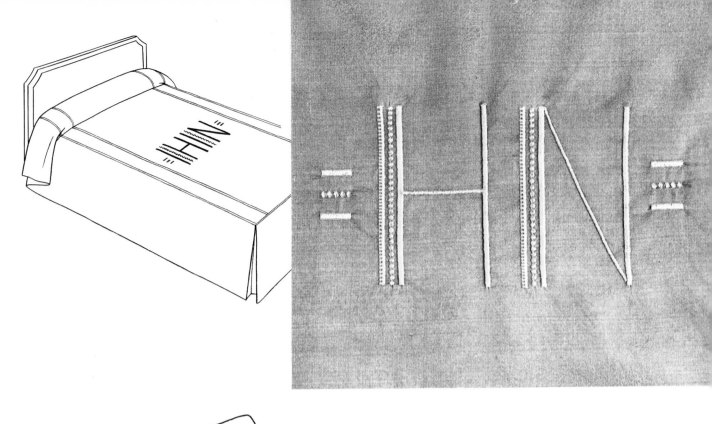

Plate 18
TWO HANDSOME MONOGRAM STYLES

ABOVE: Modern block letters formed with decorative stitch patterns.

BELOW: A graceful satin monogram appliquéd on a towel.

BELOW LEFT: Diamond-shaped cut outs, combined with decorative stitch pattern, make an attractive pillowcase border.

pattern to use within each leaf and a narrow, plain zig-zag stitch to outline the leaf. Pull the threads through to the underside and tie them after stitching each section. When completed, trim the backing close to the stitching. Press. To add a touch of glamour, sew on a few beads by hand to highlight the design.

Monograms

To monogram the 'K' shown here prepare the work as described under *Imitation Appliqué*, page 276. The first stitching is within the monogram. Select the stitch pattern, set the stitch length selector for satin stitching and stitch. Then select a narrow, plain zig-zag stitch. Align the marking for the monogram with the centre of the Presser Foot, and stitch, outlining the outer edges. Pull the threads to the underside and tie them after stitching each section. When finished, trim the backing close to the stitching. Press.

For the 'G W' monogram, prepare the work as described under *Imitation Appliqué*, page 276. Set the stitch length selector for satin stitching. First, work the individual flower petals, using the ball stitch pattern. To start stitching at the beginning of the pattern unit see page 266. Then outline the monogram with a narrow, plain zig-zag stitch. Align the marking for the design with the centre of the Presser Foot. Begin stitching at the point near the finished petals; gradually turn the fabric with both hands as you sew. When completed, pull the threads through to the underside and tie them. Trim the backing close to the stitching. Press.

Embroidery

Script monograms and satin-stitched scallops that look like hand embroidery can be made with zig-zag stitching when you use the 'free-motion' method.

In 'free-motion' stitching, you sew without a Presser Foot and control the fabric movement (and hence, stitch length) yourself using an embroidery hoop. Because you can move the hoop in any direction – forwards or backwards, from side to side, and even diagonally – free-motion stitching is well adapted to intricate embroidery designs.

To Prepare the Machine

Adjust the machine for a plain zig-zag stitch and either a medium or wide stitch width. Generally, a lighter needle thread tension is required. See page 266. Raise the stitch length selector to a short stitch. Remove the Presser Foot. Make the feed inoperative so that it will not move the fabric. (This is done by either raising the throat plate or lowering the feed. Refer to the instruction book accompanying your machine.)

Monograms

Always make a test sample first to determine the correct stitch width, spacing, tension and hoop movement.

Trace or mark the monogram on the right side of the fabric. See page 251. If the fabric is soft or loosely woven, add an underlay of crisp lawn or organdie slightly larger than the hoop used. Carefully tack the backing to the wrong side under the area where the stitching will be applied.

Use an embroidery hoop large enough to frame the whole design. The fabric must be held taut by the hoop.

Place the work under the needle. Lower the presser bar to activate the tension. Turn the hand wheel towards you and bring the bobbin thread up through the fabric to start the design.

Lower the needle into the fabric, hold both thread ends, and start stitching. Move the hoop slowly, following the outline of the design. To maintain parallel stitches, follow the monogram without turning; the work should remain straight in line with the feed at all times. The shading of stitches from wide to narrow is controlled by slowly moving the hoop to the right or left and at a slight angle. Where lines cross, make the first line of stitching less dense and the second line more prominent. This takes practice.

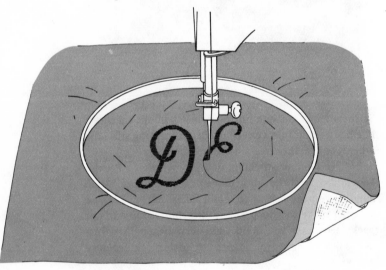

Run the machine at an even rate of speed so that the stitches are uniformly spaced. A slow motion of the hoop produces a close satin stitch; a more rapid movement produces an open stitch.

When finished, bring the threads through to the underside with a needle, and tie them. Cut away the backing close to the stitching. Press.

MONOGRAMS ON TOWELLING
(*Above right*)
Monograms can easily be applied to bath and hand towels, beach robes and other articles made of towelling.

Trace the monogram on a firm fabric, such as crisp lawn or organdie, slightly larger than the hoop used. Carefully place the lawn *on the right side of the towelling* and tack it in place. Then stitch, following the directions given above. When finished, cut away the lawn close to the stitching, using small, sharp scissors. Steam from the wrong side.

Satin-Stitched Scallops

Satin-stitched scallops provide a beautiful and durable finish for household linens as well as clothing.

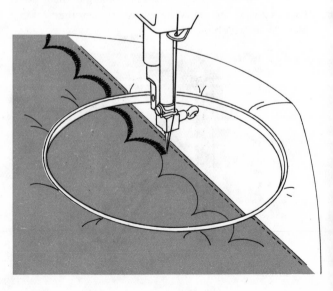

Trace the scallops on the *right side* of the fabric; *do not cut*. See page 251 for instructions. When scalloping is used as an edge finish, allow at least a 2·5-cm (1-inch) margin beyond the tracing. Machine-tack a strip of fabric to the cut edge so that the work is wide enough to fit the hoop.

If the fabric requires a backing, use crisp lawn or organdie cut slightly wider than the hoop. Machine-tack the marked scalloped edge over the centre of the backing. The lawn or organdie serves as an extension on the edge as well as a backing. Use the embroidery hoop and place it under the needle in the same way as for monograms.

To maintain parallel stitches, follow the scallops without turning; the work remains straight in line with the feed at all times. Stitch slowly, moving the hoop to the right or left, so that the needle on its left swing follows the marking for the scallops. This produces the effect of a narrow stitch at the point between the scallops; the stitch widens to its full depth at the arc. Maintain an even rate of speed so that the stitches are uniformly spaced.

To cord scallops. A fine corded edge is used as an edge finish to complete satin-stitched scallops. Use the Special Purpose Foot on the machine, and insert the filler cord into the right eyelet. See *Hairline Seam*, page 88 for threading instructions.

Position the needle close to the scalloped edge; lower the foot and stitch close to the scallops, covering the filler cord with narrow, closely spaced, plain zig-zag stitches. Stitch very close to the scallops all the way. Press.

If scallops border a hem, cut away the surplus of hem on the wrong side, close to the inside of the scallops. If scallops form an edge, cut away the surplus border and backing close to the cording stitches on the outside of the scallops. Then cut away the backing close to the inside of the scallops.

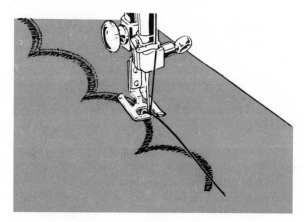

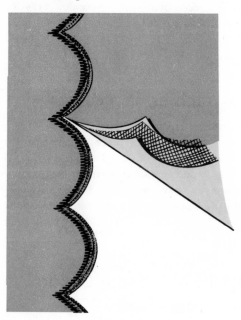

Using Your Machine Accessories

Accessories add new dimensions to machine sewing. They enable you to accomplish quickly and expertly many finishing details that would be laborious and time-consuming by hand.

Accessories are available for almost every phase of sewing. Many are standard and come with the machine; others can be purchased separately. This chapter explains how to use them all.

To Attach an Accessory

The accessories replace the regular Presser Foot on the machine. Refer to the instruction book accompanying the machine or accessory for complete information on how to place each one on your machine. If the accessory has a needle hole, draw the needle thread through it by taking a stitch in a scrap of fabric before starting to sew.

Zipper Foot, Seam Guide and Quilter

These three accessories are illustrated elsewhere in the book. For pages giving instructions on their use, consult the alphabetical index.

The *Zipper Foot* simplifies zip insertion and cording and piping. It can be adjusted to the right or left of the needle and enables you to stitch close to the teeth or coil of a zip or the filler cord in piping. It is a boon in dressmaking as well as in making furnishings.

The *Seam Guide* ensures accurate seam width and parallel lines of stitching for top stitching. It is invaluable to the beginner and even to the experienced dressmaker.

The *Quilter*, with its short, open foot and adjustable and removable space guide, is especially adapted to stitching lightly padded fabrics.

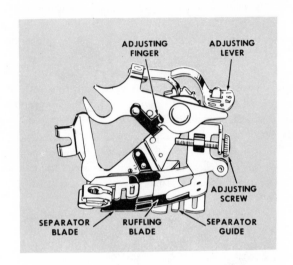

Ruffler

The Ruffler makes uniform gathered or pleated frills on light- or medium-weight fabrics. The simple settings belie the variety of work possible.

For instructions on fabric requirements and cutting of frills, and for additional information, see *Frills*, page 240.
Gathering. Adjust the Ruffler for gathering. For maximum fullness, turn the adjusting screw clockwise; for less fullness, turn it anti-clockwise. The stitch length also controls the fullness; a short stitch produces more fullness, a long stitch less.

Insert the fabric to be frilled between the two blue blades. Bring the edge under the first guide to keep the seamline even. Stitch, guiding the fabric.

Correct Position for Fabric to be Ruffled

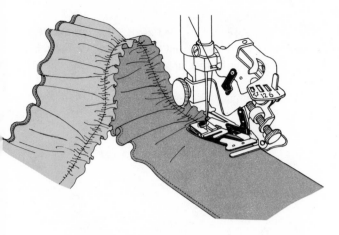

joined, right side up, between the Ruffler and feed of the machine. Bring the fabric edge under the first guide. Stitch.

Correct Positions for Fabrics

Frill with heading. Insert the fabric to be frilled between the two blades, extending the right edge beyond the needle the width of the heading. As you sew, guide the fabric to keep the heading width even.

Correct Position for Fabric to be Ruffled

Pleating. Adjust the Ruffler for pleats, either six or twelve stitches apart. Turn the adjusting screw clockwise as far as it will go. A short stitch places the pleats close together; a long stitch places them farther apart. Insert the fabric to be pleated between the two blue blades as you did for gathering. Stitch; as each pleat is formed, finger-press it the full depth of the frill.

Correct Position for Fabric

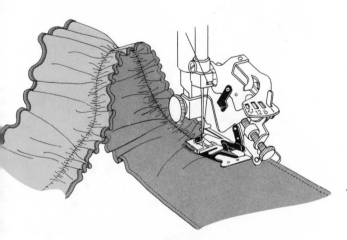

To form and attach a frill in one operation. Insert the frill strip, wrong side up, the same as for plain gathering. Place the fabric to which the frill is to be

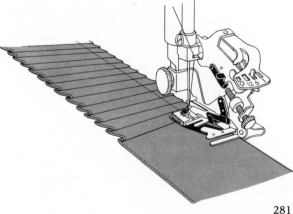

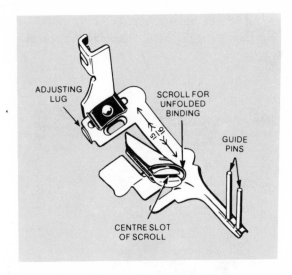

apply the binding, see *Zig-Zag Sewing,* page 268.

Inside curves are straightened as they are fed into the Binder. If the fabric is soft and has a tendency to stretch, reinforce the edge with a single row of stitching before binding.

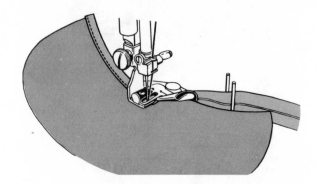

Binder

The Binder is used to apply commercial binding or self-fabric bias to an unfinished edge. Binding is a suitable finish for seam and hem edges that fray easily and a pretty trimming for frills, aprons, children's wear, curtains and novelty items. Straight or zig-zag stitching may be used with the Binder.

Cut the binding diagonally to form a long point at the end. Insert the point in the slot in the Binder and pull it through the scroll until the evenly folded binding is under the needle. Stitch just far enough to place the stitching close to the edge. To do this, move the scroll to the right or left. Do not pull the binding as it feeds through the scroll. Do not raise the presser bar after the stitching is in the correct position.

Outside curves tend to lead away from the scroll. Guide the fabric to the left in line with the needle so that the full seam width is taken. Do not attempt to pull or straighten the fabric into the full length of the scroll.

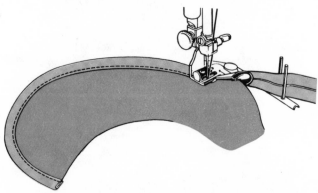

When ric-rac braid is applied to an edge as it is bound, insert the edge and ric-rac into the Binder at the same time, keeping the edges flush.

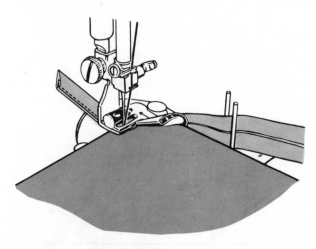

Insert the edge to be bound as far to the right as it will go in the centre scroll, and stitch.

To use decorative or plain zig-zag stitching when you

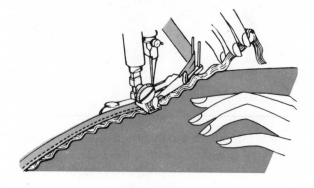

Hemmer Foot

With the Hemmer Foot you can turn and stitch narrow hems without tacking or pressing. A time-saving accessory, it is especially suited to hemming frills, sashes or any long edge where a narrow, machine-stitched hem is appropriate. Many yards may be finished as quickly as stitching a straight seam. Either straight or decorative stitching may be used. See *Narrow Hem Finishes*, page 195 for additional information.

Hemming. Form a ·3-cm (⅛-inch) double fold at the very edge of the fabric and crease it for about 5 cm (2 inches). Place the fabric under the foot and stitch through the

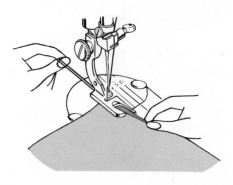

creased fold for several stitches. Hold the thread ends in the left hand and evenly guide the raw edge in front of the Hemmer into the scroll. Soft fabrics will enter the

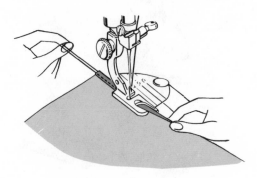

scroll best with the foot down; firm, crisp fabrics, with the foot raised. Even feeding is essential. As you sew, keep the same width of fabric in the scroll at all times.
Hemming with lace. You can make a hem and stitch lace edging in place with one line of stitching.

To apply lace over the hem, fold and start the hem in the usual way. Start about 2·5 cm (1 inch) from the end of the lace and place the selvedge under the needle; lower the needle to hold the lace firmly. Raise the foot slightly and slip the lace under the back portion of it. Stitch, guiding the hem with the right hand and the lace with the left.

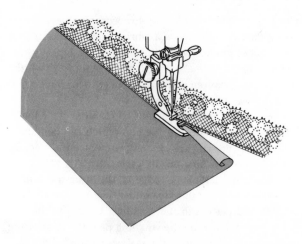

To apply lace under the hem, place the selvedge of the lace ·3 cm (⅛ inch) from the fabric edge; then fold and start the hem in the usual way. As you stitch, keep the lace ·3 cm (⅛ inch) from the fabric edge, and form the hem over the lace selvedge.

Hemmed seam. See page 85 for instructions.

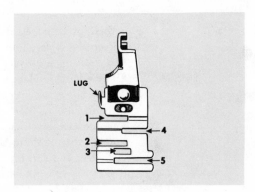

Edge Stitcher

The Edge Stitcher enables you to accurately place stitching on the extreme edge of a fabric. Using the numbered slots as your guide, you can join lace edges, fabric bands and lace insertion; make French seams of uniform width; stitch tucks from pin width to ·6 cm ($\frac{1}{4}$ inch); and edge-stitch hems, facings and seams.

The distance from the line of stitching to the edge of the fabric is regulated by the lug, which can be moved to the right or left. Test the adjustment on a piece of fabric before working on the garment.

To edge-stitch. Pink the edge of the seam allowance, facing or hem. Fold the edge under from ·3 to ·6 cm ($\frac{1}{8}$ to $\frac{1}{4}$ inch), and place it in slot 1. Adjust the lug to the left, far enough to position the stitching near the edge of the fold. Stitch, guiding the edge against the edge of the slot.

tions on forming the seam. For the first row of stitching, place the seam in slot 1 with the lug adjusted to the left

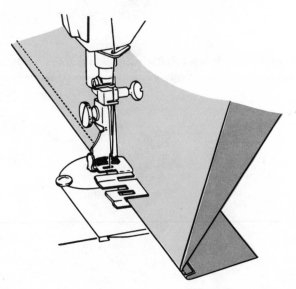

for a ·3-cm ($\frac{1}{8}$-inch) seam. For the second row of stitching, use slot 1 with the lug adjusted to its extreme right. For a wider French seam, use slot 5 and move the lug to its extreme left for the second row of stitching.

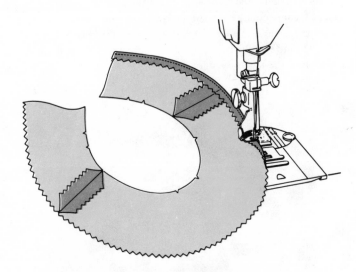

To join lace insertion and fabric bands. See page 261 for instructions.

To make a fine French seam. Trim the seam allowance to ·6 cm ($\frac{1}{4}$ inch). See *French Seam*, page 86 for instruc-

284

To make tucks from pin width to ·6 cm (¼ inch). See *Tucks*, page 235 for instructions on marking the position of the tucks on the fabric and for other information. Fold and press the fabric on the drawn thread the entire length of each tuck. The Edge Stitcher keeps the tucks uniform in width.

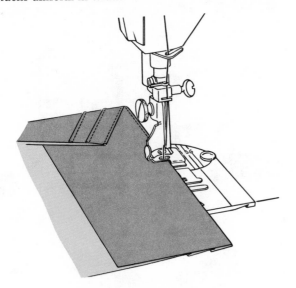

To make pin tucks, insert the creased fold in slot 1, and adjust the lug far enough to the left to position the stitching *just a few threads from the folded edge*. Guide the fold against the edge of the slot as you sew.

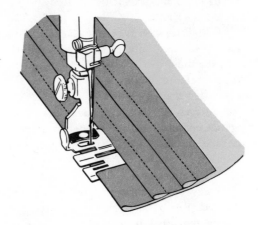

To make 6-cm (¼-inch) tucks, insert the creased fold in slot 5 and move the lug to its extreme left position.

To make tucks with lace. See page 237 for instructions.

See *Shirring*, page 242 for instructions on marking the fabric, suggestions on fabrics that are suitable for shirring and additional information.

Rows of shirring spaced ·6 cm (¼ inch) apart may be gauged by the edge of the foot. The centre of the Gathering Foot is your stitching guide. Align it with the marking for the shirring.

Gathering Foot

The Gathering Foot enables you to place single or multiple rows of shirring quickly and expertly. Since the foot is designed to lock fullness into every stitch, it ensures evenly spaced shirring.

The stitch length on the sewing machine regulates the fullness of the shirring; a long stitch produces more fullness than a short one. Tension also affects fullness; your shirring will be fuller with heavy tensions than with light. Matching thread is generally used, but thread contrasting in colour is quite acceptable for variety.

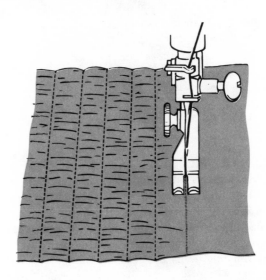

Even Feed Foot

The Even Feed* Foot is really a *must* for the following types of work:

　1. Sewing all pile fabrics, such as corduroy, velveteen, fake fur and bulky knits.

　2. Napped fabrics such as coating, suede, and tweed.

　3. Smooth surfaced fabrics such as satin, sateen, twill and gaberdine.

　4. Sticky surfaced fabrics such as leather, vinyl, and vinyl coated thermo plastics.

Other advantages of the attachment are that top stitching can be improved, the evenness of the stitch is better, and it assists with the feeding of multiple layers of fabric.

Therefore the attachment is ideal for sewing checks, stripes and any other fabric that requires matching. With the Even Feed* Foot some fabrics need only be pinned along the seams to keep the top layer of the fabric in place, with the pattern matched after machining.

A narrow hem around table linen will feed through the machine easily with the assistance of the Even Feed* attachment.

A vertical model and a model to fit the slant needle machine are available.

ATTACHING EVEN FEED FOOT

● Loosen screw and remove foot and shank.

● Guide Even Feed* Foot into position from the back of the machine, making sure the fork arm **B** of the foot fits over the needle clamp.

● Tighten screw securely with coin.

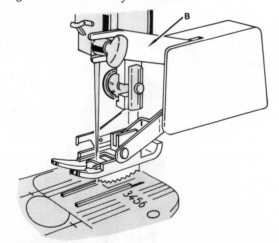

PREPARATION

● Ensure that all stripes and checks are cut out to match exactly and that the weave or grain of the fabric is 'true'. The Even Feed* Foot will *not* correct any inaccuracies in cutting or weaving. In some cases of very long or curved seams it may be advisable to tack lightly by hand before machining.

PROCEDURE

● Make sure the needle is in its highest position

● Place work under the Even Feed* Foot so that the entire needle opening is over the fabric, *Figure 1.* Lower foot firmly and stitch.

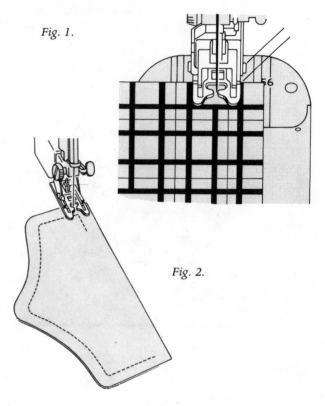

Fig. 1.

Fig. 2.

● For a reinforced seam, position needle opening about $\frac{1}{2}$ inch (1·2 cm) from the edge of the fabric, stitch in reverse to the edge; then stitch remainder of the seam forwards in the normal way.

You will observe how the upper section of the foot moves in unison with the soft-touch fabric feed on the machine to ensure a perfectly even seam of equal length on both sides.

When you are sewing intricate seams where stripe or check matching has to be perfect – use a slightly shorter stitch than usual.

Smooth Shiny Fabrics, Vinyl, Plastic, Imitation Skin or Leather

These fabrics all require careful preparation both during cutting and tacking.

Use a slightly longer stitch than usual when stitching.

Applying Pocket Flaps, Collars, or Commencing Seaming over thick Bulky Seams and Edges

● Position the work under the foot approximately $\frac{1}{2}$ inch (1·2 cm) in from the fabric edge.

● Sew backwards to exact beginning of the work – *Figure 2* – and then stitch forwards in the normal way. Stitch backwards to reinforce the end of the work.

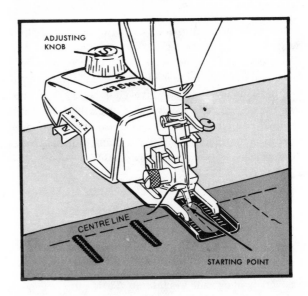

Place the fabric under the cloth clamp on the Buttonholer. (The cloth clamp will hold the fabric in position when the presser bar is lowered.) Align the buttonhole marking with the centre front and back lines of the cloth clamp, and align the centre line of the garment with the horizontal lines that are second from the back on both sides of the clamp. This alignment will accurately position the starting point of the buttonhole ·3 cm ($\frac{1}{8}$ inch)

Buttonholer

The Buttonholer makes neat worked buttonholes in a variety of fabrics in a fraction of the time required by hand. The buttonholes are firmer and stronger than those made by hand – and also more even. In addition, they are all the same length because a template controls the buttonhole length as well as style. The Buttonholer controls the stitch width and cutting space, which can be adjusted to accommodate fabric from sheer to heavy coating.

Five templates of varying lengths come with the Buttonholer – four for straight buttonholes and one for eyelet-end buttonholes for suits and coats. Five additional templates are available – three for straight buttonholes, one for an eyelet-end buttonhole, and one for eyelets for belts, studs and lacings.

beyond the centre-line marking of the garment. Follow this procedure for all succeeding buttonholes so that they are the same distance from the garment edge.

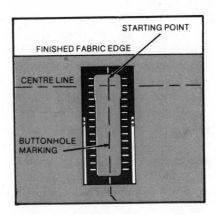

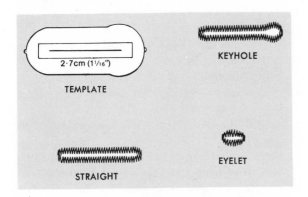

For guides on stitching the buttonholes, refer to the instruction book accompanying the Buttonholer. It gives you complete information.

Always make a test buttonhole on a piece of your fabric to determine the correct settings of the stitch width and cutting space as well as the buttonhole length. Use the number of fabric layers you will be using in the garment and include the same type of interfacing.

Work out the buttonhole length and position as described under *Worked Buttonhole*, page 116. Carefully mark the length and line of the buttonhole with chalk or hand tacking along the thread of the fabric.

Sewing for Children

Some of the greatest joys in sewing come from making well-fitting and becoming clothes for children and delicate dresses and articles for babies. Quite apart from your own satisfaction are other rewards, equally important: the individuality you can give your child's wardrobe and the money you can save. If your clothing budget is limited, you will find that you can dress your children well in better quality fabrics at a fraction of the cost of ready-made clothes in expensive children's shops.

Making Clothes for Boys and Girls

Fashion is important to children. Little girls and boys know when they are smartly dressed and when a garment fits well. They begin at an early age to develop good taste and good grooming habits.

Sewing for little girls is a mother's delight – a pastime that may develop into a truly creative hobby as the girls grow older. Sewing for little boys generally continues until the boys reach the age where their shirts and trousers require tailoring techniques.

Children's patterns are available in a variety of styles. Mother and daughter dresses and brother and sister outfits can be attractive and are often featured in fashion pages. A word of caution here: never make children's clothes too large for the child to 'grow into'. Both fit and fashion are lost along the way and the garment is worn out and discarded before the child grows to fit it. However, skirts should be made with deep hems so that they can be lengthened and worn a second year; the same is true of coats, including the sleeves.

Fabrics

Fabrics most suited for children's dresses, suits and coats are gingham, broadcloth, poplin, batiste, linen, voile, organdie, organza, denim, sailcloth, piqué, seersucker, madras cotton, flannel, lightweight wool, tweed, velveteen, corduroy, synthetic fabrics such as terylene and nylon and bonded fabrics. Drip-dry and blends of two fibres are practical and popular since they are easy to launder and require little ironing.

Look for flame-resistant fabrics for small children, and always select a fabric that will withstand the wear and laundering necessary for children's clothes. Check whether the fabric is washable or must be dry-cleaned. If it is not pre-shrunk or Sanforized, shrink it before cutting. See page 15.

Colour and Design

When sewing for children, you have an almost unlimited selection of colours from which to choose. Dark as well as pastel shades may be used. Let common sense be your guide. Select colours that are becoming to the child and practical for the outfit you are making.

As for design, plain colours, small plaids and prints, narrow stripes, little dots and tiny checks all look charming on children.

Measurements

Measure the child accurately and record the measurements on the charts; girls' opposite, boys' on page 290. If the child is very young, it is advisable to measure a garment that fits the child correctly and record those measurements on the chart. To measure the crutch for slacks and shorts, see page 49.

Here are some rules to observe in measuring:

Sleeve seams should be at the shoulder line, not dropping over the shoulder.

A round neckline and collar should fit the neckline closely; a square or V neckline should fit the neckline closely at the shoulder line.

The waistline should be midway between the hip bone and the end of the ribs and should fit with a slight ease.

Short sleeves should end halfway between the shoulder and elbow; puff sleeves should be shorter. Full-length sleeves extend to the wrist. Three-quarter length sleeves extend halfway between the elbow and wrist.

The skirt length must be correct for the dress to be fashionable. For a small girl, the skirt is short, usually midway between the knee and hip-line. As a girl grows older, the skirt should generally be longer.

Girl's Measurements

The illustrations below show you where to place the tape measure
when taking each measurement. **Measurements are taken from right side.**
(Consider seam allowance in checking with pattern.)

	Child's Measurement	Allowance for Ease	Pattern Measurement
1. CHEST		4–5 cm (1½–2 in)	
2. BREAST		4–6 cm (1½–2½ in)	
3. WAIST			
4. HIP – 7·5 cm (3 inches) below waist			
5. NECK CIRCUMFERENCE			
6. SHOULDER LENGTH – Right			
Left			
7. SHOULDER TO SHOULDER		1·2–2·5 cm (½–1 in)	
8. WAIST LENGTH –			
a – Front		1·2–2·5 cm (½–1 in)	
b – Back		1·2–2·5 cm (½–1 in)	
9. SLEEVE LENGTH –			
a – Shoulder to elbow			
b – Elbow to wrist			
c – Inside from underarm seam to wrist			
10. SKIRT FINISHED LENGTH –			
a – Front			
b – Back			
Plus allowance for hem (7·5–13 cm (3–5 inches)) . .			
Plus allowance for 'let-out tuck' (5 cm (2 inches) if desired)			

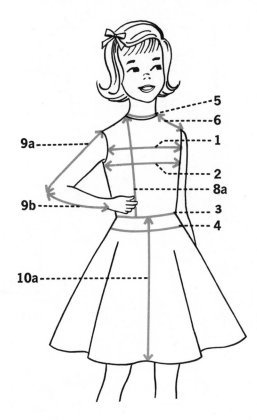
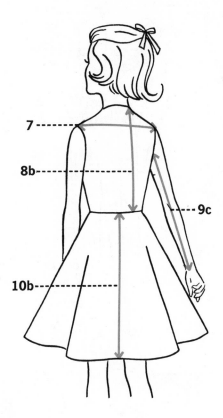

Boy's Measurements

The illustrations below show you where to place the tape measure
when taking each measurement. **Measurements are taken from right side.**
(Consider seam allowance in checking with pattern.)

	Child's Measurement	Allowance for Ease	Pattern Measurement
1. **CHEST**	_____	12·5–18 cm (5–7 in)	_____
2. **WAIST** . . . . :	_____	_____	_____
3. **HIP**	_____	_____	_____
4. **HEIGHT** – Neckline to floor	_____	_____	_____
5. **BACK LENGTH OF SHIRT**			
Neck to waistline plus 'tuck-in'	_____	4–5 cm (1½–2 in)	_____
6. **SHOULDER TO SHOULDER**	_____	1·2–2·5 cm (½–1 in)	_____
7. **FINISHED LENGTH OF TROUSERS**	_____	_____	_____
8. **FINISHED LENGTH OF SHORTS**	_____	_____	_____
9. **FINISHED LENGTH OF JACKET** –			
a – Front	_____	_____	_____
b – Back	_____	_____	_____
10. **NECK CIRCUMFERENCE**	_____	_____	_____
11. **SLEEVE LENGTH**	_____	_____	_____

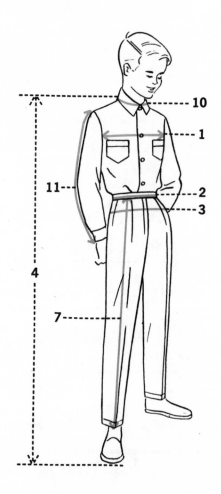

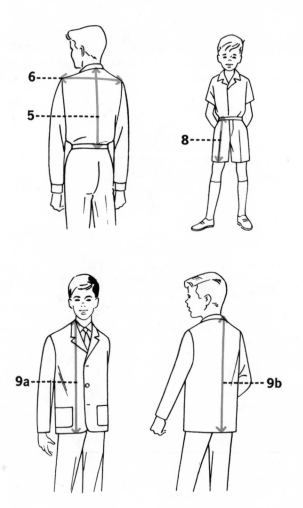

Patterns

SELECTING PATTERN SIZE

Before selecting the pattern, study the measurements in the pattern catalogues and on the back of the pattern envelope. For girls, select the pattern according to the breast measurement; for boys, chest measurement. *Never select a pattern by age.*

The size marked on the pattern will give the approximate age for which the pattern was designed. But children of the same age often differ in height, weight and proportion. A three-year-old child, for example, may need a size 4 or size 2 pattern. By using the breast and chest measurement as a guide, you will have to make very few, if any, adjustments to the pattern.

The pattern allows sufficient ease for action; however, the ease may vary with the style and make of pattern. Buy the same size coat pattern as dress or shirt pattern since the necessary ease is included.

CHECKING THE PATTERN

Always measure the pattern and make any necessary adjustments. See *Checking the Pattern against Your Measurements*, page 37.

Pin the pattern pieces together and try the pattern on right side of the figure if the child is not too young.

ADJUSTING THE PATTERN

The adjustments for children's patterns are essentially the same as for adults'. See *Adjusting the Pattern*, page 39. Shown here are adjustments for the *chubby child*.

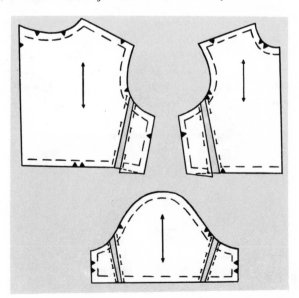

To add width across the chest, waistline and sleeves. Slash the front and back bodice and sleeve from lower edge to armhole as illustrated. Place a piece of tissue paper underneath and spread the pattern to add a quarter the width required. Pin the pattern to the tissue. Adjust the skirt in the same manner. Remember that only half the pattern is given; therefore, an adjustment of 1·2 cm (½ inch) in both the front and the back bodice sections will add 5 cm (2 inches) to the chest and waist measurement.

To add width across the shoulders, chest and waistline. Slash the front and back bodice from the centre of the dart at the lower edge to the shoulder line. Place a piece of tissue paper underneath and spread the pattern to add a quarter the width required. Pin the pattern to the tissue. Adjust the skirt in the same manner. The shoulder width will be increased the amount of the adjustment; the chest and waistline will be increased four times the amount of the adjustment.

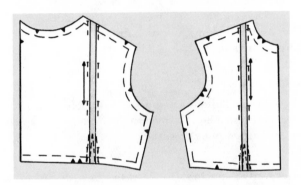

Decrease the darts the amount of the adjustment, as indicated by the dotted line. The darts should be in the correct position when the adjustment is made through their centre.

Construction Tips

Good workmanship is essential. The construction tips listed below will guide you in your sewing for children. For specific instructions on each one, consult the alphabetical index.

Seams. Make strong seams that will withstand the many washings and rough wear to which the garment may be subjected. For little girls' dresses of washable cottons, drip-dry and sheer fabrics, use French seams. For velveteen, corduroy and linen, use plain seams pressed open, and neaten the seam edges with overcasting.

Boys' shirts should be made with either a flat felled seam or a French seam. For shorts and trousers, use a flat felled seam for play clothes and a plain seam pressed open for better clothes. Finish seam edges with binding, edge-stitching or overcasting.

Layer seams the same as you would in clothing for adults. See page 89.

Interfacings. Use a washable interfacing such as muslin, batiste or lawn in boys' shirts, girls' dresses and blouses, and collars and cuffs. Always interface the waistband on shorts.

Plackets. The continuous bound placket is usual for the skirts of dresses and for boys' shirt sleeves with cuffs.

Hems. Always allow 7·5 or 10 cm (3 or 4 inches) for hems in full, gathered skirts and about 5 cm (2 inches) for hems in gored skirts. Hem finishes should be durable. Edge-stitching is excellent for most fabrics. Neaten velveteen, corduroy and linen with seam binding. Hems blindstitched by machine are satisfactory for everyday dresses and shorts; for better clothes, finish hems by hand.

Fastenings. Buttons and worked buttonholes are used for most fastenings. On pyjamas and dungarees tap-on press-studs may be substituted.

Decorative touches. To vary the look of favourite patterns, add something new. Dresses, for example, may be changed by the addition of tucks, lace, frills, appliqué, lacing, ric-rac braid, bias binding, pockets, smocking, piping or decorative zig-zag stitching. The neckline, waistline and sleeve edge of little girls' dresses may be finished with a double-fold bias binding or piping cord; these details are found only in the better ready-made dresses. An organdie pinafore may be added for charm. Your machine accessories will simplify the stitching of many decorative details. (Refer to the alphabetical index for the listing of these finishes.)

Underskirts. When a dress has a full skirt, include an underskirt to the waist seam. Make the underskirt of net and cut it by the skirt pattern. Use a French seam to join the skirt sections. Gather the underskirt and skirt fabric separately, then join them to the bodice in a single seam. For instructions on gathering, see page 106.

After hemming the skirt, trim the underskirt to the same length and finish the edge with seam binding. Use decorative zig-zag stitching or straight stitching to sew the binding in place.

Special Features in Children's Clothes

GROWTH AND SHRINKAGE TUCKS

A tuck is frequently put into children's clothes to allow for growth or fabric shrinkage. The tuck *must be on the true grain of the fabric* and can be placed in the following sections: (1) in the hem so that it is not visible on the right side; (2) on the right side just above the hem; (3) in the bodice near the waistline; and (4) vertically over the shoulder. Although you may use a regular

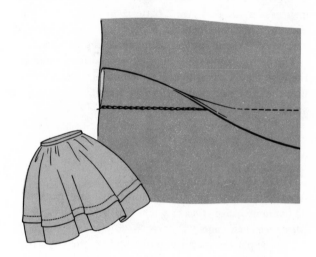

straight stitch, a chain stitch is ideal, for it makes 'letting out' a simple task – you merely unlock the last loop of the chain formed on the underside of the tuck and pull out the stitching. (If your machine has Chain Stitch Accessories, see page 63.)

SASH

The sash on a child's dress is often cut in two pieces and joined to the garment at each side seam.

To make the sash. Hem each side of the two pieces, using the Hemmer Foot. Hem one end of each piece by making a 1·5-cm ($\frac{5}{8}$-inch) double fold. Press, then stitch near the edge of the first fold.

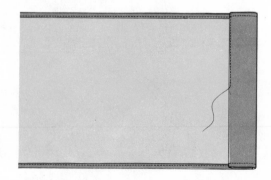

Courtesy of McCall's magazine

Plate 19
PRETTY, PRACTICAL AND YOUNG

ABOVE: In an attic room, the sloping ceiling provides a built-in base for a frilled canopy of provincial print. Matching café curtain, placed low on the window, and gathered valance and curtain give a pleasing balance to the room.

ABOVE: Sunny yellow brightens a small room. Semi-sheer patterned café curtains ensure privacy while letting in light. The same fabric is repeated in the flounce on the bed, which is topped with a quilted box coverlet.

From The American Home ©
1964 The Curtis Publishing Company

LEFT: Alice in Wonderland theme is created with printed fabric for curtains, bed flounce and headboard trim and is emphasised by cut outs from the fabric on the wall. Ball fringe makes a gay finish. The solid pink of the quilted coverlet blends perfectly with the print.

Courtesy of F. Schumacher and Company

Plate 20
QUILTING FOR LUXURY

RIGHT: A quilted print screen gives this bedroom a charming touch of distinction. The quilting outlines the handsome floral motif, giving the fabric an extra dimension of luxury. The fabric design is precisely matched in the pleated flounce. The simple coverlet can be varied for a quick change of colour scheme or for laundering.

BELOW: The smartly tailored bedspread's diamond-pattern quilting could be stitched by machine or bought by length. Luxurious blue curtains, hung on bright brass rods and held with braid and tassel tie-backs, create a Victorian feeling, which is softened by sheer, white net curtains.

Illustrations above and below from The American Home © 1964, The Curtis Publishing Company

From the American Home © 1964, The Curtis Publishing Company

BANDS FOR ELEGANCE

Bands of fabric, cut from the striped pattern used for the valance on the bed, add elegance to the brilliant orange and red tones of this room. Curtains, pelmet, coverlet and bolsters are all outlined with striking effect.

Another method is to make a point at the sash ends. Fold the end, right sides together, and stitch ·6 cm ($\frac{1}{4}$ inch) from the cut edge. Back-stitch at each end. Cut off the corner at the folded edge, and press the seam open. Turn to the right side, forming a tie point.

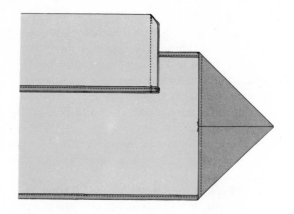

To join the sash to the bodice. Fold the unfinished ends of the sash into pleats and join them to the bodice, following one of the methods given below:

Method 1: Before stitching the side seams of the bodice. Pin the sash, right side up, to the right side of the back bodice, keeping the cut edges even at the side seam and the lower edge of the sash even with the waistline seamline. Stitch, including it in the seam as the front and back bodice sections are joined together.

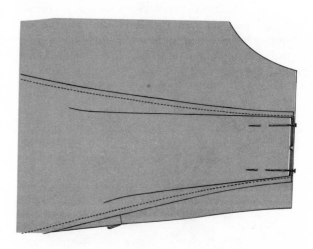

Method 2: After the dress is finished. On the right side, place the sash, right side up, at the side seam, keeping the cut edges to the front, the sash to the back and the lower edge even with the waistline. Pin, then stitch ·6 cm ($\frac{1}{4}$ inch) from the cut edge; back-stitch at each end. Trim the cut edge to ·3 cm ($\frac{1}{8}$ inch). Fold the sash to the front and stitch in place on the side seam. Back-stitch at each end. This encases the cut edges and forms a finish similar to a French seam.

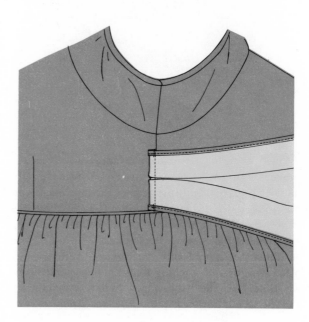

FLY FASTENING

For boys over the age of three, a fly fastening should be used on shorts and trousers. Trouser zips are available from 15 to 28 cm (6 to 11 inches) in length, but it is customary to cut off the top of the tape at the waist after it has been stitched in place, so the zip teeth are included in the waistband seam. A neckline zip can be used for small boys' shorts and trousers.

Cut the shorts or trousers by the pattern. Transfer the notches and markings to the fabric. The fly is the first construction work.

Pin the facing for the opening over the left front, right sides together. Stitch from the waistline to the marking for the crutch. Trim the seam allowance to ·6 cm ($\frac{1}{4}$ inch) and clip into it on the curve. Press. Clip into the seam allowance ·9 cm ($\frac{3}{8}$ inch) at the lower end of the opening. Turn the facing to the underside, fold on the stitching line, and press.

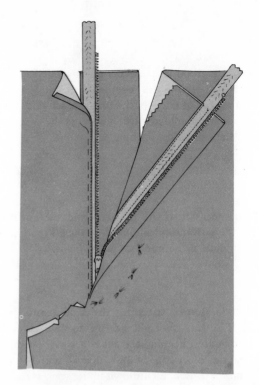

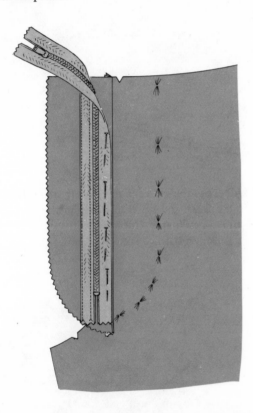

Turn the facing and seam allowance away from the garment. Place the closed zip, face down, over the right side of the facing, with the edge of the tape even with the seamline and the end stop ·6 cm ($\frac{1}{4}$ inch) above the crutch seamline. If necessary, curve the tape to fit the lower end of the opening. Pin in place.

Adjust the Zipper Foot to the right of the needle and place two rows of stitching from the lower end to the waistline. Place the first row close to the teeth of the zip and the second row near the edge of the tape.

On the right front, clip into the seam allowance ·9 cm ($\frac{3}{8}$ inch) at the lower end of the opening. Fold the edge of the opening under ·6 cm ($\frac{1}{4}$ inch) from the seamline. Open the zip and pin the folded edge to the right side of the tape, with the end stop ·6 cm ($\frac{1}{4}$ inch) above the crutch seam and matching the left front at the end of the opening and at the waistline. Make the fly underlay, then pin it in place under the zip, with the seam edges even. Tack through all thicknesses. Stitch in place from the end of the zip to the waistline, close to the fold. Remove tackings.

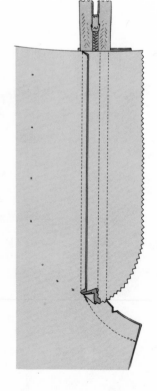

Pin the crutch seams together with the cut edges even. Stitch, joining the stitching of the left front facing seam. Back-stitch at each end.

294

Turn the left front facing to the underside and pin. Tack in place, following the markings on the right side. Stitch on the right side, close to the tacking, from the lower end to the waistline. (Do not catch the underlay in the stitching.) At the lower end, pull the threads

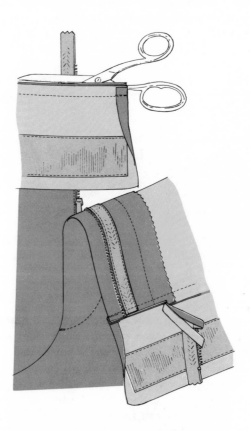

Interface the waistband, following the instructions under *Method 1*, page 154. Open the zip and pin the waistband to the waistline, right sides together, extending the band ends 1·2 cm (½ inch) beyond the opening. Stitch. Trim the seam edges to ·6 cm (¼ inch) and cut off the ends of the zip if they extend beyond the waistline seam edge. Press. Turn the band away from the garment and press the seam allowance towards the band. Turn the ends of the band under 1·2 cm (½ inch) and press.

through to the underside and tie. Make a bar tack through all thicknesses at the end of the opening. See page 337. This prevents splitting. Press the stitching, but do not press over the zip.

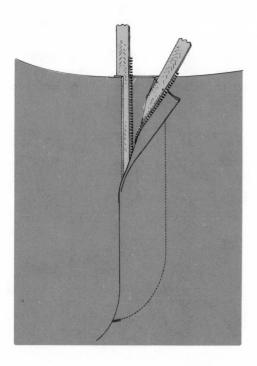

Turn under the free edge of the band and pin it in place on the underside, enclosing the seam allowances. Top-stitch round the band. Work buttonholes and sew on buttons.

ELASTIC BAND ON BOXER SHORTS

To apply elastic to the waistline of boxer shorts you may use zig-zag stitching or straight stitching. Use conventional elastic or a woven elastic made especially for boxer shorts, pyjamas and underwear.

Try the elastic round the waist for a comfortable fit, allow 2·5 cm (1 inch) for joining the ends. Lap the ends 2·5 cm (1 inch), then fold one end under ·6 cm (¼ inch) and join with two rows of narrow zig-zag stitching.

To attach the elastic to the waistline, use one of the methods described here – *Method 1* if the elastic is to show on the underside, and *Method 2* if the elastic is concealed in the hem of the garment.

Method 1: Fold under the waistline seam allowance on the garment and press. Divide both the elastic circle and the garment waistline into quarters and pin-mark the garment and each edge of the elastic at these intervals.

Place the elastic circle over the wrong side of the garment, extending the fold for the seam ·3 cm ($\frac{1}{8}$ inch) beyond the elastic. Pin each edge of the elastic to the garment at the quarter intervals.

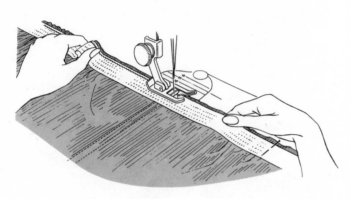

Join the two with a row of stitching placed near each edge of the elastic. Stitch from the elastic side; as you stitch, stretch the elastic between the pins so that it will remain stretchable after the stitching is completed. Use a medium-width zig-zag stitch and a 2·5 mm (10) stitch length. If you want a third row of stitching, space it evenly between the first two rows. Pull threads to the underside; tie and clip.

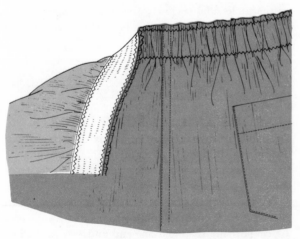

Method 2: Finish the cut edge of the waistline hem with the blindstitch zig-zag, or fold it under ·6 cm ($\frac{1}{4}$ inch) and edge-stitch. Fold the waistline hem to the underside of the garment and press. Divide both the elastic circle and the garment waistline into quarters and pin-mark the garment and each edge of the elastic at these intervals.

Turn the hem away from the garment and, on the underside, place the elastic edge to the crease for the hem. Pin each edge of the elastic to the hem at the quarter intervals. Then, with the elastic up, stitch near the top edge of the elastic. Stretch the elastic between the pins as you stitch so that it will remain stretchable after the stitching is finished. Use a medium-width zig-zag stitch and a 2·5 mm (10) stitch length.

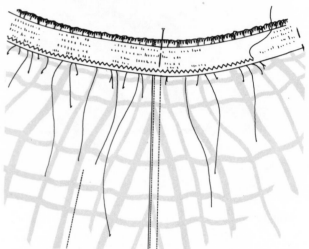

Fold the elastic and hem to the inside and pin to the garment at the quarter intervals. On the right side, place a row of zig-zag stitching close to each edge of the elastic, stretching the elastic between the pins as you sew. If you add the third row of stitching, space it evenly between the first two rows. Pull threads to the underside; tie and clip.

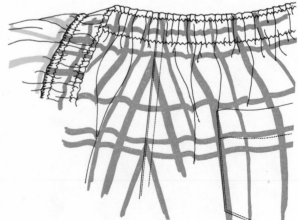

296

SHIRT-SLEEVE OPENING

The opening. Finish the opening before stitching the sleeve seams. Slash the opening as marked on the pattern. Cut the pieces for the overlapping and the underlapping edges of the slash binding.

Bind the back edge of the slash with the narrow piece, taking a ·6-cm (¼-inch) seam. Pin the overlap piece to the

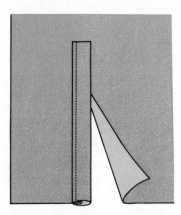

front edge of the slash with the right side next to the wrong side of the sleeve. Stitch, taking a ·6-cm (¼-inch) seam. Press, then press the seam edges towards the sleeve.

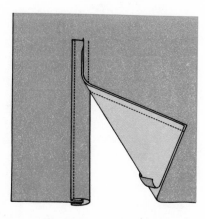

Turn the overlap to the right side of the sleeve. Turn under the cut edge and adjust the piece so that it will

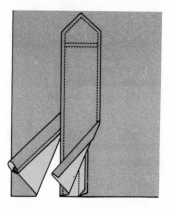

overlap the back edge. Press. Top-stitch round the overlap and stitch twice across the point to hold the underlap in position.

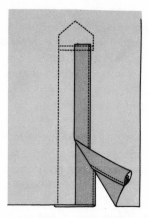

Stitch the sleeve seam, using a flat felled seam. Gather the lower edge. Turn the sleeve to the right side.

The cuff. Use a lawn interfacing. Make the cuff following the instructions on page 172, leaving the top edge open. Trim one seam edge and the interfacing to ·3 cm (⅛ inch) and the other edge to ·6 cm (¼ inch). Press. Turn the cuff to the right side, and press. Pin the underside of the cuff and interfacing to the sleeve, matching markings. Adjust the gathers to fit the cuff, and stitch. Trim the seam allowance to ·6 cm (¼ inch). Press. Turn the cuff away from the sleeve and press the seam allowances towards the cuff. Turn the cut edge under on the top side of the cuff and pin it to the sleeve at the stitching line, enclosing the gathered seam allowance inside the cuff. Top-stitch as illustrated. Press. Work buttonholes and sew on buttons.

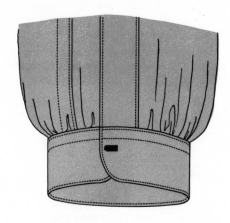

Sewing for Babies

Sewing for babies brings you into a world of soft fabrics, fine seams and dainty trimming. Choose soft cotton, silk or woollen fabrics that will withstand frequent laundering. Magyar sleeves are practical in most babies' wear except dresses. They are easy to make and their loose fit makes them comfortable for the baby and simplifies dressing for the mother.

A fine French seam, machine-stitched or hand-stitched, is the usual method for your seams. Your first stitching of the seam may be by machine and the second by hand. Since the fabric is delicate, the stitches should be short.

Trimming should be dainty. Narrow lace edging and insertion, tiny pin tucks, dainty hand stitches, small appliquéd motifs, narrow hemstitching, smocking, scallops and small zig-zag stitches that are lacy in design are all appropriate, decorative finishes for babywear.

Needle and Thread

The sewing thread should blend with the fabric in fibre, colour and size. In selecting a needle, consider both the fabric and the thread. Silk and woollen fabrics are stitched with silk thread and size 11 needle. Viyella, Clydella, batiste, lawn, flannelette, piqué, needlecord and cotton knitted fabrics, are stitched with size 50 mercerised cotton thread and size 14 needle. Threads used for embroidery stitches should be fine enough for you to make dainty stitches on the soft fabrics you will be working with.

Fastenings

Use tiny buttons and hand-made buttonholes or thread loops in dresses, slips and angel tops, use ribbon ties in matinée jackets and nightgowns. The tap-on snap fastener is practical for the crutch opening of pyjamas and play-suits. A very narrow, continuous bound placket or a hemmed placket is appropriate below the yoke of a garment. If the garment does not have a yoke, a hemmed placket is better.

Patterns

Basic layette patterns can be bought at pattern counters. Choose two or three and adapt them to your needs.

The seam allowance in layette patterns varies from ·3, ·6 to 1·5 cm ($\frac{1}{4}$, $\frac{1}{2}$ to $\frac{5}{8}$ inch), depending on the position of the seam and the make of the pattern. Check these very carefully.

Cot and Pram Blankets

Cot and pram blankets are made from flannel or flannelette. Each blanket requires 1 metre of 90 cm fabric (1 yard by 36 inches). Remove the selvedges and finish the edges following one of the methods given here.

Method 1: Turn the cut edge under ·6 cm ($\frac{1}{4}$ inch) and press. Then fold a ·9-cm ($\frac{3}{8}$-inch) hem and tack. Finish the edge with a blanket stitch or buttonhole stitch. See page 231.

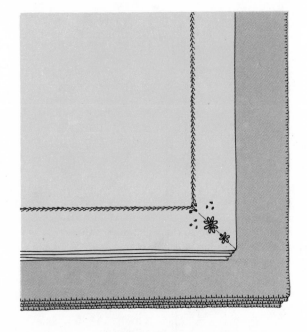

Method 2: For a wider hem, which is frequently used, turn the hem to the underside 5–6 cm ($2\frac{1}{4}$ inches) and press. Fold the cut edge under ·6 cm ($\frac{1}{4}$ inch), mitre the corners as instructed on page 195. Tack the hem in place and finish on the top side, using a featherstitch near the inside edge of the hem. A group of French knots or a small lazy daisy stitch placed in each of the corners adds a personal touch.

Nightgowns

Nightgowns are made of batiste, Viyella, Clydella, lawn, fine flannel and Winceyette.

For sturdy seams that will withstand many washings, use a fine French seam throughout the construction. Finish the neckline and sleeves with a narrow hand-rolled hem, or face the edges with narrow lace insertion. Gather the lace and hand-sew it round the neckline and sleeves. If the fabric is white or a plain colour, consider adding French knots near the neckline and sleeve edge. A small design, such as a duck, bunny or kitten may be outlined with stem stitch or small buttonhole stitch; use a pastel colour and a single strand of six-strand floss.

Hem the lower edge by turning the cut edge under ·6 cm ($\frac{1}{4}$ inch) and fold and tack the hem. Finish with a slip stitch.

If a drawstring is used at the hem, leave one underarm seam open ·9 cm ($\frac{3}{8}$ inch) at hem level. Turn the casing in the same manner as the hem and machine-stitch in place. Slot 1$\frac{1}{2}$ metres (1$\frac{1}{2}$ yards) of fine tape in the casing.

Matinée Jackets

Matinée jackets are made of fine wool, challis, needlecord, piqué, Viyella, crêpe de chine and flannelette. Whites and pastel colours are usual; magyar sleeves are easy to make. Line silk and wool with Jap silk or crêpe de chine; line cottons with batiste.

LINED JACKET

Cut the jacket and lining by the same pattern. Stitch the underarm seams separately in each. Clip into the seam

allowance at the underarm curve. Press the seams open and stay them at the curve of the underarm seam. See page 162.

Apply decorative detail round the neckline, front opening, lower edge and sleeve – for example the featherstitch, French knot, lazy daisy stitch or one of the lacy zig-zag machine stitches. A tiny appliqué may be placed near one side of the neckline or a very small pocket may be added as a finishing touch.

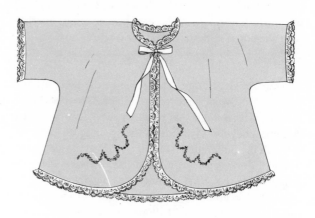

Turn the jacket to the wrong side. Place the lining inside, right sides together, matching seams and cut edges. Pin, then tack along the neckline, fronts and lower edge. Stitch in a continuous line; make one stitch diagonally across the corners and overlap a few stitches at the starting point. Leave the sleeve edges open for turning the jacket to the right side. Trim the lining seam allowance to ·3 cm ($\frac{1}{8}$ inch) and the jacket seam allowance to ·6 cm ($\frac{1}{4}$ inch). Cut diagonally across the corners, close to the stitching and clip into the seam allowance on the

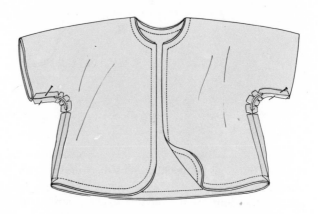

neckline curve. Notch the seam allowance of outside curves. Press.

Turn the jacket through the sleeve opening to the right side. Fold on the seamline and tack. Press. To finish the sleeve edges, turn the seam allowance of the jacket to the underside and pin. Press. Turn the edge of the lining to the underside and pin it to the jacket. Slip-stitch the folded edges together.

Narrow lace edging may be gathered and hand-stitched to the outer edges.

Cut two 23-cm (9-inch) lengths of narrow ribbon for the ties. Fold one end to the right side ·3 cm ($\frac{1}{8}$ inch) and pin to the underside of the neckline opening, overlapping the edges ·3 cm ($\frac{1}{8}$ inch). Hand-sew in place.

Zig-zag finished edge. The jacket in the illustration is made of fine wool lined with Jap silk. The neckline is finished with a single bias fold that extends about 20 cm (8 inches) beyond each side of the opening for ties.

Stitch the underarm seams separately in the jacket and lining, following the instructions given above. Place the lining inside the jacket, wrong sides together, matching seams and keeping the cut edges even. Tack near all edges. Select the small scalloped zig-zag stitch on the machine and set the stitch length for satin stitching. See *Edge-stitched Finish*, page 274. From the right side, stitch down the front, round the lower edge and up the opposite front. Stitch round the sleeve edges. Press. Trim the fabric close to the stitching.

Finish the neckline with a single-fold bias binding with ends long enough to tie. Cut off the seam allowance if binding is not specified on the pattern. Pin the neckline edges of the jacket and lining together and stitch ·3 cm ($\frac{1}{8}$ inch) from the edge.

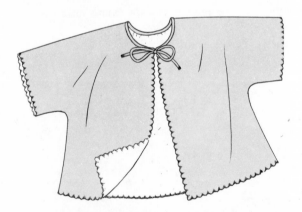

Refer to *Single-Fold Bias Binding*, page 146, for instructions on finishing the neckline. Cut the true bias strip 2 cm ($\frac{3}{4}$ inch) wide and 66 cm (26 inches) long. Begin by pinning the centre of the binding to the centre of the

back neckline. Then pin round the neckline to the centre fronts. When the neckline is finished, fold the tie ends under ·6 cm ($\frac{1}{4}$ inch) and press. Turn the long cut edges of the tie to the centre and finger-press. Bring the folded edges together and pin; then slip-stitch. Do not draw the threads taut.

UNLINED MATINÉE JACKETS
Unlined jackets are made of cotton crêpe, crêpe de chine and soft rayon, and are ideal for summer wear.

French-seam and underarm seams. Finish the neckline, fronts, lower edge and sleeve edges with a single-fold bias binding (see page 146) or with a ·3-cm ($\frac{1}{8}$-inch) rolled hem, hand-stitched in place. Gather narrow lace edging and sew it to the rolled hem, or use a blanket stitch in place of the lace. Appliqué a small design near the neckline, or use a fine featherstitch close to the hem. Use tiny buttons and thread loops for the closing.

Angel Top and Pants

Angel Tops and matching pants are made of cotton, Viyella, Clydella and broderie anglaise. The top is a short version of a traditional baby's dress, and with the addition of matching pants makes a suit ideal for boys or girls. The Angel Top can button down the back or front

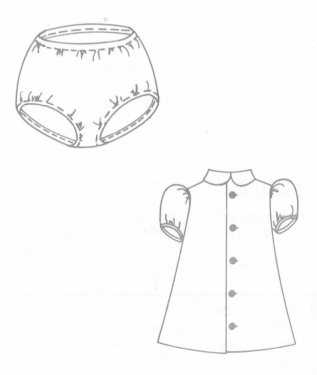

elastic. Stitch, leaving an opening through which to slot the elastic. Slot elastic through casings, join ends. Stitch openings to complete.

Dresses

Dresses are made of batiste, organdie and fine lawn. A fine French seam is used throughout the construction. If the dress has a set-in sleeve, sew in the sleeve before stitching the underarm seam whenever possible. It is much easier to work with a flat surface than with a dress that is joined at these seams, especially when it is so small. Also, complete the placket before stitching the underarm and inside seams. Use tiny buttons and hand-worked buttonholes in the back opening.

Babies' clothes can be finished in so many beautiful ways that it is impossible to list them all; a few of the prettiest finishes are illustrated here.

so the baby is easily dressed. The sleeves can be long or short according to the time of year, the neckline can have a tiny Peter Pan collar, a narrow binding or lace edging. A yoke can be embroidered, tucked or trimmed with lace. The matching pants are cut large enough to cover a nappy.

ANGEL TOP WITH YOKE
Gather front to fit yoke, tack and stitch yoke to front. Trim seam and overcast to neaten. Join shoulders using a fine French seam. On the back, press the facings to the inside.

PETER PAN COLLAR
To make a tiny two-piece Peter Pan collar, pin and tack each top collar to an undercollar, stitch, leaving neck edges open. Snip and trim turnings, turn to right side, tack and press seamed edges. Tack collar pieces to neckline matching markings and centre lines. Join collar to the garment with a 1·2-cm ($\frac{1}{2}$-inch) bias strip, following the instructions on page 148. Join side seams using fine French seams. Make up and insert sleeves (see pages 303 and 304). Turn up and neaten hem. Make buttonholes and sew on buttons.

PANTS
Join side seams using fine French seams. Fold the hem allowance on waist and leg edges to the inside, turn under new edges to form a casing the same width as the

TUCKED YOKE DRESS
Tiny pin tucks spaced ·5 cm ($\frac{3}{16}$ inch) apart in groups of four, six or eight, add a delicate beauty to the dress. Tucks may be hand- or machine-stitched. Fold, press and stitch tucks in the front and back sections. See *Tucks*, page 235. At the lower end of the tucks, pull the threads to the underside and tie them together in a single knot.

301

Placket. Make a hemmed placket in the back of the dress. Slash down the centre back to the end of the opening. At the end, snip diagonally into each side ·3 cm ($\frac{1}{8}$ inch). On one side, turn the hem on the marking and press. Then turn the cut edge under ·3 cm ($\frac{1}{8}$ inch) and pin it to the dress. Slip-stitch in place. Finish the opposite

Seaming and pleating. Join dress front and back at the shoulder line and underarm, using a fine French seam.

Some patterns show an inverted pleat at the underarm. Fold the pleat and press. Stitch in place at the armhole, just within the seam allowance.

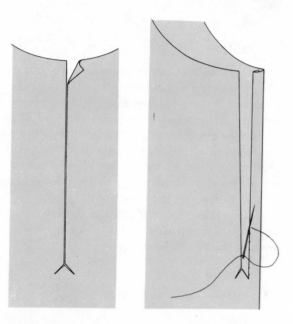

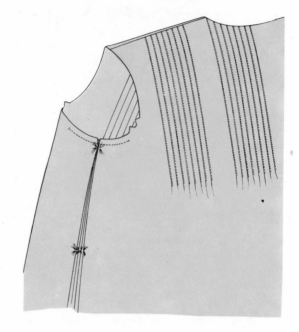

side in the same way. Lap the right hem over the left, and hand-stitch the lower ends together. This forms a soft pleat in the dress below the opening.

Neckline finish. Draw up the thread at the top edge of narrow lace edging and gather it to fit the neckline. Distribute the fullness evenly. Finish one end of the lace with a narrow hem. Tack the gathered lace, right side up, to the wrong side of the neckline. Neaten the opposite end of the lace. Trim the neckline seam allowance to ·6 cm ($\frac{1}{4}$ inch). Roll the fabric edge over the seamline, and make small whipping stitches through the lace and rolled hem. Remove tacking. Turn the lace up over the edge, and press.

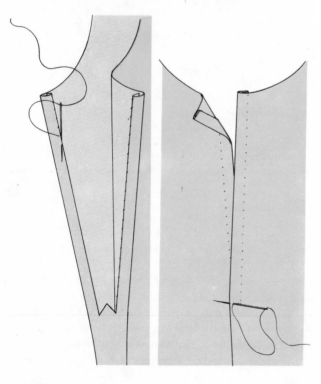

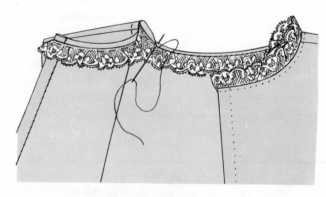

302

Sleeves. Finish the lower edge of the sleeves with narrow lace edging and a rolled hem the same as the neckline. Gather the lower edge of the sleeve, leaving a ·9-cm ($\frac{3}{8}$-

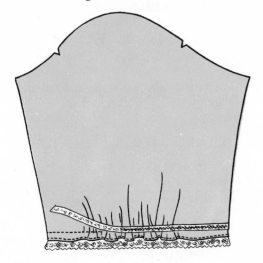

inch) heading. Pin narrow lace insertion over the gathers and hand-sew each edge of the insertion, using a hemming stitch. Use a French seam to stitch the underarm seams.

Stitch the sleeve in the armhole. See *Set-In Sleeve*, page 158. Trim the seam allowance on the sleeve side to ·3 cm ($\frac{1}{8}$ inch), and on the armhole side to ·6 cm ($\frac{1}{4}$ inch). Turn the edge of the armhole seam allowance under ·3 cm ($\frac{1}{8}$ inch); fold this seam allowance over the sleeve seam allowance to the stitching line, enclosing the cut edge. Pin. Slip-stitch in place.

Hem. A plain hem is generally used. Make it about 7·5 cm (3 inches) deep. Turn the hem to the underside and tack ·6 cm ($\frac{1}{4}$ inch) from the fold. Press. Turn the free edge under ·3 cm ($\frac{1}{8}$ inch) and tack to the dress. Slip-stitch in place. On the top side, finish the hem with fine featherstitches or French knots.

Work buttonholes in the placket and sew on buttons.

of the yoke. Press. Finish one end of the insertion with a hem the same width as the yoke opening. On the right side of the yoke, tack the insertion, right side up, with the edge on the seamline. Neaten the opposite end of the insertion. Trim the seam allowance under the lace to ·6 cm ($\frac{1}{4}$ inch). Roll the fabric edge and make small hand stitches through the rolled edge and lace.

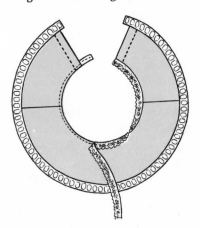

ROUND YOKE DRESS

This dainty, simple design for a dress with a yoke is traditional for babies.

Yoke. Join the yoke sections at the shoulder line, using a fine French seam. Fold and hand-stitch the hems in the back opening. See *Placket*, page 302. Finish the neckline with gathered lace applied to a ·3-cm ($\frac{1}{8}$-inch) rolled hem, as instructed on page 260.

Draw up the thread at the top edge of lace insertion and shape it to fit round the seamline of the outer edge

Joining yoke and dress. Join the shoulder seams of the dress, using a fine French seam; hem the placket, following the instructions for the tucked yoke dress. Gather the dress to fit the yoke. Pin, then tack the lace insertion on the yoke over the seam allowance of the dress. Trim the seam allowance under the lace to ·6 cm ($\frac{1}{4}$ inch). Roll the fabric edge and make small hand stitches through the lace and rolled edge. In the gathered section of the

303

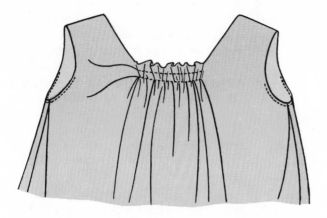

dress, sew the insertion in place from the top side, using small hand stitches over the lace edge; then overcast the fabric edges on the underside.

Sleeves. Stitch the sleeve seam, using a fine French seam. Sew gathered lace to the lower edge. See *Puff Sleeve*, page 161. After you have stitched the sleeve in the armhole, finish the seam as instructed for the sleeve, see page 303.

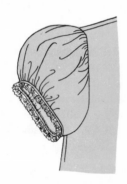

Hem. The scalloped hem is a dainty finishing touch. Transfer the scallop pattern with the points to the lower edge of the dress. (Remember, the scallops will be reversed when the hem is turned.) Cut on the scalloped line. Turn the hem to the underside and tack ·6 cm (¼ inch) from the fold. Press. On the free edge, clip ·3 cm (⅛ inch) into the curve of the scallops at even intervals. Turn the edge under ·3 cm (⅛ inch) retaining the shape of the scallops, and tack. Tack the scalloped edge to the

dress. On the right side, finish the hem with a feather-stitch or work French knots round the scallops. Gathered lace edging, hand-sewn on the right side of the scalloped edge, is also a lovely finish.

CHRISTENING ROBE

Christening robes may vary in length from 54 to 76 cm (21 to 30 inches) or longer. For this special occasion, the robe should be elaborate, yet dainty and delicate enough for an infant.

Additional Dress Finishes

Make a tiny collar of a single thickness of fabric. Either roll the collar edge and hand-sew gathered lace round it as instructed on page 260, or use a small decorative zig-

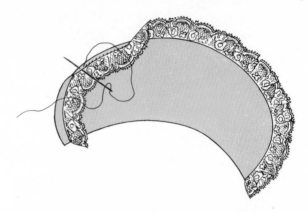

zag scallop on the edge. See *Edge-stitched Finish*, page 274. Join the collar to the garment with a 1·2-cm (½-inch) bias facing, following the instructions on page 148. Or use narrow lace insertion instead of a bias strip – especially if you are hand-sewing the collar. Steam-press the lace and shape it to fit the curve of the neckline; pin it in place and finish by hand.

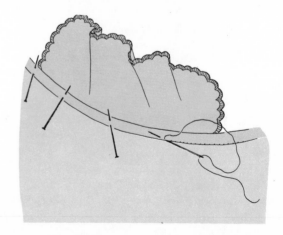

Instead of a hem, finish the lower edge of the baby's dress with edge-stitching as you did the collar above.

Cradle Cover and Skirt

The cradle skirt illustrated has seven rows of shirring at the top and is finished with a fine piping on the edge. Two 15-cm (6-inch) frills are sewn to the lower edge of the skirt. The skirt is held in place with press-fastener tape and can easily be removed for cleaning and storing.

A cradle skirt may be made in any number of ways. The construction of the one illustrated is basic to all skirts.

There should be an *overskirt* and an *underskirt*. The overskirt may be of a sheer fabric, such as nylon net, organdie, broderie anglaise, muslin or spotted voile. Taffeta, poplin, cotton satin or chintz are suitable opaque fabrics for the underskirt. The overskirt may be white and the underskirt a pastel pink or blue, or both skirts may be white.

The inside of the cradle should be lined with the same fabric used for the underskirt. The lining is quilted with a small diagonal design.

The cradle in the illustration is 229 cm (90 inches) in circumference and with the stand measures 68·5 cm (27 inches) from the top edge to the floor. The cradle itself is 30·5 cm (12 inches) deep.

FABRIC REQUIREMENTS

The skirts should be gathered. Use triple fullness in the sheer overskirt and double fullness in the opaque underskirt. Fabric width may vary from 90 to 115 cm (36 to 44 inches), and net may be 180 cm (72 inches) wide. In working out length required, consider the width of the fabric. In the cradle shown, 101·5-cm (40-inch) fabric was used; 5 cm (2 inches) were allowed for selvedge and a French seam on each side, leaving a width of 96·5 cm (38 inches).

Fabric requirements are determined as follows:
Overskirt. For the *width*, measure the circumference of the cradle and multiply this figure by the amount of fullness required. *Example*: 229 cm (90 inches) (circumference) × 3 (fullness) = 687 cm (270 inches) after seaming. (Multiply the circumference by two when twice the fullness is required.)

For the number of *lengths of fabric*, divide the circumference plus fullness by the width of the fabric after seaming. *Example*: 687 cm (270 inches) (circumference plus fullness) ÷ 96·5 cm (38 inches) (width of fabric) = just over 7 lengths of fabric. (If the division results in a fraction of a length, buy another complete length.)

For the *skirt length*, measure from the top edge of the cradle to the floor. (When the skirt is hemmed at the bottom and seamed at the top, it will be 2·5 cm (1 inch) from the floor.) *Example*: 68·5 cm (27 inches) (length of skirt) × 7 (number of lengths) = 480 cm (189 inches) or 4·8 m (5¼ yards). Allow an additional 70 cm approx.

(¾ yard) for covering the cord and straightening the ends of the fabric; purchase 5·5 m (6 yards).

If the fabric has a design, remember to allow extra for matching. See page 367.

The two 15-cm (6-inch) frills are twice as full as the overskirt. *Example*: 687 cm (270 inches) (fullness of skirt) × 2 (frill fullness) × 2 (number of frills) = 2748 cm (1080 inches), or 27·5 m (30 yards) of frill. Six 15-cm (6-inch) widths, each 96·5 cm (38 inches) long, can be cut from 1 m (1 yard) of fabric; therefore, buy an additional 4·6 m (5 yards) of fabric for the frills.

Underskirt and cradle lining. The fullness of the underskirt is twice the circumference of the cradle. Multiply the circumference by two instead of three, then work out the fabric requirements the same as you did for the overskirt. Five 68·5-cm (27-inch) lengths of 101·5-cm (40-inch) fabric, or 3·75 m (4 yards) are required for the skirt in the example.

Line the inside of the cradle with the same fabric as the underskirt. 1·5 m (1½ yards) will be needed. Buy an equal amount of domette or terylene wadding to back the fabric for quilting.

THE LINING

For the cradle in the illustration, the lining must be 38 cm (15 inches) deep and 236·5 cm (93 inches) in circumference (including seams).

Straighten the ends of the fabric as described on page 14. Then cut strips of fabric on the lengthwise grain 38 cm (15 inches) long; cut as many strips as you will need for the 236·5 cm (93 inches) (about two-and-a-half strips of 101·5-cm (40-inch) fabric). Join the strips with a 1·2-cm (½-inch) seam allowance; do not join the last ends together for the circle yet.

Cut the backing of domette or terylene wadding the same size as the lining, and quilt the two pieces together.

See *Diagonal Quilting*, page 256. When the quilting is finished, join the open ends with a 1·2-cm (½-inch) seam allowance.

Place the quilted lining inside the basket, wrong side out, with a seam at one corner, and extend the edge over the top rim of the cradle about 5 cm (2 inches). Shape the lining to fit smoothly by pinning a dart at each of the corners. Stitch the darts; then trim the dart width to within 1·2 cm (½ inch) of the stitching. Press the darts open. Sew 1·2-cm (½-inch) twill tape to the lower edge of the lining. Separate the press-fastener tape and stitch one half to the right side of the upper edge.

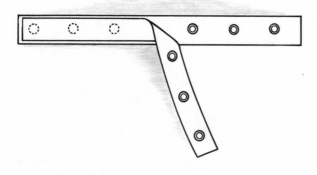

Place the lining smoothly inside the basket, right side out, and tack the twill tape to the bottom of the basket. Turn the upper edge over the top rim of the basket.

THE OVERSKIRT

Straighten the fabric. See page 14. Cut the required number of fabric lengths for the overskirt. Measure accurately and draw a thread from the fabric to indicate the cutting line and to ensure cutting on the true grain (see page 14).

Remove selvedges and join the fabric on the lengthwise grain with a fine French seam. Press. Finish the lower edge with a narrow hem, using the Hemmer Foot. Press. If net is used, you need not hem it.

Cut 15-cm (6-inch) strips on the crosswise grain of the fabric for the frills. Draw a thread from the fabric for the cutting line. Join the strips; then hem each edge, using the Hemmer Foot. (Net need not be hemmed.) Gather the frills with a 1·2-cm (½-inch) heading. Pin them to the skirt, keeping the lower edge of the first frill even with the lower edge of the skirt, and the lower edge of the second frill barely above the heading of the first frill. Stitch on the gathering stitches of the frills.

Gather the top edge of the skirt. Use heavy-duty mercerised cotton or nylon thread on the bobbin so it will not break while you are easing the fullness across the width of the skirt. Follow the instructions for

Gathering to Control Fullness on page 105. (Omit the pin tuck across the threads in this case.)

First divide the skirt into two sections and pin-mark. Then gather each section separately. After you have placed the first two rows of stitching in the seam allowance, place seven additional rows below the first, spacing them ·6 cm (¼ inch) apart. Use the Presser Foot as a guide. To gather each skirt section, pull the bobbin thread at each end of the section and ease the fullness towards the centre. Distribute the fullness evenly. Try the skirt on the cradle to be sure it fits correctly. Pull the threads to the underside and join the lines of stitching from the two sections by tying the four threads together in a single knot close to the stitching.

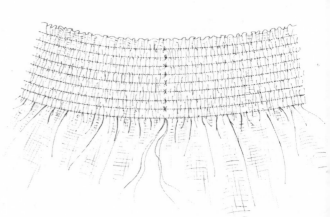

THE UNDERSKIRT

Cut the required number of fabric lengths for the underskirt. Make them the same length as the overskirt and on the same grain. Remove the selvedges, and join the fabric on the lengthwise grain, with a narrow French seam. Finish the lower edge with a narrow hem, using the Hemmer Foot.

Gather the underskirt in the same way as the overskirt. However, place only three rows of stitches below the first row; space them 1·2 cm (½ inch) apart.

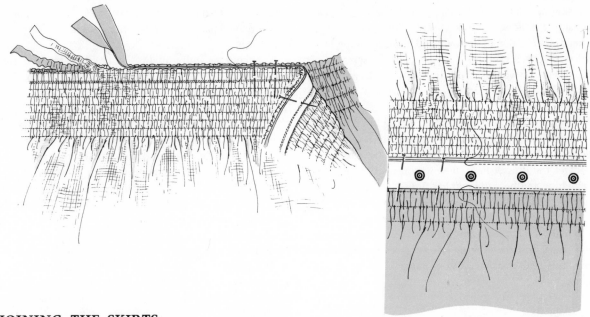

JOINING THE SKIRTS

For the piping cord around the top edge, cut a true bias of the sheer overskirt fabric and one of the opaque underskirt fabric. Cut enough lengths for the circumference of the gathered skirt plus seam allowances. Cover the cord, following the directions for sheer fabric on page 245.

Follow the instructions for cording a straight seam on page 245. Pin and stitch the piping to the right side of the overskirt. Join the ends of the piping as described on page 397. Then join the two skirt sections with the right side of the overskirt next to the wrong side of the underskirt.

Trim the piping seam allowance to ·3 cm ($\frac{1}{8}$ inch), and trim the seam allowance on both skirts to ·6 cm ($\frac{1}{4}$ inch). Press. Turn the overskirt to the right side over the underskirt. The right sides of both skirts should face in the same direction. Fold on the seamline, and press.

Turn the underskirt and seam allowance away from the overskirt and pin the remaining side of the press-fastener tape to the underskirt, barely below the piping. Stitch on each side of the tape. Turn the underskirt back in place. Place the skirt round the cradle, and fasten the press-fastener tape to hold the skirt in position.

Children Can Sew Too

While you are busy making dresses for your child or sewing for the nursery, there may be a pair of young eyes watching you work and a pair of young hands wanting to stitch a seam too. This is the moment to lay your own sewing aside and to teach your child some simple sewing skills.

As an activity for children, sewing has much to recommend it. It brings out and stimulates children's innate creative talent, builds self-confidence and gives them a sense of accomplishment. Also not to be overlooked is the value of sewing in developing dexterity and co-ordination.

Sewing is an activity in which both boys and girls can express themselves. But keep it simple at first, start small hands on hand sewing. Teach the child to make an X or sew on sequins and buttons, using a larger needle and thread and following no particular pattern. A little later show the child how to thread a needle, to knot the end of the thread and to tack two pieces of fabric together.

As you go along, teach the child that safety and care

of her sewing equipment are two good friends. Needles, for example, belong in a pin cushion when not in use. Get her a pin cushion of her own and a small sewing box fitted with other supplies – a pair of small scissors, a small thimble, two or three needles with large eyes, several spools of coloured thread, one lead pencil and one white pencil, and a ruler.

When your young beginner is old enough to sit at the sewing machine, teach her first how to stitch straight on ruled paper with the needle unthreaded, how to raise and lower the Presser Foot, how to control the speed of the machine and how to keep her fingers a safe distance from the needle. When you are satisfied that the child can control the machine safely, teach her to thread it and to make a plain seam and hem. A dressmaker visualises an idea, and the moving needle gives it shape and form. Thus real creativity can develop in each sewing project.

Sewing Projects for Children

When children do begin to sew, they should start with simple projects – things they can make quickly and without much trouble. Nothing is more discouraging to a child than to undertake a project with excitement and anticipation and then find the details beyond her skill. But if the child is taught the details gradually and systematically, she will soon master them and enjoy the thrill of seeing real results.

Doll's clothes are the first thought of many little girls. Save scraps of fabric for doll's dresses, and sequins, old buttons, short lengths of lace, braid and ric-rac, for trimmings. As your child progresses, she may want to try a real pattern for her doll's outfit. Pattern companies have created patterns for an entire wardrobe for dolls of all sizes.

To encourage individuality, let children be their own designers if they choose, cutting patterns when they need them. They may design items for gifts as well as for their own use.

Felt, flannel and towelling are three fabrics that are easy for children to handle and that lend themselves to many gift articles. Some of the possibilities are listed below. They can all be made without patterns but do require accurate measuring and the drawing of straight lines or circles:

Apron	Kettle holder
Baby bib	Needle case
Bath mitt	Pencil case
Beanbag	Pin cushion
Beach bag	Place mat
Book cover	Puppet
Bookmark	Scarf
Collar	Shoe bag
Cushion cover	Tea cosy
Dog's coat	Tray cloth

When children get into their teens they become more ambitious and adventurous in their sewing projects. They are able to sew neatly, and many are capable of making a simple dress, skirt or blouse for themselves. They should be taught how to use a thimble and how to press. This may be the time when a young girl will wish to increase her sewing skills by studying sewing at school or taking a sewing course at the Singer Centre during her summer holiday.

Tips on Mending

The mending basket is seldom empty. Just when you think you've reached the bottom it is filled again with socks, shirts, children's clothes and household linens.

Although mending is an unending task, it need not be an onerous one.

Mending is the term used to cover all types of fabric repairs – re-stitching split seams; darning socks; patching children's clothes; mending sheets and tablecloths; replacing elastic in the waistline of lingerie, pyjamas and boxer shorts; repairing girdles; and replacing blanket binding. All the small jobs that prolong the life of worn but still usable articles can easily be taken care of by hand or by machine. Whenever possible, *mend by machine*. It is quicker, easier and more durable than hand mending.

For machine mending, you may use the zig-zag machine with the Presser Foot or free-motion stitching. In free-motion stitching, the Presser Foot is removed, the feed is made inoperable and the fabric to be mended is placed in an embroidery hoop under the needle and moved manually in any direction you desire. Free-motion mending is the method to use on a straight stitch machine.

Needle and Thread

Use a fine needle for both machine mending and hand mending. The thread should match the fabric in colour and texture. You can use the warp threads of the fabric to darn small holes by hand, especially in woollens. When darning socks, separate the strands of darning thread and use only one or two in a fine darning needle.

Machine Darning with Embroidery Hoop

Free-motion darning is easier to do when the machine is designed with a throat plate that can be raised above the feed or with a feed that can be lowered below the throat plate.

Remove the Presser Foot and raise the throat plate or lower the feed. Set the stitch length lever on a close stitch.

DARNING A HOLE

Trim away any ragged edges from the area to be darned. Place the worn section, right side up, in embroidery hoop to hold it taut.

With the work under the needle lower the presser bar to activate the tension. Hold the needle thread loosely with the left hand, turn the hand wheel towards you and draw the bobbin thread up through the fabric. Hold both thread ends and lower the needle into the fabric.

For reinforcement, outline the area to be darned with a line of stitching ·6 cm ($\frac{1}{4}$ inch) from the open edge. Stitch across the opening, moving the hoop backwards and forwards under the needle at a slight angle. Overlap the outline stitching at each end of the area; keep the lines of stitching closely spaced and even in length.

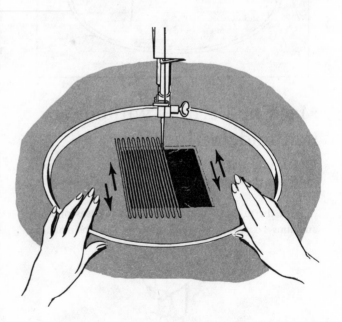

Run the machine at a moderate speed and control the hoop with a steady, continuous movement.

When the opening is filled, turn the work and cover the area with crosswise lines of stitching. Pull threads to the underside; tie and cut. Press.

DARNING TEARS

A straight tear may follow either the lengthwise or cross-wise grain of the fabric. A three-cornered tear follows both grains.

Press the area round the tear. Cut an underlay, of the same fabric if possible, for reinforcement. Bring the edges of the tear together and pin the underlay to the wrong side. Tack.

Place the worn section, right side up, in embroidery hoop. With the work under the needle pull up the bobbin thread as instructed above. Move the hoop backwards and forwards under the needle, making about six stitches across the tear until the work is finished. In a three-cornered tear, cross the stitches at the corner for extra strength. Pull the threads through to the underside; tie and clip. Trim away the underlay close to the stitching. Press.

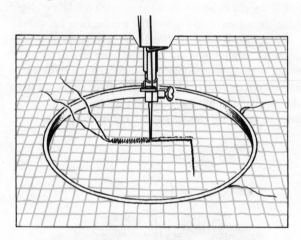

Machine Darning without an Embroidery Hoop

With a little practice, you can darn worn or torn spots easily and quickly without the aid of an embroidery hoop.

Turn the pressure dial to D, which releases pressure and allows darning with the Presser Foot on the machine.

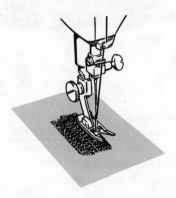

See page 25. Set the selectors on the machine for straight stitching and 2·5 to 1·5 mm (10 to 15) stitch length.

If the worn area is open, tack an underlay in place on the underside.

Place the area to be darned under the Presser Foot. Lower the Presser Foot and start stitching, alternately drawing the fabric gently away from you and pulling it gently towards you. Continue this forwards and backwards motion until the area is filled with parallel lines of stitching. For additional strength, turn the work and cover the area with crosswise lines of stitching.

Darning by Hand

Use a darning mushroom to darn socks and small embroidery hoop for flat work. Use a fine needle and do not knot the end of the thread.

Darn the sock over the mushroom, or place the flat work in the hoop. Make small running stitches, beginning about ·6 cm (¼ inch) beyond the edge of the hole; work across to the opposite side, extending the stitches ·6 cm (¼ inch) beyond the hole. Work back and forth, keeping the lines of stitching and the threads across the hole parallel and evenly spaced until the hole is covered. Then turn and work across the threads, weaving alternately over and under in parallel lines until the repair is completed. Be careful not to draw the threads taut; this will cause the work to pucker. Fasten the threads on the underside. Press.

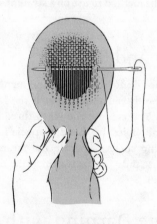

Zig-Zag Mending without an Embroidery Hoop

Zig-zag stitches are just as useful for mending as they are for creative sewing. The multi-stitch zig-zag and plain zig-zag stitch provide a firm, flexible bond for repairing tears, replacing elastic and blanket binding and mending lingerie. Select the stitch length and stitch width suitable for the work. Use the Presser Foot on the machine.

REPAIRING TEARS

Trim away the ragged edges. Cut an underlay, of the same fabric if possible, for reinforcement. Bring the edges of the tear together and pin the underlay to the wrong side. Tack.

Place the work under the Presser Foot with the needle directly over one end of the tear. Use the multi-stitch zig-zag, and stitch along the line of the tear. Shorten the stitch length at the ends and cross the stitches at the corners for added strength.

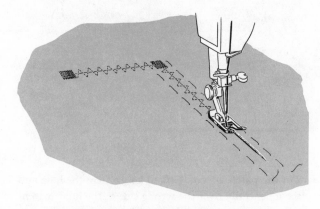

Pull threads to the underside; tie and clip. Trim away the underlay close to the stitching. Press.

APPLYING ELASTIC

Elastic is easily applied to the waistline of lingerie, pyjamas and boxer shorts with zig-zag stitching. The elasticity of the stitch prevents the stitches from breaking when the elastic is stretched.

Lingerie. Cut the elastic to fit the waist comfortably, allow 2·5 cm (1 inch) for joining the ends. Lap the ends 2·5 cm (1 inch) then fold one end under ·6 cm (¼ inch) and join the two, using two rows of narrow zig-zag stitching.

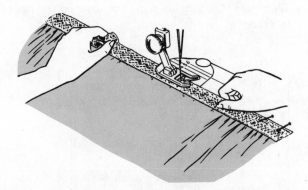

Remove the worn elastic, and press the garment. Divide the elastic circle and the garment waistline into quarters. From the right side, pin the two together at these intervals, lapping the elastic over the seam allowance of the garment. Join the layers with two rows of the multi-stitch zig-zag or a narrow, plain zig-zag stitch; stretch the elastic between the pins as you stitch so that it will remain stretchable when the stitching is completed. Pull threads to the underside; tie and cut.

Boxer shorts. Remove the worn elastic and press the garment. To apply the new elastic, follow the instructions for *Elastic Band on Boxer Shorts*, page 295.

Girdle repairs. Either the multi-stitch zig-zag or the plain zig-zag is suitable for mending girdles. Both produce an elastic stitch that will not break when the girdle is stretched. If the repair requires elasticity in two directions – that is lengthwise and crosswise – the multi-stitch zig-zag should be used.

Regulate the stitch length and stitch width to suit the garment. If you are sewing through several layers of elastic and fabric – for example, repairing the seams, suspenders or waistband on foundation garments – use a needle slightly larger in size than you would usually choose.

REPLACING BLANKET BINDING

Remove the worn binding and press the edges of the blanket. Fold under the cut ends of the new binding 1·2 cm (½ inch), and pin and tack it securely in place. Stitch, using the multi-stitch zig-zag. Adjust the pressure, if necessary, to allow for the thickness of the blanket. Remove tacking.

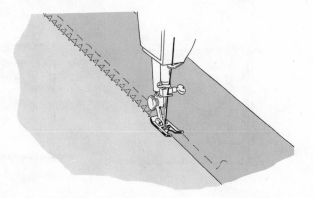

Patching

If a hole is large, a patch is better than a darn. The fabric for the patch should be the same as the garment; if no scraps are available, cut the patch from the facing or pocket, or from the under collar or cuff. If the fabric is a print, plaid or stripe, match the design of the pattern.

PATCHING WITH EMBROIDERY HOOP

Press the area round the hole. Cut the hole into a square or rectangle, following the thread of the fabric.

Cut the patch 2·5 cm (1 inch) larger than the hole and place it over the wrong side of the hole, matching the fabric grain and design. Tack.

Put the patch, right side up, in the embroidery hoop.

Prepare the machine and work as instructed in *Machine Darning with Embroidery Hoop*, page 309.

Work round the patch; move the hoop back and forth under the needle at a slight angle, making about six or eight small stitches across the cut edge. Turn the work at the corners, crossing the stitches for added reinforcement. Press. Trim the edges on the underside close to the stitching.

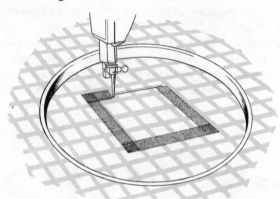

TAILORED PATCH

Press the area round the hole. Cut the hole into a square or rectangle, following the thread of the fabric. Cut diagonally into the corners about ·6 cm (¼ inch). Fold the cut edges under ·6 cm (¼ inch) and tack. Press.

Cut the patch 2·5 cm (1 inch) larger than the hole and place it centrally over the wrong side of the hole, matching the fabric grain and design. Pin.

From the right side, slip-tack the folded edge to the patch. See *Slip Tacking*, page 62.

Remove the pins and the first line of tacking which was used to retain the fold.

On the wrong side, turn both the seam allowances away from the garment and stitch through the centre of the short tacking stitch in the fold. Stitch round the patch, pivoting the fabric on the needle at the corners; overlap a few stitches at the starting point. Pull threads to the underside; tie and cut. Press.

Stitch diagonally across the corners for reinforcement. Remove slip tacking and press.

Herringbone the wide seam allowance to the garment as illustrated. The stitches must not show on the right side. Press.

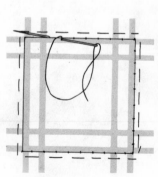
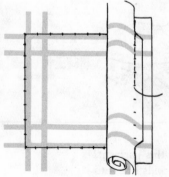
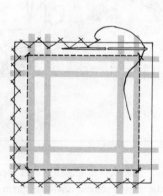

TOP-STITCHED PATCH

Top stitching is often used to hold a patch in place.

Cut the fabric for the patch and tack it in place, following the instructions for the *Tailored Patch*; use even tacking instead of slip tacking.

On the right side, stitch the patch in place near the folded edge. On the wrong side, fold under the cut edges of the patch and tack in place. Stitch again near the folded edge of the patch. Pull threads to the underside; tie and cut. Press.

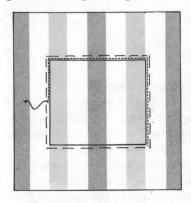 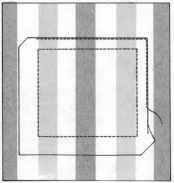 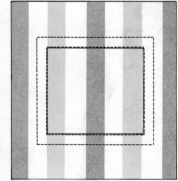

Reinforcing Worn Areas

You can add months of wear to a garment by reinforcing areas that are worn thin. Such areas occur most often at the elbow and underarm of a dress and at the knee and seat of boy's trousers. Use a piece of the same fabric or a lightweight fabric such as chiffon, nylon net or batiste. To reinforce the elbow and knee, select a fabric with some 'give'.

TO REINFORCE THE ELBOW
OR UNDERARM

Cut the reinforcement 2·5 cm (1 inch) larger than the worn spot. Place it over the wrong side of the worn section, and tack.

Use matching thread and a fine needle. Make small stitches by hand through the two layers of fabric, catching only a single thread of the fabric on the right side. Keep the rows of stitching parallel to the grain of the fabric and extend them slightly beyond the worn area. If extra body is needed, make several rows of stitches in the opposite direction. Fasten the threads on the underside; tie and cut. Press.

If the worn area is in the underarm of the garment, shape the upper edge of the reinforcement to fit the armhole and stitch it to the seam allowance.

TO REINFORCE BOYS' TROUSERS

Boys' trousers last longer if the knees and seat are reinforced with zig-zag stitching when they are worn thin. The thread must match the fabric colour exactly.

Cut the reinforcement 2·5 cm (1 inch) larger than the worn area. Place it over the wrong side of the worn section, and tack.

Select the multi-stitch zig-zag, medium stitch width, and short stitch length. Begin and end the work with backstitching. Stitch on the right side. To do this, turn the trousers to the wrong side and work on the inside. If the reinforcement is to be placed at the knee, roll up the leg to do the stitching. Place several rows of stitching parallel to the grain of the fabric, extending them slightly beyond the worn area but not beyond the reinforcement. At the end of each row of stitching, stop with the needle in the fabric, raise the Presser Foot, and turn the fabric, pivoting on the needle. Lower the Presser Foot and continue stitching.

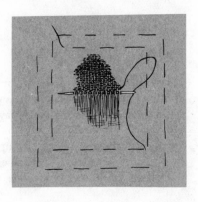 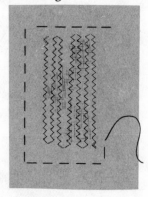

Tailoring

Tailoring is an advanced stage of dressmaking. To it you should bring a thorough knowledge of sewing techniques, good workmanship and plenty of experience. You must be able to sew with care, know how to handle fabric, respect tailor's tacks and tacking and take great care in fitting, seam layering, pressing and hand finishing. In addition, tailoring requires that you are experienced in the use of mounting and interfacing, which are important in the moulding and shaping of the garment. When you use fine fabrics, follow the correct techniques, and observe the rules of good workmanship, professional results will not be hard to achieve.

This chapter explains and illustrates the details of suit and coat construction. The principles given here are basic to tailoring and apply equally to other types of tailored wear.

Preliminaries

Pattern

Select the pattern with care. Choose one that is suitable for the fabric and classic enough to be fashionable for several years. Think of the pattern in relation to yourself and your needs and, above all, your figure proportions. Buy the same size suit and coat patterns as dress patterns as the necessary ease is included in the pattern.

Fabric

Firmly woven wool, tweed, flannel, wool broadcloth, knitted jersey fabric, raw silk, heavy cotton, linen, heavy silk, velveteen, corduroy, faille, rayon, blends of natural and synthetic fibres and many other fabrics can be used for suits. Coats are made of coating, flannel, camel hair, tweed, wool broadcloth and faille, to name a few. Although the fabric may be any one of a variety of weaves and weights, it must be heavy enough to prevent the interfacing, and the stitching securing it, from showing through, and sturdy enough to withstand several years of wear and many trips to the cleaners. See *Fabric*, page 7 for additional information.

As for colour, select one that is becoming to you. Avoid checks if you have not worked with them before. Unless checks are matched at the seams, they spoil the look of the outfit.

Lining and Interlining

To avoid bulk in suits, choose a lightweight fabric for the lining – for example, silk crêpe, rayon crêpe or Jap silk – which matches the jacket fabric in colour. Or, as a fashion note, choose a print or contrasting colour for the lining and make a matching blouse.

Line coats with heavy silk or rayon crêpe, satin, taffeta or Milium. For warmth and added body, coats are generally interlined with wool or cotton domette interlining. If Milium is used for the lining, interlining is not necessary. Milium lining fabric has an aluminium insulating treatment which increases warmth without increasing weight.

Interfacing and Mounting

Interfacing fabrics are available in many weights and textures. The weight of the garment fabric, the effect desired, and personal preference determine the choice. See *Interfacings*, page 16. For most coats and suits, hair canvas is appropriate. Lightweight suits may also be interfaced with linen canvas or a suitable Vilene.

Mount jackets and coats designed to stand away from the figure. Hair canvas and Vilene are two excellent fabrics that give the added body required for this effect. Loosely woven fabrics may be mounted on Jap silk, batiste or voile to support the fabric and give added weight. Shrink batiste and voile before using them. See *Mounting and Lining*, page 20, for additional information.

Shrinking

Most good quality fabrics are pre-shrunk and ready for cutting. This information is sometimes printed on the selvedge or label. If there is any doubt, shrink the fabric as instructed on page 15. Shrink interfacing fabrics except those that are non-woven.

Pattern Adjustments

Select the pattern pieces for the version you have chosen. Measure and adjust the pattern to fit correctly. See *Fitting the Pattern to Your Figure*, page 37, and *Adjusting the Pattern*, page 39.

Pressing

Press out any creases in the fabric before starting the construction work. See *Pressing as You Sew*, pages 66 and 67, for instructions on how to press the fabric you are using and how to press each construction detail. Before attaching the lining, press the jacket carefully on the wrong side; use the correct pressing cloth and moisture which the fabric requires. Do not press dry. Place the jacket on a hanger; lap and pin fronts and allow the jacket to dry completely before inserting the lining.

Calico Toile

If you are just starting tailoring, or are an experienced dressmaker it is a good idea to construct the suit jacket in calico before cutting into the suit fabric. The calico toile will ensure a perfect fit.

Use a good quality unbleached calico. After making the necessary pattern adjustments, cut out the jacket. Transfer all notches and markings and mark the centre lines on the front and back sections. (Use a tracing wheel and dressmaker's tracing paper to speed up the marking; on the jacket fabric, however, use tailor's tacks and tackings). Mark the balance lines on the calico. See page 77.

Stitch and press the darts, and seams within the jacket, and shoulder and side seams. Apply the facings and undercollar. Layer all seams properly and press them open. Seam the sleeves and tack them into the armholes. Fold, tack and press the hems at the lower edge of the jacket and sleeves.

A chain stitch is ideal for stitching the calico toile for a fitting because the stitching can be ripped out in seconds if adjustments are necessary. If your machine has Chain Stitch Accessories, refer to the instruction book accompanying the machine, and to page 63.

Try on the jacket. For the toile fitting, wear the blouse, lingerie and shoes you expect to wear with the finished jacket. Also wear a skirt made of a fabric similar in weight. If shoulder shapes or pads are used, slip them between the jacket and blouse. Lap the front opening, matching centre lines, and pin together at the buttonhole markings.

Check the position of the darts, buttonholes and pockets; the length of shoulder and waist; the fit across the bustline, shoulder line and hipline, allowing for the lining. Check that the waistline curve is in the correct position. The seams should hang straight from the underarm. Check the position of the balance lines. See page 77. Check the fit, the 'hang' and the length of the sleeves. The jacket length is important too; it may be necessary to lengthen or shorten the jacket, depending on your figure proportions. Pin-mark any adjustments.

Stitch the adjustments in the calico toile and try it on again to prove them. Make the same adjustments in the tissue pattern before cutting the fabric.

Layout and Cutting

Straighten the ends of the fabric as instructed on page 14.

Study the instruction sheet accompanying the pattern and select the layout suited for the fabric width you are using. Lay all the pattern pieces on the fabric in the same direction so that the sheen and colour will be uniform throughout the garment. Place the pieces on the correct grain, then pin them in place. Carefully cut out the garment, using dressmaker's shears.

Cut the notches and use tailor's tack to mark the position of the buttonholes, pockets, darts, pleats and any other seams or slashes, gussets and collars. Use different coloured threads to designate each type of marking. Tack the centre lines of the collar, skirt and jacket, both front and back. See *Transferring Notches and Markings*, page 56.

Cut the interfacing, lining and mounting, and transfer the notches, markings and centre lines the same as above.

The Skirt

Make the skirt first and wear it each time you try on the jacket. Stitch the darts and mount or line the skirt, using the method appropriate for the fabric and style. See *Mounting*, page 95.

Tack the seams, then try on the skirt to check the fit. If you are satisfied, stitch and press the seams. Neaten the seam edges according to the fabric. Use a hand finish for the final stitching of the zip. See *Skirt Placket Zip in Lapped Seam*, page 179.

Interface the skirt band: *Method 2* on page 156 is excellent. Sew on hooks and eyes to fasten.

Try on the skirt, and mark the length. Finish the hem as required by the fabric. See *Hems and Hem Finishes*, page 187.

Constructing the Jacket

Pin, tack and stitch the seams within the front and back sections, then press them open. It is not necessary to neaten the jacket seams since the lining will cover them.

Tack all darts. Tack the front and back sections together at the shoulder and underarm seams. Tack the sleeve seams. If the sleeve has a centre seam, stitch and press it open. Place a line of stitching round the sleeve head between the notches for ease. Tack the sleeves in the armhole. Stitch the centre seam of the undercollar. Pin the collar to the neckline in an overlapped seam, matching seamlines.

The Jacket Fitting

Try on the jacket with the finished skirt and the blouse and shoes that will be worn with the suit. If shoulder shapes or pads are used, slip them between the jacket and the blouse. Lap the fronts so that the centre lines match, and pin at the buttonhole markings.

Check the position of darts, buttonholes and pockets, length of shoulder and waist; the fit across the bustline,

shoulder line and hipline, allowing for the lining. Check the fit and 'hang' of the sleeve, and that the waistline curve is in the correct position. Check the position of the balance lines. Seams should hang straight from the underarm. Turn up the jacket and sleeve hems to find their correct length. Pin-mark any necessary adjustments, then pin-mark the roll line of the lapels and collar.

Remove the jacket and mark the adjustments with tackings. Try on the jacket again to prove the adjustments. If you are satisfied, continue with the other construction steps in the sequence given below.

Buttonholes

Bound buttonholes are best in tailor-made suits. Place an underlay over the wrong side of the right front section where the buttonholes will be made. Then follow the instructions given under *Bound and Corded Buttonholes*, on page 108.

Darts

Stitch all darts. Underarm, shoulder, elbow, diagonal and contour/waist darts are used in making jackets. When they are made on the right side of the jacket, they become a styling point and the 'continuous-thread' method should be used in the stitching. If the fabric is

heavy and the dart wide, slash through the centre of the dart and press it open. See *Darts*, page 100.

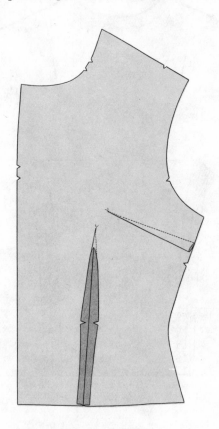

Back Underlining

Cut an underlining of pre-shrunk linen, batiste, cotton broadcloth or a similar fabric for the back section of the jacket. Use the jacket pattern as a guide. If the back has a centre seam, pin the pattern pieces together with the seamlines meeting in the centre. Cut the underlining in one piece about 25 cm (10 inches) deep at the centre and shaped to fit round the armholes. Slash through the centre of the shoulder darts. Lap one cut edge over the other with the seamline meeting in the centre; stitch, using the multi-stitch zig-zag. Back-stitch at each end. Press.

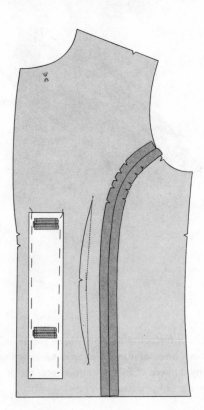

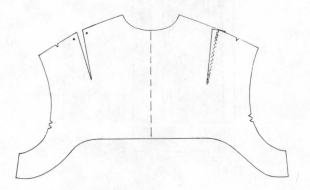

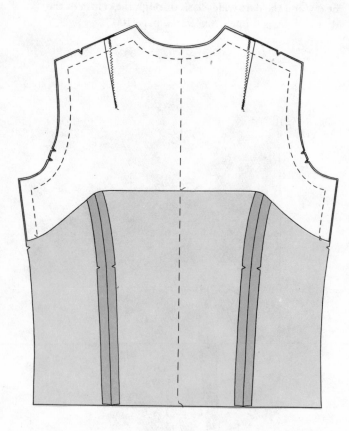

Place the underlining over the wrong side of the back section, matching centre lines and seam edges. Pin, then tack in place about 2·5 cm (1 inch) from the edges.

Front Interfacing

Use *Method 1*, page 136, to treat the seam edge of the interfacing. It ensures a thin seam since the organza instead of the interfacing is included in the seam. If the interfacing has darts, read the instructions under *Interfacing Darts*, page 104.

Pin the interfacing over the wrong side of each front jacket section, keeping the organza strip and garment edges even.

Determine the roll line of the lapels from the neckline to the top button. Place a ruler between these points, and mark the interfacing with chalk. Pin the interfacing in place along this line. Stay it to the lapels with padding stitches, catching only one thread of the fabric under the interfacing. Use thread that matches the fabric. Begin each line of stitches at the top of the lapel and end at the seamline, working from roll line to seamline. As you work, roll the lapel over the first finger, and hold it firmly with the thumb. This will shape the lapels as they will be worn.

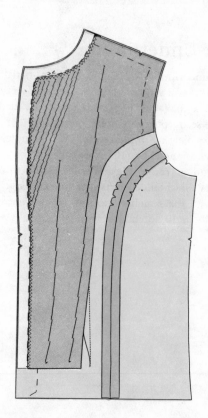

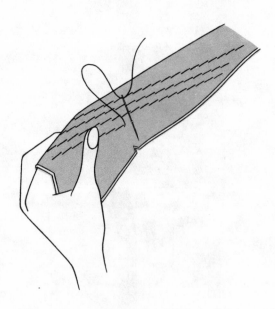

Tack the interfacing in place along the seamline; then make a few lines of long diagonal tackings within the interfacing to hold it in position as you work. Press the lapels over a tailor's ham or pressing mitt.

Shoulder Seams

Join the front and back sections at the shoulder line; make the seam through the garment fabric only. Cut off the corners of the dart in the seam allowance. Press, then press the seam open. Join the back underlining and front interfacing at the shoulder seam using either *Method 1* or *2* below.

Method 1: Lap the back underlining and front interfacing over the shoulder seam and pin. Place the shoulder seam, right side up, over the hand to be certain that the interfacing and underlining fit smoothly on the underside. On the wrong side, herringbone the lapped seam from the neckline to within 2 cm (¾ inch) of the armhole, catching only the seam allowance of the garment.

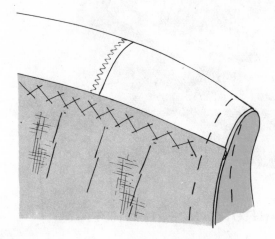

Method 2: Trim off the seam allowance on the back underlining and front interfacing, and slip the edges under the seam allowance of the jacket. Pin, then herringbone the seam edges to the back underlining and front interfacing.

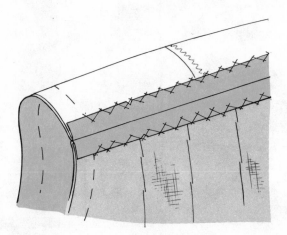

The Undercollar

INTERFACING THE UNDERCOLLAR

Stitch the centre seam of the undercollar and press it open. Lap the centre seam of the interfacing, matching the seamlines, and stitch, using the multi-stitch zig-zag. Mark the interfacing a measured 2 cm (¾ inch) from the edges. Place the markings close together to retain the shape of the collar. Trim on the marked line.

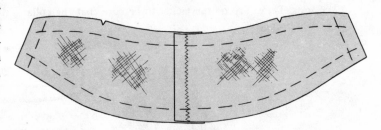

Cut a collar of organza, using the undercollar pattern and omitting the centre seam. Place the interfacing over the organza and pin. (The organza should extend 2 cm (¾ inch) beyond all edges of the interfacing.) Cut off the corners of the interfacing to eliminate bulk when the collar is turned to the right side. Stitch, using the multi-stitch zig-zag. Trim the organza under the interfacing ·6 cm (¼ inch) from the stitching. Press.

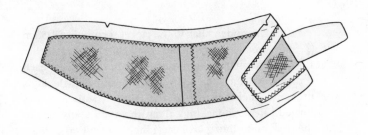

Pin the interfacing over the wrong side of the undercollar, keeping the organza and collar edges even. Tack along the roll line. Use thread matching the fabric. Stay the interfacing to the undercollar with padding stitches from the roll line to the neckline. Then stay the interfacing to the balance of the collar with rows of padding stitches as far as the seamline. As you work, roll the

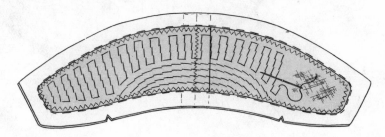

collar to shape it as you did the lapels. Tack the interfacing in place along the seamline. Press over a tailor's
ham or pressing mitt.

ATTACHING THE UNDERCOLLAR
TO THE JACKET

Pin the undercollar to the jacket, right sides together,
matching markings. Work from the garment side. Pin at
the centre, shoulder and front markings, then pin at
intervals between, easing the collar between the markings. Tack. Try on the jacket to be sure that the collar
fits properly.

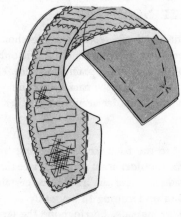

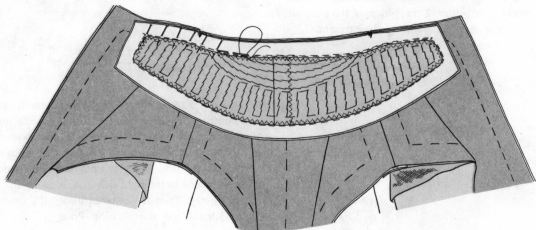

Stitch the undercollar to the jacket, beginning 1·5 cm
($\frac{5}{8}$ inch) from one collar edge and stitching to within
1·5 cm ($\frac{5}{8}$ inch) of the opposite edge. Back-stitch at each
end of the seam. (The open seam allowance at the ends
prevents puckering when the facing is stitched and
turned.) Remove tackings. Trim the seam allowance of
the back underlining to ·6 cm ($\frac{1}{4}$ inch) and cut off corners
where seams cross at the shoulder and centre back. Press.
Slash into the seam allowances at evenly spaced intervals
so that they will lie flat when pressed. Press the seam
open.

Buttonholes in Interfacing

Tack the interfacing smoothly round each buttonhole.
Follow the instructions on page 110 and cut out the
interfacing round the buttonholes.

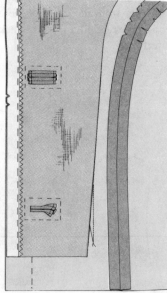

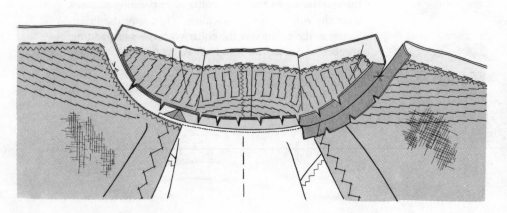

Facings and Top Collar

If a back neckline facing is not given with the pattern, cut one about 9 cm (3½ inches) deep, using the jacket tissue pattern to shape the neckline and shoulders.

JOINING FACING TO TOP COLLAR

Join the front and back sections of the facing at the shoulder seams. Press the seams open.

Pin the top collar to the facing, right sides together, matching markings. Work from the collar side and pin at the centre shoulder, and front markings, then at intervals between, easing the collar between the markings. Tack. Stitch, beginning 1·5 cm (⅝ inch) from one collar edge and stitching to within 1·5 cm (⅝ inch) of the opposite edge. Pull threads through to the underside and tie. Cut off corners where seams cross at the shoulder. Remove tackings and press. Slash into the seam allowances at evenly spaced intervals so that the seam will lie flat. Press the seam open.

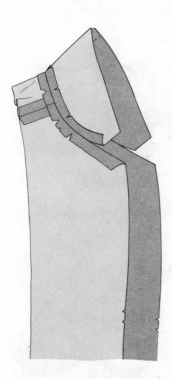

ATTACHING FACING AND TOP COLLAR TO JACKET

Place the top collar and facing over the jacket, right sides together. Work from the top collar side and keep the seam edges even. Pin the collars together, first at the centre, points and notches. Match seams where the undercollar joins the jacket and the top collar joins the front facing. Then pin at intervals between, easing the top collar between the markings.

Pin the front facing in place, first at the lapel point, notches and lower edge. Then pin at intervals between, easing the facing from the top button to the lapel point. Tack with silk thread but do not tack through the seam allowances of the crossing seams where the collars join. **To stitch the collar seam,** turn the seam allowance on both the top side and the underside away from the collar. Carefully position the needle in the seamline, exactly at the end of the stitching that joins the collar and facing. Lower the Presser Foot and stitch round the collar to the same point on the opposite side. Make one or two stitches diagonally across the points to avoid bulk when the collar is turned to the right side.

To stitch the facing seam so that it will join the collar stitching perfectly, place a needle through the seam from the collar side to the facing side. The needle should come out at the end of the stitching that joins the collar and facing. Turn the seam allowance on both the top side and the underside away from the facing. Carefully lower the machine needle in the seamline at the needle marking and stitch. Make one or two stitches diagonally across the point. Stitch the opposite side in the same manner. Check the right side to make sure the seam matches exactly.

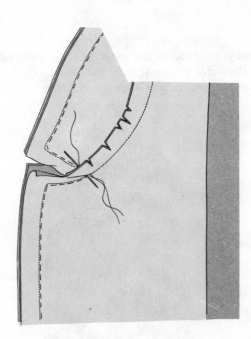

Pull the threads on the collar through to the underside and tie. Repeat the same procedure on the facing side, then use a needle to carry the threads through the seam to the collar side and fasten them in the interfacing with two backstitches. This gives added strength at the notch of the collar.

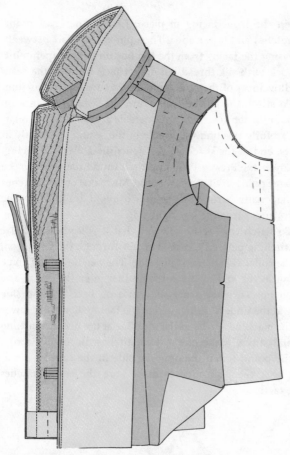

allowances on the outside curve. From the top of the lapel to the top button, trim the garment seam allowance to ·3 cm ($\frac{1}{8}$ inch) and the facing seam allowance and organza strip to ·6 cm ($\frac{1}{4}$ inch). Reverse the layering below the top button by trimming the facing seam allowance to ·3 cm ($\frac{1}{8}$ inch) and the garment seam allowance and organza strip to ·6 cm ($\frac{1}{4}$ inch). Cut diagonally across the points, close to the stitching, and cut off corners where seams cross at the outer edges. Press, then press the seams open.

Trim the seam allowances joining the undercollar and jacket to ·9 cm ($\frac{3}{8}$ inch) from the outer edge to the shoulder line. Herringbone the open seam edges to the interfacing on each side.

Turn the facing to the underside. Ease out the corners of the collar and lapels. Tack, using diagonal tacking and silk thread. As you work, ease the garment under slightly at the seamline along the lapels and collar, and ease the facing under slightly from the top button to the lower edge. Do not remove these tackings until the jacket is

Remove the tackings and press. Trim the undercollar seam allowance to ·3 cm ($\frac{1}{8}$ inch) and the top collar seam edge and organza strip to ·6 cm ($\frac{1}{4}$ inch). Notch the seam

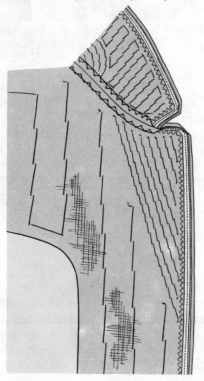

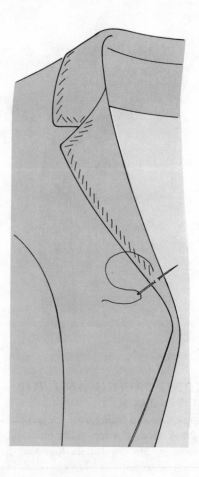

finished. Press, then press lapels and collar over a tailor's ham or pressing mitt.

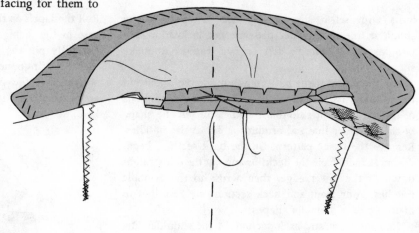

Roll the lapels and collar as they will be worn, allowing sufficient ease in the top collar and facing for them to fit smoothly over the roll. Pin the facing and top collar in place along the roll line, then near the neckline seam. Where the collars join the neckline across the back, catch the open seams together between the shoulders with loose hand stitches. (You will complete the work on the front facing after you have set in the sleeves.)

Sleeves

Before you sew in the sleeves, pin and tack the underarm seams of the jacket; include the back underlining in the seam. Try on the jacket to be sure that it fits correctly. Stitch the seams. Slash the seam allowances at the waistline just far enough so that they will lie flat. Press, then press the seam open.

Construct the sleeves. Refer to *Set-in-Sleeve*, page 158, for instructions on pinning and tacking the sleeve in the armhole. Include the back underlining, but not the front interfacing in the seam.

Try on the jacket. Check the 'hang' of the sleeve. Turn the hems in the sleeve and jacket and check their length. Pin-mark any adjustments.

Remove the jacket and adjust the sleeve if necessary. Tack the marking for the hemline of the sleeves and jacket.

Stitch the sleeve in the armhole, overlapping the stitching at the underarm seam. Remove tackings, cut off corners where seams cross at the underarm and shoulder. Trim the back underlining seam allowance to ·6 cm (¼ inch). Press. Turn the seam into the sleeve.

If the fabric is heavy and the armhole close fitting, trim the seam allowance on the sleeve side to ·9 cm (⅜ inch) over the head between the notches, then tack it loosely to the garment side of the seam. At the underarm, between the notches, trim the seam allowance to ·9 cm (⅜ inch), then sew the edges together, using either the multi-stitch zig-zag or the blindstitch zig-zag. Place the stitching between the seamline and seam edge. Hand-sew the front interfacing to the sleeve seam, barely outside the previous line of stitching, using matching thread. Trim the interfacing to within ·6 cm (¼ inch) of the hand stitching.

To maintain the roll of the sleeve head, cut wool domette on the true bias 3·1 cm (1¼ inches) wide. Fold it through the centre, then pin it to the sleeve side of the seam allowance over the head between the notches, keeping the fold even with the stitching line. Hand-stitch the domette to the sleeve seam.

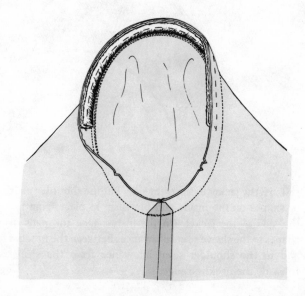

Shoulder Pads or Shapes

Suits with set-in sleeves may need support at the shoulder line. If shoulder pads are not in fashion, use two layers of tailoring felt or hair canvas to make shoulder shapes.

Use the jacket tissue pattern as a guide. Fold and pin the shoulder darts in the front and back bodice sections of the pattern. Cut a double thickness of felt the shape of the shoulder line and armhole as far as the notches. Remove the tissue pattern. On the back section, begin 2·5 cm (1 inch) from the neckline and cut the felt straight down to the lower edge, then across to the armhole notches. Four front and back sections are required to make a pair of shoulder shapes.

Join the front and back sections at the shoulder line by lapping one edge over the other, with seamlines meeting in the centre; pin. Stitch, using the multi-stitch zig-zag. Join the two layers of shapes with two lines of multi-stitch zig-zag, as illustrated. Cut off the underlayer of felt ·6 cm (¼ inch) from the outer edge; remember to trim one shape for the right shoulder and one for the left.

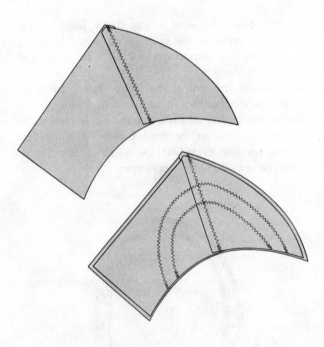

Turn the jacket to the right side. Put the shoulder pads or shapes on the inside and pin them in place from the top side of the jacket. On the inside, tack the pads or shapes to the sleeve seam allowances between the notches and to the shoulder seam allowance from the sleeve towards the neckline edge.

The Front Facings

Roll the lapels as they will be worn, allowing sufficient ease in the facing for it to fit smoothly over the roll. Carefully pin the free edge of the facing smoothly in place. Herringbone the facing to the interfacing from the shoulder to the point where the interfacing extends across the front; then tack it to the jacket as far as the hemline.

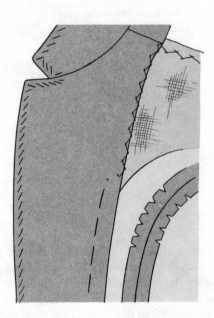

Jacket Hem

Compare the front edges of the jacket to make sure that they are the same length. Remove enough diagonal tacking to fold the hem. Turn the facing away from the jacket. Fold the hem in the jacket and facing, and pin. Ease the hem down slightly at the seams to allow for the fold over the seam allowances. (The front interfacing should extend to the hem fold.) Tack with silk thread ·6 cm (¼ inch) from the hem fold. Press. Trim the hem to an even width. Trim the hem across the facing and seam to 1·2 cm (½ inch); trim all seam allowances to half their width from hem fold to edge. Press, shrinking out any fullness. **Interface the lower edge of the jacket** with pre-shrunk linen to give extra body and weight at the hem. Cut the interfacing on the true bias 2·5 cm (1 inch) wider than the hem and the length of the lower edge of the jacket plus 2·5 cm (1 inch) for seam allowances. Remove the tacking at the lower edge of the hem after pressing, and turn the hem away from the jacket. Place the interfacing between the hem and jacket; align the lower edge of the interfacing with the crease for the hem and extend the ends 1·2 cm (½ inch) over the front interfacing. Pin, tack, then herringbone the interfacing to the jacket along each edge, catching only one thread of the fabric outside the interfacing and only the interfacing on the opposite side. Use thread to match the fabric. Press.

Turn the hem over the interfacing and pin the free edge in place, matching seams. Tack. Herringbone the hem to the interfacing as far as the facing seam. Make a stitch in the hem, then a stitch in the interfacing over the hem edge. Continue, alternating the stitches.

Turn the front facing to the underside; ease it under slightly at the lower edge and pin it to the hem. Slip-stitch in place, then herringbone over the cut edge the depth of the hem. (A soft hemline is described on page 194.)

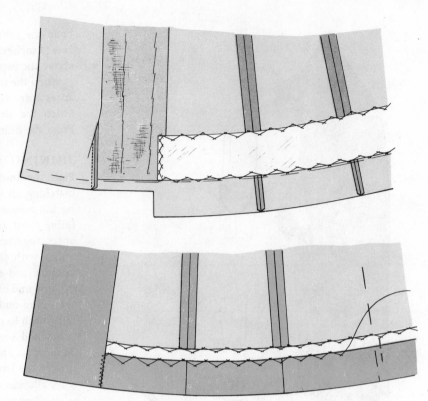

Sleeve Hem

Turn the sleeve hem and tack ·6 cm (¼ inch) from the fold, using silk thread. Trim the seam allowances to half their width from the fold to the hem edge. Interface the hem of the sleeve in the same way as the jacket. Cut the interfacing ends on the lengthwise grain and join them, overlapping about 1·2 cm (½ inch). Herringbone the interfacing in place, then complete the hem of the sleeve in the same way as the jacket.

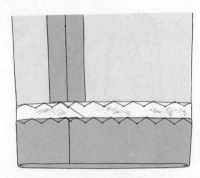

Buttonholes in Facing

Finish the back of the buttonholes, following the instructions on page 111.

Lining

Any adjustments you made in fitting the jacket must also be made in the lining.

Stay-stitch the back neckline of the lining 1·2 cm (½ inch) from the edge and stitch the shoulder darts. Fold and tack the release pleats (to provide ease in movement in the back) and waistline darts in the front and back lining. Press.

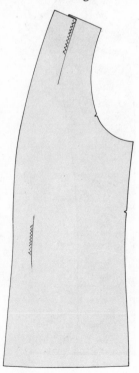

Use a fine herringbone to hold the release pleats and darts in position. Make the stitches through the three thicknesses, near the fold, on the right side of the lining. On the fronts, herringbone the release pleats from the shoulder to about 7·5 cm (3 inches) down, and the waistline darts about 2·5 cm (1 inch) above and below the waistline. On the back, herring-

bone the release pleat from the neckline down about 5 cm (2 inches), across the pleat at the waistline, and just above the hem.

Stitch the underarm seams. Slash into the seam allowances at the waistline. Press, then press the seams open. Stitch the sleeve lining seams and press them open. Press the lining thoroughly.

JOINING LINING TO JACKET

Place the lining inside the jacket, wrong sides together, matching all seams and centre back. Pin at the centre back, underarm and round the armhole. Fold back the lining front and pin the lining and jacket seam allowances together at the underarm, matching markings. Stitch with long tacking stitches, starting below the armhole and ending 7·5 cm (3 inches) above the hem.

Turn under the seam allowance on the front edge of the lining and pin it over the free edge of the facing. Slip-stitch in place.

Pin and sew the front lining to the shoulder seam. Turn under the back shoulder seam allowance, then lap it over the front lining and pin. Tack the lining to the seam allowance round the armhole. Clip into the lining seam allowance at the back neckline. Turn it under just beyond the stay stitching, and pin it to the neckline facing. Slip-stitch the lining in place from the outer edge of one shoulder to the other.

Place the jacket on a hanger, right side out. Smooth out the lining and pin it to the jacket 7·5 cm (3 inches) above the hem.

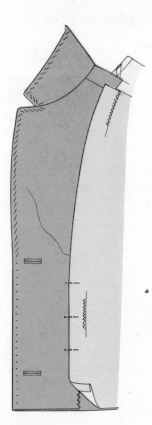

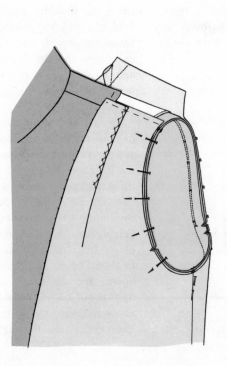

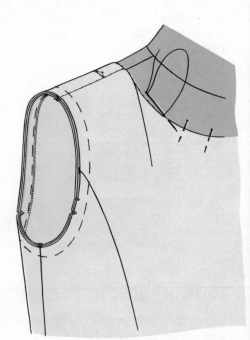

Allow 1·2 cm (½ inch) for ease in the lining length.
Turn under the edge of the lining so that it overlaps the
jacket hem 2·5 cm (1 inch). Press. Pin the lining to the
jacket hem, matching seams and darts, then tack it in
place 1·2 cm (½ inch) above the fold. Turn back the lining
on the tacking line and slip-stitch it to the jacket hem,
catching only the under layer of the lining.

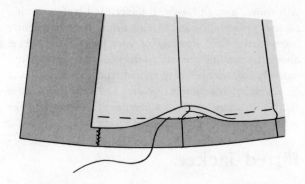

LINING THE SLEEVES

Place a line of stitching round the sleeve head of the
lining between the notches, 1·2 cm (½ inch) from the
edge. Turn the sleeve to the wrong side.

Turn the jacket sleeve to the wrong side. Pin the lining
and sleeve seam allowances together at the underarm
seams, matching markings in the seams and armhole.
Stitch with long tacking stitches, beginning about 7·5 cm
(3 inches) below the armhole and ending 7·5 cm (3 inches)
above the hem. If the sleeve is a two-piece one, catch the
back seams together.

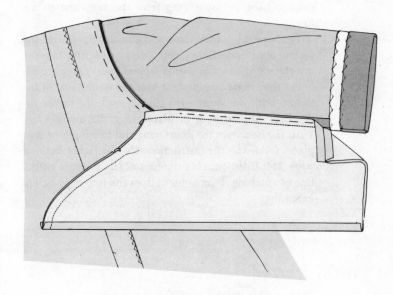

Turn the lining sleeve to the right side over the jacket
sleeve. Pull the bobbin thread round the sleeve head and
ease the lining to fit over the armhole seam allowance.
Turn the seam edge under just beyond the stitching;
overlap the armhole seam allowance and pin the sleeve
lining in place at the shoulder, notches and underarm
seam, then at intervals between. Slip-stitch in place.

Allow ·6 cm (¼ inch) for ease in the length of the sleeve
lining. Turn under the lower edge and slip-stitch it to
sleeve hem, following the instructions for the lower edge
of the lining as described at the beginning of this page.

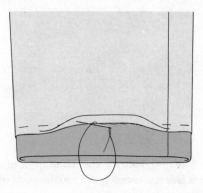

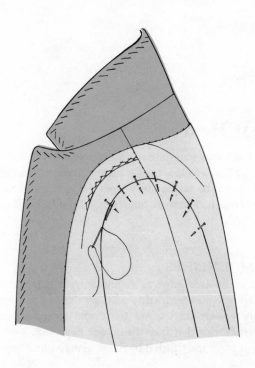

Weights

To add weight to the hemline and keep the line of the
jacket, lead weights can be stitched at intervals round
the lower edge. The lead weights to use are flat, round
discs with two centre holes, they are made in various
sizes to suit different types of fabric. When you have
chosen the weights to suit your garment, lightly hammer
them round the rim to flatten the edge so no hard outline

327

will show through the hem. Cover each weight with a piece of lining fabric and stitch it through the two centre holes to the seam turnings of your jacket, place them above the hemline and within the hem allowance. Alternatively buy a length of weighted tape, this is a series of tiny weights in a tubular covering and very supple. Use this right round the jacket hemline, catching it to the seam allowances before turning up the hem.

Fitted Jacket

In addition to front and collar interfacings, fitted jackets usually have an interfacing from the waistline to the hemline.

To shape interfacing darts and eliminate bulk, see the instructions under *Interfacing Darts*, page 104. Join the interfacing side seams with a lapped seam. See page 83.

Pin the interfacing in place over the wrong side of the jacket, with the lower edge aligned with the crease for the hem. Slip-stitch it in place along the lower edge. Turn the hem over the interfacing and herringbone it in place, following the instructions for the jacket hem on page 324. If the hem is full, control the fullness with a line of stitching ·6 cm ($\frac{1}{4}$ inch) from the free edge before hemming.

WAISTLINE STAY

To prevent stretching, stay the waistline of fitted and semi-fitted jackets and princess-line coats with straight seam binding or 1·2-cm ($\frac{1}{2}$-inch) petersham ribbon. Work with the jacket in the shape it will be worn.

On the underside, pin the tape round the waistline, extending the ends 2 cm ($\frac{3}{4}$ inch) beyond the front facings. Turn the ends of the tape under ·6 cm ($\frac{1}{4}$ inch), and pin them to the front facings and interfacings. Tack the tape in place at the ends and at all seams and darts. When interfacing is used below the waistline, tack it in place with the tape.

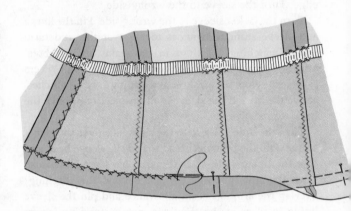

Basic Construction

Coat construction follows the same procedures and sequence as jacket construction up to the point of making the hem. Remember to fit a coat over the type of dress or suit you will wear under it.

Sleeve styles vary. One comfortable and popular style is a sleeve that has a centre seam with the back (or front) section cut in one with the bodice and the other section set into the armhole. Gussets are frequently used, so are raglan and set-in sleeves. Instructions on making the several types of sleeves are given under *Sleeve Styles and Finishes*, page 158.

Before you hem the coat, interface the sleeve hem and finish it, following the directions for the jacket, page 325.

Coat Hem

Mark the coat length. Refer to *Hems and Hem Finishes*, page 187, and follow the first three steps in forming the hem. Turn the facing away from the coat and form the hem across it. The front interfacing should extend to the hem fold.

HEM FINISHES

Neaten the free edge as required by the fabric. The neatenings most frequently used are the *Pinked Hem* for firmly woven fabrics and the *Bound Hem* for loosely woven fabrics that fray easily. See page 188. Tack the hem in place and finish it by hand, using a blind herringbone. If the fabric is heavy or the hem wide, double-stitch the hem. See page 193.

INTERFACED HEM

For added body and weight, interface the hem with a true bias strip of unbleached calico or tailor's linen, cut the width of the hem.

Press the fold for the hem, shrinking out any fullness. Finish the free edge of the hem. Remove all tacking. Place the interfacing over the underside of the hem, extending the ends 1·2 cm (½ inch) beyond the front interfacings. Shape the interfacing to the hem and herringbone it to the hem near the fold and top edge. Press.

Tack the free edge of the hem to the coat, and blind herringbone it in place. Press.

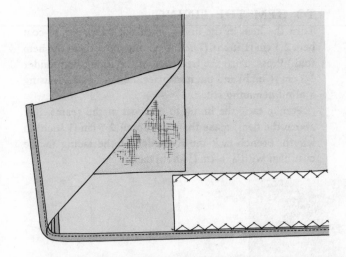

Lining and Interlining

Cut the lining and interlining by the same pattern; however, cut the interlining to extend to the turn of the lining hem at the bottom of the coat and sleeves. Make the same adjustments to the lining and interlining that you made to the coat after fitting it.

Place the interlining pieces over the wrong side of the lining pieces, matching markings; tack together along the edges. Place several rows of diagonal tacking within the sections to hold the layers together. Handle as one fabric when making the lining. See *Mounting a Dress*, page 95.

Stay-stitch 1·2 cm (½ inch) from the neckline edge. Stitch any seams within the lining; also stitch shoulder, underarm and sleeve seams. Press, then press the seams open. Sew in the sleeves. Treat the darts and pleats the same as in the jacket lining, page 325.

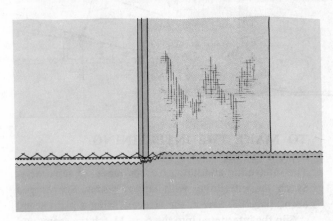

TO JOIN THE LINING TO THE COAT

Place the lining inside the coat, wrong sides together. Pin it in place at the centre back, shoulders, sleeves and underarm, matching seams and markings. Sew the lining and coat seam allowances together at the underarm and sleeve seams, following the instructions given for the jacket, page 326. Remove any pins necessary to sew the seam allowances together in the sleeves.

Slash into the lining seam allowance at the back neckline. Turn the edge under just beyond the stay stitching and pin it to the coat. Turn under the seam allowance on the front edge of the lining and pin it over the free edge of the facing. Slip-stitch in position.

Allow 1·2 cm (½ inch) for ease in the length of the sleeve lining. Turn under the lower edge and slip-stitch it to the sleeve hem, following the instructions for the jacket lining, page 327.

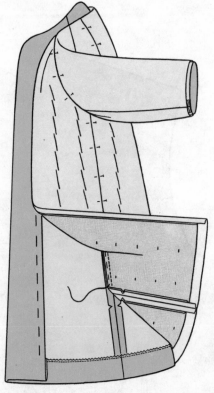

TO HEM THE LINING

Turn the hem in the lining so that it overlaps the coat hem 2·5 cm (1 inch). (The interlining extends to the hem fold.) Press. Turn the free edge of the lining hem under 1·2 cm (½ inch) and pin it in place. Finish by hand, using a blind hemming stitch.

French-tack the lining to the coat at the seams, just above the hem; make the tacks about 2·5 cm (1 inch) in length. French-tack the free edge of the facing to the coat hem with a ·6-cm (¼-inch) tack.

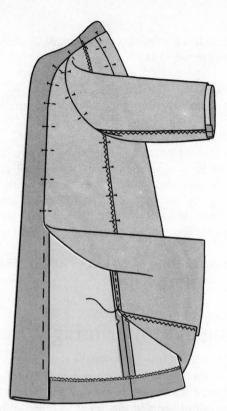

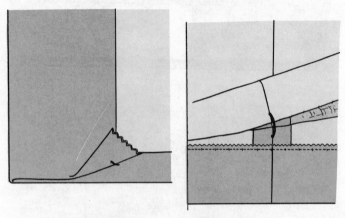

TO MAKE THE INTERLINING SEPARATELY

The interlining and lining may be made up separately. Stitch the interlining with lapped seams. See *Lapped Seam*, page 83. Sew in the sleeves, using a plain seam.

Slip the interlining into the coat. Match the seams and pin. Hand-sew the coat and interlining seam edges together at the underarm and sleeve, following the jacket lining instructions on page 326. Hand-sew the interlining to the facing edge.

Slip the lining into the coat and finish, following the lining instructions above.

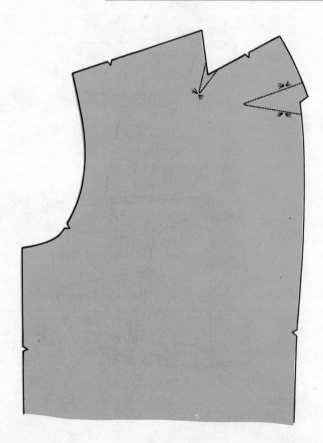

Additional Construction Techniques

To Make a Notched Shawl Collar

In a shawl collar, the top collar and facing are cut in one with a centre back seam. The tailoring technique is the same as that for the jacket collar on page 321, except for the treatment of the notches.

Tailor-tack the position of the notches in the garment, facing and interfacing. To retain the shape of the notches, do not cut them out until after the final stitching is completed.

Stay-stitch round the notched area of the garment and facing, barely outside the seamline. Use a 1 mm (20) stitch length; take one or two stitches across the point. Press. (This stitching will not show in the finished work.) Stay-stitch the slash in the neckline seam allowance.

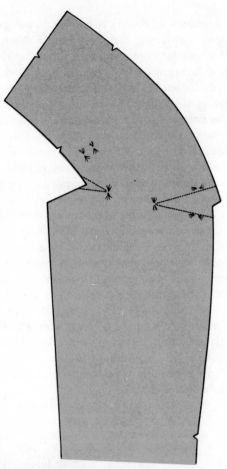

Cut a strip of organza wide enough to cover the notch, use the pattern to shape the neckline and front edges. Pin the organza strip over the interfacing, extending the edge 2 cm (¾ inch) beyond the interfacing. Cut out the notches in the interfacing only, ·3 cm (⅛ inch) beyond the seamline. Cut off the corners of the interfacing to eliminate bulk when turned. Stitch, using the multi-stitch zig-zag. Press.

Place the interfacing on the wrong side of the jacket or coat, keeping the organza strip and garment edge even. The uncut notches in the garment must coincide with those in the interfacing. Finish, following the instructions under *Front Interfacing*, page 318. Join shoulder seams, and interface the undercollar. See page 319.

Pin the undercollar to the neckline, matching markings, and slash the neckline seam at the inside corner. Tack, then stitch. Cut off the corners where seams cross, and slash into the seam allowances at evenly spaced intervals so that they will lie flat when pressed open. Remove the tacking and press the seam open. Trim the seam edges to ·9 cm (⅜ inch) from the outer edge to the corner, then herringbone the open seam edges to the interfacing on each side. Press.

Prepare the garment for a fitting following the instructions given on page 316.

Mark the neckline and front edges of the interfacing a measured 2 cm (¾ inch) from the edge (1·5 cm (⅝ inch) seam allowance plus ·3 cm (⅛ inch)). Trim off along the marked line, *but do not cut out the notches.*

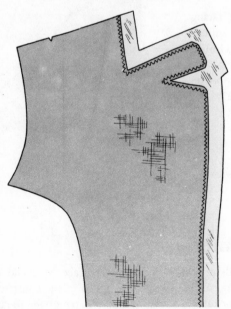

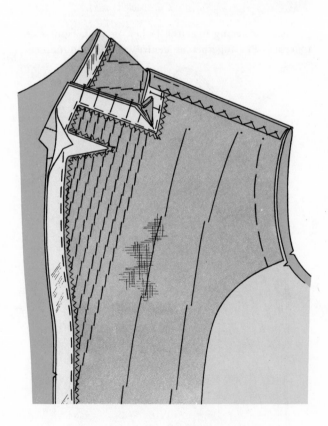

Stitch the centre back seam of the top collar and facing, then press the seam open. Attach the back neckline facing in the same manner as the undercollar. Press the seam open.

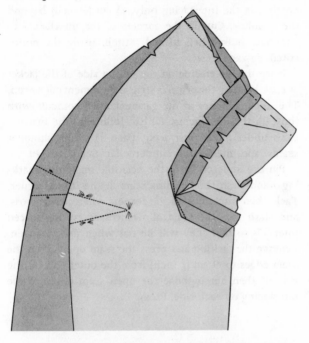

Place the facing over the jacket, or coat, right sides together. Pin together at centre, points and notches.

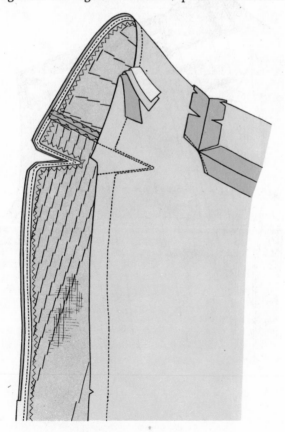

Match seamlines of the uncut notches in the garment, interfacing and facing, and pin together. Then pin at close intervals between, easing the top collar and lapel section of the facing between the markings. Tack. Stitch in one continuous line from one hem edge to the other. Take one or two stitches diagonally across the corners; stitch the notched area barely beyond the stay stitching, taking one or two stitches across the point. The width at the point provides space for cutting and prevents pulling at the point in the finished work. Remove tacking.

Trim the undercollar seam allowance to ·3 cm ($\frac{1}{8}$ inch) and the top collar seam allowance and organza strip to ·6 cm ($\frac{1}{4}$ inch). From the top of the lapel to the top button, trim the garment seam allowance to ·3 cm ($\frac{1}{8}$ inch) and facing seam allowance and organza strip to ·6 cm ($\frac{1}{4}$ inch). Reverse the layering below the top button by trimming the facing seam allowance to ·3 cm ($\frac{1}{8}$ inch) and the garment seam allowance and organza to ·6 cm ($\frac{1}{4}$ inch). Cut between the lines of stitching in the notch, almost to the point, then trim the garment seam allowance to ·3 cm ($\frac{1}{8}$ inch) and the facing seam allowance and organza to ·6 cm ($\frac{1}{4}$ inch). Cut diagonally across the corners at the lapel points and where seams cross. Press, then press the seams open.

Turn facing to the underside and finish, following the instructions on page 322.

To Interface

You will probably prefer to interface suits and coats according to the instructions given in the construction of the jacket. However, you may herringbone the interfacing in place as instructed under *Method 2*, on page 136. Or you may use the method explained here, which is suitable for loosely woven fabrics such as tweed and heavy coating.

Mark the neckline and front edge of the interfacing, just under 2 cm (¾ inch) from the edge (1·5-cm (⅝-inch) seam allowance plus ·3 cm (⅛ inch)). Trim off on the markings. Cut off corners.

Place the interfacing over the wrong side of the garment front section with the fabric extending 2 cm (¾ inch) beyond the interfacing edge. Pin. Stay the interfacing to the lapels with padding stitches; then tack the interfacing in place, following the instructions on page 318.

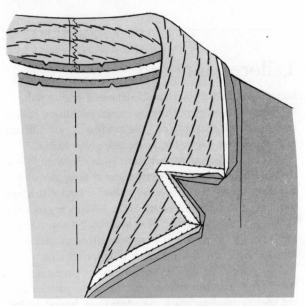

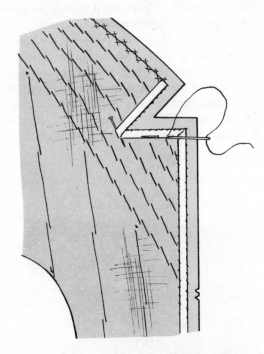

Tape the front opening, lapel and front edge of the collar with ·6-cm (¼-inch) tape. Shrink and shape the tape with steam pressing. Position the tape so that it overlaps the interfacing and the outer edge is ·2 cm (1/16 inch) from the fabric seamline. Mitre the tape at the corners. Sew the outer edge of the tape to the fabric, using a hemming stitch. Then sew the opposite edge in place, taking the stitches through the interfacing and tape edge only. Press.

Apply the facing and top collar, following the instructions on page 321.

To Stay Neckline Seam

To prevent the back neckline seam from stretching, stay it with ·6-cm (¼-inch) tape or straight seam binding folded through the centre. Steam-press the tape, shrinking and shaping it to fit the neckline. After the under-

collar is stitched in place and the seam pressed open, pin the tape over the open seam between the shoulders; then herringbone it to the seam allowance on each side.

To Stay Armhole Seam at Underarm

The armhole seam at the underarm of coats and suits is subject to extra strain. For added strength in tweed and loosely woven fabrics, tape the seam with ·6-cm (¼-inch) tape (narrower, if possible) or straight seam binding folded through the centre. Steam-press the tape, shrinking and shaping it to fit the armhole at the underarm.

Pin the tape over the right side of the seam allowance of the armhole, between the notches, with the lower edge barely above the seamline.

Stitch it in place about ·2 cm (1/16 inch) from the lower edge of the tape, using a 1·5 mm (15) stitch length.

The seamline is just below the tape; so when the sleeve is stitched into the armhole, the tape between the seam edges will carry the strain, not the seamline. Trim the armhole seam allowance at the underarm to ·9 cm (⅜ inch).

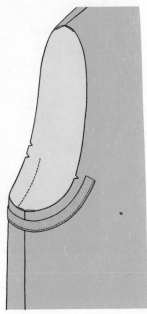

Tailored Binding

Suits, coats and dresses can be trimmed with a tailored binding on the edge of front openings, necklines, collars and cuffs and pocket flaps. The binding is not difficult to apply if you follow the procedure given here.

A good quality of slipper satin is an excellent fabric for binding as it will not show signs of wear as quickly as other fabrics. Self-fabric may also be used if it is not too heavy. The finished width of the binding is generally 1·2 cm (½ inch) but it may be as wide as 2·5 cm (1 inch). Buy enough fabric to cut long bias strips so that your binding will have the minimum number of joins.

Before applying the binding, finish the garment up to the point of attaching the interfacing. If the pattern does not specify binding, mark the edges to be bound 1·5 cm (⅝ inch) (seam allowance) from the edge and trim on the marked line. Treat the facing and interfacing the same. Tack the interfacing in place on the wrong side. Place the facing on the underside of the garment, wrong sides together, with the cut edges even; pin. Tack the layers of fabric together 1·5 cm (⅝ inch) from the edge. On a heavy fabric, it may be necessary to tack again ·6 cm (¼ inch) from the edge.

Cut the binding on the true bias, four times the finished width. See *Cutting Bias Strips*, page 244. Fold the bias strip through the centre, wrong sides together, and press lightly. Since this means pressing on the right side of the fabric, place a pressing cloth between the fabric and iron.

Do not slide the iron, but lift it from one section to the other. Open the bias and fold the cut edges to the centre, leaving a ·3-cm (⅛-inch) space between the edges. Press. This spacing allows for folding the bias over the edge of the garment.

TO BIND A STRAIGHT EDGE OR CURVE

Open the binding and carefully pin it to the edge, right sides together, keeping the cut edges even. Extend the end of the binding ·6 cm (¼ inch) beyond each end of the seam to allow for turning and finishing. Do not stretch the binding on straight edges; ease it slightly on outside curves and stretch it slightly on inside curves.

Carefully stitch in the folded crease of the binding. Trim the interfacing in the seam allowance close to the stitching. Press to the stitching, but not beyond.

Fold the ends of the binding under ·6 cm (¼ inch) then fold the binding over the seam edge to the stitching on the underside; pin. Finish by hand, using a slip stitch. Slip-stitch the folded ends of binding together.

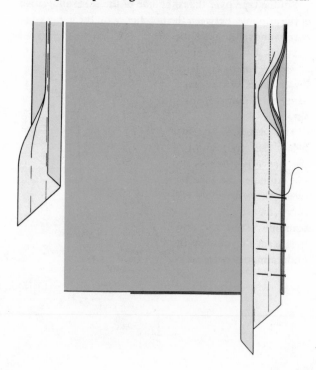

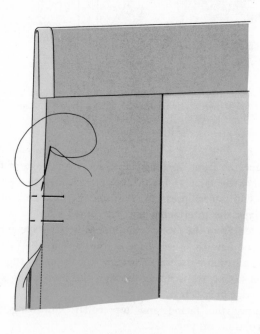

TO BIND A SQUARE CORNER

Open the binding and pin it along *one* side, following the instructions above. Stitch in the folded crease from the outer edge to the intersecting seamline at the corner.

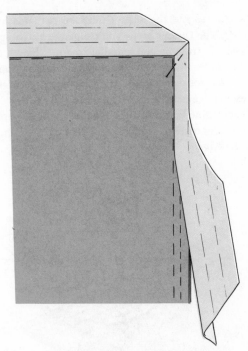

Pull the threads to the underside and tie them together in a single knot.

Fold the bias over the edge and mitre the corner from the seamline to the centre fold of the binding, as illustrated; pin. Turn the binding back over the garment, right sides together, and finish pinning the edge in place along the adjoining side. Carefully stitch in the folded crease of the binding. Press only the stitching.

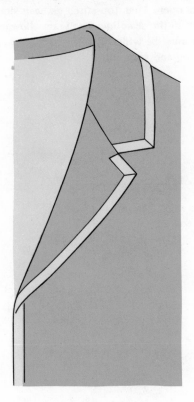

Finish, following the instructions for the straight edge. On the underside, mitre the binding at the corner, folding it in the same direction as on the top side. Slip-stitch the folds of the mitre together.

Top Stitching

Top stitching is a smart and practical way to accent the lines of a garment and at the same time add firmness. A single line of stitching on a heavy fabric, such as coating or a laminate, produces a welt effect. Single or multiple rows of parallel stitching on a lighter weight fabric lend importance to finished edges such as lapels, facing edges, collars and pockets, as well as to style seams and hemlines.

For top stitching you can use either your usual sewing thread or buttonhole twist. Buttonhole twist is frequently preferred for medium-weight and heavy-weight fabrics. Use it for the needle thread and the regular thread for the bobbin. Select a size 18 needle and a slightly longer stitch than for the regular seaming. It is generally necessary to increase the needle thread tension when stitching with buttonhole twist. To determine the best stitch length and tension, make a stitching test on a piece of your fabric; fold the fabric, duplicating the seam allowance, and include the same type of interfacing or underlining you are using in the garment.

Before applying top stitching to an edge, attach the interfacing and facing to the garment, trim the seams, and turn the facing and press as instructed on pages 318 and 321. Tack the layers of fabric together to prevent them from slipping during the stitching. Use diagonal tacking and silk thread. One line of tacking is sufficient if the top stitching will be close to the edge. Tack again just outside the stitching line if the stitching will be 1·2 cm ($\frac{1}{2}$ inch) or more from the edge.

Mark the stitching line with tacking on the right side and use it as a guide in your machine stitching. Use a gauge to measure accurately, and take tiny stitches through all thicknesses of fabric. Space the stitches about 2·5 cm (1 inch) apart; keep the slack out of the thread between them. On curved edges and seams, place the tacking stitches closer together, with the short thread on the top side and the long one on the underside.

On the right side of your garment, top-stitch very close to the tacking but not on it. Stitch slowly, using the appropriate stitch length for the fabric. Additional rows of stitching may be gauged with the Presser Foot if the spacing is less than ·6 cm (¼ inch). For wider spacing, mark each stitching line the same as the first one. At corners, pivot and turn the fabric on the needle, following the directions on page 28.

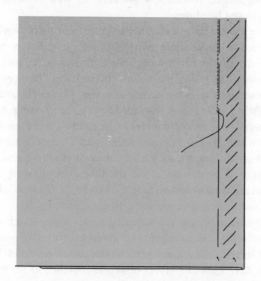

When the stitching ends at a finished edge, leave thread ends about 10 cm (4 inches) long. Then use a hand sewing needle to fasten them in the seam allowance between the facing and garment.

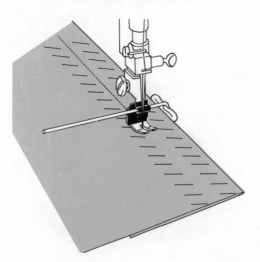

The Quilter and the Seam Guide are two aids in top stitching. The Quilter helps you gauge the stitching line and keep it straight and parallel to the edge or seam depression. See *Welt Seam*, page 88, for instructions on its use. As you sew, guide the finished edge or seam depression against the space guide of the Quilter. With the Seam Guide you can stitch parallel to the edge of the fabric at any distance from ·3 to 3·1 cm (⅛ to 1¼ inches) from the edge.

The interesting use of top stitching in the style seams illustrated is simple to achieve. After stitching the seams, press them open. Then top-stitch on each side an equal distance from the seamline. The seam allowance on the underside must be wider than the distance between the top stitching and seamline.

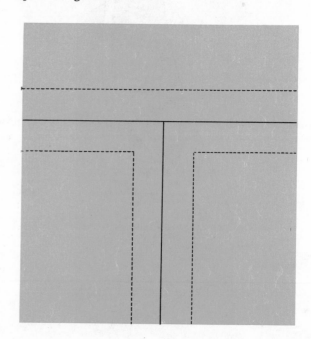

Arrowhead

The arrowhead is used in tailored suits as a decorative and secure finish at the ends of pockets and top of pleats and on fashion seams that end within the garment.

Mark the triangular shape of the arrowhead with chalk or thread. Use buttonhole twist in the needle.

Make two small stitches, bringing the needle out at the lower left corner. At the upper corner, take a stitch from right to left. Insert the needle at the right corner and bring it out at the left corner, barely inside of the previous thread. Repeat the procedure, placing the threads side by side until the triangle is completely filled in. Fasten the thread on the underside with two tiny backstitches.

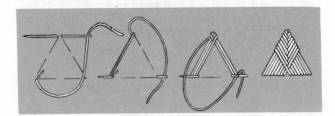

Crow's Foot

The crow's foot is used in the same places as the arrowhead. With thread or chalk, mark a triangle that is slightly curved on the sides. Use buttonhole twist in the needle.

Make two small stitches, bringing the needle out at the lower left corner. At the upper corner, take a horizontal stitch from right to left. At the lower right corner, take a diagonal stitch from left to right. Then at the lower left corner, make a diagonal stitch from left to right. Continue making stitches in the same sequence, placing them side by side until the centre is filled in. Fasten the thread on the underside with two small backstitches.

Bar Tack

Bar tacks are used to prevent splitting at the end of a fly opening and at the ends of pockets in shorts and slacks. They are also used to hold belt carriers in place. Make them by hand or by machine. Use mercerised cotton, silk or synthetic thread.

BY HAND

Make two or three long stitches the length of the bar tack. Then make small overhand stitches across the threads and through the fabric. When the bar is finished, make tiny bar stitches across each end.

BY MACHINE

Use a fine, closely spaced zig-zag stitch. Stitch the length of the bar tack. Pull the threads through to the underside and tie.

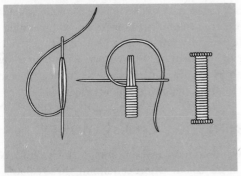

337

Introduction to Home Furnishings

Home furnishings are in many ways the most rewarding adventure in sewing. They offer you a perfect opportunity to express yourself – your design sense and your flair for colour. They give you the satisfaction of creating your own home.

The home you decorate is part of the life you share with your family, it must reflect as well as contribute to that life. Before you plunge into decorating, consult the several magazines available on the subject. They will give you many excellent ideas on style, colour and fabrics. Consider fashion trends but do not let novelties or fads influence your judgment. Aim for harmony and simplicity, for beauty and comfort, and you will give your family a home they can enjoy for many years.

In making your decorating decisions, remember that fabric furnishings should be planned in relation to the size and shape of the room, the height of the ceiling, the number and position of windows, and the effect you wish to achieve. Fabric, colour and style, as well as construction, determine the end results.

This section of the book will guide you in choosing styles and fabrics and in planning colour schemes. Its most valuable contribution, however, is the techniques it explains, through words and pictures, on construction. In made-to-measure fabric furnishings, it is not the price of the fabric that makes the greatest difference – it is the fit of a loose cover and the fullness and 'hang' of curtains.

Planning a Colour Scheme

The success of your entire decorating project may depend on how wisely you use colour. But do not let this statement intimidate you. If you follow a few basic rules, you will find that it is not difficult to assemble colours harmoniously.

The Colour System

To use colour skilfully, you should have some knowledge of the colour system. See colour wheel, Plate 21, opposite page 340. The primary colours are red, yellow and blue. They are pure colours and cannot be produced by mixing other colours. The secondary colours – orange, green and violet – are produced by mixing equal amounts of two primary colours, as illustrated in the colour wheel. The primary and secondary colours together comprise the six standard colours.

Intermediate colours or hues are produced by combining a primary colour with the secondary colour that flanks it in the colour wheel. The six intermediate hues and the six standard colours are known as the twelve 'true' colours because they are not diluted with white, black or grey.

When true colours are diluted, a shade or tint results. A shade is produced by adding varying degrees of grey or black to the true colour to give a colour value darker than the true colour. A tint is produced by adding varying degrees of white to the true colour to give a colour value lighter than the true colour. Each true colour has numerous shades and tints. A slight degree of colour value is illustrated in the colour wheel.

Warm and Cool Colours

The warm colours are red, orange and yellow. All the hues in the colour wheel containing these colours share

338

in their warmth. The cool colours are blue and all the hues grouped round it in the colour wheel. Green, which contains equal amounts of blue and yellow, and violet, which contains equal amounts of blue and red, are neither warm nor cool. As greater percentages of the warm colours are added to them, however, they gain in warmth; as the percentage of blue is increased, they grow cool.

Warm colours make the size of an object seem larger and the size of a room smaller. Cool colours behave in the opposite way, diminishing the apparent size of an object and giving an illusion of spaciousness in a room.

Neutral colours – white, grey and beige – are frequently used in home decorating. Neutral walls, ceilings, windows and floors provide an effective background for the bold, bright colours so often found in fabric furnishings. Colours appear darker than they actually are when placed against a light background, lighter against a dark background. Medium tones are less forceful than extreme light or dark tones.

Colour Harmony

Colour harmony is the art of grouping colours pleasingly in a room. Many ideas on colour combinations can be gleaned from the beauty of nature. Study a sunset or a rainbow; notice how subtly each colour blends with and accents the other. Study colour proportion, keeping in mind the colours nature used for the peacock and the elephant. In short, be aware of colour.

Shades and tints are mainstays in home decorating. They make it possible for you to repeat a colour, but to alter it slightly to retain interest without sacrificing unity and harmony. Strong contrasts may also be welcome in your decorating scheme. For example, red, blue and yellow can produce a striking and still harmonious effect, provided the tints or shades are compatible.

Here are some suggestions for you in planning colour schemes:

Think of the colour value and also of colour balance – that is, the position and quantity of the colours you are using. Concentrating dark colours on one side of the room and light colours on the other upsets the balance of a room and prevents you from achieving the harmony you seek.

Prints or florals in fabric, rug or wallpaper can add interest to the decorating scheme. However, do not mix two different figured or patterned fabrics; this creates a feeling of confusion. A wide variety of co-ordinated colours is available to you. It is also possible to buy fabric in the identical pattern or colour found in the wallpaper.

In decorating, the focal point of a room may be the window, a picture, chair or sofa. Plan your colour scheme round one dominant colour and use shades or tints of this colour in moderate amounts to give interest. Select a third colour for accent and contrast.

Repetition of a colour can be monotonous, but curtains and walls of the same colour or tone-on-tone are pleasing to the eye. White and gold produce a rich accent. Or, if you are using a print in the curtains repeat one of the colours in the sofa, another in a chair. Keep the texture and weave of the fabrics compatible.

Take into account the aspect of the room as well as the effect you wish to achieve. Some decorators advocate warm colours for north and east exposures and cool colours for south and west. Rooms that are distinctly feminine in character have pale, pastel tints and shades; those that are masculine tend towards deep, strong colours. Family rooms seem to require brighter colours. In planning colour schemes for them, however, consider the family's living habits as well as the style and purpose of the room.

When your decorating project is confined to a window, a bedspread or a chair or sofa covering, remember the colours and fabric textures already in the room.

Experiment with colour. Drape swatches of various colours together to see whether they complement one another. If you wish to use red, choose shades or tints that harmonise with the colours already selected.

Selecting Fabrics

Fabrics today are interesting and exciting. Study them carefully when you are planning your room, for the variety available is bound to influence your decorating decisions. You can choose from the traditional natural fibres, man-made fibres or a blend of natural and man-made fibres – each is offered in a variety of textures and weaves as well as colours.

The variation of weave may be the means of introducing pattern into the room. The weave may also determine where the fabric can be used – whether it will hang gracefully as curtains or be hardwearing as loose covers. (The tighter the weave, the more durable the fabric.) Both texture and weave should be suitable for the use you put it to, as well as giving a decorative effect. For more information on fabrics, see page 7.

In selecting a fabric, consider these facts about the room: its size and aspect; its purpose – whether formal or informal, whether for the entire family or only one of its members; its furniture – whether modern or traditional; and the effect you wish to achieve. Above all, make sure that the fabric is in keeping with family living as well as family likes and dislikes. Each style has its own place in good design.

For formal rooms, select antique satin, damask, brocade, brocatelle, faille, antique taffeta, furnishing satin, velvet, cut velvet or velveteen. These fabrics may be of silk or man-made fibres, or a blend of two fibres.

For informal rooms, the selection is much greater – chintz, polished cotton, antique satin, gingham, sailcloth, repp, denim, hand-blocked linen, linen cotton union, corduroy, poplin and many synthetic fabrics such as terylene, nylon and Acrilan.

Curtains. Net curtains are generally made of a soft, sheer fabric that softens and diffuses light without impeding it – for example, ninon, terylene, Tergal, sheer nylon, cotton, marquisette or loosely woven acrylics. Frilled tie-back curtains should be made of crisp organdie, lawn, voile, net, nylon, terylene, muslin, marquisette. Café curtains are made of gingham, velvet, muslin, chintz, polished cotton, voile, corduroy and nylon, to name just a few.

Curtains are constructed of medium-weight and heavy-weight fabrics, and the selection is unlimited. Some of the fabrics listed for net curtains are also suitable.

Loose covers should be made of a medium-weight or heavy-weight, closely woven fabric so that they will retain their shape.

Lining. Curtains are frequently lined. A sateen lining is available 122 cm (48 inches) wide. Generally, white, light beige or soft grey is used to blend with the neutral colour of the net curtain.

When you contemplate changing only the curtains, bedspread or loose covers, carefully consider the function and existing design of the room before you choose a fabric. Balance colour texture to maintain the character of the room.

If the entire room is to be redecorated, study it carefully before visiting the shop. Begin with your focal point of interest – a window, chair, sofa, picture or lamp. For example, if windows are the focal point, select fabrics for the curtains, then blend and harmonise all other fabrics with this selection. Drape the fabrics together while you are in the shop to make certain that the textures, weaves and colours are compatible. Then try the fabrics in the room where they will be used. If swatches large enough for this purpose cannot be borrowed, it is advisable to buy short lengths of the fabrics you are considering. In view of the ultimate cost of the fabric such a small expense is worthwhile.

Work out the quantity of fabric you need for each project before you go shopping. Take into consideration the width of the fabric as well as the length.

Last, but not least, consider how the fabric will be cleaned. Must it be dry-cleaned? Is it hand or machine washable? Will it shrink? Examine the labels for information on the fibre content and any special instructions on its care. Some fabrics are now chemically treated to resist soiling.

Thread, Needle, and Stitch Length

The selection of the thread depends on the fabric to be stitched. The thread should blend with the fabric in colour, fibre and size. Needle selection depends on both the thread and the fabric. The weight and texture of the fabric determine the stitch length.

Silk and wool fabrics are stitched with silk thread; cotton, linens and some blended fabrics, with mercerised cotton thread (however, fine linens may be stitched with silk thread). Synthetic fabrics and blends of natural and man-made fibres may be stitched with mercerised cotton or synthetic thread. Use a size 14 needle with mercerised cotton or synthetic thread, and a size 11 needle for finer threads such as nylon.

Organdie, voile, muslin, marquisette, batiste and similar fabrics used for sheer curtains should be stitched with mercerised cotton thread, size 14 needle, and 2 to 1·5 mm (12 to 15) stitch length, depending on their weight. Nylon, terylene and similar synthetic fabrics may be stitched with either nylon or polyester thread.

Damask, brocade, taffeta, satin and similar fabrics appropriate for curtains and bedspreads should be stitched with silk or mercerised cotton thread, size 14 needle and 2 mm (12) stitch length.

For lightweight or medium-weight fabrics like chintz, polished cotton, linen, percale, antique satin, corduroy and faille, use mercerised cotton thread, size 14 needle and 2 mm (12) stitch length. Heavy-weight fabric used in loose covers – linen, cotton damask, sailcloth, ticking, denim and the like – should be stitched with heavy-duty thread, size 16 needle and 2 mm (12) stitch length.

If your fabric is not listed, see page 24.

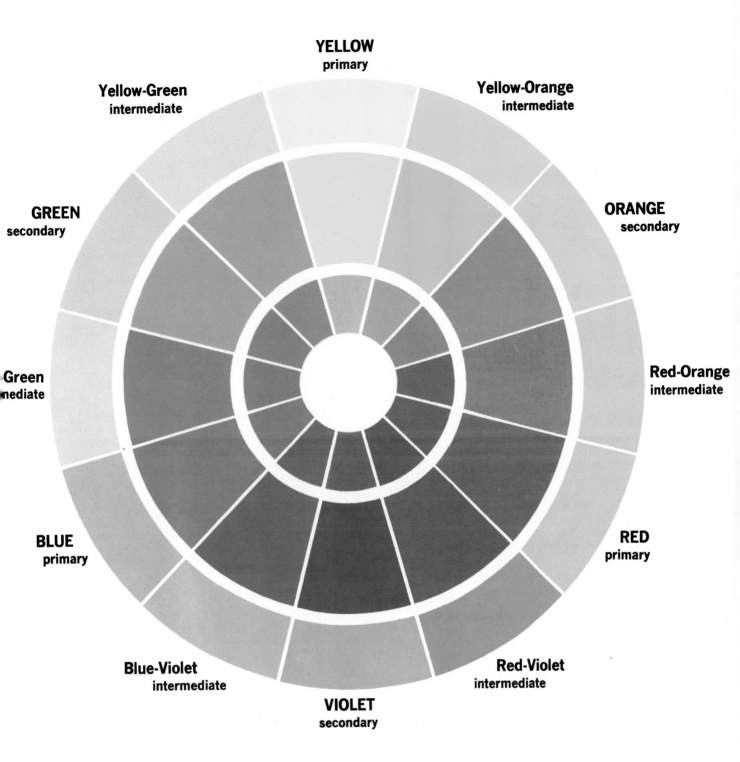

YELLOW
primary

Yellow-Orange
intermediate

Yellow-Green
intermediate

ORANGE
secondary

GREEN
secondary

Red-Orange
intermediate

Green
mediate

RED
primary

BLUE
primary

Blue-Violet
intermediate

Red-Violet
intermediate

VIOLET
secondary

Plate 21
COLOUR WHEEL

The twelve true colours shown in the centre (widest) ring,
can be varied to shades (inside ring) by adding black, or to
tints (outside ring) by adding white.
For an explanation of the colour system, see pages 338 and 339.

Plate 22
COLOUR IN FOCUS

Courtesy of George Strachan & Son Ltd. (furniture)

ABOVE: Colour is the key to success in this lilac room, the soft shiny surfaced fabrics giving a rich contrast to the other muted surfaces.

LEFT: Harmonised rose-toned prints of the blind, wallpaper and fabric are effectively used with ivory or white in this charming room. The blind featured here is from the Sunway Matchmate range designed to compliment the Sanderson Triad range of wallpapers and fabrics.

Courtesy of Sunway

A Look at Your Windows

Windows bring light and air into your home. When you look at them with a homemaker's eye, your first thoughts are to ensure privacy without obstructing the sunlight or the view if it is a pleasant one. When you look at them with a decorator's eye, your concern is to create a window treatment that is in harmony with the other furnishings of the room and still captures the light and the view. The window treatment you decide on depends mainly on your plans for the room. The style of the window may suggest or even dictate the treatment, but even that can be changed by the clever use of curtains or by simple carpentry tricks that alter inside window proportions.

There are many types of curtains you can choose from. Sheer net curtains which hang close to the window, heavier lined curtains to hang from a track, rod or pole, or café curtains which cover the lower half of a window only and usually have a decorative heading.

Changing Window Proportions

Window proportions can be changed to make them appear higher or wider or to create the illusion of an entire wall of windows.

To increase height. A window may be increased in height just a few inches or all the way to the ceiling by fixing the track at that point or by using a board.

The board should be as thick as the window frame, at least 10 to 15 cm (4 to 6 inches) wide, and cut to the same length as the window width. Use the recommended method to attach the board to the wall above the frame. Then paint or finish the board to match the finish on either the frame or the wall, whichever will look better. When dry, mount the fixtures on the extreme ends of the board, 2·5 cm (1 inch) below the top.

341

To increase width. Narrow windows can be widened to bring them into proportion to the size of the room and to admit as much light as possible. A longer track may be fitted to extend beyond the window, or boards may be used to extend the top portion of the frame on each side.

Cut the boards, one for each side, to the desired increase in width. Use the recommended method to attach the boards to the wall on each side. Then paint or finish the boards to match either the finish on the frame or the wall, whichever will look better. When dry, mount the fixtures on the extreme ends of the boards, 2·5 cm (1 inch) below the top.

To increase both height and width. Often, a better proportion can be obtained by increasing both the height and the width. Mount the fixture to the dimensions required on the wall or board, cut to the required dimensions, mounted above the window frame. Mount the fixtures at the extreme ends of the board, 2·5 cm (1 inch) below the top.

A pelmet board may also be used to change window proportions. Mount it above the track used to lengthen or widen the window. The pelmet covers the top of the curtains.

Two-way track with overlap

Poles, Rods, Tracks and Fixtures

The type of track, or rod and fixture you select depends on the style and weight of the curtains. The pole or track should be sturdy enough to prevent the curtains from sagging; it may be decorative or utilitarian. There is a track available for every window treatment, and you can generally find the kind you need in shops that specialise in curtains.

Some rods have a return at each end. 'Return' is the term used for the distance the rod projects from the wall. In the adjustable rod for sheer curtains, the return is the distance from the curve of the rod to the wall. In the straight track, it is the depth of the bracket. Always measure the return, for its depth may vary from 7·5 to 10 cm (3 to 4 inches) or more. Curtains and draperies extend round the returns.

The fixtures holding the track in place should be mounted, so that the curtains cover the entire window frame. Café curtains, however, may be recessed within the window frame and casement curtains are mounted on the window sash.

Since the measurements for your curtains are based on the position of the track or rod, this and the fixtures should be fastened in place before you take any window measurements. In this way you will be sure of measuring accurately to determine the length and width of your curtains and length of fabric required.

Installing Fixtures on a Wall

A moderate degree of skill with tools and some previous experience in mounting fixtures on walls are necessary to get a satisfactory result. If you do not have the skill or the experience, have the job done by a professional.

Fixing brackets with screws, and careful and detailed instructions for wall or ceiling fixing are usually supplied with the track or cornice pole.

Measuring Your Windows

This section explains how to measure different kinds of windows and how much to add for hems, headings, casings, seams and shrinkage tucks. In all cases, the amount you should allow depends on the style of the window treatment. You will need these measurements later to estimate the length of fabric and to cut and construct your curtains.

Sash Windows

The curtain and drapery treatment possible for sash windows is practically unlimited. Any of the styles described in the chapters that follow can be used. When two or three windows are grouped together, they are treated as a single unit.

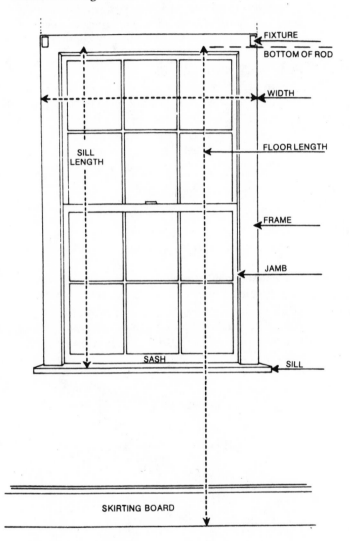

Living room and dining room curtains may be sill or floor length, depending on the style of the room and on whether there is a radiator below the window. Bedroom curtains and tie-backs may also be sill or floor length although here you will want to consider not only the effect desired but also the age and sex of the person occupying the room. Kitchen, bathroom and breakfast room curtains generally extend to the sill or just below.

To measure windows, use a steel tape or folding ruler if possible.

Length: Measure from the bottom of the rod to the sill or the floor. (The finished length should be about 1·2 cm

343

($\frac{1}{2}$ inch) above the floor. The turning of the hems will take up the fabric slightly.)

Width: Measure from edge to edge of the window frame. To this width, add the depth of the return on each side if this type of rod or track is used. (The measurement for the return will be used later for positioning the end pleat in the curtain heading.)

This gives you your basic window measurements. To them you must add the allowances given below. Café curtains are an exception. For them, see page 358.

FOR NET CURTAINS

Length: To the measured length of your window, add 5 cm (2 inches) for casing (if using a rod or stretch-wire) and 5 cm (2 inches) for heading, ·6 cm ($\frac{1}{4}$ inch) for turning, 5 cm (2 inches) for shrinkage tuck (2·5 cm per 91 cm (1 inch per yard)), and 8 cm ($3\frac{1}{4}$ inches) for lower hem and turning. If double lower hems are used, and they

are desirable for sheer fabrics, allow 15 cm (6 inches) for the lower hem instead of 8 cm ($3\frac{1}{4}$ inches).

Width: Multiply the measured width of your window by two-and-a-half or three for fullness. To this figure, add 20 cm (8 inches) for hems (2·5-cm (1-inch) double hem on each side of the two panels).

FOR CURTAINS

A pair of curtains is required for each window or group of windows. Use a two-way track or rod.

Length for lined curtains: To the measured length of your window add 2·5 cm (1 inch) if using a rod, and 5 cm (2 inches) for heading; add 10 cm (4 inches) for top hem and 9 cm ($3\frac{1}{2}$ inches) for lower hem and turning.

Length for unlined curtains: Add an extra 1·2 cm ($\frac{1}{2}$ inch) for turning on top hem.

Measure the width as instructed below for picture windows.

Picture Windows

Full length curtains are an attractive and practical treatment for picture windows. Use a two-way track or rod. Install the brackets for the track or rods on the extreme ends of the window frame, 2·5 cm (1 inch) below the top of the frame or ceiling. (Use a ceiling-mounted track if feasible.)

Length for lined curtains: Measure from the bottom of the track or rod to the floor. To this measurement, add the width of tape you propose to use, plus turning, and a lower hem (23 cm (9 inches) usually allows suffi-

cient for hems and headings and allows for average shrinkage). If using a rod allow 2·5 cm (1 inch) for rod, 5 cm (2 inches) for heading, 10 cm (4 inches) for top hem, 9 cm ($3\frac{1}{2}$ inches) for lower hem and turning.

Length for unlined curtains: Add an extra 1·2 cm ($\frac{1}{2}$ inch) for turning on the top hem. If double hems are used, and they are recommended for sheer fabrics, allow 20 cm (8 inches) for the top hem and 15 cm (6 inches) for the lower hem.

If curtains extend from the ceiling, measure from the ceiling to the floor and add only the amounts stated for top and bottom hems.

Width: Measure across the window from one end of the track or rod to the other. To this measurement, add the depth of the return on each side if included in the fitment, 25 cm (10 inches) for hems (5-cm (2-inch) hems and 1·2-cm ($\frac{1}{2}$-inch) seam allowance on each side of the two panels), 6 cm ($2\frac{1}{2}$ inches) for overlap, plus the amount required for pleats and seams within the curtain. See page 368.

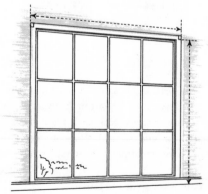

Sliding Windows or Doors

Sliding windows or doors should be treated as a single unit. Floor length curtains are an effective way to do this. Use either a two-way or one-way track or rod, depending on the position of the window. Mount the brackets for the track on the extreme ends of the window frame, 2·5 cm (1 inch) below the top of the frame or ceiling. Measure the length as instructed for the picture window and make the same allowances for top and lower hems.

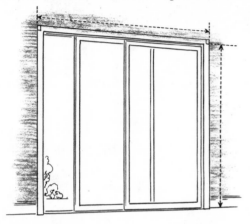

Two-way track with overlap

Corner Windows

Corner windows are treated as a single unit; however the curtains for each window should be an independent unit. Use two one-way tracks or rods (a one-way left and a one-way right) and position them so that you draw each side curtain *away from the corner* when opening it. The rods may meet at the corner, or one rod may be fully in the corner and the second rod almost against the first, as illustrated. If the second installation is used, allow enough room for the curtain on the first rod to pass by the end of the second rod.

If there is a wall space between two windows which

One-way track
(right)

One-way track
(left)

are near a corner, the windows may be treated separately or the wall and windows may be treated as a single unit as illustrated here. Install two one-way tracks or rods the same as for the corner windows above, but reverse the rods so that you draw each side curtain *towards the corner* when you open it. With this positioning of the rods, the curtains cover the wall space at the corner whether they are opened or closed. Install one bracket for the track or rod on the wall in the corner and the other bracket on the extreme end of the window frame.

Measure the length and width the same as instructed for picture windows on page 345; however, the length may be to the sill or the floor.

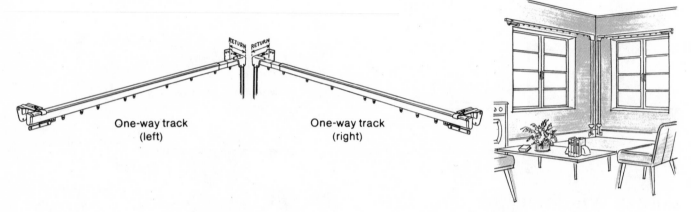

One-way track (left)   One-way track (right)

Casement Windows

If casement windows open inwards, sheer casement curtains must be mounted on the window sash so that they will swing in with the window. The curtains have a heading and casing at the top and bottom and require two stretch-wires or rods. They are stretched tightly over the glass.

With a rod use the elbow bracket. Place the brackets so that the curtain will cover the glass portion of the window.

Length: Measure from the bottom of the upper wire or rod to the top of the lower. To this measurement add, to top and bottom, 4 cm (1½ inches) for heading, 4 cm (1½ inches) for casing, 1·2 cm (½ inch) for turning, or 18 cm (7 inches) in all. Either shrink the fabric before cutting, or allow an additional 5 cm (2 inches) for a shrinkage tuck at the top.

Width: Measure across the window from one eye hook or bracket edge to the other. Allow for double or triple fullness. To this figure, add 5 cm (2 inches) for hems (1·2-cm (½-inch) double-fold hem on each side).

346

If the windows open outwards, the fixtures are mounted on the window frame so that the windows will swing free of the curtain. The curtains can be sill or floor length, depending on the style of the room and personal choice.

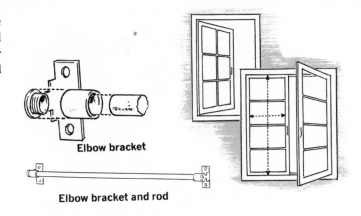

Elbow bracket

Elbow bracket and rod

Elbow bracket and rod

French Windows and Doors

French windows may swing either in or out. The window treatment is the same as for casement windows.

French doors open inwards. Use the casement curtain and follow the instructions for the casement window opening inwards.

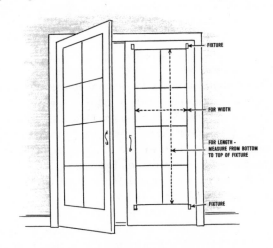

Projected Windows

Projected windows swing out and are generally placed high in a wall. A decorative two-way rod with rings is shown in the illustration. Make the curtains in two panels that meet in the centre of the window, and line them.

Install the brackets for the pole or rod on the wall, 2·5 to 5 cm (1 to 2 inches) above the window and beyond each side of the window.

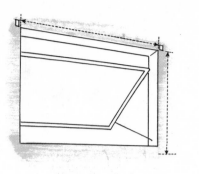

Length: Measure from the lower circle of the ring to about 5 cm (2 inches) below the window. To this measurement, add 13 cm (5 inches) for top and lower hems (5-cm (2-inch) hems and 1·2 cm (½ inch) for turning).
Width: Measure from the edge of one bracket to the other. Multiply this measurement by two for fullness. To this figure, add 25 cm (10 inches) for hems (5-cm (2-inch) hem and 1·2 cm (½ inch) for turning on each side of the two panels).

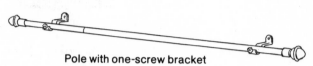

Pole with one-screw bracket

One-screw bracket

Awning Windows

Café curtains are a pleasant informal treatment for awning windows. In the illustration, café curtains are used and the tiers are uneven in length. They do not overlap and decorative rods and rings are visible above each tier. Two brass rods with matching curtain ring are required for this style of café.

Mount the brackets for the top rod on the wall, 2·5 to 5 cm (1 to 2 inches) above the window and a few inches beyond each side of the window. Mount the brackets for the second rod at the point where the top and second window sections meet; extend them the same distance beyond the window as the top brackets.

Length, top tier: Measure from the lower circle of the ring to the top of the second rod.
Lower tier: Measure from the lower circle of the ring to 5 cm (2 inches) below the window. To these measurements, add 13 cm (5 inches) to each tier for top and lower hems (5-cm (2-inch) hems plus 1·2 cm (½ inch) for turning).
Width: Follow the instruction for the projected window.

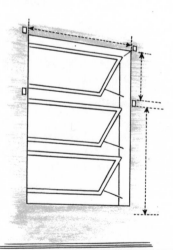

Two-screw bracket and pole

Two-screw bracket

Pivot and Hopper Windows
(opening inwards)

A two-way track or rod should be selected for these windows so that the curtains can easily be drawn to the sides when you open or close the window. Position the bracket and measure the same way as for a projected window.

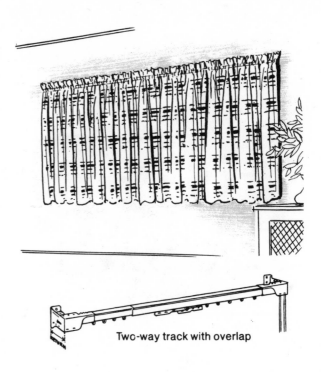

Two-way track with overlap

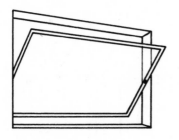

Bay or Bow Windows

A group of three or more windows placed at angles to each other and projecting outwards, forming a recess or alcove in the wall, is known as a 'bay window'. If the window or windows are curved, they are called a 'bow window'. Many pleasing treatments are possible; however, the bay or bow should always be treated as a single unit.

Curved track with overlap

Dormers

The dormer is a window in a gable rising from a sloping roof. Simple frilled tie-backs, full sheer net curtains hanging straight from a rod, or casement curtains, are all suitable.

Success with Curtains

Your success with net curtains depends on your accuracy in measuring your windows, in adding the allowances necessary for your curtain style, in estimating fabric requirements, in cutting your fabric and in sewing. This chapter will guide you through those steps for the basic curtain styles: straight-hanging net curtains, casement curtains, tie-back curtains, festoon and café curtains.

Net Curtains

Full, sheer curtains that hang straight from a track, stretch-wire or rod against the glass are usually called 'net' curtains. They often have a casing and heading at the top and are gathered on a stretch-wire or rod. Their purpose is to ensure privacy, to soften the interior and to diffuse light. They also create a uniform appearance from the outside. Net curtains are often used with floor length curtains. Both curtains should be the same length and hung on separate tracks or rods. If you use an *adjustable curtain track or rod*, secure the fixtures for the rod on the extreme ends of the window frame, 2·5 cm (1 inch) below the top.

Marquisette, ninon, voile (many with pattern borders and ready-worked decorative hems), acrylics, terylene, cotton and other gossamer or semi-sheer synthetics and blends are all appropriate fabrics for net curtains. Neutral colours are generally used – beige, white or grey; however, pastels and stronger colours are seen occasionally.

Adding Allowances to Measurements

Net curtains should hang in graceful, soft folds. To get the fullness necessary, you must allow from two-and-a-half to three times the width of the window. Ready-made curtains are often skimpy and two pairs may be required for the desired fullness. If your budget is limited, choose less expensive fabric but *do not skimp on fabric length*.

Length: If using one of the many types of curtain tapes available (pencil pleats, pinch pleats or gathered) the amount of fabric to allow for the heading will depend on

whether the tape is to be placed about 2·5 cm (1 inch) below the top in the case of gathered curtains, or whether the tape is to be fixed flush with the top of the curtain.

To the measured length of the window (see page 344), add 5 cm (2 inches) for heading, ·6 cm ($\frac{1}{4}$ inch) for turning, 5 cm (2 inches) for shrinkage tuck (2·5 cm per 91 cm (1 inch per yard)), plus 8 cm ($3\frac{1}{4}$ inches) for the hem and turning, and if a rod is used add 5 cm (2 inches) for casing. *Example*: 183 cm (72 inches) (measured length) plus 23 cm ($9\frac{1}{2}$ inches) = 206 cm ($81\frac{1}{2}$ inches). If double-fold hems are used, and they are desirable in sheer fabrics to eliminate the turned raw edge that would normally show through, allow 15 cm (6 inches) for the hem instead of 8 cm ($3\frac{1}{4}$ inches), 183 cm (72 inches) (measured length) plus 31 cm ($12\frac{1}{4}$ inches) = 214 cm ($84\frac{1}{4}$ inches).

Width: Multiply the measured width (page 344) by two-and-a-half or three for fullness. To this figure, add 20 cm (8 inches) for hems (2·5-cm (1-inch) double-fold hem on each side of the two panels). *Example*: 107 cm (42 inches) (measured width and returns) × $2\frac{1}{2}$ (fullness) = 263·5 cm (105 inches) plus 20 cm (8 inches) (hems) = 283·5 cm (113 inches). Each of the two panels is 141·7 cm ($56\frac{1}{2}$ inches) wide.

Estimating Fabric Requirements

To estimate fabric length for each window, you must consider the fabric width. *Example*: Three lengths of 101·5-cm (40-inch) fabric are required for the 283·5-cm (113-inch) width in the example above. (Remember, lengths cannot be pieced. If your figures result in a fraction of a length, such as 2½, buy 3 full lengths.) 214 cm (84¼ inches) (length required for curtain with double lower hem) × 3 (lengths of fabric) = 642 cm (252¾ inches) or 6·42 m (just over 7 yards) for *each* window. It is advisable to buy an extra 23 cm (9 inches) to allow for straightening the ends of the fabric, so you will need 6·65 m (7¼ yards) for each window.

Cutting the Curtains

Curtains must be cut on the true lengthwise and crosswise grains of the fabric so that they hang in straight, smooth lines.

Straighten the end of the fabric by drawing a single thread on the crosswise grain to indicate the cutting line. See page 14. Press the fabric and remove selvedges.

Work on a flat surface and use a tape measure to measure the lengths for your curtain. Draw a thread on the crosswise grain to mark the cutting line of each length. Cut, do not tear, the fabric. Straighten the fabric grain, following the instructions on page 14.

Constructing the Curtains

SEAMS
If it is necessary to seam the fabric to gain the width you need, use a fine French seam. See page 86.

SUGGESTIONS FOR FOLDING AND PRESSING HEMS
For convenience in folding and pressing hems and casings of your curtains, work on the ironing board. Reverse the direction of the board and place the iron on the narrow end so that you have a wider working area. If the height of the board is adjustable, lower it so that you can work in a sitting position. Use a small gauge to measure each turn of the fabric; accuracy is extremely important. As you make each fold for the hem, pin straight through the fabric into the ironing board. Place the pins far enough from the fold so that they do not interfere with your pressing.

SIDE HEMS
Finish the side hems first. Use a 2·5-cm (1-inch) double-fold hem on the side and centre hems; then the panels will be interchangeable. (A 5-cm (2-inch) hem may be used if you prefer, but make the extra allowance when cutting the curtains.)

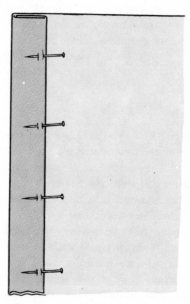

Turn 2·5 cm (1 inch) to the underside and pin along the cut edge. Press the fold. Then make a second 2·5-cm (1-inch) turn and pin in place. Press the fold. Stitch as close to the first fold as possible. Back-stitch at each end. Press.

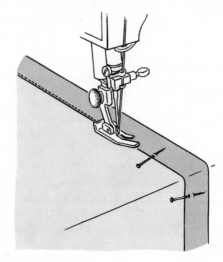

HEADING AND CASING

If using curtain tapes, tack a 2·5-cm (1-inch) hem at the top, prepare the tape cords at each end and then tack to the curtain. Stitch.

In the measurements, 11 cm (4¼ inches) were allowed for heading, turning and casing. At the top edge, turn ·6 cm (¼ inch) to the underside and finger-press. Turn 5 cm (2 inches) to the underside and pin the free edge in place. Press along the top fold. Stitch close to the first fold. Back-stitch at each end. Press.

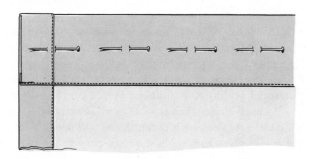

Divide the hem for the casing and heading by placing a row of pins midway between the stitching and top edge. Stitch along this line. Back-stitch at each end. Press.

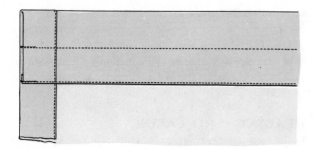

SHRINKAGE TUCK

On the right (or wrong side, if you prefer), barely below the casing, fold and pin in a 2·5-cm (1-inch) tuck. Press. Stitch close to the previous line of stitching, using a long stitch. Back-stitch at each end. If the curtain shrinks when laundered, let out the tuck the required length.

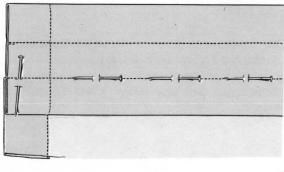

Note: if your machine is one with Chain Stitch Accessories, chain-stitch the shrinkage tuck. Then you can easily let out the tuck when necessary – merely unlock the last loop of the chain and pull out the stitching. Refer to the instruction book accompanying the machine, and to page 63.

LOWER HEM

Compare the panels to make sure that they are the same length. Place them wrong sides together, and check the length at the centre and outside hems.

In the measurements, 15 cm (6 inches) were allowed for a 7·5-cm (3-inch) double-fold hem. Turn under 7·5 cm (3 inches) and pin along the fold. Make a second 7·5-cm (3-inch) turn and pin the first fold to the curtain.

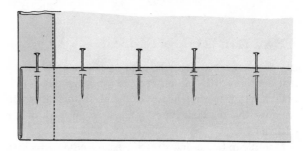

Before pressing and stitching the hem, hang the curtain on the track or rod. Adjust the fullness and check the length; the curtain should be about 1·2 cm (½ inch) above the floor. If your measurements were accurate, the length should be correct; however, if there is a slight difference in length, adjust the hem width accordingly.

Press the hem, then stitch it in place close to the fold. Back-stitch at each end. Press.

WEIGHTS

Weight the hems so that the curtains will hang evenly. Use the lightest weighted tape made of polyester fibre. Slot the weighted tape through the hem behind the double turn and secure it only at each side hem. Remove the weights when laundering the curtains by machine, it is not necessary to remove the weighted tape for hand washing.

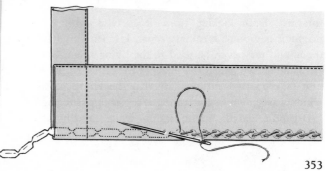

353

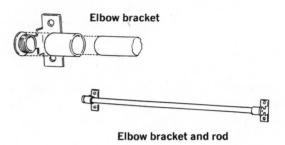

Elbow bracket

Elbow bracket and rod

Casement Curtains

Casement curtains should be used on casement windows that open inwards and on French windows and doors. They are tightly stretched over the glass portion of the window. Use the same types of fabrics suggested for net curtains.

Mount cup hooks and stretch wires or elbow brackets and rods, then measure the window as instructed on page 346.

Adding Allowance to Measurements

Length: To the measured length (bottom of upper rod to top of lower rod), add to top and bottom, 4 cm (1½ inches) for heading 4 cm (1½ inches) for casing and 1·2 cm (½ inch) for turning. *Example*: 173 cm (68 inches) (measured length) plus 18 cm (7 inches) = 191 cm (75 inches). Either shrink the fabric before cutting, or allow an additional 5 cm (2 inches) for a shrinkage tuck at the top.

Width: Measure from hook to hook or bracket to bracket. Allow for double or triple fullness. To this figure, add 5 cm (2 inches) for hems (1·2-cm (½-inch) double hem on each side). *Example*: 66 cm (26 inches) (measured width) × 2 (fullness) = 132 cm (52 inches) plus 5 cm (2 inches) (hems) = 137 cm (54 inches).

To estimate the length of fabric you will need, follow the guides given under *Net Curtains*, page 352.

Cutting and Constructing the Curtains

Straighten and cut the fabric as instructed on page 352.

SIDE HEMS
Fold and press a 1·2-cm (½-inch) double-fold hem on each side, following the instructions for net curtains on page 352.

HEADING AND CASING
In the measurements, 18 cm (7 inches) (9 cm (3½ inches) for each end) were allowed for heading, casing and turning. Turn under 1·2 cm (½ inch) at each end and press; then turn 4 cm (1½ inches) to the underside and press. Pin and stitch the casing and heading as instructed for net curtains. See page 353.

Tie-back Curtains

Informal, fresh looking tie-back curtains with frills brighten bedroom, breakfast room, kitchen and bathroom, and may even be used in the living room. They are made in two panels that meet in the centre or, in the case of crisscross curtains, overlap the width of the window as shown in illustration at top of opposite page.

Organdie, lawn, ninon, nylon, voile, muslin and similar fabrics are appropriate.

For crisscross curtains, use the adjustable crisscross or double rod. For tie-back panels that meet in the centre, use an overlap. Mount the fixtures for the rod on the extreme ends of the window frame, 2·5 cm (1 inch) below the top.

Adding Allowances to Measurements

Measure from the bottom of the rod to the floor. See page 343. (Remember to consider the width of the finished frill in the measurement and when cutting the curtains.) To this measurement, add 5 cm (2 inches) for casing, 5 cm (2 inches) for heading and ·6 cm ($\frac{1}{4}$ inch) for turning.

Allow two-and-a-half to three times the width of the window for fullness. If you are making crisscross curtains, double this figure since each gathered panel covers the entire window.

The width of the frill may be from 10 to 20 cm (4 to 8 inches), depending on the texture of the fabric. Double or triple fullness may be required, depending on the width of the frill and the texture and weight of the fabric. Sheer fabrics require triple fullness; muslin may require only double fullness.

To estimate the length of fabric you will need, follow the guides given under *Net Curtains*, page 352. Remember to include the amount for the frills.

Cutting the Curtains

Straighten and cut the fabric lengths as instructed on page 352. Usually, fabric for gathering is cut on the crosswise grain. For curtains, however, cut the fabric on the lengthwise grain since you will need a long length. Frills cut on the lengthwise grain require fewer seam joinings than those cut on the crosswise grain and will remain bouncy much longer when exposed to atmospheric conditions. It is always wise to cut and gather up more than your estimated requirement. If you are planning to make frilled tie-backs, allow sufficient length for each pair.

Constructing the Curtains

SEAMS

Use a fine French seam if it is necessary to seam the fabric to gain the required width. See page 86. Join strips for the frills with a hemmed seam, using the Hemmer Foot.

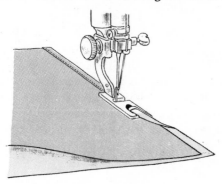

MAKING THE FRILL

Finish the edges of the frill with a narrow hem, using the Hemmer Foot. Hem each edge if there is a heading on the frill. One of the decorative zig-zag patterns may be used in the hemming.

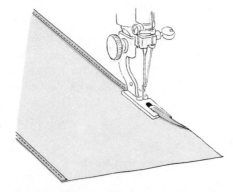

If crisp organdie or lawn is used, finish the edges with a decorative zig-zag stitch rather than a hem. See *Edge-stitched Finish*, page 274.

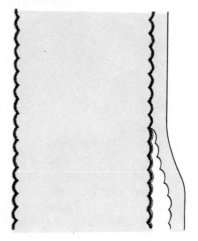

Use the Ruffler to gather the fabric. Always adjust the setting of the Ruffler and test the fullness of the frill on a piece of your fabric. To stitch organdie or chintz, dampen the fabric along the seamline with a small, moist sponge, and gather the fabric while it is still damp. Press when finished.

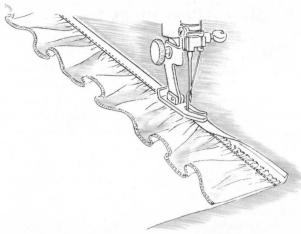

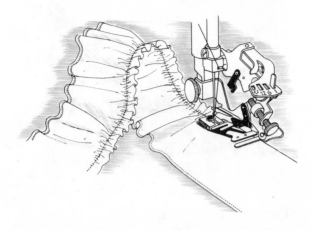

JOINING FRILL TO CURTAIN

Frill with heading. First finish the centre and lower edges of the curtain with a narrow hem. Use the Hemmer Foot or turn a ·3-cm (⅛-inch) double hem to the underside and stitch. Press. Pin the frill right side up, over the right side of the hemmed edge. Ease in extra fullness at the corners, beginning and ending about 2·5 cm (1 inch) from each side of the intersecting edge. Pin at close intervals. Stitch on the gathering stitches, with the frill side up.

the stitching line, enclosing the raw edge; pin it in place. Stitch near the first fold. Press. Turn the frill away from the curtain and press the seam towards the curtain.

SIDE HEM

Finish the hem on the outer edge of the curtain and frill with a 1·2-cm (½-inch) double-fold hem. To do this, turn the cut edge under 1·2 cm (½ inch) and press. Make a second 1·2-cm (½-inch) turn for the hem, and press. Pin the hem in place, then stitch. Back-stitch at each end. Press.

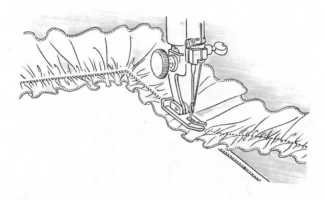

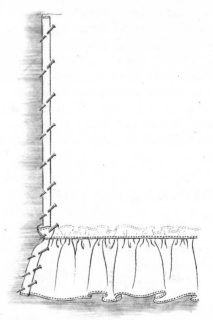

Frill without heading. Pin the frill to the curtain, right sides together, extending the curtain edge 1·2 cm (½ inch) beyond the gathering stitches. Ease in extra fullness at the corners. Stitch with the frill side up. Trim the seam allowance on the frill to ·6 cm (¼ inch). Fold the curtain edge under ·3 cm (⅛ inch), then fold it over the seam to

HEADING AND CASING

If using curtain tapes on a track follow instructions for net curtains (page 353). If using a rod, turn, press and stitch the heading and casing now, following the instructions for net curtains on page 353. In each case extend the hem through the frill, making sure that you keep it straight with the grain line of the frill.

Plate 23
COLOUR BRINGS THE OUTDOORS IN

ABOVE: Brilliant floral linen
loose covers reflect the garden
atmosphere of the patio. For
privacy and convenience,
Roman shades, taped in red to
echo the red-beamed ceiling,
solve the curtain problem for
the patio doors.

*From The American Home
© 1964, The Curtis Publishing
Company*

ROMANTIC DINING CORNER

LEFT: Scalloped pelmet lends
an air of formality to flowered
cotton-satin curtains in print
to match wallpaper. Pink ball
fringe with tiny green tassels
adds finishing touches to
curtains, pelmet and tie-backs.

Courtesy of McCall's magazine

Plate 24
LOOSE COVERS CAN RE-MAKE A ROOM

ABOVE: Spirited red-white-and-blue printed
linen carries out the Early American theme
of this room while contributing a
contemporary glow. Loose covers made
without skirt show off the clean lines of the
wing chair and sofa.

Courtesy of Good Housekeeping magazine

LEFT: The cheerful chintz chosen here for
loose covers and curtains is a lively addition
to this simple, restful room. The sofa is
covered in a fabric of similar colour to the
wall to blend into the background, yet add
some textural interest of its own.

Courtesy of Good Housekeeping magazine

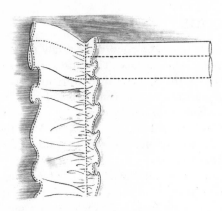

VALANCE

Finish the ends of the gathered valance with narrow hems to match those on the frills. Pin and stitch to the curtain over the top line of stitching that forms the heading.

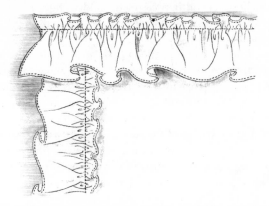

CASING AND CORD FOR DRAPING

To ensure an even drape in the curtains, you may use a cord with a casing on the underside of each panel.

Hang the curtains, then drape each side back, using a tape measure as a tie-back. (At the same time, take the measurement for the length of the tie-backs.) Pin-mark each side of the curtain for the diagonal line of the drape.

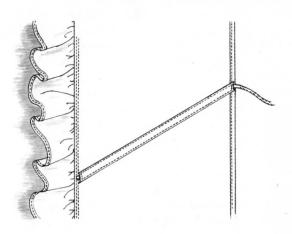

To make the casing. Cut a strip of the curtain fabric on the lengthwise grain the length of the diagonal line plus 1·2 cm (½ inch) for turning, and 2·5 cm (1 inch) wide. Fold under all edges ·6 cm (¼ inch) and press. On the wrong side of the curtain, pin the strip on the diagonal line, from the frill to the outer edge. Stitch on each side of the strip to form a casing. Do not catch the frill heading in your stitching. Back-stitch at each end. Press.

To add the cord. Slot a small cable cord (size 2) through the casing. Knot the end of the cord at the centre edge of the curtain. Then stitch across the end of the cord and casing two or three times; do not catch the gathered heading in the stitching. Tie the threads on the underside. Cut the opposite end of the cord to within ·6 cm (¼ inch) of the curtain; then wind thread round the cord to stop it unravelling.

Hang the curtains. Draw the cord to gather the curtain the required amount. Tie a loop in the end of the cord so that the gathers may be released when the curtain is laundered. The tie-back covers the casing.

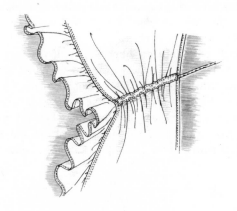

TIE-BACKS

A pair of tie-backs is used to hold the draped curtain in place. The position of the tie-back depends on fashion as well as personal choice. Generally, however, it is at the centre sash or below it.

The length of the tie-back depends on the amount of fullness in the curtain. For an average-sized window, the tie-backs are about 50 cm (20 inches) long; for a wide window, they may be 91 cm (36 inches) long. To determine the length necessary, hang the curtains, bring a tape measure round each curtain, and secure it with a drawing pin in the edge of the window frame. Drape the curtain, and adjust the tape measure for the length desired. Make one pair of tie-backs for each window.

Tie-back with one frill. Cut the band for the tie-back on the lengthwise grain the required length plus 1·2 cm (½ inch) for seam allowances, and 6 cm (2½ inches) wide. Crease the band through the centre, wrong sides together. Cut the frill the same width as the curtain frill and the same length as the band. Finish each end with a ·3-cm (⅛-inch) hem. Pin the wrong side of the frill to the

right side of the band, extending the ends of the band ·6 cm (¼ inch) beyond the frill. Stitch in place and back-stitch at each end. Press the seam allowances towards the band. Turn under ·6 cm (¼ inch) on the free side of the band and press. Turn the band, right sides together, and stitch across each end, taking a ·6-cm (¼-inch) seam. Cut diagonally across the corners. Turn the band to the right side and pin the folded edge in place at the stitching line, enclosing the seam allowance inside the band. Top-stitch close to the edge. Press.

Sew a small ring near each end of the tie-back. Place a hook in the side edge of the window frame at the position for the tie-back.

Tie-back with frill on both edges. If the frill is no more than 7·5 cm (3 inches) wide and the fabric is crisp, you can stitch a frill on each side of the band. Cut two bands on the lengthwise grain the required length plus 1·2 cm (½ inch) for seam allowance, and 4 cm (1½ inches) wide. Cut two frills the length of the band and finish each end with a ·3-cm (⅛-inch) hem. Lay the bands right

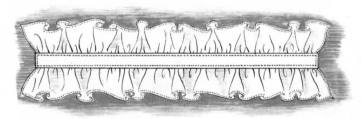

sides together, and pin one frill between the two strips, extending the ends of the band ·6 cm (¼ inch) beyond the frill at each end. Turn the ends of the band to the wrong side ·6 cm (¼ inch) and press. Stitch, backstitching at each end. Pin the second frill to the opposite edge of one band section, right sides together. The right sides of both frills should face in the same direction. Stitch. Press the seam allowances towards the band. Turn the free edge of the band under ·6 cm (¼ inch) and pin it in place at the stitching line, enclosing the seam allowances. Stitch round the band from the top side.

358

Festoons

Festoons are fascinating and surprisingly easy to make with terylene curtain tape. They are very practical to launder too, as the tape drip-dries with the curtain. Your curtain material should measure two-and-a-half to three times the *depth* of the window (measuring from the track or wire) and one-and-a-half times the *width* of the track or wire. Be sure to select the correct width of fabric for the width of window.

Hem each side but leave top and lower edges unfinished until later. Measure the total width of your fabric and decide how wide each festoon must be – e.g. if your material is 182 cm (72 inches) wide, leaving 2·5 cm (1 inch) at either side you could get seven festoons each 25 cm (10 inches) wide. You will therefore need sufficient tape for eight times the depth of each curtain. Ensure that any joining seams will be hidden under the vertical tape. Fold the fabric vertically accordion-wise to the festoon width, pressing the folded edges as you go. When unfolded the fabric will be marked evenly in vertical panels.

Sew lengths of tape along each of these vertical fold lines from top to bottom, including one along each side hem, 2·5 cm (1 inch) from the edge. Secure the draw-cords by knotting ends at the bottom. Turn up and finish lower hem, enclosing the knotted ends in the hem. Finish the top edge of the curtain with a double hem and terylene tape. Now pleat each length of vertical tape by drawing up cords until the curtain is the depth you require.

Café Curtains

Café curtains are never full-length. They may start at the centre of the window or midway down on the upper half of the window, or they may be made in tiers that start from the top of the window. The tiers may be even or uneven in length. The bottom tier can be sill or floor length. Each tier must hang on a separate rod.

Café curtains are generally made in two panels. If the curtains begin at the centre or upper half of the window, they are often used with a one-piece valance. (*Illustrated on left at top of opposite page*.) The heading may be styled in several ways. Café curtains may also be used in combination with other curtains.

Select such fabrics as chintz, sailcloth, linen, gingham, glazed cotton, organdie, muslin, nylon, corduroy and polished cotton. Plain colours, prints or stripes may be chosen for informal curtains, and antique satin, brocade, wild silk or taffeta for formal treatments.

Café curtains are not usually lined. They should be lined, however, when expensive fabric is chosen. The lining prevents the fabric from fading and ensures privacy. It also gives the windows a uniform appearance from the outside.

Poles, Rods and Fixtures

Before taking measurements and purchasing fabric, you must decide what style and heading you are going to use for the curtains and what type of pole, rod, fixture and hooks you will need. Several types are illustrated. Also shown are split rings; they are ideal for hanging the curtains because they can be removed quickly when laundering is necessary.

If the café curtains are to be pleated to control the

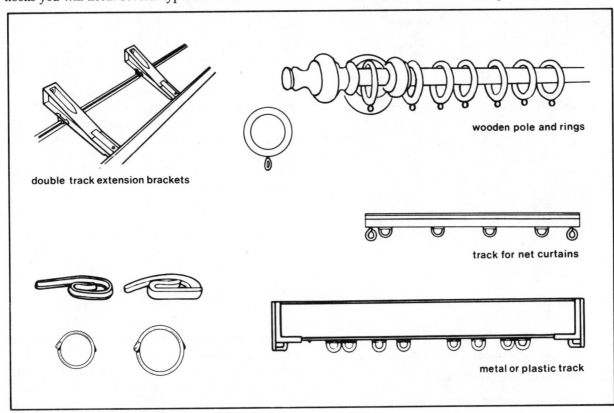

double track extension brackets

wooden pole and rings

track for net curtains

metal or plastic track

359

fullness, they are made the same way as curtains and require both rings and hooks.

Always place your rod (or rods) level with any horizontal strips between the glass panes or even with the centre sash of the window.

Secure the brackets and rods before taking measurements. If you have chosen a valance for the top of your café curtains, mount the brackets for the first rod on the extreme ends of the window frame as close to the top as possible. (If you have recessed windows, see page 364.)
One-tier. Place the brackets for the rod on the extreme ends of the window frame and at the centre of the window (C in the illustration) or midway down on the upper half of the window (B).
Two-tier. Place the brackets for the first rod on the extreme ends of the window frame as close to the top as possible. Position the rod for the second tier halfway between the first rod and sill (A in the illustration).
Three-tier. Measure from the top of the first rod to the sill. Divide the measurement by three. Position the second and third rods at one-third intervals as shown in D.

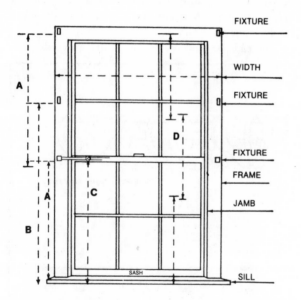

A. **Two-tier curtain–**
   To sill

B. **One-tier–**
   Midway upper half of window to sill

C. **Centre of window–To sill**

D. **Three-tier curtain–To sill**

Adding Allowances to Measurements

You must measure your windows and add allowances for hems, seams and fullness. Make a note of your measurement and the allowances added and use them when you calculate the length of fabric required and when you cut and make your curtains.

MEASURE EACH TIER OF THE CAFÉ CURTAIN AS FOLLOWS:

Length: Measure from the lower circle of the ring to the top of the next rod. To this measurement, add 13 cm (5 inches) for top and lower hems (5-cm (2-inch) hems, plus 1·2 cm ($\frac{1}{2}$ inch) for turning). *Example:* 76 cm (30 inches) (measured length) plus 13 cm (5 inches) (hems) = 90 cm (35 inches).
Width: Measure from the inside edge of one bracket to the other. Multiply this measurement by two for fullness. To this figure, add 25 cm (10 inches) for hems (5-cm (2-inch) hem and 1·2 cm ($\frac{1}{2}$ inch) for turning on each side of the two panels). *Example:* 91 cm (36 inches) (measured width) × 2 (fullness) = 182 cm (72 inches) plus 26 cm (10 inches) (for hems) = 208 cm (82 inches). Each of the two panels is 104 cm (41 inches) wide.
The valance is one piece and the finished length may vary from 15 to 45 cm (6 to 18 inches).
Measure as follows:
Length: Decide on the length you wish. To this measurement add 13 cm (5 inches) for top and lower hems (the same as for the tiers). *Example:* 30 cm (12 inches) (length of valance) plus 13 cm (5 inches) (hems) = 43 cm (17 inches).
Width: Measure from one edge of the bracket to the other. Multiply this measurement by two for fullness. To this figure add 13 cm (5 inches) for hems (5-cm (2-inch) hem and 1·2 ($\frac{1}{2}$ inch) for turning on each side of the valance). *Example:* 91 cm (36 inches) (measured width) × 2 (fullness) = 182 cm (72 inches) plus 13 cm (5 inches) (hems) = 195 cm (77 inches).

Estimating Fabric Length

The examples above are for a one-tier café curtain. If your curtains will have more than one tier, multiply your measurements by the number of tiers in each curtain you are making. Then estimate length of fabric following the directions given under *Net Curtains*, page 352.

Simple Café Curtains

Straighten and cut the fabric as instructed on page 352.

SIDE HEMS

Turn the edge under 1·2 cm (½ inch) and press. Turn under a 5-cm (2-inch) hem and press. Pin the hem in place. You may slip-stitch the hem by hand or machine-stitch it, using either straight stitching or blindstitching. If hems are blindstitched, tack them in place, ·6 cm (¼ inch) from the edge. With the wrong side of the curtain

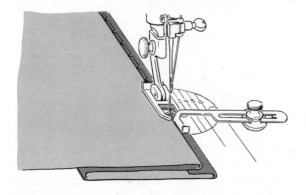

up, turn the hem under on the tacking line, forming a soft fold and exposing the ·6-cm (¼-inch) hem edge. Select the blindstitch zig-zag, a medium stitch width, and 2 to 1·5 mm (12 to 15) stitch length. Stitch so that the straight stitches are in the hem edge and the sidewards stitches pierce only a few threads of the soft fold. Press.

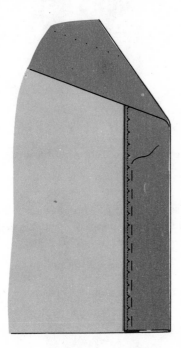

TOP AND LOWER HEMS

Turn the edge under 1·2 cm (½ inch) and press. Turn under a 5-cm (2-inch) hem and press. Pin the hem in place and mitre the corners. Finish the same way as the

side hems. If you machine-stitch the hem, begin and end the stitching at the side hems using either straight stitching or blindstitching. Mitre the corners and slip-stitch them in place. Press.

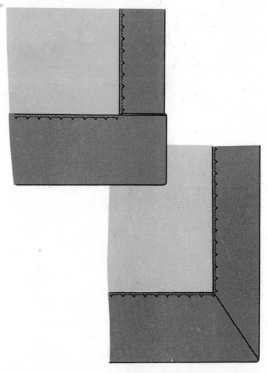

Stitch rings to the top ends of each panel, then place additional rings between them at 10- or 13-cm (4- or 5-inch) intervals. Slip the rod through the rings and hang the curtains.

Café Curtains with Decorative Trimming

Bands of decorative zig-zag stitching glamorise the café curtains illustrated here. The bands extend above the finished heading, forming loops which slip over the rod.

Turn, press and stitch the hems along the sides and top, following the instructions given. Cut 10 bands (5 for each panel) the length of the curtain plus 6 cm (2½ inches) for loops, and about 7·5 cm (3 inches) wide. Refer to *Border Designs*, page 272, for instructions on decorative stitching. When the stitching is completed, turn under each edge of the bands close to the stitching and press.

Pin the bands to the right side of the curtain, extending the ends 6 cm (2½ inches) above the top hem, following this sequence: place the first band 2·5 cm (1 inch) from the outside edge; place the second band in the same position on the opposite edge; place the third band in the centre band and the outside band. Space all bands an equal distance apart.

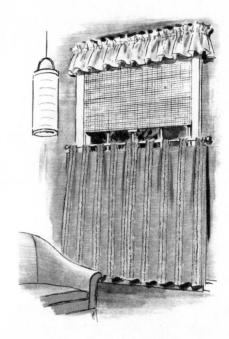

Stitch close to the folds, carrying the stitching to the end of each band.

To form the loops, fold under ·6 cm (¼ inch) at the top of each band extension and hand-sew it to the curtain, ·6 cm (¼ inch) below the finished edge.

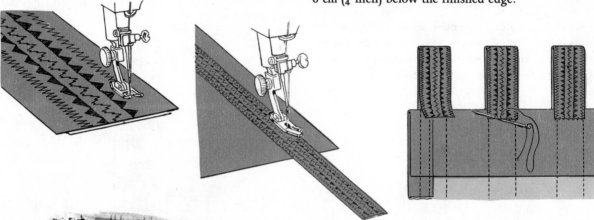

Finish the lower hem, following the instructions, on page 361.

Frills are also an attractive addition to café curtains. For a decorative touch, finish the frills with zig-zag stitching. See *Edge-stitched Finish*, page 274.

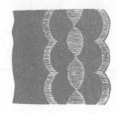

Café Curtains with Scalloped Heading and Pleats

The curtains in the illustration have alternate scallops and pleats in the heading. Select and fix a decorative café rod and bracket with a return.

Length: Measure the length of the tier as instructed on page 360; but allow 11 cm (4½ inches) instead of 6 cm (2½ inches) for the top hem and turning.

Width: Measure from the outside edge of one bracket to the other. Divide this measurement by two to determine the space each panel will cover. If the measurement is 91 cm (36 inches) then 45·5 cm (18 inches) of the window will be covered by one panel. This width allows space for four scallops 10 cm (4 inches) wide, beginning 5 cm (2 inches) from the inside edge.

ADDING ALLOWANCES TO MEASUREMENTS

For fullness, allow 12 cm (4¾ inches) for each pleat. Each panel in the illustration has five pleats. Place the first end pleat 5 cm (2 inches) from the inside edge and the second end pleat at the return, which is usually about 7·5 cm (3 inches) from the outside edge; then place three pleats between the four scallops. Five (pleats) × 12 cm (4¾ inches) (for each pleat) = 60·5 cm (23¾ inches) (required for pleats).

To one-half the measured width, add depth of return, 13 cm (5 inches) for hems (5-cm (2-inch) hem and 1·2 cm (½ inch) for turning on each side), plus the fullness required for pleats. *Example*: 45·5 cm (18 inches) (one-half window width) plus 7·5 cm (3 inches) (for return) plus 13 cm (5 inches) (for hems) plus 60·5 cm (23¾ inches) (for 5 pleats) = 126 cm (49¾ inches). This is the width of one panel; you will need two panels for the window.

CUTTING AND CONSTRUCTING THE CURTAINS

Straighten the ends of the fabric and cut the length for the curtains as instructed on page 352.

Turn under the top edge of the curtains 1·2 cm (½ inch), and stitch close to the fold. Turn and press the side hems, following the instructions on page 361.

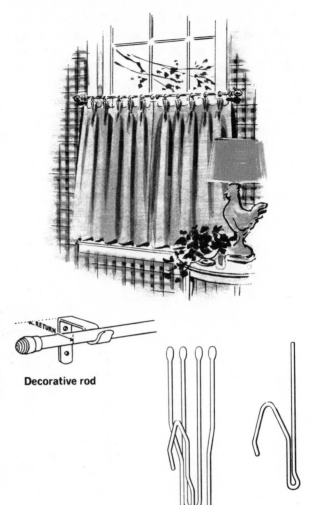

Decorative rod

High pleat hooks

Cut 10-cm (4-inch) Vilene 237 the length of the panel width. Mark the Vilene for the position of the return, pleats and scallops, beginning 5 cm (2 inches) from the inside edge as illustrated. Draw an outline for the scallops. See the example for pleats under *Adding Allowance to Measurements* above. Mark one strip of Vilene for the right panel and one for the left. Place the Vilene on the underside of the fabric, 10·5 cm (4⅛ inches) from the top edge and pin it in place.

Turn the top hem to the right side 10 cm (4 inches),

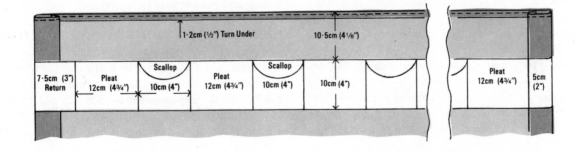

and pin. The fabric fold should be barely above the straight edge of the interfacing. Stitch the scallops, using a shorter stitch than that used in stitching the fabric. Back-stitch at each end. Cut away the Vilene close to the stitching. Cut out the scallops ·6 cm (¼ inch) from the stitching. Slash the seam allowances at evenly spaced intervals for a smooth turning. Press. Slip the top hem to the underside, over the Vilene and turn the scallops smoothly on the stitching line; press.

Finish the side hems and the lower hem by hand. Pin-mark the position for the pleats, allowing the same fullness and spacing as in your planning above. See *Adding Allowances to Measurements*, page 363. Make French pleats, following the instructions on page 380. Fix or sew a curtain hook to the back of each pleat and at each end of the curtain. Fasten the hooks in the curtain rings of the rod.

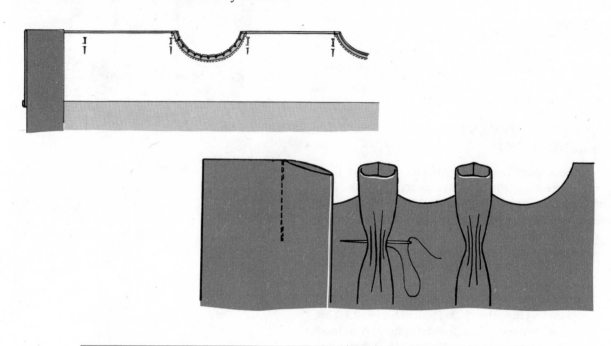

Café Curtains for Recessed Windows

Curtains for a recessed window may hang flush with the wall. The illustration here shows where the rods are placed for a three-tier café in which the tiers overlap.

ROD AND FIXTURES

Select a spring-tension socket and round rigid rod, which must be cut to measurement. (In having this done, remember to allow for the spring in the socket.) A rod is required for each tier and is recessed between the sides of the window.

Measure the length inside the window recess. Divide the measurement by three. Position the first rod in the recess close to the top; the middle rod at the one-third line; and the bottom rod at the two-thirds line. *Example*: If the window is 153 cm (60 inches) long, place the first rod at the top, the middle rod 51 cm (20 inches) from the top, and the bottom rod 51 cm (20 inches) above the sill.

ADDING ALLOWANCES TO MEASUREMENTS

In a three-tier café with overlapping tiers, the visible lengths of all tiers should be the same. To achieve that, you must allow an extra 5 or 8 cm (2 or 3 inches) on the middle and bottom tiers for an overlap.

MEASURE THE WINDOW AS FOLLOWS:

Length: Measure the top and middle tiers from the lower circle of the ring to the bottom of the next rod, and the bottom tier from the lower circle of the ring to the sill. To the measurement of each tier add 13 cm (5 inches) for top and lower hems (5-cm (2-inch) hems plus 1·2 cm (½ inch) for turning), and to the middle and

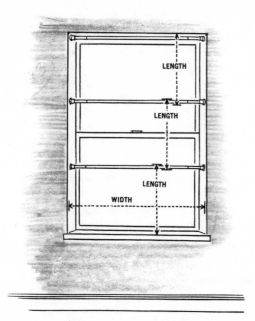

bottom tiers, add an extra 5 cm (2 inches) for overlap. *Example*: Top tier, 51 cm (20 inches) (measured length) plus 13 cm (5 inches) (hems) = 64 cm (25 inches). Middle and bottom tiers, each 51 cm (20 inches) (measured length) plus 13 cm (5 inches) (hems) plus 5 cm (2 inches) (overlap) = 69 cm (27 inches).

Width: Measure the width inside the window recess.

Multiply the measured width by two for fullness. To this figure add 25 cm (10 inches) for hems (5-cm (2-inch) hem and 1·2 cm ($\frac{1}{2}$ inch) for turning on each side of the two panels). *Example*: 89 cm (35 inches) (measured width) × 2 (for fullness) = 178 cm (70 inches) plus 25·5 cm (10 inches) (for hems) = 203·5 cm (80 inches). Each of the two panels is 101·5 cm (40 inches) wide.

Make a note of your measurements and the allowances added. Use them when you work out the fabric required and when you cut and make your café curtains.

CONSTRUCTING THE CURTAINS
Construct the curtains, following the instructions beginning on page 361.

HANGING THE CURTAINS
Mark the position of the rods and remove them. It is simple to re-position them as spring-tension sockets are used.

Stitch rings to the top ends of each panel, then place additional rings between them at 10- or 13-cm (4- or 5-inch) intervals. Slip the rod through the rings. Position the first rod at the top of the window flush with the wall, the middle rod 5 cm (2 inches) above the marking and into the window recess 2·5 cm (1 inch) from the wall, and the bottom rod 5 cm (2 inches) above the marking and into the window recess 5 cm (2 inches) from the wall.

Set the Stage with Curtains

Making curtains lures many women into sewing. The reason is not hard to find. Ready-made curtains are expensive and seldom completely satisfactory; often you have to compromise on colour or fabric because you cannot find exactly what you want. Made-to-measure curtains may be absolutely lovely to the eye – but absolutely devastating to the purse. The solution: make your own.

This chapter explains how to plan and make lined and unlined curtains. Remember accuracy is vital – accuracy in measuring, in estimating fabric requirements, in cutting and in sewing.

Full Length Curtains – Preparation

Full length curtains may be used on almost any type of window and are always used for French and picture windows.

They can be made of heavy or fine sheer fabric, and should hang in balanced, graceful folds. Pleats are the most effective means of controlling their fullness.

Cornice Poles, Rods, Tracks and Fixtures

You will need a pole, rod or track. Select a two-way track with overlap if the curtains are to overlap at the centre. See *Picture Windows*, page 344. Select a one-way straight track for corner windows and sliding doors, page 346, and other windows where the curtain is drawn to one side.

Install the brackets for the track on the extreme ends of the window frame, 2·5 cm (1 inch) below the top of the window frame, or on the wall. If the curtains are to hang from the ceiling, use a ceiling-mounted track.

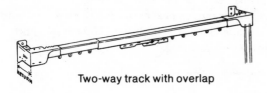

Two-way track with overlap

Adding Allowances to Measurements

Length: To the measured length (as described on page 344), add 5 cm (2 inches) for heading, 10 cm (4 inches) for top hem (see page 371 for curtains with pleat tape headings), and 9 cm (3½ inches) for lower hem and turning. *Example*: For lined curtains 221 cm (87 inches) (measured length) plus 23 cm (9½ inches) = 244 cm (96½ inches). For unlined curtains, add an extra 1·2 cm (½ inch) for turning on the top hem.

If double-fold hems are used, and they are better for sheer fabrics, allow 20 cm (8 inches) for the top hem and 15 cm (6 inches) for the lower hem. 221 cm (87 inches) (measured length) plus 40 cm (16 inches) (heading and double-fold hems) = 261 cm (103 inches).

Add 2·5 cm (1 inch) if curtains are to go on a rod. If curtains extend from the ceiling, measure from the ceiling to the floor and add only the amounts stated for top and bottom hems.

Width: Measure across the window from one end of the track to the other. To this measurement, add the depth of the return on each side. *Example*: 234 cm (92 inches) (measured width) plus 13 cm (5 inches) (two 6-cm (2½-inch) returns) = 247 cm (97 inches). This is the width the curtains must cover; each finished panel must be one-half this width plus one-half the overlap.

To the measured width you must add the allowances for hems, overlap, seams and pleats. But first you must determine the number of pleats and the space between the pleats.

Pleats in a pair of curtains must always be even in number, although the number in each panel may be even or uneven. Allow 13 or 15 cm (5 or 6 inches) for fullness in each pleat, and space the pleats about 10 cm (4 inches) apart. (You may have to estimate the number of pleats several times before arriving at the exact spacing. The paper pattern suggested below will help you here.)

To determine the exact spacing between pleats, proceed as follows: always have the end pleat at the depth of the return from the outside edge of each curtain; use the distance between these two pleats to figure the space between additional pleats. *Examples*: 247 cm (97 inches) (measured width and returns) less 13 cm (5 inches) (returns) = 234 cm (92 inches) (to be divided into space for additional pleats). Since two end pleats are predetermined, the number of spaces is one less than the number of pleats. For 24 pleats: 234 cm (92 inches) divided by 23 spaces = 10 cm (4 inches) (spaces between pleats). 24 (pleats) × 13 cm (5 inches) (for each pleat) = 304 cm (120 inches) (required for pleats). Page 379 describes how to measure and make pleats in the heading.

The diagram overleaf shows the 6-cm (2½-inch) overlap and position of the first end pleat at the centre edge of each curtain. When the spacing of the pleats is worked out before making the allowance for the overlap, the distance between pleats at the centre overlap will be the same as that between all other pleats when the curtains are drawn.

MAKING A PAPER PATTERN

You may feel more confident about your decisions if you make a pattern to fit your window and mark your spacings on that. Cut two strips of stiff paper about 15 cm (6 inches) wide and a few cm (inches) longer than the width of the window and return at each end. Lap the centre edges the amount of the overlap – usually 6 cm (2½ inches). Pin. Then mark paper 3 cm (1¼ inches) from one edge of the overlap to indicate the centre line. Measure the window width and the return at each end, and cut the paper an equal distance from centre line. *Example*: For the 247-cm (97-inch) width used above, the centre is 123·5 cm (48½ inches) from each edge of the pattern. Fit the pattern across the rod and round the return at each end to check that the width is correct. Mark the position of the returns and the spacing for pleats. Remember that the allowance for side hems, seams and fullness for pleats has not been added to the pattern.

Now you are ready to work out the width required for the curtains. To do this, add your allowances to the window width plus the return at each end. *Example*: 234 cm (92 inches) (measured width) plus 13 cm (5 inches) (two 6-cm (2½-inch) returns) plus 26 cm (10 inches) (5-cm (2-inch) hem and 1·2-cm (½-inch) seam allowance on each side of the two panels), 304 cm (120 inches) (pleats), and 6 cm (2½ inches) (overlap) = 583 cm (229½ inches) (width required). Each of the two panels is 291·5 cm (114¾ inches) wide plus seam allowances. For each seam within the curtain, allow 2·5 cm (1 inch) (1·2-cm (½-inch) seam allowance on each edge).

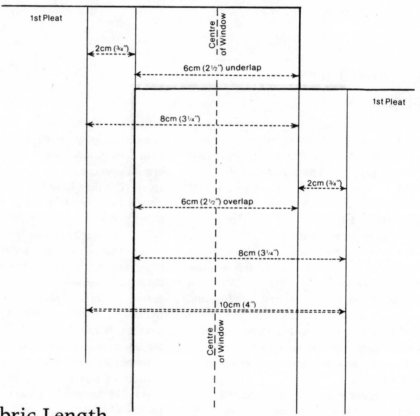

Estimating Fabric Length

When estimating quantity first consider the width of the fabric. If 122-cm (48-inch) fabric is used, it will be 117 cm (46 inches) wide after you have removed the selvedges and allowed for seaming. In the example, 583 cm (229½ inches) (width required) divided by 117 cm (46 inches) (fabric width) = 4$\frac{15}{16}$ lengths. Buy 5 lengths. Remember, lengths cannot be pieced. If your figures result in a fraction, always buy the next full length.

Example: 248 cm (97½ inches) (length of curtain) × 5 (lengths) = 1240 cm (487½ inches) or 12·4 m (13 yards 19½ inches). Buy an additional 23 cm (9 inches) to allow for straightening the ends of the fabric. If the fabric has a design, allow for matching. See page 367. If the curtains are sheer, add the allowances for double-fold hems. See page 367.

If you plan to place seams just outside pleats, you will need extra width. This is explained below in *Making Seams*. How much extra depends on the width of your curtains.

Lining. The lining is 25 cm (10 inches) shorter and 20 cm (8 inches) narrower than the curtain fabric. For the example above, the lining is 222 cm (87½ inches) long, and 5 lengths of 122-cm (48-inch) lining, or 11·1 m (12 yards 5½ inches), are required. Buy an additional 23 cm (9 inches) to allow for straightening the ends of the lining. Information on suitable lining fabric is given on page 340.

Cutting the Curtains

Curtains must be cut on the true lengthwise and crosswise grains of the fabric so that they will hang straight, fall smoothly and gracefully and clean satisfactorily.

Straighten the ends of the fabric by drawing a thread on the crosswise grain to indicate the cutting line. Steampress the fabric, then remove the selvedges.

For accuracy in cutting, work on a flat surface such as the dining-room table or a cutting board. *Use a tape measure to measure the lengths.* Draw a thread on the crosswise grain to mark the cutting line for each length; then cut the length. If the fabric has a design, match the pattern in each panel. See page 367.

Straighten the fabric grain as instructed on page 14.

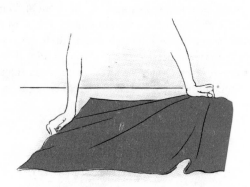

Constructing the Curtains

MAKING SEAMS

Seaming is your first construction step when you are making curtains. Seams are placed just outside pleats, where they are less noticeable than they would be if placed within a pleat or between pleats. To do this, measure and pin-mark the width of the centre hem and turning, the distance of the first pleat from the hem edge, and then the amounts for as many pleats and spaces as the fabric width will allow, plus seam allowance. Draw a thread on the lengthwise grain to indicate the cutting line. Cut on the drawn thread. Use a French seam in unlined curtains so that the cut edges will be enclosed, and a plain seam pressed open in lined curtains. Match the designs at the seamline.

For convenience in folding and pressing hems in curtains, work on the ironing board during the construction steps that follow, as suggested for net curtains, page 352.

Making Unlined Curtains

The informal mode of today's living has increased the popularity of unlined curtains. Many of the new synthetic fabrics do not require lining. The colour and design of the fabric are visible from the outside.

The allowances for heading, side and lower hems referred to overleaf are described on page 367.

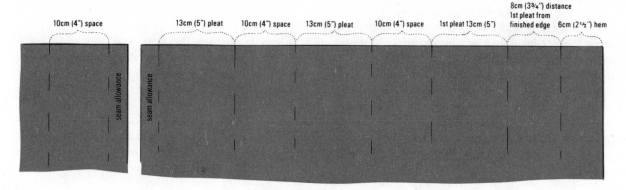

10cm (4″) space   13cm (5″) pleat   10cm (4″) space   13cm (5″) pleat   10cm (4″) space   1st pleat 13cm (5″)   8cm (3¾″) distance 1st pleat from finished edge   6cm (2½″) hem

seam allowance   seam allowance

HEADING HEM

To support the pleated heading, use Vilene or buckram of the same width as the hem at the top. In the measurements, 11 cm (4½ inches) were allowed for a top hem and turning. Turn 11 cm (4½ inches) to the underside and press.

Cut 11-cm (4-inch) interfacing 13 cm (5 inches) shorter than the width of the curtain. Place the interfacing over the underside of the hem, aligning one edge with the crease and extending the ends to within 6 cm (2½ inches) of the fabric edges. (This is the turn for the side hems.) Stitch the interfacing in place, ·6 cm (¼ inch) from the crease for the hem. Turn the cut edge of fabric over the opposite edge of the interfacing and stitch. Press. Turn the hem to the underside and press again. Pin, then tack the hem in place. *Do not stitch the hem;* when the pleats are stitched, they will hold it in place. Leave the tacking in until you have stitched the pleats.

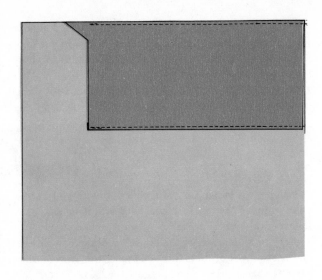

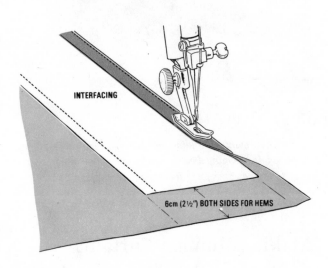

INTERFACING

6cm (2½") BOTH SIDES FOR HEMS

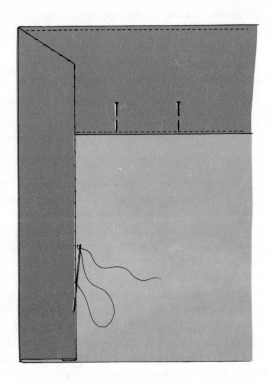

SIDE HEMS

To remove bulk, cut out the corner of the top hem edge. Begin 6 cm (2½ inches) from the outer edge (turn for the side hem) and cut upwards to within 1·2 cm (½ inch) of the top fold; then cut diagonally to the top hem fold, and on the hem fold to the outer edge.

Turn 1·2 cm (½ inch) to the underside, and press. Turn a 5-cm (2-inch) hem and pin in place. Mitre the corner at the top edge. Press.

Hems may be slip-stitched by hand or machine-stitched, using either straight stitching or blindstitching. If you finish the hem by hand, catch only a few threads of the fabric in the stitches so that they are invisible on the top side. If you machine-stitch the hem using straight stitching, place the stitching as close to the folded edge as possible.

If you blindstitch the hem, first tack it in place, ·6 cm (¼ inch) from the folded edge. With the wrong side of the curtain up, turn the hem to the right side on the tacking line, creating a soft fold and exposing the ·6-cm (¼-inch) hem edge. Select the blindstitch zig-zag, a medium stitch width and about 1·5 mm (15) stitch length. Stitch so that the straight stitches fall in the hem edge and the sideward stitches pierce only a few threads of the soft fold. Turn the hem down and press.

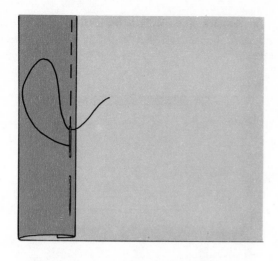

to allow for the thicknesses of fabric and to square the corners. Tack the hem in place.

Before finishing the hem, pleat the heading and attach the curtain hooks. See pages 379 and 381. Hang the curtains and check the length. The curtains should be 1·2 cm ($\frac{1}{2}$ inch) above the floor. If your measurements were accurate, the length should be correct and the change in hem, if any, will be slight.

The hem may be slip-stitched by hand or blindstitched by machine. If finished by hand, the work may be done after curtains are hung. If the hem is blindstitched, begin and end the stitching at the side hems. Then mitre the corners and slip-stitch them in place, making the stitches through the hems only.

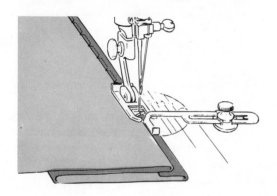

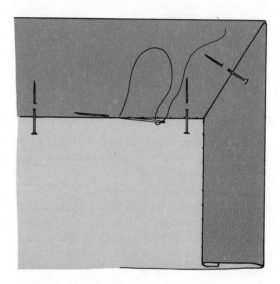

LOWER HEM

Compare both curtains, wrong sides together, and check the length at the centre and outer side hems to make sure they are identical.

In the measurements, 9 cm (3$\frac{1}{2}$ inches) were allowed for the hem and turning. Turn under 1·2 cm ($\frac{1}{2}$ inch) and press. Turn a 7·5-cm (3-inch) hem and pin in place. Mitre the corners and ease the hem down slightly at this point

Making Curtains with Pleat Tape Headings

Ready-made pleat tape with woven-in pockets for hooks to give a variety of pleated headings is available. If you decide to use it instead of interfacing at the top, omit the allowance for the 10-cm (4-inch) top hem; and allow 1·2 cm ($\frac{1}{2}$ inch) for turning. Consider if you have a return at each end and position the woven-in pockets so that a pleat falls at the turn, or the end of a straight rod.

Cut the pleat tape 13 cm (5 inches) shorter than the width of the curtain. Pin the tape across the top of the curtains, right sides together, ·8 cm ($\frac{5}{16}$ inch) from the fabric edge; extend the ends to within 6 cm (2$\frac{1}{2}$ inches) of the curtain edge. (This is the turn for the side hems.) Stitch the tape in place 1·2 cm ($\frac{1}{2}$ inch) from the fabric edge. Press.

Turn the pleat tape to the underside, fold the fabric

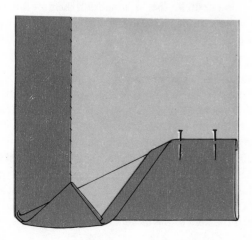

371

on the stitching line, and press. Pin the lower edge of the pleat tape to the curtain and stitch ·6 cm (¼ inch) from the edge. Press.

Form the side and lower hems as instructed above. Then insert hooks into the woven-in pockets to form the pleats.

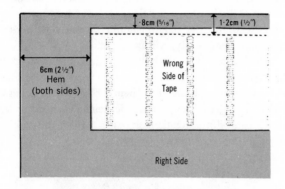

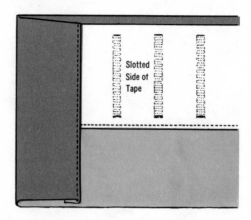

Pull-up Pleat Tape Headings

Ready-made curtain tapes are also available to give a variety of automatic pull-up pleat headings to curtains. These include deep-headed pencil pleats, triple pleats (pinch pleats) and twin pleats.

The tapes are stitched flush to the top of the curtain after folding and tacking a 1·5-cm (⅝-inch) turning (no interfacing is needed). Widths are joined and side hems made before attaching the tapes. The pocket openings to take hooks should be at the lower edge of the tape and the cords should be pulled out about 4 cm (1½ inches) at each end of the tape and knotted. The ends of the tape are turned under to neaten and the tape is then tacked

to the curtain. Stitch all round the outer edge of the tape avoiding pockets.

It is always advisable first to prepare the tape for pleats, and check against the track and the fabric, marking the pockets to be used for hooks to give you the fullness and even pleating arrangement that you wish. Remember to allow 1·2 cm (½ inch) at each end of the tape for neatening.

Making Curtains of Sheer Fabric

Curtains of sheer fabric may be used alone or with net curtains that are hung on a separate rod. The sheer over sheer imparts a cool, crisp look.

Refer to *Full Length Curtains – Preparation*, page 366, for instructions on adding allowances to your measurements and estimating fabric length. Remember that you should make double-fold hems in sheer fabrics.

SIDE HEMS

The side hems are stitched first. In the measurements, 40 cm (16 inches) were allowed for a 5-cm (2-inch)

double-fold hem on each side of the two panels. Fold, press and stitch the double-fold hems, following instructions on page 352.

HEADING HEM

Vilene can be used to support the pleated heading. It must be the same width as the heading hem. In the measurements, 20 cm (8 inches) were allowed for a 10-cm (4-inch) double-fold hem.

Cut 10-cm (4-inch) interfacing the exact length of the curtain width. Place the interfacing on the underside of the hem, keeping the edges even, and pin. Stitch along the lower edge of the interfacing. Back-stitch at each end. Press.

Turn the hem to the underside, fold along the edge of

interfacing and press. Then turn again for a double-fold hem. Pin, press and tack. Do not stitch the hem; the pleats will hold it in place when they are stitched. Do not remove this tacking until you have stitched the pleats.

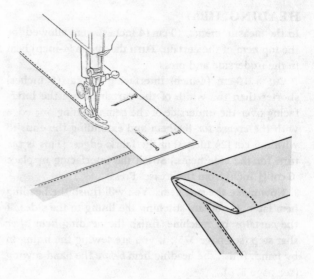

LOWER HEM

Compare both curtains, wrong sides together, and check the length at the centre and outer side hems to make sure they are identical.

In the measurements, 15 cm (6 inches) were allowed for a 7·5-cm (3-inch) double-fold hem. Fold and pin the 7·5-cm (3-inch) double hem, following instructions on page 353. Before stitching the hem, pleat the heading and attach the hooks as described on pages 379 and 381. Hang the curtains and check the length; it should be about 1·2 cm (½ inch) above the floor. If your measurements were accurate, the length should be correct and the hem width will require only a slight adjustment, if any.

Machine-stitch the hem, then add weights. See instructions on page 353.

Making Lined Curtains

Curtains are lined to protect the fabric. The lining also adds weight, ensures soft, graceful folds and creates a uniform appearance from the outside. Colour-fast sateen of light beige, eggshell, soft grey or white is generally used as the lining fabric.

The allowances for heading, side and lower hems referred to below are given on page 367.

THE LINING

The lining fabric must be cut on the true lengthwise and crosswise grains the same as the curtain fabric. Straighten the ends by drawing a thread on the crosswise grain to indicate the cutting line. Remove selvedges.

Cut the lining 25 cm (10 inches) shorter and 20 cm (8 inches) narrower than the curtain fabric. This allows 1·2 cm (½ inch) for seam allowance on each side, 1·2 cm (½ inch) for turning at the top and 5 cm (2 inches) for the lower hem plus 1·2 cm (½ inch) for turning. When the curtains are finished, the lining hem will overlap the curtain hem 2·5 cm (1 inch).

Draw a thread on the crosswise grain to indicate the cutting line of each length. See page 369.

Bolts of sateen are often rolled tighter at one end of the board than the other, with the result that the fabric threads are drawn off-grain. Straighten the fabric grain as described on page 14. Steam-press.

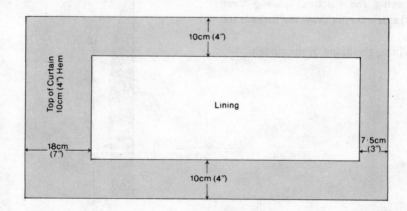

Top of Curtain
10cm (4") Hem

10cm (4")

18cm (7")

Lining

7·5cm (3")

10cm (4")

HEADING HEM

In the measurements, 10 cm (4 inches) were allowed for the top hem of the curtain. Turn the 10-cm (4-inch) hem to the underside and press.

Cut a 10-cm (4-inch) interfacing 13 cm (5 inches) shorter than the width of the curtain. Place the interfacing over the underside of the hem, aligning one edge with the crease for the hem and extending the ends to within 6 cm (2½ inches) of the fabric edges. (This is the turn for the side hems.) Stitch the interfacing in place ·6 cm (¼ inch) from the crease. Press.

Now make the side hems. You will finish the heading hem later. If you are stitching the lining to the sides of the curtains by machine, finish the heading hem *after* that step (see page 375); if you are sewing the lining in by hand, finish the heading hem *before* the hand sewing (see page 376).

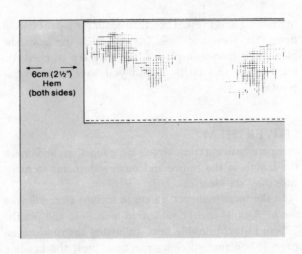

6cm (2½")
Hem
(both sides)

SIDE HEMS

In the measurements, 13 cm (5 inches) were allowed for a 5-cm (2-inch) hem and 1·2-cm (½-inch) seam allowance on each side. Turn the side hems to the underside 6 cm (2½ inches) and press. Pin the hem in place about 4 cm (1½ inches) from the fold. Place the pins parallel to the hem and leave them until you have sewn the lining in place. Turn the hem edge back on the pin line and catch the hem to the curtain. Make a stitch in the curtain about 20 cm (8 inches) below the top; loop the thread to the left; then, directly opposite the first stitch, make a stitch in the hem fold, bringing the needle out over the thread. Continue making the stitches, spacing them about 5 cm (2 inches) apart. Do not draw the threads too tight.

The next step is joining the lining to the curtain.

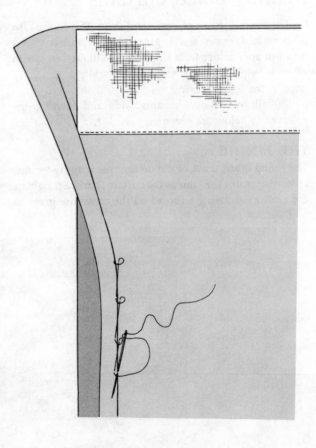

374

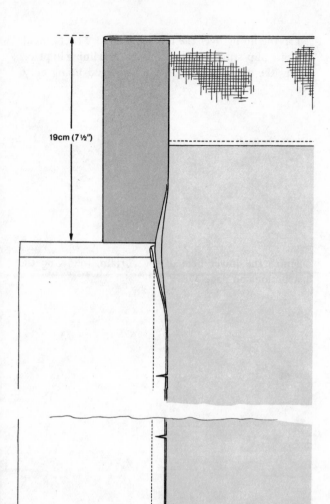

19cm (7½")

14cm (5½")

METHODS OF JOINING LININGS TO CURTAINS

The lining may be stitched to the curtain by machine as illustrated here or by hand as illustrated on page 377.

Method 1, Machine-stitched: Hem the lower edge of the lining as follows: turn the edge under 1·2 cm (½ inch) and press; then turn the hem to the underside 5 cm (2 inches) and press. Pin the hem in place, and stitch close to the top fold. Press.

At the top of the lining, turn the 1·2-cm (½-inch) seam allowance to the underside and finger-press. Pin the lining to the curtain side hem, right sides together, keeping the top fold of the lining 19 cm (7½ inches) below the top edge of the curtain, and the hem 14 cm (5½ inches) above the lower edge. Turn the seam allowance away from the curtain and stitch from the lining side, taking a 1·2-cm (½-inch) seam.

Back-stitch at each end. Stitch the lining to the hem on the opposite side of the curtain in the same way. Press, then press both seam edges towards the lining. Slash the seam allowances at 15-cm (6-inch) intervals. Turn to the right side. If measurements and seaming are accurate, the lining should fit smoothly over the curtain.

To complete the heading hem of the curtain. Turn the heading hem to the underside and press. To remove bulk, cut out the corner of the top hem edge. Begin 6 cm (2½ inches) from the outer edges (turn for the side hem) and cut upwards to within 1·2 cm (½ inch) of the hem fold, then cut diagonally to the hem fold, and on the fold to the outer edge. Mitre the corners; turn under the side seam allowance on the curtain as far as the lining, and pin.

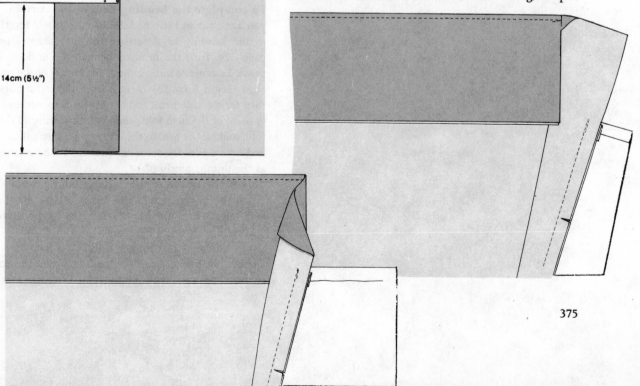

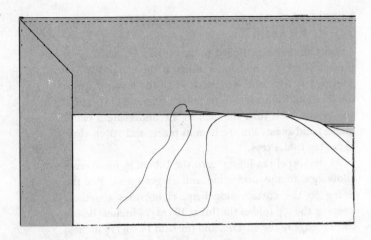

Lap the lining over the top hem edge 1·2 cm (½ inch), and pin. Slip-stitch the corner mitres and lining in place, taking the stitches through the hems and lining only. Press.

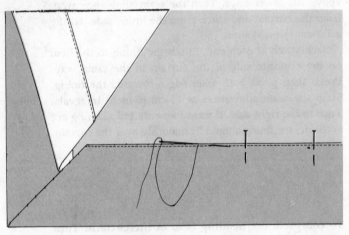

Finish the lower hem of the curtain, following the instructions on page 378.

Method 2, Hand-sewn: For wide curtains it is advisable to hand-sew the lining to the curtain. This makes it possible to catch the lining to the curtain at even intervals, to prevent it from sagging below the curtain. Before you join the lining to the curtain, you must first complete the heading.

To complete the heading hem of the curtain. After you have cut and stitched the 10-cm (4-inch) interfacing to the heading as described under *Heading Hem* on page 374, turn the heading hem to the underside and press. To remove bulk, cut out the corner of the top hem edge. Begin 6 cm (2½ inches) from the outer edge (the turn for the side hem) and cut upwards to within 1·2 cm (½ inch) of the hem fold; then cut diagonally to the hem fold, and on the fold to the outer edge. Mitre the corners and turn under the seam allowance on the curtain as far as the lining; pin in place.

To sew the lining to the curtain. Fold, press and slip-stitch the lower hem of the lining. Along the top and side edges, turn the seam allowance to the underside 1·2 cm (½ inch) and finger-press.

Lay the curtain, wrong side up, on a flat surface and smooth out the fabric. Place the lining over the curtain, wrong sides together, with the folded edges overlapping the heading and side hems of the curtain 1·2 cm (½ inch). The lining hem should extend to within 14 cm (5½ inches) of the lower edge of the curtain.

Now you must catch the lining to the curtain at about 61-cm (24-inch) intervals. Begin at the centre. Pin the lining to the curtain on a vertical line, then turn the lining back on the pin line. Make a stitch in the curtain about 10 cm (4 inches) below the top hem, loop the thread to the left, then directly opposite the first stitch, make a stitch in the lining fold, bringing the needle out over the thread. Catch only one or two threads in the fabric so that the stitches will be invisible on the top side. Continue, spacing the stitches about 15 cm (6 inches) apart. Do not draw the thread taut. About 15 cm (6 inches) above the hem, fasten the thread in the lining with a tiny backstitch and leave a 10-cm (4-inch) thread end. Then pin and stitch additional vertical lines, working from the centre towards each edge and spacing the rows about 61 cm (24 inches) apart.

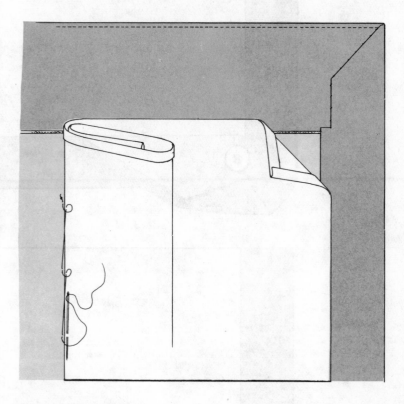

Pin the lining to the curtain hems across the top and along each side, with the folded edges overlapping the curtain hems 1·2 cm (½ inch). Slip-stitch the lining in place, making the stitches through the lining and curtain hems only so that the stitches will be invisible on the right side. Do not draw the thread tight.

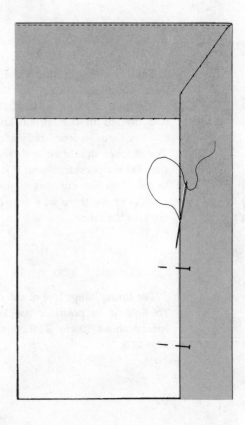

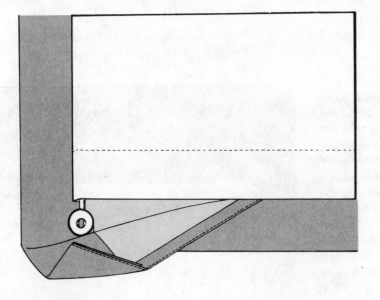

LOWER HEM

Compare both curtains, wrong sides together, and check the length at the centre and outer side hems to make sure they are identical.

Turn the lower edge of the curtain under 1·2 cm (½ inch) and press. Stitch near the fold. (The lining will cover the stitching.) Turn a 7·5-cm (3-inch) hem to the underside, and pin in place. Mitre the corners so that they fit smoothly under the lining. Ease the hem slightly at this point to allow for the thicknesses of fabric and to square the corners. Sew weights at each side seam allowance.

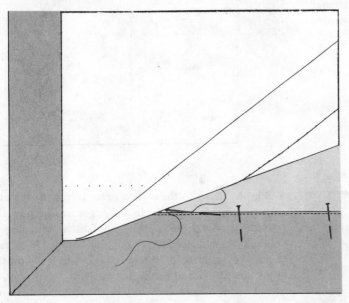

Before finishing the hem, pleat the heading and attach the hooks. See pages 379 and 381. Hang the curtains and check the length, which should be about 1·2 cm (½ inch) above the floor. Let the curtains hang for two or three days before you sew the hem because some fabrics will shrink or stretch slightly. If your measurements are accurate, the length should be correct and the change in the hem width will be slight, if any.

The hem may be finished after the curtains are hung. Slip-stitch the hem and corner mitres in place. Catch only one or two threads in the curtain and make the stitches through hems only at the corners. The stitches should be invisible on the top side. Do not press this hem. If it is necessary to lengthen the curtains slightly after six months or so, there will then be no crease mark in the fabric.

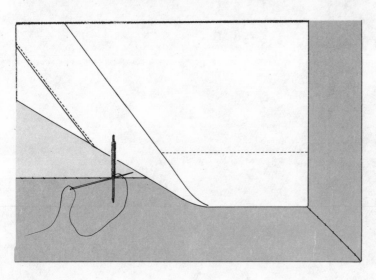

The lining hangs free of the curtain hem. To hold it in position, use French tacks spaced about 30 cm (12 inches) apart. See page 208.

DETACHABLE CURTAIN LININGS

This is an easy way to line curtains and allows the lining to be detached quickly for washing or cleaning. Ready-made lining tape is used for the lining and a curtain tape for the curtains. Curtains and linings are made separately: the lining is then attached to the curtain by the same hooks which are used to suspend the curtain from the track.

Make up the curtain lining with side and lower hems, but leave the top edge unfinished. Check against the curtain for length.

At the commencing end of the lining tape, pull free 4 cm (1½ inches) of drawcord and knot the ends. Trim the surplus tape to within ·6 cm (¼ inch) of the point where the cord enters the tape. Turn under the end of the tape including the knotted cords and stitch across the folded edge to make a neat finish. With the right side of the lining uppermost and the lining tape cord side uppermost, slip the top raw edge of the lining between the two sides of the split skirt on the tape about 2·5 cm (1 inch) from the prepared end. Pin into position.

Turn under the surplus 2·5 cm (1 inch) of the tape so that the fold is in line with the side edge of the lining. Machine-stitch the top edges of the turned under tape together. Continue stitching along the folded edge and along the bottom edge of the tape, keeping the top of the lining enclosed in the double skirt.

The underside of the skirt is slightly longer than the corded side to ensure that the stitching will not miss it even though sewing unseen. Finish the end of the tape in a similar manner to the commencing end, but leave the ends of the cords free for pulling to pleat or gather the lining as needed.

The sides of the lining and curtains can be anchored together with a few French tacks if desired.

Making a Pleated Heading

The most popular styles of pleats for curtains are the pinch pleat, box pleat, French pleat and cartridge pleat.

MEASURING FOR PLEATS

Curtains may have either an even or an uneven number of pleats in each panel, resulting in an even number in each pair. The number of pleats, the allowance for each pleat, and the spacing between pleats are matters you should decide before cutting out the fabric. See pages 367 and 368 for this information.

Always measure and pin-mark position of *all pleats and spaces* before you begin any stitching.

In curtains, the centre edges overlap 6 cm (2½ inches) when a two-way track or rod is used; therefore the *first* end pleat must be about 8 cm (3¼ inches) from the centre edge. Using the measurements in the example on page 368, measure 8 cm (3¼ inches) from the centre edge of the curtain and pin-mark. Then measure and pin-mark the width of the *first* end pleat. At the opposite end, measure and pin-mark the depth of the return. Then measure and pin-mark the width of the *second* end pleat. Continue measuring and marking the space, then the width of each pleat. All spaces between the last and first pleats must be the same; and the width of all pleats must be the same. Compare the two panels, wrong sides together, to be sure the pin-marks correspond.

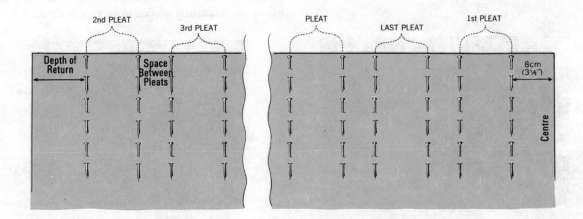

FORMING THE PLEATS

Bring the pin-marks for each pleat together and pin. Stitch from the top edge to 1·2 cm ($\frac{1}{2}$ inch) below the heading hem, placing the stitching into the pleat about ·2 cm ($\frac{1}{16}$ inch) from the pins (this allows for the width that is taken up by the layers of fabric). Back-stitch at each end.

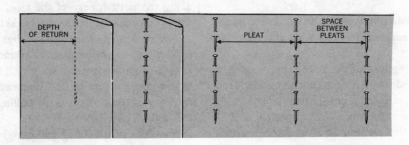

Pinch pleat. Divide each pleat evenly into three smaller pleats and crease the length of the pleat. At the lower edge, either hand-tack the three pleats together or machine-stitch across them. If they are hand-tacked, you can insert the shank of the curtain hook into the pleat.

Box pleat. Slip two fingers inside the pleat and finger-press it open. Then press flat, keeping the folds an equal distance from the stitching line. Tack the top and bottom corners of the pleat to the curtain, placing the stitches under pleat. Box pleats should be about 5 cm (2 inches) wide and require 10 cm (4 inches) of additional fabric for each pleat; the space between pleats is 10 cm (4 inches). Make this allowance in the planning stage.

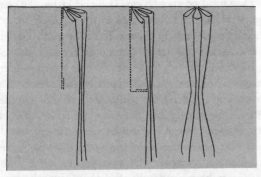

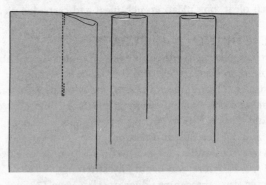

French pleat. At the lower edge of the heading, divide the pleat into three smaller pleats; then hand-sew through them several times before drawing tightly on the threads. Fasten the threads on the underside.

Cartridge pleat. This small, round pleat is filled with Vilene or buckram, which holds its cartridge shape. In the planning stage, allow about 5 cm (2 inches) for each pleat and about 5 cm (2 inches) for each space. Cartridge pleats are frequently placed in groups of three.

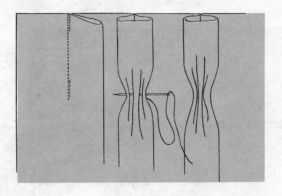

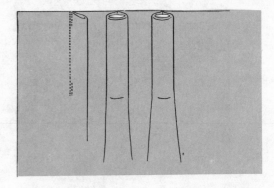

Selecting Hooks and Pins

Curtains are attached to the track or rod by hooks or pins, which are placed in the back of each pleat and at each end of the curtain. Most

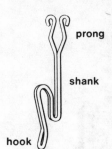

hooks are available in several sizes and in metal or plastic. When buying them, be sure to consider the position of the hook part on the shank and the length of the prong. Examine them closely and get the type best suited for the type of heading tape you propose to use.

A few of the more popular hooks are illustrated.

Hook **A.** This popular and practical **slip-in hook** has a long two-piece prong that holds the heading erect. It requires no sewing. The long prong slips between the heading hem and curtain and round the pleat. Select hooks with the hook part near the bottom of the shank if the curtains hang from a track and the heading extends above it. Select hooks with the hook part at the top of the shank if curtains hang from a decorative pole with rings, or a track mounted on the ceiling.

Hook **B.** The **pleater pin with hook** is used with ready-made pleat tape. Slip each prong into a woven-in

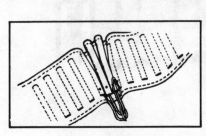

pocket in the tape to pinch the pleat in shape. Select the position of the hook part on the shank the same as hook A and suitable for the heading tape you are using – the position of the pockets may vary.

Hook **C.** This two prong hook is for use with automatic pull-up pleat tapes.

Hook **D.** Either in clear or white plastic, is for use with stiff-type pleat tapes, and is particularly suitable for net curtains.

Similar style hooks are available in metal for simple gathered headings in heavier fabrics.

Rings **E** and **F.** Solid and split rings are for use where curtains are suspended from rods or wires.

Whatever style of hook you select, insert the hook part correctly. If the curtain heading extends above the track, measure the distance from the position of the hook part on the track to 2·5 cm (1 inch) above the track. Position the top edge of the hook (not the shank) this distance from the top of the curtains.

If curtains hang from a decorative pole that is visible or from a rod mounted on the ceiling, place the hook part at the top of the curtains.

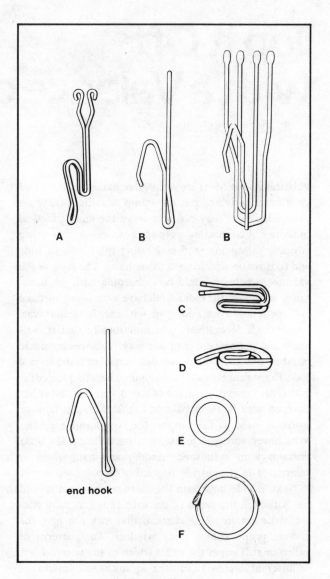

Anchoring Curtains

The outside edges of the curtains should hang against the wall in a straight, taut line. Sew small plastic rings to the heading hem in line with the track, and to the lower hem. Place cup hooks in the wall or skirting board in line with the rings. Fasten the rings over the hooks.

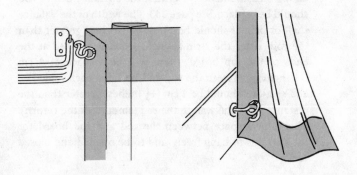

381

Top it Off
with a Valance or Pelmet

Valances and Pelmets are decorative extras at the top of your curtains which put the stamp of individuality on your windows. They can also serve the more practical functions of connecting a group of windows, increasing window dimensions and concealing the tracks or rods and fixtures on which curtains are hung. The style of the valance or pelmet should be in keeping with the decorative scheme of the room. Both have a tendency to make ceilings appear lower; use them with care in small rooms.

Although decoratively and functionally similar, valances and pelmets differ in this way. Valances are made of fabric and tacked to a wooden 'shelf' or hung from a rod; the valances may be straight, shaped, pleated or gathered. Pelmets are made of wood that may be either covered with fabric or painted to match the curtains or walls, or used as the support for swags and cascades. Whichever you plan to use, you must first make your curtains with a finished heading and hang them as instructed in the chapter beginning on page 366.

Next, decide how deep the valance or pelmet should be. Although the depth of the valance is generally one-sixth the length of the curtain, that may not give the correct proportion to your window. Cut patterns of calico or stiff paper the exact width of the window but of different depths. Hold them up to the window to see which looks best.

The Valance Shelf and Pelmet Board

The ends and top board of the valance shelf and pelmet board should be made of 2-cm ($\frac{3}{4}$-inch) pine, and the face board of the pelmet of ·6-cm ($\frac{1}{4}$-inch) plywood. Before taking measurements for either, the curtain track or rod should be in place. See page 343. The width of the valance shelf or pelmet should be 11 cm ($4\frac{1}{2}$ inches) greater than the rod. After the 2-cm ($\frac{3}{4}$-inch) wood is secured at the ends of the top board, there will be a space of 4 cm ($1\frac{1}{2}$ inches) between the rod and board at each end. The end sections should be 4 cm ($1\frac{1}{2}$ inches) greater than the distance from the wall to the rod (amount of the return). This allows space between the rod and the board for the curtains to hang freely and to be opened and closed easily.

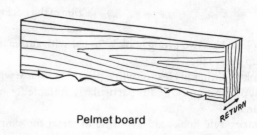

Pelmet board

RETURN

382

To make the valance shelf, join the end sections to the top board with finishing nails and a thin line of white glue. Keep the outer edges even. *To make the pelmet board*, add a face board of ·6-cm (¼-inch) plywood to the shelf with finishing nails and a thin line of white glue along both sides and top.

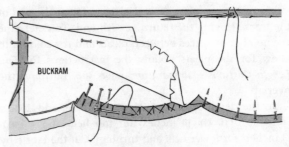

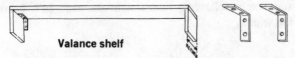

Valance shelf

Mount angle brackets, top end extending forwards, on the wall (see page 343) or frame at each end of the board. If the board is more than 100 cm (40 inches) across, mount extra brackets to give added support.

Although the valance shelf or pelmet board only rests on the brackets and is not fastened to them, it is advisable to hammer small finishing nails through one of the screw holes at each end to prevent the board from sliding forwards. The covered board can then be lifted easily off the brackets for cleaning.

Straight and Shaped Valances

Straight and shaped valances are made over a stiff foundation such as buckram and are interlined and lined. If the fabric is quilted, you may omit the interlining.

MEASURING THE VALANCE SHELF

Place a tape measure across the return at one end, across the front, then across the return at the opposite end. This is the finished width of the valance.

MAKING A PAPER PATTERN

Cut a paper pattern this exact width and the depth desired. If the lower edge is shaped, mark the amount of the return at each end; shape the valance between these markings, then at the returns. Fit the pattern to the valance shelf to be sure your measurements are correct.

MAKING THE VALANCE

Cut buckram the exact measurements of the paper pattern. Press all fabrics before cutting. Cut cotton curtain interlining and curtain fabric 2·5 cm (1 inch) wider than the pattern on all edges to allow for seams. Cut the width on the crosswise grain and depth on the lengthwise grain. Cut lining ·6 cm (¼ inch) wider than the pattern on all sides for the seam allowances.

Lay the fabric on the table, wrong side up. Place the interlining over the fabric and pin together along the edges. Place the buckram over the interlining. Turn the fabric and interlining over the buckram edge 2·5 cm (1 inch), and pin. Slash into the seam allowances at

inside curves and notch them on outside curves. With a heavy needle and heavy-duty thread, herringbone the edges of the fabric to the buckram. Turn the lining edge under 1·2 cm (½ inch) and pin to the back of valance, ·6 cm (¼ inch) from the edge. Slip-stitch in place. Hand-sew the top edge of 2-cm (¾-inch) twill tape near the top edge of the valance.

At the top and bottom edges of the valance, measure and pin-mark the amount of the return at each end. Fold the valance, wrong sides together, and crease the line of the return at each end.

Place the valance across the front and returns of the valance shelf with the twill tape over the top. Tack the tape to the shelf with upholsterer's tacks.

Pleated Valance

A pleated valance is made the same way as curtains except that it is in one piece. Also, it requires a separate rod. If the window treatment includes net curtains as well as curtains and valance, triple rods are needed for the hangings.

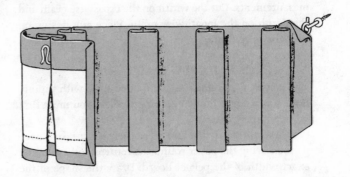

Put up the rod. The amount of the return on the top rod is greater than on the other rod or rods.

Measure the length of the rod plus the amount of the return at each end. This is the finished width of the valance. To the measured width, with the two returns, add the amount required for side hems, seam allowances and pleats. This is the width required to make the valance. Always place an end pleat to fall at the end of the track, leaving the return at each end. To determine the number of spaces between pleats and the amount to allow for the pleats, follow the instructions for *Full Length Curtains – Preparation*, page 366, but omit the overlap.

To the depth selected for your valance, add 18 cm (7 inches) (10 cm (4 inches) for top hem and 7·5 cm (3 inches) for lower hem and turning). Cut the fabric by these measurements. Cut the lining 21 cm (8½ inches) shorter and 20 cm (8 inches) narrower than the top fabric and make a 5-cm (2-inch) hem with a 1·2-cm (½-inch) turn.

To make the valance, see page 374, which describes how to make lined curtains, and page 379, which describes how to measure and make pleats in the heading. Select the proper hooks for the heading. See page 381. Anchor the valance at the top the same as the curtain.

Fabric-Covered Pelmet Board

A pelmet may be covered with a fabric identical to that used in the curtain or, if the curtain is a print, the pelmet-board may be covered with a plain colour that picks up one of the colours in the print. For an interesting contrast, the fabric may be quilted. The pelmet board should be padded and interlining should be placed between the padding and curtain fabric.

MEASURING THE PELMET BOARD
Place a tape measure across the return at one end, across the front and across the return at the opposite end. To this measurement, add 7·5 cm (3 inches) to turn under. Measure the depth at the widest and add 7·5 cm (3 inches) to turn under.

Cut the curtain fabric and cotton interlining by the measurements. Cut the width on the crosswise grain and the depth on the lengthwise grain. Place any design on the fabrics centrally.

MAKING A PAPER PATTERN
The pelmet illustrated has a scalloped edge with piping. Before you cover it or something similar, you must first make a paper pattern.

Spread the paper flat and place the pelmet board over it; then bring the paper round the returns and cut in the exact width of the pelmet board. Draw the shape of the scallops on the paper; cut on the marking.

Place the pattern over the right side of the fabric, 4 cm (1½ inches) from the edge at the deepest point of the scallops and 4 cm (1½ inches) in from each end. Lightly mark the scallops on the fabric. *Do not cut.*

COVERING THE PELMET BOARD
Before you cover the pelmet board, cover the corded

piping and stitch it to the lower edge of the fabric as follows: cut the bias strips as directed on page 244, but make the strips 5 cm (2 inches) wide plus three times the width of the cord. Bring the bias strip round the cord, right side out, with one edge 2·5 cm (1 inch) shorter than the other. Adjust the Zipper Foot to the left of the needle and stitch, following instructions on page 245. Press the seam.

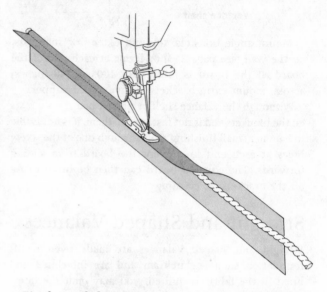

Pin the corded piping on the right side of the fabric, with the stitching on the piping over the scalloped marking. Stitch with the cording up, and stitch between the cord and previous line of stitching. Press. Trim the pelmet fabric to within 4 cm (1½ inches) of the scallops.

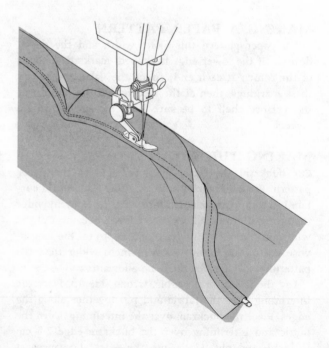

For the padding, place a layer of cotton batting, 2·5 cm (1 inch) thick, over the front and end sections of the pelmet board. Trim the padding to within ·6 cm (¼ inch) of the pelmet edges. Lay the interlining and fabric over the padding, right side up, extending all edges 4 cm (1½ inches) beyond the pelmet board. Smooth out the fabric and use drawing pins along all edges to hold it in place. (Do not push the pins in too far as you will remove them when the pelmet is finished.)

At the deepest point of the scallops, turn the fabric edges over the edge of the board and tack them to the underside with upholsterer's tacks. The piping must follow the edge of the scallops. Slash into the seam allowances at the point of the scallops and pin the edges to the underside of the board. Turn the fabric over the top edge of the board and tack it in place. Mitre the corners. Across the returns, or end sections, turn the fabric over the edges of the board and tack it to the underside. Mitre the corners. To finish the top of the board, tack 2-cm (¾-inch) twill tape over the fabric edges.

LINING THE PELMET

Line the inside of the pelmet if it can be seen from the outside.

Use sateen lining. Cut the lining by the pattern you

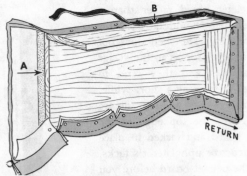

A. Layer of cotton batting
B. Cover edge of fabric with twill tape

made for the top fabric and allow 1·2 cm (½ inch) on all edges for seam allowances.

Lay the pelmet right side down. Place the lining over the inside of the pelmet and use a few drawing pins to hold the lining in place. (Do not push the pins in too far because you will remove them after you have finished the edges.) Turn under the seam allowance and place the folded edge about 1·2 cm (¼ inch) in from the edge of the pelmet; tack it in place with small upholsterer's tacks. First tack the lower edge in place, then the upper edge and finally the ends. Place a few tacks along each corner to hold the lining securely in this area.

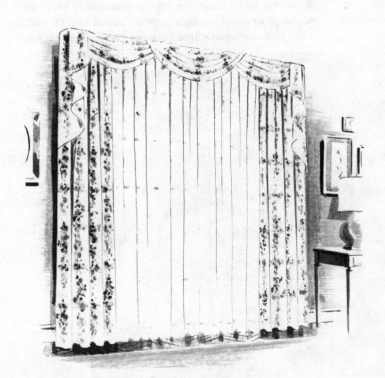

Swags and Cascades

Swags and cascades generally match the curtain fabric; the cascades may be faced with a contrasting fabric or self-fabric. The edges are often trimmed with a decorative braid or fringe. This touch is particularly attractive on swags and cascades made of a single thickness of sheer fabric.

A pelmet board rather than a valance shelf should be used for the mounting. The shelf does not offer enough support to the swags and cascades and they tend to droop after hanging a short while. The finished swag and cascade are lapped over the top edge of the pelmet board and tacked in place with carpet or upholsterer's tacks. Make the pelmet board before you begin the swag. See page 382.

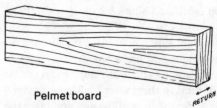

Pelmet board

RETURN

Single Swag

For a single window of average width, one swag extending the width of the window is sufficient. For a lounge window, you will need two smaller swags overlapping at the centre, and for a group of windows, three or more overlapping swags. The single swag is explained first.

MAKING A CALICO PATTERN

Straighten the ends and cut the calico 91 cm (36 inches) long on the lengthwise grain. Mark the centre line along the entire length. Measure the width of the pelmet. Subtract 25 cm (10 inches) from this measurement (13 cm (5 inches) from each end) and use this measurement to mark the top edge of the calico. *Example*: 91 cm (36 inches) (width of pelmet) less 25 cm (10 inches) = 66 cm (26 inches). Divide this measurement at the centre line so that you have the same distance 33 cm (13 inches) on each side of centre. Then mark the calico 2·5 cm (1 inch) from the top to indicate the lap over the top edge of the pelmet. At the bottom edge, mark each side 20 cm (8 inches) wider than the top measurement; keep the markings an equal distance from the centre line. On each side, draw a diagonal line between the top and bottom

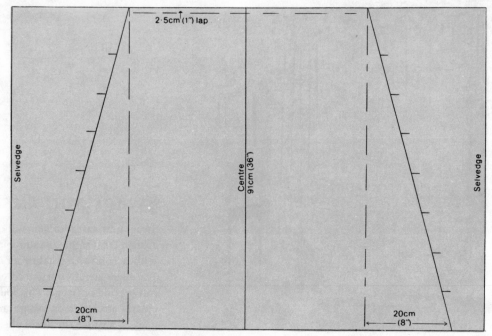

386

edges. Beginning 2·5 cm (1 inch) from the top, divide the diagonal lines into eight equal parts for seven folds and mark the calico. (If five folds are used, divide the lines into six equal parts.)

Mark the centre line on the top of the pelmet board. Lap the straight top edge of the calico 2·5 cm (1 inch) over the top of the pelmet board, matching centre lines; hold in place with drawing pins. Then tack the calico at the A markings, which are 13 cm (5 inches) from the ends, and at intervals between. Fold the calico at the first marking on the diagonal line and tack it to the top of the pelmet at A on each side. Shape the fold smoothly from the centre to each side and match the centre line. Use pins for tacking the folds; place them at an angle

and drive them slightly into the wood with a hammer. Now make a fold at the second marking on the diagonal line and tack it to the board, ·6 cm (¼ inch) from the previous fold. The fabric to the left and right of the diagonal lines lies in folds on top of the pelmet board. Continue to follow the diagonal lines and tack each fold to the board, ·6 cm (¼ inch) from the previous fold. When all folds are tacked in place, the calico swag extends the entire width of the pelmet board.

Cut off one end of the excess calico across the top 2·5 cm (1 inch) above your pin tacks. Trim off the excess calico along the lower curved edge 10 cm (4 inches) beyond the last fold, tapering gradually towards the centre.

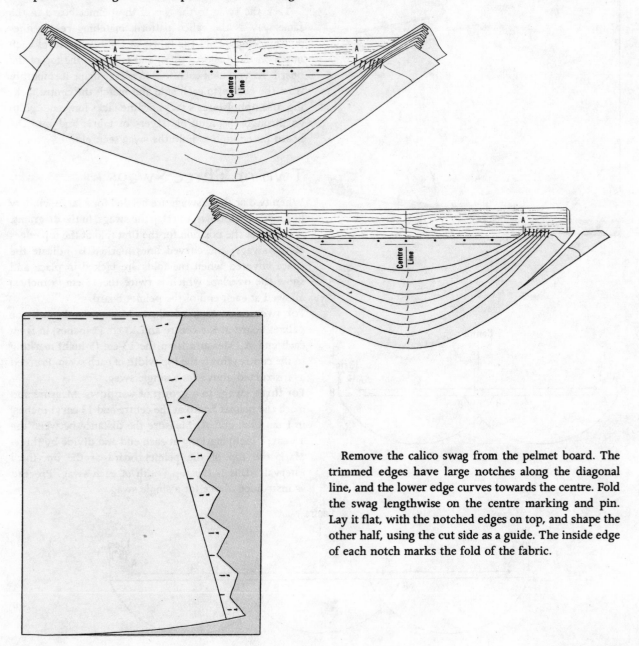

Remove the calico swag from the pelmet board. The trimmed edges have large notches along the diagonal line, and the lower edge curves towards the centre. Fold the swag lengthwise on the centre marking and pin. Lay it flat, with the notched edges on top, and shape the other half, using the cut side as a guide. The inside edge of each notch marks the fold of the fabric.

MAKING THE SWAG

Cut the curtain fabric by the calico pattern, placing the centre marking on the lengthwise grain of the fabric. If the fabric has a design, make sure it is central. Tack the centre line on the fabric. Cut a sateen lining by the same pattern but ·6 cm (¼ inch) shorter.

Turn the lower edge of the top fabric under 1·2 cm (½ inch) and press. Lay the lining over the fabric, wrong sides together; keep the top and notched edges even; pin. Turn the lower edge of the lining under 1·2 cm (½ inch) and pin it to the fabric ·6 cm (¼ inch) from the edge. Slip-stitch in place. Sew the lining and fabric together along the notched edges and top, using the multi-stitch zig-zag. Press.

Tack the swag to the top of the pelmet board in the same way as the calico pattern, matching centre lines and markings. Fold the fabric at the inside cut of each notch on the diagonal lines, and tack it to the top of the board. As you tack each fold in place, shape it smoothly from the centre to each side and match the centre tacking. Use upholsterer's tacks or fine tacks long enough to go through the multiple layers of fabric and into the board far enough to hold the swag securely.

Two or Three Swags

When two or three swags are needed for a large window or group of windows, overlap the swags. In the diagrams, A indicates the position for the first fold at the top edges of the swags; the curved lines marked B indicate the space covered when the folds are tacked in place and show the overlap, which is twice the 13 cm (5 inches) allowed at each end of the pelmet board.

For two swags to a window. Measure and mark the pelmet board at the centre and 13 cm (5 inches) in from each end A. Measure from the 13-cm (5-inch) marking to the centre; this is the top width of each swag. Proceed as instructed above for a single swag.

For three swags to a group of windows. Measure and mark the pelmet board at the centre and 13 cm (5 inches) in from each end A. Measure the distance between the 13-cm (5-inch) marking at each end and divide by three. Mark the top of the pelmet board at the one-third intervals; this is the top width of each swag. Proceed as instructed above for a single swag.

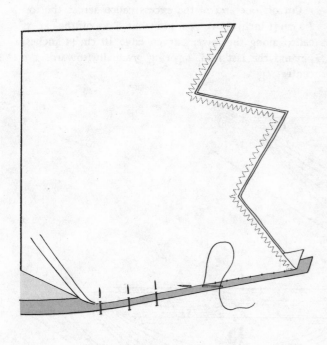

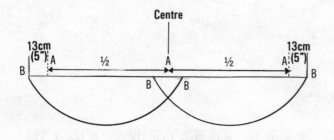

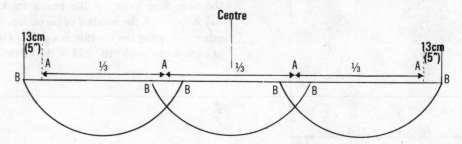

Cascades

Cascades extend round the returns of the pelmet board and overlap the swag in front about 15 cm (6 inches). The longest depth is the outside edge, which is generally between 69 cm (27 inches) and 91 cm (36 inches), depending on the height of the window; however, there is no set rule. The inside edge of the cascade matches the depth of the finished swag.

MAKING A CALICO PATTERN

Straighten the ends and cut the calico a few cm (inches) longer than the outside edge of the cascade. Measure the depth of the return across the end and add 1·2 cm ($\frac{1}{2}$ inch) for a seam allowance. Mark the top edge of the calico this distance from the outer edge. Fold the first pleat, bringing the fold to the inside edge of the return. Make the pleat 10 cm (4 inches) deep (20 cm (8 inches) of fabric). Form two more pleats of the same depth, overlapping the previous pleat about 7·5 cm (3 inches). *Example*: 11 cm (4$\frac{1}{2}$ inches) (10-cm (4-inch) return plus seam allowance) plus 61 cm (24 inches) (3 pleats) plus 5 cm (2 inches) (1·5-cm (1-inch) space between two pleats) plus 11 cm (4$\frac{1}{2}$ inches) (from last fold to inside edge and seam) = 71 cm (35 inches). If pleats are placed one on top of the other, make them at least 13 cm (5 inches) deep. Notch the folds at the top to mark the position of the folds for each pleat.

At the outside edge, 69 to 91 cm (27 to 36 inches) from the top, cut straight across the depth of the return and seam allowance. Mark the inside edge approximately 38 cm (15 inches) from the top, or the depth of the swag. Then draw a diagonal line between these two points. Cut on the drawn line.

MAKING THE CASCADE

Cut the curtain fabric by the calico pattern, placing the top edge on the crosswise grain and the outside and inside edges on the lengthwise grain. Allow 2·5 cm (1 inch) on the top edge for the overlap on the pelmet board and 1·2 cm ($\frac{1}{2}$ inch) on the lower edge for a seam allowance. Remember to cut one cascade for the right side and one for the left. If your fabric has a design, it must fall in the same place on each cascade. Cut the facing the same size as the fabric.

Pin the facing to the fabric, right sides together. Stitch 1·2 cm ($\frac{1}{2}$ inch) from the edge, leaving the top edge open. Cut diagonally across the corners, ·3 cm ($\frac{1}{8}$ inch) from the stitching. Press. Turn the fabric to the right side. Pull out the corners, fold on the seamline and press. Fold the pleats and pin them in place across the top edge. Lap the straight top edge over the top of the pelmet board 2·5 cm (1 inch) and tack it in place. The pleated section must overlap the swag across the front.

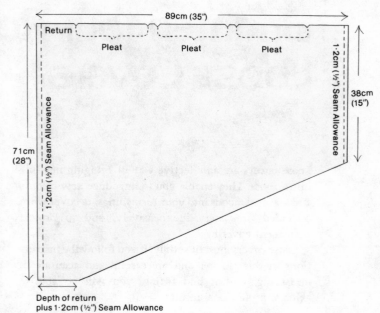

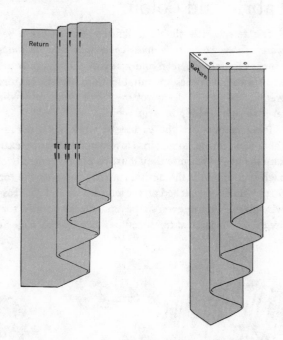

FINISHING THE TOP

To finish the top of the pelmet, cut self-fabric 2·5 cm (1 inch) longer and 7·5 cm (3 inches) wider than the top of the board. Spread the fabric over the top of the pelmet. Turn the edges under 1·2 cm ($\frac{1}{2}$ inch) along the front and ends, overlap the cut edges of the swags and cascades 2·5 cm (1 inch) and tack the cover to the board. Use steel furniture nails that are long enough to go through the multiple layers of fabric and into the board. Across the back, bring the fabric over the edge of the board and tack it to the underside.

Brighten Your Room with Loose Covers

Loose covers are an effective way of bringing new life into a room. They enable you to introduce new colours and seasonal moods into your furnishings, to cover worn or faded upholstery inexpensively, and to protect permanent coverings.

Loose covers must fit snugly. If you follow the instructions in this chapter and are careful and accurate in measuring, cutting and fitting, you will be able to achieve professional results.

Fabric and Colour

Fabric selection is almost unlimited. But *choose closely woven fabric so that the loose cover will hold its shape.* Linen, chintz, velveteen and many of the lovely cotton and synthetic fabrics are suitable. Consider the texture, weave, colour and design of the fabric. Remember that large designs belong in large rooms.

Plain colours are the easiest to work with because there is no design to match. Flower prints require extra care in cutting because they must be placed centrally on each section, with the design running towards the top. Stripes must be matched on the lengthwise and the crosswise grains. Choose even stripes and checks because they are easier to match at the seamlines. See *Checks*, page 53.

Measuring Your Chair

Record the measurements of your chair on the chart on page 392. Measure accurately, following the exact lines of the chair, and add seam allowances as indicated on the measurement chart. Always measure the lengths of the outside back, outside arms, and front section from seamline to floor; then deduct from these measurements the amount not required for finishing, see page 405.

Estimating Fabric Requirements

After you have recorded the measurements of your chair on the chart, estimate the fabric required.

To estimate how much to buy add the *lengthwise* measurements of the sections and divide by 100 cm (36 inches). If the fabric has a design that must be matched, add an extra metre (yard) for matching. If you are piping the seams, add one metre (1 yard) of fabric to cover the cord. If you are going to make a flounce or skirt for the chair, add the extra amount required, see page 400. (For zips see page 403.)

Preparing to Work

Collect all your sewing equipment together. You will need a box of sharp pins, tape measure, coloured pencil or chalk, hand sewing needles, heavy-duty thread, ironing board, iron and, of course, your sewing machine. Place the chair to be covered on a card table or low table.

Pin-Fitting a Calico Pattern or the Loose Cover Fabric

Your first step is to pin-fit the chair. If you are a beginner or if the chair has an unusual shape, it is advisable to make a calico pattern. If you have made loose covers before and feel confident about your ability, you can begin with the loose cover fabric. The sequence of steps is the same in both cases.

Cut all length measurements on the lengthwise grain of the fabric and all width measurements on the crosswise grain. Cut out the calico or loose cover fabric roughly to correspond with the measurements for each section of the chair, following the sequence in which the measurements were taken. Tear the calico; however, if you are working with the fabric in this initial 'blocking', draw a thread on the lengthwise or crosswise grain to indicate the cutting line, and cut the fabric along the drawn thread. As each section is cut, mark the centre on the lengthwise grain with a small notch at each end.

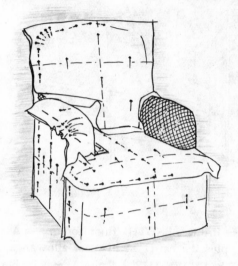

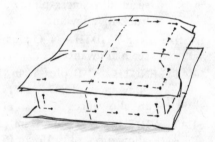

Pin-mark the centre of the chair at the top and lower edges. Then pin the section in its proper place, using one or two pins to hold it to the chair.

To pin-fit the calico pattern. Pin each section to the chair, following the sequence in which the measurements were taken. The dotted lines in the illustration indicate the lengthwise and crosswise grains of the fabric; these may be marked on the calico but not on the fabric. Centre the section on the chair and pin on the lengthwise grain and crosswise grain, then pin near the outer edges. Keep the crosswise grain parallel to the floor. At the widest points, the calico extends 2·5 cm (1 inch) beyond the seamline on each side of the chair; at narrower points, however, the extension is greater. At rounded edges, place the pins crosswise and distribute the fullness evenly between them.

Pin the sections together at the seamline, following the lines of the chair. Begin at the centre of the seams and work to the outer edges, placing pins parallel to the

(*Continued on page 394*)

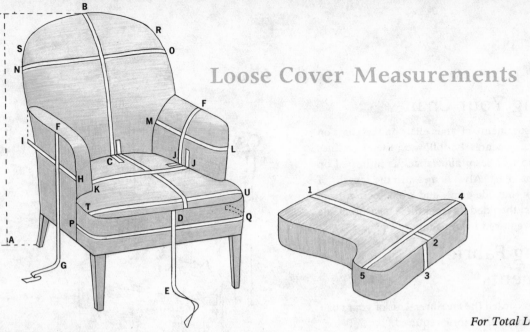

Loose Cover Measurements

For Total Length

OUTSIDE BACK LENGTH (floor to top) – **A–B**
plus 2·5 cm (1 inch) seam allowance.. _____ cm (in) _____ cm (in)

OUTSIDE BACK WIDTH – **R–S** plus 5 cm (2 inches)
seam allowance. . . . . _____ cm (in) _____ cm (in)

INSIDE BACK LENGTH – **B–C** plus 5 cm (2 inches)
seam allowances plus 7·5 cm (3 inches)
'tuck-in' allowance . . . . _____ cm (in) _____ cm (in)

INSIDE BACK WIDTH – **N–O** plus 5 cm (2 inches)
seam allowances. . . . . _____ cm (in) _____ cm (in)

SEAT LENGTH – **C–D** plus 5 cm (2 inches) seam
allowances plus 7·5 cm (3 inches) 'tuck-
in' allowance. . . . . _____ cm (in) _____ cm (in)

SEAT WIDTH – **J–K** plus 5 cm (2 inches) seam
allowances plus 15 cm (6 inches) 'tuck-
in' allowances. _____ cm (in)

SEAT WIDTH – **T–U** plus 5 cm (2 inches) seam
allowances. . . . . _____ cm (in)

FRONT LENGTH – **D–E** plus 2·5 cm (1 inch) seam
allowance. . . . . _____ cm (in) _____ cm (in)

FRONT WIDTH – **P–Q** plus 5 cm (2 inches) seam
allowances. . . . . _____ cm (in)

OUTSIDE ARM LENGTH (arm to floor) – **F–G**
plus 2·5 cm (1 inch) seam allowance _____ cm (in) × 2 = _____ cm (in)

OUTSIDE ARM WIDTH – **H–I** plus 5 cm (2 inches)
seam allowances. . . . . _____ cm (in)

INSIDE ARM LENGTH – **F–J** plus 5 cm (2 inches)
seam allowances. . . . . _____ cm (in) × 2 = _____ cm (in)

INSIDE ARM WIDTH – **L–M** plus 5 cm (2 inches)
seam allowances, plus 7·5 cm (3 inches)
'tuck-in' allowance. . . . . _____ cm (in)

CUSHION –

Length – **1–2** plus 5 cm (2 inches) seam
allowances. . . . . _____ cm (in) × 2 = _____ cm (in)

Width – **4–5** plus 5 cm (2 inches) seam
allowances. . . . . _____ cm (in)

Depth of boxing – **2–3** plus 5 cm (2
inches) seam allowances. . . . . _____ cm (in) _____ cm (in)

Additional Measurements for Wing Chair

INSIDE WING LENGTH – **A-1–B-1** plus 5 cm
(2 inches) seam allowances . . . .

For Total Length

_____ cm (in) × 2 = _____ cm (in)

INSIDE WING WIDTH – **C-1–D-1** plus 5 cm
(2 inches) seam allowances, plus 7·5 cm
(3 inches) 'tuck-in' allowance . . . .

_____ cm (in)

OUTSIDE WING LENGTH – **A-1–B-2** plus 5 cm
(2 inches) seam allowances . . . .

_____ cm (in) × 2 = _____ cm (in)

OUTSIDE WING WIDTH – **C-1–D-2** plus 5 cm
(2 inches) seam allowances . . . .

_____ cm (in)

FRONT ARM LENGTH – **E-1–F-1** plus 5 cm (2
inches) seam allowances . . . .

_____ cm (in) × 2 = _____ cm (in)

FRONT ARM WIDTH – **G-1–H-1** plus 5 cm (2
inches) seam allowances . . . .

_____ cm (in)

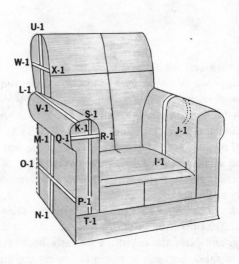
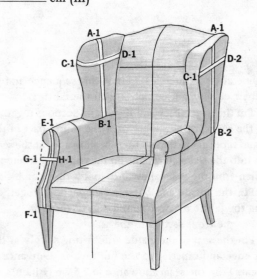

Measurements for Chair with Wide Rounded Arm and Front Section

(Take these measurements instead of arm measurements on preceding page.)

INSIDE ARM LENGTH – **I-1–J-1** plus 5 cm (2
inches) seam allowances, plus 7·5 cm
(3 inches) 'tuck-in' allowance . . . .

For Total Length

_____ cm (in) × 2 = _____ cm (in)

INSIDE ARM WIDTH – **K-1–L-1** plus 5 cm (2
inches) seam allowances . . . .

_____ cm (in)

OUTSIDE ARM LENGTH – **M-1–N-1** plus 2·5 cm
(1 inch) seam allowance . . . .

_____ cm (in) × 2 = _____ cm (in)

OUTSIDE ARM WIDTH – **O-1–P-1** plus 5 cm
(2 inches) seam allowances . . . .

_____ cm (in)

FRONT ARM LENGTH – **S-1–T-1** plus 5 cm (2
inches) seam allowances . . . .

_____ cm (in) × 2 = _____ cm (in)

FRONT ARM WIDTH – **Q-1–R-1** plus 5 cm (2
inches) seam allowances . . . .

_____ cm (in)

SIDE-BACK LENGTH – **U-1–V-1** plus 5 cm (2
inches) seam allowances . . . .

_____ cm (in) × 2 = _____ cm (in)

SIDE-BACK WIDTH – **W-1–X-1** plus 5 cm (2
inches) seam allowances . . . .

_____ cm (in)

393

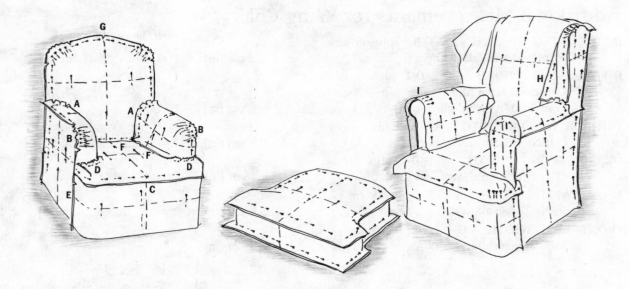

seamline at close intervals. Follow this sequence and fit the chair closely but do not stretch the fabric:

A Pin the inside back and inside arm sections together with the seam fitting snugly over the round part of the arm and tapering to the full tuck-in allowance at the seat. Slash into the seam allowance on the curve for a smooth fit, then trim the seam allowance to 2·5 cm (1 inch).

B Pin the inside and outside arm sections together, easing the fabric over the round part of the arm.

C Pin the front section to the seat.

D Pin the seat to the inside arm, fitting snugly at the outer edge and tapering to the full tuck-in allowance at the seat. Trim the seam allowance to 2·5 cm (1 inch) and slash into it for a smooth fit.

E Pin the outside arm to the front section.

F Join the seat to the inside arm and inside back sections, allowing for the full tuck-in allowance.

G Begin at the centre and pin the outside back to the inside back and outside arm sections.

A wing chair or a *chair with front arm sections* requires additional seams:

H A tuck-in allowance should be made between the wing and the back, tapering from the 2·5-cm (1-inch) seam allowance at the top to the tuck-in at the seat.

I Pin small calico or fabric pieces to the front of each arm section. As the seams are joined, ease the arm section slightly at the seamline.

Block the calico for the cushion sections the same way as for the chair sections. Cut one continuous strip for the boxing, and place the seam in the centre back. Pin the calico or fabric sections in place, following the lines of the cushion.

When the pin-fitting is completed, examine the chair carefully to be sure that the cover fits snugly and that the seams are in the correct position. Make any necessary adjustments. Trim all seam allowances to 2·5 cm (1 inch).

You can follow the above procedure for all types of chairs and sofas. The method of fitting and assembling the cover is the same regardless of the number of sections to be covered.

Before removing the pin-fitted cover from the chair, mark the seamlines and label each section.

MARKING THE SEAMLINE

Cut small notches in the seam allowances at centre points and on each side of the eased sections. Open the seams with the fingers and, with coloured chalk, mark the seamline on the wrong side of the fabric over the parallel pins. Mark both sides of the seam allowance. Match these markings in seaming the loose cover fabric.

Label the calico so that you can identify each section – for example, 'inside back', 'left inside arm', 'right inside arm' and so on. If the loose cover fabric is pinned to the chair, write the identifications on pieces of paper and pin them to the fabric.

Leave all seam pins in place. Remove the pins holding the calico or fabric to the upholstered chair. Mark the length of the opening at one back seam where inside and outside backs join, then remove the calico pattern from the chair.

Cutting the Fabric

If you blocked and pin-fitted the cover fabric instead of the calico, you are ready to proceed with the construction. If you made a calico pattern, you are now ready to cut the fabric.

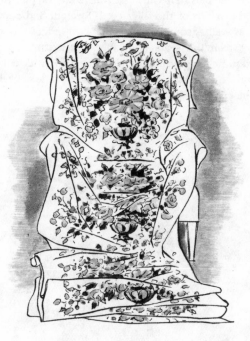

Remove the seamline pins. Lay the calico pattern, right side up, on the right side of the cover fabric. The lengths of all sections must be on the lengthwise grain. *Place flower prints centrally; match stripes on the lengthwise grain; match checks on both the lengthwise and the crosswise grains.* Pin the pattern in place along the edges, then cut. Notch the seam allowances to correspond with the pattern.

Pin-Fitting the Fabric

It is important to pin-fit the loose cover fabric even though you pin-fitted the calico pattern. The texture and weight of the calico differ from those of the fabric, and pin-fitting now may save time and trouble later.

Follow the same sequence of steps as for the calico pattern. Pin-fit the cut out sections to the chair *right side out* to ensure proper matching of the design and a good fit. One arm of a chair or sofa may be slightly lower or fuller than the other. Match notches and place pins at close intervals, parallel to the 2·5-cm (1-inch) seams. Fit closely, but do not stretch the fabric. Very few adjustments should be necessary.

Mark the seamlines as instructed above. Remove pins controlling the ease. With a needle and double strand of heavy-duty thread, place small running stitches on the seamline between the notches, and gather the fabric to fit the joining section. Fasten the thread ends.

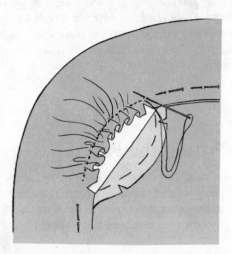

Before removing the pin-fitted cover from the chair, measure the seams to be trimmed with piping or braid to determine the length required. All seams should be trimmed except those joining the seat and those with a tuck-in allowance. An arm chair or wing chair may require 12 to 14 metres (yards), a sofa with three cushions, approximately 25 metres (yards). Remember that the cushion has two trimmed seams – those that join the top and bottom sections to the boxing; so double the measurement round the cushion. If piping is used at the top of the flounce, measure the circumference of the chair.

When you have completed the seam measurements, remove the pins holding the fabric to the upholstered chair; then remove the seamline pins in the zip area only. Carefully remove the loose cover.

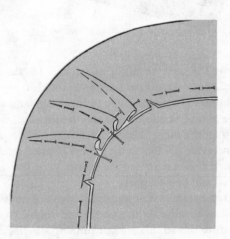

If darts are used instead of gathers to control the fullness, pin the darts to follow the curve or corner of the chair. A word of caution: darts may break the continuity of a striped or check design; avoid using them if you can ease in the fullness.

Accenting Seams

Seams in loose covers are accented to emphasise the lines of the chair, to give added strength to the seam itself, and to ensure a professional finish.

PIPED SEAM

The most popular seam in loose covers is the piped seam. Either self or contrasting fabric may be used. The size of the filler cord used depends on the size of the chair or sofa and the weight of the fabric covering the cord.

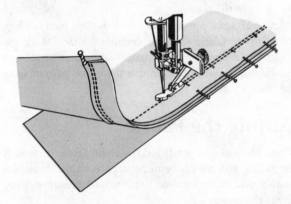

Cut the bias strips, cover the cord and form the seams, following the instructions beginning on page 244. The width of the bias strips must be 5 cm (2 inches) plus three times the width of the filler cord. Straight and curved seams as well as square corners are used in loose covers. Do not trim the seam allowances after stitching the corded piping in place but do slash them on inside curves and square corners and notch them on outside curves so that the cord will lie smoothly.

To join ends of piping in a seam. Overlap the ends of the corded piping 2·5 cm (1 inch) as you pin the piping to the single seamline. Cut the cord and bias fabric even at the first end. Pull out the cord at the second end and cut off 2·5 cm (1 inch) so that the ends of cord will just meet. Smooth the bias fabric back over the cord, unpick the stitching as far as the end of the cord. Turn the end of the bias fabric under ·9 cm ($\frac{3}{8}$ inch) and lap it round the first end, with the ends of cord meeting; pin. Stitch the cording in place.

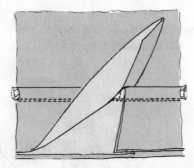

To match stripes and checks. Join the seams from the right side of the fabric as follows: stitch the corded piping to the seamline of one section; then turn the seam allowance of the second section to the underside, and pin. Lay both sections right side up, and lap the folded edge over the second seam allowance to the cording; pin in place. Slip-tack from the right side. See page

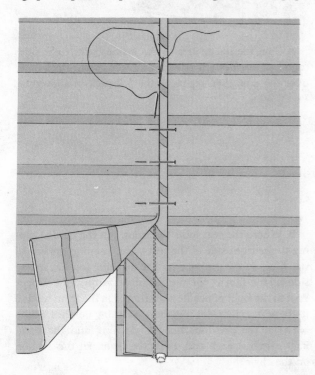

62. Stitch the seam from the wrong side, following the centre of the short tacking stitch. (Many people slip-tack the seams in *all* fabrics so that they can fit each section to the chair before stitching.)

BRAID SEAM
Braid may be used on almost any type of cover to lend interest and colour. If the loose cover is casual, select braid that is simple in style. Pin the braid to the single seam allowance, right sides together, extending the heading slightly over the seamline. Stitch just outside the seamline. Pin the second seam edge over the braid with the fabric right sides together. Place the work under the needle with the first line of stitching up so that you can use it as a guide. Stitch on the seamline, just beyond the previous stitching.

BOUND SEAM
This seam is an attractive finish for simple covers where lightweight fabrics are used and where there is little stress or strain on the seam. Pin and stitch the seam, right sides together. Press. Then follow the instructions for *Plain Bound Seam*, page 93.

SEAM FINISH

After the seams of loosely woven fabrics are stitched, the edges should be finished to prevent fraying. Use the blindstitch zig-zag on the machine, or overcast by hand. See pages 93 and 94. Although seam edges are turned in the same direction, finish each edge separately.

Making the Loose Cover

Before you begin, be sure identifying labels are securely pinned to each section, as suggested on page 395.

DARTS

If darts are used, mark the line on the wrong side of the fabric over the pins; then remove the pins. Fold the dart, right sides together, matching markings; pin and stitch, following the instructions on page 100.

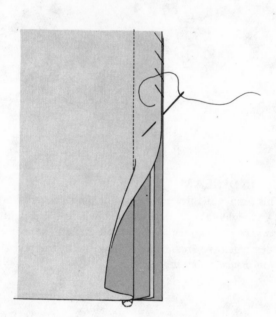

BASIC RULES FOR SEAMS

– Seams that will be crossed by other seams are stitched first.

– Always pin and stitch the corded piping or braid to a single seam allowance; then pin and stitch to the joining section. Place the pins at right angles to the seamline with the heads towards the cut edge. Do not attempt to join sections and trimming in one operation.

– If striped or check fabric is used, slip-tack the sections together from the right side; then stitch from the wrong side. See page 397.

SEQUENCE OF SEAMS

Remove seamline pins and join the sections, right sides together, in the following sequence:

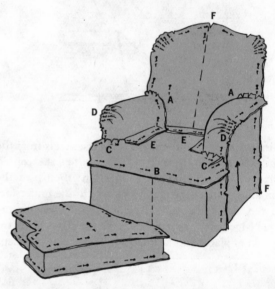

A Join the inside arm to the inside back, right sides together. Back-stitch at each end. This seam fits snugly over the arm, then tapers to the full tuck-in allowance. Press.

B Where the seat joins the front, pin the corded piping to the right side of the seat seam, keeping the line of stitching on the piping over the marking (on the wrong side of the fabric) for the seamline. Adjust the Zipper Foot to the right of needle and stitch. Pin the front section to the seat, right sides together, matching notches. Stitch between the previous line of stitching and the cord. Back-stitch at each end. Press the seam. Fit this section on the chair.

C Join seat to inside arm, as instructed in 'A' on opposite page.

D Pin; then stitch piping to the seamline of the inside arm and front sections, as instructed in 'B'. Join outside arm to inside arm and front sections, right sides together, matching notches. Back-stitch at each end. Press. Try the assembled sections on the chair; make any necessary adjustments.

E Pin, then stitch seat to inside arms and back sections, right sides together. Press.

F Pin piping to inside back and outside arms in a continuous line, as instructed in 'B' above. Stitch, leaving the piping free in the zip opening (see page 403). Try assembled sections on the chair; make any necessary adjustments. Press.

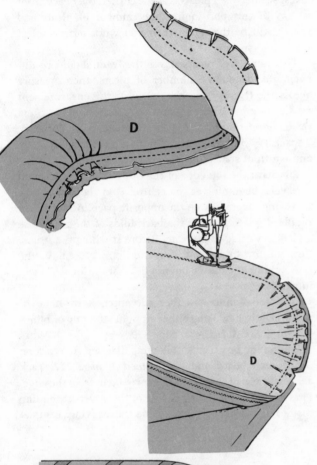

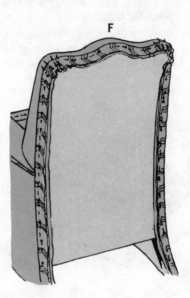

G Pin outside back to inside back and outside arm sections, right sides together. Stitch from the top of the zip opening (see page 403), to the lower edge on the opposite side, as instructed in 'B' above. Remove the pins holding the piping to the outside arm and inside back sections in the zip opening; then pin and stitch the piping to the outside back section. Press. Try the loose cover on the chair for inspection.

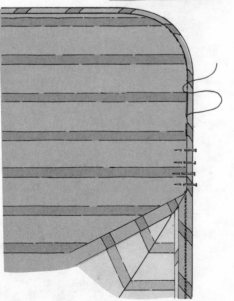

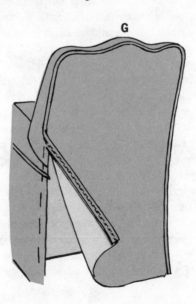

399

Adding a Skirt or Flounce

PREPARATORY STEPS

Leave the loose covers on the chair until you are ready to stitch the flounce in place. Pin-mark the position of the flounce an even distance from the floor, using a ruler. After the flounce has been stitched in place, cut off the excess fabric 2·5 cm (1 inch) below the marking for the flounce, and press the seam allowances of both the cover and the flounce towards the top of the cover to eliminate bulk. (Keep these seam allowances turned towards the top when the finished cover is placed on the chair.)

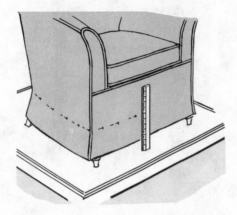

The flounce on the average chair is 18 or 20 cm (7 or 8 inches) deep and should clear the floor by approximately 2·5 cm (1 inch). For an 18-cm (7-inch) flounce, pin-mark the cover 20 cm (8 inches) from the floor. To the depth of the flounce, add 4 cm (1½ inches) for hem and turning plus 2·5 cm (1 inch) for a top seam allowance. If you are planning to make a heading (as for spaced box pleats, described below), add an extra 2·5 cm (1 inch).

To determine the length required for the flounce, measure round the chair, over the pin line. To this measurement, add the amount for pleats or gathers, plus 15 to 20 cm (6 to 8 inches) for seaming of strips, ease and hems at the opening. *Example*: If the circumference of the chair is 2·7 m (3 yards), twice this measurement, 5·5 m (6 yards), plus 15 or 20 cm (6 or 8 inches) is required for evenly spaced box pleats; three times this measurement, or 8·2 m (9 yards), plus 15 or 20 cm (6 or 8 inches) is required for closed box pleats or side pleats.

Cut the flounce on the crosswise grain of the fabric. Draw a thread from the fabric to indicate the cutting line. Before you begin, study the instructions for the flounce you have selected so that you can plan where to place the seams. They should not be noticeable in the finished flounce.

FLOUNCE WITH SPACED BOX PLEATS

The heading illustrated requires an extra 2·5 cm (1 inch) in the depth of the flounce. Turn the top edge under 2·5 cm (1 inch) and press.

In the illustration, the pleats and the spacing between pleats are identical in width. The back folds of each pleat meet at the centre. Plan the flounce so that the centre of a pleat is at the centre of the chair front and the centre of a space between pleats is at the corner, over each front leg. With this positioning, the number of pleats and spaces will be the same when you work out the pleat width and spacing.

The number of pleats across the front should be uneven. Decide on the number of pleats, then measure across the front of the chair. Divide this measurement by the number of pleats and spaces. *Example*: 70 cm (28 inches) (front measurement) divided by 14 (7 pleats, 7 spaces) = 5 cm (2 inches) (width of each finished pleat and width of spacing).

Pin-mark the top edge of the flounce at 5-cm (2-inch) intervals, beginning at the centre. Fold the box pleats, following diagram A on the opposite page. As seams are required, place them at the back folds of the pleat; use a plain 1·5-cm (⅝-inch) seam. Before stitching the seams, turn the top fold away from the flounce. Remove the pins holding the pleats, but not those at the 5-cm (2-inch) intervals.

Hem the flounce – either slip-stitch it by hand or machine-stitch it, using either straight stitching or blind-stitching. See *Side Hems*, page 370.

Fold in the box pleats, following diagram A. Work on the ironing board and use *Method 3*, page 212. Tack across the top of the pleats, 1·2 cm (½ inch) from the edge. Pin the flounce to the right side of the cover, extending the heading 1·2 cm (½ inch) above the marking. Begin at

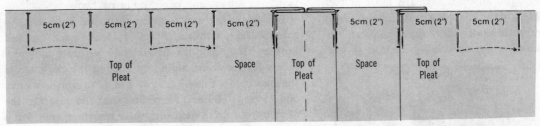

| 5cm (2″) | 5cm (2″) | 5cm (2″) | 5cm (2″) | | | 5cm (2″) | 5cm (2″) | 5cm (2″) |
| Top of Pleat | | | Space | Top of Pleat | Space | Top of Pleat | | |

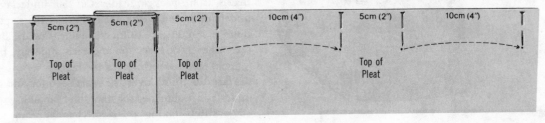

| 5cm (2″) | 5cm (2″) | 5cm (2″) | 10cm (4″) | 5cm (2″) | 10cm (4″) |
| Top of Pleat | Top of Pleat | Top of Pleat | | Top of Pleat | |

the centre front and align the centre of the pleat with the centre of the loose cover. Ease the flounce slightly and extend the ends at least 5 cm (2 inches) beyond the sides of the opening. Stitch the flounce in place, 1·2 cm (½ inch) below the top edge. Finish the seam edge on the loose cover.

FLOUNCE WITH SIDE PLEATS

The flounce illustrated here has no spacing between pleats. In the 70-cm (28-inch) measurement in the example for spaced box pleats, 14 pleats, 5 cm (2 inches) deep, will fit across the front of the chair. Pin-mark the top and bottom edges of the flounce alternately at 5- and 10-cm (2- and 4-inch) intervals. Fold the pleats, following diagram **B** above. Work on the ironing board and use *Method 3*, page 212. Place the seams at the back fold of the pleats.

Sew corded piping to the right side of the flounce. Pin the flounce to the loose cover, right sides together, keeping the line of piping stitching on the marking that

designates the position of the flounce. Ease the flounce slightly and extend the ends about 5 cm (2 inches) beyond the sides of the opening. Place the work under the needle with the flounce and previous stitching uppermost so you can use the stitching as a guide. Stitch, crowding the stitching between the cord and previous line of stitching. Trim the seam allowance on the loose cover to 2·5 cm (1 inch). Press the seam towards the top of the cover. Although seam edges are turned in the same direction, finish each edge separately.

GATHERED FLOUNCE

A gathered flounce is used for an informal effect in cottages or living rooms. Allow one and one-half or twice the circumference of the chair for fullness, plus 15 to 20 cm (6 to 8 inches) for seaming of strips, ease and a hem at the opening. Hem and gather the flounce. Stitch the flounce to the loose cover, following the instructions above.

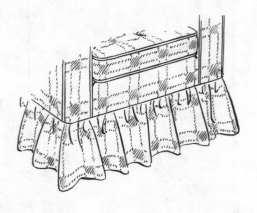

401

SKIRT WITH OPEN INVERTED PLEAT

A straight skirt, with an open inverted pleat at each corner over the legs of the chair, is a neat, tailored finish. An underlay forms the underside of the open pleat. This means that each pleat has an opening instead of back

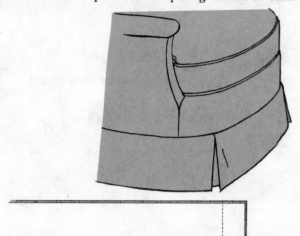

fold, and bulk is thus eliminated. The skirt is lined with matching sateen, and needs no lower hems.

Decide on the depth of the skirt. See page 400. To this measurement, add 4 cm (1½ inches) for top and bottom seams. For the length, take separate measurements for the front, sides and back of the chair across the marking for the skirt. To each of these measurements, add 25 cm (10 inches) for pleat, seams and ease. Cut the skirt in four sections, using these measurements. Pin a label to the right side of each section for identification; that is, front, back and sides. Cut four underlays for the underside of the pleats, making them the depth of the flounce and 25 cm (10 inches) wide. Cut the lining the same as each skirt section and each underlay, but ·6 cm (¼ inch) less in depth. Press the fabric.

Place the lining over the skirt sections and over the underlays, right sides together, and pin along the lower edge. Stitch, taking a 1·2-cm (½-inch) seam. Trim the seam allowance to ·6 cm (¼ inch). Press; then press the seam allowances towards the lining. Turn the right sides together again, fold the skirt and underlay fabric ·6 cm (¼ inch) from the stitching line, and pin the lining in place across the ends. Stitch; then back-stitch at each end. Trim the seam allowances to ·6 cm (¼ inch) and cut diagonally across the corners. Turn to the right side and pull out the corners to square them. Fold the skirt and underlay fabric across the bottom ·6 cm (¼ inch) from the stitching line and press. Fold the ends on the seamline and press.

Fold the ends of each skirt section under 10 cm (4 inches) to form the top folds of the pleats; pin. Do not press the folds at this time. Place the skirt sections wrong

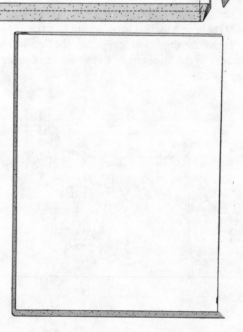

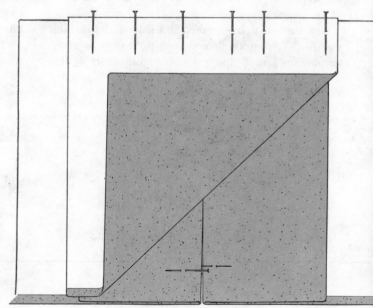

side up. Bring the folded edges together in the following sequence: join sides to front skirt, and back to sides. Place the underlays over the joining folds, wrong side up, and pin across the top. The underlays should extend about 1·2 cm (½ inch) beyond the outer edges of the pleats.

Try the skirt on the chair, over the pin marking, to be sure it fits correctly. The centre of inverted pleats should be over the legs and there should be a slight ease in the skirt to allow for the thicknesses of fabric. Make any necessary adjustments in the pleat folds. Press the pleats; then stitch the underlays in place 2·5 cm (1 inch) from the top edge. At the side of the fastening, stitch the underlay to the side skirt only.

Cut off the excess loose cover fabric 2·5 cm (1 inch) below the marking for the skirt. Before stitching the skirt in place, insert the zip following the directions below; however, extend the open end of the zip only to the seamline of the skirt.

Pin the skirt to the cover, right sides together, keeping the seam edge 2·5 cm (1 inch) below the marking on the loose cover. At each side of the zip opening, the pleat folds extend to the seamline and the underlay on the side skirt extends beyond the seamline. Stitch with the skirt uppermost, taking a 2·5-cm (1-inch) seam. Back-stitch at each end. Press the seam; then press the seam allowances towards the top of the loose cover. Although seam edges are turned in the same direction, finish each edge separately. Use press fasteners to hold the underlay in position under the back skirt.

Inserting the Zip

For an average chair, one fastening on the left side is sufficient; for a sofa, two fastenings, one at each side, are necessary. Select either a 45-, 50- or 60-cm (18-, 20- or 24-inch) zip, depending on the length of the closing required.

SIDE FASTENING

The following instructions explain how to apply the zip when the fastening is on the left side of the loose cover. When the fastening is on the right side, reverse the right and left sides in the instructions as well as the adjustment of the Zipper Foot.

Trim the flounce even with the seam edge on the left side of the opening. If corded piping is used in the seam that joins the flounce to the cover, pull out the end of the cord and cut off 2·5 cm (1 inch) (width of the seam allowance). Turn the seam allowances towards the top of the loose cover.

On the left side of the opening, fold the seam allowance under ·5 cm (³⁄₁₆ inch) from the seamline; carry the fold to the edge of the flounce. Close the zip. Pin; then tack

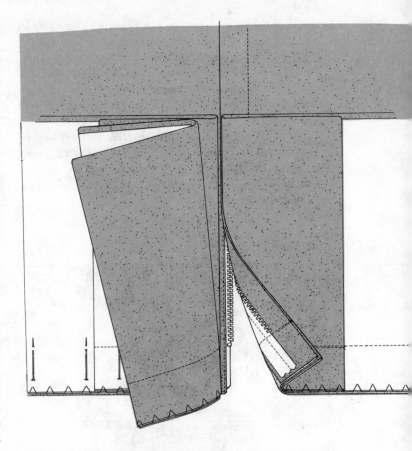

the folded edge to the right side of the zip tape, ·3 cm (⅛ inch) from the teeth; keep the pull-tab about 5 cm (2 inches) above the bottom of flounce. Adjust the Zipper Foot to the left of the needle and stitch near the fold from the top of the opening to the lower edge of the flounce.

On the right side of the opening, fold the seam allow-

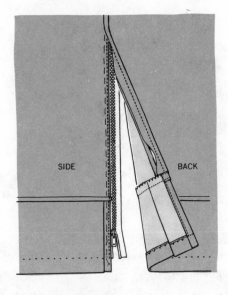

403

ance under on the seamline; carry the fold to the bottom of the flounce. Press. In the flounce area, turn the cut edge under 1·2 cm (½ inch) and pin it to the flounce. Lap the folded edge over the zip to the seamline on the opposite side, and pin. (The right side will overlap the left ·7 cm ($\frac{5}{16}$ inch) beyond the zip teeth; the piping will extend beyond the seamline.) Tack through all thicknesses a measured 1·5 cm ($\frac{5}{8}$ inch) from the fold. Adjust the Zipper Foot to the right of the needle; stitch across the top end and down the side to the hem of the flounce, following the even line of tacking. Tie the threads on the underside.

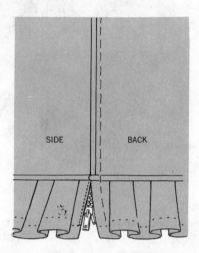

Blindstitching the final step of the zip insertion gives a finish that is almost invisible. Follow the instructions on page 178.

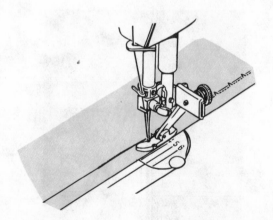

Work a bar tack across the top of the closing to prevent splitting. See page 337.

CENTRE BACK FASTENING

A fastening at the centre back of the loose cover is frequently used in sofas and chairs that will be placed against a wall or in a corner.

In a sofa the outside back section generally has one or two seams in which a zip may be inserted. In a chair the outside back is usually in one section and it is necessary to make a centre back seam. Refer to the chart on page 392. Measure the *Outside Back Width – R to S,* and add 10 cm (4 inches) instead of 5 cm (2 inches) for seam allowances. The additional 5 cm (2 inches) are for the centre seam allowances. Block the calico or fabric as instructed on page 391. Fold the outside back lengthwise through the centre, right sides together, then cut on the fold. Pin these edges together. Stitch from the top edge to the top of the zip opening, making a 2·5-cm (1-inch) seam. Reinforce with backstitching. Machine-tack the seam in the opening. Press the seam; then press it open.

Construct the loose cover up to the point of inserting the zip; then follow the instructions given under *Neckline or Sleeve Zip in Channel Seam,* page 181. However,

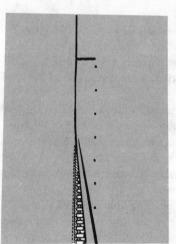

place the open end of the zip about 1·2 cm (½ inch) above the hem of the flounce, and place the tacking and stitching 1·2 cm (½ inch) from the centre tacked seam.

Finishing a Loose Cover without a Flounce

If you do not add a flounce or skirt to your loose cover, allow 7·5 or 10 cm (3 or 4 inches) on the lower edge for a turn under. Mark the seamline across the legs, following the contour of the chair frame. Cut out the fabric over the legs to within 1·2 cm (½ inch) of the seam marking. Stitch piping on the 1·2-cm (½-inch) seamline round

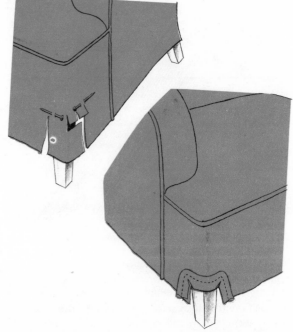

the cut out, as illustrated. Slash into the corners, almost to the stitching. Press. Turn the seam allowance to the underside. Turn the cut edges of the loose cover under 1·2 cm (½ inch) and stitch near the fold.

Place the cover on the chair. Make sure the cover fits smoothly and the seams are straight. Close the zip. Turn the lower edge of the cover over the chair frame to the underside and tack it to the frame.

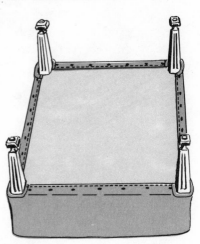

Holding the Loose Cover Securely

Here are two further suggestions.

– Sew 1·2-cm (½-inch) twill tape to the loose cover seams next to the chair legs. Cut the tape long enough to lap twice round the legs. Tie securely.

– Push a heavy cotton cord, 2 to 2·5 cm (¾ to 1 inch) in diameter, into the tuck-in to hold it in place. Or use a roll of cotton batting, 4 to 5 cm (1½ to 2 inches) in size, covered with calico, or a roll of brown paper. Any one of these will help prevent the loose cover from sliding.

Covering the Cushion

Cushions should be reversible (top to bottom). Floral designs should be in the centre on both sides of the cushion. Match stripes and checks, on both sides of the cushion, with the inside back and front sections of the chair. Checks must also match the inside arms. Match stripes and checks across the front of the boxing with those on both sides of the cushion.

CONSTRUCTING THE COVER

Pin-fit the fabric to the cushion, right side out, following the instructions for the calico pattern, page 391. Corners may be round or square; follow the exact shape of the cushion. Trim seam allowances to 2·5 cm (1 inch); mark the seamline and stitch piping or braid to the top and bottom sections, as in loose covers. Pin the boxing to the top and under sections. Join the ends of boxing at

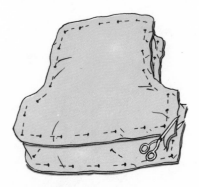

the back of the cushion. Stitch the boxing in place, but leave the seam open across the back and round the corners of the bottom section the entire length of the zip. Back-stitch at each end. Cut into the seam allowances on inside curves and notch them on outside curves. Press, then turn to the right side.

INSERTING THE ZIP

Two methods of zip insertion are explained here.

Method 1: Fold the boxing on the seamline of the opening and press. Open the zip. Pin the piped seam to the zip tape, right sides together, keeping the seamline about ·3 cm ($\frac{1}{8}$ inch) from the teeth or coil of the zip. Stitch on the seamline. Close the zip and turn it away from the seam. Lap the folded edge of the boxing over the zip to the piped seam, and pin through all thicknesses. Open the zip and tack a measured 1·5 cm ($\frac{5}{8}$ inch) from the fold. Stitch across the end, along the side, following the tacking, and across the opposite end.

inches) for centre seam allowances. Fold lengthwise through the centre, right sides together; then cut on the fold. Tack the cut edges together, making a 2·5-cm (1-inch) seam. Press the seam, then press it open. Place the teeth of the closed zip over the wrong side of the tacked seam, right side down, and pin through all thicknesses. Turn right side up and tack, on each side, a measured ·9 cm ($\frac{3}{8}$ inch) from the centre seam. Adjust the Zipper Foot to the left of the needle and stitch round the zip,

Method 2: Make a separate back section of the boxing and insert the zip before joining the boxing to the top and bottom sections. To do this, cut the back section the length of the zip, plus 5 cm (2 inches) for seam allowances, and the same width as the boxing plus 5 cm (2

following the tacked line. Join the ends of this separate back section to the rest of the boxing with a 2·5-cm (1-inch) seam. Stitch the boxing in place as instructed above.

406

Covering a Studio Bed or Couch

A loose cover for a studio couch conceals a spare bed for an extra guest. A tailored couch is illustrated here.

In covering the mattress, treat it as the cushion for a chair or sofa – in other words, make it reversible. Make a separate fitted cover for the divan base. Flower prints should be in the centre on both sides of the mattress. Match stripes or checks on the boxing with those on both sides of the mattress; also match the stripes or checks on the boxing and on the flounce for the divan base with those of the mattress. Cut each section on the true lengthwise and crosswise grains of the fabric. Draw a thread from the fabric to indicate the cutting line.

Covering the Mattress

Measure the length and width of the mattress and add 5 cm (2 inches) to each measurement for seam allowances. Cut two sections (one for each side of the mattress) by these measurements.

Measure the depth of the mattress and add 5 cm (2 inches) for seam allowances. Then measure round the mattress (both sides and ends) and add at least 20 cm (8 inches) for seam allowances. Cut the boxing on the lengthwise grain by these measurements; place seams at the back corners. If the fabric has a floral or one-way design, cut the boxing on the crosswise grain.

TO CURVE THE CORNERS

The corners of both top and bottom sections must be curved to fit the mattress. Here is a simple and easy method:

Place a piece of cardboard (about 20 by 28 cm (8 by 11 inches)) between the mattress and divan base, with the edges extending about 2·5 cm (1 inch) beyond the

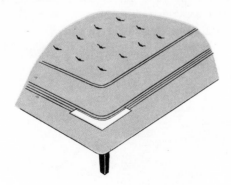

side and end of the mattress. Hold the cardboard securely, and mark it to indicate the curve of the mattress corner as well as the straight line of the side and end. Then cut off the cardboard edge along the marking.

Place the cardboard over the corners of the fabric (one at a time) with the fabric extending 2·5 cm (1 inch) (seam allowance) beyond the straight side and end of the cardboard. Hold the cardboard firmly in position and chalk-mark the shape of the corner of the fabric. *Do not cut.* This is the seamline in construction.

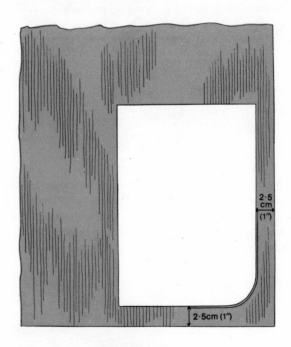

2·5 cm (1")

2·5cm (1")

TO MAKE THE COVER

Carefully study *Making the Loose Cover*, beginning on page 398; and *Covering the Cushion*, page 405. Then proceed with the construction of the mattress cover.

Stitch piping or braid to the 2·5-cm (1-inch) seamline

of both the top and bottom sections of the cover. Join the ends of the piping at the centre back, following the instructions on page 397. Try the sections over the mattress to make sure they fit correctly. Press. Join the boxing to the top and bottom sections, leaving the bottom seam open across the entire back and about 10 cm (4 inches) round the corners.

Trim the corner seam allowances to 2·5 cm (1 inch). Press; then press the seam allowances towards the boxing. Use two zips in the opening and place them so that the pull-tabs meet in the centre back. Insert the zips in the seam, following the instructions on page 406. Place the cover on the mattress and turn the seam allowances towards the boxing.

If you are not using zips, turn under the 2·5-cm (1-inch) seam allowance on the boxing the length of the opening, and press. Place the cover on the mattress and turn the seam allowances towards the boxing. Lap the folded edge of the boxing over the second seam allowance to the piping, and pin at about 10-cm (4-inch) intervals. Slip-stitch in place, using a curved needle and heavy thread.

Covering the Divan Base

Measure the length and width of the divan base and add 5 cm (2 inches) to each measurement for seam allowances. Cut the fabric; then *curve the corners* as instructed for the mattress. Stitch piping or braid to the seamline.

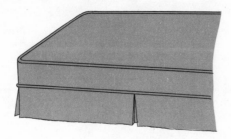

Measure the depth of the divan base and add 5 cm (2 inches) for seam allowances. Then measure round the divan base (both sides and ends) and add about 20 cm (8 inches) for seam allowances. Cut the boxing by these measurements. Join the boxing to the top section and try it over the divan base to make sure the fit is correct. Stitch piping or braid to the free edge of the boxing.

Measure the depth of the flounce from the bottom of the divan base to the floor and add 2·5 cm (1 inch) for seam allowance plus 4 cm (1½ inches) for the lower hem and turning. Measure the length round the divan base and add 30 cm (12 inches) for seam allowances plus the amount required for inverted pleats (40 cm (16 inches) for each) at the four corners and at the centre front and back. Cut the flounce by these measurements: place the seams in the back fold of the pleats. Hem the lower edge. Join the flounce to the boxing, right sides together; fold in the inverted pleats, making each fold 10 cm (4 inches) deep.

Covering the Pillows

You can choose from several pillow styles – box or wedge pillows, or round or square bolsters. You may need two or three pillows of the same style. To cover the pillows, follow the instructions for the cushion, page 405. Decorative scatter cushions may be added for colour contrast.

Making a One-Piece Fitted Cover

Take measurements over sheets and blankets. Measure the top section of the mattress and boxing as instructed above: cut one section to cover the mattress top. Curve the corners; then stitch piping or braid to the seamline. See *Covering the Mattress*, page 407. Join the boxing to the top section. Stitch piping or braid to the lower edge of the boxing.

Measure the depth of the flounce from the bottom of the mattress to the floor and add 2·5 cm (1 inch) for seam allowance plus 4 cm (1½ inches) for the lower hem and turning. Measure the length round the mattress and add the amount required for pleats. Cut the flounce by these measurements. Construct the flounce; then join it to the boxing, right sides together.

Cover the pillows, following the instructions for the cushion, page 405.

Make Your Own Bedspreads

Whether austerely tailored or frivolously feminine, bedspreads or counterpanes are often the focal point of your bedroom. The style, of course, depends on the other fabric furnishings in the bedroom. Bedspreads may match curtains or loose covers, or they may introduce a new colour note. As bedspreads cover an article of furniture not easily overlooked, the texture and design of the fabric, as well as the styling and colour, should all complement each other.

Bedspread Preliminaries

What to Know Before You Start

Many fabrics are suitable for bedspreads. To name a few: rayon or silk taffeta, chintz, velveteen, polished cotton, antique satin, faille, sailcloth, hand-printed linen, corduroy, gingham and organdie. The fabric may consist of natural or synthetic fibres or a blend of two fibres such as terylene and cotton.

Bedspreads are often underlined with taffeta, polished cotton, chintz, batiste, muslin or a similar fabric. The choice depends on the fabric used in the bedspread. If you are planning to use an underlining, select one the same width as the bedspread fabric so that seams will be in the same places. If lightweight or medium-weight fabric is used in the bedspread, only the centre section covering the mattress may require underlining. If sheer fabric is used, the entire bedspread must be underlined. A style with a gathered frill is usual in this case. The sheer fabric and underlining are hemmed and frilled separately and then both are attached to the centre section with one line of stitching.

A full width of fabric is always placed down the centre of the bed, and the seams joining it to the other sections must fall in the same place on each side. When the bedspread has a flounce, the joining strips extend to the edge of the mattress, and the flounce extends from the top edge of the mattress to the floor; when the bedspread is plain, the strips joining the centre section extend over the edge of the mattress to the floor. In every style of bedspread, most of the seams are straight lines of stitching, and a 1·5-cm ($\frac{5}{8}$-inch) seam allowance is adequate. The seams should be emphasised with piping, braid, binding or decorative bands of zig-zag stitching. See *Accenting Seams*, page 396.

Bedspread Measurements

To Measure the Bed

Before you take any measurements, make up the bed with sheets, blankets and pillows. Decide on the style of bedspread, then measure accurately and add the amounts specified below. Pin-mark each edge of the mattress (**A, C** and **D** in the illustration) to indicate the points of the measurements. Since the tape measure may not extend the entire length or width of the mattress, pin-mark the mattress at the point where the tape measure ends; then move the tape and continue your measurements.

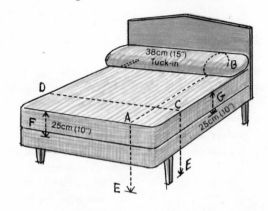

Bedspread

LENGTH – **A–B.** Measure from the foot end, along the length of the mattress, over the pillow, and down well under the pillow. ADD 38 cm (15 inches) for pillow 'tuck-in' allowance plus 1·5 cm ($\frac{5}{8}$ inch) for seam allowance plus 2·5 cm (1 inch) for hem and turning at the headboard. _____ cm (in)

WIDTH – **C–D.** Measure from one side of the mattress to the other. ADD 9·5 cm ($3\frac{3}{4}$ inches) for seam allowances . . . . _____ cm (in)

Flounce

DEPTH – **C–E.** Measure the side overhang from the top edge of the mattress to the floor. ADD 1·5 cm ($\frac{5}{8}$ inch) for seam allowance plus 4 cm ($1\frac{1}{2}$ inches) for hem and turning . . . . _____ cm (in)

LENGTH – **A–B.** Measure as for the bedspread length above. ADD 38 cm (15 inches) for pillow 'tuck-in' × 2 (sides) plus **C–D** (width across foot) plus allowances for pleats or gathers.

For Box Flounce – ADD depth of 2 inverted pleats, 40 cm (16 inches) each, plus 6 cm ($2\frac{1}{2}$ inches) for seam allowances plus 5 cm (2 inches) for hems and turnings at the headboard end . . . . _____ cm (in)

For Gathered Flounce – Multiply the measured length by $2\frac{1}{2}$ or 3 for fullness. ADD to this figure at least 20 cm (8 inches) for seam allowances plus 5 cm (2 inches) for hems and turnings at the headboard end . . . . _____ cm (in)

410

Coverlet

LENGTH – **A–B.** Measure from the foot end, along the length of the mattress, over the pillow, and down well under the pillow. ADD 38 cm (15 inches) for pillow 'tuck-in' allowance plus 25 cm (10 inches) for foot overhang (indicated by **F**) plus 1·5 cm ($\frac{5}{8}$ inch) for seam allowance plus 2·5 cm (1 inch) for hem and turning at the headboard end . . . .   _____ cm (in)

WIDTH – **C–D.** Measure from one side of the mattress to the other. ADD 51 cm (20 inches), 25 cm (10 inches) overhang on each side, indicated by **G**, plus 16 cm (6$\frac{1}{4}$ inches) for seam allowances . . . .   _____ cm (in)

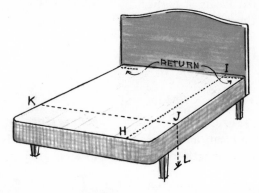

Valance Covering for Divan Base

This is a covering that is placed between the mattress and divan base. Remove the mattress and measure the divan base.

LENGTH – **H–I.** Measure from one end of the divan base to the other. ADD 1·5 ($\frac{5}{8}$ inch) for seam allowance at the foot end plus 2·5 cm (1 inch) for hem and turning at the headboard end . . . .   _____ cm (in)

WIDTH – **J–K.** Measure from one side of the divan base to the other. ADD 3 cm (1$\frac{1}{4}$ inches) for seam allowances . . . .   _____ cm (in)

Valance

DEPTH – **J–L.** Measure the overhang from the top edge of the divan base to the floor. ADD 1·5 cm ($\frac{5}{8}$ inch) for seam allowance plus 4 cm (1$\frac{1}{2}$ inches) for hem and turning . . . .   _____ cm (in)

LENGTH – **H–I.** Multiply the length measurement by 2 (sides) plus **J–K** (width across foot). ADD 30 cm (12 inches), (15 cm (6 inches) on each side), for returns at the headboard end; then multiply by 2$\frac{1}{2}$ or 3 for fullness. ADD to this figure at least 20 cm (8 inches) for seam allowances plus 5 cm (2 inches) for hems and turning at the headboard end . . . .   _____ cm (in)

The average measurements of finished bedspreads are:
Double – 240 × 280 cm (94 × 110 inches)
Single – 188 × 280 cm (74 × 110 inches)
King-size – 255 × 305 cm (100 × 120 inches)

Remember, the necessary allowances for seams and hems must be added to these finished measurements. The average height of a bed (from top of mattress to floor) is 51 cm (20 inches); however it may vary from 45–57 cm (18–22$\frac{1}{2}$ inches).

FABRIC REQUIREMENTS
Estimates for Bedspreads

	Fabric 90 cm (36 inches)	Fabric 122 cm (48 inches)
DOUBLE BED – 137 × 190 cm (54 × 75 inches) or 198–203 cm (78–80 inches)		
METRIC DOUBLE – 150 × 200 cm (59 × 78¾ inches)		
Plain	9·45 m (10⅓ yards)	6·4 m (7 yards)
Box Sides with Inverted Pleats at corner	9·4 m (10¼ yards)	7·8 m (8½ yards)
Gathered Flounce (2½ times length for fullness)	18·8 m (20½ yards)	12·35 m (13½ yards)
SINGLE BED – 100 × 190 cm (39½ × 75 inches) or 198 cm (78 inches)		
METRIC SINGLE – 100 × 200 cm (39½ × 78¾ inches)		
Plain	9·45 m (10⅓ yards)	6·4 m (7 yards)
Box Sides with Inverted Pleats at corner	9·4 m (10¼ yards)	6·9 m (7½ yards)
Gathered Flounce (2½ times length for fullness)	17·85 m (19½ yards)	11·45 m (12½ yards)
KING-SIZE BED – 198 × 214 cm (78 × 84 inches) or 203 cm (80 inches) OR 183 × 214 cm (72 × 84 inches) or 203 cm (80 inches)		
Plain		9·65 m (10½ yards)
Box Sides with Inverted Pleats at corner		9·4 m (10½ yards)
Gathered Flounce (2½ times length for fullness)		14·05 m (15⅓ yards)
QUEEN-SIZE BED – 152 × 203 cm (60 × 80 inches)		Same as King-Size

If you are planning to use piped seams, add an extra metre (yard). If the fabric has a large floral design or check allow one full length of the repeat for each additional length required after cutting the centre length.

The above figures are the approximate requirements. To be on the safe side, measure your own bed carefully. Remember it is better to have extra fabric than not enough.

Making the Bedspread

Box Bedspread

Refer to the *Bedspread Measurements chart*, page 410, and measurements **A** to **B**, **C** to **D** and **C** to **E**. Check your measurements to be sure that they are accurate and that you have added the correct allowances for seams, hems and pillow tuck-in.

THE CENTRE SECTION

Cut one length of fabric for the centre section, using the full width. Remove selvedges. The full width of the fabric is seldom as wide as the bed, so cut two additional strips (one for each side) the length of the centre section and wide enough to give the amount required to cover the top of the mattress plus 9·5 cm (3¾ inches) for seam allowances. If you have 122-cm (48-inch) fabric, cut both of these strips from one length, and use the remaining width for the end section of the flounce. If you have 90-cm (36-inch) fabric, cut the strips from two lengths of fabric so that sufficient width remains in each length for the flounce. If you are going to underline the bedspread, cut the underlining fabric the same length and width as each section. Pin the underlining to the top fabric, wrong sides together. Tack 1·2 cm (½ inch) from the edges if necessary.

Join a strip to each side of the centre section, right sides together. Accent the seams with corded piping. See page 396. Try the section on the bed to make sure it fits properly. The 1·5-cm (⅝-inch) seam allowance should extend beyond the foot and each side of the mattress. Curve the corners at the foot, following instructions on page 407. Pin corded piping, in a continuous line, to the right side of the 1·5-cm (⅝-inch) seamline: begin at the headboard end and pin the piping in place along the side, across the end, and along the opposite side to the headboard. Stitch.

THE FLOUNCE

Cut the flounce in three sections: cut two side sections (on the lengthwise grain) the length of the centre section plus 32 cm (12⅝ inches) for pleat and seam allowances, and the depth of measurement **C** to **E** plus 5·5 cm (2⅛ inches) for seam allowances and hem; cut one end section (on the crosswise grain) the length of measurement **C** to **D** plus 23·5 cm (9¼ inches) for pleats and seam allowances, and the same depth as the side sections. This allows for two seams, one at the back fold of each corner pleat. If 122-cm (48-inch) fabric is used, cut both side lengths from one length of fabric; if 90-cm (36-inch) fabric is used, cut the side lengths from the fabric left from the strips that join the centre section (see above).

Join the three sections of the flounce with a 1·5-cm

(⅝-inch) seam. Hem the lower edge. Turn the edge to the underside 1·2 cm (½ inch) and press; then turn a 2·5-cm (1-inch) hem and press. The hem may be slip-stitched by hand or machine-stitched, using either straight stitching or blindstitching. See *Side Hems*, page 370.

TO JOIN THE FLOUNCE AND CENTRE SECTION

Pin-mark the centre of each of the following: the foot of the centre section, the curved corners and the end section of the flounce. Pin the flounce in the centre section, right sides together, matching the centre pin marks. Fold the inverted pleats at the corners, making each fold 10 cm (4 inches) deep. (Seams joining the sides of the flounce to the end section should fall at the back fold of the pleats.) Then pin each side of the flounce in place. Stitch, following the directions for *Corded or Piped Seams*, page 245. Finish the headboard end with a 1·2-cm (½-inch) double-fold hem.

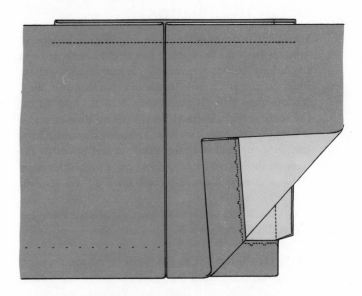

If the bed has a footboard, make an opening in the back seam of each corner pleat so that the flounce will fit over the frame joining the footboard.

Pin a band to each side of the centre section, right sides together. Stitch, taking a 1·5-cm ($\frac{5}{8}$-inch) seam. Press the seams open.

THE SIDE SECTIONS

Cut two side sections the length of the centre section and wide enough to complete the overhang on each side of the bedspread plus 5·5 cm ($2\frac{1}{4}$ inches) for seam allowances and a hem at the lower edge. (If you are adding a frill, make the allowance for its width.) Pin a side section to the band on each side of the centre section, right sides together. Stitch, taking a 1·5-cm ($\frac{5}{8}$-inch) seam.

Place the bedspread on the bed; the edges even with the floor. *To shape the corners* of the spread, pin-mark them in line with the floor. Remove the bedspread and check the evenness of the pin-marks to make sure the curves are identical. Finish the lower edges with a narrow hem.

THE FRILL

The bedspread in the illustration has a frill. Cut the frill on the lengthwise grain of the fabric, allowing for double or triple fullness. Finish each edge of the frill with decorative zig-zag. See *Edge-Stitched Finish*, page 274. Gather the frill with a 1·2-cm ($\frac{1}{2}$-inch) heading; then stitch it in place. See *Frill with Heading*, page 281. Finish the headboard end with a 1·2-cm ($\frac{1}{2}$-inch) double-fold hem.

Bedspread with Appliqué Monogram

A monogram is an individual and distinctive touch on a plain or tailored bedspread.

The centre of the monogram should measure about 30 or 45 cm (12 or 18 inches). Work the monogram in the centre section of the bedspread and complete the appliqué joining the flounce or overhang. See *Appliqué Monograms*, page 252.

Plain Bedspread with Decorative Bands

For a plain bedspread, the entire length of the bedspread – that is from the floor at the foot to the headboard end (including tuck-in allowance) – is cut in one section. Refer to the *Bedspread Measurements chart* and illustration, page 410. Measure from **E** to **B.** Add 43 cm (17 inches) for a 38-cm (15-inch) pillow tuck-in and a 2·5-cm (1-inch) hem at each end. Measure the width from the floor, up and over the mattress and down to the floor on the opposite side. Add 13 cm (5 inches) for seam allowances plus 5 cm (2 inches) for a 2·5 cm (1-inch) hem on each side.

Cut the centre section the length required, using the full width of the fabric. Remove selvedges.

THE DECORATIVE BANDS

Cut two strips of fabric the length of the centre section and about 9 cm ($3\frac{1}{2}$ inches) wide. Place the decorative stitching as explained in *Border Designs*, page 271. Allow 2 cm ($\frac{3}{4}$ inch) on each side of the decorative stitching for a border.

Coverlet and Valance

The overhang on a coverlet extends only a little below the mattress, not to the floor. The coverlet is used with a valance, which covers the divan base and extends to the floor.

For a pleasing contrast, the coverlet may be of a quilted or floral fabric and the valance of a plain colour that matches the quilting or the background of the floral design. For instructions on quilting, see page 256.

THE COVERLET

Refer to measurements **A** to **B** and **C** to **D** on the measurement chart on page 411. Check that your measurements are accurate and that you have added the correct allowances for seams, hems and pillow tuck-in.

Cut and make the centre section of the coverlet, following the instructions for the box bedspread on page 413. Use piped seams, and stitch the piping to the outer edges. Try the section on the bed to check the fit. The 1·5-cm ($\frac{5}{8}$-inch) seam allowance should extend beyond the foot end and sides of the mattress.

The overhang in the coverlet illustrated is lined and has an open inverted pleat at each corner of the footboard end. An underlay forms the underside of the open pleat. This means that each pleat has openings instead of back folds so that bulkiness is eliminated. The edges of the overhang are finished with tailored binding.

Cut the overhang in three sections: cut two side sections (on the lengthwise grain) the length of the centre section and 25 cm (10 inches) deep (or more) plus 1·5 cm ($\frac{5}{8}$ inch) for seam allowances; cut one end section (on the crosswise grain) long enough to extend across the width of the centre section and the same depth as the side sections. Cut two underlays 25 cm (10 inches) wide and 25 cm (10 inches) deep plus seam allowance. Cut a sateen

lining the same length and depth as each section of the overhang and underlay; then pin the lining to the fabric sections, wrong sides together. Finish these edges with tailored binding: the lower edge of the underlays; the lower edge and both ends of the end section; and the lower edge and end at foot end of each side section. Finish one section of the overhang for the right side and one for the left. For instructions on applying the binding, see *Tailored Binding*, page 334. Overcast the side edges of the underlays.

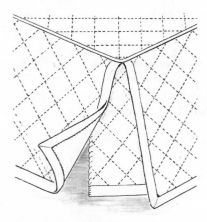

Pin the end section, then the side sections, of the overhang to the centre section, right sides together, with the bound edges meeting at the corners. (Keep the ends the same depth.) Place an underlay, right side down, over each joining; pin. Refer to *Corded or Piped Seams*, page 245, and stitch. Finish the headboard end with a 1·2-cm ($\frac{1}{2}$-inch) double-fold hem.

415

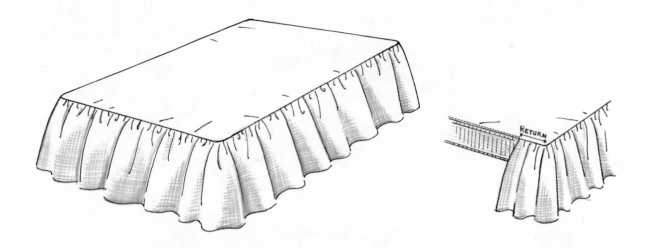

VALANCE COVERING FOR DIVAN BASE

Refer to measurements **H to I, J to K** and **J to L**, page 411. Measure accurately and add allowances for seams, hems and returns at the headboard end.

The section covering the box spring, **H to I** and **J to K**, may be cut from cotton sheeting; it is placed between the divan base and mattress, and the coverlet overlaps the edges joining the valance. Shape the four corners of the sheeting, following the contours of the mattress. See the instructions on page 407. Pin-mark the centre of the corners.

Cut the valance on the crosswise grain the length and depth required. See *Valance* on the chart, page 411. Seam the strips, using a French seam. Press. Hem the lower edge; then gather the frill. See page 280.

Pin the frill to the centre section, right sides together, placing the gathering stitches on the seamline. Begin at the headboard end and extend the frill 18 cm (7 inches) round the corner at the headboard end. (The returns at the headboard prevent the cover from slipping out of place.) Finish the ends of the frill with a 1·2-cm (½-inch) double-fold hem. Stitch the frill in place, with the frill

side up, barely beyond the gathering stitches. Hem the end of the sheeting centre section between the returns. **If the bed has a footboard,** you must make an opening in the frill at each corner so that the frill will fit over the frame joining the footboard. Cut the frill as instructed above but add 50 cm (20 inches) to the length for the underlap and turn-under at the corners of the foot end.

Join the strips for the frill. Hem, then gather, the frill as instructed above.

Pin the gathered frill to one side of the centre section, right sides together, extending it 18 cm (7 inches) round the corner (the return) at the headboard end. At the footboard end, extend the frill 13 cm (5 inches) beyond the corner; then cut it off at this point. Turn the end of the frill to the underside 13 cm (5 inches). (The turn-under is not gathered.) Finish the cut end with a 1·2-cm (½-inch) double-fold hem. Pin the frill to the opposite side in the same manner. Pin the frill across the foot end, extending it 13 cm (5 inches) round each corner for the under-lap. Neaten the cut edges. Stitch the frill in place, and finish the headboard end between the returns with a 1·2-cm (½-inch) double-fold hem.

416

The Many Faces of
Knitted Fabrics

The Many Faces of Knitted Fabrics

Flattering, comfortable, and easy to care for, knitted fabrics are an increasingly important part of the fashion scene. Indeed, they play a larger role than most people realise. In addition to the familiar types of knits used in dressmaking, an ever-growing variety is available for lingerie, clothes for active sports and even fake fur and leather coats.

The great variety of knitted fabrics presents the home dressmaker with an equally great variety of sewing challenges. No single set of sewing guidelines can be applied to all knitted fabrics. It is possible, however, to classify them into groups, each of which calls for a specific set of sewing procedures.

This section first presents a comprehensive picture of knitted fabrics and what they mean to the home dressmaker, and then deals with the specific guidelines for sewing each of eight groups of knits.

Table of Contents

About Knitted Fabrics

What is a Knitted Fabric?

Knitted fabrics function differently from woven fabrics. Woven fabrics are rigid; they resist stress. Knitted fabrics are mobile and 'give' with stress. Good knitted fabrics are elastic in the sense that they can be stretched and will return to their original form.

Knitted and woven fabrics function differently because they are of two *different structures*. Woven fabrics are structured from two systems of yarns that cross each other and are interlaced. See page 10.

Knitted fabrics are structured from only one system of yarns. The single system of yarns is looped either in the lengthwise direction of the fabric (warp knitting) or across the width of the fabric (weft or circular knitting). **Warp knitteds,** which are made on flat-bed machines, are generally tighter, flatter and less elastic than weft knitteds. In warp knitting, multiple yarns (but all part of a single system of yarns) run vertically and parallel to each other. The fabric is constructed by manipulating all these warp yarns at the same time into interconnected loops.

The two most familiar types of warp knits are *tricot* and *raschel*. Until a few years ago, tricot was used mainly as a lingerie fabric or as backing for bonded fabrics, and raschel as lace for curtains. But today, so many advances have been made in both tricot and raschel knitting machines that the fashion fabric potential in warp knits is beyond simple classification.

Weft knitteds, which are made on either circular or flat-bed knitting machines, are constructed in much the same way as hand knitting. In weft knitting, the fabric is constructed with one yarn at a time running in a horizontal direction, with the needles forming loops in

Tricot: Warp knitting — yarns run up and down

Tricot: A system of vertical yarns interlocks loops vertically and horizontally, producing a smooth-surfaced fabric, resistant to runs, and with little lengthwise but considerable crosswise stretch

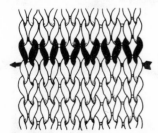

Plain Knit: Weft or circular knitting — yarns run across fabric

Raschel: Rows of plain knit resembling chain stitch run vertically, interlocking crossing insertion yarns, to form lace-like or looped surface patterns

419

horizontal courses, building one on top of the other.

The most familiar types of weft knits are jersey, rib knits, double knits and jacquards. Double knits appear to have been knitted twice; the effect is produced by two-needle construction, which interlocks two fabrics into one. Double-knit fabrics have become familiar to most women who sew because there are many on sale and they have proved easy to work with and to wear. **The differences in knitted fabrics** come from many things: the capabilities of the knitting machine; the design of the needle; the number of sets of needles; the gauge or number of needles per 2·5 cm (1 inch); the stitch formation or pattern; the type of yarn (filament, textured filament or spun); the kind of fibre the yarn is made of; the size of yarn; and the finishing processes applied to the fabric.

To sew knitted fabrics successfully, you need to recognise that they have just as many different faces, textures and characteristics as woven fabrics.

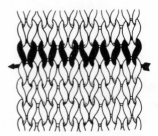

Jersey: Plain knit with a face of flat, smooth, vertical ribs and a back of horizontal loop segments

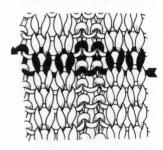

Ribbed Knit: A combination of sets of knit and purl stitches, which form prominent vertical ribs separated by receding spaces. The back of the fabric shows a reverse of the face ribs and spaces

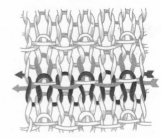

Double Knit: A smooth-surfaced face and back produced by interlocking stitches from two sets of both yarns and needles

Jacquard: A figured surface produced by two or more sets of both yarns and needles working periodically together and separately to produce designed fabric

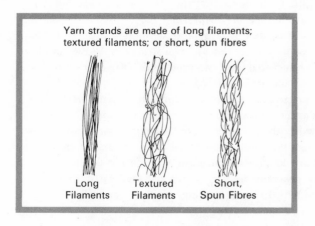

Yarn strands are made of long filaments; textured filaments; or short, spun fibres

Long Filaments   Textured Filaments   Short, Spun Fibres

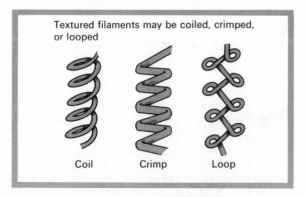

Textured filaments may be coiled, crimped, or looped

Coil   Crimp   Loop

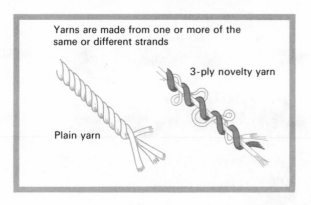

Yarns are made from one or more of the same or different strands

3-ply novelty yarn

Plain yarn

420

Your Sewing Machine and Knitted Fabrics

Knitted fabrics place a greater demand on your sewing machine than wovens. Knowing more about your sewing machine and how it reacts will help you to sew knitted fabrics easily and well.

Machine Care

Because knitted fabrics contain more yarn than wovens, they tend to drop more lint, fibres and finishing granules into the machine; so frequent cleaning and light oiling are important. Your cleaning tools are: a lint brush; a piece of clean muslin or any soft cloth; and a tube of SINGER* sewing machine oil. Disconnect the electric cord for safety and then brush out lint, wipe off residue or film, and oil lightly.

The upper threading points collect sticky film and fine lint because friction from the flow of thread creates heat and static electricity. To ensure an even flow of the needle thread, brush and wipe these threading points with a cloth, but do not oil them.

The **feed and bobbin-case area** collects a surprising amount of lint, fibres and granules. A clean bobbin case is essential. Remove the throat plate and open the slide plate to expose the working parts. Brush out all of the

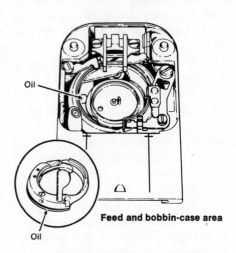

Feed and bobbin-case area

lint you can see. Then turn the hand wheel slowly, stop and brush out additional lint as it appears. Remove the bobbin case and repeat the brushing procedure. Then, with a soft cloth, wipe the bobbin case and the surfaces it touches. If the metal parts feel sticky, put a little oil on the cloth to enable you to rub off the residue. Place a drop of oil at each point indicated in the instruction book for your machine. Replace the bobbin case and throat plate carefully when finished.

Open the face plate and brush out the small amount of lint that may have accumulated. Lightly oil the points indicated in the machine instruction book. Turn the hand wheel slowly to reveal the oiling points. Give special attention to the presser bar. Raise and lower the Presser Foot so that you can see which parts move. A freely moving presser bar improves the feeding of seam layers.

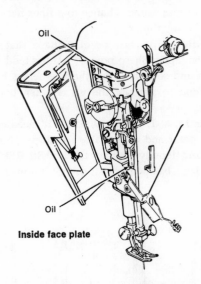

Inside face plate

When you have finished, close the face plate and wipe again round the lower part of the presser bar and needle bar to remove any excess oil. Then run the machine slowly to distribute the oil round the parts as they move.

The Needle

The importance of the sewing machine needle takes on a new dimension when one is sewing knitted fabrics.

The correct *needle size* depends on the fabric thickness (consider both plain and crossing seams) and on the diameter of the needle thread. The needle should be large enough, and therefore strong enough, to penetrate seam layers without being deflected; it should have an eye large enough to allow the thread to pass through it freely.

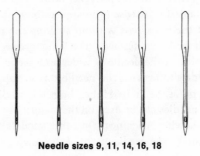

Needle sizes 9, 11, 14, 16, 18

421

Loosely constructed knitted fabrics present no unusual problems; but closely constructed ones of nylon or polyester fibres; or those with a heat-set or fused surface, resist the needle's penetration. As a result, the needle forces the fabric downwards, loosening it under the foot, before it penetrates; and this loosening of fabric may cause skipped stitches. Closely constructed fabrics also cling to the needle, impeding the flow of needle thread and causing skipped stitches. To overcome skipping from these causes, change to a finer needle and a finer but strong thread.

The needle point must be of a shape that will not damage the fabric. Sharp-pointed needles tend to pierce the yarns and sometimes cut them, whereas ball-point needles tend to separate the yarns when penetrating the fabric.

Regular *15 × 1, No. 2020,* SINGER* needles have a modified point and are suitable for all-purpose use on wovens and loosely knitted fabrics. SINGER* needle *No. 2021* has a ball point and is suitable for many knitted fabrics.

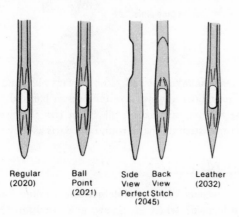

Regular (2020) Ball Point (2021) Side View / Back View Perfect Stitch (2045) Leather (2032)

A special needle for knitted fabrics is the SINGER* Perfect Stitch needle *No. 2045.* In addition to the ball shape of the point, it has other features which enable it to stitch knitted fabrics well. It has a deeply cut flat side at the top, which brings the needle close to the point of the sewing hook and thus prevents skipped stitches; and it has a slanted crosswise groove just above the needle eye to let the hook pass without striking the needle as the stitch is being formed. The long groove on the opposite side of the needle is wider and deeper than on other needles to prevent the needle-thread supply from being cut off as the knitted fabric hugs the needle. These *No. 2045* needles can be used on the majority of the later SINGER* sewing machines. On other models they are likely to strike the needle guard of the sewing hook.

Jersey-backed vinyl, synthetic leather or thermoplastic-coated fabrics should be sewn with a special *wedge-point needle,* style *15 × 2, No. 2032.* These needles make a small, clean slash in the fabric. This kind of penetration is ideal for leather and leather-like coated fabrics but not for other knitted fabrics.

Blunt, bent or out-of-set needles can cause stitching problems. A needle is blunt when its point has been flattened or burred. Tightly constructed polyester or nylon knitted fabrics wear off the needle point amazingly fast. A blunt needle will cause snagged or broken yarns and will make a thumping sound as you stitch.

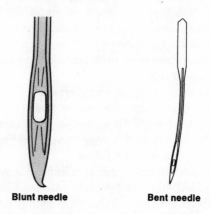

Blunt needle   **Bent needle**

A bent needle is usually caused by striking a pin, the presser foot or a non-yielding crossing seam. Or it may be caused if fabric is removed from the machine by pulling it when the needle thread is above the presser foot. A needle can also be bent by changing from a straight-stitch to a zig-zag setting while the needle is in the fabric. A bent needle will cause skipped stitches and it may cause the seam to pull to the side as you stitch.

An out-of-set needle is one in which the lower part is angled in a different direction from the top part. To test for correct set, remove the needle from the machine and place it flat side down on the slide plate, holding it at the top. You should be able to see an even space between the needle and the plate for the full length of the needle blade. If the space is uneven, the needle will cause skipped stitches and should be replaced.

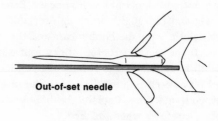

Out-of-set needle

A **sticky or coated needle** can cause skipped stitches after several seams have been stitched. The solutions used to stabilise the stretch or to give crease-resistance often remain in fabrics and rub off. (Excess finishing solutions can be removed by laundering before the fabric is cut.) Sometimes, the synthetic fibres themselves cause the needle to be coated. This coating results from the heat generated by the friction of the needle penetrating the fabric at a fast and constant speed.

Regardless of cause, the resulting skipped stitches can be corrected by cleaning or replacing the needle. To clean the needle, wipe it with a cloth moistened with SINGER* oil. Clean the long groove carefully and thoroughly.

The Thread

The correct type and thickness of thread is essential. The thread size is most important, so you cannot always match the fibre of the thread with that of the fabric. The most reliable rule to follow is to use the strongest fine thread available so that you can use a fine needle for stitching. This rule is especially important when you sew firm, tightly knitted fabrics. The following comments on thread types will help you to make a wise choice.

Silk is often the best available thread for nylon and polyester knitted fabrics; it is fine and strong, and it allows you to use a size 11, fine needle.

Fine spun polyester 'Drima' is a little more wiry and harsh than silk but it allows you to use a size 11, fine needle.

General-purpose spun polyester 'Trylko', which is suitable for heavier knits, must be used with a size 14 needle.

Mercerised cotton 'Sylko' size 50, is generally available in all colours and should be used in a size 14, medium needle. (Occasionally, you can break the rule and use mercerised cotton thread in a size 11, fine needle, but the thread may fray or break.) Mercerised cotton lacks strength and stretch for knits. It is satisfactory only for seams that are stayed with tape or woven mounting, or seams that are stitched with the straight stretch stitch.

Silk twist, known also as buttonhole twist, should be used with a size 16 or 18 needle for top-stitching seams, collars and faced edges where a heavy thread accent is desired.

Boldstitch or polytwist, a heavy-weight polyester thread, should be used with a size 16 or 18 needle for top-stitching synthetics.

The Stitch

A balanced straight stitch will produce a smooth strong seam that will 'give' slightly as the fabric stretches; when this stitch is made with silk or synthetic thread, it will stretch a little more.

By regulating the needle-thread tension, you can achieve a balanced straight stitch on almost every kind of fabric. A straight stitch is balanced if it looks the same on both sides.

Both tensions correct

Before making any change in your tension setting, however, make a test stitching on two layers of the fabric, using the thread and needle you have selected for stitching the garment. Start with a 2 mm (12) stitch length and a straight-stitch setting. Inspect the stitching. Both sides should look the same. If the seam is puckered, shorten the stitch and test again. Seam puckering caused by too long a stitch should then disappear.

To correct an unbalanced stitch when the thread on the *upper* side of the fabric looks straight and tight, loosen the needle-thread tension by turning the dial to a lower number and test again.

Tight upper tension

To correct an unbalanced stitch when the thread on the *under* side looks straight and tight, tighten the needle-thread tension by turning the dial to a higher number and test again.

Loose lower tension

If thread loops appear on the underside, the needle-thread tension is too loose; tighten it and test again.

Very loose upper tension

Some nylon jerseys require a higher needle-thread tension than you would ordinarily choose for thin supple fabrics. The reason is that nylon clings to the needle and retards the flow of thread.

Once the bobbin-thread tension is set at a normal and versatile setting, you should seldom need to change it on most machines, and never on *Touch & Sew** machines.

There are some things you should not do. One is to attempt to test the bobbin-thread tension by pulling and feeling it. This test is invalid because every machine has a bobbin-thread pull-off device that supplies an increment of thread for each stitch; thus, what you feel is not the same tension as when the stitch is being formed. Neither should you set the needle-thread tension so low that there is no tension on it at all. With little or no tension on the needle thread, the take-up lever will pull thread from the spool instead of retrieving the thread loop from the bobbin case. The result, at best, is short thread loops on the underside of the seam and, at worst, a thread jam in the bobbin case.

Do not assume that puckering seams are caused by tensions balanced at too high a level. Seam puckering on knitted fabrics is more often caused by too long a stitch, or too heavy a thread, or too coarse a needle.

Starting to Stitch

Many home dressmakers are careless when starting to stitch. The combination of soft, tightly knitted fabric and strong synthetic thread makes it necessary to start seams carefully if you are to avoid the machine stalling from tangled threads on the underside of the seam or in the bobbin case. In extreme cases, threads will jam tightly under the bobbin case and pull the soft fabric down into the throat-plate needle hole.

When stitching knitteds with strong synthetic threads, always place both bobbin thread and needle thread under the Presser Foot, across the feed diagonally to the right and back. Position the fabric and lower the needle

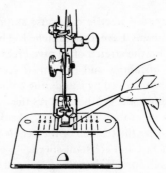

into it *before* lowering the Presser Foot. The needle should enter the fabric at least 1·2 cm ($\frac{1}{2}$ inch) from the end of the seam. Before starting to stitch, grasp both the

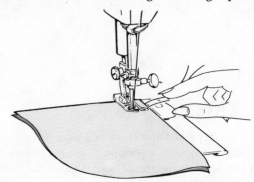

needle and bobbin threads; hold them securely in a position to the right and back of the Presser Foot; and then begin to stitch forwards slowly for one or two stitches. When backstitching, stitch only to within ·6 cm ($\frac{1}{4}$ inch) of the end of the seam and then stitch forwards.

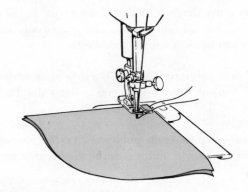

Handling the Fabric

'Fabric handling' refers to the way the seam layers pass under the Presser Foot. Three elements affect fabric handling: the choice of sewing machine accessories, the degree of presser-foot pressure, and the way you control the seam layers by hand when stitching.

Machine accessories. Select the correct machine accessories for the work you are doing. (For the various types of stitches suitable for knitted fabrics, see page 427.) Plain and stretch straight stitching should be done with the Straight-stitch Presser Foot and throat plate. These accessories hold the fabric very close to the needle; the small opening in the throat plate supports the fabric upon penetration of the needle; the Presser Foot strips the fabric from the needle as it is withdrawn.

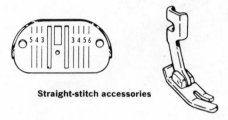

Straight-stitch accessories

Zig-zag stitching must be done with the zig-zag throat plate and the General-purpose Presser Foot or one of the special feet that accommodate the stitch width.

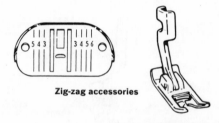

Zig-zag accessories

Loosely knitted fabrics – such as sweater, chenille, raschel and novelty-yarn jersey – sometimes catch over the toes of the General-purpose Presser Foot. To overcome this, simply cut a short strip of sellotape ·6 cm (¼ inch) wide and wrap it round the foot, encasing both toes. Remove the tape after the garment has been completed.

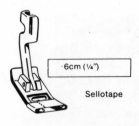

·6cm (¼")

Sellotape

The Even Feed* Foot is a very important accessory that solves many of the stitching problems presented by knitted fabrics. By providing top feeding action, which works with the feed of the machine, it ensures that all seam layers feed evenly, with no puckers. At the same time, it prevents skipped stitches by providing a per-

fectly timed 'hold' and 'lift' action: the frame of the foot holds the fabric firmly when the needle is down and lifts on the feeding stroke. This foot also eliminates the need to hold the fabric under tension during stitching.

The Even Feed* Foot can be used for straight and zig-zag stitching, as well as for forward and reverse stitching. Use it for stay stitching, machine tacking, stitching seams and top-stitching through several layers of fabric.

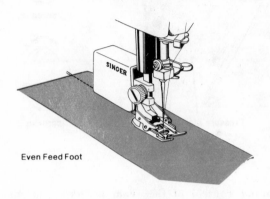

Even Feed Foot

Presser-foot pressure is the force that the Presser Foot exerts against the seam layers. It is regulated by a dial inside the face plate or a dial or screw at the top of the presser bar. Presser-foot pressure holds the fabric in place while the stitch is being formed. When the pressure is correct, both layers of fabric move as one layer under the Presser Foot.

When the pressure is too heavy, the top layer will lag behind the underlayer, the underlayer will pucker and the seam will be uneven. Also, the Presser Foot or feed may make a permanent impression on the fabric. Pressure that is too light causes other problems on heavy, spongy knits, the stitch length will be shorter than the setting indicates; the seam will not feel firm when you guide it; and crossing seams will stall under the foot. On firm, tightly knitted fabrics, the fabric will loosen under the foot, causing skipped stitches.

Most knitted fabrics should be stitched at a normal or medium pressure setting, even those that appear soft and supple but are tightly constructed.

To arrive at the best pressure setting for a specific fabric, cut two 30-cm (12-inch) strips and 'stitch' a seam without thread. If the two seam layers come out evenly at the ends, the pressure setting is correct for the feeding stroke. Then thread the machine and stitch with thread. If the stitch length is uniform, with no skipped stitches, the pressure setting is correct. However, if the seam ends come out unevenly in the first test, try decreasing the pressure a little at a time. If, on the second test with thread, there are skipped stitches, increase the pressure to see if skipping can be eliminated. If this does not work, check the other possible causes of skipping discussed earlier.

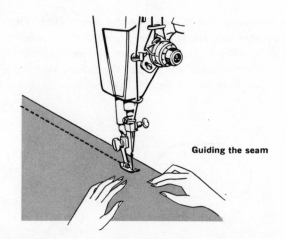

Guiding the seam

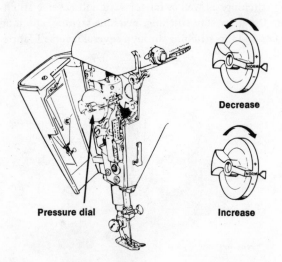

Pressure dial   Decrease   Increase

seam when it is relaxed to its normal length; (3) it enables you to put ease in one seam layer and not the other when the construction calls for it. The recovery characteristic of most knitted fabrics makes this method of handling ease possible; on woven fabrics, it does not.

Manual control of the seam layers is sometimes necessary to improve stitching if you are not using the Even Feed* Foot. Such control is called 'guiding and supporting' the seam. The illustration shows the hand position for guiding the seam and applying tension to the fabric while you stitch. This control does three things: (1) prevents the fabric from loosening under the foot as the needle penetrates and is withdrawn from the fabric, preventing skips; (2) it stretches the seam while the stitch is being formed and puts more stretch into the

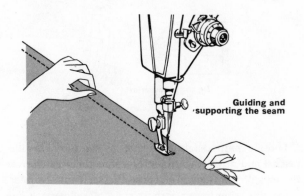

Guiding and supporting the seam

The Eight Knit Groups

The following chapter gives sewing guidelines for four of the eight basic groups of knitted fabrics; these four are the types traditionally thought of as knitted, such as single and double knits, raschel and sweater weight.

Guidelines for the four special groups – tricot, towelling and stretch towelling, leather-look and fur fabrics – begin on page 456.

Types of Stitches

Today's sewing machines offer a wide variety of stitches that are suitable for sewing knitted fabrics. Take advantage of this variety for the special purposes described below.

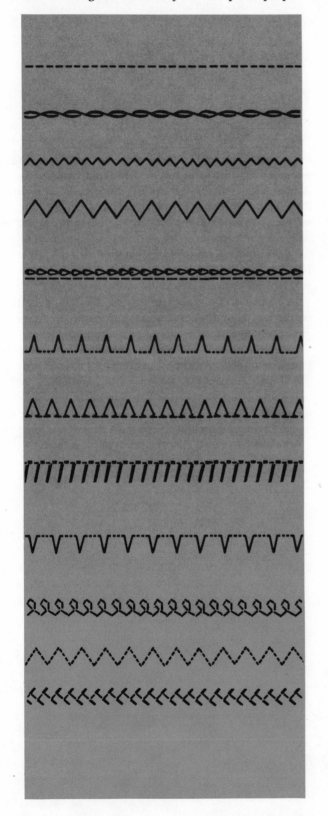

Straight stitch. Use with strong thread for stitching plain, pressed-open and double-stitched seams.

Straight stretch† stitch. Use for stitching plain, pressed-open and double-stitched seams.

Narrow zig-zag, 1 to 2 stitch width. Use for stitch-pressed-open and double-stitched seams.

Wide, open zig-zag, 3 to 5 stitch width. Use for neatening seam, facing and hem edges.

Chain stitch. Use double row, made from opposite directions, for double-stitching seams in thin knitted fabrics. Use single row for stay stitching where some 'give' is desired.

Over-edge†† stitch. Use for finishing seam, hem and facing edges and for seams stitched and finished with one row of stitching.

Over-edge stretch† stitch. Use for finishing seam, hem and facing edges and for seams stitched and finished with one row of stitching.

Slant over-edge††† stitch. Use for finishing seam, hem and facing edges and for seams stitched and finished with one row of stitching.

Blindstitch. Use a 5 stitch width for finishing seam, hem and facing edges; a 2 to 3 stitch width for blindstitching hems. When guided with seam allowance to left, the blindstitch duplicates the over-edge stitch.

Multi-stretch† stitch. Use for neatening and flattening seam, hem and facing edges.

Multi-stitch zig-zag stitch. Use for neatening and flattening seam, hem and facing edges.

Featherstitch† for top stitching and flattening seams.

† Made with a *Flexi-Stitch** disc, built in or inserted.
†† Can be obtained with disc 32, available separately for all SINGER slant- and straight-needle zig-zag machines with interchangeable *Fashion** discs.
††† Available on SINGER* sewing machine Models 413, 416, 438, 513, 514 and 538.

427

Knitted Fabrics for Dressmaking

Identifying Your Knitted Fabric

Both the type of garment and the characteristics of the fabric must be considered when choosing a pattern and a sewing procedure. It is important to consider the amount of stretch, recovery ability, thickness and surface texture of the fabric. The following four groups of knitted fabrics have both similarities and differences, and some fashion fabrics will fall on the borderline between groups. However, by treating knitted fabrics in groups, instructions can be simplified and made easier to understand.

- Firm Dress-Weight and Suit-Weight Knitted Fabrics and Bonded Knits
- Raschel and Rough-Textured, Medium-Firm Knitted Fabrics
- Sweater and Loose, Stretchable Knits
- Single and Thin, Supple Knitted Fabrics

Determine the degree of stretch in your fabric so that you can identify the group into which it falls. Measure and mark exactly 20 cm (8 inches) on the width of your fabric. Do this at least 15 cm (6 inches) from all edges. Mark each point with a thread marking, made with a

single stitch, and tie the thread ends together. Hold the fabric at one width mark between the thumb and fingers of your left hand, and at the other width mark between the thumb and fingers of your right hand. Then gently stretch the fabric against a ruler, stretching the fabric only as far as it will go without distortion. Take a reading for the amount of stretch in the width. With the fabric relaxed, measure it again and take another reading; this will indicate the recovery ability in the width.

In another area of your fabric, mark 20 cm (8 inches) on the length, and follow the same procedure to determine the degree of stretch and recovery in the length.

Using the reading for the amount of stretch in the crosswise direction (width), classify your fabric according to the scale below.

If a 20-cm (8-inch) portion stretches in the crosswise direction:
- to 23·5 cm (9¼ inches) or less, it is a firm, stable knit;
- to more than 23·5 cm (9¼ inches) but less than 27·5 cm (10½ inches), it has medium or moderate stretch;
- to 27·5 cm (10½ inches) or more, it is a stretchable knit.

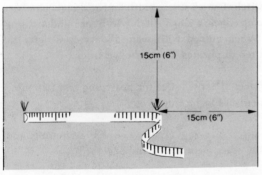

15cm (6")

15cm (6")

The amount of crosswise stretch is the primary factor in determining the suitable pattern classification, the amount of fitting ease needed, and the sewing methods to use.

Knowing the amount of lengthwise stretch will give you an idea of how much lengthwise ease you may need to allow in the bodice of a garment with a waist seam, or in the crutch of trousers. It will help you decide the kind of stitch, thread and seam construction needed to prevent lengthwise seams from breaking, and it will guide you in deciding whether to tape seams.

Knowing the degree of recovery, or the ability of your fabric to return to its original length or width after being stretched, will tell you how well your fabric will hold its shape when you wear it. It will help you decide whether to line or mount it to prevent bagginess.

Paper patterns made by the major pattern companies for knitted fabrics may be classified in three categories:

Those that are designed primarily for woven fabrics but that list specific firm, stable knits that are also suitable. These patterns include standard ease allowances beyond actual body measurements and design ease allowances appropriate for the specific style.

Those designated as 'Recommended for Knits' or 'Suitable for Knits'. These patterns have standard ease plus appropriate design ease allowances. They differ from the first group only in that the styling elements and lines are especially suitable for knitted fabrics. They, too, will indicate specific fabrics on the pattern envelope.

Those designated for 'Stretch Knits Only'. These patterns are smaller in comparison with other patterns of the same type and size. Less total ease, both basic and design, has been incorporated into the pattern; and shaping, normally achieved by seams and darts, is minimal. They are designed to utilise the stretchability of the fabric for both shaping and ease. These patterns should not be used for woven fabrics or firm and medium-firm knits. And they are suitable only for those with slim figures.

Preparing, Cutting, and Pressing Knitted Fabrics

Preparing the Fabric

Double knits and warp knits made of **polyester** or polyester and cotton have a crease-resistant finish, so they cannot be straightened by diagonal pulling. Simply fold, right side out, on a lengthwise rib. Place fold along table edge and cut crosswise ends square with the end of the table. Tack crosswise ends together and lengthwise edges together. To shrink and to remove excess finish, wash the tacked fabric in the same way you will wash the garment. Set your washing machine for gentle motion and warm water, and use a mild soap or detergent. An anti-static fabric softener is a good idea. After washing put the fabric and a dry turkish towel in a dryer set for low temperature. (The towel will help to remove moisture from the fabric.) Remove fabric from dryer before completely dry. If you do not have a washing machine with a gentle-motion cycle, wash fabric by hand. If you do not have a dryer, roll fabric in towels to take off most of the moisture and dry over the bath. Pressing before cutting is seldom necessary.

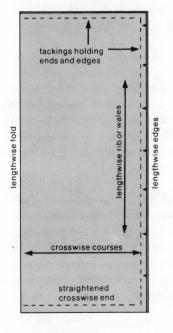

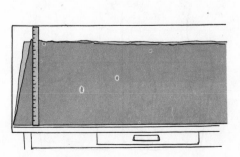

Wool jersey and double-knit fabrics can usually be straightened by pulling them diagonally. Fold, right side out, on a lengthwise rib. Lengthwise edges may not match exactly because tubular knits are sometimes cut crookedly. Single knits are more likely to be crooked than double knits. If the fabric is extremely crooked, there is no way to straighten it perfectly. Just square the ends by placing the lengthwise fold along a table edge, and cut the crosswise ends square with the table end. Tack crosswise ends and lengthwise edges.

If a fabric that cannot be straightened has a *prominent crosswise* stripe or pattern, shrink it without squaring or tacking the ends and edges.

Raschel knits with a soft finish are often made of acrylic fibre, which is washable. With right sides together, fold at centre along a lengthwise chain. Lengthwise edges will be straight because they are knitted on flat-bed machines. The crosswise yarns are very prominent and can be followed when cutting the ends straight.

Raschel knits with a sheen are usually polyester and can be treated the same way as acrylics.

Lace-patterned raschel knits should be handled in accordance with the fabric-label instructions. Some are washable, others must be dry-cleaned. Washable lace-patterned raschel knits should be shrunk before cutting; dry-cleanable ones should not.

Soft, loosely constructed raschel knits should be machine-stitched singly along crosswise edges before laundering to prevent fraying. Fold in centre, tack ends and edges together and launder.

Bonded fabrics should be straightened according to the rules for the face fabric. They are usually not washable and so do not need to be shrunk. Cut bonded knits folded right side out to make it easier to match designs.

Sweater knits labelled washable can be hand-washed before cutting, but they should be dried on a flat surface to prevent stretching out of shape. Wool sweater knits should not be washed before cutting. Machine-stitch along crosswise edges in a single layer to prevent fraying. If fabric is tubular, do not cut on lengthwise rib before shrinking, or when laying out the pattern, unless the layout calls for it.

Single knits that are labelled hand-washable should be shrunk in warm water. Those labelled machine-washable can be machine-washed. It is a good idea to test-launder a 15-cm (6-inch) square of the fabric to find out if it shrinks and whether the colours run or fade. If there is no shrinkage, do not shrink; if the colour fades, dry-clean the garment.

Cutting

There are seven rules that apply to cutting all knitted fabrics.

1. If the fabric has a prominent lengthwise rib, fold the fabric right side out along a lengthwise rib.

2. If a knitted fabric has a prominent crosswise stripe, yarn or pattern, treat it as you would a woven fabric with a crosswise stripe, matching stripes at corresponding notches.

3. Do not let fabric hang over the table edge because it will stretch out of shape.

4. Follow 'with nap' pattern layout diagram. Because of their loop construction, knits have an up-and-down way.

5. When pinning pattern to fabric, use fine steel pins. Pin sparingly and only within seam and dart allowances.

6. Use heavy, sharp shears and long cutting strokes.

7. Cut notches outwards on firm knitteds and mark notches on loosely knitted fabrics with tailor's tacks.

If a *knitted fabric with a prominent crosswise stripe* or pattern cannot be straightened, cut it in a single layer, giving the crosswise detail precedence over the lengthwise rib. To reproduce the additional half of the pattern, cut duplicate pattern sections in plain tissue paper. Mark a crosswise grain line at right angles to the lengthwise grain line on all pattern pieces and place the crosswise grain line parallel to the crosswise stripe. Match crosswise details at corresponding seamlines. To produce right and left sleeves, lay the sleeve pattern on the fabric twice, once face down and once face up.

Knitted fabrics with a sharply pressed fold should be cut so that the fold is not used within a pattern piece. A sharply pressed fold can seldom be entirely removed with pressing. When parts of the pattern must be placed on a fold, create a new fold and place pattern edges on it.

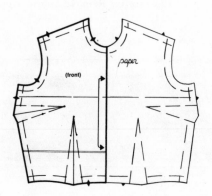

Pressing

Pressing during construction is essential with all knitted fabrics.

Iron temperature must be regulated according to the fibre content. When pressing blends, do not exceed the iron-temperature setting for the fibre that has the lowest heat tolerance. Always test-press a fabric scrap in which you have made a dart and a seam. Test for heat setting and amount of steam needed.

Never use the iron directly on the fabric. Protect the fabric with a dampened pressing cloth of thin cotton.

A softly padded ironing board is better than a firmly padded one. Final pressing on the right side of the garment, and with the fabric protected from direct contact with the iron, will give a smoothly pressed surface because the impressions of seams, darts and hems will be made in the soft surface of the ironing board rather than in the garment.

Trimming excess bulk from seam allowances and darts on knits is just as important as careful pressing. Slash narrow darts and press them open; then trim seam allowances diagonally within the crossing seam allowance.

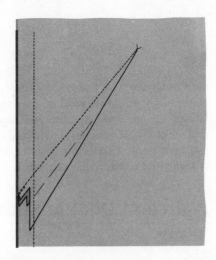

Square-cut the dart seam allowances at the crossing seam.

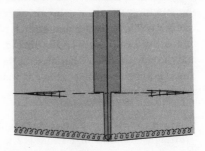

In hems, trim the seam allowances to half width from hem fold to hem edge.

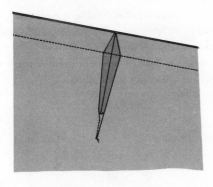

Press bustline darts downwards and trim the layer next to the garment to 1·2 cm ($\frac{1}{2}$ inch); trim the other layer on the fold line. This method of trimming will hold the seam allowances of the dart in position and reduce bulk.

On loose, bulky fabrics, use a blocking, rather than a conventional, pressing technique. 'Blocking' means creating steam without iron pressure on the fabric. Cover the fabric with a moist cloth. Apply the iron to produce steam but do not allow the full weight of the iron to rest on the fabric. Move the iron from one position to another by lifting it rather than sliding it. Remove pressing cloth. Use a pounding block to flatten seams and eliminate steam. Do not move the garment section until it is dry.

Yarn-pulls may show up as you press. To repair a yarn-pull, hold the fabric and stretch it along the pull to work as much yarn back in place as possible. Then insert the wire of a wire-loop needle threader through the fabric at the yarn-pull from the wrong side of the fabric. Pass the pulled yarn through the wire loop and draw it to the inside of the fabric.

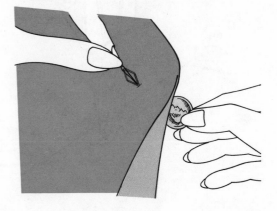

431

Seams and Special Techniques

Conventional sewing and sweater construction methods, either singly or in combination, are used to sew knitted fabrics. The method you select will depend on both the characteristics of your fabric and the type of garment you are making. This section describes the various types of seams and construction methods that can be used.

Plain and Double-Stitched Seams

Seam allowances should be wide enough to support the structure of the garment, but not too wide, or they will roll and have excessive bulk. Seams should stretch but the stitching should not break with the movements of the body. The strength and stretch of a seam are determined by the strength of the thread, the type of stitch and the way the seam is handled. In the following instructions, wherever strong thread is indicated, use silk or synthetic thread.

PLAIN SEAM – STRAIGHT STITCH

● Straight stitch, 2 to 1·5 mm (12 to 15) stitch length; or straight stretch stitch.
● Straight-stitch Presser Foot or Even Feed* Foot; straight-stitch throat plate.
● Strong thread; ball-point needle of appropriate size, or Perfect stitch needle.
● Prepare seam with hand tacking if necessary.
● Stitch seam under tension by guiding and supporting, except when using the Even Feed Foot.

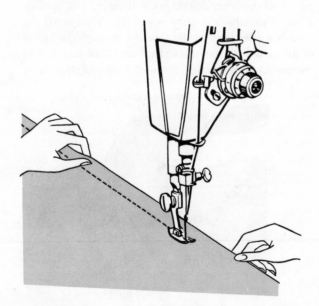

● Press seam as stitched, then press open; cut off notches and leave edges unfinished.

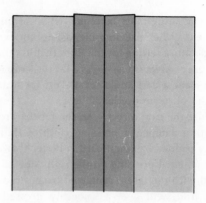

PLAIN SEAM – NARROW ZIG-ZAG STITCH

● Narrow zig-zag stitch, 1 to 2 width, 1·5 to 1 mm (15 to 20) stitch length.
● General-purpose Presser Foot or Even Feed* Foot; zig-zag throat plate.
● Strong thread, ball-point needle of appropriate size, or Perfect stitch needle.
● Prepare seam with hand tacking if necessary.
● Stitch seam under tension by guiding and supporting, except when using the Even Feed Foot.
● Press seam as stitched, then press open; cut off notches and leave edges unfinished.

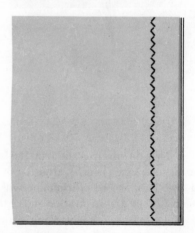

DOUBLE-STITCHED SEAM

● Stitch on seamline with straight, straight stretch or narrow zig-zag stitch.
● Stitch again ·3, ·6 or ·9 cm ($\frac{1}{8}$, $\frac{1}{4}$ or $\frac{3}{8}$ inch) outside seamline. Width depends on fabric weight, garment and desired width of finished seam allowance.
● Trim seam allowances near second stitching.

● Press seam as stitched, then towards the front on side and shoulder seams and towards the sleeve on armhole seams.

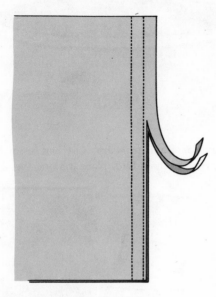

DOUBLE-STITCHED SEAM, MOCK OVER-EDGED

● Stitch on seamline with straight, straight stretch or narrow zig-zag stitch.

● Stitch again ·3†, ·6 or ·9 cm ($\frac{1}{8}$, $\frac{1}{4}$ or $\frac{3}{8}$ inch) outside seamline. Width depends on fabric weight, garment and the desired width of the finished seam allowance.

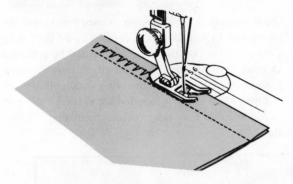

● Use blindstitch (illustrated) or one of the following stitches:

Over-edge stretch†	Multi-stretch zig-zag††
Multi-stitch zig-zag††	Slant over-edge†††
	Plain zig-zag†

● Use zig-zag throat plate and General-purpose Presser Foot or Even Feed* Foot.

● Trim seam allowances near stitching and press.

  † Use a stitch width less than 5 for seam-allowance widths less than ·6 cm ($\frac{1}{4}$ inch).
  †† Use to neaten and flatten seam allowances in bulky knits.
  ††† Available on SINGER* sewing machine Models 413, 416, 438, 513, 514 and 538.

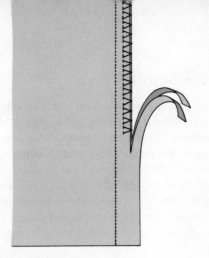

DOUBLE-STITCHED SEAM, OVER-EDGED (*Above*)

● Stitch on seamline with straight, straight stretch or narrow zig-zag stitch.

● Trim seam allowance to ·3†, ·6 or ·9 cm ($\frac{1}{8}$, $\frac{1}{4}$ or $\frac{3}{8}$ inch), depending on fabric weight and type of garment.

● Use zig-zag throat plate and General-purpose foot.

● Stitch over the trimmed edges with over-edge, slant over-edge or over-edge stretch stitch.

† Use a stitch width less than 5 for seam widths less than ·6 cm ($\frac{1}{4}$ inch).

SEAM STITCHED AND NEATENED IN ONE OPERATION

● Use only for seam allowances ·6 cm ($\frac{1}{4}$ inch) or less† in width.

● Hand-tack on seamline if necessary.

● Trim seam allowances to ·6 cm ($\frac{1}{4}$ inch) or less.††

● Use general-purpose throat plate and General-purpose foot.

● Stitch over seam-allowance edges, placing straight edge or over-edge, slant over-edge or over-edge stretch stitch on seamline.

  † Use a stitch width less than 5 for seam-allowance widths less than ·6 cm ($\frac{1}{4}$ inch).
    Seam-allowance widths less than ·6 cm ($\frac{1}{4}$ inch) are suitable for sheer nylon tricot only.
  †† Place seam allowance to left when stitching.

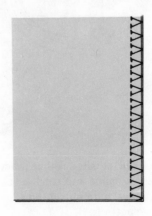

Stayed Seams

Neckline, shoulder and waistline seams usually need to be stayed to prevent stretching and to support the shape of the garment. Other seams may also need to be stayed, depending on garment styling. Seam binding and ·6-cm (¼-inch) wide twill tape are firm and do not stretch. Bias seam binding of mercerised cotton is pliable and allows for some stretch, and it prevents the seams slipping on loosely knitted fabrics. Shrink seam binding and twill tape and, if seamline is curved, press it to shape before applying it.

Front shoulder seam. Tack seamline, place the centre of the stay tape on the seamline and stitch through stay and seam at the same time. Press seam as stitched, then press open.

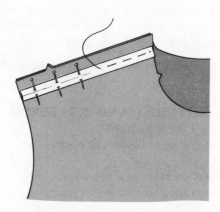

Neckline. Tack neckline including interfacing, garment facing and stay tape (pressed to shape and tacked to seamline). Stitch on seamline. Press. Then trim seam allowances to uneven widths. Press seam open, then turn and under-stitch facing to seam allowances.

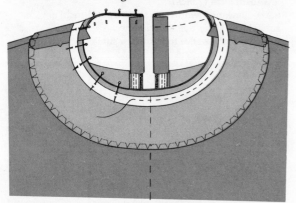

Waistline. Tack and stitch waistline seam. Place edge of stay tape near seamline and stitch along edge. Trim seam allowances level with outside edge of tape. Finish

tape and seam allowances together with multi-stitch zig-zag.

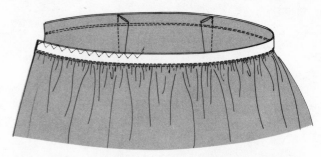

Bias stay for flexible seam. Cut bias seam binding through centre. Open fold, place it along the seamline, and stitch.

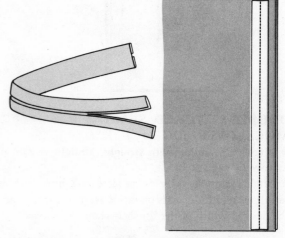

The seam may be a plain seam pressed open; and the edges may be neatened or not, depending on the fabric and construction. Or the seam edges may be trimmed level with the stay tape. Turn all edges towards seam edge and form a double-stitched seam with a blindstitch edge finish. This is recommended for raschel knits and other open knits that tend to lose their shape under strain.

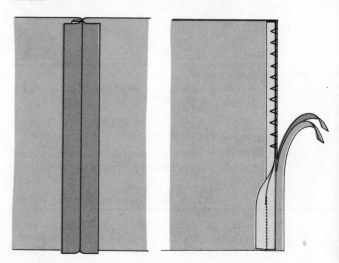

434

Interfacing Knitted Fabrics

Interfacing in collars and facings is just as important for firm and medium-firm knitted fabrics as it is for woven fabrics. You should omit interfacing only when you use sweater construction methods. The interfacing fabric may be a soft woven fabric, when you need only to increase the stability of the interfaced section; it may be a non-woven fabric like terylene non-woven interfacing, when you need to increase the stability and add extra body to the section; or, it may be linen or hair canvas when you want a crisp, tailored look in a lapel or collar detail. Handling the interfacing so as to eliminate seam bulk is especially important with knitted fabrics.

SOFT WOVEN AND NON-WOVEN INTERFACING

● Tack interfacing (soft woven or terylene non-woven) to wrong side of under collar.†
● Tack upper collar to under collar, right sides together, and ease upper collar slightly along seamline.

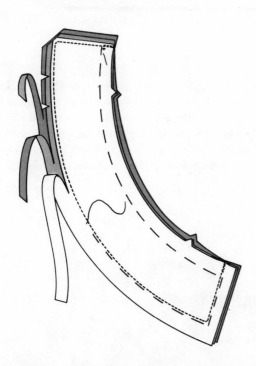

● Stitch on seamline, making blunt corners by taking one or two stitches diagonally across corners.
● Trim seam allowances to uneven widths, keeping the upper collar seam allowance widest. Notch seam allowances along outside curves.
● Press seam, then steam-press seam allowances open over a seam board.

● Turn seam allowances towards under collar and understitch from facing side through facing, interfacing and all seam allowances.

† To reduce collar thickness, under collar may be made of colour-matched taffeta or another crisp, woven fabric.

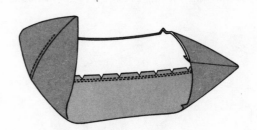

LINEN OR HAIR CANVAS INTERFACING

Where a firm, crisp texture is desired – as in faced-front and open-neckline styles, collars, pockets, pocket flaps and cuffs – either of the canvas interfacings can be handled in three different ways:

METHOD 1: ORGANZA STRIP

● Measure, mark and cut the seam allowance from the interfacing.
● Attach canvas to a shaped section of organza (or Victoria lawn), 4 cm (1½ inches) wide, with multi-stitch zig-zag stitching.
● Tack interfacing to wrong side of garment section and facing to right side with right sides together.
● Stitch on seamline near the edge of the interfacing.

METHOD 2: HERRINGBONE

● Measure, mark and cut the seam allowance from the interfacing.
● Tack interfacing to garment with the edge along the seamline.
● Herringbone interfacing to seamline.
● Tack and stitch facing as described in *Method 1*.

METHOD 3: IRON-ON

● Cut iron-on interfacing from pattern and carefully cut off all seam allowances.
● Iron-on the interfacing to the upper collar; to the upper side of cuff, pocket or pocket flap; and to the facing of a neckline, lapel or garment-front, depending on the design, using the correct iron temperature.
● Stitch facing and garment section on seamline near edge of interfacing.

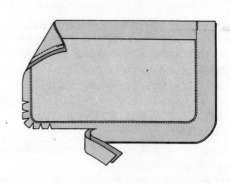

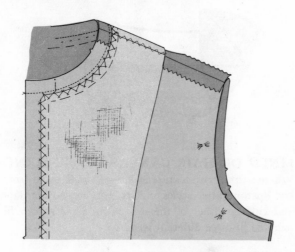

Bound Buttonholes

Bound, piped or corded buttonholes are suitable for firm knitted fabrics. Make them according to your favourite method. Finish them through the facing in a way that reduces the seam layers to a minimum. Tack the facing securely with a lengthwise tacking along the inner edge. Make crosswise tackings above and below each buttonhole. Using a 1 mm (20) stitch length and the Straight-stitch Presser Foot, stitch round the buttonhole from the right side, on the seamline of the buttonhole stitching. Slash through the facing at the centre of the buttonhole from the right side. Then turn the garment and trim the facing close to the stitching line on each side of the buttonhole. The result will be a smooth strong finish on the facing side and almost invisible stitching on the right side.

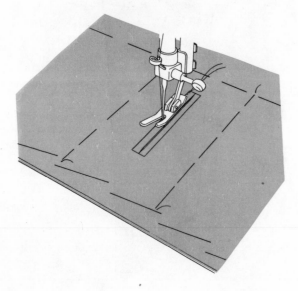

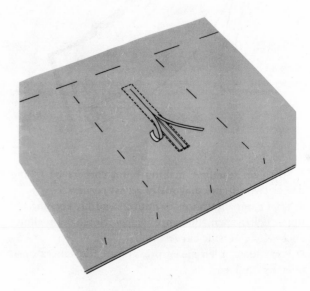

Bands and Bindings

Fabric bands, shaped facings and edge bindings are especially suited to knitted fabric designs. They eliminate the bulk of conventional facings and add a special interest. Knowing how to apply them will enable you to vary simple patterns in ways that add a professional touch to your clothes.

Shaped Bands

● Appropriate for firm, stable knits.
● Cut shaped band by pattern, 4 to 6 cm (1½ to 2½ inches) wide plus seam allowance.
● Cut interfacing for band from crisp, thin, colour-matched fabric.
● Stitch and trim edge as illustrated. (*Below left*)

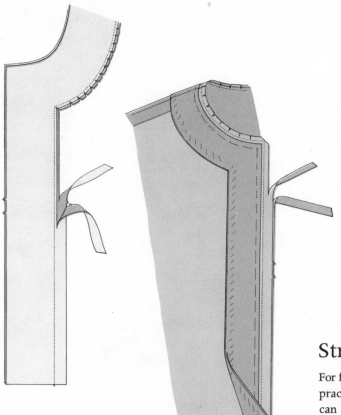

● Press. Turn the band and interfacing to right side. Ease the interfacing under slightly at the seamline and tack using diagonal tacking.
● Tack 2.5 cm (1 inch) from neckline and front edges through band and interfacing to keep edges in place.
● Trim seam allowance plus ·3 cm (⅛ inch) from interfacing near 2·5-cm (1-inch) tacking line.

● Place band on wrong side of garment with right side of band facing the garment.
● Pin, tack, stitch and trim neckline and front seam allowances. Press and turn band to right side of garment.
● Diagonally tack neckline and front edge.
● Tack free edge to garment and slip-stitch invisibly.
● Remove all tacking and press.

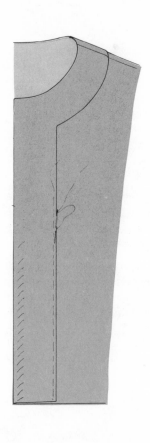

Straight Bands

For firm and medium-firm knits, straight-cut bands form practical finishes for V necklines and sleeve hems. They can also be used instead of a hem at the lower edge of the garment. Cut the fabric lengthwise twice the width of the finished band plus two 1·2-cm (½-inch) seam allowances.

V NECKLINES

Three methods for completing the band at the point of a V neckline are: seamed and opened, hidden seam and crossed. The preparations are the same for all three methods. Do not cut the front of a neckline on the seamline, but cut as a high round neckline.

Using a piece of tissue paper, mark the outline of the V, both the seamline and the cutting line, marking a 1·2-cm (½-inch) seam allowance. Pin the marked paper to the

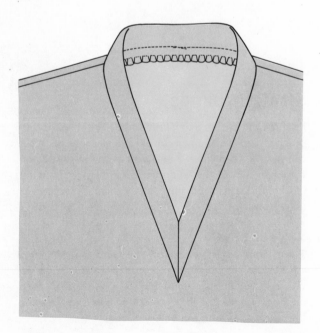

wrong side of the front section and stitch with a straight stitch, 1·5 mm (15) stitch length, on both the seamline and the cutting line; pivot at the point and make one stitch across it. Tear away the paper and slash the centre

front as far as the cutting line, leaving the extra fabric beyond the seamline until the entire band is completed. Stay-stitch the back neckline exactly on the seamline and trim seam allowance to 1·2 cm (½ inch). Then stitch and press shoulder seams. The V neckline must be deep enough to allow the finished neckline to slip over your head without strain, unless there is a centre-back zip.

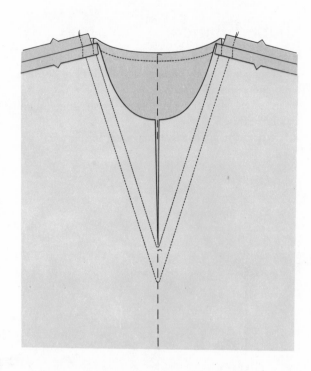

SEAMED AND OPENED

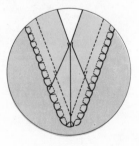

- Fold strip in centre, right side out, to form band; press.
- Pin-mark centre back of band.
- Starting at centre of both back and band, with right sides together, pin together along seamline. Slash back

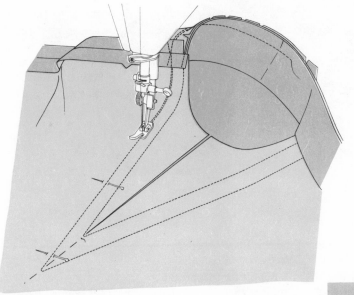

- Turn garment to wrong side and fold on centre front tacking, carrying fold through the band, matching the pin marks through point of V and along centre front fold. Tack band ends together along this line to form a mitre.
- To stitch mitre, lower needle ·3 cm ($\frac{1}{8}$ inch) from point where band folds meet. Carefully back-stitch two stitches, then stitch forwards only far enough to meet the seamline stitching that joins the band at the V. Back-stitch two stitches. Tie the thread ends at both ends of this stitching.

neckline seam allowance in several places almost to stay stitching. Do not ease or stretch. Continue pinning one side to V point. Tack if necessary.

- Stitch, garment-side up, from centre back to V just inside the seamline stay stitching; stop exactly at the end of the V. Carefully back-stitch three stitches and tie threads.
- Slash V to stitching line.
- Repeat for second side.
- Place the front of garment right side up over the end of the ironing board. Extend folded edges of band towards neck opening and extend seam allowances towards garment. Let the ends of the band fold under, adjusting the fold to form a centre line above the V point. Pin-mark the band at the edges where the centre folds meet.

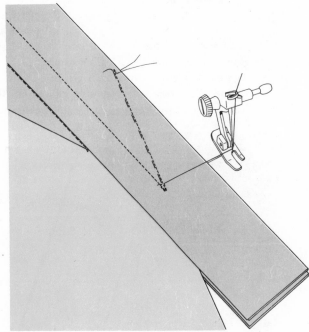

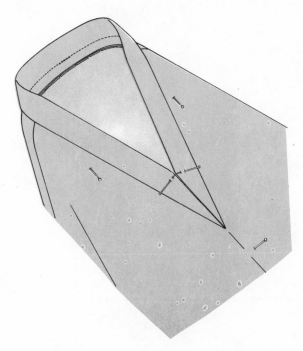

- Press band ends open along mitred seam and pin ends to seam allowances. Trim excess length from bands.
- Working with garment wrong side up, extend seam allowances and stitch ·2 cm ($\frac{1}{16}$ inch) outside seamline through all layers including end of band. Do this on both sides of V. See detail in circle on opposite page.
- Trim seam allowances to uneven widths and finish with an over-edge stitch.
- Press from right side over a padded surface to give a soft seam, and prevent the seam allowances making an impression on the right side. Do not press with iron directly on fabric; use a pressing cloth and light steam.

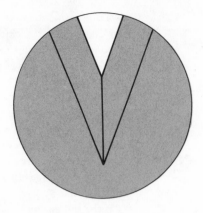 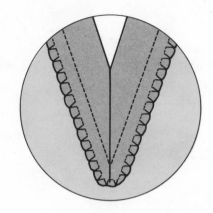

MITRE, ENCLOSED SEAM

● Cut strip for band, but do not fold. Mark centre back of band with tacking.

● With right sides together, start at centre back to pin one edge of band to garment along seamline. Slash seam allowance almost to stay stitching in several places at back neckline curve. Do not ease or stretch. Continue pinning one side to V point. Tack if necessary.

● With garment-side up, stitch from centre back to V just inside seamline stay stitching; stop exactly at the end of the V. Carefully back-stitch three stitches and tie threads.

● Slash V to stitching line.

● Repeat for second side.

● Turn garment wrong side out, fold entire front on centre tacking, and pin. Open out band, letting seam allowances extend towards the garment. Cut off ends of band straight and level, ·6 cm (¼ inch) beyond end of V. Pin seamlines of band together along V and pin un-stitched edges of band together for 10 cm (4 inches). Pin along exact centre of band.

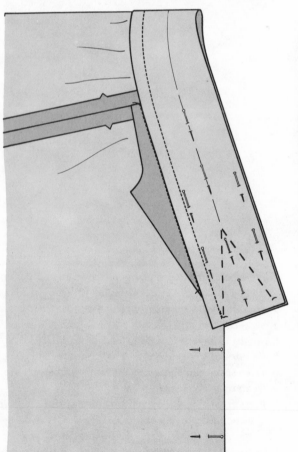 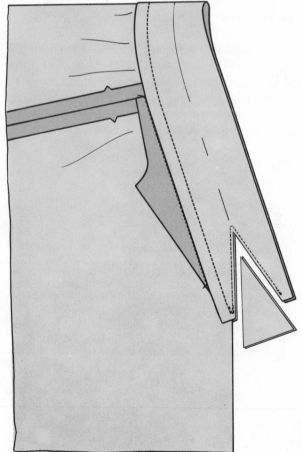

440

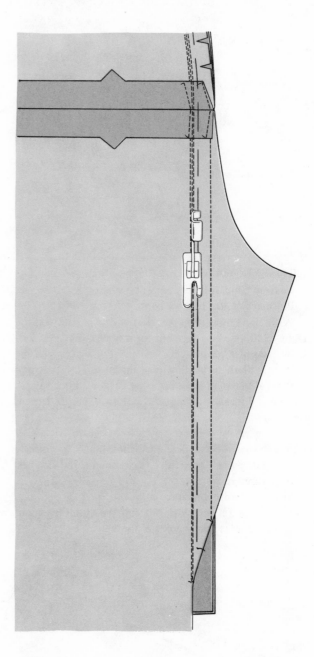

● To form a stitching line for the V mitre, tack through the band in a straight line following the centre-front fold, from point of V to centre of band. Turn and continue tacking from the centre of band in a straight line to the seamline of the band (1·2 cm ($\frac{1}{2}$ inch) from outer edge, ·6 cm ($\frac{1}{4}$ inch) from end), forming a V.

● Stitch along tacking, at mitre point of V; take one stitch across point. Back-stitch at both ends of this stitching.

● Trim seam allowance to ·6 cm ($\frac{1}{4}$ inch) and press seam open.

● Unpin and unfold garment.

● Pin bottom ends of band together with mitre seams matching, and continue pinning the seam allowances of the band together along the entire neckline. Tack.

● Stitch through seam allowances of neckline and band, from wrong side of garment ·2 cm ($\frac{1}{16}$ inch) outside neckline stitching.

● To reduce bulk, trim seam allowances to uneven widths – garment to ·6 cm ($\frac{1}{4}$ inch) inside band seam edge to ·3 cm ($\frac{1}{8}$ inch), and outside band to ·9 to 1·2 cm ($\frac{3}{8}$ to $\frac{1}{2}$ inch). Neaten seam allowances.

● Place garment right side up over a soft surface; cover with a pressing cloth and lightly steam-press the neckline.

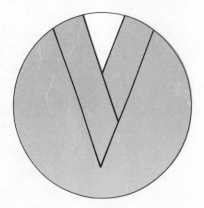

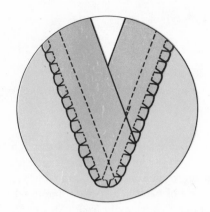

CROSSED BANDS

- To form band, fold strip in centre, right side out; press.
- Pin-mark centre back of band.
- With right sides together, start at centre back (on the right-hand side of a garment for a woman and the left-hand side of a garment for a man). Pin together along seamline. Slash seam allowance almost to stay stitching in several places at back neckline curve. Do not ease or stretch. Continue pinning one side to V point. Tack if necessary.
- With garment-side up, stitch from centre back to V barely inside the seamline stay stitching. Stop exactly at the end of the V, carefully back-stitch three stitches, and tie threads.
- Slash V to stitching line.
- Repeat for second side, but end the stitching about 4 cm (1½ inches) above point of the V.

- Turn the garment right side out and slip it over the end of the ironing board; let the band extend towards the neckline and the seam allowances towards the garment. Cross the ends of the band at the V point by letting the end of the band on the stitched side pass over the band on the unstitched side and into the unstitched seam.

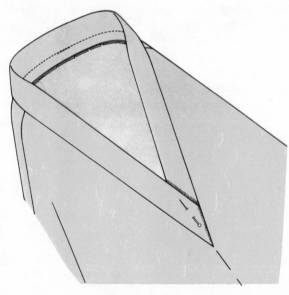

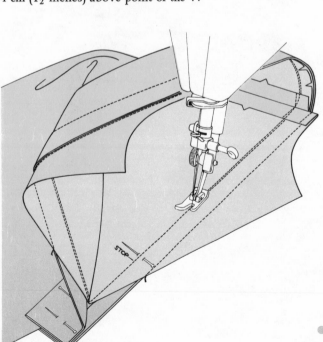

Arrange the garment-front so that it is smooth and the V is not distorted. Place a pin through both layers of the band at the V. Using a pressing cloth and steam, press lightly along the stitched seamline, but avoid pressing over the pin and unstitched seam.

- Turn the garment inside out and stitch the open portion of the seam just inside the stay stitching from the garment side to the point of the V. On second side, stitch ·2 cm ($\frac{1}{16}$ inch) outside the seamline through all seam layers, including the extended portion of the crossed band.

● Trim seam allowances to uneven widths, leaving the under seam allowance the widest.

● Neaten with machine over-edging. See detail of underside of neckline, in circle on opposite page.

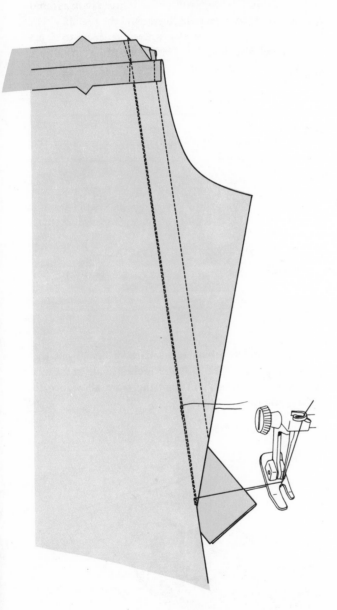

finished width. Cut a continuous strip or, if necessary, make joins to match crossing seams. Leave ends unstitched until later. The band may be interfaced.

● Fold band in centre right side out, and press lightly.

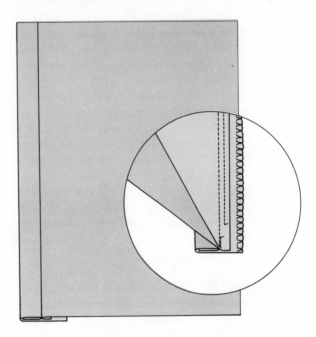

● Open band and, with right sides facing, pin one edge to the garment, starting with the centre of the band. Do not ease or stretch. With garment-side up, stitch to within 5 cm (2 inches) of the end of the band.

● Repeat for second side.

● Work out the exact position to stitch the ends of the band together (or for finishing each end of an open band). Stitch, trim seam allowances to ·6 cm ($\frac{1}{4}$ inch), and press seam open.

● Stitch open portion of band, overlapping stitching lines.

● Press seam open and trim seam allowance of band to ·6 cm ($\frac{1}{4}$ inch) for bands wider than 1·2 cm ($\frac{1}{2}$ inch). Do not trim seam allowance on 1·2-cm ($\frac{1}{2}$-inch) bands.

● Fold band along centre crease, match the seam edges of the band and the garment, and pin them together. Tack through seam allowances only. Steam-press from right side, using a pressing cloth.

● Extend seam allowances and stitch from the wrong side, garment-side up, through the seam allowances only, ·2 cm ($\frac{1}{16}$ inch) outside the previous stitching.

● Machine-over-edge the seam edges together, or trim garment seam allowance to ·6 cm ($\frac{1}{4}$ inch) and over-edge one edge only.

OPEN-FRONT, SLEEVE OR HEM EDGE FINISH

● Estimate length needed for band and add 2·5 cm (1 inch). Width of finished band may be from 1·2 to 7·5 cm ($\frac{1}{2}$ to 3 inches), depending upon the style. To work out cutting width, add 2·5 cm (1 inch) to twice the

Stretched Bands

Stretched bands, sold as 'ribbing', are usually made of rib knit or one made of textured yarn that has a great deal of stretch and a strong recovery. Stretched bands are used: (1) at sleeve wrists to ease or gather a wide sleeve into a smaller band; (2) at or below the waistline of a sweater, overblouse or jacket to fit the edge to the figure; (3) at the neckline to form a crew neck, turtleneck or polo neck finish; and (4) round the armhole of a sleeveless dress.

In all cases, the length of the band is determined by: (1) the body measurement it is to fit or pass over and (2) the amount of tension that you want on the band in wear. The seam allowances for both band and garment are ·6 cm ($\frac{1}{4}$ inch). Cut the band so that the direction of greater stretch is on the length of the band.

If the band is to form a circle (which is always the case except for the waistline of a cardigan), seam the band ends together with a narrow double-stitched seam. Then, fold the band right side out and pin the seam allowances together.

To ensure even distribution of fullness or ease, pin-mark both the band and the garment in four equal parts. The joining should be where it will show least. Pin the band to the right side of garment, all seam edges level, matching pin markings of the equal parts.

Place garment under Presser Foot, band up, eased side towards feed. Set machine for a straight stretch stitch or an over-edge stretch stitch, which seams and finishes at the same time. Stretch and stitch simultaneously; keep

the work under tension by holding the seam both in back and in front of the Presser Foot, but allow the feed to carry the fabric. Stretch the band until the edge it is being applied to lies flat but is not stretched. Steam the seam by holding the iron above the fabric so the seam and band will recover their unstretched length.

For a crew neck, cut the band 7·5 cm (3 inches) wide and, if you are working with a basic pattern with a round neckline, cut the crew neckline below the seamline, cut it 2 cm ($\frac{3}{4}$ inch) lower at centre front tapering to ·6 cm ($\frac{1}{4}$ inch) lower at shoulder. This new cutting line allows for ·6 cm ($\frac{1}{4}$ inch) seam allowance.

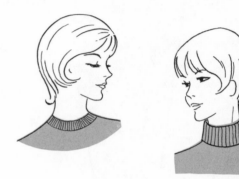

For a polo-neck, which turns back on itself, cut the band or ribbing about 23 cm (9 inches) wide and use a basic round neckline, but trim the seam allowance to ·6 cm ($\frac{1}{4}$ inch).

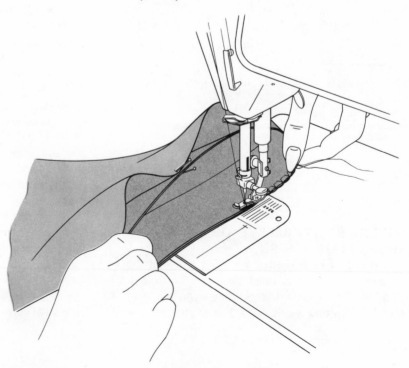

444

For a turtleneck, which does not turn back, cut the band or ribbing 10 to 11·5 cm (4 to 4½ inches) wide and use a basic round neckline, but trim the seam allowance to ·6 cm (¼ inch).

Bands Blocked-to-shape

Double knits of polyester, wool or blends of these fibres, as well as some warp knits and single knits of these fibres, can be steam-pressed or blocked into shapes for accenting curved pocket flaps, U necklines, yokes and patch pockets.

● Trace the outline of the finished edge on a large piece of laundered calico or sheeting. Pin this to your ironing board cover to use as a shaping guide.

● Cut the strip for the shaped band twice the finished width plus two 1·2-cm (½-inch) seam allowances. Cut either lengthwise or crosswise, after testing a short length to see which will hold the shape best.

● Tack edges of strip together, leaving one end of tacking thread long and unknotted. Press lightly to form crease.

● Pin-mark band at centre and place centre of band at centre of the marked shaping guide. Tack band to guide across centre.

● Use the surface of the band that is upwards as the underside in the garment in case some shine develops during pressing.

● Using a damp cloth over the band and working from the centre tacking, apply steam, stretch the band and pin it along the cut edges, keeping the fold edge level with the marked line. Working with only a few cm (inches) of the band at a time, slightly ease the fold edge and stretch the cut edge. Place pins along the outside edge into the padding of the ironing board so that you can press over them without marking the band. When the entire band has been shaped and pinned, steam-press again to give it a permanent set. Polyester knitted fabrics will retain this shaping after laundering, and so will wool after dry cleaning.

● Apply as described on page 443, *Open-Front, Sleeve or Hem Edge Finish*.

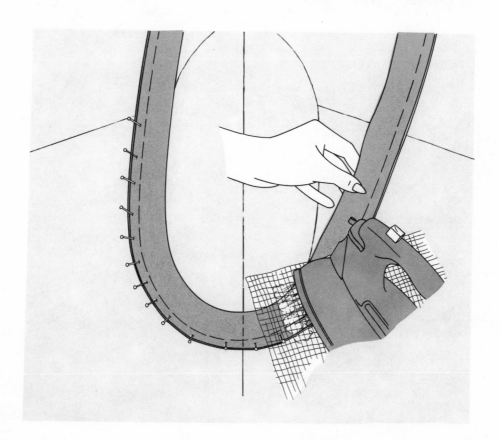

Bound, Piped and Corded Edges

Bound, piped and corded-edge finishes on knitted fabrics are different from those on woven fabrics: the free edge may be finished with an over-edge stitch; but on wovens, the free edge is turned to the inside or covered with a facing. Fabric strips, which may be cut lengthwise, crosswise or bias, are perfect for knitteds because they eliminate facings that often show an impression on the right side. These strips can be applied to an unstitched edge, to an edge that has been stay-stitched on the seamline for moderate control, or to an edge stayed with woven seam binding for firm control.

BOUND EDGE

For a ·6-cm (¼-inch) wide bound edge, cut a strip 3·2 cm (1¼ inches) wide, and over-edge one edge. Trim garment on seamline. Place bias strip over garment, edges level and right sides facing. Stitch ·6 cm (¼ inch) from edges, as at **A**. Press seam allowances open. Turn strip over one seam allowance and hand-tack through centre of binding, as in **B**. Turn garment wrong side up; extend both the seam allowance and the finished edge of strip. Stitch ·2 cm ($\frac{1}{16}$ inch) outside first stitching line, as at **C**.

Remove tacking and steam-press to shape binding and free edge, as in **D**. Catch edge to crossing seams.

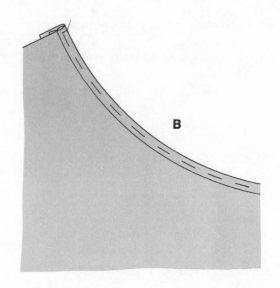

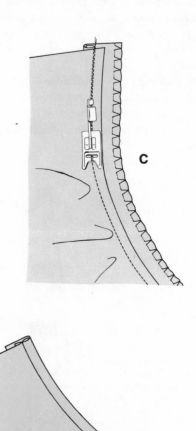

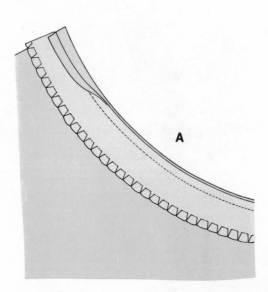

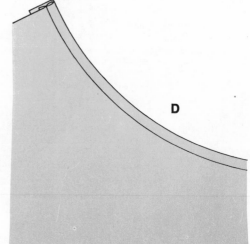

446

PIPED EDGE

For a piped edge, cut a strip 4 cm (1½ inches) wide and neaten one edge with the over-edge stitch. Fold back the other edge 1·2 cm (½ inch) and steam-press, as in E. Trim garment on seamline. Place prepared strip right side down and garment edge over it, also right side down. Pin garment edge to strip, matching edges as at F. With General-purpose Presser Foot on machine, straight-stitch, 1·5 mm (15) length, ·6 cm (¼ inch) from edges, using edge of foot as a guide. See G. Remove pins before stitching over them. Fold strip to underside, letting piping extend from stitching line. See H. Steam-press to shape the piping and the free edge of strip. Catch the edge to crossing seams.

CORDED EDGE

For a corded edge, cut strip 4 to 5 cm (1½ to 2 inches) wide, depending on diameter of cord. Fold strip over cord, right side out, near one edge of strip; allow ·6 cm (¼ inch) to extend beyond the stitching line at the cord on one side and 2 cm (¾ inch) on the other. Machine-tack using the Zipper Foot, as in I. Neaten the wider edge of the strip with machine over-edging. Trim garment edge on seamline. Place prepared strip right side down with garment edge over it also right side down, edges match-ing as in J. Pin; then stitch, using the Zipper Foot adjusted to the left of the needle and very close to the cord as shown. Remove pins as you stitch. Fold strip to underside, letting the cording extend, as in K. Steam-press to shape the cording and the free edge of the strip. Catch edge to the crossing seams.

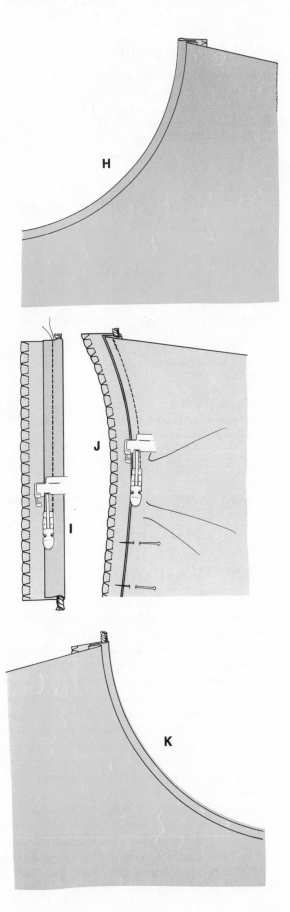

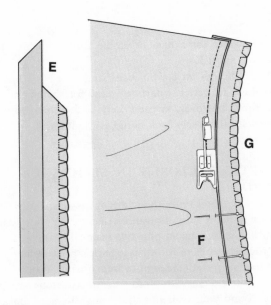

Soft-Roll Edge Finish

A bound edge with a bold, soft roll is an attractive finish for the neckline and armholes of tank tops and jumpers. Trim the garment edges to allow for a 1·2-cm ($\frac{1}{2}$-inch) seam allowance. Cut the strip for binding 7 cm ($2\frac{3}{4}$ inches) wide on the crosswise direction of the fabric. Set your sewing machine for a 1·5 mm (15) stitch length and attach the Straight-stitch Presser Foot. Then, with right sides together, stitch the binding strip to the garment 1·2 cm ($\frac{1}{2}$ inch) from edge; stretch the strip slightly at the curves, as in **A**.

Press seam allowances and stitching to remove any 'ringing' along the curve. Then roll the binding over both seam allowances and place pins at right angles to the edge along the seamline catching the unfinished side of the binding, as in **B**.

Stitch in the seamline from the right side, using the Zipper Foot adjusted to the left side of the needle, and a 1·5 to 1 mm (15 to 20) stitch length, as at **C**. When stitching is completed, trim the seam allowance of the binding close to the stitching.

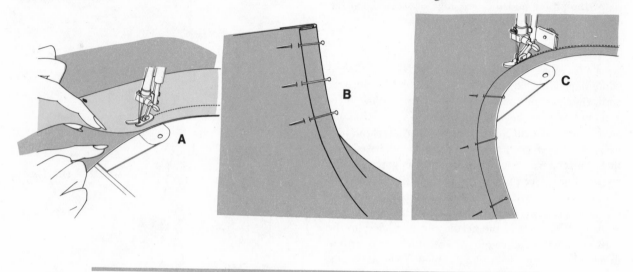

Elastic Waistbands

In most knitted fabric skirts and trousers, you may omit the zip unless you have a larger-than-average difference between your waist and hip measurements. Test the fabric by making a test waistband. In the direction of the greatest stretch, cut a strip of fabric 7·5 cm (3 inches) wide and long enough to go round your waistline. Stitch the ends together, making the band the same measurement as your waistline. Fold the band right side out and tack edges together, leaving ends of tacking thread free. Step into the waistband and bring it up over your hips to the waistline. If it does not stretch enough to go over your hips without undue strain, you should use a zip fastening.

If the waistband does slip over your hips easily, you can make an elastic waistband.

There are two basic types of elastic waistbands: (1) those in which the elastic is enclosed in a separate band, which is then applied as a unit to the garment; and (2) those in which the garment fabric is cut to provide an allowance for a hem or casing through which the elastic is slotted.

Even though an elastic waistband is used, trousers and skirts fit better if darts are used for shaping at the waistline; however, sweater knits and knitted fabrics which stretch freely look better without darts.

ELASTIC ENCLOSED IN SEPARATE BAND

● Cut waistband twice the width of the elastic plus two 1·5-cm ($\frac{5}{8}$-inch) seam allowances, and the length of your waistline measurement plus two seam allowances.
● Stitch the ends of the strip together, press seam open and fold strip right side out to form a band. Press.
● Cut 2- to 2·5-cm-wide ($\frac{3}{4}$- to 1-inch) elastic long enough to go round your waistline under slightly more tension than you need for a close fit, as some tension in the elastic will be lost in the construction.

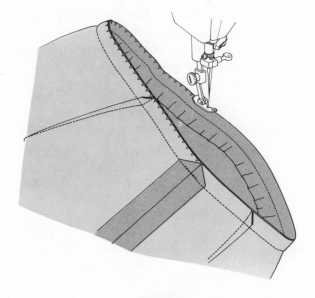

Add 2·5 cm (1 inch) to the length, overlap ends 1·2 cm (½ inch) and stitch together.

● Divide and pin-mark both the waistband and the garment into four equal portions.

● Place elastic inside band and pin seam allowances of band together at 5-cm (2-inch) intervals.

● Pin waistband unit to garment waistline, right sides together, matching the four points that divide the two edges into equal portions. Place waistband seam at centre back or at a side seam.

● Use the Zipper Foot or the General-purpose Foot, and set the machine for a narrow zig-zag or a straight stretch stitch. Test-stitch to see that machine settings are correct and that the needle does not strike the foot.

● Place garment under foot, right side down, with open edge of foot against the elastic.

● Stitch slowly, stretching the band if necessary and easing the garment seam to the band.

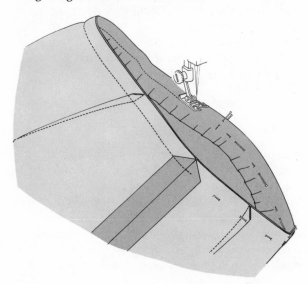

● Trim the centre seam allowance to ·6 cm (¼ inch) and machine-over-edge the remaining seam allowances together. See illustration left below.

● Catch seam allowances to crossing seams.

ELASTIC ENCLOSED IN HEM OR CASING

● Measure waistband elastic to fit closely round your waistline and add 2·5 cm (1 inch); overlap ends 1·2 cm (½ inch) and stitch together.

● Machine-over-edge waistline seam allowance of garment.

● Turn garment hem over the elastic and pin at lower edge of elastic at 5-cm (2-inch) intervals. Hand-tack if necessary. Stitch with garment right side up, open side of Zipper Foot against elastic, and use a straight stretch stitch.

● To prevent elastic from turning, distribute ease evenly over the elastic, pinning through casing and elastic at crossing seams. Stitch in the seamline of each crossing seam through the casing and the elastic from the right side. Tie thread ends.

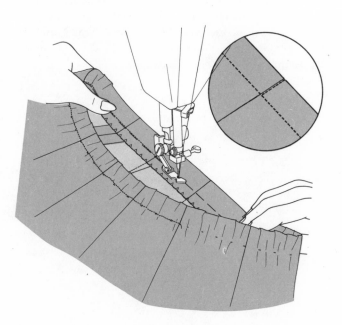

ELASTIC STITCHED TO CASING

● Measure and cut 2-cm (¾-inch) waistband elastic to 2·5 cm (1 inch) less than your waist measurement.

● Overlap ends 1·2 cm (½ inch) and stitch together.

● Divide elastic and waistline into four equal parts and mark with pins.

● Place top edge of the elastic ·3 cm (⅛ inch) from edge on inside of the garment.

● Using the General-purpose Presser Foot and the straight stretch stitch, stitch near the lower edge of the elastic while holding the garment and elastic under enough tension to stretch the elastic to fit the fabric.

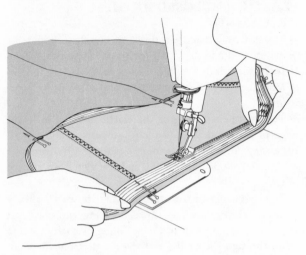

● Turn the elastic and fabric once to the inside. The elastic will then be covered.

● While holding the fabric and elastic under tension, stitch near the edge of the elastic through the turned fabric, the elastic and the garment. Again, use the General-purpose Presser Foot and the straight stretch stitch.

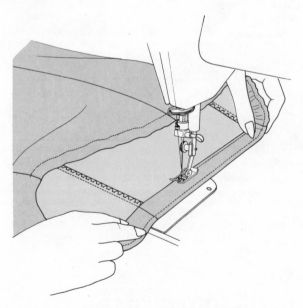

Sleeves

Always set sleeves in firm and medium-firm knits by the conventional method for woven fabrics, and neaten the seam allowances, ·9 cm (⅜ inch) wide, together.

On stretchable knits, follow the sweater method. Stitch the open sleeve to an open armhole and stitch the underarm and sleeve seams later as one continuous seam. Patterns that are designed for stretchable knits and recommend this method have a sleeve with less ease than regular patterns. Work with ·9-cm (⅜-inch) seam allowances on both the armhole and the sleeve head.

● Pin sleeve to armhole, matching dots, notches and underarm seams.

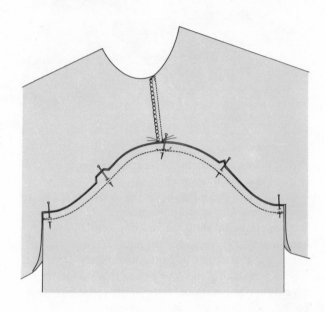

● Using the straight stretch stitch, Straight-stitch Presser Foot and throat plate, and with garment side up, stitch from top of sleeve head to underarm seam. Stretch the seam as you stitch.

● Overlap the stitching at the top of the sleeve head and stitch the second side of the sleeve.

● Neaten with an over-edge finish. On thin fabrics where a less than ·9-cm (⅜-inch) seam allowance is used, trim seam, then neaten.

● Stitch underarm and sleeve seam the same way, matching crossing seams at the underarm.

● Apply steam to regain shape.

Hems

Follow the same preparatory steps for hemming as for hemming woven fabrics. Choose a hem finish that has the least bulk for your knitted fabric. Use either the blind hemming stitch or the blind herringbone, both of which go between the hem edge and the garment and not over the edge. For most firm or heavy knits, use the double-stitched hem in which two rows of blind hemming stitches support the weight of the hem.

Firm Dress- and Suit-weight and Bonded Knitted Fabrics

FABRICS

Characteristics. These knitted fabrics are stable and can be handled like woven fabrics. Minimum lengthwise stretch, and crosswise stretch of less than 3·2 cm in 20 cm (1¼ inches in 8 inches).

Types. Double knits; bonded knits; firm, untextured warp knits; jacquard knits.

Fibre content. All polyester, all wool, fibre blends and yarn mixtures of wool/nylon, wool/polyester, cotton/polyester, nylon/acrylic, etc.

PATTERN CHOICE

Dresses – look for simple style lines; darted or seamed shaping; pocket details; top-stitched seams; soft pleats; collars, cuffs, facings; eased fullness; A-line, princess line; waistline seaming.

Also – separates, trouser suits, jackets, dressmaker suits, children's wear, light- or medium-weight coats, some slacks and jackets for men.

PREPARATIONS

- Fold on lengthwise wale or rib, square ends, tack ends and edges for shrinking (unless fabric is labelled 'preshrunk').
- Woollens – shrink very carefully unless marked 'washable'.
- Polyesters – launder to remove excess finishing solution.
- All other washables – launder by hand or machine according to label.
- Bonded knits – straighten according to face fabric; shrinking is not usually necessary.

PATTERN FITTING

- Buy your usual pattern type and size.
- Allow no less than basic ease allowance.
- Fit pattern accurately to reduce garment fittings during construction.

CUTTING AND MARKING

- Fold fabric right side out on lengthwise rib.
- Follow 'with nap' layout.
- Pin with new steel pins.
- Cut with sharp shears.
- Cut notches outwards.
- Mark centre front and back lines with hand tacking.
- Mark internal details with tailor's tacks.

STAY STITCHING

- Stay neckline and waistline seams with straight stitching (2 mm (12) stitch length) or chain stitching.
- Use Even Feed* Foot to avoid easing or stretching seamline.

STITCHING

- These fabrics are generally easy to stitch.
- Use size 14 regular or ball-point needle with spun-polyester thread.
- Use size 11 regular or ball-point needle with silk thread.
- Balance tensions.
- Use normal or regular presser-foot pressure.
- Set stitch length at 2 mm (12) for straight seams, at 1·5 mm (15) for curves.
- Kinds of stitches: straight stitch with strong thread; straight stretch stitch; narrow zig-zag (1 to 1½ stitch width).
- Guide and gently support seam while stitching, holding it under tension with both hands, or
- Use the Even Feed* Foot.

SEAMS AND SEAM FINISHES

- For general use: use plain seams pressed open, no seam neatening.
- For unlined jackets, coats, pants, armhole of set-in sleeves: use straight-stitched seam, pressed in one direction, cut to ·9 cm (⅜ inch) or half-width, and edges finished together with machine-over-edge.
- To accent style lines: top-stitch seams with buttonhole twist or heavy thread. Use the Even Feed* Foot to reduce need for tacking.
- For seams that must not stretch, such as shoulder and waistline seams: use stayed seams.

FACINGS, INTERFACINGS, LININGS AND MOUNTINGS

- Neaten shaped facings with machine-over-edge stitch. Always understitch facing to seam allowances.
- Use lightweight woven or non-woven interfacing for dresses.
- Use lightweight tailor's canvas in the conventional way to interface jackets or coats.
- For a quick method, use an iron-on interfacing of a recommended quality, but cut off seam allowances.
- Mounting or lining is optional for dresses, but recommended for tailored jackets or coats.

PRESSING

- Limit iron temperature to that for fibre with lowest heat requirement.
- Use damp cloth to produce steam.
- Press at each construction step.   *(continued)*

451

● Place heavy paper under seams and darts to prevent them marking the right side when pressed.

HEMS AND EDGE FINISHES
● For fashion garments – use blind hemming methods; consider also the double-stitched hem.
● For trousers, sleeves, children's dresses and straight hems in fashion garments, use machine blindstitch.
● Edge finishes, such as folded straight-cut bands and cross- and diagonal-cut bindings, may be used instead of conventional hems.

Raschel and Rough-textured, Medium-firm Knitted Fabrics

FABRICS
Characteristics. These knitted fabrics have:
– firmness with rigidity
– depth without cumbersome bulk
– soft supple handling
– parallel rows of chain stitching on back of fabric, which hold filling yarns together.
Types. Raschel (often with embroidery-like surface) and other textured knitteds that have medium stretch in both directions.
Fibre content. Wool, polyester, acrylic cotton blend. Yarn may be smooth, looped or chenille type.

PATTERN CHOICE
Dresses – look for simple lines, ease for shaping (gathers disappear as ease), soft unpressed pleats, set-in or raglan sleeves.
Culottes – long and graceful or short.
Waistcoats – long, sleeveless.
Skirts – wrap-round, gathered or softly pleated.
Also – scarves, stoles, coats, hooded capes.

PREPARATIONS
● Fold lengthwise on chain stitch visible on back of fabric, right sides together.
● Cut ends crosswise along single filling yarn.
● Pull diagonally to square ends.
● Tack ends and edges for shrinking when necessary.
● Polyesters – launder to remove finishing solution.
● Woollens – shrink very carefully.
● Acrylics – usually need no shrinking.
● Cottons – refer to label; should be drip-dry.

PATTERN FITTING
● Buy your usual pattern type and size.
● Allow no less than basic ease allowances. (Remember, these fabrics have minimum-to-medium stretch.)
● Fit pattern accurately, to reduce garment fittings during construction.

CUTTING AND MARKING
● Fold right sides together on lengthwise chain.
● Match patterns or designs.
● Check which end of chain will unravel and use that end for the top of all pattern pieces.
● Lay out pattern according to 'with nap' directions.
● Place pins close together; do not allow fabric to hang over table edge.
● Cut with long, even strokes, using sharp shears. Do not cut notches.
● Mark with tacking lines and tailor's tacks.

STAY STITCHING
● Do *not* use conventional stay stitching.
● Through a single layer of fabric, stitch ·6 cm ($\frac{1}{4}$ inch) from seam edges to prevent unravelling, using straight stitch, 1·5 mm (15) stitch length.
● Do this on all edges except lower edge of sections before you begin any construction.

STITCHING
● These fabrics are generally easy to stitch.
● Use size 14 regular or ball-point needle with polyester thread.
● Use size 11 regular or ball-point needle with silk thread.
● Balance tensions.
● Set stitch length at 2 mm (12) for straight seams, at 1·5 mm (15) for curves.
● Use normal or regular presser-foot pressure.
● Wrap presser-foot toes with a ·6-cm ($\frac{1}{4}$-inch) wide sellotape to prevent loops of fabric yarn catching on Presser Foot.

SEAMS AND SEAM FINISHES
● You do not need to stay seams that are stitched with the straight stretch stitch.
● Stay seams that are stitched with regular straight stitch to prevent pulling or 'slipping'. Use seam tape or bias seam binding, or twill tape. Shrink before using.
● Trim seam edges to remove stay thread.
● Neaten seam edges separately when open, or together when pressed in one direction, with a zig-zag seam finish:
  (1) over-edge (Disc 32).
  (2) multi-stitch zig-zag.
  (3) blindstitch pattern.
  (4) over-edge stretch.

FACINGS, INTERFACINGS, LININGS AND MOUNTINGS

● Facings – standard shaped facings for less bulky varieties; colour-matched taffeta or soft-surfaced woven fabric for bulky knits. Understitching is necessary. Optional: instead of using facings, finish edges with braid, bindings or self-fabric bands.
● Interfacing – non-woven or woven, soft or crisp depending on styling. Test see-through effect and colour-match interfacing to fabric or mounted portion.
● Lining – optional, depending on styling.
● Mounting – optional, depending on styling. If you use mounting, preserve soft, supple effect of combined fabrics and colour-match.

PRESSING

● Limit iron temperature to that for fibre with lowest heat requirement.
● Use damp cloth to produce moisture.
● When pressing soft-surfaced raschels: stop pressing before fabric is dry; brush surface with soft brush or piece of same fabric; do not move fabric until dry.
● Press at each construction step.

HEMS AND EDGE FINISHES

● For fashion garments – use blind hemming methods; consider also the double-stitched hem.
● For casual garments – straight-stitch hem by machine, but hem edge should be machine-finished rather than turned.

Sweater and Loose, Stretchable Knitted Fabrics

FABRICS

Characteristics. These knits look and act like hand knitteds; stretch freely in both directions; adjust to the body; and have a loose, soft look.
Types. Patterned, plain or rib knits.
Fibre content. Wool, polyester or acrylic fibre or blends of these fibres.

PATTERN CHOICE

Choose patterns marked 'for knits only' or with close-to-the-body styling.
Dresses – straight and slim with few or no darts, set-in or raglan sleeves, scoop or high neckline.
Waistcoats – long, sleeveless.
Sweaters – cardigan or turtleneck.
Trouser outfits – with sweater overblouse.
Scarves, ponchos.

Note: *sweater knits can also be used for couturier two-piece, tailored outfits if they are made over a firm, layered base of mounting, thin hair canvas and lining. In this case, construction methods are the same as for woven fabrics.*

PREPARATIONS

● Relax fabric by allowing it to lie flat on floor or table overnight.
● Cut ends along crosswise courses.
● Fold on lengthwise rib, right side out.
● Pull diagonally to straighten crosswise ends.
● Square ends with table edges.

PATTERN FITTING

● Pattern should measure the same as body measurements. All ease can come from the fabric itself.
● Often, one size smaller than you normally wear is adequate.

CUTTING AND MARKING

● Observe grain-line principles.
● Pin sparingly.
● Do not let fabric hang over table edge.
● Lay out pattern according to 'with nap' directions.
● Cut with strong, sharp shears.
● Do not cut notches.
● Mark with tacking lines and tailor's tacks.

STAY STITCHING

● Do *not* use conventional stay stitching.
● Through a single layer of fabric, stitch ·6 cm ($\frac{1}{4}$ inch) from seam edges to prevent unravelling, using straight or chain stitch, 2 mm (12) stitch length. Stitch slowly and neither ease nor stretch edges. The Even Feed* Foot helps with this stitching.
● Mount very loosely knit fabrics on tissue paper for this stitching. Tear away paper after stitching.

STITCHING

● Requirements: (1) a stitch that will give, such as a straight stretch stitch, plain zig-zag ($\frac{1}{2}$ to 1 stitch width, 1 mm (20) stitch length), or a plain straight stitch (1·5 mm (15) stitch length) done under tension, (2) strong thread, such as spun polyester with size 14 needle; or silk thread with size 11 needle.
● Use normal or regular presser-foot pressure.
● Balance tensions.
● Use ball-point needle or the Perfect stitch needle to prevent snags.

SEAMS AND SEAM FINISHES

● Usually, seam edges are pressed and finished together.
● Pressed-open seam edges tend to roll.   *(continued)*

● Most seams should *not* be stayed, so that they will stretch with body movement.

● To prevent puckered seams, hand-tack. Leave thread ends long and free. Allow garment sections to hang overnight. Then stitch.

● Seams which should not stretch, such as some shoulder, back-of-neck or waistline seams, should be stayed with straight seam binding or narrow twill tape (both shrunk).

● Seams that should stretch but need some support can be stayed with ·6-cm (¼-inch) soft elastic.

● Select a seam-finishing stitch that will stretch, flatten and retain the yarn ends but will not be harsh.

● Apply the seam-finishing stitch first, then trim seam allowance to 1·2-to-·6-cm (½-to-¼-inch) width. Heavy fabrics usually have wider seam allowances than medium-weight fabrics.

FACINGS, INTERFACINGS, LININGS AND MOUNTINGS

● Not used, except for unusual styling; e.g. couturier 2-piece outfits are mounted over colour-matched mounting, lightweight canvas interfacing and a soft lining.

PRESSING

● Limit iron temperature to that for fibre with lowest heat requirement.

● Block rather than press. Steam, holding iron above the pressing surface, and allow fabric to dry before moving it with both hands.

HEMS AND EDGE FINISHES

● For dress hems – use a machine seam finish for edge and blind hemming for stitching hem; consider also the double-stitched hem.

● For sweater hems – use seam finish for edge and machine blindstitch for hemming.

● Apply finishing bands or folds of knitted fabric, cut for greatest stretch, to neaten neckline, sleeve ends, armhole or lower edge. These bands may be applied with or without being stretched, depending on styling.

Single and Thin, Supple Knitted Fabrics

FABRICS

Characteristics. Knitted fabrics in this group are thin and supple; have moderate to maximum crosswise stretch and moderate lengthwise stretch; and tend to cling to the figure.

Types. Plain colour, printed or knitted with a design.

Surface may be brushed, dull or lustrous. Yarns may be filament, textured or crimped.

Fibre content. Cotton, wool, triacetate, polyester, acrylic or nylon.

PATTERN CHOICE

Fashion uses these fabrics for three distinctive 'looks' – skinny and covered, elegantly draped and comfortably supple.

Dresses – sportswear, casual, formal or high-fashion.

Leisure wear – turtleneck tops, gathered and scoop-neckline tops, shirts, draped cat-suits. Children's dresses and fitted tops and men's shirts.

PREPARATIONS

● If fabric is tubular, cut on lengthwise rib.

● Plan not to use fold, which seldom will press out.

● Re-fold on lengthwise rib for cutting.

● Square and cut ends of fabric with table edges.

● Launder to shrink washable fabrics.

● Have dry cleaner shrink wool.

● Before cutting out pattern, relax fabric by allowing it to lie flat on table or floor overnight.

PATTERN FITTING

● Buy your usual pattern type and size for supple or draped styling.

● Buy patterns labelled 'For stretchable knits only' for the skinny and covered look.

● Fit and alter pattern carefully before cutting to reduce number of fittings during construction.

● Adapt the 'ease' on the pattern to the type of design.

CUTTING AND MARKING

● Cut on soft surface.

● Do not let fabric hang over table edge.

● Pin fabrics which are difficult to control to tissue for cutting.

● Use ball-point or fine, steel pins, placed within seam allowances.

● Cut notches outwards.

● Mark internal details with tailor's tacks.

● Use a whole pattern piece, rather than a half, for cutting crosswise stripes that cannot be squared.

STAY STITCHING

● Stay-stitch only neckline and waistline seams.

● Use chain stitch or regular straight stitch, 1·5 mm (15) stitch length. Even Feed* Foot eliminates the need for easing or stretching.

STITCHING

● For lightweight wool jersey, use silk thread, size 11 needle, regular straight stitch, 2 to 1·5 mm (12 to 15) stitch length.

- For cotton knits, use fine spun polyester thread, size 11 needle and regular straight stitch; or ball-point needle, straight stretch stitch and mercerised cotton thread.
- For shiny-surfaced synthetics, use silk or nylon thread, ball-point needle or regular size 9 or 11 needle, and straight stretch stitch or regular straight stitch, 2 mm (12) stitch length.
- Stitch all seams under tension by holding them in back and front of Presser Foot, or use the Even Feed* Foot.
- Normal or above-normal presser-foot pressure.
- Use Straight-stitch Presser Foot and throat plate for all straight stitching.
- If you encounter stitching problems, remember: *Missed stitches* result from too coarse a needle, too heavy thread, too little tension on the fabric while stitching, or a bent needle. *Fabric pulls* result from too heavy needle and thread or blunt needle. *Puckered seams* result from not supporting fabric while stitching, un-balanced tensions, too tight tensions, too long stitches. *Stitching through paper* next to feed helps to eliminate some puckering and skipping.

SEAMS AND SEAM FINISHES
- Kind of seaming depends on kind of garment.
- Fashion garments are made with plain, pressed-open seams with no seam finish.
- Casual garments are made with seam edges pressed in one direction, trimmed to ·6-to-1-cm (¼-to-⅜-inch) width and neatened together.

- Blindstitch, multi-stitch zig-zag, regular over-edge (Disc 32), plain zig-zag (3 to 5 stitch width) are preferred for seam finishing.

FACINGS, INTERFACINGS, LININGS AND MOUNTINGS
- Skinny-look garments need none.
- Slim, straight-line dresses need none in body of garment but require soft interfacing in cuffs, collars or faced necklines.
- Softly draped fashions usually require soft, firm mounting as a foundation.
- A firm edge is achieved with non-woven terylene interfacing.

PRESSING
- Limit iron temperature to that for fibre with lowest heat requirement.
- Pressing should be gentle and of a blocking nature.
- Use moist cloth to produce steam.
- Do not over-press.

HEMS AND EDGE FINISHES
- For fashion garments – finish the hem edge with straight stitching, 1·5 mm (15) stitch length, placed ·6 cm (¼ inch) from straight cut edge, and use blind hemming stitch.
- For casual garments – machine-blindstitch hems.
- Folded bands may be substituted for hems.
- Narrow self bindings are suitable for necklines and armholes.

Lingerie Tricot

Now that nylon tricot can be bought by the metre or yard, many women are finding that making lingerie can be both fun and economical.

Lingerie can be made amazingly fast because it requires little if any hand tacking, pressing or hand finishing. Most garments have very few seams, and the elastic and lace finishes are simple to apply with a zig-zag sewing machine.

The very simplicity of lingerie sewing may seem a little strange to you at first. But, once you relax, develop a light touch, and realise that a cut edge is acceptable (because tricot does not unravel), you will quickly learn to stitch seams and finishes on your machine without hand tacking.

Tricot Fabrics

Tricot is a two-thread warp knit that will not run or fray because of its interlocking yarns. It has fine vertical ribs, or wales, on the right side and crosswise courses on the wrong side; the direction of greatest stretch is crosswise. The fabric is usually 140 cm (54 inches) wide or 90 cm (36 inches) but you may find it 115 cm (45 inches) wide.

The fibre content can be all nylon, a blend of nylon and acetate, or triacetate. The surface may be smooth, satin-like, crêpe-like or napped, depending on the texture of the yarn used in knitting.

Tricot comes in different weights, ranging from very sheer to heavy, depending on the size of the yarn and how closely it is knitted. Heavy tricots are used for housecoats, pyjamas and opaque slips. Medium tricots are used for panties, slips, nightgowns, pyjamas and the underlayer of nightgowns and negligées designed for two-layer construction. Sheer tricot resembles chiffon and is used for the outer layer of nightgowns and negligées, for mounting lace sections and insertions, and for edge trims. Brushed nylon, which has a napped surface, is suitable for warm nightgowns and pyjamas.

Stabilised nylon tricot has a special finish that limits its stretch and the amount of static it generates. Thus it is suitable for slips that are to be worn under dresses where non-cling characteristics are essential; it is labelled 'anti-stat'.

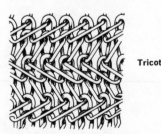

Tricot

456

Patterns

You can use two sources for lingerie patterns: commercial paper patterns, and your own favourite garments.

Patterns for slips, half-slips, panties, nightgowns, housecoats and negligées are available from your favourite pattern company and in the usual size ranges. Patterns that are marked 'for stretchable knits only' are close fitting and rely on the stretch of the knit for comfort. Patterns that are marked 'suitable for knits' have enough ease for woven fabrics, but their style lines are also suitable for knits.

The most challenging type of pattern is the one you cut yourself from a favourite garment. There are two ways to proceed.

Method 1: Cut apart a discarded garment. Cut on the seamlines and carefully lay each section on paper, keeping lengthwise and crosswise lines true. Mark the edges and then mark a ·6-, 1·2- or 1·5-cm ($\frac{1}{4}$-, $\frac{1}{2}$- or $\frac{5}{8}$-inch) seam allowance, whichever is most appropriate for the garment, and cut out the pattern on the cutting lines. Check corresponding seam lengths and cut notches to identify the seamlines that join.

Method 2: Transfer the shape of each garment section to paper without destroying the garment. Make either a half or a whole pattern for each major section and a whole pattern for small sections. Work on a padded surface such as an ironing board or table. Fold the garment at the centre front. For a half pattern, pin the fold to the straight edge of the paper; for a whole pattern, pin the garment fold to the folded edge of the paper. Keeping lengthwise and crosswise lines straight, plunge pins through the garment seamlines into the paper and padded surface at short intervals (every 1·2 cm ($\frac{1}{2}$ inch) on straight seams; every ·3 cm ($\frac{1}{8}$ inch) on curved seams). Remove the garment and draw the seamlines, following the pinholes in the paper. Add seam allowances and mark cutting lines. Follow the same procedure for each large section, and mark all edges for small sections.

If the tricot is very wide, you may cut two or more garments at one time; you will find this easier if you lay out whole, rather than half, patterns.

Notions and Trimmings

Needles and thread must be fine; thread must also be strong. Silk, and fine spun polyester are the best threads for stitching tricot because they can be used with fine needles. Choose size 11 ball-point needles, SINGER* *No. 2021*, or *2045*, the Perfect stitch needle. Size 11 regular needles will also work satisfactorily in many cases, but ball-point needles are recommended because they are especially designed for stitching knitted fabrics.

Lace is an important edge finish for tricot garments and for decorative sections and insertions. Choose nylon or polyester lace because it requires no ironing and wears well. Lace comes in three forms. Lace for edging has one selvedge edge and one decorative edge; it comes in widths from ·9 cm ($\frac{3}{8}$ inch) to more than 7·5 cm (3 inches). Lace for insertions has two selvedge edges and comes in widths from ·9 cm ($\frac{3}{8}$ inch) to more than 7·5 cm (3 inches). A third form, galloon lace, has two decorative edges and comes in a variety of widths.

Edging   Insertion   Galloon

Elastic in lingerie is primarily functional but it can also be decorative. The following descriptions of the different kinds of elastic and their uses will enable you to select the one that is best for your purpose.

Elastic. The most familiar type looks the same on both sides and on both edges. It has lengthwise cords of rubber, Lycra or Spanzelle. When stretched, elastic braid becomes narrower. It comes in widths of ·6, ·9, 1·2, 2 and 2·5 cm ($\frac{1}{4}$, $\frac{3}{8}$, $\frac{1}{2}$, $\frac{3}{4}$ and 1 inch) and is usually described by the number of 'cords' it has. The yarn may be rayon, nylon, mercerised cotton or a blend. Rayon elastic braid relaxes when wet and should not be used for swimwear. Elastic is usually slotted through a hem or casing rather than stitched to an edge. Stitching should always be done between the lengthwise cords; when stitching penetrates the lengthwise cords, they are damaged or broken and the elasticity is weakened.

Elastic braid

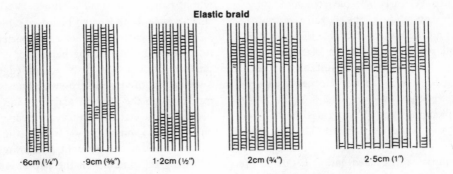

·6cm (¼")   ·9cm (⅜")   1·2cm (½")   2cm (¾")   2·5cm (1")

Elastic edging for lingerie can be of either braid or web construction. Braid becomes narrower when stretched; webbing does not. Edging always has one decorative edge that resembles a frill or picot. Widths of 1·5 or 1·2 cm (⅝ or ½ inch) are suitable for waistbands of half-slips and panties; widths of ·9 or ·6 cm (⅜ or ¼ inch) for leg edges of panties and briefs. Elastic edging is not enclosed in a casing; it is applied to either the outside or the inside edge of the garment. Refer to page 466.

Elastic edging

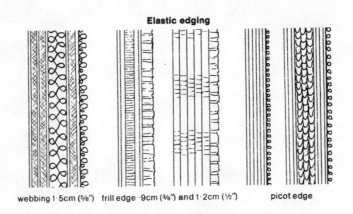

webbing 1·5cm (⅝")   frill edge ·9cm (⅜") and 1·2cm (½")   picot edge

Preparations

Launder nylon tricot before cutting the garment to prevent shrinkage later and to remove any finishing solution, which could cause stitching problems. Use an anti-static fabric softener to reduce the tendency of nylon tricot to cling to the needle during stitching. After laundering, place fabric and a dry Turkish towel in a dryer set at low temperature. (The towel will help to absorb moisture.) Remove fabric when not quite dry. If you do not have a low-heat dryer, roll the fabric on a Turkish towel to remove as much moisture as possible and finish drying by draping the fabric over the bath.

Pressing should not be necessary; but if there are creases, press at a low temperature, moving the iron in a lengthwise direction only.

Prepare your pattern carefully. Patterns for tricot garments that fit the figure closely should measure at least as much as your figure and preferably 2·5 to 5 cm (1 to 2 inches) more at the hipline to allow ease. If you usually need to increase or decrease the crutch depth on trousers, apply the same alteration to lingerie pants patterns. Nightgowns should be roomy enough for comfort. All fitting changes should be made at the pattern-alteration step so that construction can be completed without further fitting.

458

Layout and Cutting

The right side of tricot is the side with fine lengthwise ribs. On sheer tricot, it is sometimes difficult to see the ribs. For a quick test, stretch a crosswise edge. Tricot always rolls to the right side. Mark the wrong side with strips of sellotape.

Lay out the fabric on a large table and do not let the fabric hang over the edge. If you are using an extra wide tricot, cutting out on the floor may be necessary when a large table is not available. Four layers can be cut at once if you are making a number of identical garments. A layer of tissue paper placed between fabric layers will help you to cut a smooth edge.

Tricot stretches most in the crosswise direction; always cut it with the stretch running across the figure. Cut gusset sections with the stretch running from back to front. Use sharp pins and pin sparingly, preferably within seam allowances. Placing a strip of sellotape, instead of pins, at the top and bottom edge of each pattern piece is useful in holding the pattern on grain.

Cut extended notches to mark corresponding seams, and trim them off as you approach them when stitching. Cut with sharp scissors and be careful to cut all edges smoothly, especially if your pattern has narrow seam allowances.

Preparing to Stitch

Start your sewing with a lint-free, carefully oiled sewing machine. Put in a new ball-point needle and thread it with fine, strong thread. Set the presser-foot pressure at normal or medium and the stitch length between 2 and 1 mm (12 and 20), depending on the kind of stitch you have chosen to use. Refer to page 427 for appropriate stitches. If you are using a plain straight stitch or a straight stretch stitch, use the straight-stitch throat plate and the Presser Foot recommended for the kind of stitch and seam you will use. Regulate the needle-thread tension to produce a balanced stitch that looks the same on both sides. The best tension setting is usually a point or two lower than your regularly use for other fabrics. If your sewing machine has a 'fast' and 'slow' speed setting, use the slow setting because you should stitch slowly enough to control the untacked seam edges. Remember to guide and support all lengthwise seams with one hand in front and one hand at the back of the Presser Foot to keep the seam under tension during stitching.

Test-stitch seams on fabric scraps before stitching your garment. This will enable you to get the feel of handling the fabric. Also, it will indicate whether your tension, pressure, stitch length, needle and thread sizes are correct.

Always place the needle in the fabric at the start of a seam, then lower the Presser Foot. Hold the thread ends until a few stitches have been made. This procedure is essential to prevent thread and fabric from jamming at the start. The softness of the fabric, coupled with the strength of the thread, makes this necessary.

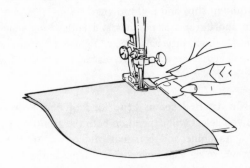

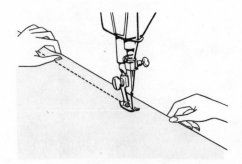

If skipped stitches appear, look first at thread and needle size and remember they must be 'fine'. To rule out the needle as the cause, it is always a good idea to change the needle. Presser-foot pressure may not be heavy enough, so increase it slightly and also increase the tension under which you are holding the fabric while stitching. Needle-thread tension, unless it is very high, is seldom a cause of skipped stitches.

If skipped stitches appear after you have been stitching for some time, the cause may be that the needle has lost its set and has become slanted away from the sewing-hook point, which picks up the thread loop from the needle. Sometimes you can correct an out-of-set needle by drawing your thumb down the long-groove side of the needle, exerting slight pressure to flex the needle back into its original position. *Do not* try to bend the needle, merely stroke it a few times, flexing the lower part back slightly. Before testing the stitching, turn the hand wheel by hand to make certain the needle enters the hole in the throat plate without rubbing or striking the edge. Then test-stitch on a fabric scrap.

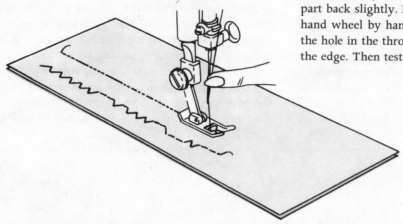

Seams and Darts

SEAMS

The following guidelines will help you to handle seams in tricot lingerie.

● Seams in tricot lingerie are always either double-stitched or stitched and neatened with a single row of machine over-edge stitching.

● Always stitch seams under tension by guiding and supporting the fabric.

● Almost all seams are lengthwise on both the fabric and the garment. The few exceptions are gusset seams in briefs and the horizontal seams at or above the waistline in slips and nightgowns.

● Pin short seams at notches and ends; long seams at 30-cm (12-inch) intervals.

● Finish crosswise edges with elastic, lace or decorative edge finishes.

Double-stitched seams. The kind of double-stitched seam you select will depend on both the abilities of your sewing machine and personal preference. In the two seams where zig-zag or over-edge stitches are placed over the seam edges, the straight stitching may be done either before or after the finishing stitch. When the straight stitching is done last, the Zipper Foot may be substituted for the Straight-stitch Presser Foot.

Straight or straight stretch stitch. Use the Straight-stitch Presser Foot and throat plate, centre needle position, and a 1·5 mm (15) stitch length or straight stretch settings. Stitch on the seamline and again ·3 cm (⅛ inch) outside the seamline. Trim seam allowances near second stitching.

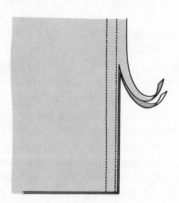

Straight and zig-zag stitches. Straight-stitch on the seamline as above. Trim seam allowances to ·3 cm (⅛ inch). Use zig-zag throat plate and General-purpose Foot, a zig-zag stitch, right needle position, 2½ to 3 stitch width, and 1 mm (20) stitch length. Guide seam edges along the right edge of the foot.

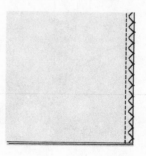

Straight and over-edge stitches. Straight-stitch on seamline as above. Trim seam allowances to ·3 cm ($\frac{1}{8}$ inch). Use zig-zag throat plate and General-purpose Foot; over-edge stitch or over-edge stretch stitch, right needle position, $2\frac{1}{2}$ to 3 stitch width, and 1 mm (20) stitch length. Guide seam edges along right edge of foot. Seams may be double-stitched before trimming.

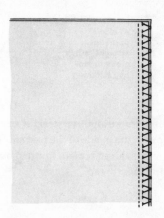

Chain stitch. Use chain stitch accessories and 1·5 mm (15) stitch length. Stitch on the seamline. Stitch second row close to first row, outside the seamline and in the opposite direction from the first stitching. Stitch the third row close to the second row, outside the seamline and in the opposite direction from the second stitching.

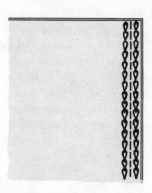

SEAMS STITCHED AND NEATENED IN ONE OPERATION

Some sewing machines are capable of stitching and finishing in one step.

Over-edge stretch stitch. Trim seam allowances to ·6 cm ($\frac{1}{4}$ inch) or slightly less for a seam narrower than ·6 cm ($\frac{1}{4}$ inch). Use the over-edge stretch stitch and the General-purpose Presser Foot. Set stitch width at 5 for ·6-cm ($\frac{1}{4}$-inch) seam or between 3 and 5 for a narrower seam. Guide the edges of the seam under the General-purpose Presser Foot so that the needle goes over the right-hand seam edge rather than through it.

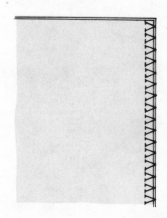

Over-edge stitch. Follow the same procedure as described for the over-edge stretch stitch above, but use a 1·5 to 1 mm (15 to 20) stitch length and the over-edge stitch.

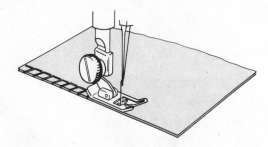

Slant over-edge stitch. Some models of sewing machines make a slant over-edge stitch instead of the over-edge stretch stitch. Refer to your sewing machine instruction book for machine settings. Trim seam allowances to ·6 cm ($\frac{1}{4}$ inch). Place trimmed seam under General-purpose Presser Foot with seam edges to your left. For a slightly narrower seam, use a stitch width setting less than 5.

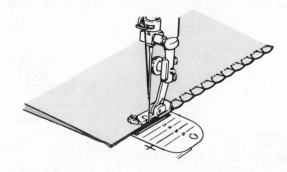

Darts

In tricot lingerie, darts are usually in the bodice sections of slips, nightgowns, pyjama tops, and bras. Trim away the fold of the dart by cutting ·6 cm ($\frac{1}{4}$ inch) inside the stitching lines. Treat the stitching lines as seams. Where the darted section is of more than one layer, stitch all

461

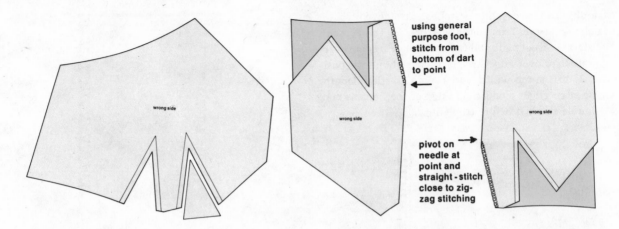

using general purpose foot, stitch from bottom of dart to point

pivot on needle at point and straight - stitch close to zig-zag stitching

layers as one. With a seam-finishing stitch, stitch from the widest end of the dart to the point, then pivot on the needle and turn the fabric round half circle for the second stitching. Lower the Presser Foot and raise the needle.

Set the machine for straight or straight stretch stitching, and stitch close to the inside of the first stitching. Threads used for lingerie seldom remain knotted and in this way you can secure the thread.

Seams in Pants

BRIEFS WITH GUSSET

Briefs are made from three pattern sections: front, back and gusset. The gusset section is double with the length-

wise rib running across the section.

Stitch the side seam first to make it clear which are the right and wrong sides of these sections, they can easily be confused if gusset seams are stitched first.

Join front gusset seam, placing right sides of gusset sections next to the front section, front section in between. Stitch with straight stretch stitch and trim seam allowance to ·6 cm; or trim seam allowances first and stitch with stretch over-edge stitch.

Pin back seam of outside gusset section to the right side of the back.

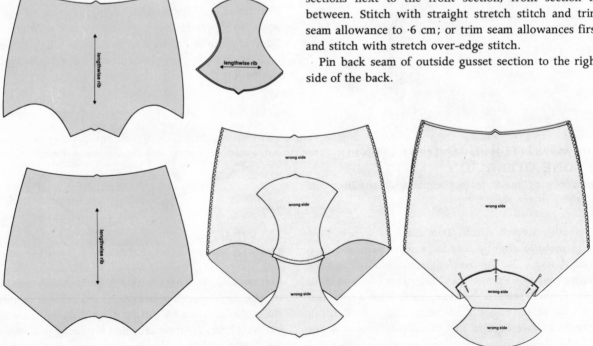

Pin back seam of inside gusset section to the wrong side of the back by bringing it right round the top of the briefs. Stitch in the same way as the front gusset seam.

Pull the body of the garment through one open side of the gusset section and turn it right side out. Seams will be concealed inside gusset sections.

To finish briefs, refer to *Elastic Finishes* on page 465.

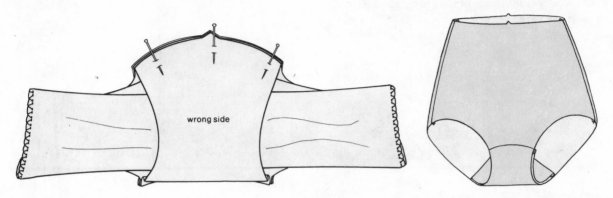

FRENCH KNICKERS – GUSSET SEAMS

These garments differ from briefs in that they are usually cut with centre front and back seams instead of side seams. This makes the gusset section easier to insert.

There are three shapes that may be used for gusset sections. One is a two-piece construction designed with a curved seam from front to back. The other two shapes, the diamond and the modified diamond, are one-piece constructions. All styles have a double-layered gusset, and the sections are cut with the lengthwise rib running from side to side, placing the crosswise rib (the direction of greatest stretch) from front to back. All three types are inserted in the same way, but the two-piece gusset requires one preparatory step that the others do not.

To prepare the two-piece gusset, place the sections right sides together. Fold, matching the curved edges, which will form four seam layers. Stitch on the seamline, using the straight stretch stitch, and trim seam allowances to ·3 cm ($\frac{1}{8}$ inch) or use the stretch over-edge stitch. Hold the two centre layers and pull them out of one side opening; this places the seam allowances between the remaining two layers. Reverse the fold in the outside layers to flatten the seamed sections. The folds become the lower edges of the inside portion of the legs. Apply lace to finish the outside leg sections before taking the next step.

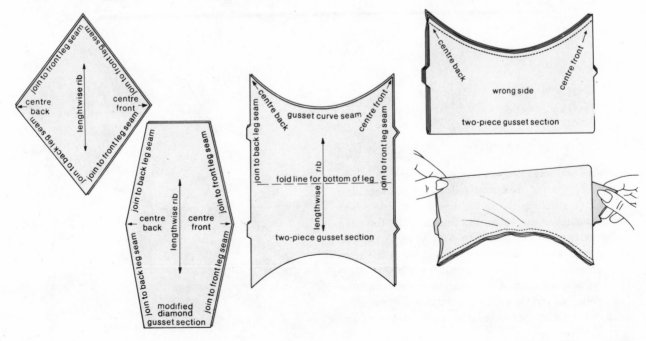

To assemble the gusset section and garment, stitch one leg front seam to the corresponding side of the gusset section. Then stitch the entire front seam, continuing across the seam joining and down the other leg seam, joining the remaining side of the gusset. Repeat the same steps at the back.

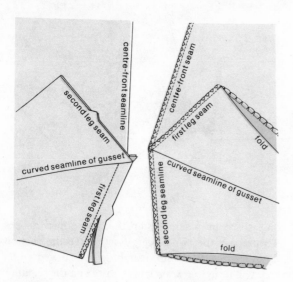

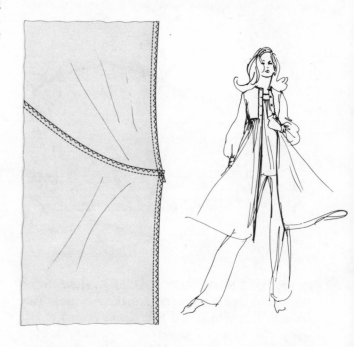

SEAMS IN PYJAMA PANTS

Tricot pyjama pants are usually cut without side seams. If you need to lengthen or shorten a pattern above the crutch level for trousers, you should do the same for pyjamas, although pyjamas should have at least 2·5 cm (1 inch) more ease at this point than trousers. Stitch the centre front and centre back seams before stitching the leg seams, using one of the double-stitched seams or the over-edge stretch seam. Then stitch the leg seams, starting at the crutch and stitching down one leg first and

then the other. Turn the centre back seam in one direction and the centre front seam in the other, and overlap the stitching at least 2·5 cm (1 inch). Finish the waistband with elastic (page 465). Finish the hem as described on page 470.

Setting in Sleeves

There are two ways to set-in sleeves in housecoats, negligées and pyjamas. You may follow the conventional method of stitching the sleeve seams and side seams before putting in the sleeve, and trimming and finishing the seam allowances together to ·6 cm (¼ inch). Or, you may use the open construction method. Trim the seam allowances on both the armhole and the sleeve to ·6 cm (¼ inch). Stitch and finish the seam allowances together before the side and sleeve seams are stitched. Then stitch each side seam and sleeve seam as one continuous seam.

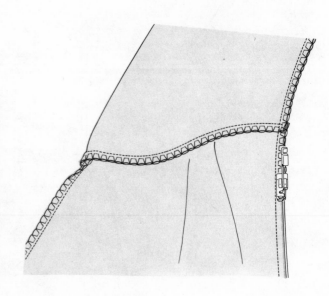

Elastic in Casing

For children's panties, use ·9-cm ($\frac{3}{8}$-inch) elastic for the waistline and ·6-cm ($\frac{1}{4}$-inch) elastic for the legs. For women's briefs or panties, use 1·5- or 1·2-cm ($\frac{5}{8}$- or $\frac{1}{2}$-inch) elastic for waistline and ·6- or ·9-cm ($\frac{1}{4}$- or $\frac{3}{8}$-inch) elastic for legs. Measure elastic round waistline and legs at a comfortable degree of tension, allowing 1·2 cm ($\frac{1}{2}$ inch) for overlap.

Method 1: Overlap the elastic at the ends and hand-whip them together along the overlapped edges and ends. Fold top of garment over the elastic to the wrong side. Let the edge extend beyond the elastic at least

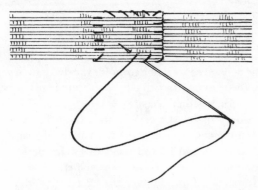

·6 cm ($\frac{1}{4}$ inch). The stitching may be done in one or two ways. Using the adjustable Zipper Foot and the straight stretch stitch, stitch through the tricot layers alongside the elastic. Or, using a narrow zig-zag stitch (width 3, length 1·5 mm (15), and right needle position), stitch along the elastic through the tricot layers. Trim the seam allowance close to the stitching. Finish the legs the same way.

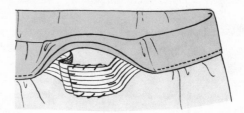

Method 2: Fold waistline or leg edge to the inside, and turn again to form a hem or casing the same width as the elastic. Stitch along the turned edge with a narrow zig-zag or straight stretch stitch. Leave a 2·5-cm (1-inch) opening through which to slot the elastic into the hem. Join the ends of the elastic as above. Then stitch the 2·5-cm (1-inch) opening.

To prevent elastic from twisting inside casing, distribute the fullness evenly and pin through the fabric and elastic at centre front and back and midway between these points. Stitch, holding the fabric and elastic under tension, using plain zig-zag (5 stitch width, 2 mm (12) stitch length) or multi-stitch zig-zag stitch (5 stitch width, 1·5 mm (15) stitch length). Test this stitching on a scrap before stitching the garment because elastic with a heavy rib may be unsuitable for this technique.

465

Nylon Elastic Lace Webbing

Measure elastic round waistline at a comfortable tension and allow 2·5 cm (1 inch) for joining. Machine-stitch

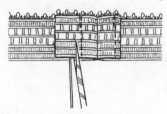

across ends, wrong sides together. Open seam and stitch ·6 cm ($\frac{1}{4}$ inch) on each side of seam. Trim ends near stitching.

Place seam at centre front. Divide elastic in four equal sections and mark with pins. Do the same to the garment. Then pin together at corresponding points, pinning elastic over right side of tricot, bottom edge on seamline. Stitch, using a 1·5 to 1 mm (15 to 20) stitch length and a narrow zig-zag stitch (2 to 3 stitch width) that is just wide enough to cover the elastic cord near the edge. Trim seam allowance near stitching.

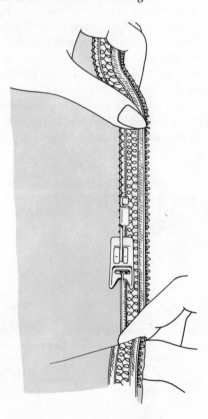

Cover elastic join at centre front with 1·2-cm ($\frac{1}{2}$-inch) satin ribbon folded over the elastic and top-stitched on the sides and the lower edge.

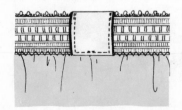

Frill-Edge and Picot-Edge Elastic

Apply narrow elastic to the legs of briefs as described above. Allow 2·5 cm (1 inch) for overlapping the ends at the side seams for comfort. Catch the ends into the stitching as illustrated.

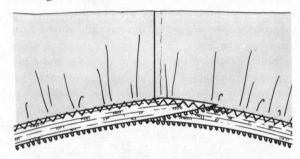

For a more feminine treatment at the waistline, the elastic may be concealed except for the decorative edge. Place the elastic with frill edge on seamline of garment, right sides together, elastic covering seam allowance. Stitch over the elastic cord nearest the frill, using the General-purpose Presser Foot and a narrow zig-zag stitch (2 stitch width and 1·5 to 1 mm (18) stitch length). Hold elastic and tricot under tension as you stitch, and guide the stitching uniformly over the elastic rib. Trim seam

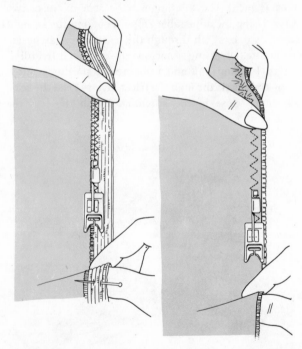

allowance to ·6 cm ($\frac{1}{4}$ inch). Turn elastic to the inside of the garment and, using the multi-stitch zig-zag stitch (5 stitch width and 1·5 mm (15) stitch length), top-stitch through the tricot and the centre of the elastic while holding it under tension.

Lace Edging

Method 1: The easiest and quickest way to apply lace edging is to hold it on top of the tricot, lace selvedge edge along the seamline. Use the General-purpose Presser Foot and a narrow zig-zag stitch ($1\frac{1}{2}$ to $2\frac{1}{2}$ stitch width and 1·5 to 1 mm (15 to 18) stitch length). Allow the starting end of the lace to extend ·6 cm ($\frac{1}{4}$ inch) beyond the starting point, which will also be the joining point for the ends of the lace. After stitching all but 5 or 7·5 cm (2 or 3 inches) of the lace edging, and without removing the work from under the needle, measure and cut the free end of the lace 1·2 cm ($\frac{1}{2}$ inch) beyond the starting point. Fold ·6 cm ($\frac{1}{4}$ inch) of the lace over the first end and fold both ends another ·6 cm ($\frac{1}{4}$ inch). Whip over-lapped lace seam edges together by hand. Continue the zig-zag stitching, overlapping the starting point a few stitches. Pull thread ends to underside and tie. Cut away tricot seam allowance near stitching on inside of garment.

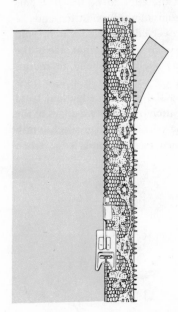

Method 2: Place lace over tricot, right sides together, with selvedge of lace on seamline and decorative edge away from the seam edge. Stitch over selvedge with a narrow zig-zag stitch ($1\frac{1}{4}$ to 2 stitch width, 1·5 mm (15) stitch length) or along selvedge with a 1·5 to 1 mm (15 to 20) length straight stitch. Turn lace towards the edge, seam allowance towards garment, and top-stitch along tricot fold with a narrow zig-zag or straight stitch. Trim seam allowance near stitching on underside. This method is also suitable for lace insertions.

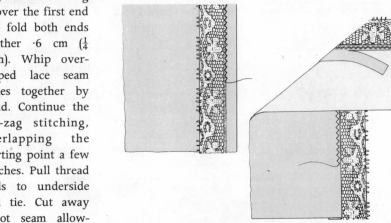

Tricot appliqué. Place tricot right side up over right side of lace and pin. Hand-tack, if necessary. Stitch near

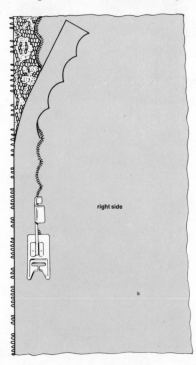

right side

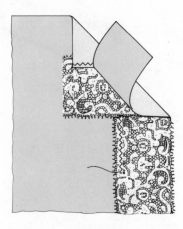

Lace without a selvedge can be applied in the same way, but let the decorative edge extend slightly above the zig-zag stitching.

selvedge of lace, using a decorative satin stitch (close stitch length, 5 stitch width), such as the open scallop or crescent pattern. Trim tricot seam allowance outside decorative stitching and trim lace inside decorative stitching from the underside. Any width of lace with or without a selvedge may be used.

Folded Tricot Appliqué

A fold of sheer tricot or net may be used for an edge finish instead of lace. Hand-tack the fold underneath the tricot edge above the seamline. Using a decorative zig-zag stitch, such as the crescent pattern, stitch on the seamline. Trim tricot along the outside edge of the stitching, and trim the underneath edges of the applied fold straight along the top edge of the decorative stitching.

Applied Band

An applied 2·5- to 4-cm (1- to 1½-inch) band or false hem makes a smooth, tailored finish for legbands and the hem edge of slips. Cut a lengthwise strip of tricot twice the finished width plus ·9 cm (⅜ inch) for two seam allowances, and the length of the edge to be finished plus ·9 cm (⅜ inch) for two seam allowances. Stitch ends of strip together with the over-edge stretch stitch. Fold band and place the edges even with the right side of the tricot edge. Off-set seams slightly in band to reduce number of layers at a single point. Pin in at least four places to avoid stretching the garment edge and band unequally as you stitch. Stitch over the two edges of the band and one edge of the tricot. Regulate stitch width to suit fabric weight. Turn band towards edge when completed.

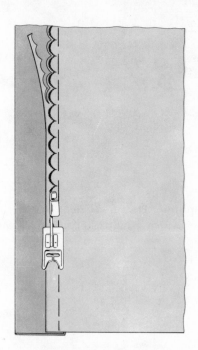

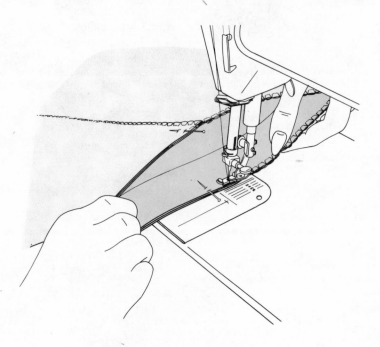

Shell Edge

The shell edge can be made with the blindstitch, *Flexi-Stitch** (Disc 32). Use the General-purpose Presser Foot; 5 stitch width, and 1·5 mm (15) stitch length. Fold the tricot edge to underside 1·2 cm (½ inch). Guide edge to your right with *Flexi-Stitch** (Disc 32), and to the left with the blindstitch. Stitch from the right side of the fabric, guiding it so that the needle passes over the fabric fold at the zig-zag stitch. Tighten needle-thread tension slightly if shell formation is indistinct.

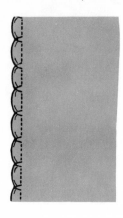

Tricot Bound Edge

For a self-fabric finish on tricot, a ·6-cm (¼-inch) edge is a long-lasting tailored finish on a slip, nightgown, French knickers or pyjama top. Cut tricot binding 3·2 cm (1¼ inches) wide on the lengthwise direction for straight edges or on the crosswise direction for curved edges.

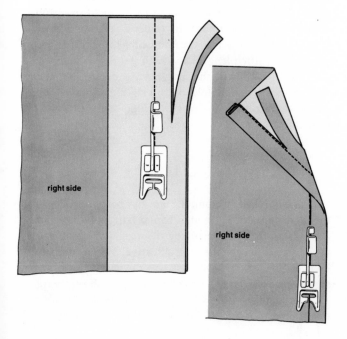

With right sides together, place binding along garment edge and straight-stitch a 1·2-cm (½-inch) seam, using a 1·5 to 1 mm (15 to 20) stitch length. Trim both seam allowances to a level ·6 cm (¼ inch). Fold the binding round the seam edges, and stitch near the line of the first seam through the garment and the single free edge of the binding strip. Trim the seam allowance of the binding strip near the stitching. This finish is practical and durable for tricot because it does not fray.

Simulated Rolled Edge

To finish the edge of a tricot frill, turn the edge under 1·2 cm (½ inch). Stitch over the turned edge from the right side, using the General-purpose Presser Foot, a plain zig-zag stitch, 3 stitch width and 2 mm (12) stitch length. Trim seam allowance on underside near stitching.

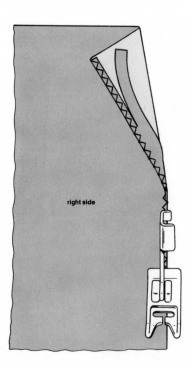

Double Collar with Decorative Edge

Place collar sections wrong sides together and stay-stitch ·3 cm (⅛ inch) outside neckline seamline through both layers. If you prefer more firmness than two layers of tricot give, use one layer of terylene, non-woven interfacing between the layers. Hand-tack outer edges. Stitch outer edges together on seamline, using a satin stitch, 5 stitch width and open scallop or crescent stitch pattern. Trim seam allowances near outside edge of scallop.

There are many other decorative stitch patterns that can be used in place of the crescent. A bound edge and lace edging are also suitable finishes. The conventional faced collar is not as attractive as other finishes.

Tailored Hem

Suitable for pyjama sleeves and legs, the tailored hem is 2·5 to 3·2 cm (1 to 1¼ inches) wide and is formed after the sleeve and leg seams have been stitched. Turn and press the full hem width to the wrong side of the garment. Turn and press the full hem width again, keeping the edge inside the second fold. Stitch ·6 cm (¼ inch) from the fold, hem side up, through the three thicknesses with a straight 1·5 mm (15) length stitch and the General-purpose Presser Foot. Turn hem fold downwards when stitching is completed.

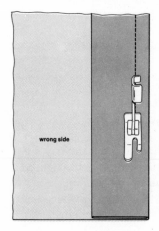

right side

wrong side

Machine-Blindstitched Hem

Suitable for pyjama tops, housecoats, nightgowns and general use where a hem is required; the machine-blindstitched hem is easy to make. Measure and fold hem the width desired. Press lightly. Hand-tack ·6 cm (¼ inch) from top edge. With garment right side out, fold hem to right side, forming a soft fold ·6 cm (¼ inch) from top edge of hem. Place under the General-purpose Presser Foot with machine set for the blindstitch (2½ stitch width, 1·5 mm (15) stitch length) and with the needle entering the single edge during the straight stitching interval and just piercing the soft fold on the zig-zag stitch, When completed, trim edge near stitching and turn hem downwards.

Buttonholes

Machine-stitched buttonholes are the best type to use for tricot garments, although bound buttonholes can be made in tricot. Those made by the manual method on a zig-zag machine are the most effective. The Buttonhole Foot or Special-purpose Foot will not mark the fabric surface, as sometimes happens with an attachment with a cloth clamp, and the stitch length can be set to space the stitches far enough apart to avoid stretching the buttonhole with too-dense stitching. Always use an interfacing of either non-woven terylene or a crisp, fine woven fabric. Stitch width settings of 2½ and 4½ are correct on most machines.

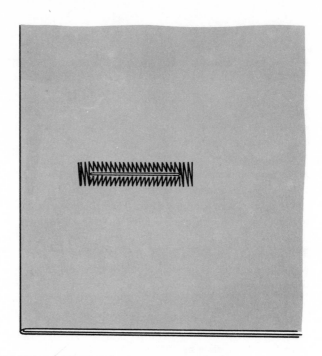

Lingerie Tricot

FABRICS
Characteristics. Crosswise is direction of greater stretch.
Types. Tricot comes in different weights, depending on yarn size and number of loops per inch. 40-denier is a medium weight. 15-denier is a sheer light weight.
Fibre content. Nylon, acetate, triacetate.

PATTERN CHOICE
Choose from the growing selection of commercial patterns.
Or, cut apart a favourite discarded garment and make a pattern of its sections.†
Or, make a pattern from a favourite garment without cutting it apart. Lay each section, one at a time, over paper on a soft surface. Mark outline by plunging pins through fabric and paper along seamlines at short intervals; then cut paper along pin marks.†

† Add seam allowances when cutting new fabric.

PREPARATIONS
● Test-stitch a scrap before cutting to test the stitching. If stitches are skipped, launder fabric before cutting, using fabric softener to remove excess finish and static.
● Relax fabric by allowing it to lie flat on floor or table overnight.
● Fold, right sides together, and square and cut ends with table edge.

● To find right side, stretch a crosswise edge; tricot will roll to the right side.

PATTERN FITTING
● Buy your usual pattern type and size.
● Alter pattern before cutting.
● Garments are usually made up without a fitting.

CUTTING AND MARKING
● Fold fabric, right sides together.
● As crosswise direction has greater stretch, cut with the stretch going round the figure and to run from front to back on gusset sections of panties or briefs.
● Use sharp, smooth pins. Pin sparingly, within seam allowances.
● Patterns may be anchored with sellotape instead of pins. (Some patterns allow only ·6-cm (¼-inch) seam allowances; others 1·5-cm (⅝-inch).)
● Do not let edges of fabric drape over table edge.
● Observe lengthwise grain-like markings on pattern and place on lengthwise rib.
● Cut with sharp shears and keep cut edges even and regular.
● Cut notches outwards.
● Mark internal details with tailor's tacks. *(continued)*

471

STAY STITCHING
● Usually omitted.
● Used occasionally to hold two layers together.

STITCHING
● Use ball-point or size 11 needle and very fine thread (silk or fine polyester).
● Balanced tensions.
● Normal to above-normal presser-foot pressure.
● For straight stitching, use straight-stitch (round-hole) throat plate and Straight-stitch Presser Foot. (Rigid Presser Foot – not hinged – helps to prevent skipped stitches.)
● 1·5 mm (15) stitch length for straight stitching.
● Guide and support fabric, keeping seam under tension while stitching.
● Kinds of stitches: regular straight, straight stretch, stretch over-edge, plain zig-zag (narrow widths), chain stitch (2 or 3 rows in alternating directions), over-edge with Disc 32 or plain narrow zig-zag.

SEAMS AND SEAM FINISHES
● Narrow, machine-finished seams are generally used.
● Choose from three different procedures: (1) stitch, finish and trim; (2) stitch, trim and finish; or (3) trim and stitch, using the stretch over-edge.
● Pin seams at ends and centre; do not hand-tack; trim off notches before stitching; stretch short side of seam where ease is indicated.

FACINGS, INTERFACINGS, LININGS AND MOUNTINGS
● Use double layer of same weight tricot for gusset.
● Mount lace inserts or sections with sheer tricot.
● Face collar with same weight tricot.
● Interfacing is often omitted.

PRESSING
● Limit iron temperature to that for nylon.
● Press lightly with moist cloth to generate steam to remove stretched portions.

HEMS AND EDGE FINISHES
● Hems may be finished with:
  – machine blindstitching (2·5- or 4-cm (1- or 1½-inch) hem).
  – shell edging (1·2-cm (½-inch) hem).
  – machine stitching with Hemmer Foot (·4-cm (⅛-inch) hem).
● Hems or edges may be finished with:
  – folded, cross-cut matching or sheer tricot.
  – applied lace.
  – appliquéd lace with finished selvedge, sometimes mounted on sheer tricot.
  – taffeta or satin binding cut on bias (suitable also for rouleau straps or ties).
● Waistline may be finished with lingerie elastic encased or stitched and turned to underside with picot edge extending.

Towelling and Stretch Towelling

Knitted towelling, with its looped surface and stretchable back, has become a favourite for all ages, from babies to grown-ups. It is a companion fabric to knitted velour, which has a cut pile surface. There is considerable range within this fabric type, and the appearance and density can vary, depending on the kinds and sizes of yarns, size and number of needles used in knitting and whether the fabric also contains elastofibre yarn, which strengthens its recovery after being stretched.

Preparing to Stitch

Use the general-purpose throat plate and Presser Foot, or the Even Feed* Foot for most stitching. Use normal presser-foot pressure, a size 14 ball-point needle (catalogue *2021* or *2045*), and strong thread such as spun polyester.

Unless you use an Even Feed* Foot, guide and support the seam layers by holding the seam taut at the back of the Presser Foot with one hand and in front of the needle with the other.

If the looped surface catches over the toes of the General-purpose Foot, wrap it with ·6 cm ($\frac{1}{4}$ inch) wide sellotape (see page 425).

Seams

When seaming towelling and stretch towelling, the important points to remember are: most seams must stretch with the fabric. Seams that should not stretch should be stayed with twill tape or straight seam binding. And seams should be made in ways to keep bulkiness to a minimum because pressing cannot sharpen seams.

Stitching and neatening in one operation. The most frequently used seam is the one that uses the over-edge stretch stitch. Stitch on the seamline while holding the seam taut. Trim the seam allowances near the outside edge of the stitching. The stitching-then-trimming sequence retains the garment shape better than the reverse sequence.

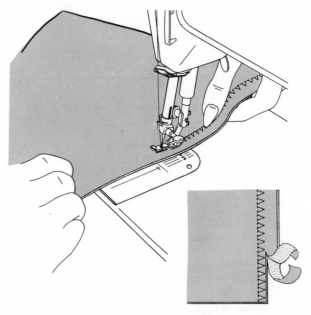

Stitched and finished in two steps. Another favourite is the narrow seam that is first stitched on the seamline with the straight stretch stitch and either the General-purpose Presser Foot or the Even Feed* Foot and then finished with a flattening stitch such as the multi-stretch as illustrated.

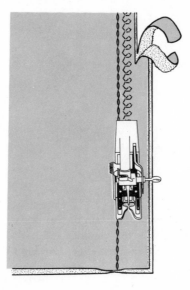

Alternative stitches you can use are the regular straight stitch or a narrow zig-zag stitch (2 stitch width, 1·5 mm (15) stitch length) instead of the straight stretch stitch, and multi-stitch zig-zag or wide plain zig-zag (5 stitch width, 2 mm (12) stitch length) instead of the multi-stretch zig-zag stitch.

473

Flat-felled seam. For men's wear and baby clothes, a flat seam is sometimes preferred. Stitch first as a plain seam on the seamline, using the straight stretch stitch and the Even Feed* Foot, or the regular straight stitch and the General-purpose Presser Foot. (Hold seam taut if you use the General-purpose Presser Foot.) Finger-press both seam allowances in one direction and top-stitch from the right side of the fabric an even distance (·6 to ·9 cm ($\frac{1}{4}$ to $\frac{3}{8}$ inch) from the seamline through both seam allowances. Trim both seam allowances near the stitching. The seam may appear slightly stretched when finished, but it will recover after light steam pressing or when the garment is worn.

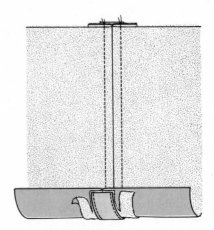

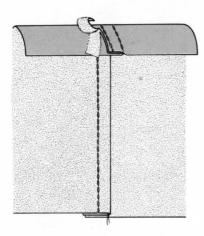

Plain seam, double top-stitched. Where a flat, seam is necessary, a plain seam, top-stitched ·3 cm ($\frac{1}{8}$ inch) from the seamline on both sides, is used. Seam allowances can be trimmed near the top stitching to further reduce bulk.

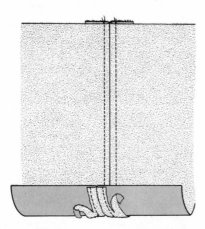

Plain seam, double top-stitched, taped. For seams that should not stretch, such as the shoulder and back-of-neck or yoke seams, include woven-edge seam binding or twill tape on the underside when top-stitching.

Collars and Band Finishes

Garments made of knitted towelling and velour should retain their soft, supple, stretchable characteristics, but collars and finishes of some garments must have body and shape. Beach robes, men's sports shirts, bath robes and V-neck pullovers, are a few examples. Terylene, non-woven interfacing will supply the shape and body needed in these areas without robbing the towelling of its softness or washability.

A firm band suitable for a beach robe, V-neck pullover or cardigan cover-up is cut twice the width of the finished band plus two 1·5-cm ($\frac{5}{8}$-inch) seam allowances on the lengthwise direction of the fabric. Cut the interfacing the same length and width. With a plain, straight-stitch seam, join one edge of the interfaced band to the garment edge. Finger-press seam allowances open and trim the seam allowances of the band and interfacing band to ·6 cm ($\frac{1}{4}$ 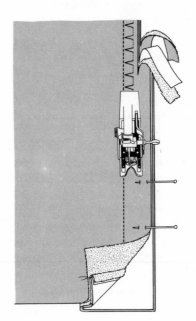 inch). Pin free edges of interfaced band to the extended seam allowance of the garment. Stitch with either the Even Feed* Foot, or the General-purpose Presser Foot, using the blindstitch (5 stitch width, 1·5 mm (15) stitch length). Place the stitching with the left edge slightly outside the seamline.

Trim the seam allowances near right-hand edge of the blindstitching.

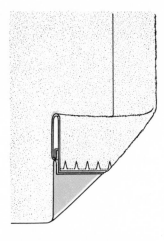

A tailored collar interfacing should be attached to both the upper and under collar sections. Cut both upper and under collar sections on the lengthwise rib from the upper collar pattern. The fabric has adequate give for shaping. Cut also two collar sections of terylene non-woven interfacing. Stitch one interfacing to the wrong side of each collar section 1·2 cm (½ inch) from all edges.

Place right sides of interfaced collar sections together; pin and stitch 1·5 cm (⅝ inch) from edges, taking 3 stitches diagonally across the points to blunt them.

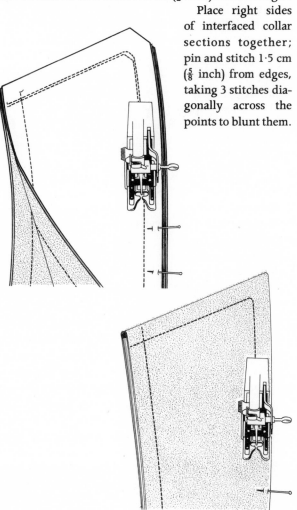

Trim seam allowances on upper collar and interfacing to ·6 cm (¼ inch) and on under collar and interfacing to ·3 cm (⅛ inch). Turn the collar right side out, finger-press and pin edges to turn sharply on seamline. Top-stitch ·9 cm (⅜ inch) from edge.

A round collar, interfaced with one layer of terylene, non-woven interfacing and with a self-binding, makes a feminine finish. Cut two collar sections and one interfacing section. With collar sections right sides out, place the interfacing between them. Cut a binding strip, on crosswise direction of the fabric for greatest stretch, twice the width of the finished binding plus two seam allowances. Pin the binding to the collar unit, edges matching and binding stretched slightly. Stitch with multi-stitch zig-zag stitch (5 stitch width, 1 mm (20) stitch length), inside edge of stitching on seamline. Trim all seam allowances near outside edge of stitching. Fold

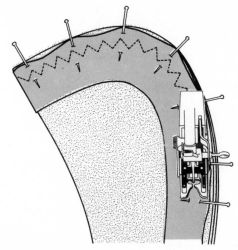

free edge of binding over seam allowances and pin. Top-stitch with Even Feed* Foot and straight stitch, 1·5 mm (15) stitch length, in the stitch line of the seam through collar layers and free edge of binding on underside. Trim binding seam allowance near the stitching.

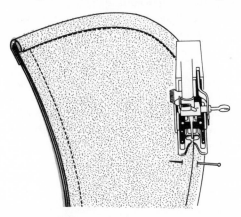

Soft finishes applied as bands or bindings are for garments that should look soft and moulded to the body.

475

Remember that lengthwise-cut bands or bindings have greater control of an edge than crosswise-cut strips because knitted towelling stretches less lengthwise. Also, as with tricot, a cut edge near a line of stitching is acceptable. Many of the techniques suggested for lingerie apply to towelling.

Hems

Machine-blindstitched hems are ideal for towelling, as are multi-row top-stitched hems and applied bands instead of hems.

Buttonholes and Fasteners

Machine-stitched buttonholes can be made in an interfaced area. (See *Buttonholes*, page 470.) Metal press fasteners, which are attached with a tool, are more usual for young children.

Towelling and Stretch Towelling

FABRICS
Characteristics. Greater stretch in crosswise direction.
Types. Plain, printed or striped. Some have a velour surface and jersey back.
Fibre content. All-cotton, nylon, polyester or blends of these fibres. Some include elastofibre yarn.

PATTERN CHOICE
Casual wear – jumpsuits, trousers or shorts, swimwear, hooded cover-ups, robes, dresses.
Children's wear, baby wear.
Men's wear.

PREPARATIONS
● Relax stretch towelling by allowing it to lie flat on floor or table overnight.
● Pin crosswise edges of stretch towelling to tissue to control, since they tend to roll.
● Cut ends on crosswise course.
● Pull diagonally to straighten.

PATTERN FITTING
● Buy your usual pattern type and size.
● Patterns for 'Stretchable Knits Only' are suitable.
● Alter pattern before cutting.
● Stretch towelling may be fitted with no ease in the stretch direction.

STAY STITCHING
● Instead of using conventional stay stitching, stitch seam allowances with chain stitch or straight stitch, 2 to 1·5 mm (12 to 15) stitch length, ·6 cm ($\frac{1}{4}$ inch) from cut edge to prevent crosswise-cut edge unravelling or rolling during construction.

STITCHING
● Use size 14 ball-point needle. Needles may become blunt quickly because of yarn density.
● Spun polyester thread.
● Normal presser-foot pressure.

● Guide and support seam by holding fabric taut behind and in front of Presser Foot, except with Even Feed* Foot.
● Wrap toes of Presser Foot with ·6-cm ($\frac{1}{4}$-inch) strip of sellotape to prevent snagging.
● Kinds of stitches: regular straight stitch, straight stretch stitch or narrow zig-zag. For finishing: wide zig-zag, over-edge stretch, multi-stretch stitch, multi-zig-zag stitch, blindstitch.
● Even Feed* Foot handles seam layers evenly.

SEAMS AND SEAM FINISHES
● Stitched and over-edged seams, ·6 to ·9 cm ($\frac{1}{4}$ to $\frac{3}{8}$ inch) wide, are generally used.
● Plain seams, opened and top-stitched, are used to reduce bulk and, when taped, to give stability.
● Flat-felled seams are used for some men's wear.

FACINGS, INTERFACINGS, LININGS AND MOUNTINGS
● Generally not used.
● For some garments, terylene, non-woven interfacing is suitable.
● Facings are often cut in one with garment.
● Applied bands may replace facings.
● Ribbing is a popular finish.

PRESSING
● Press sparingly.
● Finger-pressing is adequate in many cases.

HEMS AND EDGE FINISHES
● Finish hem edge with over-edge stitch, turn once and machine-stitch hem.
● Or, finish edge as above and machine-blindstitch hem.
● Or, finish edge as above and oversew hem by hand.
● Or, finish edge with decorative braid or fabric binding.
● Use worked or bound buttonholes, or fabric or cord button loops.

Leather-Look Fabrics with Knitted Backs

Leather-look fabrics have reached a high place in fashion. Those with a knitted back are more supple than those with a woven back. The knitted back fake leathers consist of a plastic layer of polyurethane or vinyl over a knitted base fabric. Polyurethane produces a soft, spongy fabric; vinyl (P.V.C.) tends to be more rigid. Whether they are made to look like patent or grained leather or like fabric, the new plastics are still handled in the same way.

Preparing to Stitch

Stitch plastic-coated fabrics with spun polyester thread, a style *15 × 2* (catalogue *2032*) needle, size 14, and a 2·5 mm (10) stitch length.

Use the Straight-stitch Presser Foot and throat plate for straight stitching, or the General-purpose Presser Foot and throat plate for zig-zag stitching, or the Even Feed* Foot for either straight or zig-zag stitching. The top feeding action of the Even Feed* Foot overcomes the natural tendency of plastic-coated fabrics to adhere to the underside of the Presser Foot and thus retard the movement of the top seam layer. When you do not use the Even Feed* Foot on polyurethane or vinyl fabrics for top stitching, use clear oil†, powder†† or a silicone sewing spray as you stitch to keep the top layer from adhering to the underside of the Presser Foot. Test before applying to the garment that it will not mark the fabric.

† SINGER* oil or clear baby oil.
†† Talcum powder or French chalk.

Test-stitch seams. Usually, you will need to increase the needle-thread tension slightly to compensate for the lack of porosity of these materials. Medium or normal presser-foot pressure is usually adequate. However, if the stitch length appears shorter than set for, increase the pressure slightly; or if feed marks show on the underside and the machine runs hard, decrease the pressure. Use your test-stitched seams to test the new ways of treating seams that follow in the next section.

Darts and Seams

Preparations. Leave the pattern on the cut out sections and do not mark until you are ready to use the section. Mark seam widths that differ from the standard 1·5 cm ($\frac{5}{8}$ inch), and mark notches with a pencil or chalk.

Darts. Fold right sides together, matching markings. If you use pins, place them within the dart allowance because of the permanent holes they will leave, or use paper clips over the fold.

Darts, which are placed over rounded parts of the figure, should be stitched on a slight outwards curve, and the last few stitches near the point should be on the edge of the fold. Tie threads at both ends. Slash through the fold as far as possible, finger-press the allowances open and trim to ·6 cm ($\frac{1}{4}$ inch).

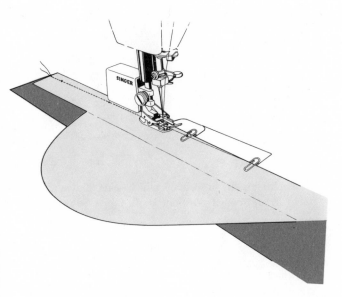

Pounding, rolling and sticking. Pounding seams open on leather-like fabrics is equivalent to pressing to embed the stitches, and to pressing a seam open with the point of the iron. With the garment held over a padded and rounded hard-wood surface (or a firm tailor's ham), use a wooden mallet to pound along the stitching line with

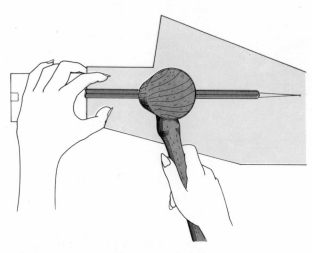

Copydex. Place a thin line of adhesive under the seam allowance slightly inside the seam edge. Finger-press the seam allowance against the garment. Pound lightly or roll to compress the two layers, and allow to dry.

Do as much sticking at one time as possible. Be meticulous and avoid smears. A fine, stiff-pointed brush for applying the adhesive will help you. To protect the shiny face of the fabric, work with the garment section over a Turkish towel.

short, staccato strokes. Pound near the dart point to flatten the fold, distributing it equally on each side of the stitching.

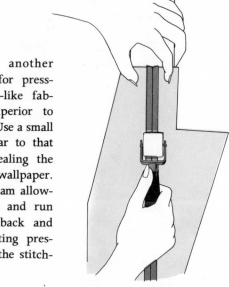

Rolling, another substitute for pressing leather-like fabrics, is superior to pounding. Use a small roller similar to that used for sealing the edges of wallpaper. Hold the seam allowances open and run the roller back and forth, exerting pressure along the stitching line.

Plain seam. Place garment sections right sides together. Match edges, if seam allowances are equal, or seamlines, if seam allowances are unequal. Match seam ends and notches first, and hold together with paper clips or small strips of sellotape. Add more clips or sellotape as needed.

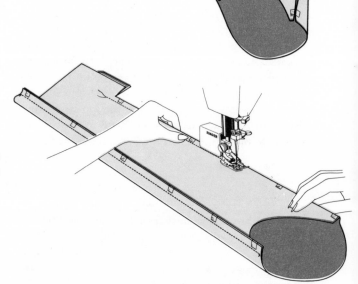

Sticking is the process by which seam allowances are held in an opened position. Use a fabric adhesive like

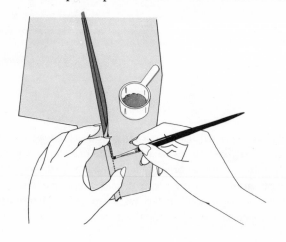

If there is slight ease in one layer of the seam, stitch with that side against the feed. Stitch slowly and keep a firm hold on the seam. Remember, you cannot remove stitches without leaving holes. Tie threads at both ends, remove tape and finger-press seam open. Pound or roll along stitching line, and stick seam allowances open.

Taped seam. When extra strength is required, include pre-shrunk twill tape or straight seam binding in the seam as you stitch. Pound or roll along the stitching line, and stick seam allowances open the same as a plain seam.

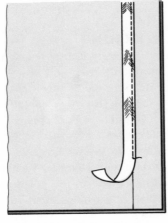

Double-top-stitched seam. Straight-stitch a plain seam, pound or roll it open, but do not stick. Top-stitch an equal distance from centre on each side through garment and seam allowance.

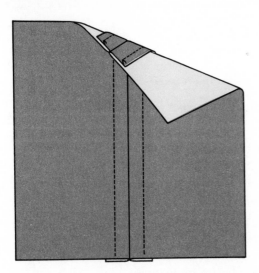

Welt seam. Seam allowances may be equal or unequal for the welt seam. Stitch a plain seam on the stitching line. Pound or roll seam open first. Then turn seam allowances to one side and pound or roll again. Trim the seam allowance next to the garment to ·6 cm ($\frac{1}{4}$ inch). Top-stitch through garment and one seam layer. Use no adhesive.

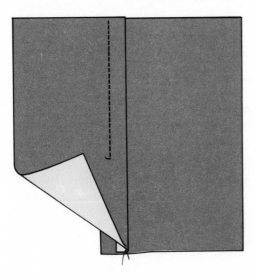

Channel seam. Turn both seam allowances under along seamline. Pound or roll and stick. Cut a strip of fabric twice the seam width plus 1·2 cm ($\frac{1}{2}$ inch). Place the strip, right side against one seam allowance, and top-stitch one side. Hold the strip and abutted edges in place with strips of sellotape, as illustrated, and stitch second side. Do not stitch through the tape.

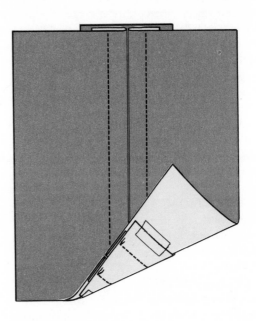

Clipping, notching and trimming seam allowances. Straight seam allowances present few problems in handling, but curved seam allowances must be carefully clipped or notched to form a smooth and continuous line. Cut out small notches to flatten seam allowances that ripple, and slash into seam allowances to release any tightness that restricts the shape of the garment. Cut seam allowances diagonally at cross seams. Cut seam allowances that are inside faced edges to unequal widths, such as ·6 and ·3 cm ($\frac{1}{4}$ and $\frac{1}{8}$ inch).

Pockets and Buttonholes

Pockets and bound or corded buttonholes should be completed before garment sections are interfaced and assembled; hand-worked buttonholes should be made after the garment is completed.

Leather-look Fabrics with Knitted Backs

FABRICS

Characteristics. Thermoplastic or vinyl coating gives knitted-back fabrics a shiny, water-repellent surface and makes them highly stable, with little or no give. Supple and soft, they are easy to sew.

Types. Surface may be smooth, crinkled or marked with reptile-skin pattern.

Fibre content.

Face – vinyl or polyurethane.

Back – cotton, polyester.

PATTERN CHOICE

Select patterns with a tailored look.

- Avoid gathers, sharp pleats or tucks.
- Choose styles with shaped seams rather than darts.
- Top stitching is a good fashion accent and is also functional (substitutes for pressing).
- Raglan sleeves are easiest to handle.

All-weather coats, capes, jackets, jumpers, trouser outfits.

Children's wear.

Men's wear.

Home furnishings, cushions, chair covers, tablecloths and mats.

PREPARATIONS

- Store rolled. Do not fold or crease.
- Fold face out.
- Square and cut ends with table edges.

PATTERN FITTING

- Buy your usual pattern type and size.
- Fit pattern carefully, preserving standard basic ease and design ease.
- Test-fit calico or non-woven interfacing fabric.
- Convert ease to darts.
- Eliminate added facings if possible.
- Remove excessive ease in sleeve head.
- Once stitched, the garment cannot easily be refitted.

CUTTING AND MARKING

- Lay out pattern on grain of fabric.
- Observe pattern-matching rules required by the design.
- Avoid pinning into garment areas; pin marks will show.
- Pin only within seam allowances and sparingly.
- Weights and sellotape can be substituted for pins.
- Mark fabric back with chalk or marking pencil.

STAY STITCHING

- Do *not* stay-stitch.

STITCHING

- Use size 14 leather-sewing needle, style 15 × 2, and polyester thread.
- Increase needle-thread tension to balance stitch.
- 2·5 mm (10) stitch length for straight stitching.
- Normal or regular presser-foot pressure.
- When stitched from right side, the shiny surface will adhere to Presser Foot. To prevent sticking, dust the surface with a powder such as talcum powder, French chalk or one of the powders used for spot cleaning. These brush off without stain. Try a silicone sewing spray.
- The Even Feed* Foot will enable you to stitch without need for the above precautions.

SEAMS AND SEAM FINISHES

- Pin only within seam allowances or hold edges together with paper clips.
- Top-stitched seams and darts are best because they control and hold the seam allowances in place.
- Or, use a thin line of fabric adhesive.
- No seam finish is required.
- Shoulder and neckline seams should usually be taped to prevent stretching.

FACINGS, INTERFACINGS, LININGS AND MOUNTINGS
INTERFACING

- Hair canvas for sharp support.
- Non-woven for soft support.

LINING

- Line for comfort.
- Washable fabric that does not show the dirt.
- Fake fur for zip-in type.
- Interline for warmth and to prevent harsh seams damaging the lining.
- Machine-stitch lining to facing.

MOUNTINGS

- Generally not used except at back across shoulders and in front to anchor interfacing.

PRESSING

- Do *not* press with an iron.
- Instead, finger-press, weight or top-stitch.
- 'Press' seams open with a small roller.

HEMS AND EDGE FINISHES

- Turn and top-stitch.
- Use adhesive to hold hem.
- Or, stitch on a folded band for hem substitute.
- Bound or worked buttonholes.
- Reinforce buttons with small support buttons on the inside.

Fur Fabrics with Knitted Backs

Many fur fabrics have a knitted backing. They are more flexible, and more responsive to easing and easier to sew than fur fabrics with a woven back.

Cutting

Cut fur fabrics with sturdy shears and cut through the backing only, not the pile. The way you cut is entirely different from the way you cut other fabrics. Cut with the tips of the shears only, taking one short snip at a time. Do not rest the shears on the table but hold them up enough to allow the underneath blade to separate the pile. Fur fabrics can also be cut with a single-edge razor blade, a Stanley knife or a special fur cutting knife, but most women find it far easier to cut them with shears.

Preparing to Stitch

For most fur fabrics, select a strong thread, like spun polyester. For lightweight fur fabrics use silk thread.

For all knitted-back fur fabrics, use a size 14 ball-point needle, style *15 × 1*, (catalogue *2021* or *2045*).

The Even Feed* Foot gives the best results on most fur fabrics for both zig-zag and straight stitching; on very thick types, however, the Zipper Foot is better.

The Straight-stitch or General-purpose Presser Foot also can be used for straight stitching and the General-purpose Presser Foot only for zig-zag stitching.

Stitch lengths of 2·5 to 2 mm (10 to 12) are best for straight stitching. Use the shorter length, 2 mm (12), for short pile and 2·5 mm (10) for long pile fur fabrics. Stitch lengths of 2 to 1·5 mm (12 to 15) are best for zig-zag stitching. Use the shorter length, 1·5 mm (15), for short-pile and 2 mm (12) for long pile furs.

Needle-thread tension should be regulated to produce an evenly set stitch. In most fabrics, it must be regulated at a slightly higher setting than for fabrics of similar weight without pile.

Presser-foot pressure should be tested at a regular or normal setting first and then increased slightly if the stitch length appears shorter than the setting indicates, or if the fabric is not firmly held under the Presser Foot.

Seams

For a lined garment, you have a choice of two basic types of seams: (1) plain, straight-stitch seams with 1·5-cm (⅝-inch) seam allowances pressed open; and (2) zig-zag seams with seam allowances trimmed to narrow width before stitching. Procedures vary for making each of these basic types of seams, depending on the bulk and length of the fur pile and whether you use tape to support the seam.

For an unlined fur garment, you have a choice of straight-stitch or zig-zag seams with a decorative covering, or a flat-felled seam.

Using scraps, test-stitch different kinds of seams and procedures described in this section in order to decide which ones are best for your fur. You may need to use two or more different kinds of seams in a single garment.

PLAIN STRAIGHT-STITCH SEAMS
(1·5-cm (⅝-inch) seam allowances)
In short-pile furs, pin, hand-tack (optional) and stitch in the same direction as the pile. Finger-press the seam

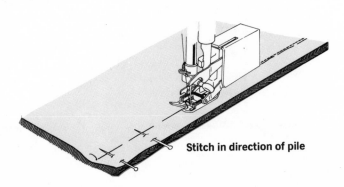

Stitch in direction of pile

open. Check the right side and, with the eye end of a heavy, long darning needle, raise pile threads caught in the stitching. Then apply steam by holding the steam iron level, just above the fabric. Roll along the seamline to press. Use long, loose padding stitches to hold seam allowances open.

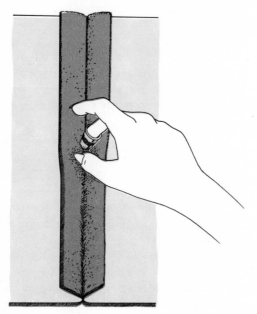

Finger-press seam open

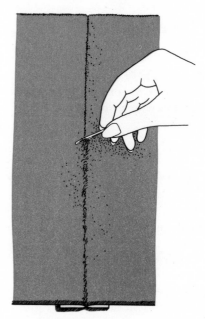

Raise pile-threads
caught in stitching

Steam,
holding iron above fabric

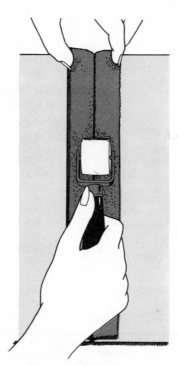

Roll along seam line

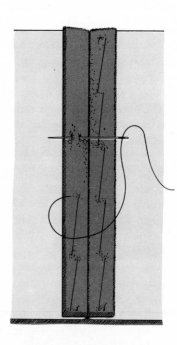

Hold seam allowances
open with padding stitches

In medium-length-pile furs, pin, hand-tack (optional), and stitch in the direction of the pile, working the pile away from the seamline with a long needle. Finger-press seam allowances open. Check both sides of the seam and raise the pile threads caught in the stitching from both

In long-pile furs, trim pile from 1·2 cm ($\frac{1}{2}$ inch) of the seam allowances and tack on the seamline. Check the outside and then raise pile caught in the tacking. Stitch on the seamline in the direction of the pile, and, if necessary, use the Zipper Foot adjusted to the right of the needle to avoid the bulk of the fur. Finger-press seam

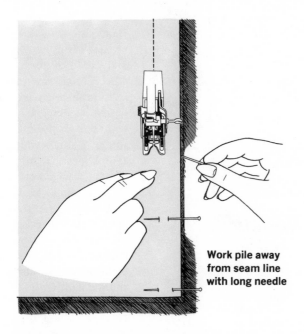

Work pile away from seam line with long needle

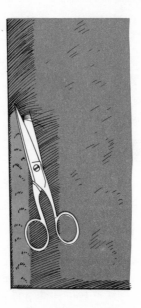
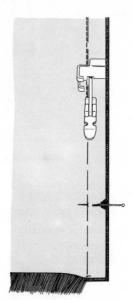

inside and outside. Trim pile from seam allowances with scissors, cutting it close to the backing. Steam, holding the iron just above the fabric. Roll along the seamline to press.

Use long, loose padding stitches to hold seam allowances open.

allowances open. From the outside, raise pile threads along both sides of stitching with a long needle. Press seam allowances with steam iron, allowing it to rest on the two layers of seam allowance only. Cover the seam allowances with a thin pressing cloth if testing indicates a fibre content which needs protection.

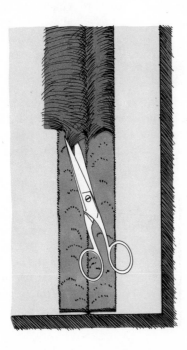

Open the seam allowances with your fingers and roll to hold them open temporarily. Use long, loose padding stitches to hold seam allowances open permanently.

483

To tape straight-stitch seams which should not stretch, include a ·6-cm (¼-inch) shrunk twill tape in the seam as it is being stitched. This procedure applies to furs of any pile length.

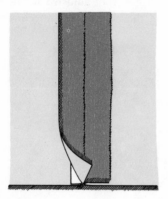

ZIG-ZAG SEAMS

(*·3-to-·6-cm (⅛-to¼-inch) seam allowances*)

In sparsely covered, short-pile furs, do not use a zig-zag seam.

In short-but-dense-pile furs, trim seam allowances to ·3-cm (⅛-inch) width, transferring notches to new seam-allowance edge. Pin edges together at seam ends and at notches. Use a plain zig-zag stitch, 3 stitch width and 1·5 mm (15) stitch length, stitch in the direction of the pile, letting the needle enter at the seamline on one side and beyond the seam edge on the other side. Back-stitch at both the start and the finish of the seam. Finger-press seam allowances open. From the outside, raise pile caught in the stitching. Steam, holding the iron above the inside of the fabric, and roll lightly.

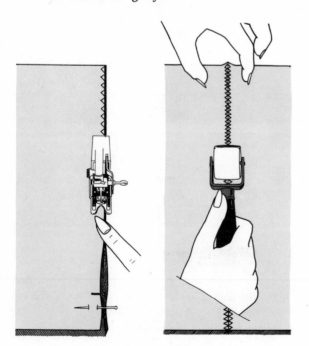

In medium-pile and long-pile furs, trim seam allowances to ·6-cm (¼-inch) width, taking special care to snip with the points of shears through the backing only. Do not cut off the fur. Transfer notch markings as you work. Pin seam-allowance edges together at ends and notches, and at shorter intervals if necessary. Hand-tack with thread of matching colour, and use an overcasting stitch. From the outside, raise pile caught in the tacking. Stitch with the plain zig-zag stitch, 5 stitch width, and 2 mm (12) stitch length, back-stitching at both ends of the seam. Finger-press seam open. Raise pile caught in stitching. Steam, holding the iron above the inside of the fabric, and roll lightly

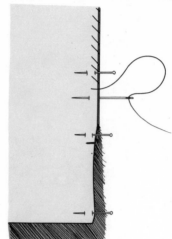

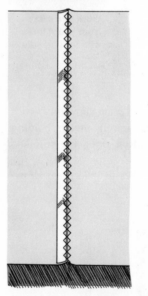

To tape zig-zag seams that should not stretch, add ·6-cm (¼-inch) pre-shrunk twill tape to the tacking step of the above seam preparation, catching only the outside edge of the tape in the tacking and allowing the greater width of the tape to extend towards the garment.

To cross a zig-zag seam, make sure that the stitching at the end of the seam being crossed is reinforced. Trimming the seam allowance before crossing is likely to remove the backstitching that reinforced the seam end.

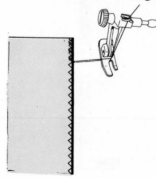

When this has happened, reinforce the seam end again. Place the seam under the needle 1·2 cm (½ inch) from the new seam end and stitch backwards 1·2 cm (½ inch), then forwards 1·2 cm (½ inch).

To cover seams with tape, use 1·2-cm (½-inch) pre-shrunk twill tape and herringbone it over the seam. This taping method prevents abrasion of the lining and gives a slightly more flexible seam than the taping method described above. A covering is usually better for side seams and other major structural seams.

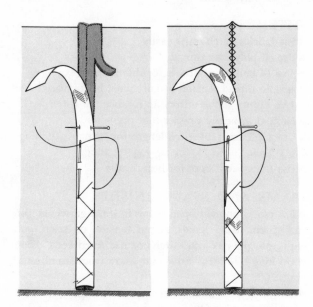

To tape folds, such as the fold of a soft pleat or the fold line of a pocket set in a seam, herringbone 1·2-cm (½-inch) twill tape on the underside of the fabric, bringing the outside edge of the tape to the fold line. The taping is to prevent the fabric stretching. For a pocket set in a seam, tape both back and front sections alike for firmness, although only the front section is folded.

SEAMS IN UNLINED FURS

Straight-stitch or zig-zag seams can be covered with petersham ribbon, leather or leather-like fabric, braid or folded bias-cut bands of fabric. Edges can be finished with contrasting ribbon that has been pressed to shape before being applied. This kind of detail is usually applied to the fabric side of fur fabric by hand or machine. Experiment and adapt the method to suit the garment you are making.

Flat-felled seams can be used for unlined garments made from fur fabrics that are boldly printed on the back and have a matted lamb's wool face. The printed side is usually used as the outside of the garment so that the lamb's wool side becomes the lining. Often, the lamb's wool is turned to the right side for trimming bands on front, sleeve and hem.

To make a flat-felled seam, straight-stitch the seam

first. Trim the seam edge that will be covered to ·6 cm (¼ inch); shear the pile from it and from 1·2 cm (½ inch) of the garment area underneath it. Also, trim the pile from the wide seam allowance for ·3 cm (⅛ inch) so that you can turn it under and top-stitch. These fabrics are often polyester and can be steam-pressed like other fabrics, using a moist cloth to protect the fabric.

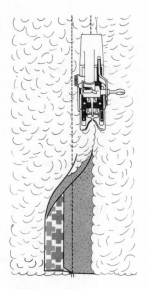

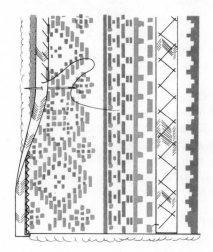

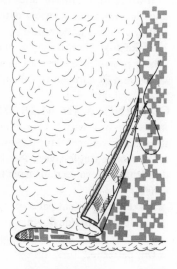

Above. Neaten fold-back facing edges with twill tape. Apply the tape with a narrow zig-zag stitch. Turn tape and stitch it to the backing with an over-casting stitch.
Right. Slip-stitch the finished taped edge to the garment.

DARTS

Darts can be straight-stitched in your fur fabric in the same way as the seams. Narrow zig-zag stitching is better for all fur fabrics except those with very short pile.

Fur Fabrics with Knitted Backs

FABRICS

Characteristics. These fabrics are highly stable, with little give in either lengthwise or crosswise direction. Some are washable; others must be dry-cleaned.

Types. Range is great, from thin ones that handle like corduroy to long-pile ones that require special handling. Some are printed on the backing and are reversible.

Fibre content. Backing – cotton, acrylic or polyester. Face – rayon, modacrylic, polyester, acrylic or wool.

PATTERN CHOICE

Look for simple lines, few seams and raglan or set-in sleeves. Choose patterns recommended for fur fabrics, if possible. Remember, fur-lined garments must be cut generously to allow for fur on the inside. These fabrics combine well with leather, suede, tweed or bulky wool knits.

Coats and capes – casual, country or dressy.

Children's – coats, capes, jackets.

Men's wear – car coats, jackets.

PREPARATIONS

● Store suspended from a hanger.

● Relax fabric by allowing it to lie flat on floor or table overnight, fur-side up.

● Take great care with stripes, animal-like markings, shadings and any special design or pile characteristics.

● Square and cut ends with table edge.

PATTERN FITTING

● Buy your usual pattern type and size.

● If using fur on inside, add up to 2 cm (¾ inch) to side and sleeve seams; or, use a pattern one size larger than usual; or, use a pattern designed for fur lining.

● Make fold back facing sections to garment sections where possible, to eliminate seams.

● Cut and fit garment in calico.

CUTTING AND MARKING

● Cut one-way with fur running downwards except for sheared beaver or seal types, which should run upwards.

● Cut from a single-layer. (Purchase two patterns or cut duplicate pattern sections from tissue, or cut from fitted calico.)

● Make sure you cut pairs, not two for same side.

● Lay fabric fur side down.

● Lay pattern on fabric side, right side down.

● On patterned furs, follow pattern-matching procedures.

● Cut fur with cutting knife, razor-type cutter or tips of shears, through backing only and with very short strokes.

● Mark notches with chalk or thread.

● With your vacuum cleaner, pick up fall-out of fur fabric as you cut.

STAY STITCHING

● Do *not* stay-stitch.

STITCHING

● Fur fabrics stitch quite easily.

● Use all-polyester thread.

● Size 14 ball-point needle for thinner weights.

● Needle-thread tension usually must be increased one or two points above normal to balance the stitch.

● Normal to heavy presser-foot pressure.

● Use a 2·5 mm (10) stitch length for straight stitching, 2 to 1·5 mm (12 to 15) for zig-zag stitching.

● Use Even Feed* Foot for best results.

SEAMS AND SEAM FINISHES

● For plain, pressed-open seams in lined garments, pin and stitch, using hands to put tension on seam, and withdraw pins as you stitch; or use Even Feed* Foot.

● On long-pile furs, stroke fur away from seamline as you stitch.

● Pull long pile threads from seam on right side with coarse darning needle.

● To reduce seam-allowance bulk, shear the fur.

● Stitch seam allowances to backing with padding stitches.

● For zig-zag seams, trim seam allowances to ·6 or ·3 cm (¼ to ⅛ inch), use plain zig-zag, 5 or 3 stitch width.

● For two-faced fur fabrics in unlined garments, use flat-felled seams and trim fur from all under-layers of the seam allowances. Hand-stitch the second stitching where stitching will not embed.

FACINGS, INTERFACINGS, LININGS AND MOUNTINGS

● Fur fabrics styled for conventional construction – use these fabrics in the usual way.

● Two-faced fabrics – when using reverse side for trimming, stitch, turn back, and oversew twill tape to edge of fur facing used for trimming, then slip-stitch to garment.

PRESSING

● Limit iron temperature to that for fibre with lowest heat requirement.

● Fur fabrics can be tacked and pad-stitched without the stitches showing on outside.

● Many fur fabrics should not be pressed at all.

● Press only all-polyester lamb's wool types with steam from moist cloth and with low temperature.

- Embed stitching and shape seams with a small roller.
- Stitch sheared seam allowances to backing instead of pressing.

HEMS AND EDGE FINISHES
- Lined garments – turn hem only 2·5 cm (1 inch), stitch twill tape to edge, hand-oversew to garment and face hem with 5-cm (2-inch) bias of lining fabric.
- Edges may be trimmed decoratively with suede, leather, plastic or woven binding.
- For long furs, fasten with button loops, toggles or metal fasteners rather than buttonholes.
- Reinforce buttons with a small support button on the inside.

EQUIVALENT MEASURES
approved by the Pattern Fashion Industry

Millimetres and Centimetres into Inches (slightly rounded)

mm		cm	inches	cm	inches	cm	inches
3 mm			$\frac{1}{8}$	18	7	73·5	29
6 mm			$\frac{1}{4}$	20·5	8	76	30
10 mm	or	1 cm	$\frac{3}{8}$	23	9	79	31
13 mm	or	1·3 cm	$\frac{1}{2}$	25·5	10	81·5	32
15 mm	or	1·5 cm	$\frac{5}{8}$	28	11	84	33
20 mm	or	2 cm	$\frac{3}{4}$	30·5	12	86·5	34
22 mm	or	2·2 cm	$\frac{7}{8}$	33	13	89	35
25 mm	or	2·5 cm	1	35·5	14	91·5	36
32 mm	or	3·2 cm	$1\frac{1}{4}$	38	15	94	37
38 mm	or	3·8 cm	$1\frac{1}{2}$	40·5	16	96·5	38
45 mm	or	4·5 cm	$1\frac{3}{4}$	43	17	99	39
50 mm	or	5 cm	2	46	18	101·5	40
65 mm	or	6·5 cm	$2\frac{1}{2}$	48·5	19	104	41
75 mm	or	7·5 cm	3	51	20	106·5	42
90 mm	or	9 cm	$3\frac{1}{2}$	53·5	21	109	43
100 mm	or	10 cm	4	56	22	112	44
115 mm	or	11·5 cm	$4\frac{1}{2}$	58·5	23	114·5	45
125 mm	or	12·5 cm	5	61	24	117	46
140 mm	or	14 cm	$5\frac{1}{2}$	63·5	25	119·5	47
150 mm	or	15 cm	6	66	26	122	48
				68·5	27	124·5	49
				71	28	127	50

Metres to Yards (slightly rounded)

metres	yards	metres	yards	metres	yards	metres	yards	metres	yards
0·15	$\frac{1}{8}$	0·70	$\frac{3}{4}$	2·75	3	5·05	$5\frac{1}{2}$	7·35	8
0·25	$\frac{1}{4}$	0·95	1	3·20	$3\frac{1}{2}$	5·50	6	7·80	$8\frac{1}{2}$
0·35	$\frac{3}{8}$	1·40	$1\frac{1}{2}$	3·70	4	5·95	$6\frac{1}{2}$	8·25	9
0·50	$\frac{1}{2}$	1·85	2	4·15	$4\frac{1}{2}$	6·40	7	8·70	$9\frac{1}{2}$
0·60	$\frac{5}{8}$	2·30	$2\frac{1}{2}$	4·60	5	6·90	$7\frac{1}{2}$	9·15	10

Available Fabric Widths

cm	inches	cm	inches
65	25	127	50
70	27	140	54/56
90	35/36	150	58/60
100	39	175	68/70
115	44/45	180	72
122	48		

Available Zip Lengths

cm	inches	cm	inches	cm	inches
10	4	25	10	55	22
12	5	30	12	60	24
15	6	35	14	65	26
18	7	40	16	70	28
20	8	45	18	75	30
22	9	50	20		

mm = millimetres   cm = centimetres   m = metres

Glossary of Sewing Terms*

abutted seam – Two cut seam edges joined edge to edge with an underlay of a lightweight fabric. Usually used in interfacing and interlining.

appliqué – To sew a design of a small piece of fabric over the main fabric. The design or motif may be applied either by machine with a zig-zag stitch or by hand with the blanket stitch.

armholes – The garment opening for the arm and sleeve.

backstitch – 1. The reverse stitch on the machine. Used to reinforce the stitching at the beginning and ending of seams. 2. A hand sewing stitch.

balance lines – The horizontal level on which the crosswise grain of the fabric falls at a right angle to the lengthwise grain in each dress section.

belt backing – Stiffening used as interlining or backing in a belt and inside a waistband.

bias – The diagonal line of fabric that is on neither the lengthwise nor the crosswise grain. A 'true bias' is the diagonal line formed when the lengthwise grain of the fabric is folded to the crosswise grain.

binding – A single or double bias finish used to encase raw edges. It may be applied without top stitching or with top stitching, using the Binder Foot.

Bishop sleeve – A long sleeve with fullness gathered at the wrist.

blindstitch – 1. A hand stitch used for hemming and finish which is invisible, on the right side. 2. A zig-zag machine stitch pattern. See Zig-Zag stitches.

block – To outline on calico, paper or fabric, the principal sections of a chair, sofa or cushion before the loose cover fabric is cut. Sections of dress fabric also are often blocked to ensure a perfect matching of design.

block – To pin to shape and steam, rather than press. Steam, holding iron above surface, and allow fabric to dry before handling – used with some kinds of embroidery and also knitted fabrics.

bodkin – A heavy needle with a blunt point and large eye. Used to slot tape, elastic, ribbon, cord, etc., through a casing or heading; also used to help form a thread shank in button sewing.

boning – See Featherbone.

buckram – A coarse, stiff cotton fabric used to hold the heading erect in curtains and to give body to contour belts, and similar constructions.

cable cord – Soft cotton cord used for cording and piping; available in several sizes.

canopy – 1. Fabric hung or draped over a frame attached to a four-poster. 2. A decorative treatment above a headboard.

casing – 1. A hem or tuck through which ribbon, tape, cord or elastic can be drawn. 2. Opening at the top of a curtain through which a rod is run.

catch – to attach one piece of fabric to another with tiny hand stitches – generally with several backstitches over the first stitch; for example a facing to seam allowance.

centre line – The vertical centre of the bodice, skirt or yoke section of a garment. It is marked on the pattern pieces and is transferred to the fabric sections with a tacking thread.

clip – To cut a short distance into a seam allowance or selvedge with the point of the scissors. Used in curved seams, square corners, buttonholes and the like, so that seams will lie flat when pressed.

controlled fullness – The gathering necessary on a long seam edge so that it can be joined to a shorter seam edge.

crease – 1. A line or mark made by folding the fabric and pressing the fold. 2. The line or mark that may result when the manufacturer folds the fabric and rolls it on the bolt.

dart – A short fold or tuck in the fabric which is tapered; used to shape a garment.

decorative stitching – 1. A zig-zag machine stitch that is ornamental in design. 2. Hand embroidery stitches.

directional stitching – Stitching of seams in the correct direction of the grain so that the fabric will not stretch during the stitching.

drape – 1. A property many fabrics have of falling easily into graceful folds; a soft silk, for example. 2. An attractive arrangement of folds in a garment or curtains. The folds may be controlled by means of gathers, tucks or pleats.

dress form (shape) – A body shape (dummy) which is used to fit a garment. Made from various materials and often adjustable for size.

dressmaker's cutting board – A board marked in squares used for cutting fabrics where table space may not be available. Folds for storage. Marked every 2·5 cm (1 inch) in each direction – usual size 180 × 101·5 cm (72 × 40 inches), folding to 101·5 × 31·5 cm (40 × 12½ inches).

dressmaker's squared paper – Used for making a pattern by copying from a miniature diagram. Diagrams are usually scaled with one square equalling 2·5 cm (1 inch). Squared paper has either 2·5 or 5 cm (1 or 2 inch) squares so that the pattern shape can be easily drawn to the correct size. (Alterations required in size of pattern, etc. should be made on the miniature.)

dressmaker's tracing paper – A coloured carbon (copying) paper used to trace a shape or pattern markings on to fabric. Usually used with a tracing wheel.

Many of the terms defined here are explained more fully in the text. Consult the alphabetical index.

drop shoulder – Shoulder line located below the normal line.

ease – The even distribution of fullness when one section of a seam is joined to a slightly shorter section without forming gathers or tucks. Used to shape set-in sleeves, the shoulder line and other areas.

ease allowance – The amount added to body measurements to make garments comfortable and allow for movement.

edge-stitch – 1. To stitch close to a finished edge or seam from the right side of the fabric. 2. To stitch close to the edge of a fold after the fabric edge is turned to the underside. Used to finish hems and facings.

embroidery hoop – Two narrow circles of wood, the smaller of which is placed under the fabric and the larger over it on the top side – used to hold fabric taut.

facing – The second layer of fabric used to finish necklines, front and back openings and sleeves.

featherbone – A narrow strip of boning used to stiffen the seams and edges of closely fitted garment sections to prevent them from slipping or rolling; for example, the bodice of strapless dresses, and cummerbunds.

fibres – Natural or man-made filaments from which yarns are spun.

finger-press – To press flat (as a turning or seam) using fingers and thumbnail.

finishing – The sewing techniques used in garment construction to finish seams, facings, hems, necklines and other sections.

fly – A neatened opening that conceals the zip or buttons. Generally used in shorts, men's pants and topcoats.

footboard – The upright board at the foot of a bed.

gather – To control fullness by a running stitch through the fabric; the thread is fastened at one end and then pulled up from the other end.

grain – In woven fabrics, the lengthwise and crosswise direction of the yarn. The lengthwise yarn forms the lengthwise grain; the crosswise yarn, the crosswise grain. When these two threads or grains are at right angles, the fabric is 'on the true grain'.

guidelines – Tacked stitches to be followed for the final stitching (for buttonholes, pockets, etc.).

gusset – A small shaped piece of matching fabric set into a slash or seam for added width and ease. Found at the underarm when sleeve and bodice are cut in one, and in briefs and knickers.

haberdashery – Small sewing needs, such as thread, needles, pins, zips, press fasteners, hooks and eyes, bias binding, etc., available at haberdashery and notion counters in department stores.

headboard – The upright board at the head of a bed.

heading – 1. A fabric tuck above the casing or at the top edge of curtains. 2. A narrow edge above a line of gathers that form a frill.

hemline – The line on which the hem is marked and turned to the underside. This line is an even distance from the floor.

hem-marker – See skirt marker.

interfacing – A third thickness of carefully selected fabric which is placed between the garment and facing fabrics for added body, shaping and support.

interlining – A fabric placed between the lining and outer fabric. Used in coats, jackets and the like to add warmth or bulk; in bedspreads to give body; in curtains to add body and to prevent light from showing through and fading the fabric.

intersecting seams – Seams that cross one another when garment sections are joined together at the waistline, shoulder line, set-in sleeve and similar points.

'iron-on' – A term used to describe chemically treated fabric which is joined or applied to another fabric by using a warm iron (for hem facings); also an embroidery transfer design (on tissue paper) which is placed face down on the fabric – the heat of a warm iron then transfers the design to the fabric.

joinings – The points at which one garment section is joined to another, such as skirt and bodice.

lap – To extend or fold one piece of fabric or garment section over another.

lapel – The section of a garment which is turned back between the top button and collar.

layout – The position in which pattern pieces are laid on the fabric for cutting.

layering – Trimming all seam allowances within a seam to different widths. Layering removes bulk so that the seam will lie flat.

link buttons – Two flat buttons held together by several threads covered with blanket stitch (as a French tack or button shank) forming a cuff link.

lining – A carefully selected fabric that covers the underside of another fabric, adding body to the article. 1. In dress construction, the lining is cut the same as the dress fabric and constructed separately. It adds a finished look to the inside. 2. In tailoring, the lining is constructed to fit into the jacket or coat and prevents the unfinished seam allowance from showing. 3. In home decorating, the lining is used to finish curtains and protect the top fabric. It is also used in bedspreads.

made-to-measure – Professionally made and fitted garments, loose covers, bedspreads and curtains.

markings – The symbols shown on the pattern for darts, buttonholes, tucks and other construction details. They are transferred from the pattern to the fabric by means of tailor's tacks, chalk, tackings or tracing wheel.

mercerised – A finish for cotton that adds strength and lustre and makes the fabric more receptive to dyes.

mitre – 1. The diagonal line formed when fabric is joined at a square corner. After stitching the excess fabric is generally cut away on the underside where the hems meet. Used where hems join at the corner as in a vent in a jacket, curtains and linens. 2. The diagonal fold made when applying a band, lace or the like to square or pointed shapes.

mounting – The second thickness of a carefully selected fabric which is cut by the same pattern as the garment and is stitched in place with the garment seams. Used to give added body and shape.

multi-stitch zig-zag – See Zig-Zag stitches.

nap – A soft fabric surface made by short fibres brushed in one direction.

neaten – To finish: i.e. to pull threads through to the wrong side and tie, or stitch in the ends and trim neatly so that they are almost invisible.

notches – V-shaped cutouts in the cut edge of the seam allowance that indicate which edges are to be seamed together. Matching notches are always joined.

notions – Small items used in sewing such as thread, needles, pins and buttons, (haberdashery).

overwrap or overlap – The part of the garment that extends over another part, as the opening of a blouse, jacket, coat or waistband.

pattern layout guide – The instruction sheet that shows how to arrange the pattern pieces on the fabric before cutting. It includes the most economical layout for different types and widths of fabrics and for the various pattern sizes.

pattern stitching – Zig-zag stitching of designs on a zig-zag machine which is made possible by setting selectors in a certain position or by inserting specific cams or discs.

pile – Raised loops or tufts on the surface of a fabric.

pinking – A serrated-edge seam-finish, cut with pinking shears (used where fabrics do not fray).

pivot – To turn the fabric on the machine needle while the needle is still in the fabric. Used when stitching square corners such as in buttonholes, pockets and notched sections.

placket – A finished opening that is generally closed by means of a zip, press fasteners or other fastening. Used in dresses, skirts, shorts and other garments to make them easy to put on and to assure a good fit at the waistline, sleeve, etc.; also used in such fabric furnishings as loose covers and cushions.

pleats: dressmaking – Folds in the fabric to give fullness (usually at the hemline) often partly stitched down.

　　Accordion pleats – Fine narrow pleats made by a machine process.

　　Box pleats – Two knife pleats which turn away from each other. (Also used in loose cover flounces and curtain valances.)

　　Inverted pleat – Two knife pleats which turn towards each other.

　　Kick pleat (Dior pleat) – A short pleat at the hemline of a skirt formed by an additional layer of fabric placed under an opening.

　　Knife pleats – A series of pleats which are the same width and fall in the same direction. (Also used in loose cover flounces.)

　　Release pleat – A partly stitched pleat (at top and/or bottom) in the back of a coat or jacket lining to give freedom of movement.

　　Sunray pleats – Commercially pleated – wider at the bottom than the top.

pleats: curtain – Folds in the heading made into pleats by using a tape with woven-in pockets and hooks.

　　Cartridge pleats – A small round pleat filled with rolled vilene – usually placed in groups of three.

　　French pleats – One large pleat divided into three at the lower edge of the heading, hand sewn and drawn together, leaving pleats uncreased. Arranged in groups at intervals.

　　Pencil pleats – Narrow pleats arranged close together to form a deep firm top heading.

　　Pinch pleats – One large pleat divided into two or three and creased the length of the pleats. Formed at intervals and fanning out at the top.

pleat tape – A stiffened tape with woven-in pockets used for curtains; also available with draw cords to pull up and form pleats at various distances apart. Made from various fabrics, including nylon and terylene for net curtains, and in different widths.

pre-shrunk – To shrink the fabric before cutting so that its dimensions will not be altered by laundering or dry cleaning. Many fabrics are pre-shrunk by the manufacturer.

pressure – The force the presser foot exerts on the fabric during the machine stitching. The pressure can – and should – be regulated to suit the fabric.

reinforce – To strengthen an area that will be subjected to strain. The area may be reinforced with an underlay or patch of fabric or with extra rows of stitching.

regular stitch – The machine stitch length best suited to the fabric being stitched; usually applied to straight stitching.

return – In curtain fixtures, the distance from the curve of the track or rod to the wall. Curtains are constructed so that they extend round the return.

revers – Wide, shaped lapels on coats and suits.

reversible – Describing: 1. A fabric that is woven so that either side may be used for the right side – for example damask or double-faced wool. 2. A garment finished so that it may be worn with either side out.

rip – 1. To remove machine stitching. 2. To tear, usually along the seam.

rouching – Several lines of stitching forming a puckered area – see shirring.

sag – To hang or drop below the normal line or level. A seam sags when it is stretched or pulled down from the normal position through weight of the fabric (for example, a bias seam).

seam allowance – The amount of fabric allowed for seams in joining sections of a garment or other article together – generally 1·5 cm ($\frac{5}{8}$ inch).

seam edge – The cut edge of the seam allowance.

seam neatening – The finish used on the edge of the seam allowance to prevent the fabric unravelling or fraying.

seamline – The line designated for stitching the seam – generally 1·5 cm ($\frac{5}{8}$ inch) from the cut edge.

selvedge – The finished edges on all woven fabrics which are parallel to the lengthwise thread.

shank – The stem between the button and the garment to which the button is sewn. The shank can be made with thread or it can be a part of the button. It allows room for the buttonhole side of the garment to fit smoothly over the button.

shirring – Gathering with three or more parallel rows of stitching, to control fullness – used as a fashion detail. Also used to rouch a complete bodice or top with special elastic thread which allows it to give with the figure.

shrink – To relax the fibres of the fabric through moisture or steam to prevent subsequent shrinking.

sizing – A finish applied to fabrics to add body and stiffness.

skirt marker – A rule standing from the floor (or attached to a door) with cm/inches marked and attached to it a press bulb with chalk to mark the fabric for a hem; can be self-operated. Also available with a pin apparatus which requires a second person to operate.

slash – A cut in the fabric along a straight line. A slash is longer than a clip. Examples are: a finished slit in a garment that is faced, and an opening into which a gusset is inserted.

snip – A small cut into the fabric (see clip).

stay – A small piece of fabric or tape that is sewn to an area of the garment for reinforcement. Use at the point of a slash, under bound buttonholes, and at the waistline.

stitch pattern – See Pattern Stitching.

straight stitch – A plain straight stitch made with the Straight-stitch Presser Foot.

straight-stretch stitch – Appears like a loose outline stitch, made with a Flexi-stitch disc, especially suitable for knitted and stretch fabrics.

tacking stitch – A long stitch made by hand or machine to hold two pieces of fabric together temporarily. Used to join garment sections before fitting and to prevent the fabric from slipping during stitching of seams.

tailoring – A method of sewing characterised by classic lines; in suits, coats, dresses and trousers.

tailor's tacks – Markings made of thread which are used to transfer symbols from the pattern to the fabric.

tension – The degree of looseness or tightness of the needle and bobbin threads that interlock to form the sewing machine stitch. There are two tensions – the upper (needle thread) and the lower (bobbin thread). When the two are balanced both the needle and the bobbin threads are drawn into the fabric to the same degree.

thread count – Number of threads (yarns) per cm (inch) in the warp and weft of woven fabric.

top stitching – A row of stitching on the right side, or top side, of a garment near to the finished edge as a decorative accent. Can be made by machine or hand. Hand stitches include:

> **glove stitch** – Even small stitches on both sides of fabric.
>
> **saddle stitch** – Longer stitches on top and shorter underneath.

tuck – A stitched fold of fabric which provides fullness or a decorative feature (as pin tucks); also a shrinkage or growth tuck (in children's clothes) to allow for letting out (removing the stitches) as a child grows (especially used to lengthen a garment).

underlap or underwrap – The edge of a garment that extends under another edge, as in the opening of a coat, jacket or waistband.

underlay – 1. A strip of fabric that is placed on the underside of the main fabric for reinforcement. Used in stitching buttonholes, pockets and similar sections; in mending; in decorative zig-zag stitching. 2. A piece of fabric placed under finished shirring to prevent strain on the shirring stitches.

up and down – The direction of the nap, pile or design of a fabric. On napped and pile fabrics, the shading varies depending on the angle from which the fabric is viewed. On prints, the design may run in one direction – for example, flowers with 'heads up', or uneven checks.

unravel – 1. To separate or pull the woven threads away from the cut edges of the fabric, leaving long threads; to unweave. 2. To fray, as unfinished seam edges.

vent – A lapped opening. Used in hems of tailored jackets and sleeves and in other garment sections.

warp – The threads or yarns that run lengthwise in the weaving of the fabric.

weft (old term woof) – The threads or yarns that cross the warp. Also called 'filler'.

zig-zag stitches:

blindstitch zig-zag – A stitch pattern that produces four straight stitches separated by a single sidewards stitch to the left. Used in finishing seam edges, in stitching hems and in decorative stitching.

closely spaced stitch pattern – A decorative zig-zag stitch pattern that places all stitches close together when the stitch length selector is set for satin stitching.

multi-stitch zig-zag – A stitch pattern that makes four stitches to the left, then four to the right in a zig-zag shape. Used to finish hem and seam edges, mend, stitch darts and seams in interfacing and sew elastic and blanket binding in place; also used for decorative stitching and other sewing.

open-spaced stitch pattern – A decorative zig-zag stitch pattern that does not place the stitches close together although the stitch length selector is set for satin stitching.

plain zig-zag stitch – A regular zig-zag stitch where all stitches are of the same width and in a straight line. The stitch length and stitch width selectors may be set for various lengths and widths.

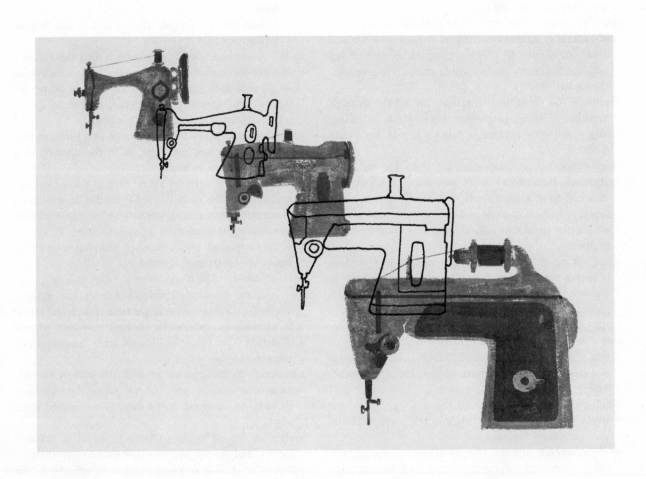

Index

493

Index for 'The Many Faces of Knitted Fabrics'

*Trademark of THE SINGER COMPANY